Third Edition

GERMAN
A STRUCTURAL APPROACH

Walter F.W. Lohnes
F.W. Strothmann

STANFORD UNIVERSITY

Third Edition
GERMAN
A STRUCTURAL APPROACH

W·W·NORTON & COMPANY

New York   London

Frontispiece: Tübingen.

"Klatsch am Sonntagmorgen" by Horst Bienek, "der tisch ist oval" by Franz Mon, and "Reisen" by Peter Otto Chotjewitz, from *Die Meisengeige*, ed. Günter Bruno Fuchs. Copyright © 1964 Carl Hanser Verlag, Munich.

"Wenn die Haifische Menschen wären" and "Freundschaftsdienste," from *Prosa I* by Bertolt Brecht. Copyright 1965 by Stefan S. Brecht. All rights reserved by Suhrkamp Verlag, Frankfurt/Main.

"If Sharks Were People" and "Good Turns," trans. Yvonne Kapp. Reprinted from the copyrighted works of Bertolt Brecht by permission of Pantheon Books, a Division of Random House, Inc., and Methuen & Company, Ltd. Copyright © 1962 by Methuen & Company, Ltd. Translation copyright © 1962 by Stefan S. Brecht.

"Die Moritat von Mackie Messer" by Bertolt Brecht, aus *Gesammelte Werke*. © Copyright Suhrkamp Verlag, Frankfurt am Main, 1967. Alle Rechte Vorbehalten.

"Mack the Knife," trans. Mark Blitzstein. ©1928 Universal Edition. Copyright renewed and assigned to Weill-Brecht-Harms Co., Inc. © 1955 Weill-Brecht-Harms Co., Inc. All rights reserved. Used by permission of Warner Bros. Music.

"Sachliche Romanze," "Die Entwicklung der Menschheit," and "Das Eisenbahngleichnis" by Erich Kästner, from Kaestner fuer Erwachsene. Copyright © Atrium Verlag, Zurich.

"Heimkehr" and "Gibs auf!" Reprinted by permission of Schocken Books Inc., from *Beschreibung eines Kampfes* by Franz Kafka. Copyright ©1946 by Schocken Books Inc. Copyright renewed © 1974 by Schocken Books Inc.

"Das Gleichnis vom verlornen Sohn." Reprinted from *Die Heilige Schrift (Zürcher Bibel)*, Verlag der Zürcher Bibel, 1954.

"Demokratie," by Mathias Schreiber. Reprinted by permission of the author.

"Ostkontakte" and "Grünanlage" from *Neues (& altes) vom Rechtsstaat & von mir*. Alle Epigramme. Copyright © 1978 by Arnfrid Astel, Vertrieb Zweitausendeins, Frankfurt a.M.

"Zugauskunft" by Peter Handke from Die Innenwelt der Außenwelt der Innenwelt © Copyright 1969 Suhrkamp Verlag, Frankfurt am Main.

"Ein Tisch ist ein Tisch" by Peter Bichsel, from *Kindergeschichten*. Copyright © 1969 by Hermann Luchterhand Verlag, Darmstadt and Neuwied.

Layout by Ben Gamit

Copyright © 1980, 1973, 1968, 1967 by W. W. Norton & Company, Inc.

Printed in the United States of America.

ALL RIGHTS RESERVED

Published simultaneously in Canada by Stoddart, a subsidiary of
General Publishing Co. Ltd, Don Mills, Ontario.

Library of Congress Cataloging in Publication Data
Lohnes, Walter F. W.
  German: a structural approach.
  Includes index.
   1. German language—Grammar—1950- I. Strothmann
Friedrich Wilhelm, 1904- joint author.
II. Title.
PF3112.L6 1980   438.2'421   80–403

ISBN 0-393-95059-X

W.W. Norton & Company, Inc., 500 Fifth Avenue, New York, N.Y. 10110
W.W. Norton & Company Ltd., 37 Great Russell Street, London WC1B 3NU

3 4 5 6 7 8 9 0

Contents

Unit 3   The Structure of German Sentences—Verbal Complements— Negation by **kein** and **nicht**.   **55**

Verbal Complements.   The Structure of German Assertions.   The Position of Verbal Complements.   The End Field.   Word Order in German Questions.   Sentence Intonation: Shifting the Stress Point.   *no, not*: **kein, nicht.**   Negation by **nicht.** Professional Status Negated.   **schon** and **noch nicht; noch** and **nicht mehr.   nicht ein. nicht wahr?** and **nicht?** as Complete Questions.   **doch.   doch** as Answer to a Negative Question.   **aber, denn, oder, und.**   Sentence Adverbs.

Unit 4   Modal Auxiliaries—Contrast Intonation—Imperative.   **87**

Infinitives with and without **zu.**   Modal Auxiliaries.   The Six German Modals and Their Meaning.   The Forms of the German Modals.   Position of Dependent Infinitives. The Two-Box Second Prong.   Replacement or Omission of the Dependent Infinitive. Contrast Intonation. Word Order under Contrast Intonation.   The Imperative.

Unit 9 The Subjunctive.   **247**

Unit 10 Prepositions with Dative or Accusative—The Genitive
Case—**ein**-Words without Nouns.   **279**

Unit 11 Indirect Discourse—The Conjunctions **als, ob, wann,**
wenn.   **311**

The Passive Voice.   Action and State.   Dative Objects and the Passive Voice.   Use of the Actional Passive to Express Activity as Such.   The Use of **von, durch,** and **mit** in Passive Sentences.   The Impersonal **es** in the Front Field.   **jetzt** and **nun.**   Pre-Noun Inserts.

Preface

THIS NEW EDITION OF *German: A Structural Approach* has been a long time in the making. What was originally intended as a routine revision became considerably more. For we recognized that a language text cannot simply count on its record of success to continue unabated; it must reflect recent changes in teaching strategy. And we believe this one does. It has been tailored to meet the needs of the college student of the 1980s.

Teachers familiar with previous editions will immediately notice the changes in content. We have not, however, altered our basic approach to contemporary German; we still believe that an adult learner is best served by combining active use of the language with an intellectual understanding of grammatical structure. Thus, we employ some features of the audio-lingual method as well as what is now often referred to as the "cognitive approach." But the shift in methodology during the past decade, from the language teacher to the language learner, can be detected in these modifications, among others: new types of conversational material allow the student to use the spoken language in a less controlled and more natural fashion; simpler pattern sentences now provide a narrative flow; and readings are far less tied to the formal study of grammar than they were in previous editions.

Because of these changes, the book can be used in a greater variety of teaching situations than before. It can still be used for a global approach in which all four skills are given equal emphasis, but it can also be employed when the goal is reading competence, in which case the conversational material can simply be left out; conversely, since vocabulary and grammar of most reading selections are not so closely tied to the rest of the book as before, they need not be used in a more conversational approach. This flexibility of the third edition, we hope, will make it more readily usable in courses that meet less than three or four times a week.

The book lays a solid foundation for the student who plans to continue German beyond the first year. But, given the fact that many students have far less time for language study in their curriculum today than they had ten or twenty years ago, especially where the language requirement has been dropped, the book provides a self-contained introduction to German language and culture that need not necessarily be followed by additional courses. Furthermore, it can serve in self-study and individualized programs.

The third edition is divided into eighteen rather than thirteen units. We have redistributed the material into a more balanced sequence and have split up some grammatical topics, for example subjunctive and adjectives, to avoid occasional tedium. Each unit now has a brief English introduction calling attention to the most significant features in the unit. The grammatical analysis is less detailed; many of the pattern sections have been rewritten, often as consecutive texts to provide contexts for individual sentences. Most of the illustrations are new and even more closely integrated into the text than before, especially in the early units. The vocabulary was completely reworked and carefully checked against the frequency lists compiled by J. Alan Pfeffer and H.-H. Wängler, as well as the word list for *Zertifikat Deutsch als Fremdsprache* (Goethe-Institut, Munich).

No introductory language text could at the same time be a complete introduction to the entire foreign culture. We have selected certain aspects of the culture of Central Europe which we felt to be of special interest to American students. They can be used for further excursions into *Kultur- und Landeskunde*, both present and past, and thus offer another possible goal for the teaching of German. Tante Amalie and Johannes Schmidt-Ingelheim, however, are still alive and well. For aficionados, the two Ingelheim stories have been retained as "additional reading."

Again, we wish to express our gratitude to all those who helped us in the preparation of this third edition. Many helpful suggestions and criticisms came from users of the second edition, and, wherever possible, we have altered the text accordingly. Peter Schmidt, of UCLA and Mississippi State College, and Eugene Weber, of Swarthmore College, carefully read the manuscript and frequently improved our own formulations. Nancy Ferguson Handels provided us with valuable inside information on the West German education system. Our repeated tours of duty at Stanford-in-Germany enabled us to get to know a small region of the Federal Republic extremely well, and we are grateful to the people of Beutelsbach who unknowingly provided us with a wealth of material. Without Jutta McCormick, who became a cut-and-paste artist par excellence, our scribbles might never have seen the light of day. At our publisher's, Josepha Gutelius has worked tirelessly on the editing of the new edition.

From our first contact with Norton until his untimely death, Jack M. Stein, as consulting editor, was critic, cajoler, contributor, and, ultimately, faithful shepherd to *German: A Structural Approach*. In one of his last letters, Jack wrote, "I enclose Xeroxes of the pages I have had comments on and, as usual, I have to ask you to overlook any peremptoriness in them. The substance is what counts and we have known one another long enough so that I do not feel the need of careful phraseology to avoid injuring your sensibilities," and he signed off with "Excelsior!"·

We dedicate this third edition to his memory.

W.F.W.L.
F.W.S.

Stanford, California
January 1980

Introduction

THIS THIRD EDITION OF *German: A Structural Approach* has the same aims as its parent volume: developing the skills of listening, speaking, reading, and writing, while at the same time giving students a clear understanding of the principles underlying their language performance. Our experience has shown that the combination of the "how" and the "why" of language acquisition produces good results. An introductory course that makes students aware of how language is organized and why speech patterns develop systematically can be far more stimulating than one that is limited to language practice alone.

In learning our native language, we absorb its syntactical principles without any clear conceptual knowledge of many of these principles, and we certainly do not think of them every time we utter a sentence. Nevertheless, we know when to say *He thinks not* and when to say *He doesn't think*. By a series of "pattern drills" that stretches from birth into adulthood we learn how to use a linguistic code without necessarily having a conceptual understanding of that code. The learning of a second language resembles this process in some ways, but we can never really repeat our first performance.

It is true that one can drill the structural patterns of German intensively over a long period of time and thus gradually acquire fluency. But since college students are linguistic adults who already speak one language, they should not be exposed to the nonconceptual learning process of a child.

In the first place, there is not that much time. In one year of college German, an American student cannot afford to learn the language by trial and error and from context only; he or she has to resort to grammar in order to master German quickly.

Secondly, the linguistic code of English acts as a source of interference; it prevents the students from understanding many German sentences they hear and from actively using German sentence patterns correctly. This is to be expected, for once we have absorbed one linguistic code, we cannot learn a totally different code without some contrastive analytical knowledge of that new code. In learning this new code, we construct a hypothetical "learner's language," initially full of errors, which we constantly revise and refine as we absorb more of the new language, until finally the learner's language matches the new code in every detail. When this happens, the learner is no longer a learner, but has become bilingual.

Thirdly, college students have reached an age at which they are both able and eager to grasp the systematic concept behind the individual phenomenon. When they encounter the simple sentence **Ich bleibe heute natürlich zu Hause,** they want to know why it is perfectly acceptable to say **Zu Hause bleibe ich heute natürlich nicht**, but not **Zu Hause bleibe ich heute natürlich.** A conceptual understanding of German sentence structure is a time-saving short cut, and we see no virtue in postponing the immediate comprehension of German syntax by refusing to tell students, as they manipulate structural patterns, what the principles underlying these patterns are.

PATTERN SENTENCES make up the first part of each unit. They systematically introduce elements of German which are described in corresponding analysis sections and give students an immediate chance to work with sentence structures that are typically German. Each pattern group contains a sufficient number of examples to illustrate a grammatical point, and there are marginal cross-references to the analysis.

From the very beginning, we aim at the students' ability to acquire not only the German they will see in formal print, but also the German they will hear in informal speech, and we have not shied away from the colloquial German used by educated people in everyday speech. Colloquial as well as literary German is recognized as equally acceptable, and the students are taught that **Wo kommen Sie denn her?** and **Wo willst du denn hin?** are just as correct as **Woher kommen Sie?** and **Wohin willst du?**

We have tried not to write typical classroom German, and we have never yielded to the temptation to produce unidiomatic expressions for the sake of making our patterns fit into a preconceived mold. For instance, the use of the attributive genitive must obviously be illustrated, but this is no excuse for introducing sentences like **Die Farbe meines Kugelschreibers ist blau** as long as there is available a wealth of idiomatic phrases such as **ein Freund meines Mannes, gegen Ende des Jahres,** and **der Erfolg der neuen Methode.** We have mitigated the rigidity of many drills by insisting that the student create sentences that could occur in actual speech. It serves no purpose to have a substitution drill end with **Sie werden ihre Tränen getrocknet haben.** On the other hand, we do expect the student to be able to handle complex structures such as **Seine Frau soll sehr aufgeregt gewesen sein** or **Ich hätte natürlich auch zu Hause bleiben können,** for such structures do belong to the living language as it is actually spoken and written.

Most pattern sections in this third edition have been revised or entirely rewritten. In many instances, we have created a kind of narrative flow in these sections in order to show sentences in a more natural context and to increase student interest in their content. Some sections contain built-in variations or are followed by a separate set of variations. These are designed in such a way that they can be used in class immediately after a group of pattern sentences has been introduced.

ANALYSIS is the intellectual core of each unit. The analysis sections have intentionally been written as detailed and unhurried discussions of grammatical points. Pains have been taken to explain grammar in terms the student will understand. We have avoided short, terse rules that cannot be applied without elaboration in the classroom. The analysis sections should be assigned as outside reading as the new patterns are introduced in class, so that the students, while they work on the patterns, will have the feeling that they know what they are doing and why they are doing it.

In the analysis, our first and foremost concern is syntax. After an introductory section on the pronunciation of individual sounds, Unit 1 deals with sentence intonation; in the following units, the basic structure of German sentences is developed. A discussion of the two-part predicate, the most characteristic feature of German syntax, is followed by an analysis of word order in the inner field of a sentence. Negation and time phrases are dealt with at length. Modal auxiliaries and the subjunctive—indispensable in "real" German—are introduced very early. A number of sections deal with sentence adverbs like **doch, ja,** or **denn.** Other sections are devoted to principles of word formation. In order to contrast German structures with corresponding English structures, we have spent much time analyzing English usage from a German point of view. We want to call attention to those features of English that differ from German, and are therefore a significant cause of error.

The broad coverage of the analysis section reflects our desire to avoid unidiomatic German. This should not detract from the fact, however, that the major building blocks of German grammar have received the greatest emphasis. Some important grammatical categories, for example the subjective use of modals or the relationship of tenses and time phrases, are not treated in other introductory grammars; some have been considered "too advanced" for the beginner. We firmly believe that these categories must be included in a beginning text, for without them the student cannot acquire a totally satisfactory knowledge of basic German.

EXERCISES are provided in addition to the variations in order to reinforce the student's control of each structural element. Their sequence is the same as that of the patterns and the analysis sections and they too are cross-referenced in the margins. Unlike the variations, however, the exercises should not be done until the student has thoroughly drilled and studied the corresponding patterns. We have intentionally included more exercises than most teachers will want to use, in order to save teachers the time-consuming effort of writing practice drills of their own.

A separate set of laboratory exercises appears in the Study Guide. These exercises are keyed to each unit; the student is given full instructions for these exercises, but their texts appear only in the Teacher's Manual. Thus their use is not restricted to the language laboratory; they can also be used for further oral drill in the classroom.

On the assumption that the only time students are *forced* to speak German is when they encounter a German speaker who knows no English, we have provided a number of situations in which the teacher is asked to play the role of a native German who, unaware of the extent of the students' knowledge, can test their ability to communicate to the utmost. Also, as the book progresses, we have added an increasing number of skeletal conversational materials for the student to flesh out, and finally, in the last few units, topics are suggested for discussions of a more substantive nature.

READING German is a major concern throughout the book. In contrast to earlier editions, many of the reading selections are not as closely tied to the grammatical topics of a unit as before, thereby allowing the students to push their reading comprehension at a faster pace. Some new literary selections have been added, and much of the new material, both in the reading and in the pattern sections, serves as an introduction to the contemporary culture of all German-speaking countries. All early reading selections are fully translated; later on, marginal glosses have been used.

WRITING should be practiced from the very beginning. At first the student should be encouraged simply to copy from the text. Dictations should be given regularly. A number of the lab exercises are dictations as well. In the second half of the book we have provided a number of structured compositions, based on the material of the conversations and the reading.

VOCABULARY study is essential to the successful completion of a German course. In the pattern sentences the vocabulary has purposely been restricted so that the student can concentrate on learning the sentences introduced; the conversations and reading selections provide most of the new words and phrases. All vocabulary is introduced in the context of whole sentences, and vocabulary should be *practiced* in context only. We do, however, recommend very strongly that the student memorize the "basic vocabulary" at the end of each unit. Less frequently used words and phrases appear under the heading "Additional Vocabulary."

ILLUSTRATIONS for this edition have been integrated into the text even more than before. We have favored posters, signs, and other material that show language in action in contrast to typical "tourist" pictures, devoid of any linguistic message.

THE STUDY GUIDE for the third edition contains not only lab exercises, but also a series of programmed exercises which should be used in conjunction with the study of the analysis. Through these exercises, the students can check their own progress as they study, and can use them for quick review. All answers to the programmed exercises are contained in the Study Guide. In addition, there are a number of tear-out exercises that can be assigned as homework and handed in, if the instructor so chooses. For each unit, the Study Guide also contains a summary of important grammatical points under the heading "Grammar in a Nutshell."

A TEACHER'S MANUAL is available which contains a number of detailed suggestions on how to teach individual parts of this book, outlines for typical lesson plans, and the scripts for all those lab exercises that do not appear in the printed text.

The Sounds of German

THROUGHOUT THIS BOOK, major emphasis is placed on the intonation of entire utterances, on the characteristic sound of whole German sentences. The pronunciation of the individual sounds that make up those complete sentences is dealt with only in this section. It is imperative that you practice these sounds, with the help of your teacher, and that you listen to the accompanying tapes until you have mastered the sounds. You should review this section frequently as you work your way through the book. After four weeks or four months you will find that this section on pronunciation may be even more useful to you than at the outset.

We have avoided all technical discussion of the German sounds; instead, we have provided a large number of contrastive drills to show the distinction between two or more different German sounds which, to the ear of an American student, very often sound alike when he first hears them. Many German sounds are sufficiently similar to English sounds so as not to cause the beginner great trouble. Our main concern will be those German sounds which either have no equivalent at all in English or tend to cause an American accent if pronounced like their English spelling equivalents. In many cases, an American accent will not make the German sound unintelligible (though you shouldn't take this as an excuse to retain an American accent); in some cases, however, the wrong pronunciation of certain sounds will produce unintended results. If you mispronounce the **ch**-sound in **Nacht**, as many Americans tend to do, you will not produce the German word for *night*, but the word **nackt**, which means *naked*.

Good pronunciation is essential if you want to speak German correctly and naturally. With patience and lots of practice, you should easily be able to overcome your initial difficulties. Don't worry about making mistakes at the beginning; you'll learn more from them than from not speaking at all.

German Vowels

German has long and short vowels, and diphthongs. The distinction between long and short vowels is very important, but unfortunately it is not always indicated by spelling. As a rule of thumb, however, you can assume that a vowel is short if it is followed by a double consonant (for example, **bitte**) or by two or more consonants (**binde**). German vowels are either quite long or very short.

In the following table, all German vowel sounds appear in words. On the tape, this is Pronunciation Drill 1. All the pronunciation drills in this section appear on tape. You should listen to them repeatedly and review them periodically. It is just as important, however, that you listen carefully to your instructor as he drills these exercises with you in class.

PRONUN- CIATION DRILL 1

	LONG	SHORT	UNSTRESSED ONLY
a	Saat	satt	
e	Beet	Bett	
/ə/*			-be (gebe)
/ʌ/*			-ber (Geber)
i	ihn	in	
o	Ofen	offen	
u	Buhle	Bulle	
ä	bäte		
ö	Höhle	Hölle	
ü	fühle	fülle	DIPHTHONGS
au			Baum
ei (ai)			kein (Kain)
eu (äu)			Heu (Häuser)

Note: The two dots over **ä, ö,** and **ü** are called Umlaut. Occasionally, especially in names, these sounds are spelled **ae, oe, ue.**

As the table shows, there are twenty different vowel sounds, of which two occur only in unstressed positions. These two are here represented by the symbols /ə/ and /ʌ/, which are not letters in the German alphabet, but are written as **-e** and **-er.**

All German vowels are "pure"; that is, they are monophthongs and do not have any diphthongal glide at the end as do the English letters *a* and *o*. As you hear the following examples, the difference will become clear.

PRONUN- CIATION DRILL 2

ENGLISH *a*	GERMAN LONG **e**		ENGLISH *o*	GERMAN LONG **o**
gay	geh		moan	Mohn
ray	Reh		tone	Ton
stay	steh		tote	tot
baited	betet		boat	Boot

Long **a** vs. short **a**

Many American students have real difficulty in hearing the difference between these two sounds and consequently have trouble pronouncing them. Yet very often the difference between long **a** and short **a** is the difference between two totally unrelated words, as the following examples show.

* We are using phonemic symbols here; in the alphabet /ə/ is **-e** and /ʌ/ is **-er.**

LONG a VS.	SHORT a
Saat (planting)	satt (satisfied)
rate (guess)	Ratte (rat)
Rabe (raven)	Rappe (black horse)
Wahn (insanity)	wann (when)
fahl (pale)	Fall (fall)
kam (came)	Kamm (comb)
Maße (measures)	Masse (mass)
Bahn (track)	Bann (ban)

Now say these words again, but stretch the long a sound. Instead of **Saat**, say **Saaaat,** etc. You cannot do this with the short a: if you stretch the words in the second column, you have to stretch the consonant; for example, **Kamm** will become **Kammmm.**

Long e, long ä, short e and ä, unstressed e /ə/ and er /ʌ/

This group of vowel sounds will need your special attention.

Remember that the long **e**, like all other vowels, does not end in a glide: **geh,** not *gay.*

Some Germans do not really distinguish long ä from long **e**, except where there is a difference in meaning, for example, in **Gräte** (fishbone) vs. **Grete** (the girl's name Greta).

Short **e** and short **ä** represent the same sound: the **e** in **Kette** is indistinguishable from the **ä** in **hätte.**

The unstressed /ə/ occurs most frequently in endings and in prefixes; it is quite similar to the unstressed English *a* in *the sofa.* If /ə/ appears in front of final -n, it often all but disappears; thus **nennen** sounds like **nenn'n** and **kommen** like **komm'n.** These forms are hard to hear and hard to distinguish from forms without the -en ending. Yet very often it is essential to realize the distinction, as in **ihn** vs. **ihn(e)n, den** vs. **den(e)n.**

The unstressed /ʌ/, which is written as **er,** is one of the most difficult sounds for most Americans to produce. At first, you will have difficulty hearing the difference between /ə/ and /ʌ/, but the distinction is there and may be crucial, as in **bitte** (*please*) vs. **bitter** (*bitter*).

The following drills are designed to show you the differences between the various sounds of this group.

LONG e VS.	SHORT e		LONG e VS.	SHORT e
Beet	Bett		wen	wenn
Wesen	wessen		den	denn
reden	retten		stehen	stellen

Note again that short **e** and **ä** represent the same sound:

PRONUN-CIATION DRILL 5

SHORT e	VS.	SHORT ä
Wetter		Blätter
kenne		sänne
hemme		Kämme
Schwemme		Schwämme

PRONUN-CIATION DRILL 6

LONG ä	VS.	LONG e	VS.	SHORT e OR ä
Gräte		Grete		rette
Ähren		ehren		Herren
bäte		bete		bette
wähne		Vene		Wände

PRONUN-CIATION DRILL 7

/ə/	VS.	/ʌ/		/ə/	VS.	/ʌ/
bete		Beter		gute		guter
Rede		Reeder		Güte		Güter
nehme		Nehmer		Liebe		Lieber
gebe		Geber		Spitze		Spitzer
Esse		Esser		Pfarre		Pfarrer
Messe		Messer				
Summe		Summer		gehören		(erhören)
Hüte		Hüter		gearbeitet		(erarbeitet)
führe		Führer		gegessen		vergessen
Kutte		Kutter		gestört		zerstört

Long i and ü, short i and ü, long and short u

The two i-sounds are not very difficult to produce. They resemble the English vowel sounds in *bean* and *bin*.

The ü-sound, on the other hand, does not exist in English. To produce it, say **i** (as in English *key*); then freeze your tongue in that position and round your lips; or, to put it another way, say English *ee* with your lips in the English *oo* position. If you are musical and can get B above C above middle C on a piano, whistle it, and your tongue and lips will be in perfect ü-position. The letter y, which occurs mostly in foreign words, is usually pronounced like **ü**.

The long u-sound is similar to English *oo* in *noon;* the short u-sound is—to oversimplify matters a bit—just a very short version of the same English *oo*-sound, but again both sounds are much more clearly articulated in German.

LONG i	vs.	SHORT i			PRONUN-CIATION DRILL 8
Miéte		Mitte			
biete		Bitte			
riete		ritte			
ihnen		innen			

LONG i	vs.	LONG ü (y)			PRONUN-CIATION DRILL 9
Miete		mühte			
Miete		Mythe			
Kiel		kühl			
schiebe		Schübe			
Stiele		Stühle			

SHORT i	vs.	SHORT ü	SHORT i	vs.	SHORT ü	PRONUN-CIATION DRILL 10
Kissen		küssen	Liste		Lüste	
missen		müssen	Gericht		Gerücht	
sticken		Stücken	springe		Sprünge	
Bitte		Bütte	Kiste		Küste	

LONG ü	vs.	SHORT ü	LONG ü	vs.	SHORT ü	PRONUN-CIATION DRILL 11
Hüte		Hütte	Wüste		wüßte	
rügen		rücken	Düne		dünne	
pflügen		pflücken	Füßen		Füssen	
kühnste		Künste	fühle		Fülle	

LONG u	vs.	SHORT u	LONG u	vs.	SHORT u	PRONUN-CIATION DRILL 12
Mus		muß	schuf		Schuft	
Ruhm		Rum	spuken		spucken	
sucht		Sucht	Buhle		Bulle	
Fuder		Futter	Buße		Busse	

LONG u	vs.	LONG ü	LONG u	vs.	LONG ü	PRONUN-CIATION DRILL 13
Mut		Mythe	Schub		Schübe	
Hut		Hüte	tuten		Tüten	
gut		Güte	Huhn		Hühner	
Schwur		Schwüre	Kuhle		Kühle	

SHORT u	vs.	SHORT ü	SHORT u	vs.	SHORT ü	PRONUN-CIATION DRILL 14
Mutter		Mütter	mußte		müßte	
Kunst		Künste	wußte		wüßte	
durfte		dürfte	Bund		Bünde	
kurze		Kürze	Luft		Lüfte	

Long and short o, long and short ö

Remember that the German o-sound does not end in a glide toward **u:**
Mohn, not *moan.* To produce an **ö,** say a long German **e,** then freeze your
tongue and round your lips. Note also the clear distinction between German
a and German **o.** An American would be likely not to distinguish between
Bann, Bahn, and **Bonn,** but the three sounds are clearly different.

PRONUN-CIATION DRILL 15	LONG o	VS.	SHORT o
	wohne		Wonne
	Schote		Schotter
	Ton		Tonne
	Lote		Lotte

PRONUN-CIATION DRILL 16	SHORT o	VS.	LONG a	VS.	SHORT a
	Bonn		Bahn		Bann
	komm		kam		Kamm
	Sonne		Sahne		Susanne
	hoffen		Hafen		haften
	Schollen		Schalen		schallen
	locken		Laken		Schlacken
	ob		gab		ab

PRONUN-CIATION DRILL 17	LONG e	VS.	LONG ö
	redlich		rötlich
	heben		höben
	bete		böte
	lege		löge

PRONUN-CIATION DRILL 18	LONG o	VS.	LONG ö
	Ton		Töne
	Lohn		Löhne
	Hof		Höfe
	Not		Nöte
	Bogen		Bögen

PRONUN-CIATION DRILL 19	SHORT e	VS.	SHORT ö
	stecken		Stöcken
	Recke		Röcke
	westlich		östlich
	helle		Hölle

LONG ö	VS.	SHORT ö
Goethe		Götter
Schöße		schösse
Öfen		öffnen
Höhle		Hölle

LONG ö	VS.	LONG ü	VS.	LONG i
Söhne		Sühne		Kusine
löge		Lüge		liege
Öl		kühl		Kiel
schöbe		Schübe		schiebe

SHORT ö	VS.	SHORT ü
Stöcke		Stücke
schösse		Schüsse
Röcken		Rücken
Hölle		Hülle

SHORT u	VS.	SHORT ü	VS.	SHORT i
mußte		müßte		mißte
Stuck		Stück		Stickstoff
Kummer		Kümmel		Kimme
Kunde		künde		Kinder

Diphthongs

There are three German diphthongs, two of which can be spelled in two different ways: **ei (ai)**, **eu (äu)**, and **au**. They will not present much of a problem. They are similar to *i* in English *light,* *oi* in English *foible,* and *ou* in English *mouse,* but, like all German vowels, they are more precise, more clearly defined, and not as drawn-out as their English counterparts.

ei (ai)	eu (äu)	au
leiten	läuten	lauten
freien	freuen	Frauen
zeigen	zeugen	saugen
leise	Läuse	Laus
Meise	Mäuse	Maus

You will be bothered by the fact that the combination **ei** represents a diphthong, but the combination **ie** is simply a long **i**. The following drill should help you overcome this difficulty. To keep the two sounds straight, think of the English phrase *The hEIght of my nIEce* or of the German phrase **wEIn und bIEr.**

ei	vs.	ie		ei	vs.	ie
meine		Miene		Zeit		zieht
deine		diene		bereiten		berieten
leider		Lieder		keimen		Kiemen
reimen		Riemen		verzeihen		verziehen

Read the following words, distinguishing carefully between **ei** and **ie**:

Viel, Kleid, sieben, Liebe, Leib, leider, Lieder, Seife, siegen, zeigen, liegen, schieben, scheiden, Tier, einheitlich, einseifen, einfrieren, vierseitig, Bierseidel, Zeitspiegel, Spieglein, Meineid, Kleinigkeit.

Vielerlei aus einem Ei

German Consonants

In presenting the German vowel system, we have, of necessity, had to use almost all German consonant sounds. As you worked through the preceding section, you doubtless noticed that some German consonants, such as **m** and **n**, differ hardly at all from their English equivalents. Others, such as **z**, have probably surprised you because they are not pronounced the way you expected them to sound. The combination of sounds represented by German **z**, however, does exist in English: if you can say *cats* in English, you should be able to say "Tsoh" in German, even though it is spelled **Zoo.**

There are only two consonant sounds in German which have no equivalent in English; they are both graphically represented by **ch**. The following notes and drills will introduce the German consonants and show you where you will encounter difficulties. We shall start with the two **ch**-sounds.

ch after **a, o, u, au**

This sound is relatively easy for Americans to produce; it corresponds to the **ch** in the Scottish word *loch*. To produce it, start with the sound **h**, let the air flow freely, and then, without diminishing the air flow, reduce the space between the back of your tongue and the roof of your mouth.

Most Americans tend to substitute a *k* for this **ch**-sound. The following drill will show you the difference. Note that the vowels preceding the **ch** are sometimes long and sometimes short.

LONG VOWEL	SHORT VOWEL	DIPHTHONG	
nach	Bach	auch	PRONUN-CIATION DRILL 26
hoch	noch	Lauch	
Buch	Bruch	Bauch	

k	vs.	ch	k	vs.	ch	
nackt		Nacht	Kokken		kochen	PRONUN-CIATION DRILL 27
Akt		acht	Pocken		pochen	
Laken		lachen	zuckt		Zucht	
lockt		locht	pauken		brauchen	
dockt		Docht				

ch in combination with other letters; **chs**

For most Americans, this is the most difficult German consonant to produce. There are several ways of learning how to produce it. Say the English word *you* with an extended *y: y-y-y-you*. This *y* is a voiced sound; if you take the voice out of it, you'll produce something very close to this second **ch**-sound. (You can figure out the difference between a voiced and an unvoiced consonant by comparing the *s*-sounds in English *see* and *zee* (the letter *z*) or *Sioux* and *Zoo*.) Another way of getting at this second German **ch** is by starting with a word like *Hubert* or *huge*. Strongly aspirate the *h* and stretch it out: *h-h-huge;* the result will be quite similar to the **ch**-sound. Try the following combinations:

a human
say Hugh
the hue
see Hubert

PRONUN-CIATION DRILL 28

Again, you must be careful not to substitute *k* for **ch**:

k	vs.	ch	k	vs.	ch	
Bäcker		Becher	siegt		Sicht	PRONUN-CIATION DRILL 29
Leck		Lech	nickt		nicht	
schleckt		schlecht	Brücke		Brüche	
häkeln		hecheln				

The following drill contrasts the two **ch**-sounds. The words in the second column are the plurals of the words in the first column.

PRONUN-CIATION DRILL 30

Dach	Dächer		Buch	Bücher
Bach	Bäche		Bruch	Brüche
Loch	Löcher		Brauch	Bräuche

In the following drill, the **ch**-sound occurs after consonants.

PRONUN-CIATION DRILL 31

München	solcher
mancher	Milch
welcher	Furcht

Another difficulty arises when the **ch**-sound appears initially, as in the suffix **-chen**. Note that if the preceding consonant is an **s** or **sch**-sound, the **ch** in **-chen** is pronounced almost like an English *y*.

PRONUN-CIATION DRILL 32

Männchen	bißchen
Frauchen	Häuschen
Säckchen	Tischchen

Finally, the combination **chs** is pronounced like English *x*.

PRONUN-CIATION DRILL 33

sechs	Sachsen
Luchs	wachsen
Lachs	Büchse

b, d, g and p, t, k; pf, ps, ng, kn

You will have no trouble pronouncing these sounds, but there is one area where you must watch out: if **b, d, g** appear at the end of a syllable or in front of **t**, they are pronounced like **p, t, k.** In the following drill, the German words are not translations of the English words.

PRONUN-CIATION DRILL 34

ENGLISH *b, d, g*	vs.	GERMAN **b, d, g**
glib		gib
glide		Kleid
lied		Leid
lead		Lied
bug		Bug

Compare the pronunciation of **b, d, g** in the following two columns:

PRONUN-CIATION DRILL 35

b, d, g	vs.	p, t, k	b, d, g	vs.	p, t, k
lieben		lieb, liebt	kriegen		Krieg, kriegt
heben		hob, hebt	fliegen		flog, fliegt
sieben		Sieb, siebt	lügen		log, lügt

b, d, g	vs.	p, t, k		b, d, g	vs.	p, t, k
Abend		ab		beobachten		Obdach
loben		Lob, lobt		aber		abfahren
leiden		Leid		radeln		Radfahrer
Lieder		Lied		Tage		täglich
baden		Bad		sagen		unsagbar
Süden		Süd				

Now read the following words:

Bad Soden, Abendland, wegheben, abheben, Aberglaube, Staubwedel, Abwege, Feldweg, Feldwege, Waldwege, Laubwald, Laubwälder.

The **p** in the combinations **pf** and initial **ps** is always pronounced; the latter occurs only in foreign words:

PRONUN-
CIATION
DRILL 36

Pfeife	Psychologie
Pfarrer	Psychiater
hüpfen	Psalm
Köpfe	Pseudonym
Topf	
Napf	

The combination **ng** is pronounced as in English *singer,* not as in *finger.*

PRONUN-
CIATION
DRILL 37

Finger	lange
Sänger	England
Ringe	

The **k** in **kn** must be pronounced.

PRONUN-
CIATION
DRILL 38

ENGLISH	GERMAN	ENGLISH	GERMAN
knave	**Knabe**	knee	**Knie**
knack	**knacken**	knight	**Knecht**
knead	**kneten**	knob	**Knopf**

z

The German letter **z** represents the combination **ts,** which, in English, does not occur at the beginning of words. To learn to produce it in initial position start with the English word *cats;* say it again, but make a break between *ca-* and *-ts.* Then do the same with *Betsy: Be/tsy.* If you only say *tsy,* you almost have the first syllable of the German word **Ziege.**

PRONUN-
CIATION
DRILL 39

INITIAL	MEDIAL	FINAL
ziehen	heizen	Kranz
zog	duzen	Pfalz
gezogen	geizig	Salz

INITIAL	MEDIAL	FINAL
zu	Lanze	Kreuz
Zug	Kanzel	Malz
Züge	Kerze	Pelz
Zahn	Kreuzung	stolz

However, if it occurs in the middle or at the end of a word, the ts-sound is usually represented by **tz**.

Katze	Platz
putzen	Fritz
sitzen	

s, ß, sp, st, sch

German **s** does not present much of a problem. It is neither as strongly voiceless as the English *s*-sound as in *see* nor as strongly voiced as the *s*-sound as in *zoo*.

INITIAL	MEDIAL	FINAL
so	lesen	das
sie	blasen	los
sagen	gewesen	Glas
sicher	Käse	Mus

The *s*-sound may be represented by the symbol **ß** (instead of **ss**). It is called an **s-z** (**ess-zet**) and is used:

(a) between two vowels of which the first is long:

LONG VOWEL + ß	SHORT VOWEL + ss
Maße	Masse
Buße	Busse
Straße	Rasse
große	Rosse

(b) after a vowel or a diphthong before a consonant (mostly in verbs whose stem ends in **-ss**):

weißt	paßt
mußt	heißt

(c) in final position:

Fuß	weiß
Roß	daß

Many Germans no longer use the ß symbol, but write ss instead.

The s in German **sp** and **st** at the beginning is pronounced like English *sh*.

Spaß	Start	Strand
Sport	stehen	Strom
spät	still	streng
Spinne	Stock	streichen
Spule	Stück	streuen

PRONUN-
CIATION
DRILL 43

German **sch** is pronounced like English *sh*.

schön
waschen
Busch

PRONUN-
CIATION
DRILL 44

sch	vs.	ch
Tisch		dich
mischen		mich
Esche		Echo
Büsche		Bücher

w, v, f

There is no German equivalent of the English *w*-sound as in *water*. German w is pronounced like English *v*.

wann	wie
wer	warum
wo	

PRONUN-
CIATION
DRILL 45

German v is usually pronounced like English *f*.

Vater	voll
verliebt	von
viel	

In some foreign words, German v corresponds to English *v*.

Vase
Villa

German f always corresponds to English *f*, as does the *ph*-sound in foreign words.

fallen	fünf
Fell	Philosophie
fliegen	Physik

w	vs.	f	w	vs.	f
Wein		fein	Wort		fort
Wand		fand	Wunde		Funde
winden		finden			

l and r

These two consonants are mispronounced by most Americans. Such mispronunciations will not normally lead to a misunderstanding, but they do in large measure contribute to a "typical American accent." Constant practice with these two consonants is therefore essential.

The English *l* is a "dark," back *l,* and the German l is a "clear," front l. Listen to the difference:

PRONUN-CIATION DRILL 46

ENGLISH *l*	vs.	GERMAN l	ENGLISH *l*	vs.	GERMAN l
feel		viel	hell		hell
stool		Stuhl	lewd		lud
mall		Mal	light		Leid
fall		Fall	long		lang
toll		toll	bald		bald
still		still	built		Bild

In some parts of Germany, the **r** is trilled, but the preferred sound is a uvular **r.** To produce it, say **Buchen,** with the **ch**-sound as far back as possible. Then add voice to it and you should be saying **Buren.**

PRONUN-CIATION DRILL 47

ENGLISH *r*	vs.	GERMAN r	ENGLISH *r*	vs.	GERMAN r
run		ran	fry		frei
rudder		Ruder	fresh		frisch
reef		rief	creek		Krieg
rest		Rest	warn		warnen
ray		Reh	start		Start
row		roh	stork		Storch
brown		braun	worst		Wurst
dry		drei			

We introduced the **er**-sound (ʌ) under the vowels. Many Germans use this same sound for **r** before **t.**

PRONUN-CIATION DRILL 48

er fährt   er bohrt   er knurrt
er lehrt   er irrt

INITIAL r	r AFTER CONSONANT	MEDIAL r	r BEFORE t	FINAL r (ʌ)
raffen	graben	fahren	fahrt	fahr'
Rebe	Bregenz	Beeren	fährt	Bär
riefen	Friesen	vieren	viert	vier
rot	Thron*	Toren	bohrt	Tor
Ruhe	Bruder	Uhren	fuhrt	Uhr

PRONUN-
CIATION
DRILL 49

ch	vs.	r		ch	vs.	r
Buchen		Buren		Sucht		surrt
suchen		Suren		Dach		dar
fachen		fahren		Loch		Lohr
Acht		Art		Tuch		Tour
Docht		dort				

PRONUN-
CIATION
DRILL 50

l	vs.	r		l	vs.	r
wild		wird		Spalt		spart
Geld		Gert		spülen		spüren
halt		hart		fühlen		führen
hold		Hort		fallen		fahren
bald		Bart		tollen		Toren

PRONUN-
CIATION
DRILL 51

h

At the beginning of a word or syllable, **h** is pronounced as in English *house*. It is never silent as in English *honor*. The symbol **h,** however, is also used to indicate that the preceding vowel is long.

sehen	seht	steh'
fehlen	fehlt	geh'
Lehrer	lehrt	Reh

PRONUN-
CIATION
DRILL 52

q

As in English, **q** appears only with a following **u,** but it is pronounced like English *kv*, not *kw*.

ENGLISH	GERMAN
quicksilver	Quecksilber
quadrant	Quadrant
Quaker	Quäker
qualify	qualifizieren
quality	Qualität
quarter	Quartier

PRONUN-
CIATION
DRILL 53

* The combination **th,** which occurs in a few German words, is always pronounced as **t:** English *throne*, German **Thron.**

j

This letter is pronounced like English *y*.

ENGLISH	GERMAN
yes	ja
year	Jahr
young	jung
youth	Jugend
yacht	Jacht
yoke	Joch

The Glottal Stop

The glottal stop is a phenomenon much more common in German than in English. In certain parts of the eastern United States, the word *bottle* is pronounced *bo-'l* with a very short open *o*, after which the glottis is closed and then suddenly reopened. This sudden release of air occurs in German in front of all initial vowels: **ein alter Affe.** Most Americans tend to run these words together: **[einalteraffe]**; this is another contributory factor in a "typical American accent." If you neglect to use the glottal stop, you may get yourself into embarrassing situations. For instance, if you don't use the stop in front of -'au, you will interpret the name of the village of **Himmelsau** as *Celestial Pig* instead of *Heavenly Meadow.*

ein alter Affe	**alle anderen Uhren**
Himmelsau	**es erübrigt sich**
der erste Akt	**es ist aber veraltet**
ein alter Omnibus	**eine alte Eule sitzt unter einer alten Ulme**
er aber aß Austern	

Note the difference in

vereisen (*to get covered with ice*)   and   **verreisen** (*to go on a trip*)
verengen (*to narrow*)   **verrenken** (*to sprain*)

Sentence Intonation

Since sentence intonation is closely connected with syntax, it is dealt with in various units of this book, as new syntactical patterns are introduced. A few prefatory remarks, however, are in order, to explain the symbols used in the intonation graphs.

Like English, German is spoken on three basic levels of pitch; these levels are indicated by three horizontal lines:

Unstressed syllables are indicated by dots (•), stressed syllables by short lines with a stress mark (∕). Thus the English sentence *He lives in Munich* would be diagrammed as follows:

He   lives   in   Munich

If this same sentence is spoken as a question, the last syllable, though un-stressed, shows a rise in pitch. This rise is indicated by the symbol (♪). If the last syllable is stressed, rising pitch is indicated by (∕) and falling pitch by (∕).

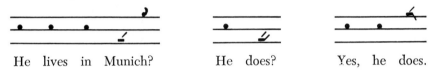

He   lives   in   Munich?   He   does?   Yes,   he   does.

Syllabication

German syllabication is considerably simpler than English syllabication. A few basic rules will suffice to see you through this book.

German words are divided before single consonants and between double consonants.

Va - ter   kom - men
Da - me   reg - nen
Te - le - fon   Mün - chen

The only exception to this rule is st, which is never separated.

fe - ster
mei - stens
Fen - ster

Unlike English, German does not consider suffixes independent units; thus it is **Woh - nung**, not [**Wohn - ung**].

Compound words are divided according to their individual parts.

Brief - trä - ger
Glas - au - ge
Sams - tag

Punctuation

Generally speaking, most German punctuation marks are used as in English. Only the use of the comma is different. The comma may be used to separate main clauses if the second clause contains a new subject, especially in front of coordinating conjunctions. The comma *must* be used to separate dependent clauses from main clauses. Relative clauses are dependent clauses, and German does not distinguish between restrictive and nonrestrictive relative clauses. In contrast to English, the comma is not used in front of **und** in series: **Männer, Frauen und Kinder.**

The first of a pair of quotation marks in German appears below the base line in writing or printing, the second appears at the top: "Be quiet!" „**Sei ruhig!**"

Third Edition

GERMAN
A STRUCTURAL APPROACH

UNIT 1 Personal Pronouns—The Present Tense of Verbs—Basic Sentence Structure—Sentence Intonation

The German language has existed in written form for over a thousand years—though its earliest documents are as different from modern German as the language of *Beowulf* is from that of James Joyce or Art Buchwald. Today, German is spoken by over one hundred million people, some scattered all over the globe, but most living in an area that is best described as Central Europe.

The German language area is not identified with, nor identical to, a single nation state. German is spoken in five different countries: the tiny principality of Liechtenstein, Austria, the German-speaking parts of Switzerland, and the two states into which Germany was divided after the Second World War: the Federal Republic of Germany (West Germany; Bundesrepublik Deutschland, or BRD for short) and the German Democratic Republic (East Germany; Deutsche Demokratische Republik, or DDR).*

While there are many differences between these countries in their political and economic systems, in regional customs and local dialects, they are still all bound together by one common element, the German language. This German language is not so far removed from English as it might appear. Deriving from the same Proto-Germanic ancestor two thousand years ago, German and English are rather closely related, as becomes obvious when you compare such pairs of words as English *winter* and German **Winter,** or English *summer* and German **Sommer.** You will find that English *father* corresponds to German **Vater,** *mother* to **Mutter,** *ship* to **Schiff,** *come* to **kommen,** *green* to **grün.**

The existence of all these cognates, that is, of words that have the same origin, does not mean that, in order to produce a German sentence, you simply replace each English word by its German equivalent. There are major, and crucial, differences in the structure and the vocabulary of the two languages. Germans order their words quite differently into sentences. For example, a German will express the idea "I went to the movies last night" by the seemingly outlandish "I am yesterday evening to the movies gone." Thus you should not think in terms of "What is the word in German for X?" but rather, "How does German convey the idea of X or the feeling of X?" Each language has a unique way of dividing up experience, and these divisions find their expression in words and phrases. Frequently, perfectly commonplace words in German will strike you as quaint or amusing, such as the word for *thimble*, **Fingerhut** (*finger hat*), or for *glove*, **Handschuh** (*hand shoe*), but they are really quite accurate names for the things they represent.

---

*See map on end papers.

1

The same is true of idiomatic expressions, that is, of turns of phrase that are peculiar to a given language: expressions that are often metaphorical (*He kicked the bucket*), euphemistic (*He passed away*), or just plain idiosyncratic (*How are you doing?*). In some cases, German uses the same idiom, but usually Germans will use completely different expressions.

In this first unit, you will discover that a people's customs and social conventions are often mirrored in their language. Germans, for example, must differentiate their relations with one another by choosing from among three different pronouns of address, **du, ihr,** and **Sie,** all of which correspond to English *you.* Also, Germans, and especially Austrians, use titles much more frequently than Americans, and a letter addressed to "Herrn Prof. Dr. Hans Schmidt" does not raise any eyebrows.

Small talk is the same all over the world. People talk about the weather, their health, food, and drink; they step on each other's toes—literally and otherwise —and have to apologize. German has its own stereotyped phrases for such basic social intercourse, and you will learn some of these in this unit. Try to use this small talk with your fellow students, in class and outside. Don't be shy about making mistakes; you won't be able to speak German until you have made a good number of mistakes. Just talk, and above all talk with as strong a German accent as you can, because that is precisely how Germans speak German.

Patterns

[1] Personal Pronouns and the Present Tense of Verbs

Practice and read aloud the following sentences until you have memorized them. Then restate all sentences of the first group, except **Es regnet,** starting with each of the personal pronouns; change endings accordingly.

SEE
ANALYSIS
1-7
(pp. 7-10)

Ich	wohne	hier.	I live here.
Du	trinkst	Bier.	You drink beer. You are drinking beer.
Er	geht	nach Berlin.	He goes to Berlin. He is going to Berlin.
Sie	kommt	heute.	She is coming today.
Es	regnet.		It is raining.
Wir	lernen	Deutsch.	We are learning German.
Ihr	studiert	Medizin.	You are studying medicine.
Sie	bleiben	zu Hause.	They stay at home. They are staying at home.
Ich	bin	Hans Schmidt.	I am Hans Schmidt.
Du	bist	zu Hause.	You are at home.
Er	ist	Lehrer.	He is a teacher.
Sie	ist	Ärztin.	She is a doctor.
Es	ist	kalt.	It is cold.
Wir	sind	in Köln.	We are in Cologne.
Ihr	seid	in München.	You are in Munich.
Sie	sind	hier.	They are here.

[2] Assertions: Basic Intonation Pattern

Practice and read aloud the following sentences until you have mastered the intonation pattern.

| Intonation sample: | Es *regnet.* |

Er *wohnt* hier.   He lives here.
Sie *kommt* schon.   There she comes.
Sie *trinken.*   They are drinking.
Es *regnet.*   It is raining.

SEE
ANALYSIS
8, 10–12
(pp. 11, 13–14)

[3] Assertions: Enlarged Pattern

| Intonation sample: | Das ist Fritz *Müller.* |

After you have studied the sentences, cover up the print and repeat the sentences from memory as you look at the pictures.

Das ist Erika *Mü*ller.
  This is Erika Müller.

Erika ist heute zu *Hau*se.
  Erika is at home today.

Sie trinkt *Kaf*fee.
  She is drinking coffee.

Das ist *Fritz* Müller.
  This is Fritz Müller.

Fritz ist *auch* zu Hause.
  Fritz is at home too.

Er liest die *Zei*tung.
  He is reading the paper.

SEE
ANALYSIS
9, 12
(pp. 11,14)

[4] Assertions: Syntactical Stress on Last Syllable

Intonation sample: ● ● ●   Er ist in *Köln.*

SEE
ANALYSIS
12
(p. 14)

Das ist *Milch.*   This is *milk.*
    Wein.   *wine.*
    Bier.   *beer.*
    Tee.   *tea.*

Der Mann trinkt *Bier.*   Sie lernt *Deutsch.*
Er _____ _____.   She is learning *German.*
Die Frau _____ _____.   Er _____ *auch* Deutsch.
Sie trinken _____ und _____.   *He* is learning German *too.*
                                               Sie _____ *beide* _____.
                                                   They are *both* learning German.

Das Wetter ist *gut.*   Das Wetter ist *schlecht.*
    The weather is good.   The weather is bad.
Es ist *warm* (*heiß*).   Es ist *kalt.*
    It is warm (hot).   It is cold.

[5] Assertions: Syntactical Stress on First Syllable

Intonation sample: 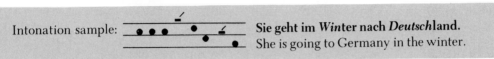 *Fritz* ist schon hier.
Fritz is here already.

SEE ANALYSIS 12 (p. 14)

Hans kommt. Hans is coming.
Erika ist hier. Erika is here.

[6] Syntactical Stress on More than One Syllable

Intonation sample: 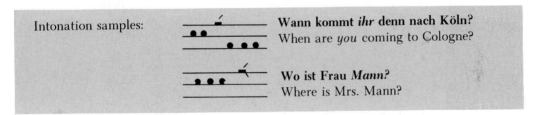 Sie geht im *Winter* nach *Deutsch*land.
She is going to Germany in the winter.

Fritz und Erika *Müller* wohnen in *Köln*. Fritz and Erika Müller live in Cologne.
Herr *Mey*er bleibt heute zu *Hause*. Mr. Meyer is staying at home today.
Peter studiert *Deutsch* und Psycholo*gie*.* Peter is studying German and psychology.
Erika studiert Medi*zin*. Erika is studying medicine.

SEE ANALYSIS 12 (p. 14)

[7] Word Questions

Intonation samples: Wann kommt *ihr* denn nach Köln?
When are *you* coming to Cologne?

Wo ist Frau *Mann?*
Where is Mrs. Mann?

Wie *heißen* Sie, bitte? What's your name, please?
—Ich heiße *Müller*. —My name is Müller.
Wie *heißt* du denn? What's your name?
—Ich heiße *Erika* —My name is Erika.
Was *ist* das? What is that?
—Das ist *Kaf*fee. —That's coffee.
Wer *ist* das denn? Who is that?
—Das ist Fritz Müller. —That's Fritz Müller.
Wo *wohnt* er denn? Where does he *live?*
—Er wohnt in *Köln*. —He lives in *Cologne*.

SEE ANALYSIS 13-14 (pp. 16-17)

*Some English words are spelled with an initial ps-, but drop the p when pronounced; in German, however, both the **p** and the **s** are sounded. Try to say *harpsichord* without the initial *har-*, and you get the **ps-** of **Psychologie.**

Wann kommt er denn nach *Hause?*   When is he coming *home?*
—Um *eins.*   —At one o'*clock.*
—Um ein *Uhr.*
Wann kommt *sie* denn nach *Hause?*   When is *she* coming home?
—Um *zwei.*   —At *two* o'clock.
—Um *zwei* Uhr.

[8] Yes-or-No Questions

Ist Frau *Bertram* schon hier?
Is Mrs. Bertram here already?

Bist du al*lein?*
Are you alone?

SEE
ANALYSIS
13-14
(pp. 16-17)

Ist Hans heute zu Hause?   Ja, er ist heute zu Hause.
Ist er heute zu Hause?   (Nein, er ist morgen zu Hause.)

Wohnt Peter in Hamburg?   Ja, er wohnt in Hamburg.
Wohnt er in Hamburg?   (Nein, er wohnt in Berlin.)

Ist Inge Ärztin?   Ja, sie ist Ärztin.
Ist sie Ärztin?   (Nein, sie ist Lehrerin.)

Lernt Anna jetzt Deutsch?   Ja, sie lernt jetzt Deutsch.
Lernt sie jetzt Deutsch?   (Nein, sie lernt jetzt Englisch.)

Ist das Wetter gut?   Ja, das Wetter ist gut.
                                           (Nein, das Wetter ist schlecht.)

Ist es heute warm?   Ja, es ist heute warm.
                                           (Nein, es ist heute kalt.)

Sind Hans und Inge hier?   Ja, sie sind hier.
Sind sie hier?   (Nein, sie sind zu Hause.)

Kommen Peter und Anna heute?   Ja, um ein Uhr.
Kommen sie heute?   (Nein, morgen.)
                                           Ja, sie kommen heute.
                                           (Nein, sie kommen morgen.)

[9] Assertions Intonated as Questions

Intonation sample:

Du wohnst *auch* in München?
You are living in Munich too?

Read the questions aloud, then supply answers starting with "**Ja, . . .**" or "**Nein, . . .**"

> **Sie wohnen *auch* in München?**
> **Ja, ich wohne *auch* in München.**
> **Nein, ich wohne in *Köln*.**

Sie studieren Psycholo*gie*, Fräulein *Müller*?

_____

Ihr *ar*beitet heute?

_____

Du trinkst *Kaf*fee?

_____

Erika ist heute in *Stutt*gart?

_____

Erika ist *heu*te in Stuttgart?

_____

*E*rika ist heute in Stuttgart?

_____

SEE
ANALYSIS
13–14
(pp. 16–17)

[10] Brief Utterances without Verbs

Invent statements and questions to which the following brief utterances could be reactions. Note that these can follow various intonation patterns, depending on the number of syllables and the speaker's intention.

Ja.
Ja?

Danke.
Bitte.

Nach *Köln?*
In *Frank*furt.
Zu *Hause.*

Nein.
Nein?

Heute *a*bend.
*Mor*gen abend?

*Kaf*fee.
Tee?
Wein.

SEE
ANALYSIS
11–14
(pp. 13–17)

Analysis

1 Personal Pronouns

SINGULAR		PLURAL		
1.	**ich** I	1.	**wir**	we
2.	{**du** / **Sie**} you	2.	{**ihr** / **Sie**}	you
	er he			
3.	**sie** she	3.	**sie**	they
	es it			

English *you* : German **du, ihr, Sie**
_____

Modern English has just one form (*you*) for the second person. English *you* is both singular and plural, formal and informal. In German, there are three mutually exclusive forms:

1. **du** (corresponding to the archaic English *thou*) is the familiar singular. It expresses intimacy and is therefore used in the family and with close friends. It is also used with *all* children up to the age of about fourteen and with animals (pets). In recent years, the use of **du** has spread considerably, especially among young people. University students, for example, now commonly address each other with **du,** where only ten or fifteen years ago **Sie** was the accepted norm.

2. **ihr** is the plural of **du,** that is, it is used when speaking to two or more people whom one addresses individually by **du.**

3. **Sie** is used in speaking to all those one does not address by **du,** that is, the vast majority of people one comes in contact with. It *must* be used with anybody addressed as **Herr, Frau, Fräulein,** or with other titles. The more formal **Sie,** which is used whether addressing a single person or more than one, corresponds to the plural **sie** (*they*) and it takes the same verb form. When written, it is always capitalized.

Trinkst du Tee, Maria?	Do you drink tea, Mary?
Trinkst du Kaffee, Karl?	Do you drink coffee, Karl?
Trinkt ihr Milch, Kinder?	Do you drink milk, children?
Trinken Sie Bier, Frau Meyer?	Do you drink beer, Mrs. Meyer?
Trinken Sie Wein, Herr Doktor?	Do you drink wine, Dr. Meyer?

Beware!	[**Trinkst du Wein, Herr Meyer?**]	
Americanism!	[**Trinkst du Bier, Frau Meyer?**] *	DO NOT USE!

NOTE: Germans are fond of titles. If **Herr Meyer** has earned any kind of doctorate, he is addressed as **Herr Doktor** (no last name), and he is referred to as **Herr Dr. Meyer** or as **Dr. Meyer.**

Herr, Frau, Fräulein. Whereas someone addressed as **Herr Meyer** may be married or unmarried, **Frau Meyer** is ambiguous: it may mean **Mrs. Meyer** or **Ms. Meyer.** The choice of **Frau** vs. **Fräulein** used to be clear-cut: a **Frau** was married, a **Fräulein** was not, except that older unmarried women could elect to call themselves **Frau.** In recent years, that age limit has been lowered considerably so that today a single woman in her twenties may legitimately and properly be called **Frau Meyer,** the closest German has come to the American *Ms.*

_____

*Brackets are used to indicate unacceptable forms—either Germanisms in English or Americanisms in German.

2 The Infinitive

The *infinitive* is that form of the verb which is used as a dictionary entry. Thus the English forms *am*, *is*, and *was* are found in the dictionary under *be; bought* is found under *buy*; and *does* is found under *do*.

Most German infinitives end in **-en: arbeiten, bleiben.** The infinitives **sein, tun,** and certain others to be introduced later end in **-n.** That part of the verb which precedes the infinitive ending **-en** or **-n** is called the *stem*. Thus:

STEM	+	INFINITIVE ENDING	=	INFINITIVE
arbeit-		-en		arbeiten
bleib-		-en		bleiben
tu-		-n		tun

3 Inflected Verb Forms

The predicate verb of a sentence or a clause is always an *inflected* form—that is, a form modified by a personal ending. (With the exception of *-s*, as in *he lives*, all personal endings have been dropped in English.)

The present tense of regular verbs is formed as follows:

		PRONOUN	STEM	+	PERSONAL ENDING	=	INFLECTED FORM
SINGULAR	1.	ich	lern-		e		ich lerne
	2.	du	lern-		st		du lernst
		Sie	lern-		en		Sie lernen
	3.	er / sie / es	lern-		t		er / sie / es lernt
PLURAL	1.	wir	lern-		en		wir lernen
	2.	ihr	lern-		t		ihr lernt
		Sie	lern-		en		Sie lernen
	3.	sie	lern-		en		sie lernen

4 Absence of Progressive and Emphatic Forms in German

A native speaker of English will always differentiate between the *simple present* and the *progressive form*. The simple present usually expresses either a timeless fact:

Water boils at 100 °C

or some habitual attitude or activity:

She is usually funny.
He only smokes cigars.
I like science fiction.

Use of the progressive form, on the other hand, expresses the idea of "being in the middle of" a temporary activity. Thus, it would make no sense to say *I am liking science fiction*, but it *is* possible to say:

> The water is boiling.
> She is being funny again.
> He is smoking a cigar.

German cannot express the difference between *boils* and *is boiling* by verb forms. You should not "translate" *he is having, he is being, he is working* into German. Otherwise you will start by saying **er ist** . . . and end up with an Americanism. **Er arbeitet** means both *he works* and *he is working*, and **es regnet** means both *it rains* and *it is raining*.

German also has no emphatic form. It cannot express the difference between *I go* and *I do go* by different verb forms. Thus **er arbeitet** also expresses the notion *he does work*.

5 Future Meaning of Present-Tense Forms

Just as the progressive form *I am going* has a future meaning in *I am going to Germany next year*, so the present tense of German verbs frequently assumes a future meaning.

> **Morgen abend gehen wir ins Kino.**   We are going to the movies tomorrow night.

6 Variations in Personal Endings

In the case of **er lernt** or **er kommt**, the ending **-t** is easily pronounced and heard. However, in the case of such verbs as **arbeiten** and of all other verbs whose stems end in **-d** or **-t**, the vowel **-e-** is inserted between the stem and the endings **-st** and **-t** to make these endings clearly audible. For similar reasons (so that the second syllable of all forms of **regnen** starts with an **n-**), it is **es regnet**, not [**es regnt**].

NORMAL VERBS		VERBS WITH STEMS IN -d OR -t	
du	lernst	du	arbeitest
er		er	
sie }	lernt	sie }	arbeitet
es		es	
ihr	lernt	ihr	arbeitet

Since the infinitive **tun** ends in **-n** and not in **-en**, the **wir**-form and the **sie**-form also end in **-n: wir tun, sie tun.**

7 sein and haben

A few of the most frequently used German verbs are quite irregular. In this unit, we introduce **sein** (*to be*) and **haben** (*to have*). In the present tense, they are inflected as follows:

ich	bin
du	bist

er ⎫
sie ⎬ ist
es ⎭

wir	sind
ihr	seid
sie	sind
Sie	sind

ich	habe
du	hast

er ⎫
sie ⎬ hat
es ⎭

wir	haben
ihr	habt
sie	haben
Sie	haben

8 The Position of the Inflected Verb and of the Subject

In English assertions, the subject is usually position-fixed: it precedes the inflected verb. Some other elements may also precede the inflected verb, so that it may be the second, third, or even the fourth element in the sentence.

	She	*lives*	in Munich.
	She now	*lives*	in Munich.
Now	she	*lives*	in Munich.
Fortunately, she now		*lives*	in Munich.

In German, the inflected verb is always the second syntactical unit. There are no exceptions. This means that one cannot imitate the word order of the English sentences above and say:

Beware!   [Sie jetzt wohnt in München.]   DO NOT USE!
Americanism!   [Jetzt sie wohnt in München.]

A German verb can be preceded by the subject *or* by a time phrase, but not by the subject *and* a time phrase. The sentences

Jetzt wohnt sie in München
Morgen gehen wir ins Kino

where the subject *follows* the verb, are just as idiomatic as

Sie wohnt jetzt in München.
Wir gehen morgen ins Kino.

If pronoun subjects like **ich, er, wir** do not precede the inflected verb, they *must* follow it immediately. Noun subjects usually also follow directly after the inflected verb.

9 The Element in the Front Field

The area preceding the inflected verb is called the front field. A number of elements other than the subject can occupy the front field of German sentences, but some elements cannot. In order to determine which elements *can* appear in the front field, follow this rule of thumb.

Only those elements that can precede an *English* verb can also precede a German verb:

> Of course, we are going to the movies.
> By the way, we are going to the movies.
> Tonight we are going to the movies.

Thus, the German equivalents of *of course*, *by the way*, and *tonight* can be placed in the front field:

Natürlich
Übrigens⎫ **gehen wir ins Kino.**
Heute abend⎭

Phrases like these are *never* set off by a comma.

Conversely: Any syntactical element that cannot precede an *English* verb cannot normally precede a German verb either:

> [To the movies we are going tonight.]

What determines whether the subject or another element will occupy the front field? The choice is by no means arbitrary. For example, you cannot start a sentence with **In München** if you are answering the question

> **Wo ist Fritz heute?**

The answer must be

> **Fritz ist heute in München.**

But **In München** can stand in the front field if you ask someone **Was wissen Sie über München?** (*What do you know about Munich?*) The answer could be that well-known German drinking song, **In München steht ein *Hof*bräuhaus.** On

the other hand, the sentence **Das Hofbräuhaus steht in München** must be the answer to **Wo steht das Hofbräuhaus?**

If the question is **Wann gehst du ins Kino?** the answer could be **Ich gehe morgen *a*bend ins Kino.** But if you ask the more general question **Was machst du heute *a*bend?** then the answer could be **Heute abend gehe ich ins Kino.**

Rule of thumb: The element containing the answer to a question starting with question words like **wo** (*where*) and **wann** (*when*) does not appear in the front field, but follows the inflected verb. Very frequently, of course, the answer consists of only the specific information asked for rather than a complete sentence.

> **Wo seid ihr heute abend?**—**Zu *Hause*.**
> **Wir sind zu *Hause*.**
> **Heute abend sind wir zu *Hause*.**
> **Wir sind heute abend zu *Hause*.**

This rule does not apply to questions with **Wer** (*who*). Such questions ask for the subject of a sentence and can be answered in two ways:

> **Wer kommt morgen?**—***Fritz* kommt morgen.**
> **Morgen kommt *Fritz*.**

In both cases, the subject has the main stress.

10 Word Stress

Almost all simple (noncompound) German words stress the first syllable: **A'bend** (*evening*), **ar'beiten** (*to work*), **heu'te** (*today*). Words composed of two nouns stress the first noun much more strongly than the second: **Haus'frau** (*housewife*), **Haus'hund** (*house dog*), **Hun'dehaus** (*doghouse*). Words of non-German origin frequently do not stress the first syllable: **natür'lich, die Natur', studie'ren.** The vocabulary will indicate which syllable is stressed in these cases.

11 Syntactical Stress

Word Stress versus Syntactical Stress

If one analyzes the stress situation in a short sentence like

August wohnt in Berlin   Gus lives in Berlin

one can either look at the individual words as words, or one can look at the sentence as a whole.

Looking at the words **Au'gust** and **Berlin'**, we find that **Au'gust** is stressed on the first and **Berlin'** on the second syllable. This is a question of word stress. Word stress is fixed, and it is simply a mistake to say **August'** or **Ber'lin.** In fact, **Au'gust** is a personal name and **August'** is the name of a month.

Looking at the sentence as a whole—that is, as one single unit of thought—we find it ambiguous in its written form. The speaker may want to say:

1. *August* **wohnt in Berlin.**   *Gus* lives in Berlin.
2. **August** *wohnt* **in Berlin.**   Gus *lives* in Berlin.
3. **August wohnt in Ber***lin.*   Gus lives in *Berlin.*

The one written sentence turns out to be at least three spoken sentences, which are not interchangeable. Each of them is used in situations where the other two cannot be used.

In all three sentences, **August** is stressed on the first, and **Berlin** on the second syllable. But the stress on **Au'gust** in the first sentence above is so strong that, in comparison, the stress on **Berlin'** becomes insignificant. For in each sentence the speaker singles out at least one word into which he packs the major news value and upon which he therefore places such a strong emphasis that, as far as the sentence as a whole is concerned, all other syllables can be regarded as unstressed. Syntactical stress, by which the speaker distinguishes between important and unimportant words, overshadows word stress; and whereas word stress is fixed, syntactical stress can shift from one word to another, depending on which word is chosen by the speaker to be the important one in a certain situation. The stressed syllable of this important word is called the *stress point* of a sentence.

12 Intonation of Assertions

<u>The Basic Pattern</u>

As long as only one syllable of an assertion receives syntactical stress, this one syllable (the stress point) is also the syllable with the highest pitch.

Pitch in German (and English) is usually distributed over three levels, symbolized by the three lines below.* An assertion usually starts on level 2, moves up to level 3 for the stress point, and then falls to level 1. By using dots for the syllables without syntactical stress, and a short line with an accent over it for the stress point, the pitch distribution can be diagrammed as follows:

Sie   *wohnt*   **hier**   She   *lives*   here

<u>The Enlarged Pattern</u>

Depending on which syllable is selected by the speaker to assume the role of the stress point, the sentence **Erika wohnt in München** can be pronounced with

*For a full explanation of the symbols used in the intonation diagrams, see the introductory section on the sounds of German.

the following three intonations:

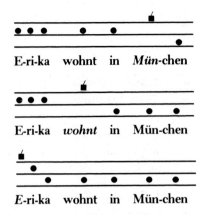

Erica lives in *Munich*.
(Question: Where does Erica *live?* or
Does Erica live in *Berlin?*)

Erica *lives* in Munich.
(Question: What's Erica doing in *Mu-nich?*)

Erica lives in Munich.
(Question: *Who* (did you say) lives in Munich?)

Observe that all the unstressed syllables preceding the stress point may be spoken with even level-2 pitch, and that all the unstressed syllables following the stress point show level-1 pitch.

Syntactical Stress on the Last Syllable

The drop from level 3 to level 1 functions as a signal meaning "This is the end of the sentence." This drop must therefore be maintained, even if the last syllable is the stress point. The last syllable itself must then show a downward glide.

Compare the difference between *No!* (↖) as an answer and *No?* (↗) as a question.

Assertions with More than One Stressed Syllable

Many German sentences contain more than one syllable which carries a strong syntactical stress. The sentence **Sie arbeiten alle in München,** for instance, may be pronounced as follows:

They *all* work in *Munich*.
(Question: What do they do for a *living?*)

If a German sentence contains more than one stressed syllable, the first one has level-3 pitch, and the ones following are lower than the first. The end of the sentence provides the usual signal: the intonation falls to level 1 and thereby indicates the end of the assertion. All stressed syllables express items which have significant news value for the specific situation in which the sentence is spoken.

13 The Structure of Questions

As far as grammatical structure is concerned, German, like English, uses three types of questions.

Yes-or-No Questions

Questions which can be answered by **ja** (*yes*) or **nein** (*no*) may start with an inflected verb in both English and German. However, there is an important difference. The opening verb in English can only be (1) a form of *to be* (*Is Bob here?*), (2) a form of *to have* (*Has he gone?*), (3) a modal auxiliary verb like *must, may, will* (*Can he play?*), or (4) a form of *to do* (*Does he want to play?*). In German, *any* verb can open a yes-or-no question, and the use of **tun** as an auxiliary is impossible. The German questions

    Regnet es heute?   **Arbeitet er in Berlin?**   **Trinkst du Milch?**

correspond in English to the unacceptable Germanisms

    [Rains it today?]   [Works he in Berlin?]   [Drink you milk?]

Conversely, the English questions

    Does he work?   Do you drink milk?

correspond in German to the unacceptable Americanisms

Beware!	**[Tut er arbeiten?]**	
Americanism!	**[Tust du trinken Milch?]**	DO NOT USE!

Word Questions

Questions that start with interrogatives (question words) such as **wer** (*who*), **wann** (*when*), **wo** (*where*), or **wie** (*how*) are called word questions. In word questions, the inflected verb follows immediately after the interrogative.

Wann kommt ihr?	When are you coming?
Wer ist das?	Who is that?
Wo wohnt sie?	Where does she live?
Wie ist das Wetter?	How is the weather?

NOTE: Any German verb can follow the interrogative, and the use of **tun** as an auxiliary is again impossible.

Beware!	**[Wann tust du kommen?]**	
Americanism!	**[Wo tut sie wohnen?]**	DO NOT USE!

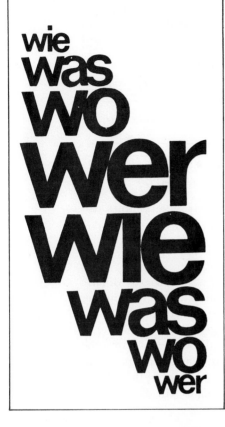

Zeitungen + Zeitschriften
aus der Deutschen Demokratischen Republik

wie was wo wer wie was wo wer

Newspapers + Magazines
from the German Democratic
Republic.

Questions Structured like Assertions

German assertions are characterized by the fact that the inflected verb is
always the second unit in the sentence. Any such assertion can be changed into
a yes-or-no question by changing its intonation (see Analysis **14**).

14 The Intonation of Questions

Word Questions

Normally, German word questions follow the intonation pattern of assertions.

Wo *wohnst* **du?**
Where do you *live?*

Wann kom-men *Sie* **nach Köln?**
When will *you* come to Cologne?

Yes-or-No Questions

Yes-or-no questions can, like word questions, follow the intonation pattern of assertions, or they can be "inverted," as it were, by moving downward from level 2, by placing the stressed syllable on level 1, and then moving upward again.

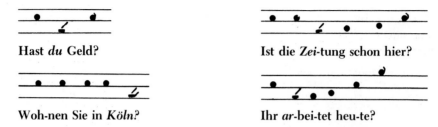

Hast *du* **Geld?**   **Ist die Zei-tung schon hier?**

Woh-nen Sie in *Köln?*   **Ihr** *ar-***bei-tet heu-te?**

Note that after a stressed syllable on level 1 no other stressed syllables can follow.

15 Gender and Plural of Nouns

Indo-European, the ancestor of most modern European languages, including English, distinguished between three classes of nouns, which we call masculines, feminines, and neuters. Modern English has given up the difference almost completely, but German has kept all three classes alive. Usually, the German nouns themselves can no longer be recognized as masculine, feminine, or neuter just by looking at their dictionary forms. However, the articles (and also the pronouns and the adjectives) used with nouns still show the old differences:

MASCULINE	*der* **Winter**	(*the* winter)	*der* **Löffel**	(*the* spoon)
FEMININE	*die* **Butter**	(*the* butter)	*die* **Gabel**	(*the* fork)
NEUTER	*das* **Wetter**	(*the* weather)	*das* **Messer**	(*the* knife)

"Gender" is a linguistic, not a biological term. There is obviously nothing "masculine" about a spoon, nothing "feminine" about a fork, and nothing "neuter" about a knife. To be sure, it is **der Mann** (the man), **die Frau** (the woman), and **das Kind** (the infant), and this is the reason why the term "masculine" came to be applied to *all* nouns used with **der**, the term "feminine" to *all* nouns used with **die**, and the term "neuter" to *all* nouns used with **das** even if this is biologically wrong, as in the neuter noun **das Mädchen** (the girl). There is only one thing to do: learn the article together with the noun.

The pronouns corresponding to **der**, **die** and **das** are **er**, **sie**, and **es**. Thus, **der Löffel** is referred to as **er**, **die Gabel** as **sie**, and **das Messer** as **es**; in all three cases, of course, the English equivalent of the pronoun is *it*.

All German nouns are capitalized; but note that the pronoun **ich** is never capitalized except at the beginning of a sentence.

With a few exceptions, English nouns form the plural by adding -s or -es to the singular: *house, houses; glass, glasses;* but *foot, feet.*

In German, the plural form of a noun usually does not end in **-s.** It may be the same as the singular form, as in the case of English *sheep,* or it may be different from the singular form, as in the case of English *mouse, mice* or *child, children.*

Since there are no rules by which to tell the plural form of a given singular, there is only one safe way to learn the plural: memorize it together with the singular, beginning with this unit.

The plural forms are indicated in the vocabulary as follows:

der Vater, ̈ means that the plural of **der Vater** is **die Väter**
das Kind,-er   **das Kind   die Kinder**
der Hund,-e   **der Hund   die Hunde**

The articles preceding plural nouns are the same for all three genders; the nominative plural is **die.**

Nouns of non-German origin may have a plural ending in **-s:**

das Auto,-s   **das Büro,-s**   **das Kino,-s**

16 denn

Idiomatic German is characterized by the very frequent use of "particles" which, in addition to their definable dictionary meaning, have a psychological meaning sometimes hard to define. One of these is **denn.**

The unstressed **denn** occurs most frequently in word questions. It expresses either impatience or interest.

IMPATIENCE	A: **Ist Meyer hier?**	Is Meyer here?
	B: **Nein, Meyer ist noch nicht hier.**	No, Meyer is not here yet.
	A: **Wo bleibt er denn?**	Well, where is he? (I have been waiting long enough.)
INTEREST	A: **Fritz ist hier!**	Fritz is here!
	B: **Wo ist er denn?**	Where is he? (I am interested in finding out.)

The use of this **denn** is so frequent in spoken German that most word questions contain it. It follows the inflected verb and the personal pronouns, and it may even follow unstressed nouns, but it precedes the first stressed element of importance unless the inflected verb is stressed.

Wo *ist* das Büro denn?
Wo ist denn das Büro?

In yes-or-no questions, **denn** implies a feeling of surprise or incredulity.

Arbeitet ihr denn heute?	You are *working* today? (I can't believe it.)
Hat er denn Geld?	Does he have *money?* (I thought he was on relief.)

Conversations

In German, as in English, conversations do not always consist of strings of questions followed by answers in "complete sentences," but of series of utterances that can be either assertions or questions. Frequently, the verb is assumed, not spoken. Thus, if someone says **Ich bleibe heute abend zu Hause**, do not hesitate to reply **Ich auch** (*Me too*), rather than **Ich bleibe heute abend auch zu Hause**; and if you are asked **Gehen Sie morgen nach Köln?**, you might answer, **Nein, nach Bonn.**

Memorize the following brief exchanges; then recombine their elements into new exchanges. Don't worry about the form of these statements for the time being; the main purpose is to get you to say a few sentences in genuine conversational German.

Guten Tag, Hedi. Wie geht's?

A:	Guten Morgen, Fritz.	Good morning, Fritz.
B:	Guten Morgen, Dieter. Wie geht's?	Good morning, Dieter. How are you?
A:	Danke, gut.	OK, thanks.
C:	Guten Tag, Herr Schulz. Wie geht's Ihnen denn?	Hello, Mr. Schulz. How are you?
D:	Danke, gut. Und Ihnen, Fräulein Braun?	Fine, thanks, and you, Miss Braun?
C:	Danke, auch gut.	Thanks, I'm OK.

E: Auf Wiedersehen, Peter. Bis morgen.
F: Wiedersehen, Fritz. Mach's gut.

Good-bye, Peter. See you tomorrow.
Good-bye, Fritz. Take care.

G: Entschuldigung! Sind Sie Herr Dr. Klein?
H: Ja,—und Sie sind Fritz Müller, nicht wahr?

Excuse me, are you Dr. Klein?
Yes—and you are Fritz Müller, aren't you?

I: Bitte, wie heißen Sie?
J: Ich heiße Müller, Erika Müller.

Excuse me, what is your name?
My name is Müller, Erika Müller.

K: Wie ist denn das Wetter heute?
L: Schlecht. Es regnet schon wieder.
(Gut. Es ist warm und die Sonne scheint.)

How is the weather today?
Bad. It's raining again.
(Good. It is warm and the sun is shining.)

M: Wohnen Sie hier in Frankfurt?
N: Ja, ich wohne hier. Fichardstraße 23.
(Nein, ich wohne in Mainz.)

Do you live here in Frankfurt?
Yes, I live here. 23 Fichardstraße.
(No, I live in Mainz.)

Fragen an Sie persönlich (Questions to you personally)

Each unit contains a set of questions addressed "an Sie persönlich"—to you personally. These questions are designed to elicit your own responses and thus to contribute to the beginning of real conversations. If at times you are hard put to answer these questions, feel free to invent; a little cheating here won't do any harm as long as you cheat in German.

1. Wie heißen Sie?
2. Wo wohnen Sie?
3. Wo sind sie denn zu Hause (Where are you from)?
   In Los Angeles? In Wichita? In New Jersey?
4. Was studieren Sie?
   Mathematik? Physik? Biologie? Chemie? Philosophie? Psychologie?
   Soziologie? English? Geschichte (history)?
   Politikwissenschaft (political science)?
5. Haben Sie ein Auto?
   ein Fahrrad (a bicycle)?
   ein Motorrad (a motorcycle)?
6. Was machen Sie (What are you doing) heute abend?
   morgen abend?
7. Gehen Sie nächsten Sommer nach Deutschland?
   nach Europa?

Exercises

A. Give the German equivalent. Remember that German does not have emphatic and progressive forms.

1. He is coming today.
2. We are going to Cologne.
3. She is learning German.
4. He works here.
5. We do work.
6. She does go.
7. I am going home.
8. You are coming today. (3 forms)

SEE
ANALYSIS
4
(p. 9)

B. Write out, and say aloud, the following German sentences. Be prepared to go through these sentences in class without your book.

SEE
ANALYSIS
3
(p. 9)

1. Ich arbeite heute, und du _____ heute *auch*.
   Du _____ heute, und er _____ heute *auch*.
   Er _____ heute, und sie (*she*) _____ heute *auch*.
   Sie (*she*) _____ heute, und wir _____ heute *auch*.
   Wir _____ heute, und ihr _____ heute *auch*.
   Ihr _____ heute, und sie (*they*) _____ heute *auch*.

2. Ich bin allein. _____ du *auch* allein, Erika?
   Er _____ allein. _____ Erika *auch* allein?
   Wir _____ allein. _____ ihr *auch* allein?
   Ihr _____ allein. _____ Meyers *auch* allein?
   Wir _____ allein. _____ Sie *auch* allein, Frau Meyer?

3. Ich habe Geld. _____ du *auch* Geld?
   Du _____ Geld. _____ er *auch* Geld?
   Er _____ Geld. _____ sie (*she*) *auch* Geld?
   Wir _____ Geld. _____ ihr *auch* Geld?
   Ihr _____ Geld. _____ sie (*they*) *auch* Geld?
   Frau Fischer _____ Geld. _____ Sie *auch* Geld, Frau Meyer?

4. Ich gehe *heute* ins Kino, und ich _____ auch *morgen* ins Kino.
   Du _____ *heute* ins Kino, und du _____ auch *morgen* ins Kino.
   Er _____ *heute* ins Kino, und er _____ auch *morgen* ins Kino.
   Wir _____ *heute* ins Kino, und wir _____ auch *morgen* ins Kino.
   Ihr _____ *heute* ins Kino, und ihr _____ auch *morgen* ins Kino.
   Sie _____ *heute* ins Kino, und sie _____ auch *morgen* ins Kino.

C. Form statements and questions from the following elements:

> **Fritz arbeitet in Bonn.**
> **Er arbeitet hier.**

SEE
ANALYSIS
13
(p. 16)

Fritz	arbeiten	heute abend
sie		hier
Herr Dr. Schöne		schon
wir		in Berlin
Frl. Müller		Bonn
ihr		Stuttgart
du		München
er		Hamburg

Note that in the following set not all combinations make logical sense:

Herr Dr. Schmidt	wohnen	in Berlin
du	studieren*	hier
Fritz Müller	lernen	zu Hause
wir	bleiben	Medizin

*studieren means *to be enrolled at a university*; lernen means *to acquire a skill*: **Er lernt Deutsch,** *He is learning German*, but **Er studiert Deutsch,** *He is a German major* and **Er studiert in Frankfurt,** *He goes to the University of Frankfurt*.

er   Psychologie
Frau Koch   Deutsch
ihr   in Köln

D. Write down the answers to the following questions. Be prepared to answer these questions in class, orally and at normal speed, without looking at your book or paper.

Wohnen Sie in Berlin?	**Ja, ich wohne in Berlin.**
	Nein, ich wohne in München.
Wo ist Fritz?	**Fritz ist zu Hause.**
	Er ist in Bonn.

1. Ist Fritz zu Hause? Ja, _____. Nein, _____ im Büro.
2. Wer ist das? Das _____.
3. Arbeiten Sie in Köln? Ja, ich _____. Nein, ich _____ in Bonn.
4. Wo arbeiten Sie? Ich _____.
5. Bleibst du heute abend zu Hause? Ja, _____. Nein, ich gehe _____ ins Kino.
6. Studiert sie in Heidelberg? Ja, _____. Nein, _____ in Hamburg.
7. Wann kommt ihr denn? Wir _____.
8. Wohnen Schmidts *auch* in Köln? Ja, _____. Nein, _____ in München.

SEE
ANALYSIS
13
(p. 16)

E. Write down one *yes-or-no* question which could be answered by the assertions printed. Copy the assertions also. Be prepared to ask these questions orally in class.

Haben wir (habt ihr, haben Sie) Geld?	**Ja, wir haben Geld.**

1. _____ Nein, wir wohnen in Berlin.
2. _____ Ja, sie arbeiten heute.
3. _____ Nein, das ist Frau Meyer.
4. _____ Natürlich ist das Wetter schlecht.
5. _____ Ja, sie (die Zeitung) ist schon hier.
6. _____ Ja, sie (Erika) wohnt *auch* in München.
7. _____ Nein!
8. _____ Ja!

F. Repeat each sentence, starting as indicated.

1. Ich bleibe zu Hause. Heute _____.
2. Er bleibt morgen zu Hause. Morgen _____.
3. Es regnet. Hier _____.
4. Im Winter regnet es hier. Hier _____.
5. Wir arbeiten. Heute _____.
6. Meyer trinkt Bier. Übrigens _____.
7. In Kalifornien regnet es im Winter. Im Winter _____.
8. Nächsten Sommer gehen wir nach Deutschland. Wir _____.

SEE
ANALYSIS
8
(p. 11)

G. Write down the *word questions* which could be answered by the statements printed. Be prepared to ask these questions in class at normal speed when you hear the statement.

Wo arbeitet Herr Meyer?	**Er arbeitet in Berlin.**

SEE
ANALYSIS
13
(p. 16)

1. Wo _____   Wir wohnen in Berlin.
2. Wo _____   Zu Hause!
3. Wo _____   Ich bin in Köln.
4. Wer _____   Herr Meyer.
5. Wann _____   Ich komme morgen.
6. Was _____   Er studiert Psychologie.
7. Wer _____   Herr Meyer kommt heute.
8. Wer _____   Ich bin Anna Meyer.

H. Express in German. Be prepared to give the German equivalents instantly without using book or
   paper.

SEE
ANALYSIS
1–16
(pp. 7–19)

1. I am at home.
2. The sun is shining.
3. Hans will come tomorrow.
4. It is cold today.
5. Where does Dr. Meyer live?
6. We are studying psychology.
7. Hans is here, too.
8. Tomorrow night we are staying home.

9. They are both drinking tea.
10. Does Hans *also* live here?
11. Hans also *lives* here.
12. We are also going to *Munich*.
13. Is it raining in Hamburg?
14. When are you coming to Bonn, Mr. Koch?
15. Do you live in Bonn? (Use **du, ihr,** and **Sie.**)
16. What is your name? (Use **du, ihr,** and **Sie.**)

I. Form sentences from the following elements:

SEE
ANALYSIS
8
(p. 11)

1. Hans / heute / nach Berlin / gehen.
2. Natürlich / ich / Milch / trinken.
3. Heute / Wetter / schlecht / sein.
4. Erika / in Stuttgart / wohnen.
5. Hans und Erika / beide / Deutsch / lernen.
6. Du / auch / Deutsch / lernen?

7. Fritz / schon / hier / sein?
8. Wie / Sie / denn / heißen?
9. Um drei Uhr / er / nach Hause / kommen.
10. Morgen / ich / zu Hause / bleiben.
11. Du / Bier / haben?
12. Ihr / in Köln / arbeiten?

Vocabulary

Verbs

arbeiten	to work
bleiben	to stay, remain
danken	to thank
danke	thanks, thank you
gehen	to go; to walk
Wie geht's?	How are you?
Wie geht es dir / euch / Ihnen?	How are things going?
haben	to have
heißen	to be called
Wie heißen Sie?	What's your name?
ich heiße Meyer	my name is Meyer; I am Mr. Meyer
kommen	to come
lehren	to teach, instruct
lernen	to learn

machen	to do; to make
mach's gut	so long; take care; see you
regnen	to rain
der Regen	the rain
scheinen	to seem; to shine
es scheint zu regnen	it seems to be raining
die Sonne scheint	the sun is shining
sein	to be
studie′ren	to study, to attend a university, to be a student (at a university)
trinken	to drink
tun	to do
wohnen	to live, to reside

Nouns*

MASCULINE

der Abend, -e	evening
abends	evenings, in the evening
Guten Abend	good evening
der Arzt, ⁀e	physician, doctor
die Ärztin, -nen	female physician
der Dok′tor, die Dokto′ren	doctor, physician
(der) Hans	Jack; John (abbrev. for Johannes)
der Herr, -en	man; gentleman; Mr.
Herr Meyer	Mr. Meyer
der Kaffee (no pl.)	coffee

der Lehrer, -	teacher (male)
die Lehrerin, -nen	teacher (female)
der Mann, ⁀er	man; husband
der Morgen, -	morning
Guten Morgen	good morning
heute morgen	this morning
morgen	tomorrow
morgen abend	tomorrow night
der Sommer, -	the summer
nächsten Sommer	next summer
der Tee (no pl.)	tea
der Wein, -e	wine
der Winter, -	winter
im Winter	during the winter

FEMININE

die Entschuldigung, -en	excuse
Entschuldigung	excuse me
entschuldigen Sie	
die Frau, -en	woman; wife; Mrs., Ms.
Frau Meyer	Mrs. Meyer, Ms. Meyer
das Fräulein, -	young (unmarried) woman, Miss
Fräulein Meyer	Miss Meyer
die Medizin′	medicine; science of medicine; study of medicine

die Milch (no pl.)	milk
die Natur′	nature
natür′lich	natural, naturally; of course
die Psychologie′	psychology
die Sonne, -n	sun
die Straße, -n	street
die Uhr, -en	clock, watch
um ein Uhr	at one o'clock
um eins	

NEUTER

das Auto, -s	car, automobile
das Automobil, -e	
das Bier, -e	beer
das Büro′, -s	office
(das) Deutsch	German (language)
(das) Deutschland	Germany
(das) Englisch	English (language)
(das) England	England
Euro′pa	Europe
europä′isch	European
das Fräulein, -	young (unmarried) woman

Fräulein Meyer (abbreviated: Frl.)	Miss Meyer
das Geld, -er	money
das Haus, ⁀er	house
ich gehe nach Hause	I am going home
ich bin zu Hause	I am at home
das Kino, -s	movie theater
wir gehen ins Kino	we are going to the movies
das Rad, ⁀er	the wheel; bicycle
das Fahrrad, ⁀er	bicycle
das Motorrad, ⁀er	motorcycle
das Wetter (no pl.)	weather

*Although no plural forms of nouns are used in Unit 1, all nouns are listed here with their plurals, as they will be in all other units. Learn the plurals with the singular forms; they will be practiced in Unit 2.

Adjectives

allein	alone	**schlecht**	bad
beide	both	**wahr**	true
gut	good; OK	**nicht wahr?**	isn't that so? aren't
heiß	hot		you? don't you?
kalt	cold		etc.
nächst-	next	**warm**	warm
nächsten Sommer	next summer		

Articles and Pronouns

der	the (*masc.*)	**du**	you (*sing.*)
die	the (*fem.*)	**er**	he; it
das	the (*neuter*)	**sie**	she; they; it
ein, eine, ein	a; one (*indef. article*)	**Sie**	you
eins	one (*number*)	**es**	it
das	that (*demonstrative*)	**wir**	we
ich	I	**ihr**	you (*pl.*)

Interrogatives

wann	at what time, when	**wie**	how
was	what	**wo**	where
wer	who		

Prepositions

bis	until; up to; as far as	**um**	at; around
bis morgen	until tomorrow; see	**um ein Uhr**	at one o'clock
	you tomorrow	**zu**	to; at; too
in	in	**es scheint zu regnen**	it seems to be
nach	to, toward; after		raining
nach Deutschland	to Germany	**zu Hause**	at home
nach zwei Uhr	after two o'clock	**zu warm**	too warm

Adverbs

heute	today	**morgen**	tomorrow
heute morgen	this morning	**schon**	already, earlier than
heute abend	this evening,		expected
	tonight	**wieder**	again
hier	here	**auf Wiedersehen**	see you again;
jetzt	now		good-bye

Numbers

eins	one	**drei**	three
zwei	two		

Other Words

auch	also, too	**nein**	no
bitte	please	**übrigens**	by the way, incidentally
denn	(see **16**)	**und**	and
ja	yes		

Unit 2 Topic, Comment, and News Value—Plural of Nouns—Irregularities in the Present Tense of Verbs—The Nominative and Accusative Cases

If German and English had one common Germanic source, what has caused the two languages to be so different today? Passage of time and geographical separation have been major factors, of course, but in spite of the isolation of the British Isles, the English language has been much more strongly subjected to non-Germanic influences than the German language ever was. On a typical page of an English dictionary perhaps fifty percent of all words will have French/Latin origin.

Christian missionaries brought many Latin words into both England and Germany, but it was the Norman conquest of England in 1066 that brought French words into English usage. For several centuries, French was the language of the court and the upper class; at about the time of Chaucer, the highbrow French and the lowbrow English meshed and modern English was born, though from the Renaissance on, the steady flow of French and Latin words into English continued unabated.

Much of the basic English vocabulary (the peasants' language of the Norman period) is still Germanic; among the most frequently used two or three hundred English words there are few of Romance origin. In some of them you can observe umlaut, that is, a vowel change from singular to plural, just as in many German words, for example, in *foot-feet* / **Fuß-Füße** or *mouse-mice* / **Maus-Mäuse.** The plural *houses*, on the other hand, has lost the umlaut; German **Häuser** has retained it.

German, too, has borrowed from French and Latin, but to a much lesser degree, and many of the borrowings—for example, **Revolution** or **Sozialismus** —are still considered **Fremdwörter**, foreign words. Since World War II, there has been a veritable invasion of American words into German: words like **der Manager, der Computer, die Pipeline, der Trend, der Pop Star, der Top Hit** can be found in all German newspapers.

The basic Germanic character of English is evident not only in its vocabulary. English sentence intonation, for example, is much more similar to that of German than that of French. Even English syntax is still close to German, although, as you are discovering, considerable differences in details have evolved in the course of time. One difference is in the use of grammatical cases. About a thousand years ago, old English, like old German, had a complete set of endings indicating case. This older English case system disappeared as the endings first coalesced into an indistinct *e*-sound and then vanished altogether. This lack of case endings is the major reason for the rigidity of English word order; without endings, case—and thus function—can only be indicated by position within the sentence. German, on the other hand, still retains four clearly recognizable cases: nominative, accusative, dative, and genitive. The nominative and the accusative are discussed in this unit, the dative and the genitive are introduced later.

Sekretärin

für den Leiter unseres **Project Team Terminal.**

Mobil

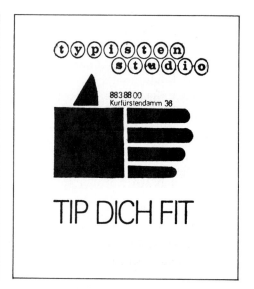

Americanisms in German.

Patterns

[1] Front Field Elements

Practice and memorize the following sentences, taking special note of the position of the subject.

SEE
ANALYSIS
17
(p. 38)

TOPIC		COMMENT
Die Milch	**ist**	*hier.*
Hier	**ist**	*die Milch.*
Hans	**geht**	heute ins *Kino.*
Heute	**geht**	Hans ins *Kino.*
Erika	**kommt**	um ein Uhr nach *Hause.*
Um ein Uhr	**kommt**	Erika nach *Hause.*
Fritz Müller	**wohnt**	jetzt in *Köln.*
Jetzt	**wohnt**	Fritz Müller in *Köln.*

[2] Plural of Nouns

SEE
VOCABU-
LARY OF
UNIT 1
(p. 24)

Herr Meyer hat zwei Büros, ein Büro in Köln, und ein Büro in Bonn.

Mr. Meyer has two offices, one office in Cologne and one office in Bonn.

Schmidts haben zwei Kinder. Der Sohn heißt Peter, und die Tochter heißt Sylvia.

The Schmidts have two children. The son's name is Peter, and the daughter's name is Sylvia.

Meyers haben zwei Söhne. Sie heißen Paul und Gerhardt.

The Meyers have two sons. Their names are Paul and Gerhardt.

Paul ist ein Junge. Paul und Gerhardt sind Jungen.

Paul is a boy. Paul and Gerhardt are boys.

Müllers haben zwei Töchter.—Wie heißen sie denn?—Sie heißen Andrea und Ingrid.

The Müllers have two daughters.—What are their names?—Their names are Andrea and Ingrid.

Andrea ist ein Mädchen. Andrea und Ingrid sind Mädchen.

Andrea is a girl. Andrea and Ingrid are girls.

Wir bleiben zwei Jahre in Deutschland.

We are staying in Germany for two years.

Wir bleiben zwei Tage in Berlin.

We are staying in Berlin for two days.

Sind Herr Schmidt und Herr Müller schon hier?—Ja, Herr Doktor, die Herren sind schon hier.

Are Mr. Schmidt and Mr. Müller here already?—Yes, Doctor, the gentlemen are already here.

Der Mann arbeitet in München. Die Männer arbeiten alle in München.

The man is working in Munich. The men are all working in Munich.

Frau Meyer und Frau Schmidt sind zu Hause. Die zwei Frauen bleiben heute zu Hause.

Mrs. Meyer and Mrs. Schmidt are at home. The two women are staying at home today.

[3] Verbs with Vowel Change

Some of the most common German verbs show irregularities in the present tense. As you read and practice the following pattern sections, note what these irregularities are and in which forms they occur.

SEE
ANALYSIS
18
(p. 39)

Wohin* fahren die Leute?	Where are the people going?
Wohin fährt der Zug?	Where is the train going?

Fahren die Leute nach Stuttgart?—Nein, sie fahren nach München. Er fährt nach München. Sie fährt auch nach München.

Ich fahre nach Köln.	I am going (driving; taking the train) to Cologne.
Fährst du auch nach Köln?	Are you going to Cologne too?
Fahrt ihr nach Hamburg?	Are you going to Hamburg?
Nein, wir fahren nach Bremen.	No, we are going to Bremen.
Ich laufe jeden Morgen eine Stunde.	I run for an hour every morning.
Warum läufst du denn so schnell?	Why are you walking so fast?
Er läuft die 100 m (hundert Meter) in neun Sekunden.	He runs the 100-meter dash in nine seconds.
Das Wetter ist so gut; wir laufen heute in die Stadt.	The weather is so good; we'll walk downtown today.
Fahrt ihr oder lauft ihr?	Are you going to drive, or will you walk?
Wir starten in zwei Minuten; die Motoren laufen schon.	We'll be taking off in two minutes; the engines are running already.

*German must use **wohin** rather than **wo** if it corresponds to English *where = whereto, whither.*

Was essen sie?—Sie essen Brot und Wurst. Er ißt Brot und Wurst und trinkt Bier. Sie ißt auch Brot und Wurst, aber sie trinkt Wein.

Was ißt du?—Ich esse Brot und Käse.

Und was trinkst du?—Milch.
Wann eßt ihr heute?—Wir essen um zwölf.

Herr und Frau Anders sind zu Hause und lesen. Herr Anders liest ein Buch, und Frau Anders liest die Zeitung.
Frau Anders fragt: „Was liest du denn?" Herr Anders antwortet: „Ich lese *Gruppenbild mit Dame.*"

Was lest ihr denn jetzt in der Schule?
Wir lesen *Deutschstunde* von Siegfried Lenz.

What are you eating?—I am eating bread and cheese.
And what are you drinking?—Milk.
When are you eating today?—We'll be eating at noon.

Mr. and Mrs. Anders are reading at home. Mr. Anders is reading a book and Mrs. Anders is reading a newspaper.
Mrs. Anders asks, "What are you reading?" Mr. Anders answers, "I am reading *Group Portait with Lady*" (a novel by Heinrich Böll).

What are you reading in school now?
We are reading *Deutschstunde* (*German Class*) by Siegfried Lenz.

[4] sein and werden

Margret Baum und Kurt Schmitz studieren Medizin; sie sind Medizinstudenten. Margret wird Ärztin. Kurt wird Arzt.

Willi Baumgärtner ist Lehrling bei Braun und Co.; er wird Automechaniker.
Die Lehrlinge bei Braun und Co. werden alle Automechaniker.

Margret Baum and Kurt Schmitz are studying medicine; they are medical students. Margret is becoming (going to be) a doctor. Kurt will be a doctor.
Willi Baumgärtner is an apprentice with Braun and Co.; he'll be an auto mechanic.
All apprentices with Braun and Company are going to be auto mechanics.

SEE ANALYSIS 18 (p. 39)

Ursula Nagel wird Laborantin.

Und was wirst du, Lilo?—Ich werde Lehrerin.

Wie wird das Wetter morgen?

Heute ist das Wetter schlecht; es ist kalt und es regnet. Morgen wird es aber bestimmt gut; morgen scheint sicher die Sonne.

Wie alt ist Rudi?—Rudi wird morgen fünf Jahre alt.—Er wird morgen fünf.

Ursula Nagel is going to be a lab technician.

And what are you going to be Lilo?—I'll be a teacher.

How is the weather going to be tomorrow?

Today the weather is bad; it is cold and it is raining. But tomorrow it'll probably be good; I'm sure tomorrow the sun will be shining.

How old is Rudi?—Rudi will be five years old tomorrow.—He'll be five tomorrow.

Wir gratulieren

80 Jahre alt wird heute Frau Martha Naber, Delmenhorst, Deichhorster Straße 12.

---

[5] wissen and kennen: to know

Wer ist das?

Wissen Sie, wer das ist?

Nein, das weiß ich nicht.*

Das ist Fritz Müller. Kennen Sie Fritz?

Nein, ich kenne Fritz nicht; ich weiß nicht, wer er ist.

Ich weiß, wer du bist.

Weißt du, wer ich bin?

Er weiß, wer wir sind.

Who is that?

Do you know who that is?

No, I don't know (that).

That's Fritz Müller. Do you know Fritz?

No, I don't know Fritz; I don't know who he is.

Wir wissen nicht, wo er ist.

Wißt ihr, wo er ist?

Sie wissen es auch nicht.

[6] Nominative and Accusative of Personal Pronouns

Practice the sentences aloud until you can say them rapidly, without having to pause for the correct pronoun.

SEE
ANALYSIS
20–21
(pp. 41–42)

you know me, and I know you

du kennst *mich*, und *ich* kenne *dich*
er kennt *mich*, und *ich* kenne *ihn*
sie kennt *mich*, und *ich* kenne *sie*
ihr kennt *mich*, und *ich* kenne *euch*
sie kennen *mich*, und *ich* kenne *sie*
Sie kennen *mich*, und *ich* kenne *Sie*

ich kenne dich, und du kennst *mich*
er kennt *dich*, und du kennst *ihn*
sie kennt *dich*, und du kennst *sie*
wir kennen *dich*, und du kennst *uns*
sie kennen *dich*, und du kennst *sie*

*For the time being, do not use **nicht** in your own sentences.

ich kenne *ihn*, und *er* kennt *mich*
du kennst *ihn*, und *er* kennt *dich*
sie kennt *ihn*, und *er* kennt *sie*
wir kennen *ihn*, und *er* kennt *uns*
ihr kennt *ihn*, und *er* kennt *euch*
sie kennen *ihn*, und *er* kennt *sie*
Sie kennen *ihn*, und *er* kennt *Sie*

du kennst *uns*, und *wir* kennen *dich*
er kennt *uns*, und *wir* kennen *ihn*
sie kennt *uns*, und *wir* kennen *sie*
ihr kennt *uns*, und *wir* kennen *euch*
sie kennen *uns*, und *wir* kennen *sie*
Sie kennen *uns*, und *wir* kennen *Sie*

ich kenne *sie*, und *sie* kennen *mich*
du kennst *sie*, und *sie* kennen *dich*
er kennt *sie*, und *sie* kennen *ihn*
wir kennen *sie*, und *sie* kennen *uns*
ihr kennt *sie*, und *sie* kennen *euch*

ich kenne *sie*, und *sie* kennt *mich*
du kennst *sie*, und *sie* kennt *dich*
er kennt *sie*, und *sie* kennt *ihn*
wir kennen *sie*, und *sie* kennt *uns*
ihr kennt *sie*, und *sie* kennt *euch*

ich kenne *euch*, und *ihr* kennt *mich*
er kennt *euch*, und *ihr* kennt *ihn*
sie kennt *euch*, und *ihr* kennt *sie*
wir kennen *euch*, und *ihr* kennt *uns*
sie kennen *euch*, und *ihr* kennt *sie*

I know he knows me.

Ich *weiß*, er *kennt* mich.
Du *weißt*, er *kennt* dich.
Er *weiß*, ich *kenne* ihn.
Sie *weiß*, er *kennt* sie.
Wir *wissen*, er *kennt* uns.
Ihr *wißt*, sie *kennen* euch.
Sie *wissen*, wir *kennen* sie.
Sie *wissen*, er *kennt* Sie.

Ist das Herr Meyer?—
Das weiß ich nicht;
ich kenne ihn nicht.

[7] Nominative and Accusative of **der**-Nouns*

Wer fragt wen? Who is asking whom?
  Was fragt die Frau den Mann?   **Was fragt der Junge das Mädchen?**
  Was fragt der Mann die Frau?   **Was fragt das Mädchen den Jungen?**

Sehen Sie den Wagen?   Do you see the car?
Ja, der Wagen ist da drüben.   Yes, the car is over there.
Seht ihr die Straßenbahn?   Do you see the streetcar?
Ja, die Straßenbahn ist hier.   Yes, the streetcar is here.

SEE
ANALYSIS
22
(p. 42)

*The term "**der**-nouns" is used for all nouns preceded by *any* form of the definite article, and "**ein**-nouns" (see [8]) for all nouns preceded by *any* form of the indefinite article.

Siehst du das Motorrad?
Ja, das Motorrad ist da drüben.
Seht ihr die Fahrräder?
Ja, die Fahrräder sind da drüben.
Wo ist der Wagen? Sehen Sie ihn?
Ja, er ist da drüben.
Wo ist die Straßenbahn? Sehen Sie sie?
Ja, sie ist hier.
Wo ist das Motorrad? Sehen Sie es?
Ja, es ist hier.
Wo sind die Fahrräder? Sehen Sie sie?
Ja, sie sind da drüben.

[8] Nominative and Accusative of **ein**-Nouns

SEE
ANALYSIS
23
(p. 43)

Ich brauche einen Löffel.
Hier ist ein Löffel.
Ich brauche ein Messer.
Hier ist ein Messer.
Ich brauche eine Gabel.
Hier ist eine Gabel.

der Löffel,- spoon
das Messer,- knife
die Gabel,-n fork
brauchen   to need

Ich brauche _____ Teller.
Hier ist _____ Teller.
Ich brauche _____ Glas.
Hier ist _____ Glas.
Ich brauche _____ Tasse.
Hier ist _____ Tasse.

der Teller,- plate
das Glas,-̈er glass
die Tasse,-n cup

Haben Sie Kinder?
Ich habe einen Sohn.   Ich habe eine Tochter.   Ich habe ein Kind.

Wen siehst du?
Ich sehe einen Herrn.   Ich sehe eine Dame.   Ich sehe ein Mädchen.
Ich sehe Herrn Nagel.   Ich sehe Frau Engel.   Ich sehe Fräulein Hahn.

What does he read? A novel? A newspaper? A book?

Was liest er?
Er liest einen Roman.   Er liest eine Zeitung.   Er liest ein Buch.

Was lest ihr?
Wir lesen Romane.   Wir lesen Zeitungen.   Wir lesen Bücher.

Was ist das?
Das ist ein Roman.   Das ist eine Zeitung.   Das ist ein Buch.
Das sind Romane.*   Das sind Zeitungen.   Das sind Bücher.

[9] Nominative and Accusative of Possessive Adjectives

NOMINATIVE   **SEE
                                                                                        ANALYSIS
MASC.   FEM.   NEUT.   23
                                                                                        (p. 43)
This is my husband.   This is my wife.   This is my child.

Das ist mein Mann.   Das ist meine Frau.   Das ist mein Kind.
Ist das dein Sohn?   Ist das deine Tochter?   Ist das dein Kind?
Peter ist sein Sohn.   Gabriele ist seine Tochter. Das ist sein Kind.
Peter ist ihr Sohn.   Gabriele ist ihre Tochter. Das ist ihr Kind.
Das ist unser Sohn.   Das ist unsere Tochter.   Das ist unser Kind.
Ist das euer Sohn?   Ist das eure Tochter?   Ist das euer Kind?
Ihr Sohn heißt Peter.   Ihre Tochter heißt Gabriele. Das ist ihr Kind.
Ist das Ihr Sohn, Herr   Ist das Ihre Tochter, Herr Ist das Ihr Kind, Herr
   Klein?   Klein?   Klein?

PLURAL
My sons are living in Lübeck.

Meine Söhne wohnen in Lübeck.
Wo wohnen denn deine Töchter jetzt?
Seine Freundinnen wohnen jetzt alle in Wien.
Ihre Freundinnen wohnen auch alle in Wien.
Unsere Kinder wohnen in Mannheim.
Wo wohnen denn eure Kinder jetzt?
Jetzt wohnen ihre Kinder in Salzburg.
Wo wohnen Ihre Freunde denn jetzt, Herr Lehmann?

*Note that **das** is followed by a plural verb form to identify a plural noun.

ACCUSATIVE

MASC.

I'm taking my car, and you take your car.

Ich nehme *meinen* Wagen, und *ihr* nehmt *euren* Wagen.
Du nimmst *deinen* Wagen, und *wir* nehmen *unseren* Wagen.
Er nimmt *seinen* Wagen und *sie* nehmen *ihren* Wagen.

FEM.

Do you know my daughter?

Kennst du meine Tochter?   Kennst du unsere Tochter?
Ich kenne deine Tochter nicht.   Natürlich kenne ich eure Tochter.
Erika kennt seine Tochter.   Wir kennen ihre Tochter nicht.
Hans kennt ihre Tochter.

NEUT.

I read my book, and you read your book.

Ich lese *mein* Buch, und *du* liest *dein* Buch.
Du liest *dein* Buch, und *er* liest *sein* Buch.
Er liest *sein* Buch, und *sie* liest *ihr* Buch.
Sie liest *ihr* Buch, und *wir* lesen *unsere* Bücher.
Wir lesen *unsere* Bücher, und *ihr* lest *eure* Bücher.
Ihr lest *eure* Bücher, und *sie* lesen *ihre* Bücher.

PLURAL

I buy my books in Frankfurt.

Ich kaufe meine Bücher in Frankfurt.
Wo kaufst du deine Bücher?
Er kauft seine Bücher bei Brentano.
Sie kauft ihre Bücher auch bei Brentano.
Wir kaufen unsere Bücher in Bonn.
Wo kauft ihr eure Bücher?
Sie kaufen ihre Bücher in Deutschland.

Analysis

17 Topic, Comment, and News Item

Most sentences consist of a "topic" and of some information, or comment, on that topic. For example, if you are asked, *Where did John go last night?* you could answer, *Last night John went to the movies*, or *John went to the movies last night*. While the two sentences contain the same information, they are focused in different ways: in the first one, you are implying, "Now I am going to say something about last night, and here is what happened: John went to the movies," whereas the implication of the second sentence is, "I'm going to talk about John, and here is what he did: He went to the movies last night." Thus, the first answer to the original question would be the more logical one, though, since the topic has already been set in the preceding question, the answer would probably be only, (*He went*) *to the movies.*

Topicalization, that is, choosing one element of the sentence as "the thing to talk about," accounts for the choice of a given element to occupy the front field. Within the comment on this topic, there are usually one or more stressed elements, or stress points (see Analysis **11**, p. 13) which contain the news the speaker wants to convey; these elements are referred to as "news items," and if there are several, we speak of "increasing news value." In the above example, the news item is *to the movies.*

EXAMPLES:

Fritz fährt morgen nach *Ham*burg.
    Topic: **Fritz**
    Comment: **fährt morgen nach *Ham*burg**
    News item: **nach *Ham*burg**
    Implied question: **Was macht *Fritz?***
Morgen kommt *Fritz*.
    Topic: **Morgen**
    Comment: **kommt *Fritz***
    News Item: ***Fritz***
    Implied question: **Wer kommt *morgen?***
Hier in Hamburg *regnet* es.
    Topic: **Hier in Hamburg**
    Comment: ***regnet* es**
    News Item: ***regnet***
    Implied question: **Wie ist das Wetter in Hamburg?**

18 Irregularities in the Present Tense of Verbs

Verbs with Vowel Change

The English verb *do* changes the sound of its stem vowel in the third person singular: *I do, you do,* but *he does.* In German, a number of very common verbs change their stem vowel in the second and the third person singular (the **du-** and the **er-**form), indicated in the vocabulary as follows: **fahren (du fährst, er fährt).** There are two major types of changes: from **e** to **ie** (or **i**) and from **a** to **ä** (or **au** to **äu**).

lesen	**nehmen**	**essen**	**fahren**	**laufen**
to read	to take	to eat	to drive	to run
ich lese	**ich nehme**	**ich esse**	**ich fahre**	**ich laufe**
du liest	**du nimmst**	**du ißt**	**du fährst**	**du läufst**
er liest	**er nimmt**	**er ißt**	**er fährt**	**er läuft**

wir lesen	wir nehmen	wir essen	wir fahren	wir laufen
ihr lest	ihr nehmt	ihr eßt	ihr fahrt	ihr lauft
sie lesen	sie nehmen	sie essen	sie fahren	sie laufen

NOTE: English *to go* has a much wider range of meaning than German **gehen**. The basic meaning of **gehen** is *to walk, to go (on foot)* (**zu Fuß gehen**), but **laufen** (*to run*) is also used with the meaning *to walk*, especially in southern Germany; **fahren**, on the other hand, always implies that a vehicle is used: *to drive, to go* (by car, etc.).

Ich gehe in die Stadt.	I'm going downtown. (means undetermined)
Ich laufe in die Stadt.	I'm walking downtown.
Ich fahre in die Stadt.	I'm driving downtown.
	or: I'm going downtown. (by streetcar, bus, etc.)

Stems Ending in an s-Sound

After a stem ending in **-s, -ss, -ß, -z,** or **-tz,** the **du**-form adds **-t** rather than **-st.** Thus, **du**-form and **er**-form are identical.

lesen to read	**sitzen** to sit	**essen** to eat	**verreisen** to go on a trip
ich lese	ich sitze	ich esse	ich verreise
du liest	du sitzt	du ißt	du verreist
er liest	er sitzt	er ißt	er verreist

werden and wissen

The verbs **werden**, *to become*, and **wissen**, *to know*, have peculiarities of their own. Note that the **er**-form **er wird** is the only third-person singular form in German that ends in **-d.**

ich	werde	ich	weiß
du	wirst	du	weißt
er	wird	er	weiß
wir	werden	wir	wissen
ihr	werdet	ihr	wißt
sie	werden	sie	wissen

19 *to know:* wissen and kennen

Both these verbs correspond to English *to know*, but German makes a clear distinction between *to know facts* (**wissen**) and *to be acquainted with persons* *or things* (**kennen**). The use of **wissen** in main clauses is largely restricted to such sentences as

> **Das weiß ich.**
> **Ich weiß es.**

Frequently, the object of **wissen** is a short clause, such as

> **Ich weiß, Meyer wohnt in München.**
> **Ich weiß, er kommt morgen.**

If **Ich weiß** is followed by a question word like **wer, wo, wann**, as in

> **Ich weiß, wer er ist.**
> **Er weiß, wo wir sind.**
> **Weißt du, wann er kommt?**

then the second clause is a dependent clause in which the conjugated verb *must* stand at the end. For the time being use only the few examples introduced here.

The verb **kennen** expresses personal acquaintance with people or objects.

> **Kennen Sie Herrn Meyer?**
> **Kennen Sie Deutschland?**
> **Kennen Sie das Buch?**

Note the difference:

> **Ich weiß, wer er ist, aber ich kenne ihn nicht.**
> I know who he is, but I don't know him (haven't made his acquaintance).

20 The Nominative and Accusative Case

In English, the notion of "case"—that is, the use of special forms to indicate functions such as subject or object—is of no significance with nouns. Function, in English, is indicated by position and not by a change of form; we know who did the biting in *The dog bit the cat*, because position fixes the dog as the subject and the cat as the object that was bitten. Reversing the words *dog* and *cat* automatically reverses their roles.

The personal pronouns, *I*, *he*, etc. are referred to as the "subjective case" in English grammars, and *me*, *him*, etc. as the "objective case." (The pronoun *you* shows no distinction.) The subjective case is reserved for the subject of a sentence; the objective case for direct and indirect objects (He visited *her* and gave *her* a book) and for the object of a preposition (He relied on *her*).

German indicates case much more frequently than English. Not only do personal pronouns show case, but the combination of article plus noun (or possessive adjective plus noun) is usually also a clear signal of case. Thus, not only are **Er liebt mich** and **Mich liebt er** totally unambiguous, but

> **Die Inge liebt den Hans**

and

> **Den Hans liebt die Inge***

both mean "Inge loves Hans." The word **Inge,** regardless of its position, must be the subject (in the nominative case), because **Hans,** preceded by the accusative **den,** can only be the object. Conversely, in **Der Hans liebt die Inge, Inge** must be the object, again regardless of position, because the nominative **der** automatically makes **Hans** the subject.

In addition to the nominative and the accusative, German has two more cases: dative and genitive, which will be introduced in later units.

21 The Nominative and Accusative Forms of Personal Pronouns

	SINGULAR					PLURAL			Sie
NOM.	ich	du	er	sie	es	wir	ihr	sie	Sie
ACC.	mich	dich	ihn	sie	es	uns	euch	sie	Sie

There is no difference in form between the nominative and the accusative of **sie** (*she-her*), **sie** (*they-them*), **Sie,** and **es.**

Agreement between Nouns and Pronouns

Since **der Kaffee** is a masculine noun, it must be represented by the masculine pronouns **er** and **ihn.**

> **Er (der Kaffee) ist gut. Wo kaufst du ihn?**

Similarly, **die Zeitung** must be referred to by using the feminine pronoun **sie.**

> **Sie (die Zeitung) ist uninteressant. Ich lese sie nie.**

Both **das Geld** and **das Kind** are neuter nouns. If these nouns are replaced, **es** must be used.

> **Ich brauche es (das Geld).**
> **Ist es (das Kind) zu Hause?**

22 The Nominative and Accusative of **der**-Words plus Noun

The term "**der**-words" is used for all words which indicate gender, case, and number in the same way in which the definite article **der,** by changing its

*In colloquial German, the article is very frequently used with both first and last names.

form, indicates gender, case, and number. For instance, **dieser** (*this*) and **jeder** (*each*) are **der**-words.

	MASC.	FEM.	NEUT.	MASC.	FEM.	NEUT.
NOM. SING.	**der** Mann	die Frau	das Kind	**dieser** Mann	diese Frau	dieses Kind
ACC. SING.	**den** Mann	die Frau	das Kind	**diesen** Mann	diese Frau	dieses Kind

NOM. PL.	die Männer
	die Frauen
ACC. PL.	die Kinder

	diese Männer
	diese Frauen
	diese Kinder

Only the masculine singular of the **der**-words distinguishes the nominative from the accusative.

In the plural, all three genders of the **der**-words have the same forms.

23 The Nominative and Accusative of ein-Words plus Noun

The term "**ein**-words" is used for all words which indicate gender, case, and number in the same way in which the indefinite article **ein** shows gender, case, and number. Other **ein**-words are **kein** (the negation of **ein**: *no, not a*) and the possessive adjectives:

mein	my	**unser**	our		
dein	your	**euer**	your	**Ihr**	your
sein	his				
ihr	her	**ihr**	their		
sein	its				

	MASC.	FEM.	NEUT.	MASC.	FEM.	NEUT.
NOM. SING.	**ein** Mann	eine Frau	ein Kind	**mein** Roman	meine Zeitung	mein Buch
ACC. SING.	**einen** Mann	eine Frau	ein Kind	**meinen** Roman	meine Zeitung	mein Buch

NOM. PL.	Männer
	Frauen
ACC. PL.	Kinder

	meine Romane
	meine Zeitungen
	meine Bücher

NOTE:

1. Only the masculine singular of the **ein**-words distinguishes the nominative from the accusative.

2. There is no plural of **ein**; for example, the plural of **ein Kind** is **Kinder**.

3. In the accusative of **unser** and **euer,** the **-e-** before the **-r-** is frequently dropped.

unseren or **unsren**   **unsere** or **unsre**

4. In the plural, all three genders have the same forms.

24 The Accusative of Nouns: Special Forms

Only very few nouns distinguish between nominative and accusative—for example, **der Mensch, der Student,** and **der Junge,** which add -(e)n in all cases but the nominative singular. **Der Herr** adds an **-n** in all singular forms and an **-en** in all plural forms.

NOM. SING.	der Mensch	der Student	der Junge	der Herr
ACC. SING.	den Menschen	den Studenten	den Jungen	den Herrn
NOM. PL.	die Menschen	die Studenten	die Jungen	die Herren
ACC. PL.	die Menschen	die Studenten	die Jungen	die Herren

25 auch

German **auch,** meaning *also* or *too,* is one of the most frequently used words. The stressed **auch** refers *back* to a preceding unit, regardless of whether that unit is stressed or not. The unstressed **auch** refers *forward* to a *stressed* unit, except in one case: Since the inflected verb is always the second unit in a German sentence, one cannot imitate the English sentence *He also lives in Munich.* Instead, the stressed verb precedes the unstressed **auch.**

Er *wohnt* auch in München.	He also *lives* in Munich.
	He *lives* in Munich, too.

Here are some further examples:

Er ist *auch* intelligent.	*He, too,* is intelligent.
Er ist auch intellig*ent.*	He is also *intelligent.*
Sie hat *auch* ein Büro in Köln.	*She, too,* has an office in Cologne.
Sie hat auch ein B*üro* in Köln.	She also has an *office* in Cologne.
Sie hat auch ein Büro in *Köln.*	She also has an office in *Cologne.*

26 Cardinal Numbers

The cardinal numbers from 1 to 12 are:

1	eins	4	vier	7	sieben	10	zehn
2	zwei	5	fünf	8	acht	11	elf
3	drei	6	sechs	9	neun	12	zwölf

The numeral **eins** is used only for counting, for telephone numbers, in arithmetic, etc; it is never used together with a following noun. In front of a noun, the numeral looks like the indefinite article **ein** and is declined like **ein.** In the sentence **wir haben eine Tochter, eine** means *one* if it is stressed, and *a* if it is not stressed.

NUMERAL	**Ich glaube, Meyers haben zwei *Söhne.*—Nein, sie haben nur *einen* Sohn.**	I believe the Meyers have two sons.—No, they have only *one* son.
INDEFINITE ARTICLE	**Ich glaube, Meyers haben jetzt auch eine *Tochter.*— Nein, sie haben nur einen Sohn.**	I believe the Meyers now have a *daughter*, too.—No, they have only a *son*.

If the other numbers are followed by a noun, they are not changed.

Wir haben drei Kinder, zwei Autos und einen Hund.

Note also:

Es ist jetzt ein Uhr.	It is now one o'clock.
but:	
Es ist jetzt eins.	It is now one (o'clock).

27 Professional Status

Certain nouns, such as **Arzt, Lehrling,** and **Student,** can be used to express legal or professional status, and in this function they are used without any article.

Ich bin Arzt. Mein Sohn wird Arzt.
Ich bin Lehrling bei Braun und Co.; ich werde Automechaniker.
Ich bin Medizinstudentin; ich werde Kinderärztin.

But:

Wir brauchen einen Arzt.
Ich kenne den Lehrling.

Many nouns indicating profession or occupation have both masculine and feminine forms, the latter ending in **-in**; in some of these, the stem vowel has an umlaut.

der Arzt	die Ärztin
der Lehrer	die Lehrerin
der Biologe	die Biologin
der Pro*f*essor	die Pro*f*ess*or*in (shift of stress)

Conversations

I

Practice reading this conversation aloud until you have memorized it.

SCHMIDT (answering the telephone):

	Alfred Schmidt!	Alfred Schmidt.
MEYER:	Hier Meyer. Guten Morgen, Herr Schmidt! Also, Sie sind noch in Hamburg! Wie ist denn das Wetter in Hamburg?	Meyer speaking. Good morning, Mr. Schmidt. So, you are still in Hamburg. How is the weather in Hamburg?
SCHMIDT:	Hier in Hamburg regnet es, schon seit Sonntag. Und kalt ist es auch.	It's raining here in Hamburg; it has been since Sunday. And it is cold, too.
MEYER:	Hier in Köln regnet es auch! Kommen Sie heute zurück?	Here in Cologne it's raining, too. Are you coming back today?
SCHMIDT:	Nein, heute noch nicht! Aber morgen! Morgen um elf bin ich im Büro.	No, not today. But tomorrow. I'll be at the office tomorrow at eleven.
MEYER:	Gut, also dann bis morgen!	OK, until tomorrow then.

II

The following conversation demonstrates the use of American terms in contemporary German. You are not expected to memorize this conversation, but you should use it for dramatic reading, and you can act it out with another student. Two young men, who haven't seen each other for quite a while, meet in the street.

HELMUT:	Tag, Jochen.	Hello, Jochen.
JOACHIM:	Tag, Helmut. Wie geht's dir denn?	Hi, Helmut. How are you?
H:	Danke, mir geht's immer gut, und dir?	Thanks, I'm always fine, and you?
J:	Auch gut. Aber sag mal, man sieht dich ja nie mehr. Wohnst du nicht mehr in der Bettinastraße?	I'm OK too. Say, I don't ever see you around anymore. Don't you live in the Bettinastraße anymore?
H:	Nein, ich wohne jetzt im Ostend. Ich habe einen neuen Job.	No, I live in the East End now. I have a new job.
J:	Wirklich, was denn für'n Job?	Really, what kind of a job?
H:	Bei Siemens. In der Datenverarbeitung. Als Programmierer.	With Siemens. In data processing. As a programmer.

J:	Computer, das ist ja dein Hobby. Hobby als Job, das ist gut.	Computers, that's your hobby, isn't it. Your hobby as a job, that's good.
H:	Na ja, ich habe schließlich Mathematik studiert.—Und du, was machst du?	Well, I've studied mathematics, after all.— And you, what are you doing?
J:	Ich bin immer noch bei Schöninghausen und verkaufe Hi-Fi's. Meine Spezialität sind jetzt Kassettenrecorder.	I'm still with Schöninghausen selling hi-fi's. My specialty now is cassette recorders.
H:	Aha, also auch Hobby als Job.— Hast du Zeit für ein Bier?	Aha, so you have made your hobby into a job, too.—Do you have time for a beer?
J:	O.K.	OK.

Möchten Sie das stärkste Argument für Telefunken-Cassetten-Recorder hören? Anhören.

Fragen an Sie persönlich (Questions to you personally)

1. Wo wohnen Sie hier auf dem Campus?
           in der Stadt?
2. Wo wohnen Ihre Eltern? (**die Eltern** parents)
      Was ist ihr Vater (What does your father do)?
           ihre Mutter?
3. Haben Sie Geschwister? (**die Geschwister** brothers and sisters, siblings)
      Brüder?
      Schwestern?
   Wie heißen Ihre Geschwister?
   Wie alt sind Ihre Brüder?
           Ihre Schwestern?
   Wo wohnen Ihre Geschwister?
4. Wen kennen Sie schon hier in der Klasse?
5. Was machen Sie heute abend?
      Bleiben Sie zu Hause?
      Arbeiten Sie?
      Gehen Sie ins Kino?
           ins Theater?
           in die Stadt?

6. Haben Sie einen Wagen?
     ein Fahrrad?
     ein Motorrad?
7. Wie ist das Wetter heute?
8. Was ist heute? Montag   Dienstag   Mittwoch   Donnerstag   Freitag
                  Samstag   Sonntag

Reading

In the following passage, you will find many words and grammatical features that are unfamiliar. But, with the aid of the parallel English translation, you will be able to "decode" the German text.

Read the text aloud several times to improve your pronunciation and sentence intonation; then compare the German text with the English translation; finally, read the German again for comprehension.

Mitteleuropa

Mitteleuropa ist das Gebiet „in der Mitte von Europa", aber „Mitteleuropa" ist nicht identisch mit „Deutschland". Es gibt heute kein Land mehr, das Deutschland heißt. Es gibt zwei Staaten, die das Wort „deutsch" in 5 ihrem Namen haben, die Bundesrepublik Deutschland (BRD) und die Deutsche Demokratische Republik (DDR). Aber nicht nur in der BRD und in der DDR spricht man Deutsch; die Republik Österreich ist ein 10 deutschsprachiges Land, und drei Viertel der Menschen in der Schweiz sprechen Deutsch.

Diese vier Länder sind ungefähr das, was wir Mitteleuropa nennen. Aber dieses Mittel- 15 europa ist keine politische Einheit: die Bundesrepublik gehört zum Westen, zur Europäischen Gemeinschaft (EG); die DDR gehört zum sozialistischen „Ostblock", und Österreich und die Schweiz sind politisch 20 neutral. „Mitteleuropa" ist eher ein kulturelles Konzept; seine historische Tradition basiert auf der Sprache, die alle Mitteleuropäer sprechen: der deutschen Sprache. Wenn

Central Europe

Central Europe is the area "in the middle of Europe," but "Central Europe" is not identical with "Germany." There is (literally: It gives) no country today that is called Germany anymore. There are two states which have the word "German" in their name, the Federal Republic of Germany (FRG) and the German Democratic Republic (GDR). But not only in the FRG and in the GDR is German spoken (lit.: does one speak German); the Republic of Austria is a German-speaking country, and three-quarters of the people in Switzerland speak German.

These four countries are approximately what we call Central Europe. But this Central Europe is not a political entity: the Federal Republic belongs to the West, to the European Community (E.C.)*; the GDR belongs to the socialist "East Bloc," and Austria and Switzerland are politically neutral. "Central Europe" is, rather, a cultural concept; its historical tradition is based on the language which all Central Europeans speak: the German language. If, therefore,

*Also referred to as the "Common Market."

also Mitteleuropa, so wie wir es definieren, mit irgendetwas identisch ist, dann ist es identisch mit dem deutschen Sprachraum.

Central Europe, as we define it, is identical with anything, then it is identical with the German language area.

Exercises

A. Restate the following sentences by starting with the element in italics.

1. Herr Schulte ist *morgen* in Hamburg.
2. Natürlich ist *er* zu Hause.
3. Ich bleibe morgen abend *natürlich* zu Hause.
4. Übrigens gehen *wir* morgen ins Kino.
5. Morgen fährt *Sigrid* nach Köln.

SEE
ANALYSIS
17
(p. 38)

B. Form questions that could precede the following sentences. Note that news items are in italics.

1. Erika trinkt *Wein*.
2. *Erika* trinkt Wein.
3. Fritz studiert *Medizin*.
4. *Fritz* studiert Medizin.
5. Ernst Reuter wohnt in *Stuttgart*.
6. *Ernst Reuter* wohnt in Stuttgart.
7. Wir sind *um zwei Uhr* zu Hause.
8. Um zwei Uhr sind wir *zu Hause*.

SEE
ANALYSIS
9, 17
(pp. 11, 38)

C. Supply the correct plural form.

1. Ich bleibe ein Jahr in Deutschland. Fritz bleibt zwei _____ in Deutschland.
2. Herr Meyer hat ein Büro. Schmidt hat zwei _____.
3. Meyers Sohn heißt Peter. Meyers _____ heißen Peter und Paul.
4. Der Mann arbeitet in München. Die _____ arbeiten alle in München.
5. Frau Meyer und Frau Schmidt sind zu Hause. Die zwei _____ bleiben heute zu Hause.
6. Mein Bruder ist auch Arzt. Wir sind _____, und unsere Schwester ist _____.
7. Hier ist nur ein Glas, aber wir brauchen doch drei _____.
8. Meyer hat nicht nur ein Haus, er hat drei _____.
9. Mein Fahrrad ist hier. Wo sind denn eure _____?
10. Herr Schobler und Herr Reinicke sind nicht hier; die _____ sind heute beide in Berlin.

SEE
ANALYSIS
15
(p. 18)

D. Insert the correct forms.

1. Ich fahre morgen nach Berlin. Wann _____ du nach Berlin?
2. Ich lese Günter Grass, und was _____ du?
3. Ich esse ein Wiener Schnitzel. Was _____ du?
4. _____ du dieses Jahr? Wir verreisen dieses Jahr nicht.
5. Unser Fritz _____ morgen fünf Jahre alt; wann _____ du denn fünf, Rudi?
6. Wann kommt er denn?—Ich weiß es nicht; _____ du es?
7. Ich kenne Frau Brandt nicht. _____ du sie?
8. Ich nehme ein Bier. Was _____ du?
9. Ich sitze zu Hause und arbeite, und du _____ im Hofbräuhaus und trinkst Bier.

SEE
ANALYSIS
18
(P. 39)

E. In the following sentences, replace the subject by a pronoun.

1. Erika ist jetzt meine Frau.
2. Dieses Buch ist interessant.
3. Der Zug fährt nach Frankfurt.
4. Seine Frau hat auch einen Wagen.
5. Karl Meyer ist mein Freund.
6. Herr und Frau May sind hier.

SEE
ANALYSIS
20-24
(pp. 41-44)

F. Replace the object by a pronoun.

1. Ich kenne Herrn Lenz nicht.
2. Er liest diese Zeitung nicht.
3. Liebst du Inge?
4. Ich kenne Hans und Erika gut.
5. Kennen Sie seine Kinder?
6. Ich brauche den Wagen.

G. Formulate affirmative answers to the following questions, using personal pronouns.

Kennen Sie Frau Bertram?	Ja, ich kenne sie gut.

1. Kennen Sie Fritz Bertram?
2. Kennen Sie mich?
3. Kennst du die Frauen da?
4. Hast du das Geld?
5. Arbeitet dein Vater in Wien?
6. Kennst du ihre Mutter?
7. Liebst du Sylvia?
8. Brauchst du den Wagen heute abend?
9. Siehst du morgen den Arzt?
10. Lesen Sie die Zeitung heute?

H. Form sentences from the elements given; supply the article where necessary.

1. Fritz / morgen / fünf Jahre alt / werden.
2. Er / nicht / wissen // wo / wir / sein.
3. Er / um zwei Uhr / nach Hause / kommen.
4. Ich / natürlich / heute abend / zu Hause / bleiben.
5. Wohin / du / heute / fahren?
6. Er / Brot / essen / und / Milch / trinken.
7. Morgen / gut / bestimmt / Wetter / werden.
8. Du / Wagen / sehen?
9. Ich / 1 Löffel, 1 Messer und 1 Gabel / brauchen.
10. Mein / Freundin (pl.) / in Wien / alle / wohnen.

I. Give the correct articles and plural forms of the following nouns.

der Mann, die Männer

SEE
ANALYSIS
15
(p. 18)

1. Arzt
2. Lehrer
3. Haus
4. Winter
5. Kino
6. Herr
7. Frau
8. Büro
9. Sohn
10. Kind
11. Tochter
12. Mädchen
13. Jahr
14. Tag
15. Stunde

J. Express in German. This is not a "translation exercise"; you should be able to produce the German equivalents of these short sentences quite spontaneously. If you have trouble, review the preceding pages once more.

1. He has money.
2. We are eating bread and cheese.
3. What is he eating?
4. They have children.
5. They have a son.
6. This is their son.
7. Is this their daughter?
8. They have one daughter.
9. This is my doctor.
10. He is a doctor.
11. Do you see the streetcar?
12. Do you see it (the streetcar)?
13. Do you see her?
14. I see you, Mr. Meyer.
15. I know this student (male).
16. I know this student (female).
17. Do you have our books?
18. We are reading a book.
19. It is a novel.
20. We are reading a novel.

Vocabulary

Verbs

antworten	to answer
brauchen	to need
er braucht nicht zu arbeiten	he doesn't have to work
essen (du ißt, er ißt)	to eat
fahren (du fährst, er fährt)	to drive; to go (by train, boat, plane, car)
fragen	to ask
geben	to give
es gibt	there is, there are
gehören zu	to belong to
kaufen	to buy
kennen	to know (by acquaintance)
laufen (du läufst, er läuft)	to run, to walk
lesen (du liest, er liest)	to read
lieben	to love
nehmen (du nimmst, er nimmt)	to take
nennen	to call; to name
sagen	to say; to tell
sag mal	tell me, say
sehen (du siehst, er sieht)	to see
sitzen	to sit
sprechen (du sprichst, er spricht)	to speak
werden (du wirst, er wird)	to become
wissen (du weißt, er weiß)	to know (facts)

Nouns

MASCULINE

der Bruder, ¨	brother
der Dienstag, -e	Tuesday
der Donnerstag, -e	Thursday
der Freitag, -e	Friday
der Freund, -e	(male) friend
die Freundin, -nen	(female) friend
der Junge, -n	boy
der Käse	cheese
der Lehrling, -e	apprentice
der Löffel, -	spoon
der Mechaniker, -	mechanic
der Mensch, -en	human being
der Mittwoch, -e	Wednesday
der Montag, -e	Monday
der Motor', -en	motor
der Name, -n	name
der Roman', -e	novel
der Samstag, -e (Sonnabend), -e	Saturday
der Sohn, ¨e	son
der Sonntag, -e	Sunday
sonntags	on Sundays
der Staat, -en	state
der Student', -en	university student (male)
die Studen'tin, -nen	university student (female)
der Tag, -e	day
der Teller, -	plate
der Vater, ¨	father
der Wagen, -	car, cart
der Zug, ¨e	train

FEMININE

die Dame, -n	lady
die Gabel, -n	fork
die Klasse, -n	class
die Minu'te, -n	minute
die Mutter, ¨	mother
die Schwester, -n	sister
die Sekun'de, -n	second
die Sprache, -n	language
deutschsprachig	German-speaking
der Sprachraum, ¨e	language area
die Stadt, ¨e	town, city
die Stunde, -n	hour
die Tasse, -n	cup
eine Tasse Kaffee	a cup of coffee
die Tochter, ¨	daughter
die Wurst, ¨e	sausage
die Zeitung, -en	newspaper

NEUTER

das Brot, -e	bread, loaf
das Buch, ¨er	book

das Glas, ¨er	glass	das Mädchen, -	girl
das Jahr, -e	year	das Messer, -	knife
das Kind, -er	child	das Thea′ter, -	theater
das Land, ¨er	country; land	das Wort, ¨er (or: -e)	word

PLURAL ONLY

| die Eltern | parents | die Leute | people |
| die Geschwister | brothers and sisters, siblings | | |

Adjectives

		kein, keine, kein,	no, (not any)
alle	all, all of us	plural: keine	
alt	old	kein Geld	no money
bestimmt	certain, certainly	neu	new
fremd	strange; foreign	schnell	fast
das Fremdwort, ¨er	foreign word, non-German word	sicher	certain, certainly
		wirklich	real, really

Articles and Pronouns

		jeder, jede, jedes	each
		man	you, we, people, they, one (indefinite third-person pronoun)
dieser, diese, dieses,	this		
plural: diese			
irgendetwas	anything, something		

Interrogatives

| warum | why | Was für einen | What kind of a car do you have? |
| was für ein | what kind of | Wagen hast du? | |

Prepositions

		beim Essen	while eating
auf	on	mit	with
bei	at; with, at the home of; near; while	seit	since
		seit einer Woche	this last week, since a week ago
Potsdam bei Berlin	Potsdam near Berlin	von	from

Adverbs

also	therefore; well; in other words	mehr	more
		nicht mehr	no longer
da	there; then; under these circumstances; (conj.) since	nicht	not
		nie	never, not ever
		nie mehr	not ever anymore
dann	then	noch	still
dort	there	noch nicht	not yet
drüben	on the other side	noch nie	never yet
da (dort) drüben	over there	nur	only
immer	always	so	so
immer noch, noch immer	still	ungefähr	approximately
		zurück	back

Numbers

vier	four	neun	nine
fünf	five	zehn	ten
sechs	six	elf	eleven
sieben	seven	zwölf	twelve
acht	eight	hundert	hundred

Other Words

aber	but, however	wohin	where (to)
wenn	when; if		

Additional Vocabulary

als	as
die Bahn, -en	track; car (on a track)
die Autobahn	freeway, turnpike, superhighway
die Straßenbahn	streetcar
basieren auf	to be based on
das Datum	date (on a letter)
pl. die Daten	data, dates
die Datenverarbeitung	data processing
der Datenverarbeiter, -	data processor
definieren	to define
eher	rather
die Einheit, -en	entity; unit
der Fuß, ¨e	foot
das Gebiet, -e	area
die Gemeinschaft, -en	community
Europäische Gemeinschaft	European Community (E.C.)
die Gruppe, -n	group
histo'risch	historical
das Hobby, -s	hobby
iden'tisch	identical
intelligent'	intelligent
der Job, -s	job
die Kasset'te, -n	cassette
kulturell'	cultural
die Laboran'tin, -nen	lab technician
die Mathematik'	mathematics
die Maus, ¨e	mouse
der (or das) Meter, -	meter
das Thermome'ter, -	thermometer
der Kilome'ter, - (km)	kilometer
die Mitte	middle, center
(das) Mitteleuropa	Central Europe
der Mitteleuropäer, -	Central European
neutral'	neutral
der Ostblock	East Bloc
(das) Österreich	Austria
persön'lich	personal, personally
poli'tisch	political
das Programm', -e	program
der Programmie'rer	programmer
programmie'ren	to program
die Republik'	republic
die Bundesrepublik Deutschland	Federal Republic of Germany
die Deutsche Demokratische Republik	German Democratic Republic
schließlich	finally, after all
die Schweiz	Switzerland
soziali'stisch	socialist
die Spezialität', -en	specialty
starten	to start
die Tradition', -en	tradition
verreisen	to go on a trip
das Viertel, -	quarter
der Westen	west

Die
Eule
spricht:

Kein Feuer-
Rauchen-
offenes Licht...!

Württ. Gemeinde-Versicherungsverein a.G. Stuttgart

Schutzgemeinschaft Deutscher Wald · Landesverband Baden-Württemberg

Unit 3 The Structure of German Sentences—Verbal Complements—Negation by **kein** and **nicht**

If it were not for the existence of modern standard English and German, both languages would have fragmented into a multitude of local and regional dialects whose speakers would barely be able to communicate with one another.

In the German-speaking countries, there would be at least five large dialect regions. But over the last five hundred years, a common standard language has evolved as a means of communication within what used to be the Holy Roman Empire. This standard language is called **Hochdeutsch**, *High German*, and in its written form varies very little from the BRD to the DDR, to Austria and to Switzerland. However, if you talk with a native speaker of German, you can almost always tell where he or she is from, just as in the United States you can recognize, for example, Southerners or New Englanders from their way of speaking. Genuine dialects—which are quite separate from High German—have largely vanished, but regional, and often local, intonation remains, such as the typical sing-song of Swabian, spoken in the southwest. If you visit the German-speaking countries, you will immediately notice the variations and deviations from standard German in the speech and vocabulary of many people, though you will find that most of them can speak the standard language you are now learning, especially if you identify yourself as a foreigner.

The reading selection of this unit describes a "typically German" situation, seen through the eyes of a foreigner who has trouble understanding the local speech and who, quite naturally, notices cultural differences much more than cultural similarities. While you might come upon this scene anywhere in Germany, the term for "butcher" localizes it to an extent (see map on p. 56). There are a number of German terms that are expressed with different words in different parts of the country; for example, there are two words for *Saturday*: **Sonnabend** in the north, **Samstag** in the south.

In this unit, you will also learn how to tell people that you have *not* understood them. Negation is a major element in human discourse, and it is important that you learn thoroughly how to say *No* in German.

The owl says: No fire, no smoking, no open light . . . !

How do you say "butcher" in German?

Adapted from Jürgen Eichhoff's *Wortatlas der Deutschen Umgangssprachen* (Francke Verlag Bern und München, 1977).

Patterns

[1] The Two-Pronged Predicate

This section demonstrates the arrangement of elements in normal German sentences. Go through the model sentences carefully and note that the elements following the conjugated verb form often come in an order that is exactly the opposite of what you would expect in English.

COMPLETE PATTERN

FRONT FIELD	1ST PRONG OF PREDICATE	INNER FIELD	2ND PRONG OF PREDICATE	END FIELD
Das Bier	**ist**	**wirklich**	**gut**	**hier in München.**

SEE ANALYSIS 28–33 (pp. 61–66)

Es	*regnet.*	
Die *Sonne*	scheint.	
Karl	**kommt**	heute abend.
Heute abend	**kommt**	*Karl.*
Herr Anders	**liest**	einen *Roman.*

Heute	ist	das Wetter	sehr *schlecht.*
Leider	ist	die Milch	*sauer.*
Der Kaffee	ist		zu *süß.*
Herr von Creglingen	ist	schon	sehr *alt.*
Adelheid	ist	noch	sehr *jung.*

Ursula	ist	jetzt	*Lehrerin.*
Margret	wird		*Ärztin.*
Dieser Roman	wird	be*stimmt*	ein *Erfolg.*
Mein Freund	heißt		*Stein.*

Herr Dr. Wagner	ist	heute leider	in *Stutt*gart.
Heute abend	bin	ich be*stimmt*	zu Hause.

Ernst	kommt	heute um zwölf	nach *Hause.*
Meine Freundin	geht	heute abend be*stimmt*	ins Kino.

Frau *Lüders*	trinkt		*Kaf*fee.
Gudrun	studiert	jetzt in Hamburg	*Psychologie.*
Er	wohnt	jetzt	in *Berlin.*
Hoffentlich	lernt	Otto jetzt	*fahren.*
Er	lernt	jetzt *doch*	fahren.
Jetzt	lernt	er doch	*fahren.*
Der Zug	fährt	um 6 Uhr 5	*ab.*
Wann	fährt	der Zug denn	*ab?*
	Fährt	der Zug jetzt	*ab?*

Das Bier	ist	wirklich	*gut*	hier in München.
Wir	schalten	jetzt	*um*	nach *Ham*burg.

[2] Negation with **kein**

The following sentences demonstrate the use of **kein.** Study these sentences first; then practice until you can say the sentences with **kein** when you hear the sentences without **kein,** and vice versa.

Das ist Wein.	Das ist kein Wein.	SEE ANALYSIS 34-35 (p. 67)
Ich trinke Wein.	Ich trinke keinen Wein.	
Du trinkst Milch.	Du trinkst keine Milch.	
Er ißt Käse.	Er ißt keinen Käse.	
Sie ißt Brötchen.	Sie ißt keine Brötchen.	
Haben Sie einen Sohn?	Nein, wir haben keinen Sohn.	
Hat er eine Tochter?	Nein, er hat keine Tochter.	
Hat sie ein Kind?	Nein, sie hat kein Kind.	

[3] Negation with **nicht**

Be prepared to produce the answers orally when you hear the questions.

SEE
ANALYSIS
36–37
(pp. 68–70)

Regnet es?	Nein, es regnet	**nicht.**	
Liebst du ihn?	Nein, ich liebe ihn	**nicht.**	
Hast du mein Buch?	Nein, ich habe dein Buch	**nicht.**	
	Nein, ich habe es	**nicht.**	
Ist die Milch sauer?	Nein, die Milch ist	**nicht**	sauer.
	Nein, sie ist	**nicht**	sauer.
Ist Ihr Mann Arzt?	Nein, mein Mann ist	**nicht**	Arzt.
Wohnen Sie in Nürnberg?	Nein, ich wohne	**nicht**	in Nürnberg.
Fährt der Zug ab?	Nein, der Zug fährt	**nicht**	ab.
	Nein, er fährt	**nicht**	ab.
Geht Ihr heute schwimmen?	Nein, wir gehen heute	**nicht**	schwimmen.

VARIATIONS ON NEGATION

Study the picture and give negative answers to the questions. Then state the correct facts.

Example: **Regnet es?—Nein, es regnet nicht; die Sonne scheint.**

1. Ist das Wetter schlecht?
2. Ist es Winter?
3. Ist es schon Abend?
4. Ist der VW-Bus grün?
5. Ist der Mann jung?
6. Raucht er eine Zigarette?
7. Trägt er einen Hut?
8. Kennen Sie den Mann?
9. Arbeitet er?
10. Liest er ein Buch?

Was sehen Sie nicht?—
Ich sehe kein Auto.

der Bus, -se
die Straßenbahn, -en
das Motorrad, ¨-er
das Kind, -er
der Polizist, -en

[4] schon and noch nicht, noch kein, noch and nicht mehr, kein . . . mehr

Be prepared to produce orally the sentences in one column when you hear the sentences in the other column.

Regnet es schon?
   Is it raining yet?

Regnet es noch?
   Is it still raining?

Ist er schon hier?
   Is he here already?

Ist er noch *hier*?
   Is he still *here*?

Ist er *im*mer noch hier?
Ist er noch *im*mer hier?
   Is he *still* here?

Ist er noch Student?
   Is he still a student?

Ist er schon Arzt?

   Is he a doctor yet?

Nein, es regnet noch nicht.
   No, it isn't raining yet.

Nein, es regnet nicht mehr.
   No, it isn't raining anymore.

Nein, er ist noch nicht hier.
   No, he isn't here yet.

Nein, er ist nicht mehr hier.
   No, he isn't here anymore.

Nein, er ist kein Student mehr.
   No, he isn't a student anymore.
   No, he is no longer a student.

Nein, er ist noch nicht Arzt.
         noch kein Arzt.
   No, he isn't a doctor yet.

SEE ANALYSIS 38 (p. 70)

Ist es schon vier Uhr?
Ja, es ist vier Uhr elf.

Fährt der Zug schon ab?
Nein, noch nicht;
es ist doch erst neun
   Uhr fünf.

Haben wir schon Milch?
   Do we have milk yet?
   (Is the milk here yet?)

Haben wir noch Milch?
   Do we still have milk?
   (Is there any milk left?)

Trinken Sie noch ein *Bier*?
   Would you like another beer?

Nein, wir haben noch keine Milch.
   No, we don't have any milk yet.
   (No, the milk isn't here yet.)

Nein, wir haben keine Milch mehr.
   No, we don't have any milk anymore.
   (No, there isn't any milk left.)

Nein danke, ich trinke jetzt kein Bier mehr.
   No thanks, I won't drink any more beer now.

[5] mehr, mehr als, nicht mehr als

In the following sentences **mehr** refers to quantity and not to time, as in [4] above.

SEE
ANALYSIS
38
(p. 70)

Die Firma Braun braucht mehr Lehrlinge.	The Braun firm needs more apprentices.
Auto-Braun hat mehr Mechaniker als Auto-Müller.	The Braun auto firm has more mechanics than Auto-Müller.
Er arbeitet mehr als ich.	He works more than I do.
Er weiß mehr, als er sagt.	He knows more than he says.
Er hat mehr Geld, als er braucht.	He has more money than he needs.
Ich habe nur zehn Mark; ich habe leider nicht mehr.	I only have ten marks; unfortunately, I don't have any more.
Das kostet nicht mehr als fünf Mark.	That doesn't cost more than five marks.
Ich habe nicht mehr Geld als du.	I don't have more money than you (have).

[6] nicht ein

SEE
ANALYSIS
39
(p. 72)

Ich kenne hier auch nicht *ein*en Menschen.	I really don't know a *single* soul here.
Meyers haben *fünf Töch*ter, aber auch nicht *ein*en Sohn.	The Meyers have *five daughters*, but not *one* son.

[7] nicht, nicht wahr

SEE
ANALYSIS
40
(p. 72)

Wohnen Sie in *Köln?*	Do you live in *Cologne?*
Sie wohnen doch in *Köln*, nicht *wahr?*	You live in *Cologne*, don't you?
Sie wohnen doch in *Köln, nicht?*	You live in *Cologne*, don't you?

[8] doch as Answer to a Negative Question

Study these sentences as questions and answers. Be prepared to formulate the answers orally when you hear the questions, and vice versa.

SEE
ANALYSIS
41–42
(pp. 72–73)

Fahren Sie heute nach *Düsseldorf?*	Nein, ich fahre erst *morgen.*
Fahren Sie *nicht* nach Düsseldorf?	*Doch*, natürlich fahre ich nach Düsseldorf.
Trinken Sie *Kaf*fee, Frau Schmidt?	Nein, ich *trinke* keinen Kaffee.
Trinken Sie *kein*en Kaffee?	*Doch*, natürlich trinke ich Kaffee.
Haben Meyers schon *Kinder?*	*Ja*, einen *Sohn* und eine *Toch*ter.
Haben Meyers noch keine *Kinder?*	*Doch*, einen *Sohn* und eine *Toch*ter.
Gehst du heute abend ins *Kino?*	*Ja*, mit *Inge.*
Gehst du heute abend *nicht* ins Kino?	*Doch*, aber *nicht* wieder mit *Inge.*

[9] aber, denn, oder, und

SEE
ANALYSIS
43
(p. 73)

Dieses Jahr bleiben wir zu *Hause.*	*This* year we'll stay at *home.*
Aber *näch*stes Jahr fahren wir nach *Deutsch*land.	But *next* year we are going to *Germany.*

*Näch*stes Jahr fahren wir aber nach *Deutsch*-
land.

Meyer geht ins Büro, aber er arbeitet nicht.	Meyer goes to the office, but he doesn't do any work.
Ich gehe jetzt schlafen, denn ich bin sehr müde.	I'm going to sleep now, for I'm very tired.
Ißt du Wurst, oder ißt du Käse?	Are you going to eat sausage, or are you going to eat cheese?
Ißt du Wurst oder Käse?	Do you eat sausage or cheese?
Ich esse den Käse, und du ißt die Wurst.	I'm going to eat the cheese, and you'll eat the sausage.
Er ißt Käse und Wurst, und er trinkt eine Flasche Bier.*	He is eating cheese and sausage, and he is drinking a bottle of beer.
Meyer geht ins Büro und arbeitet.	Meyer goes to the office and works.

Analysis

28 Verbal Complements

Although there are many one-word statements like *Sure* or *Thanks* (**Bestimmt** or **Danke**), most utterances contain some verb form and usually a subject: *I understand* (**Ich verstehe**) or *He died* (**Er starb**).

But one-word predicates like *understand* and *died* are rather rare. Most verbs cannot, by themselves, form a complete and meaningful predicate. We cannot answer the question *Where is Joe?* by saying *Joe is* or *Joe got*; we have to add at least something like *at home* or *sick*:

Joe is at home.
Joe got sick.

Forms like *is* and *got* demand some other element to complete their meaning. These additional elements are called *verbal complements*. Consider the sentence

Fritz wohnt in Zürich.   Fritz lives in Zurich.

Since **wohnen** means *to live* only in the sense of *to reside* or *to dwell*, **Fritz wohnt** would be an incomplete statement. It would not make any sense in English either to tell somebody, *Fritz is residing*. To form a complete predicate, **wohnen** needs an additional element. The phrase **in Zürich** satisfies that need; and **in Zürich**, therefore, is a verbal complement.

Verbal complements also appear in combination with verbs that can very well form a complete predicate by themselves. Thus

Johanna geht   Joan is leaving

---

*eine Flasche Bier corresponds to *a bottle of beer*; also: **eine Tasse Kaffee, ein Glas Wein**, etc.

is a complete statement. However, in the sentence

Die Lichter gehen an   The lights go on

the inflected forms **gehen** and *go* do not express the complete predicate. The verb **gehen** now no longer means *to be leaving*; in fact, **gehen** by itself now has no meaning at all, for the statements **Die Lichter gehen** and *The lights are leaving* make no sense. Only the combinations **gehen an** and *go on* complete their meaning; they are "irreducible verbal patterns" in which neither of the two parts makes sense without the other. These irreducible patterns constitute the predicate of a sentence; the predicate, in other words, consists of the verb plus its complements, that is, those elements that complete the meaning of the verb:

> **Er arbeitet.**
> **fährt . . . ab.**
> **wohnt . . . in X.**
> **ist . . . zu Hause.**

With normal intonation, sentence stress usually falls on the complement rather than on the verb:

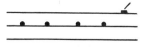

Der Zug fährt jetzt *ab*.   **Wir gehen heute *schwim*men.**

In a German dictionary, most verbs with one-word complements are listed with the complement preceding the infinitive. Thus the infinitive belonging to **Der Zug fährt jetzt *ab*** is *ab*fahren. Note that the stressed complement **ab** does not become an unstressed prefix. Even when joined to a following infinitive, **ab** can be recognized as a complement by the fact that it is stressed, while the infinitive remains unstressed. Prepositions like **an** or **aus**, and other one-word complements like **ab** or **wieder**, or even a noun like **Rad** (**radfahren**—*to bicycle*) are always joined to the infinitive. However, expressions like **nach Hause gehen**, in which complement and verb are not written as one word, are not dictionary entries.

EXAMPLES:

> *an*gehen   Das Licht geht an.   The light goes on.
> *fahr*en lernen   Sie lernt jetzt fahren.   She's learning to drive now.
> zu *Hau*se bleiben Ich bleibe heute abend zu Hause. I'll stay home tonight.
> nach *Hau*se gehen Wir gehen jetzt nach Hause. We're going (We'll go) home now.

Predicate Adjectives and Adverbs
_____

In the English sentences

> He lived happily ever after
> He was happy as long as he lived

the word *happily* is an adverb and characterizes the verbal act, the mode of living. The word *happy* is a predicate adjective. It characterizes the subject, not the verbal act.

German normally makes no distinction in form between a predicate adjective and an adverb:

PREDICATE ADJECTIVE	**Der Mensch ist gut.**	Man is good.
ADVERB	**Er fährt gut.**	He drives well.

If the verb is a form of **sein** or **werden**, the complement is always a predicate adjective, never an adverb:

> **Heute ist das Wetter schlecht.**
> **Morgen wird das Wetter gut.**

For the time being, do not use adjectives attributively—that is, in front of the noun to which they belong. Attributive adjectives require a special set of endings, which will be introduced later.

Predicate Nouns

If nouns are complements of the verbs **sein** or **werden**, they are always predicate nouns in the nominative.

> **Ich bin auch nur ein Mensch.**
> I am only human myself.

> **Dieser Roman wird bestimmt ein Erfolg.**
> This novel will surely be a success.

Directives

The question **Wohin?** (*Where to?*) is frequently answered by a prepositional phrase.

> **Wohin fährt er denn?—Er fährt nach Köln.**

Such prepositional phrases are called *directives*. They are always verbal complements.

Das Bier ist aber gut hier in München.

29 The Structure of German Assertions

The sentence

Das Bier ist wirklich *gut* hier in München

exemplifies the structure of all German assertions. This unvarying structure can be represented by the following schematic diagram:

FRONT FIELD	INFLECTED VERB	INNER FIELD	VERBAL COMPLEMENT	END FIELD
Das Bier	ist	wirklich	gut	hier in München.

Not all German assertions use this pattern in its entirety, but *no German assertion will disregard it.* The following patterns are possible:

Front Field and Inflected Verb Only

Ich	lese.
Es	regnet.
Sie	kommen.

Front Field, Inflected Verb, and Inner Field

Da	kommt	Frau Meyer.
Das	weiß	ich.
Heute	kommt	Fritz.

Front Field, Inflected Verb, Inner Field, Verbal Complement

There are several distinct types of verbal complements:

PREDICATE ADJECTIVES

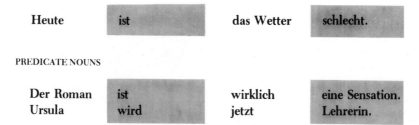

Heute	ist	das Wetter	schlecht.

PREDICATE NOUNS

Der Roman	ist	wirklich	eine Sensation.
Ursula	wird	jetzt	Lehrerin.

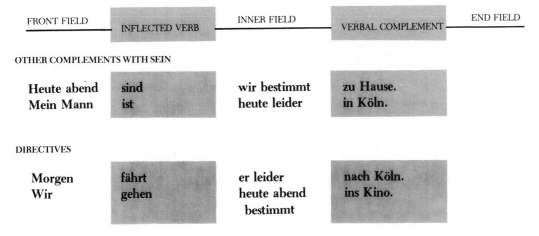

FRONT FIELD	INFLECTED VERB	INNER FIELD	VERBAL COMPLEMENT	END FIELD

OTHER COMPLEMENTS WITH SEIN

| Heute abend | sind | wir bestimmt | zu Hause. | |
| Mein Mann | ist | heute leider | in Köln. | |

DIRECTIVES

| Morgen | fährt | er leider | nach Köln. | |
| Wir | gehen | heute abend bestimmt | ins Kino. | |

OTHER COMPLEMENTS

This group includes all other complements which, together with a verb, form fixed verbal patterns.

Hans	trinkt		Kaffee.	
Erika	studiert	jetzt in Köln	Medizin.	
Heute	gehen	wir bestimmt	schwimmen.	
Der Zug	fährt	um sechs Uhr	ab.	
Die Lichter	gehen	hier um fünf Uhr	an.	

Front Field, Inflected Verb, Inner Field, Verbal Complement, End Field

| Das Bier | ist | wirklich | gut | hier in München. |
| Wir | schalten | jetzt | um | nach Hamburg. |

30 The Position of Verbal Complements

The two parts of the predicate embrace the inner field like a pair of parentheses, or like the prongs that hold the jewel of a ring in place. Since it is inconvenient to always speak of "the first part of the predicate" and "the second part of the predicate," we call them the *first prong* and the *second prong*.

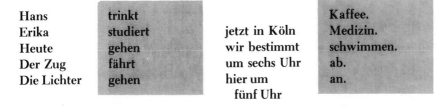

| Im Winter | gehen | hier um vier die Lichter | an. |

During the winter the lights go on here at four.

In German sentences which do not use the end field (and most of them don't), the verbal complement is the last element of the sentence.

English sentence structure is different. In most sentences, the verbal complement immediately follows the inflected verb, and it can be separated from the inflected verb by only one element.

Music turns me on.
He turned the music off.

31 The End Field

Most German sentences end with the second prong and therefore have no end field. The end field is frequently used for specifications or amplifications, especially if the amplifying element contains a preposition. It may also be used to introduce an afterthought.

| Wir | schalten | jetzt | um | nach Hamburg. |
| Das Bier | ist | wirklich | gut | hier in München. |

32 Word Order in German Questions

German questions follow the pattern of word order found in assertions. In word questions, the front field is *always* occupied by an interrogative, and personal pronoun subjects are always placed at the beginning of the inner field.

| Warum | bleibst | du heute abend | zu Hause? |

Yes-or-no questions have no front field, and again pronoun subjects are placed immediately after the opening verb.

| Bleiben | Sie heute abend | zu Hause? |

33 Sentence Intonation: Shifting the Stress Point

In German sentences which do not imply or intentionally express a contrast, the verbal complement carries the main stress—just as in English.

| Morgen | fliegen | wir | nach *Mün*chen. |
| Wir | fliegen | morgen | nach *Mün*chen. |

Any other intonation implies a contrast. The sentence

Morgen fliegen *wir* nach München

means "Tomorrow it's *our* turn to fly to Munich." The sentence

Nein, wir fliegen *morgen* nach München

means "No, not next week! Tomorrow!" Without the preceding **Nein** the sentence could also be the answer to a **wann**-question. Finally

Morgen *fliege*n wir nach München

implies "Usually we take the train (bus, car, etc.)."

34 *no, not:* **kein, nicht**

Consider the difference in the structure of the following two sentences:

    (a) That is certainly no fun.
    (b) He is not at home today.

Sentence (a) is negated by placing *no* in front of a noun; in sentence (b), *not* is placed behind the finite verb.

In German, these are the only two ways of negating a sentence. There is no German equivalent of constructions like *That isn't any fun* or *He does not (doesn't) go home today.* The *no* in (a) corresponds to German **kein:**

    (a) **Das ist bestimmt kein Vergnügen.**

The *not* in (b) corresponds to German **nicht:**

    (b) **Er ist heute nicht zu Hause.**

German **nichts** means *nothing* or *not anything;* it is the antonym (opposite) of **etwas,** *something.*

Hast du etwas gegen Erika?	Do you have anything against Erika?
Nein, ich habe nichts gegen Erika.	No, I have nothing against Erika.

35 Negation by **kein**

The noun following **kein** is either a predicate noun (in the nominative) or an object.

PREDICATE NOUNS

SING. MASC.	**Das ist kein Wein.**	That isn't wine. That's no wine.
SING. FEM.	**Das ist keine Milch.**	
SING. NEUT.	**Das ist kein Wasser.**	
PLURAL	**Das sind keine Brötchen.***	Those aren't rolls.

*Note that the verb form in sentences of this type is determined by the predicate noun; it is **sind** even though the subject **das** is singular.

    ***Das sind* meine Brüder.**   *Those are* my brothers.

OBJECTS

SING. MASC.	**Ich habe keinen Bruder.**	I have no brother.
		I don't have a brother.
SING. FEM.	**Ich habe keine Schwester.**	
SING. NEUT.	**Ich habe kein Kind.**	
PLURAL	**Wir haben keine Kinder.**	We have no children.
		We don't have any children.

The examples show:

$$\textbf{kein} + \text{noun equals} \begin{cases} no & + \text{ noun} \\ not\ any & + \text{ noun} \\ not\ a & + \text{ noun} \end{cases}$$

English no longer strictly separates *no* from *not a*. In German, this separation is still obligatory.

kein after the Inflected Verb

With normal word order, **kein** *must* be used in front of a noun object or in front of a predicate noun, *if* in the corresponding affirmative statement the noun would be used *either* with the indefinite article **ein** *or* by itself without any article or possessive adjective.

POSITIVE	NEGATIVE

Meyers haben einen Sohn. — **Meyers haben keinen Sohn.**
Meyers haben Geld. — **Meyers haben kein Geld.**
Meyers haben Kinder. — **Meyers haben keine Kinder.**
Das ist Wasser. — **Das ist kein Wasser.**

But if the noun is preceded by a possessive adjective, **nicht** must be used.

Das ist mein Sohn. — **Das ist nicht mein Sohn.**
Das ist mein Geld. — **Das ist nicht mein Geld.**
Das sind meine Kinder. — **Das sind nicht meine Kinder.**

NOTE: The plural of **ein Kind** is **Kinder**, the plural of **kein Kind** is **keine Kinder**.

kein in the Front Field

Occasionally, **kein** plus noun is found in the front field: **Kein Mensch weiß, wo Meyer wohnt**—*Nobody knows where Meyer lives.* However, such usage is very restricted. To be safe, *do not use* **kein** *in the front field.*

36 Negation by nicht

To form a negative statement, **nicht** is used whenever **kein** does not have to be used. For instance, the sentences

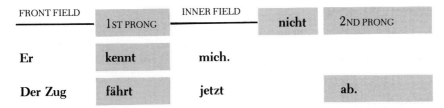

FRONT FIELD	1ST PRONG	INNER FIELD	nicht	2ND PRONG
Er	kennt	mich.		
Der Zug	fährt	jetzt		ab.

do not contain a predicate noun like **Wasser** or a noun object like **einen Sohn** (cf. **35**). Therefore, they cannot be negated by **kein**; they have to be negated by **nicht**. The problem is where this **nicht** should be placed.

The first sentence does not contain a second prong. In such cases, **nicht** stands at the very end of the sentence.

Er	kennt	mich	nicht.

The second sentence has a verbal complement, **ab**, and **nicht** must precede this complement.

Der Zug	fährt	doch	nicht	ab.

You will see later that **nicht** can also precede other elements. For the time being, however, follow this rule: **nicht** follows the inner field and precedes the second prong.

Sentences without a Second Prong

Meyer	arbeitet		nicht.
Ich	verstehe	dich	nicht.
Warum	kommt	er heute	nicht?
	Kennst	du mich	nicht?

Sentences with a Second Prong

nicht PRECEDES PREDICATE ADJECTIVES

Er	ist	leider	nicht	gesund.
Leider	ist	er	nicht	gesund.
Warum	ist	er denn	nicht	glücklich?
	Ist	sie wirklich	nicht	glücklich?

nicht PRECEDES PREDICATE NOUNS

Sie	ist	doch	nicht	meine Mutter.
Warum	werden	Sie	nicht	Arzt?
	Sind	Sie	nicht	Frau Meyer?

nicht PRECEDES DIRECTIVES—THAT IS, THE ANSWER TO *wohin*-QUESTIONS*

Nächstes Jahr	fahren	wir	nicht	nach Deutschland.
Wir	gehen	sonntags	nicht	ins Kino.
Warum	geht	ihr sonntags	nicht	in die Kirche?

nicht PRECEDES OTHER VERBAL COMPLEMENTS

Morgen abend	bleibe	ich natürlich	nicht	zu Hause.
Warum	bleibst	du morgen abend	nicht	zu Hause?
Warum	fährt	denn der Zug	nicht	ab?
Warum	lernt	sie denn	nicht	fahren?

37 Professional Status Negated

Verbal complements expressing professional or legal status can be negated by either **kein** or **nicht**.

Ich bin Arzt.
Ich bin kein Arzt

or

Ich bin nicht Arzt.

38 schon and noch nicht; noch and nicht mehr

Consider the following pairs of English sentences:

1a. It is raining already.
1b. No, it isn't raining yet.

2a. It is still raining.
2b. No, it isn't raining anymore.

Statements 1a and 2a are contradicted by statements 1b and 2b:

| 1a | 1b: | already | ⟷ | not yet |
| 2a | 2b: | still | ⟷ | not anymore |

NOTE: If 1a were a question, you would probably say, *Is it raining yet?*, but *yet* can be replaced by *already: Is it raining already?*

German expresses the same situations with the following pairs:

| 1a | 1b: | schon | ⟷ | noch nicht |
| 2a | 2b: | noch | ⟷ | nicht mehr |

1a. **Es regnet schon.**   2a. **Es regnet noch.**
1b. **Es regnet noch nicht.**   2b. **Es regnet nicht mehr.**

*Both **wo** and **wohin** correspond to English *where*. **Wo** asks for the place at which an entire action takes place; **wohin** asks for a goal toward which an action is directed and at which it ends.

If you put German and English together, you get the following system:

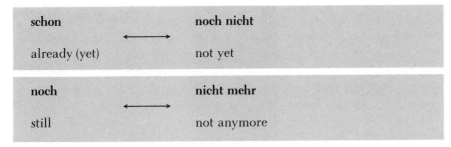

schon	noch nicht
already (yet)	not yet

noch	nicht mehr
still	not anymore

Keep in mind that
(a) **noch** and **noch nicht** are not opposites and don't belong in the same set, and
(b) *already* can be used both in assertions and in questions, but *yet* is used only in questions.

If a noun is used in these patterns, **noch nicht** becomes **noch kein,** and the noun is inserted between **kein** and **mehr.**

1a. Hast du schon Hunger?   Are you hungry yet?
1b. Nein, ich habe noch keinen Hunger.

2a. Hast du noch Hunger?
2b. Nein, ich habe keinen Hunger mehr.

1.	schon	⟷	noch kein
2.	noch	⟷	kein . . . mehr

NOTE:
1. **schon** often implies an element of surprise; something is happening sooner than expected:

Ist er denn schon *hier?*
Er hat schon drei *Kinder.*

German uses **schon** much more frequently than *already* is used in English.

2. The same surprise effect can be achieved with **noch** by adding **immer:**

Er ist *immer* noch hier

or

Er ist noch *immer* hier.

If **immer** is used, **noch** cannot be stressed. English achieves the same effect by strongly stressing *still:*

He is *still* here.

3. Frequently, **noch ein** means *another:*

Ich trinke noch eine Tasse Kaffee.   I'll have another cup of coffee.

4. While **mehr** and *more* in the sentences above have a *temporal* meaning, they can also have a *quantitative* meaning, which always involves a comparison, even if only implied; *more than* is expressed by **mehr als.** If negated, **mehr als** becomes **nicht mehr als.**

Er arbeitet mehr als ich.	He works more than I do.
Er hat mehr Geld (als ich).	He has more money (than I do).
Er hat nicht mehr Geld als ich.	He doesn't have any more money than I do.

39 nicht ein

German **nicht ein** does not correspond to English *not a* (see **35**). The **ein** in **nicht ein** is the numeral *one* and is usually stressed. German **nicht ein** therefore means *not one* or *not a single.*

Er hat nicht *einen* Freund hier.	He doesn't have a *single* friend here.

This **nicht ein** is frequently strengthened by a preceding unstressed **auch,** which may be translated by *even.*

Ich kenne hier auch nicht *einen* Menschen.	I don't know even *one* person around here.

40 nicht wahr? and nicht? as Complete Questions

Nicht wahr? (an abbreviation of **ist das nicht wahr?**—*isn't that true?*) corresponds to English *isn't that so?, don't you?, haven't you?, weren't you?,* etc. This **nicht wahr?** is frequently shortened to **nicht?** Since **nicht?** or **nicht wahr?** asks for confirmation, the preceding sentence usually contains **doch** (see **41**).

Sie *kommen* doch heute abend, nicht *wahr?*	You are coming tonight, aren't you?
Sie *kommen* doch heute abend, *nicht?*	

41 doch

The word **doch** may be stressed or unstressed. The stressed **doch** stands between inner field and second prong. It corresponds to English *after all* and expresses that the fact reported is contrary to expectations. This stressed **doch** is frequently preceded by **also,** which adds the flavor of *so* when used at the beginning of English sentences.

Er kommt *doch!*	He is coming after all! (He said he wouldn't.)
Es regnet also *doch!*	So it's raining after all! (I had hoped it wouldn't.)
Er fährt morgen *doch* nach München!	He is going to Munich tomorrow after all! (He first said he wouldn't.)

The unstressed **doch** is a sentence adverb. In assertions it adds the note "Don't you know that . . ." or "Don't forget that . . ." or simply "but."

Morgen fliegt er doch nach _Mün_chen!   But he is flying to _Munich_ tomorrow!

When assertions become questions by intonation, the unstressed **doch** expresses the speaker's hope that the opposite is not true.

Sie _kommen_ doch heute abend?   You are _coming_ tonight, aren't you?

Do not use the unstressed **doch** in regular questions.

42 doch as Answer to a Negative Question

If a negative question is answered in the affirmative, **doch** with a strong stress is used instead of **ja**.

Fährst du nicht nach Köln?   _Doch_, na_tür_lich fahre ich nach Köln.
Fährst du nicht nach Köln?   _Doch_, aber nicht _heute_.

Doch is also used to contradict a negative statement with an affirmative statement.

Ich bin doch kein Kind mehr.   _Doch_, du _bist_ noch ein Kind.

43 aber, denn, oder, und

Aber, denn, oder, and **und** are coordinating conjunctions—that is, conjunctions that connect two clauses of the same type. They precede the front field and are not counted as syntactical units. Of these four conjunctions, only **aber** can also be placed in the inner field. It then follows pronoun subjects and pronoun objects. If **denn** stands in the inner field, it is not the coordinating conjunction **denn** (_for_), but the particle **denn** discussed in **16**.

44 Sentence Adverbs

In most cases, adverbs modify

a verb:	He lived _happily_ ever after.
an adjective:	He is _unusually_ intelligent.
another adverb:	It happened _very_ suddenly.

However, certain adverbs, called _sentence adverbs_, express the attitude of the speaker toward the content of the whole sentence.

Thus, _unfortunately, naturally,_ and _obviously_ are used as sentence adverbs in

Unfortunately he died.
(It is, in my opinion, unfortunate that he died.)

Naturally, he was not at home.
(As I had expected, he was not at home.)

He was obviously not stupid.
(It was clear to all of us that he wasn't stupid.)

Three German sentence adverbs were used in Unit 1: **denn, natürlich**, and **übrigens**. Three more—**doch, hoffentlich**, and **leider**—are introduced in this unit. In both English and German, these sentence adverbs count as *independent syntactical units* as far as word order is concerned.

If a German sentence adverb stands in the front field, nothing else can occupy the front field. The sentence adverbs **doch** and **denn** can appear only in the inner field.

    Leider wohnt Tante Amalie wieder bei uns.
    Tante Amalie wohnt leider wieder bei uns.

If a sentence adverb stands in the inner field, it follows unstressed pronouns and, normally, other unstressed elements; it precedes stressed elements, that is, elements with news value, and it precedes the second prong, even if the second prong is unstressed.

    Liebt **sie ihn denn?**
    Bleibt er denn zu *Hause*?
    Bleibt sein Vater denn zu *Hause*?
    Bleibt denn sein *Vater* zu Hause?

    Sie lernt doch *fah*ren.
    Sie *lernt* doch fahren.

Conversations

I

A: Erikas Freund heißt Max. Kennst du ihn?

Erika's friend's name is Max. Do you know him?

B: Nein, ich kenne ihn nicht.

No, I don't know him.

A: Aber ich weiß, er kennt dich.

But I know that he knows you.

B: Nein, er kennt mich nicht.

No, he does not know me.

A: Erichs Freundin heißt Irene. Kennst du sie?

Erich's friend's name is Irene. Do you know her?

B: Nein, ich kenne sie nicht.

No, I don't know her.

A: Aber sie sagt, sie kennt dich.

But she says she knows you.

B: Nein, sie kennt mich nicht.

No, she does not know me.

II

JOHN RAY: Bitte, wie komme ich zum Hauptbahnhof?

Excuse me, how do I get to the main (railroad) station?

EINE FRAU:	Da gehen Sie gleich hier rechts um die Ecke, dann drei Straßen geradeaus, dann links immer die Theodor-Heuss-Allee runter, und dann sind Sie gleich da.	Go around the corner right here, then straight ahead three blocks, then turn left down Theodor-Heuss-Allee, then you'll be right there.
JOHN RAY:	Bitte, sprechen Sie etwas langsamer. Ich kann Sie nicht verstehen; ich bin Ausländer.*	Please speak a little more slowly. I can't understand you; I'm a foreigner.
FRAU:	Sind Sie Engländer?	You're an Englishman?
JOHN RAY:	Nein, Amerikaner. Ich bin erst eine Woche in Deutschland.	No, I'm an American. I've only been in Germany for a week.
FRAU:	Also gut. Hier rechts, dann drei Straßen weiter, dann kommt die Theodor-Heuss-Allee. Gehen Sie links zum Bahnhof.	OK. (Turn) right here, then (go) three blocks, then comes Theodor-Heuss-Allee. You turn left to the station.
JOHN RAY:	Jetzt verstehe ich. Vielen Dank.	Now I understand. Thank you.
FRAU:	O.K. Wiedersehn.	OK. Good-bye.
JOHN RAY:	Auf Wiedersehen.	Good-bye.

III

Construct some mini-conversations, using the elements below and phrases like "Guten Tag" or "Entschuldigung," and act them out in class.

Bitte, wo ist hier eine Bäckerei?	bakery
eine Metzgerei?	butcher's (shop)
ein Supermarkt?	supermarket
eine Drogerie?	drugstore
eine Apotheke?	pharmacy
eine Bank?	bank
ein Kaufhaus?	department store
ein Sportgeschäft?	sporting goods store
ein Lebensmittelgeschäft?	grocery store

Sagen Sie, gibt es hier keine Apotheke? (Tell me, is there no pharmacy here?)
        kein Kaufhaus?
        keinen Supermarkt?
        etc.

---

*Note that the words **Ausländer, Engländer, Amerikaner** are used here without the indirect article. (See *Professional Status*, Analysis 27, p. 44, and 37, p. 70.)

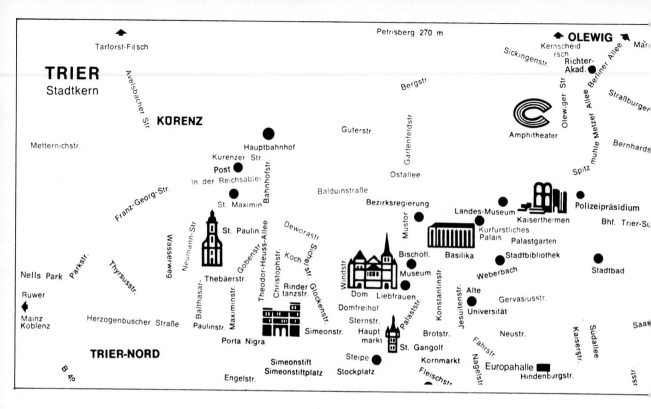

Bitte, wie komme ich zum Bahnhof?
　　　　　　　　　zum Autobus?
　　　　　　　　　zum Flughafen?
　　　　　　　　　zur Bank?
　　　　　　　　　in die Bettinastraße?

Da gehen Sie hier rechts um die Ecke.
　　　　　　　　　zwei Straßen weiter und dann links.
Dort auf der anderen Seite.
Hier immer geradeaus (always straight ahead).
Das weiß ich nicht. Ich bin hier auch fremd (I'm a stranger here myself).

Fragen an Sie persönlich

Geben Sie positive oder negative Antworten.

1. Haben Sie ein Fahrrad?
　　　　　　ein Motorrad?
　　　　　　einen Wagen?
　　　　　　ein Segelboot? (**das Boot** boat, **das Segelboot** sailboat)
　　　　　　ein Flugzeug? (**das Flugzeug** airplane)

2. Was machen Sie heute abend?
　　Gehen Sie ins Kino?
　　　　　　ins Theater?
　　　　　　ins Konzert?

in den Zirkus?
ins Museum?
Sind Sie heute abend zu Hause?
Arbeiten* Sie heute abend?

3. Sind Sie aus (Do you come from) Neu-England?
Idaho?
Südamerika?
Walla-Walla, Washington?

4. Gibt es in Ihrer Stadt ein Theater?
ein Konzerthaus?
einen Zirkus?
ein Museum?
Kinos?

5. Sind Sie schon zwanzig (20) Jahre alt?

6. Fahren Sie nächsten Sommer nach Europa?
nach Afrika?
nach Australien?
nach Asien?

7. Haben Sie (schon) einen Freund hier in der Klasse?
eine Freundin
Haben Sie schon Freunde (Freundinnen) im College?
an der Universität?

8. Haben Sie einen Bruder?
Brüder?
eine Schwester?
Schwestern?
Geschwister?
Sind Ihre Brüder schon auf dem College?
Schwestern nicht mehr auf dem College?
auf der High School?
schon verheiratet (married)?
Haben sie schon Kinder?

9. Lesen Sie Romane?
Schreiben Sie viele Briefe (many letters)?
Trinken Sie Milch?
Kaffee?
Tee?
Orangensaft (orange juice)?
Trinken Sie keinen Wein?
kein Bier?
Ist das Bier gut hier?

*arbeiten is used here in the sense of *to study:* "Are you going to study tonight?"

10. Scheint heute die Sonne nicht?
    Ist das Wetter nicht gut?
    Regnet es heute?
    Ist das Wetter schlecht?
    Gehen Sie heute schwimmen?
                          schilaufen (to ski)?

11. Haben Sie Geld?
    Brauchen Sie Geld?

Reading

Schweinefleisch

Ein Amerikaner, John Ray aus Detroit, zwanzig Jahre alt, Collegestudent und neu in Deutschland, steht in einer Metzgerei in Ulm (oder Stuttgart oder Sindelfingen) und wartet. Es ist zehn Uhr morgens, und alle 5 deutschen Hausfrauen kaufen ein. Vor ihm stehen zehn Frauen und sprechen Dialekt. Er versteht kein Wort, denn er ist ja noch nicht lange in Deutschland. Aber er liest: „Heute besonders billig—Schweinefleisch, 500 g 10 DM 5,80."*

Schweinefleisch, das versteht er nicht. Er nimmt sein Taschenwörterbuch und sucht: **das Schwein,-e,** *swine,* und **das Fleisch,** *flesh.* „Brrr", denkt er, „und die Deutschen 15 essen das?"

(Die Deutschen sagen aber nicht „brrr", wenn sie Schweinefleisch essen, denn für *pork* gibt es im Deutschen kein anderes Wort.)   20

Dann findet er, daß *Schwein* nicht nur *swine,* sondern auch *pig* und *pork* ist, und *Fleisch* ist auch *meat.* „Aha", denkt er, „also *pork meat,* oder einfach *pork.*" Aber er wartet immer noch, und vor ihm stehen noch 25 immer fünf Hausfrauen und sprechen Schwäbisch.

An American, John Ray from Detroit, twenty years old, college student and new in Germany, stands in a butcher's shop in Ulm (or Stuttgart or Sindelfingen), waiting. It is ten in the morning, and all the German housewives are out shopping. In front of him are ten women, speaking dialect. He doesn't understand a word, for he hasn't been in Germany very long. But he reads: "Especially cheap today—Schweinefleisch, 500 g. DM 5,80."*

"Schweinefleisch" he doesn't understand. takes his pocket dictionary and searches: *das Schwein,-e, swine,* and *das Fleisch, flesh.* "Yuk," he thinks, "and the Germans eat that?"

(But the Germans don't say "Yuk" when they eat *Schweinefleisch,* for there is no other word for "pork" in German.)

Then he finds that *Schwein* is not only *swine,* but also *pig* and *pork,* and *Fleisch* is also *meat.* "Aha," he thinks, "thus *pork meat,* or simply *pork.*" But he is still waiting, and in front of him there are still five housewives, speaking Swabian.

*Read as: **fünfhundert Gramm, fünf Mark achtzig**—500 grams, five marks eighty.

„Ja, bitte, der Herr", sagt plötzlich die Metzgersfrau, „*auch* ein Pfund Schweinefleisch? Ganz frisch—und sehr billig heute, nur fünf Mark achtzig das Pfund. Oder lieber ein Roastbeef oder ein Steak?" (Sie sagt „Rost-⁵behf" und „Schtehk".)

„Nein, danke", sagt er, „kein Schweinefleisch, aber geben Sie mir bitte 100 g Leberwurst."

„Gern", sagt die Metzgersfrau.—„So, das¹⁰ macht eine Mark achtzig."

„Bitte", sagt John jetzt, „sagen Sie, wo ist hier eine Bäckerei? Ich brauche Brötchen. Ich habe heute noch nichts gegessen."

„Brötchen kriegen Sie hier bei uns, ganz¹⁵ frisch, von heute morgen." Jetzt versteht er sogar ihren schwäbischen Dialekt.

Er bezahlt und geht. Zehn Minuten später sitzt er im Park auf einer Bank (gegenüber ist ein Supermarkt), ißt seine Brötchen und²⁰ seine Wurst und trinkt eine Flasche Bier. Beim Essen studiert er sein Wörterbuch. Er sagt jetzt nicht mehr „brrr" (die Wurst ist sehr gut), er sagt jetzt, „Aha : Ochsenfleisch ist nicht *ox flesh*, es ist *beef*, und Kalbfleisch²⁵ ist *veal*. Aha," denkt er wieder, „*pork*, *beef*, *veal*, diese Wörter kommen aus dem Französischen, und *swine*, *ox* und *calf* sind germanisch."

"Yes, sir, (may I help you) please," the butcher's wife says suddenly, "you'd like a pound of pork, too? Very fresh, and very inexpensive today, only five marks eighty a pound. Or would you rather have roast beef or a steak?" (She says "Rostbehf" and "Schtehk.")

"No, thanks," he says. "No pork, but please give me 100 grams of liverwurst."

"Sure," says the butcher's wife. "There, that's one mark eighty."

"Please," John says now, "tell me, where is there a bakery around here? I need some rolls. I haven't eaten anything yet today."

"Rolls you get right here from us, very fresh, from this morning." Now he even understands her Swabian dialect.

He pays and leaves. Ten minutes later he is sitting on a bench in the park (there is a supermarket across the street), eating his rolls and his sausage and drinking a bottle of beer. While he eats he studies his dictionary. Now he doesn't say "Yuk" anymore (the sausage is very good); now he says, "Aha: *Ochsenfleisch* is not ox flesh, it is *beef*, and *Kalbfleisch* is veal. Aha," he thinks again, "pork, beef, veal, these words are from the French, and swine, ox, and calf are Germanic."

Vom Denken und vom Essen und Trinken wird er müde. Bald liegt er auf der Bank, eine Zeitung über dem Gesicht, und schläft ein. Dann träumt er von dicken, fetten, rosigen Schweinen auf einer grünen Wiese.

All the thinking and eating and drinking make him tired. Soon he lies on the bench, a newspaper over his face, and falls asleep. Then he dreams of big, fat, rosy pigs in a green meadow.

Exercises

A. Complete the following conjugation samples. Be prepared to go through these sentences in class without your book.

SEE ANALYSIS 7, 16–19 (pp. 10, 39–40)

1. Ich bin zu Hause. _____ du zu Hause?
   Du _____ zu Hause. _____ er zu Hause?
   Er _____ zu Hause. _____ wir zu Hause?
   Wir _____ zu Hause. _____ ihr zu Hause?
   Ihr _____ zu Hause. _____ sie zu Hause?

2. Ich weiß es. _____ du es *auch?*
   Du _____ es. _____ er es *auch?*
   Wir _____ es. _____ ihr es *auch?*
   Ihr _____ es. _____ sie es *auch?*

3. Ich fahre morgen nach Berlin. _____ du morgen *auch* nach Berlin?
   Du _____ morgen nach Berlin. _____ er morgen *auch* nach Berlin?
   Er _____ morgen nach Berlin. _____ wir morgen *auch* nach Berlin?
   Wir _____ morgen nach Berlin. _____ ihr morgen *auch* nach Berlin?
   Ihr _____ morgen nach Berlin. _____ sie morgen *auch* nach Berlin?

4. Ich lese ein Buch. _____ du *auch* ein Buch?
   Du _____ ein Buch. _____ er *auch* ein Buch?
   Er _____ ein Buch. _____ wir *auch* ein Buch?
   Wir _____ ein Buch. _____ ihr *auch* ein Buch?
   Ihr _____ ein Buch. _____ sie *auch* ein Buch?

B. For all sentences in Patterns [1], p. 56, list the complete predicate in lexical (infinitive) form, with the second prong preceding the infinitive.

regnen
sehr schlecht sein
Lehrerin werden
in Stuttgart sein
etc.

SEE
ANALYSIS
28–30
(pp. 61–65)

C. Negate the following sentences by using **kein.** Do not stress **kein.**

1. Das ist Wasser.
2. Haben Sie einen Wagen?
3. Sie hat eine Tochter.
4. Brauchst du Geld?
5. Trinken Sie Kaffee, Frau Meyer?

SEE
ANALYSIS
34–35
(p. 67)

D. Negate the following sentences by using **nicht.**

1. Du bist doch meine Mutter.
2. Er liebt mich aber.
3. Sie wohnen in Düsseldorf.
4. Das Wetter ist gut.
5. Er ist zu Hause.

SEE
ANALYSIS
36
(p. 70)

E. Give appropriate answers to the following questions, using **noch, schon, noch nicht,** and **nicht mehr** as needed.

1. Gehst du schon schlafen? Nein, ich _____.
2. Ist er noch nicht hier? Doch, er _____.
3. Ist er noch zu Hause? Ja, _____.
4. Wie alt ist er denn? Er ist _____ jung.
5. Rauchst du noch? Nein, _____.
6. Geht ihr schon essen? Nein, _____.
7. Trinken Sie keinen Kaffee mehr? Doch, _____.
8. Lebt eure Tante Amalie noch? Ja, _____.

SEE
ANALYSIS
38
(p. 70)

F. Transform the following sentences by substituting **kein** for **nicht ein.** Say each pair of sentences aloud to practice the shift in intonation. Do not stress **kein,** but the inflected verb.

> **Ich kenne hier nicht *einen* Menschen.**
> **Ich *kenne* hier keinen Menschen.**

1. Er hat auch nicht einen Freund.
2. Wir haben hier nicht einen Arzt.
3. Heute abend fährt auch nicht ein Zug nach Garmisch-Partenkirchen.

SEE
ANALYSIS
39
(p. 72)

G. Express in German.

1. He is intelligent, isn't he?
2. He lives in Vienna, doesn't he?
3. She has a house in Cologne, doesn't she?
4. You are a doctor, aren't you?
5. They have a son, don't they?

SEE
ANALYSIS
40
(p. 72)

H. Insert first a stressed and then an unstressed **doch** into the following sentences. Explain the difference in meaning.

SEE
ANALYSIS
41
(p. 72)

1. Wir fahren nach München.
2. Meyer hat Geld.
3. Herr Lenz wohnt in Köln.
4. Er ist zu Hause.

I.   Insert the correct form of the possessive adjective.

> **Ich habe ein Buch; es ist mein Buch.**

1. Der Mann heißt Müller; ich kenne _____ Sohn.
2. Rolf ist Erikas Sohn, und Else ist _____ Tochter.
3. Herr Graber, wo sind _____ Kinder?
4. Helmut und Wolfgang, wo sind _____ Bücher?
5. Wir wissen nicht, wo _____ Bücher sind.
6. Kennen Sie Herrn Müller?—Nein, aber ich kenne _____ Tochter.
7. Frau Schmidt, wo ist _____ Sohn?
8. Frau Schmidt, wo ist _____ Tochter?
9. Ja, das ist Herr Weber; aber ist das _____ Wagen?
10. Warum trinkt ihr _____ Kaffee nicht?

J.   Form sentences from the elements given; supply articles where necessary.

1. Ich / Sie / nicht verstehen // ich / Ausländer / sein.
2. Bitte // wie / ich / zum Bahnhof / kommen?
3. Wir / in Deutschland / 12 Tage / bleiben.
4. Warum / du / denn / so schnell / laufen?
5. Heute abend / er / sein Wagen / nicht / nehmen.
6. Morgen / Sonne / hoffentlich / scheinen.
7. Ich / wissen // wer / er / sein // aber / ich / er / nicht / kennen.
8. Heute / wir / nicht / schwimmen gehen // denn / Wetter / schlecht / sein.

K.   Express in German.

1. The train is leaving.
2. Is the beer good here?
3. The milk, I hope, is not sour?
4. Do you have my novel?
5. She doesn't have a child.
6. She is not a doctor.
7. Is it raining yet?
8. Is it still raining?
9. He isn't here yet.
10. I'll drink another cup of coffee.

Vocabulary

Verbs

bezahlen	to pay (a bill)	**fliegen**	to fly
denken	to think	**hoffen**	to hope
einkaufen	to shop	**hoffentlich**	I hope; hopefully
einschlafen (du schläfst ein, er schläft ein)	to fall asleep	**kosten**	to cost
		kriegen	to get *(colloq.)*
finden	to find	**leben**	to be alive, live

liegen	to lie (flat); to be situated	schwimmen gehen	to go swimming
		stehen	to stand
rauchen	to smoke	suchen	to look for, seek, search
schlafen (du schläfst, er schläft)	to sleep	verheiratet sein	to be married
		verstehen	to understand
schlafen gehen	to go to bed	warten	to wait
schwimmen	to swim		

Nouns

MASCULINE

		der Flughafen, ⸚	airport
der Ausländer, -	foreigner	der Markt, ⸚e	market
der Bahnhof, ⸚e	train station	der Supermarkt	supermarket
der Brief, -e	letter	der Park, -s	park
der Erfolg, -e	success, result	der Stein, -e	stone

FEMININE

die Apothe'ke, -n	pharmacy	DM = die Deutsche Mark	basic unit of German currency
die Bank, ⸚e	bench		
die Ecke, -n	corner	die Seite, -n	page, side
um die Ecke	around the corner	die Tante, -n	aunt
die Firma, (pl. die Firmen)	firm, company	die Tasche, -n	pocket
		die Universität, -en	university
die Hausfrau, -en	housewife	die Wiese, -n	meadow
die Mark	mark (money)	die Woche, -n	week

NEUTER

das Fleisch (no pl.)	meat	das Konzert, -e	concert
das Flugzeug, -e	airplane	das Licht, -er	light
das Geschäft, -e	business, store	das Pfund, -e	pound
das Sportgeschäft	sporting goods store	das Wasser, ⸚	water
das Gesicht, -er	face	das Wörterbuch, ⸚er	dictionary
das Kaufhaus, ⸚er	department store		

Adjectives

anders	different	frisch	fresh
ein anderes Wort	a different word	ganz	entire; quite
billig	cheap	ganz gut	not bad
dick	thick; fat	gleich	equal, same, like; right
fett	fat		
französisch	French		
(das) Frankreich	France	gleich hier um die Ecke	right here around the corner
der Franzose, -n	Frenchman	grün	green

jung	young	**rechts**	to the right
lang	long	**sauer**	sour
lange	for a long time	**spät**	late
langsam	slow	**später**	later
link-	left	**süß**	sweet
links	to the left	**viel**	much
müde	tired	**weit**	far
plötzlich	suddenly	**weiter**	further
recht-	right		

Prepositions

an	at, on	**gegenüber**	opposite
an'gehen	to go on	**über**	over
aus	out	**vor**	in front of
aus'gehen	to go out	**vor ihm**	in front of him

Adverbs

ab	off	**gern(e)**	gladly
abfahren	to depart	**ich esse gern**	I like to eat
bald	soon	**leider**	unfortunately
besonders	especially	**lieber**	rather
doch	(see **41**)	**sehr**	very
erst	only	**sogar**	even
geradeaus	straight, straight ahead		

Other Words

etwas	something, somewhat	**sondern**	but
etwas langsamer	somewhat slower	**zwanzig**	twenty
oder	or		

Additional Vocabulary

der Amerikaner, -	American	**das Brötchen, -**	(hard) roll
der Autobus, -se	bus	**der Dialekt', -e**	dialect
der Bäcker, -	baker	**die Drogerie', -n**	drugstore
die Bäckerei, -en	bakery	**der Engländer, -**	Englishman
das Boot, -e	boat	**die Flasche, -n**	bottle
das Segelboot, -e	sailboat	**eine Flasche Bier**	a bottle of beer

germanisch	Germanic
das Gramm, *(no pl.)*	(metric) gram
fünfhundert Gramm (500 g)	500 grams
das Kalb, ̈er	calf
Kalbfleisch	veal
die Lebensmittel	groceries, food
das Lebensmittelgeschäft, -e	grocery store
die Leber	liver
die Leberwurst	liverwurst
der Metzger, -	butcher
die Metzgerei, -en	butcher's (shop)
die Metzgersfrau	butcher's wife
das Muse′um, *pl. die* Muse′en	museum
der Ochse, -n	ox

das Ochsenfleisch	beef
die Orange, -n	orange
der Orangensaft	orange juice
die Rose, -n	rose
rosig	rosy
runter (= hinunter, herunter)	down
die Straße runter	down the street
schalten	to switch (electr.)
umschalten	switch over (to a different station)
schilaufen	to ski
das Schwein, -e	pig, swine
das Schweinefleisch	pork
träumen	to dream
der Zirkus,-se	circus

Jeden Donnerstag
20 Uhr
Live Jazz
im Exhaus
Jazz
Club
Trier eV
13. Juli
HOLZWURM
Rock - Jazz
Jazz
Club
Trier eV
MIT
UND
BREAK
Samstag,
Hein & Oss

UNIT 4 Modal Auxiliaries—Contrast Intonation—
Imperative

The pork-story in Unit 3 has perhaps given the impression that Germany is a backward place with quaint and odd customs. But while it is true that this scene is "typically German," it is also true that, since the end of World War II, Germany has become a thoroughly modern, highly industrialized, and very affluent country. Some West Germans will tell you that their country has been "Americanized" beyond recognition, and many East Germans, officially referred to as "citizens of the DDR," will say that their part of the country has been "Sovietized" beyond repair. Advanced technology, tremendous industrial output, and gleaming new high-rise buildings are part of the scene in both countries.

There is no doubt that all of Central Europe went through a quarter century of unprecedented economic growth, and it is understandable that the older generation regrets the passing of the good old ways, often forgetting that the Nazi period stands between the hectic present and those halcyon days they remember. To the uninitiated, however, to an American student on his first trip to Europe, for example, the "old" Germany is still so apparent that he stumbles across it with every step he takes. He will notice the so-called Americanization, but it will also be obvious to him that West Germany, or Switzerland, or Austria, are not mirror images of the United States.

Studying the German language, you constantly encounter German culture in the broadest possible sense. No translation of individual words or of sentences is totally accurate, for it always represents the foreign culture in terms of one's own culture. For example, you will learn the word **Mittagessen,** which we have quite inaccurately translated as *dinner* because the term "midday meal" means nothing to Americans. But Germans do eat their main meal at midday, a custom so strongly ingrained that even today many people still take a two-hour "lunch break" and many small shops are closed from twelve to two.

Department stores, supermarkets, and many other shops in the big cities, of course, stay open. However, Germans cling tenaciously to the old neighborhood stores. The butcher and the baker, and sometimes even the candlestick maker, still run their own shops, although at least some of the baker's bread comes from a bread factory, and most butchers no longer slaughter their own meat. How long they will be able to continue is an open question; few young people want to become baker's apprentices who have to start work at 3:30 A.M. in order to have today's **Brötchen** ready for today's breakfast.

Another bit of cultural contrast can be found in what the Germans call
Drogerie. This kind of establishment operates on a much narrower scale than
the American drugstore and does not carry many items that you routinely expect to find in a drugstore. If you need a prescription filled, you will have to go
to an **Apotheke;** and you will never find a lunch counter in a **Drogerie.**

You will have an opportunity in this unit to use the names of some of these specialized stores in conversations, so that you get used to the fact that they are
part and parcel of all Germans' everyday life. Continue to use them, as well as
all other expressions that do not have exact equivalents in English.

Patterns

[1] können

Study the following sentences, which contain all the present-tense forms of **können**.

SEE
ANALYSIS
45–51
(pp. 95–99)

I can come today.

Ich kann heute kommen.
Kannst du heute kommen?
Hans kann heute kommen.
Wir können heute kommen.
Könnt ihr heute kommen?
Schmidts können heute kommen.

Können Sie Deutsch, Ms. Jones?—Ja, ich
kann Deutsch; ich kann auch Französisch.

Kann John auch Deutsch?—Nein, er kann
leider kein Deutsch; aber ich weiß, er
kann Spanisch und Italienisch.

Emily Jones kann Deutsch sehr gut verstehen;
sie kann Deutsch lesen und sprechen,
aber sie kann es nicht sehr gut schreiben.

I can't come today.

Ich kann heute nicht kommen.
Kannst du heute nicht kommen?
Hans kann heute nicht kommen.
Wir können heute nicht kommen.
Könnt ihr heute nicht kommen?
Schmidts können heute nicht kommen.

Do you know German, Ms. Jones?—Yes, I
know German; I also know French.

Does John also know German?—No, he
doesn't know German; but I know (that)
he knows Spanish and Italian.

Emily Jones can understand German very
well; she can read and speak German,
but she can't write it very well.

VARIATIONS

Ich kann heute kommen.
Er _____.
Er _____ nicht _____.
_____ Sie _____?
Warum _____ du denn _____ nicht _____?
Warum _____ ihr denn _____ nicht _____?
Wir _____ leider nicht _____.
Könnt _____ nicht _____?
Doch, ich _____.
Nein, wir _____ nicht _____.

Form the same variations using (1) **das Haus kaufen** and (2) **morgen nach München fahren**. Note that **nach München** is second prong, but **das Haus** is not.

[2] müssen

The following sentences contain all present-tense forms of **müssen**. Note that **nicht brauchen zu** is used in the negated sentences.

Ich muß *arbeiten*.	I have to *work*.	**SEE ANALYSIS 45–51**
Ich brauche nicht zu *arbeiten*.	I don't have to *work*.	(pp. 95–99)
Du mußt *kom*men.	You have to *come*.	
Du *brauchst* nicht zu kommen.	You don't *have* to come.	
Er muß morgen nach *Wien* fahren.	He has to go to *Vienna* tomorrow.	
Er *braucht* morgen nicht nach *Wien* zu fahren.	He does not *have* to go to *Vienna* tomorrow.	

Ich muß leider draußen bleiben

Wir müssen morgen leider *arbeiten*.	Unfortunately, we have to *work* tomorrow.
Wir *brauchen* morgen nicht zu arbeiten.	We don't *have* to work tomorrow.
Ihr müßt Tante *Amalie* besuchen.	You have to visit Aunt *Amalie*.
Ihr *braucht* sie nicht zu be*suchen*.	You don't *have* to visit her.
Sie müssen morgen alle früh aufstehen.	You will all have to get up early tomorrow.
Morgen brauchen Sie nicht früh aufzustehen.	Tomorrow you don't have to get up early.
Warum wollen Sie denn bei dem Regen nach *Hamburg* fahren?—Ich *muß!*	Why do you want to drive to *Hamburg* in this rain?—I *have* to!
Sie sagen, Sie arbeiten auch *sonn*tags? Das *brauchen* Sie aber nicht.	You say you work also on *Sundays?* You don't *have* to do that.
Sie *arbeiten* heute? *Müssen* Sie das?	You are *working* today? Do you *have* to?

VARIATIONS

Mußt du morgen arbeiten?	Nein, morgen _____ ich nicht zu arbeiten.
Ich hoffe, du brauchst morgen nicht zu arbeiten.	Doch, leider _____ ich auch *morgen* arbeiten.
Braucht er denn heute nicht zu arbeiten?	Nein, heute _____.
Müßt ihr heute arbeiten?	Ja, wir _____.
Muß Erika immer noch arbeiten?	Nein, sie _____ nicht mehr _____.

Deutsch lernen muß nicht ganz so schwierig sein ...

Form the same variations with (1) **nach Berlin fahren**, (2) **zu Hause bleiben**, and (3) **mit Tante Amalie ins Museum gehen**. Note that **mit Tante Amalie ins Museum** is one verbal complement.

Note the difference in the use of **nicht brauchen zu** and **nicht müssen** in the following examples.

Gottseidank brauche ich nächste Woche nicht zu *ar*beiten, und wir können end-lich in die *Ber*ge fahren.

Nein, ich *muß* Sonntag nicht arbeiten, aber ich will nächste Woche in die *Ber*ge fahren und brauche *Geld*.

Thank goodness I don't have to *work* next week, and we can go to the *mountains* at last.

No, I don't *have* to work on Sunday, but I want to go to the *mountains* next week and (I) need *money*.

[3] wollen

Be prepared to produce orally the negative sentences when you hear the affirmative sentences and vice versa.

SEE ANALYSIS 45–51 (pp. 95–99)

Ich will jetzt *schla*fen.
  I want to *sleep* now.

Ich *will* noch nicht schlafen.
  I don't *want* to sleep yet.

Willst du jetzt *essen*?
  You want to *eat* now?

Willst du noch *nicht* essen?
  Don't you want to eat yet?

Sie will *immer schwim*men gehen.
  She *always* wants to go *swimming*.

Sie *will* heute nicht schwimmen gehen.
  She doesn't *want* to go swimming today.

Wir wollen heute abend einen *Freund* besuchen.
  We want to visit a *friend* tonight.

Wir wollen ihn heute abend *nicht* besuchen.
  We *don't* want to visit him tonight.

Warum wollt ihr denn die *Straßen*bahn nehmen?
  Why do you want to take the *streetcar*?

Warum wollt ihr nicht mit dem *Bus* fahren?
  Why don't you want to go by *bus*?

Sie wollen vier Wochen ver*rei*sen.
  They want to go on a four-week trip.

Sie wollen nicht mehr so viel verreisen.
  They don't want to go on trips so often any-more.

München ist im Sommer besonders attraktiv.

VARIATIONS

Hans und Erika wollen essen gehen.
Hans _____ essen gehen.
Ich _____ noch nicht _____.
Wir _____ erst um zwei Uhr _____.
Du _____ schon _____?
Wann _____ ihr denn _____?

[4] sollen

For each sentence, form a parallel example according to the translation on the right.

Ich soll heute abend zu *Hause* bleiben.

_____

Aber *Hans!* Du *sollst* doch keinen Kaffee trinken.

_____

Sie *soll* sonntags nicht mehr arbeiten.

_____

Was sollen wir denn *tun?*

_____

Warum sollt ihr ihn denn schon wieder be*su*chen?

_____

Herr Meyer, Sie sollen morgen nach Hanno*ver* fahren.

_____

I am supposed to stay *home* tonight.	**SEE ANALYSIS 45–51** (pp. 95–99)

I am supposed to visit Aunt *Amalie* tonight.

But Hans, you're not *supposed* to drink coffee.

But Hans, you're not *supposed* to work so much.

She's not *supposed* to work on Sundays anymore.

She's not *supposed* to go to the movies anymore.

What are we supposed to *do?*

When are we supposed to *visit* them?

Why are you supposed to *visit* him again?

Why aren't you supposed to *read* this book?

Mr. Meyer, you are supposed to go to *Hanover* tomorrow.

Mr. Meyer, you are supposed to stay *here* tomorrow.

[5] möchte

After studying these sentences, practice the forms of **möchte** as indicated below.

SEE
ANALYSIS
45–51
(pp. 95–99)

Ich *möchte* jetzt nichts essen; ich möchte *schlafen.*	I don't *want* to eat anything now; I want to *sleep.*
Möchtest du Frau *Mey*er kennenlernen?	Would you like to meet Mrs. *Meyer?*
Er möchte *Augen*arzt werden.	He would like to become an *eye* doctor.
Sie möchte nächstes Jahr *hei*raten.	She would like to *marry* next year.
Wir möchten Sonntag mal in die *Berge* fahren.	We would like to go to the *mountains* next Sunday for a change.
Wann möchtet ihr denn *hei*raten?	When would you like to get *married?*
Alle Menschen möchten *glück*lich werden.	*Everybody* wants to become *happy.*
Ich möchte eine Tasse *Kaf*fee trinken.	I should like to have (drink) a cup of *coffee.*
Möchten Sie *auch* eine Tasse Kaffee?	Would you *also* like to have a cup of coffee?

VARIATIONS

Ich gehe essen.	Ich möchte essen gehen.
Ich fahre nächstes Jahr nach Italien.	_____
Morgen gehe ich nicht ins Kino.	_____
Gehst du nach Hause?	_____
Meyer kauft unser Haus.	_____
Wir essen heute abend mal im Regina.	_____

[6] dürfen

After studying these sentences, go through the variations below.

SEE
ANALYSIS
45–51
(pp. 95–99)

Ich darf ihn nicht be*su*chen.	I am not permitted to *visit* him.
Ich darf ihn noch nicht be*su*chen.	I am not yet permitted to *visit* him.
Ich darf ihn nicht mehr be*su*chen.	I am no longer permitted to *visit* him.
Darfst du *Kaf*fee trinken?	Can you drink *coffee?*
Darf er jetzt wieder *Kaf*fee trinken?	Can he drink *coffee* again (now)?
Hier *darf* man nicht baden.	Swimming is not *permitted* here.
Das darfst du aber nicht *tun*, Rudi.	You mustn't *do* that, Rudi.
Dürfen wir euch morgen be*su*chen?	May we *visit* you tomorrow?
Dürft ihr uns be*su*chen?	May you *visit* us?
In Deutschland dürfen die Geschäfte sonntags nichts verkaufen.	In Germany, stores may not sell anything on Sundays.

VARIATIONS

Vary each sentence with the new subjects indicated.

Ich darf morgen meinen Mann besuchen.   Du _____.

Frau Meyer _____.

Wir dürfen keinen Kaffee mehr trinken. Er _____.
                                          Erika _____.
Ich darf sonntags nichts verkaufen.   Meyer _____.
                                          Wir _____.

[7] Second Prong after Modals

| | | | | 2ND PRONG | |
FRONT FIELD	1ST PRONG	INNER FIELD	NICHT	1ST BOX	2ND BOX
Ich	möchte	das Buch			lesen.
Ich	möchte	das Buch	nicht		lesen.
Ich	darf	Kaffee			trinken.
Ich	darf	keinen Kaffee			trinken.
Morgen	kann	sie ihren Mann	noch nicht		besuchen.
Wir	dürfen	sonntags	nicht mehr		arbeiten.
Er	scheint	jetzt			zu schlafen.
Er	scheint	jetzt	nicht		zu schlafen.
Er	kann		nicht mehr		schlafen.
Er	scheint		noch nicht		zu schlafen.
Warum	brauchst	du morgen	nicht		zu arbeiten?
Das	muß			seine Frau	sein.
Das	kann	doch	nicht	seine Frau	sein.
Das	scheint			seine Frau	zu sein.
Erika	möchte	heute abend	nicht	zu Hause	bleiben.
Ich	möchte	sie wirklich		kennen-	lernen.
Meyer	muß	heute		nach Bonn	fahren.
Er	braucht	heute	nicht	nach Bonn	zu fahren.

SEE ANALYSIS 49-50 (p. 98)

[8] Contrast Intonation

Read these sentences aloud until you have thoroughly mastered this intonation pattern.

Du fährst morgen nach It*al*ien? *Ich* kann *nicht* nach Italien fahren.

You are going to *Italy* tomorrow? *I cannot* go to Italy.

Hast *du* Geld? Ich habe *kein* Geld.

Do *you* have *money?* *I don't* have any money.

Trinken Meyers *Kaf*fee?—*Sie ja*, aber *er nicht*.

Do the Meyers drink *coffee?*—*She does*, but *he* does *not*.

Ist er intelli*gent* oder interes*sant?*—Intelli*gent ist* er, aber interes*sant* ist er *nicht*.

Is he *intelligent* or *interesting?*—He is *intelligent* all right. But *interesting?* No!

SEE ANALYSIS 52-53 (pp. 99-100)

Ich höre, dein Bruder studiert Psychologie. Was studierst *du?—Ich* studiere Medizin.

I hear your brother is majoring in *psychology*. What are *you* majoring in?—*I* am in *med school*.

Kennen Sie Fritz *Ender*s, Frau *Holl*mann?—Nein, seine *Mut*ter kenne ich *gut*, aber *ihn* kenne ich *nicht*.

Do you know Fritz *Enders*, Mrs. *Hollmann?*—No, I know his *mother well*, but I do *not* know *him*.

Warum gehst du nie mit *Inge* ins *Kino?* Sie ist doch *so* intelli*gent.—Ja*, intelli*gent ist* sie.

Why don't you ever go to the *movies* with *Inge?* She is *so* intelligent!—*Yes*, she is *intelligent* all right.

Warum gehst du so oft mit *Hans* ins *Kino?* Ist er intelli*gent?—Nein*, intelli*gent* ist er *nicht*.

Why do you go to the movies with *Hans* so often? Is he *intelligent?—No*, he's not *intelligent*.

[9] Contradiction and Contrast

SEE
ANALYSIS
52-53
(pp. 99–100)

Das ist *Wasser*. Das ist *kein* Wasser. *Wasser* ist das *nicht*.

This is *water*. This is *not* water. This is *no water*.

Wir trinken *Wein*. Wir trinken *keinen* Wein. *Wein* trinken wir *nicht*.

We drink *wine*. We do *not* drink wine. *Wine* we do *not* drink.

Meyers haben einen *Sohn*. Meyers haben *keinen* Sohn. Einen *Sohn* haben Meyers *nicht*.

The Meyers have a *son*. The Meyers do *not* have a son. The Meyers have *no son*.

Wir gehen ins *Kino*. Nein, wir gehen *nicht* ins Kino. Ins *Kino* gehen wir *nicht*.

We're going to the *movies*. No, we're *not* going to the movies. To the *movies* we *won't* go.

Er ist intelli*gent*. Er ist *nicht* intelligent. Intelli*gent* ist er *nicht*.

He is *intelligent*. He is *not* intelligent. *Intelligent he's not*.

Du fährst morgen nach *München?* Nein, ich fahre morgen *nicht* nach München. Nein, *ich* fahre morgen *nicht* nach München. Nein, nach *München* fahre ich morgen *nicht*.

You are going to *Munich* tomorrow? No, I'm *not* going to Munich tomorrow. No, *I* am *not* going to Munich tomorrow. No, to *Munich* I am *not* going tomorrow.

VARIATIONS

Vary the following sentences in the same manner as above.

Sie haben eine *Toch*ter.
Wir trinken *Bier*.
Ich kenne hier einen *Arzt*.

Wir gehen nach *Hause*.
Er ist zu *Hause*.
Das ist *unser* Hund.

[10] Imperative

SEE
ANALYSIS
54
(p. 101)

Arbeiten Sie nicht soviel!
Bleiben Sie doch hier!
Kommen Sie doch morgen!

Don't work so much.
Why don't you stay here?
Why don't you come tomorrow?

Lernen Sie Deutsch!	Learn German.
Sagen Sie doch etwas!	Say something.
Tun Sie das doch bitte nicht!	Please don't do that.
Machen Sie bitte das Licht an!	Please turn on the light.
Kaufen Sie doch einen Volkswagen!	Why don't you buy a VW?
Schlafen Sie gut!	Sleep well!
Lassen Sie mich in Ruhe!	Leave me alone.
Seien Sie nicht so egoistisch!	Don't be so selfish.

Analysis

45 Infinitives with and without **zu**

Infinitives are not merely used as dictionary entries. It is virtually impossible to talk for a minute in either German or English without using an infinitive or a participle in connection with an inflected form of some preceding auxiliary verb.* A few of these auxiliaries—like **scheinen zu**, *to seem to* and **nicht brauchen zu**, *not to need to*, demand that the following infinitive be preceded by **zu**.

Er scheint hier zu wohnen.	He seems to live here.
Er braucht heute nicht zu arbeiten.	He doesn't need to work today.

If the auxiliaries do not require **zu** or *to* before the infinitive, they are called *modal auxiliaries* or simply *modals*.

46 Modal Auxiliaries

Modals usually express not a specific action, but an attitude toward the action expressed by the infinitive. Thus English *shalt* and *must* in *Thou shalt not steal* and *I must go home* view the action expressed by *steal* and *go home* as forbidden or necessary.

Modals are conjugated irregularly both in English and in German: *he must*, not *he musts*; **er kann**, not **er kannt.**

The English modals are incomplete: they have, for instance, no infinitive and no compound tenses. The German system, though grammatically complete, has pecularities of its own.

47 The Six German Modals and Their Meaning

It is definitely unwise to attempt to equate each form of a modal with a corresponding English modal. Instead, you should master the basic meaning of each modal.

---

*Auxiliary verbs, or helping verbs, are verbs used together with a following participle or infinitive. Examples: *has* arrived, *is* finished, *will* come, *must* go. The participle or infinitive always carries the main meaning.

können	to be able to		
Ich kann lesen.		I can read.	} *expresses ability*
müssen	to have to		
Ich muß nach Hause gehen.		I have to go home.	} *expresses necessity*
dürfen	to be allowed to		
Ich darf hierbleiben.		I have permission to stay here.	*expresses permission*
Das darfst du nicht tun.		You mustn't do that.	
mögen	would like to		
Ich möchte hierbleiben.		I would like to stay here.	*expresses desire*
wollen	to want to		
Ich will ins Kino gehen.		I intend to go to the movies.	*expresses intention*
sollen	to be (supposed) to		
Ich soll nach Bonn fahren.		I am (supposed) to go to Bonn.	*expresses imposed obligation; in questions it may express a suggestion*
Sollen wir ins Theater gehen?		Shall we go to the theater?	

Good books don't *have* to be expensive.

NOTE:

1. When **müssen** is negated, it is usually stressed and expresses the absence of a compelling necessity. The text in the picture above.

   Gute Bücher *müs*sen nicht teuer sein

means

   Good books don't *have* to be expensive (though they usually are).

However, the far more common negation of **müssen** is with **nicht brauchen zu**, which expresses the idea that there is no need to do something. Compare the following two sentences:

Nein, ich *muß* heute nicht nach München fahren.
No, I don't *have* to go to Munich today.

Nein, ich brauche heute *nicht* nach München zu fahren.*
No, I *don't* need to go to Munich today.

English *to have to* as in *I have to go now* (*I must go now*) cannot be expressed in German by **haben zu**, but only by **müssen**; **haben zu** is used only in constructions such as **Ich habe heute viel zu tun**, where **viel zu tun** is the object of **haben**.

Security during illness—Modern illness protection need not be expensive.

2. English *must not* (*mustn't*) is expressed by **nicht dürfen**.

Das darfst du nicht tun, Rudi.
You mustn't do that, Rudi.

3. English *to know* corresponds to **kennen**, *to be acquainted with*, or **wissen**, *to know facts* (see **19**); *to know a language* is expressed by **können**.

Er kann Deutsch (verstehen, lesen, sprechen, schreiben).
Können Sie Englisch, Herr Braun?

48 The Forms of the German Modals

	KÖNNEN	WOLLEN	MÜSSEN	MÖGEN†	SOLLEN	DÜRFEN
ich	kann	will	muß	möchte	soll	darf
du	kannst	willst	mußt	möchtest	sollst	darfst
er	kann	will	muß	möchte	soll	darf
wir	können	wollen	müssen	möchten	sollen	dürfen
ihr	könnt	wollt	müßt	möchtet	sollt	dürft
sie	können	wollen	müssen	möchten	sollen	dürfen
Sie	können	wollen	müssen	möchten	sollen	dürfen

*The basic meaning of **brauchen** is *to need:* **Ich brauche ein Buch (kein Buch).** As a modal, it can only be used in negative sentences, as above, whereas English *need* can be used as a modal in positive sentences as well: *I need to go,* **Ich muß gehen.**

†These forms of **mögen** will be explained in Unit 13.

49 Position of Dependent Infinitives

When infinitives like **arbeiten** or **zu arbeiten** depend on modals or on verbs like
brauchen, they form a second prong, follow the inner field, and are preceded
by **nicht.**

MODAL IN FIRST PRONG, INFINITIVE IN SECOND PRONG

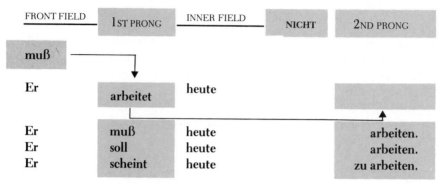

FRONT FIELD	1ST PRONG	INNER FIELD	NICHT	2ND PRONG
muß				
Er	**arbeitet**	**heute**		
Er	**muß**	**heute**		**arbeiten.**
Er	**soll**	**heute**		**arbeiten.**
Er	**scheint**	**heute**		**zu arbeiten.**

Questions are treated in the same way.

Warum	**willst**	**du heute**		**arbeiten?**
	Arbeitet	**er heute?**		
	Kann	**er heute**		**arbeiten?**

The procedure is the same if **nicht** stands at the end of the inner field.

Er	**möchte**	**heute**	**nicht**	**arbeiten.**
Er	**kann**	**heute**	**nicht**	**arbeiten.**
Er	**scheint**	**heute**	**nicht**	**zu arbeiten.**
Warum	**will**	**er denn heute**	**nicht**	**arbeiten?**
Warum	**braucht**	**er denn heute**	**nicht**	**zu arbeiten?**

50 The Two-Box Second Prong

If a simple verb like **arbeiten** is pushed out of the slot for the first prong by a
modal, it moves into the slot for the second prong. But what happens if the
verb displaced by the modal or by an auxiliary such as **brauchen** and **scheinen**
is a compound verb with some complement already filling the slot for the second prong? The second prong has two boxes, so to speak, and the infinitive
dependent on an auxiliary verb always goes into the second box, whereas all
complements go into the first box. The following diagram shows what
happens:

FRONT FIELD	1ST PRONG	INNER FIELD	1ST BOX	2ND BOX
Er	**geht**	**heute**	**ins Kino.**	

A modal comes in and pushes **gehen** into the second box.

FRONT FIELD	1ST PRONG	INNER FIELD	1ST BOX	2ND BOX
Er	**will**	heute	**ins Kino**	**gehen.**

This two-box second-prong pattern, in which the verbal complement precedes the infinitive without **zu,** is used so frequently in German that dictionaries list many compound verbs, especially if the complement is a preposition or an adverb, in the form in which they appear in this two-box sequence. Thus **fahre zurück** in **Ich fahre morgen zurück** is listed under **zurückfahren,** because it occurs so frequently in such sentences as **Ich will morgen zurückfahren.**

If an infinitive with **zu** is required with compound verbs like **zurückfahren,** this **zu** is inserted between complement and infinitive, and the whole thing is written as one word.

> **Er braucht nicht zurückzufahren.**
> **Er braucht das Licht nicht auszumachen.**

But if complement and infinitive are not written as one word, **zu** remains separate as well.

> **Er braucht nicht nach München zu fahren.**

51 Replacement or Omission of the Dependent Infinitive

An infinitive can be replaced by **das,** if the verb was mentioned in the sentence immediately preceding.

> **Sie arbeiten heute? Dürfen Sie das?**

The infinitives **gehen, fahren,** and others, if clearly understood, are frequently omitted. Compare English *He wants out.*

Ich muß nach Hause.	(**gehen** omitted)
Ich will heute nach Köln.	(**fahren** omitted)
Du brauchst nicht zu arbeiten, wenn du	
nicht willst.	(**arbeiten** omitted)

52 Contrast Intonation

Contrast intonation is characterized by the fact that the first stressed syllable, usually in the front field, has rising pitch starting on level 1, and the second stressed syllable has falling pitch starting on level 3.

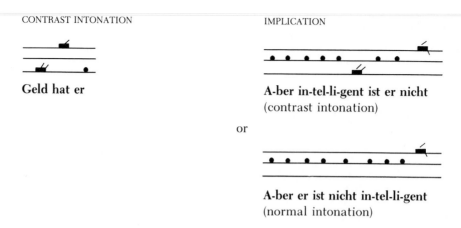

CONTRAST INTONATION

Geld hat er

IMPLICATION

A-ber in-tel-li-gent ist er nicht
(contrast intonation)

or

A-ber er ist nicht in-tel-li-gent
(normal intonation)

53 Word Order under Contrast Intonation

Under contrast intonation, the second prong frequently appears in the front field. The two sentences

Er ist in-tel-li-gent   and   **In-tel-li-gent ist er**

are not interchangeable. The first one is a remark of praise, the second is a sophisticated insult. Likewise,

Er ist nicht zu Hau-se   and   **Zu Hau-se ist er nicht**

are not interchangeable; for only the second contains some implication like "Let's try to reach him somewhere else!"

Under contrast intonation, **kein** is replaced by **(ein) . . . nicht.**

> **Meyer ist kein *Dumm*kopf.**
> **Ein *Dumm*kopf ist Meyer *nicht*.**
>
> **Ich habe kein *Geld*.**
> ***Geld* habe ich *nicht*** or ***Geld* ha*be* ich nicht.**

Observe that contrast intonation is not the same as contradiction intonation. If speaker A asserts:

> **Meyer ist intelli*gent***

Speaker B can contradict him bluntly and say:

> **Nein, er ist *nicht* intelligent.** (contradiction)

Speaker B could also say:

Ja, intelli*gent ist* **er.**   Yes, he is *intelligent* all right, (but . . .).

54 The Imperative

The English imperative is identical with the infinitive. One can say *Be my guest* no matter whether one calls the person addressed *Jack* or *Dr. Able.* German distinguishes between the **du**-form, the **ihr**-form, and the **Sie**-form of the imperative. At this point, we introduce only the **Sie**-form, which looks like the infinitive plus an immediately following **Sie: Kommen Sie! Gehen Sie! Sehen Sie!** The imperative of **sein** is **Seien Sie!**

Imperatives, like yes-or-no questions, have verb-first position; they are distinguished by intonation.

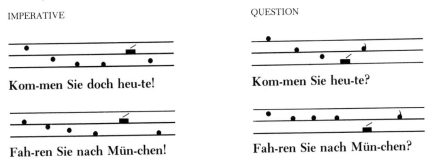

IMPERATIVE

Kom-men Sie doch heu-te!

Fah-ren Sie nach Mün-chen!

QUESTION

Kom-men Sie heu-te?

Fah-ren Sie nach Mün-chen?

In a polite request, the stress point of an imperative sentence is placed on level 2, as in the examples above. If **bitte** (*please*) is used, it must be placed either at the very beginning or after the unstressed elements following the first prong.

Bitte besuchen Sie uns doch!
Besuchen Sie uns doch bitte!

If the stress point is raised to level 3, the request, in spite of the use of **bitte**, is changed into a command.

Kom-men Sie bit-te heu-te!

Conversations

I

In a crowded restaurant. A student is looking for an empty chair.

STUDENT: Entschuldigung, ist der Platz hier noch frei?
MANN: Bitte nehmen Sie Platz.

STUDENT: Ist es hier immer so voll?

MANN: Den ganzen Tag, aber besonders von zwölf bis zwei, zum Mittagessen.

STUDENT: Herr Ober, bitte die Speisekarte.

    STUDENT: Excuse me, is this seat taken (still free)?

    MAN: Please, sit down.

    STUDENT: Is this place always so crowded?

    MAN: All day, but especially from 12 to 2, for dinner.

    STUDENT: Waiter, the menu, please.

While the student studies the menu:

STUDENT: Sie scheinen hier Stammkunde zu sein.

MANN: Ja, ich esse sehr oft hier.

STUDENT: Können Sie etwas empfehlen? Was schmeckt am besten?

MANN: Ich nehme Menü* Nummer eins. Das ist sehr gut und nicht sehr teuer.

STUDENT: Suppe, Schweinebraten, Rotkohl und Knödel. Das klingt gut. Und zum Nachtisch kriegt man Eis. Ich glaube, das nehme ich auch.

    STUDENT: You seem to be a regular customer here.

    MAN: Yes, I eat here quite often.

    STUDENT: Can you recommend something? What tastes best?

    MAN: I'm having dinner No. 1. That's good and not very expensive.

    STUDENT: Soup, roast pork, red cabbage, and dumplings. And for dessert you get ice cream. Sounds good. I think I'll take that too.

OBER: Bitte, der Herr, was darf ich Ihnen bringen?

STUDENT: Ich bekomme Menü eins.

OBER: Einmal Menü eins,—und was trinken Sie?

STUDENT: Ein Glas Bier.

OBER: Hell oder dunkel?

STUDENT: Hell, bitte.—Dauert es lange?

OBER: Nein, höchstens fünf Minuten.

    WAITER: Yes, sir, what can I bring you?

    STUDENT: I'd like dinner No. 1.

    WAITER: One number one—and what will you have to drink?

    STUDENT: A glass of beer.

    WAITER: Light or dark?

    STUDENT: Light, please.—Will it take long?

    WAITER: No, five minutes at the most.

II

The following statements could be answers. Construct questions (usually more than one) that would fit them. Then write mini-conversations around these questions and answers and act them out in class.

1. Müller, Fritz Müller.
2. Es regnet schon wieder.
3. In der Römerstraße.
4. Nein, ich wohne jetzt in der Bettinastraße.
5. Mathematik.
6. Ich bleibe hier.
7. Nein, noch nicht.
8. Mein Vater ist Ingenieur.
9. Ins Theater.
10. Donnerstag.
11. Da rechts um die Ecke.
12. Das weiß ich nicht.

*Menü does not mean *menu*, but *complete dinner*; it usually includes soup, a main course, and dessert. English *menu* is expressed by **die Speisekarte.**

Fragen an Sie persönlich

1. Sie lernen jetzt Deutsch. Können Sie auch andere Sprachen (other languages)?
    verstehen, lesen, sprechen, schreiben?
    Französisch? Spanisch? Italienisch? Russisch? Chinesisch? Japanisch?
    Arabisch?
2. Was essen Sie gern (What do you like to eat)?
    Was trinken Sie gern (What do you like to drink)?

Fleisch oder Fisch?	meat or fish?
Suppe? Salat?	soup? salad?
Kartoffeln, Nudeln, Reis?	potatoes, noodles, rice?
Wurst, Käse?	sausage (cold cuts), cheese?
Obst? Kuchen? Eis? Pudding?	fruit? cake? ice cream? pudding?

Reading

Vernunft und Intelligenz

Der Mensch, das kann man schon bei Aristoteles lesen, ist ein Tier. Aber dieses Tier, sagt Aristoteles, hat Vernunft.

Und was ist Vernunft? Vernunft ist nicht Intelligenz. Vernunft ist mehr als Intelligenz. 5

Wer nur intelligent ist, glaubt: „Alle Menschen sind egoistisch. Ja, sie müssen egoistisch sein. Denn jeder Mensch will glücklich werden. Das heißt aber, der Emil möchte haben, was Fritz hat; und der Fritz möchte 10 sein, was Emil ist. Aber der Emil kann nicht immer alles haben, was er möchte; und Fritz kann nicht sein, was Emil ist. Und darum haßt der Fritz den Emil, und der Emil den Fritz. Darum haßt ein Sohn seinen Vater, 15 und darum haßt Nation A Nation B. Der Krieg zwischen Fritz und Emil, zwischen Sohn und Vater und zwischen Nation A und Nation B ist also natürlich. So ist es, und so bleibt es. Leider!"

Aber warum „leider"? Was ist, ist, und es kann nur so sein, wie es ist. Warum also „leider"?

Hier spricht nicht unsere Intelligenz. Hier 25 spricht unsere Vernunft. Unsere Intelligenz

Reason and Intelligence

Man, one can read already in Aristotle, is an animal. But this animal, says Aristotle, has reason.

And what is reason? Reason is not intelligence. Reason is more than intelligence.

Whoever is merely intelligent believes: "All human beings are egoistic. Indeed, they have to be egoistic. For every human being desires to become happy. But this means: Emil would like to have what Fritz has; and Fritz would like to be what Emil is. But Emil cannot always have what he would like (to have); and Fritz cannot be what Emil is. And for this reason Fritz hates Emil, and Emil hates Fritz. Therefore, a son will hate his father, and Nation A will hate Nation B. War between Fritz and Emil, between father and son, and between Nation A and Nation B is therefore natural. That's the way it is, and that's the way it will remain, unfortunately."

But why "unfortunately"? Whatever is, is, and it can only be as it is. Why, therefore, "unfortunately"?

Here [through this "unfortunately"] speaks not our intelligence, but our reason. Our in-

sieht nur, was ist. Unsere Vernunft sieht mehr. Sie sieht: Das, was ist, soll und darf nicht so sein, wie es ist.

Natürlich will jeder Mensch glücklich werden. Er will es instinktiv. Er muß es wollen. 5 Der Hans will *sein* Glück, und ich will *mein* Glück. Er will also nur, was ich auch will. Ich habe ein Haus und bin glücklich. Hans hat kein Haus und ist unglücklich. Aber, so sagt meine Vernunft, ich kann nicht glück- 10 lich sein, wenn Hans unglücklich ist. Denn wenn Hans sagt: ,,Du hast ein Haus und ich habe kein Haus", dann sagt er auch bald: ,,Warum sollst du ein Haus haben, und ich habe kein Haus?" Und so beginnen alle 15 Kriege. Aber ich will keinen Krieg; Hans will auch keinen Krieg, er will ein Haus. Ich muß also etwas für ihn tun. Er braucht mich und kann ohne mich nicht glücklich werden; und ich brauche ihn und kann ohne ihn 20 nicht glücklich bleiben. Also muß ich für ihn tun, was ich kann.

Das heißt aber: Ich muß ihn lieben. Denn ,,lieben" heißt ja ,,für den Mitmenschen das tun, was gut für ihn ist". Der Krieg, so sagt 25 meine Vernunft, ist nicht natürlich. Natürlich ist nur die Liebe.

Aber leider zwingt mich meine Vernunft nicht. Ich weiß jetzt, was ich soll, aber meine Vernunft läßt mich frei, zu tun oder 30 nicht zu tun, was ich soll. Und das ist unsere Tragik. Wir wollen oft nicht, was wir sollen; und wir können, wenn wir wollen, auch tun, was wir nicht sollen.

Aber wir müssen lernen zu wollen, was wir 35 sollen. Ja, der Mensch ist nur dann wirklich frei—frei zu tun, was er will—wenn er will, was er soll.

telligence sees only what exists. Our reason sees more. It sees that what is, should not and must not be as it is.

Naturally every human being desires to become happy. He desires it instinctively. He must desire it. Hans wants *his* happiness and I want *my* happiness. Thus he only wants what I want, too. I have a house and am happy. Hans does not have a house and is unhappy. But, my reason tells me, I cannot be happy if Hans is unhappy. For if Hans says, "You have a house and I have no house," then he will soon say also, "Why should (shall) you have a house, and I don't have a house?" And thus begin all wars. But I don't want a war; Hans wants no war either, he wants a house. Therefore I have to do something for him. He needs me and cannot become happy without me; and I need him and cannot remain happy without him. Therefore I must do for him what I can.

But this means: I must love him. For "to love" means, after all, "to do that for a fellow man which is good for him." War, says my reason, is not natural. Only love is natural.

But unfortunately my reason does not force me. I now know what I ought to do, but my reason leaves me free to do or not to do what I ought (to do). And that is our tragic fate. We often do not want to do what we ought to do; and we can, if we want to, also do what we ought not to do.

However, we must learn to want to do what we ought to do. Indeed, man is only then really free—free to do what he wants to do— when he wants to do what he ought to do.

Ein Gedicht

Franz Mon (born 1926 in Frankfurt) is a serious contemporary writer; however, the following poem is from a collection of nonsense verse entitled *Die Meisengeige*. A *Meisengeige*, literally translated, is a "titmouse fiddle"; obviously, Mon wrote it in that spirit.

das Gedicht,-e poem

Franz Mon

der tisch ist oval	**der Tisch,-e** table
das ei ist oval	**das Ei,-er** egg
nicht jeder tisch ist oval	
jedes ei ist oval	
kaum ein tisch ist oval 5	**kaum** hardly
kaum ein ei ist nicht oval	
dieser tisch ist viereckig	**viereckig** rectangular
dieses ei ist nicht viereckig	
viele tische sind viereckig	
viele eier sind nicht viereckig 10	
die meisten tische sind viereckig	
die meisten eier sind nicht viereckig	

Eine Reklame

die Reklame (*no pl.*) advertisement

die Ferien (*pl.*) vacation
die Insel,-n island

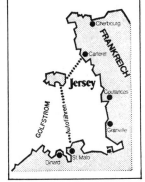

FERIENINSEL IM GOLFSTROM

Jersey

English spoken here.

Englisch spricht man überall auf
unserer Insel. Auch die Leute mit
den französischen Namen. Und
viele mit den englischen Namen
sprechen auch französisch.
Aber Sie werden erstaunt
sein, wieviele Leute mit
englischen oder franzö-
sischen Namen auch
deutsch verstehen und
sprechen. Jersey ist
„Klein-Europa". Wenn Sie
mit dem eigenen Wagen
kommen – per Auto-
fähre – dann müssen
Sie sich ein bißchen
umgewöhnen. In
Jersey ist Linksverkehr. Dafür verwöhnen wir
Sie aber mit guten Straßen und sehr günstigem
Benzinpreis.

Direkt-Flug ab Düsseldorf. In gut 2 Stunden sind Sie hier.

spricht man*
überall everywhere

viele many

werden erstaunt sein will be astonished

eigen own
die Fähre,-n ferry
bißchen a bit
sich umgewöhnen to change one's habits
der Verkehr traffic
verwöhnen to spoil
günstig favorable
das Benzin gasoline
der Flug flight

Exercises

A. Restate the sentences by using the modal indicated in parentheses.

1. Ich verstehe Italienisch, aber ich spreche es nicht. (können)
2. Kommst du heute abend? (können)
3. Herr Rücker fliegt heute nach Düsseldorf. (müssen)

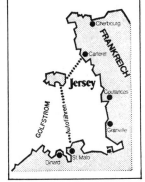

SEE
ANALYSIS
45–51
(pp. 95–99)

*one speaks = is spoken; constructions with the impersonal third-person **man** are often
expressed by the English passive. Also, note contrast intonation in this sentence.

   4. Tante Amalie besucht uns bald wieder. (wollen)
   5. Kurt und Rudi gehen jetzt schlafen. (sollen)
   6. Gehst du heute schwimmen? (mögen)
   7. Morgen stehe ich früh auf. (müssen)
   8. Heute gehe ich nicht ins Kino. (wollen)
   9. Was tue ich denn jetzt? (sollen)
  10. Heute arbeitet Hans nicht. (brauchen)

B. Fill the blanks with appropriate forms of modals, **brauchen**, or **scheinen**.

SEE
ANALYSIS
45–51
(pp. 95–99)

   1. Danke, ich _____ jetzt keinen Wein.
   2. Ich _____ heute leider nicht kommen; es geht mir nicht gut.
   3. Hans studiert Medizin; er _____ Arzt werden.
   4. Das Schwimmen ist hier verboten; hier _____ wir nicht schwimmen.
   5. Der Arzt sagt, ich _____ nicht mehr rauchen.
   6. Das _____ du aber nicht tun, Rudi.
   7. Gottseidank _____ wir heute nicht früh aufzustehen.
   8. Ich _____ sonntags nicht zu arbeiten, wenn ich nicht _____.
   9. Was _____ sie trinken, Fräulein Hannemann,—Kaffee oder Tee?
  10. Alle Menschen _____ glücklich werden.
  11. Italienisch _____ ich leider nicht, nur Spanisch.
  12. Irmgard _____ noch zu schlafen.

C. Tell somebody:

> that you have to go home. — **Ich muß nach Hause gehen.**

SEE
ANALYSIS
45–51
(pp. 95–99)

   1. that you would like a cup of coffee.
   2. that he mustn't do that. (Use **du** and **Sie**.)
   3. that he has to work on Sunday. (Use **du** and **Sie**.)
   4. that he doesn't *have* to work on Sunday.
   5. that he doesn't need to work on Sunday.
   6. that you aren't able to come today.
   7. that you know Japanese.
   8. that he isn't permitted to smoke here. (Use **Sie**.)
   9. that you don't want to eat anything now.
  10. that you'd like to become an auto mechanic.
  11. that she is supposed to come home soon. (Use **du**.)
  12. that you (*plural*) want to stay home tonight.

D. For each of the following sentences, invent a preceding sentence with contrast intonation.

> _____, und *ich* bleibe zu *Hause*.
> *Du* kannst ins *Kino* gehen, und *ich* bleibe zu *Hause*.

SEE
ANALYSIS
52–53
(pp. 99–100)

   1. _____, und *ich* muß *arbeiten*.
   2. _____, aber intelli*gent* ist er *nicht*.
   3. _____, aber eine *Toch*ter haben sie *nicht*.
   4. _____, aber ihr *Freund hat* Geld.
   5. _____, aber *ich* studiere *Deutsch*.
   6. _____, aber *arbeiten will* er nicht.

E. Negate the following sentences; use contrast intonation and move the second prong into the front field. Do not use **doch** in the answers.

> Das ist doch Wein.
> Nein, Wein ist das nicht.

1. Das ist doch Fritz *Schu*mann.
2. Sie können doch Französisch, Herr Braun.
3. Sie essen *Leber*wurst?
4. Er will doch nach *Ham*burg.
5. Ihr fahrt doch Sonntag in die *Ber*ge?
6. Ich *ken*ne hier einen Arzt.
7. Sie nehmen die *Stra*ßenbahn, nicht wahr?
8. Er will heute *ar*beiten.

SEE
ANALYSIS
52-53
(pp. 99–100)

F. Form sentences from the elements given; supply additional necessary elements.

1. Erich / nach Wien / morgen / wollen / fahren.
   Er / Wien / noch nicht / kennen.
   Sein Bruder / in Wien / jetzt / wohnen // ihn / besuchen wollen.
   Mit dem Wagen / fahren?
   Nein // fliegen.
   Wie lange / bleiben?
   Nicht wissen.
2. Herr Müller / jetzt / Französisch lernen.
   Nächstes Jahr / nach Paris / müssen.
   Dort / zwei Jahre / arbeiten / sollen.
   Er / allein / nach Frankreich / gehen?
   Nein / Frau und Kinder / auch.
   Kinder / wie alt?
   Sohn 12, Töchter 8, 6.

G. Form imperatives from the following verbs; use **doch** or **bitte** where indicated. Then repeat each sentence, without **doch** or **bitte**, changing to yes-or-no question intonation.

> nach Österreich fahren (doch) — Fahren Sie doch nach Österreich!
> Fahren Sie nach Österreich?

1. Lehrer werden (doch)
2. langsamer sprechen (bitte)
3. immer geradeaus gehen
4. Schweinefleisch kaufen
5. ein Steak essen (doch)
6. noch ein Glas Wein trinken (doch)
7. früh aufstehen (bitte)
8. schlafen gehen (doch)
9. den Bus nehmen (doch)
10. Philosophie studieren

SEE
ANALYSIS
54
(p. 101)

H. Develop the following sentences in stages, as indicated. Pay attention to the reminders in parentheses.

> I have to get up early tomorrow, unfortunately.
> (a) I have to get up.　　　　　Ich muß aufstehen.
> (b) add: *early*　　　　　　　Ich muß früh aufstehen.
> (c) add: *tomorrow*　　　　　Ich muß morgen früh aufstehen.
> (d) start sentence with *Unfortunately*　Leider muß ich morgen früh aufstehen.

1. Thank goodness I don't need to work today in this rain.
    (a) I have to work.
    (b) negate (**brauchen** + **zu!**)
    (c) add: *today*
    (d) add: *in this rain* (end field!)
    (e) start sentence with *Thank goodness . . .* (front field!)
2. Next summer, Aunt Amalie wants to go on an eight-week trip again.
    (a) Aunt Amalie wants to go on a trip. (**verreisen**)
    (b) add: *eight weeks*
    (c) add: *already again*
    (d) start sentence with *Next summer . . .*
3. I believe their daughter Monika would like to become a doctor.
    (a) Monika becomes a doctor. (professional status, feminine!)
    (b) change to *Monika would like to . . .*
    (c) add: *their daughter*
    (d) introduce sentence with *I believe . . .*
4. In Germany, stores may unfortunately not sell anything on Sundays.
    (a) Stores sell (**die Geschäfte!**)
    (b) Stores may sell
    (c) add: *nothing*
    (d) add: *on Sundays* (one word only!)
    (e) add: *unfortunately*
    (f) start sentence with *In Germany . . .*

I.   Express in German.

1. He is supposed to be home at six o'clock.
2. We want to eat at seven.
3. Tonight we'd like to go to the movies.
4. Karl unfortunately can't go.
5. He still has to work.
6. But tomorrow he doesn't need to work.
7. Tomorrow we want to go to the mountains.
8. Our train is going to leave at 8:10.
9. At ten o'clock we'll be in Garmisch.
10. When are you going to come back?

Vocabulary

alles	everything	**der Bus, -se**	bus
aufstehen	to get up (out of bed)	**darum**	therefore, for that reason
das Auge, -n	eye		
der Augenarzt, ⸚e	eye doctor	**dauern**	to last
baden	to bathe; to swim	**dunkel**	dark
beginnen	to start, to begin	**dürfen**	to be permitted to
bekommen	to get, to receive	**das darfst du nicht**	you mustn't do that
der Berg, -e	mountain		
in die Berge	to the mountains	**das Ei, -er**	egg
besuchen	to visit	**empfehlen (empfiehlst, empfiehlt)**	to recommend
braten (brätst, brät)	to roast		
Schweinebraten	pork roast	**das Ende, -n**	end
bringen	to bring	**endlich**	finally

der Fisch, -e	fish	das Mittagessen	noon meal, dinner
frei	free	mögen	to like to
früh	early	müssen	to have to
der Frühling	spring	das Obst	fruit
(no pl.)		oft	often
das Gedicht. -e	poem	ohne	without
glauben	to believe	der Platz, ⁓e	place
das Glück	luck, fortune	Platz nehmen	to sit down
glücklich	happy	die Ruhe	peace, quiet
hassen	to hate	laß mich in Ruhe	leave me alone
heiraten	to marry	der Salat, -e	salad
hell	light	schmecken	to taste
hören	to hear	schreiben	to write
der Ingenieur', -e	engineer	sollen	to be supposed to
interessant'	interesting	speisen	to eat (formal)
un'interessant	uninteresting	die Speisekarte, -n	menu
die Kartoffel, -n	potato	die Suppe, -n	soup
kaum	hardly	teuer	expensive
kennenlernen	to get acquainted with	das Tier, -e	animal
können	to be able to	der Tisch, -e	table
der Krieg, -e	war	verbieten	to prohibit
der Kuchen, -	cake	Baden verboten	no swimming
der Kunde, -n	customer	verkaufen	to sell
der Stammkunde	regular customer	voll	full; crowded
lassen (läßt, läßt)	leave; let, allow	wollen	to intend to
die Liebe	love	zwingen	to force
mal (einmal)	once, for a change	zwischen	between

Additional Vocabulary

anmachen	to switch on (light)	der Kohl	cabbage
best- (adj. or adv.)	best	der Rotkohl	red cabbage
am besten	best (adv.)	meist-	most
eckig	cornered	meistens	in most cases
viereckig	rectangular	das Menü, -s	complete dinner
egoi'stisch	egotistic	der Mitmensch, -en	fellow human
das Eis	ice; ice cream	der Nachtisch, -e	dessert
die Eiskrem	ice cream	die Nudel, -n	noodle
gottseidank	thank goodness	der Ober, -	waiter
höchstens	at the most	die Philosophie'	philosophy
instinktiv'	instinctive (ly)	der Reis	rice
die Intelligenz'	intelligence	(das) Rußland	Russia
(das) Ita'lien	Italy	russisch	Russian
italie'nisch	Italian	die Tragik	tragedy
der Knödel, -	dumpling	die Vernunft	reason (intellect)
Leberknödel	liver dumplings		

17. Sept.

Motorsportclub Rottenegg

14 Uhr

Auto- u. Solo-
Moto-Cross

ROTTENEGG

Das Rennen findet bei jeder Witterung statt

Orbis Druck, 4053 Haid

Unit 5 The Dative—Prepositions with Dative and Accusative—Word Order in the Inner Field

The Federal Republic of Germany is about the size of the state of Oregon; and the tiny principality of Liechtenstein would easily fit into the District of Columbia. From the vastness of the American perspective, these dimensions are almost incomprehensible and have to be experienced to be really believed. Of course, it is equally difficult for a European to understand that, for example, the Navajo reservation in the American Southwest is one and a half times the size of Switzerland, or nearly as large as Austria. Another surprising aspect of Central Europe is that it is located much further north than most people realize; most of the BRD and all of the DDR lie north of the 49th parallel (the U.S.-Canadian border).

This unit again introduces a number of small bits of cultural information, very much in the fashion in which you will encounter such phenomena when you first arrive in Europe. Most of them are in themselves insignificant, but the totality of culture is made up of a myriad of tiny bits of language and behavior patterns, of objects, and of facts which together produce a mosaic unique to that culture.

Some examples: Germans invariably wish each other **Guten Appetit** at the beginning of a meal, and though this, of course, means *"good appetite,"* it is not part of American table manners and hence untranslatable. The same is true of the gesture of raising one's glass (but only with alcoholic beverages) toward one's companions and saying **Auf Ihr Wohl** or **Prosit**; this is a routine habit, not to be confused with an American toast. In this category we also find the German custom of saying **Gesundheit** (*health*) every time someone sneezes. If a German tells you that he lives **im ersten Stock** (*on the first floor*), beware, because he really lives on the second floor. **Stock** does not mean *"floor"* (though all dictionaries will lead you to believe that it does), but implies that something has been put on top of something else, hence it cannot refer to the first "floor."

When you hear a German speak of the second day of Christmas, you may think of a Christmas carol, but the German is referring to December 26, which is an official holiday, as is the Monday after Easter (**Ostern**) and the Monday after Pentecost (**Pfingsten**), a holiday that is not observed in the U.S. at all. These examples could be multiplied by the hundreds; they have to stand here as random samples of what constitutes German culture.

Rottenegg in Austria: The race will take place in any weather.

This unit introduces the dative case, which presents a learning problem for the native speaker of English. It is easy to see the relationship of *I* to *him*, but in German you must relate **ich** to either **ihn** or **ihm.** The matter is further complicated by the fact that some German prepositions go with the accusative, others with the dative, and still others, such as **in** (to be discussed later) can be used with either accusative or dative. Prepositions are difficult for another reason: Though English and German often use the same preposition to express the same idea (*coffee with sugar,* **Kaffee mit Zucker**), they also very frequently use different prepositions (**bei** virtually never corresponds to *by*). If you *wait for* somebody, a German **wartet auf. Warten auf** looks suspiciously like *wait on;* however, *to wait on* has nothing at all to do with **warten,** but is expressed by **bedienen** with an accusative object. Prepositions therefore require your close attention and careful memorization.

Patterns

[1] The Dative of the Personal Pronouns

This drill contains all the dative forms of the personal pronouns. After memorizing these pronouns, follow the system used in this drill and recite these sentences until you can do them automatically.

SEE
ANALYSIS
55
(p. 118)

Heute helfe ich *dir,* und morgen hilfst du *mir.*
Heute helfe ich *ihm,* und morgen hilft er *mir.*
Heute helfe ich *ihr,* und morgen hilft sie *mir.*
Heute helfe ich *euch,* und morgen helft ihr *mir.*
Heute helfe ich *ihnen,* und morgen helfen sie *mir.*

Heute hilfst du *mir,* und morgen helfe ich *dir.*
Heute hilfst du *ihm,* und morgen hilft er *dir.*
Heute hilfst du *ihr,* und morgen hilft sie *dir.*
Heute hilfst du *uns,* und morgen helfen wir *dir.*
Heute hilfst du *ihnen,* und morgen helfen sie *dir.*

Heute helfen wir *dir,* und morgen hilfst du *uns.*
Heute helfen wir *ihm,* und morgen hilft er *uns.*
Heute helfen wir *ihr,* und morgen hilft sie *uns.*
Heute helfen wir *euch,* und morgen helft ihr *uns.*
Heute helfen wir *ihnen,* und morgen helfen sie *uns.*

[2] Verbs with both Dative and Accusative Objects

SEE
ANALYSIS
55–56
(pp. 118–119)

Die Verkäuferin zeigt dem Kunden einen Photoapparat.	The saleswoman is showing the customer a camera.
Ich möchte meinem Sohn eine Kamera zum Geburtstag schenken.	I'd like to give my son a camera for his birthday.

Geben Sie Ihrem Sohn doch eine Filmkamera.	Why don't you give your son a movie camera.
Nein, zum Geburtstag habe ich ihm einen Photoapparat versprochen.	No, for his birthday I've promised him a (still) camera.
Eine Filmkamera will ich ihm zu Weihnachten kaufen.	I want to buy him a movie camera for Christmas.
Darf ich Ihnen diese 35* mm-Kamera anbieten?—Ein Bestseller, und gar nicht teuer.	May I offer you this 35mm camera?—A bestseller and not at all expensive.
Diesen Apparat empfehle ich vielen Kunden.	I recommend this camera to many customers.
Ich kann Ihnen den Apparat leihen, Herr Schulte,—zum Ausprobieren.	I can lend you the camera, Mr. Schulte, to try out.
Sie können ihn mir morgen zurückbringen.	You can return it to me tomorrow.
Ja, geben Sie mir die Kamera bis morgen. Vielen Dank.	Yes, give me the camera until tomorrow. Thank you very much.
Ich wünsche Ihnen viel Erfolg beim Fotografieren.	I wish you much success with your picture taking.

[3] Verbs with Accusative Objects

Bitte, was bekommen Sie?	Can I help you, please? (literally: What do you get?)
Ich suche einen Roman von Schmidt-Ingelheim.	I am looking for a novel by Schmidt-Ingelheim.
Haben Sie den *Flamingo*?	Do you have *The Flamingo*?
Den Roman kenne ich leider nicht. Ist er neu?	I don't know that novel. Is it new?
Ja, ganz neu. Meine Frau liest ihn gerade.	Yes, quite new. My wife is reading it just now.
Brauchen Sie das Buch sofort, Herr Doktor Müller?	Do you need the book immediately, Dr. Müller?
Ja, ich möchte es gern gleich mitnehmen.	Yes, I'd like to take it along right away.
Ich will mal sehen; vielleicht finde ich es doch.	Let me see; perhaps I'll find it after all.
Sie haben Glück, Herr Doktor. Hier ist es.	You're in luck, Dr. Müller. Here it is.
Und bezahlen Sie das Buch dann bitte dort an der Kasse.	And please pay for the book over there at the cashier's.

SEE ANALYSIS 20–24 (pp. 41–44)

[4] Verbs with Dative Objects

Ich *weiß*, er hilft mir *gern*. Aber wie kann ich ihm *danken*?
Ich *weiß*, sie hilft mir *gern*. Aber wie kann ich ihr *danken*?
Wir helfen ihnen *immer*, aber sie *danken* uns *nie*.

Na*tür*lich könnt ihr mich fragen! Aber ich brauche euch nicht zu *ant*worten!
Na*tür*lich können Sie mich fragen! Aber ich brauche Ihnen nicht zu *ant*worten!

SEE ANALYSIS 57 (p. 121)

*fünfunddreißig.

„Das glaubt mir doch keiner."

[5] The Dative with **gehören**; Replacement of **er, sie, es** by **der, die, das**; Plural Verb Forms after **es** and **das**

SEE
ANALYSIS
51, 62-63
(pp. 99, 127)

Das ist mein Wagen.—Der gehört mir.

Das sind meine Zeitungen.—Die gehören mir.

Das ist sein Auto.—Das gehört ihm.

Das sind eure Häuser?—Die gehören euch?

Das ist unsere Zeitung.—Die gehört uns.

Das sind Ihre Blumen.—Die gehören Ihnen.

Das Haus gehört dem *Vater*.—Das Haus gehört meinem *Vater*.—Das Haus gehört *ihm*.—Es ist *sein* Haus.—Das ist *sein* Haus.

Der Wagen gehört der *Tante*.—Er gehört meiner *Tante*.—Er gehört *ihr*.—Es ist *ihr* Wagen.—Das ist *ihr* Wagen.

Die Bücher gehören den *Kind*ern.—Sie gehören unseren *Kind*ern.—Sie gehören *ih*nen.—Es sind *ih*re Bücher.—Das sind *ih*re Bücher.

VARIATIONS

Produce sentences based on the vocabulary given below, according to this pattern:

> **Der Mann trägt einen Mantel. Der Mantel gehört ihm. Es ist sein Mantel.**

tragen to wear (clothing)
der Mantel, ̈ coat
das Kleid,-er dress
der Schuh,-e shoe
    das Paar Schuhe
die Jacke, -n jacket
die Hose, -n pants
der Rock, ̈e skirt
das Hemd, -en shirt
der Pullover, - sweater

[6] The Dative in **Wie geht es Ihnen?**

SEE ANALYSIS 57 (p. 121)

Guten Tag, Herr Schmidt. Wie geht es Ihnen?
Danke, es geht mir gut.

Hello, Mr. Schmidt. How are you?
Thanks, I'm fine.

Guten Tag, Edgar. Wie geht's dir denn?
Danke, es geht mir gut.
    Danke, mir geht's gut.
    Danke, gut.
Und dir?

Hi, Edgar. How are you?
Thanks, I'm fine.

And you?

Meyer? Dem geht's immer gut.

Meyer? He's always in good shape.

Mir geht's heute sehr schlecht. Ich habe Kopfschmerzen.

I am not very well today. I have a headache.

Wie geht's denn deinem Großvater?
Danke, ganz gut.
Und deiner Großmutter?
Nicht schlecht.

How is your grandfather?
Thanks, quite well.
And your grandmother?
Not bad (i.e., pretty well).

[7] Adjectives with the Dative

Form variations by changing the pronouns.

SEE ANALYSIS 58 (p. 122)

Ist Ihnen das recht, Frau Meyer?
Natürlich ist mir das recht.
Ist das Ihrem Mann recht, Frau Meyer?

Is that all right with you, Mrs. Meyer?
Of course that's all right with me.
Is that all right with your husband, Mrs. Meyer?

Natürlich ist ihm das recht.

Of course that's all right with him.

Das ist neu.
Das ist mir neu.

That's new.
That's news to me.

Die Uhr ist teuer.
Die Uhr ist zu teuer.
Die Uhr ist mir zu teuer.

That watch is expensive.
That watch is too expensive.
That watch is too expensive for me.

Das dauert uns zu lange.

That takes too long for us.

[8] Prepositions with the Accusative

Form variations of your own, but do not replace nouns by pronouns.

SEE ANALYSIS 59 (p. 122)

Wir müssen	durch	die Stadt fahren.
Herr Lenz arbeitet	für	meinen Vater.
Hast du etwas	gegen	mich?
Ich muß	ohne	ihn fahren.
Ich kann	ohne	dich nicht leben.
Ich komme	um	sechs Uhr.
Ich wohne gleich hier	um	die Ecke.

Vor und nach dem Theater immer wieder ins

„SPATENHAUS"

Warme Küche bis 23.30 Uhr

Bei Tischbestellung
Telefon 22 78 41/42

Die Erde kreist nicht	um	den Mond;
der Mond kreist	um	die Erde.
Fahren Sie hier	um	den Dom und dann die erste Straße rechts.

[9] Prepositions with the Dative

SEE
ANALYSIS
60
(p. 123)

Woher *kommst* du?	Aus dem *Kino!*
	Aus der *Stadt!*
Wir sind *alle* hier	außer meinem *Vater.*
	außer *ihm.*
	außer *Ihnen,* Herr Lenz.
Hans ist heute	bei seinem *Vater.*
	bei seiner *Mut*ter.
	bei *uns.*
Mit wem gehst du ins Kino?	Mit Frau *Hoff*mann!
	Mit *ihr?*
	·Mit *der?*
Wann wollt *ihr* denn nach Bonn?	Nach diesem Wochenende.
Er fährt	nach Österreich.
	nach *Hause.*
	nach Amerika.

Ich komme heute sehr spät nach *Hause.—Wann?—*Um *neun.*
Wie *spät* ist es jetzt?—*Zehn* nach *sechs.*

Seit wann bist *du* denn hier?   Seit einer *Stun*de!
                                         Seit drei *Wo*chen!
                                         Seit einem *Jahr!*

Von wem hast du das *Buch?*   Von meinem *Bru*der!
                                         Von meiner *Tan*te!
                                         Ich habe es von meinem *Va*ter!

Wohin *gehst* du?   Zu meinem *Va*ter!
                                         Zu *ihm*!
                                         Zur Universi*tät*!
                                         Zu meiner *Tan*te!
                                         Zum *Es*sen!

[10] Word Order in the Inner Field

Study the following sentences and observe the word order. Note that if an answer is a
complete sentence, the element containing the answer always stands at the end of the
inner field unless the verb itself is the answer.

Ich gebe meiner Frau eine *Uhr*.
Ich gebe ihr eine *Uhr*.
Ich gebe die Uhr meiner *Frau*.
Ich gebe sie meiner *Frau*.
Ich gebe ihr die *Uhr*.
Ich *ge*be sie ihr.

SEE
ANALYSIS
61
(p. 124)

Was willst du denn deiner Mutter *schi*cken?
Ich glaube, ich schicke ihr *Blu*men.
Was willst du denn mit diesen *Blu*men hier machen?
Die schicke ich meiner *Mut*ter.
Ich glaube, ich schicke sie meiner *Mut*ter.
Ich glaube, ich schicke diese Blumen meiner *Mut*ter.
Bringst du sie ihr?—Nein, ich *schi*cke sie ihr.

Fritz möchte seiner Freundin ein *Buch* schicken.
Was will Fritz seiner Freundin schicken?
Ein *Buch!*
Er will ihr ein *Buch* schicken!
Wem will Fritz das Buch schicken?
Seiner *Freun*din!
Er will das Buch seiner *Freun*din schicken.
Er will es seiner *Freun*din schicken.

Warum will Fritz seiner Freundin denn ein *Buch* schicken?
Warum will er seiner Freundin denn ein *Buch* schicken?
Warum will er ihr denn ein *Buch* schicken?
Willst du das Buch deiner *Freun*din schicken?
Willst du es deiner *Freun*din schicken?
Willst du es ihr *schi*cken?

Willst du deiner Freundin ein *Buch* schicken?
Willst du ihr ein *Buch* schicken?
Nein, ich will ihr *Geld* schicken.
Wann willst du ihr das Geld denn *schic*ken?
Wann willst du es ihr denn *schic*ken?

Analysis

55 The Forms of the Dative Case

INTERROGATIVE PRONOUNS

NOM.	**wer**	who
ACC.	**wen**	whom
DAT.	**wem**	to whom

NOTE: The interrogative pronouns **wer, wen,** and **wem** have the same endings as the corresponding forms of the masculine definite article **der, den, dem.**

der-WORDS

	MASC.	FEM.	NEUT.	PLURAL
NOM.	**der**	**die**	**das**	**die**
ACC.	**den**	**die**	**das**	**die**
DAT.	*dem*	*der*	*dem*	*den*

ein-WORDS

	MASC.	FEM.	NEUT.	PLURAL
NOM.	**kein**	**keine**	**kein**	**keine**
ACC.	**keinen**	**keine**	**kein**	**keine**
DAT.	*keinem*	*keiner*	*keinem*	*keinen*

NOTE: There is no difference between the dative endings of the **ein**-words and those of the **der**-words.

PERSONAL PRONOUNS

SINGULAR	NOM.	**ich**	**du**	**er**	**sie**	**es**	**Sie**
	ACC.	**mich**	**dich**	**ihn**	**sie**	**es**	**Sie**
	DAT.	*mir*	*dir*	*ihm*	*ihr*	*ihm*	*Ihnen*

PLURAL	NOM.	**wir**	**ihr**		**sie**		**Sie**
	ACC.	**uns**	**euch**		**sie**		**Sie**
	DAT.	*uns*	*euch*		*ihnen*		*Ihnen*

NOUNS

In the singular, nouns have no special ending for the dative. Occasionally, masculine and neuter nouns of one syllable use -e (**dem Manne**), but this ending is obsolescent and no longer required, except in such idiomatic expressions as **zu Hause** or **nach Hause.**

A number of masculine German nouns have the ending **-en** in all cases except the nominative singular:

NOM.	**der Student**	**der Junge**	**der Mensch**
ACC.	**den Studenten**	**den Jungen**	**den Menschen**
DAT.	**dem Studenten**	**dem Jungen**	**dem Menschen**
PLURAL	**die Studenten**	**die Jungen**	**die Menschen**

The noun **Herr** is declined as follows:

SINGULAR	NOM.	**der Herr**	PLURAL	NOM.	**die Herren**
	ACC.	**den Herrn**		ACC.	**die Herren**
	DAT.	**dem Herrn**		DAT.	**den Herren**

In the dative plural, all German nouns must end in **-n**, except those foreign words the plural of which ends in **-s.** If the nominative plural already ends in **-n,** no additional **-n** is required.

NOM. SING.	NOM. PLURAL	DAT. PLURAL
der Mann	**die Männer**	**den Männern**
die Frau	**die Frauen**	**den Frauen**
die Freundin	**die Freundinnen**	**den Freundinnen**
das Auto	**die Autos**	**den Autos**

NOTE: Nouns ending in **-in** double the **-n** in the plural in order to keep the **-i-** short: **die Freundin, die Freundinnen.**

56 Verbs with both Dative and Accusative Objects

Both English and German have a group of verbs that take two objects, a "direct" and an "indirect" object.

English differentiates between these two objects in either of two ways:
(1) by position: the indirect object *precedes* the direct object.

She gave her friend a book.

(2) by adding the preposition *to* to the indirect object when the indirect object *follows* the direct object.

She gave the book to her friend.

Whenever you have a genuine dative object in English, you can, by rearranging the sentence, force the form with *to* to appear or to disappear.

She gave him the book.
She gave the book to him.

The *him* in *She gave him the book* is therefore syntactically not the same kind of *him* as that in

She loves him

for only the first *him* can be changed into a *to him*. The *him* which can be replaced by *to him* corresponds to the German dative. Note also that the *to* in

He took Charlie to the station

cannot be eliminated, since *to the station* is not an object but a directive.

German differentiates neither by position nor by adding a preposition, but uses the dative case forms (**mir, dem,** etc.) for the indirect object and the accusative case forms (**mich, den,** etc.) for the direct object. The indirect object may precede or follow the direct object and never uses the preposition **zu.**

EXAMPLE:
    A. UNSOLICITED STATEMENT: **Ich schenke meinem Freund einen Roman zum Geburtstag.**
    B. QUESTION: **Was machst du denn mit dem Roman?**
      ANSWERS: **Den Roman schenke ich meinem Freund.** (topic: **Den Roman,** direct object; accus. case; **meinem Freund,** indirect object, dative case)
       or: **Ich schenke ihn meinem Freund.**
       or: **Ich schenke den Roman meinem Freund.** (sequence of objects determined by increasing news value)
    C. QUESTION: **Was schenkst du denn deinem Freund?**
      ANSWERS: **Meinem Freund schenke ich einen Roman.** (topic: **Meinem Freund)**
       or: **Ich schenke ihm einen Roman.**
       or: **Ich schenke meinem Freund einen Roman.**

Some important verbs that can take two objects are:

anbieten	to offer	**schenken**	to give (as a present)
bringen	to bring	**schicken**	to send
empfehlen	to recommend	**schreiben**	to write
geben	to give	**versprechen**	to promise
kaufen	to buy	**wünschen**	to wish
leihen	to lend	**zeigen**	to show

NOTE:

1. The English phrases *to take something to somebody* and *to take somebody home* are expressed in German by using **bringen.**

Er bringt ihr eine Tasse Kaffee.	He is taking her a cup of coffee.
Er bringt sie nach Hause.	He is taking her home.

2. **Glauben** sometimes takes only a dative object and sometimes only an accusative object.

Ich glaube dir.	I believe you.
Das glaube ich nicht.	I don't believe that.

But, unlike English, German can combine these two sentences into one.

Das glaube ich dir nicht.	I don't believe what you say.

The dative object represents the person and the accusative object represents the facts.

3. **Antworten** and **sagen** can also be used with two objects.

Was hat er dir geantwortet?	What answer did he give you?
Was hat er dir gesagt?	What did he tell you?

But **fragen** takes two accusatives.

Was hat er dich gefragt?	What did he ask you?

4. With some of these verbs, the dative object can be left out without changing the meaning of the verb. But it is *never* possible to leave out the accusative object and retain the dative object.

Er kauft einen Wagen.	He buys a car.
Er kauft seinem Sohn einen Wagen.	He buys a car for his son.

But not:

[Er kauft seinem Sohn.]	[He buys for his son.]

57 Verbs with Dative Object Only

Many English verbs take direct objects; some take both direct and indirect objects, but there are no verbs in English that take only an indirect object. The word *him* in *They helped him* and *They thanked him* is clearly a direct object in English. However, the German equivalents of *help* and *thank*, **helfen** and **danken**, express the notions *to give help to* and *to give thanks to*; therefore, they take indirect (dative) objects.

Ich helfe dir.	I help you.
Ich danke dir.	I thank you.

The verb **gehören** may express either ownership (with dative) or membership (with **zu** plus dative).

Das Haus gehört mir.	The house belongs to me.
Ernst gehört zu uns.	Ernst is one of our group.

In contrast to German, English must use *to* with both meanings.

The verb **gefallen** (*to please, be pleasing to*) is often used as the equivalent of English *to like*. But the subject of *like* appears as a personal dative, and the object of *like* becomes the subject of **gefallen**.

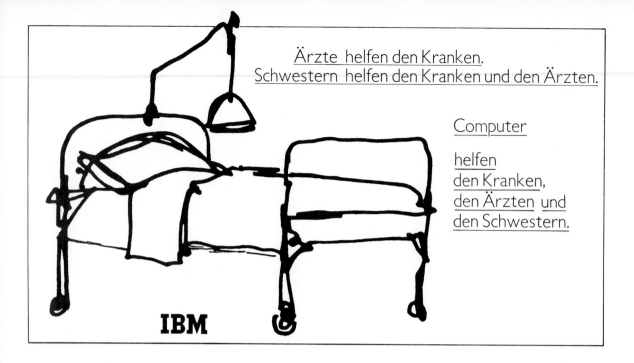

Ärzte helfen den Kranken.
Schwestern helfen den Kranken und den Ärzten.

Computer

helfen
den Kranken,
den Ärzten und
den Schwestern.

IBM

I like your novel very much, Mr. Ingelheim.
= Your novel pleases me very much, Mr. Ingelheim.
Ihr Roman gefällt mir sehr gut, Herr Ingelheim.

To express English phrases like *How are you?* and *I am fine*, German uses the impersonal construction **es geht . . . gut** with a personal dative.

Wie geht es Ihnen, Herr Weber?   How are you, Mr. Weber?
Danke, es geht mir gut.   Thanks, I am fine.

58 Adjectives Governing the Dative

Certain adjectives like **interessant, böse,** and **recht,** as well as most adjectives preceded by **zu,** can be used with the dative to point out the person for whom the grammatical subject has the quality denoted by the adjective.

Das ist neu.   That's new.
Das ist mir neu.   That's news to me.

Er ist böse.   He is angry.
Er ist mir böse.   He is angry with me.

Der Wein ist zu teuer.   The wine is too expensive.
Der Wein ist ihm zu teuer.   The wine is too expensive for him.

59 Prepositions Governing the Accusative

Some prepositions are *always* used with the accusative. This group includes: **durch** (*through*), **für** (*for*), **gegen** (*against*), and **ohne** (*without*). The preposition **um** also belongs in this group. In its most frequent use, however, in time phrases like **um sechs Uhr,** the accusative is not recognizable. In these time phrases, **um** means *exactly at*; *at about* is expressed by **gegen.** In other uses, **um** means *around*.

Er kommt um sechs Uhr.	He is coming at six o'clock.
Er kommt gegen sechs Uhr.	He is coming around six o'clock.
Fahren Sie um den Dom und dann immer geradeaus.	Drive around the cathedral and then continue straight ahead.

60 Prepositions Governing the Dative

Some prepositions are *always* used with the dative case. All the important prepositions of this group are introduced in this unit: **aus** (*out of*), **außer** (*except*), **bei** (see note 2 below), **mit** (*with*), **nach** (*after, to*), **seit** (*since*), **von** (*from*), **zu** (*to*).

NOTE:

1. A third group of prepositions, which includes **in** and **vor,** is used with either dative or accusative. These prepositions will be introduced in Unit 10.

2. **Bei** does not normally correspond to English *by*; it expresses the idea of close proximity, and frequently means *at the house of.*

Er wohnt in Potsdam bei Berlin.	He lives in Potsdam near Berlin.
Er wohnt bei seiner Tante.	He is living with his aunt.

3. Some prepositions are normally contracted with the following article into a single word, as long as the article is not stressed.

von dem	**Ich komme vom Bahnhof.**	I am coming from the station.
zu dem	**Ich gehe zum Bahnhof.**	I am on my way to the station.
zu der	**Ich gehe zur Universität.**	I am on my way to the university.
durch das	**Er geht durchs Haus.**	He is going through the house.
für das	**Er hat kein Geld fürs Kino.**	He has no money for the movies.
bei dem	**Meine Frau ist beim Arzt.**	My wife is at the doctor's.

But

Bei *dem* Regen kommt er nicht.	He won't come in *this* rain.

4. **Nach** is used to indicate time.

Nach dem Abendessen gehen wir ins Kino.	After supper, we'll go to the movies.
Er kommt nach acht Uhr.	He will arrive after eight o'clock.

Nach indicates *place* if a geographical proper name is mentioned:

Er geht nach Amerika	He is going to America
nach Deutschland	to Germany
nach Bayern	to Bavaria
nach Berlin	to Berlin

and in the idiom:

> **Er geht nach Hause.**

5. If no geographical proper name is used, **zu** is normally used to express direction.

> **Er geht zum Bahnhof.**   He goes to the station.
> **Er geht zur Universität.**   He is walking to the university.

Zu must be used with persons:

> **Er geht zu Karl.**   He goes to Karl.
> **Ich gehe zu meinem Vater.**   I go to my father.

and in the idiom:

> **Er ist zu Hause.**   He is at home.

61 Word Order within the Inner Field

Word order within the inner field is largely governed by *one* principle: The various elements are arranged in the order of increasing news value. The following rules govern most normal situations and are therefore safe to use.

The Position of the Subject

If a pronoun subject like **er, sie,** or **wir** stands in the inner field, it follows the verb immediately.

> **Morgen will er es ihm sagen.**   He wants to tell it to him tomorrow.

Since nouns generally have more news value than pronouns, noun subjects in the inner field are usually preceded by pronoun objects.*

> **Heute *gehört* ihm das Haus.**

Accusative Pronouns Precede Dative Pronouns

Accusative personal pronouns *always* precede dative personal pronouns.

> **Warum will er es ihm nicht sagen?**   Why doesn't he want to tell him that?
> **Leider kann ich es Ihnen nicht schenken.**   Unfortunately, I can't give it to you.
> **Ich soll es ihm schicken.**   I am supposed to send it to him.

Pronoun objects stand at the beginning of the inner field and can be preceded only by a subject.

> **Heute gehört es *ihm*.**
> **Heute gehört das Haus *ihm*.**

---

*However, **Heute gehört das Haus *ihm*** is also possible, if there is a strong stress on **ihm**.

Nouns and Pronouns

Nouns have more news value than pronouns. A noun object therefore follows a pronoun object.

Ich muß es meinem Vater sagen.	I must tell that to my father.
Ich kaufe mir morgen einen Hut.	I am going to buy myself a hat tomorrow.

Dative and Accusative Nouns

Nouns preceded by definite articles or by possessive adjectives usually refer to something already known or mentioned before. Nouns preceded by indefinite articles (**ein Buch**, plural **Bücher**), on the other hand, usually introduce something not mentioned before—something, therefore, of news value.

Since the sequence of elements in the inner field is determined by increasing news value, noun objects preceded by definite articles are usually placed before nouns preceded by indefinite articles.

Ich will meiner Freundin einen *Pu*del schenken.
Ich will den Pudel einer *Freun*din schenken.

If *both* nouns are preceded by either a **der**-word or a possessive adjective, the sequence is also determined by news value. In the sentence

Kannst du bitte dem Kind seine Medizin geben?	Could you please give the child his (her) medicine?

the news item is **seine Medizin;** but in the sentence

Darf ich diese Medizin auch meinem Kind geben?	May I give this medicine to my child, too?

the news item is **meinem Kind.**

Time Phrases

The position of time phrases in the inner field is again determined by news value, but they must precede **ein**-objects, which are position-fixed at the end of the inner field.

Ich soll ihm morgen das *Buch* geben.
Ich soll ihm das Buch *mor*gen geben.
Ich soll ihm *mor*gen ein Buch geben.

Several time phrases follow each other in the order of increasing specificity.

Er will morgen abend um neun nach München fahren.	Tomorrow evening at nine he wants to go to Munich.

Place Phrases
_____

There are two types of place phrases: those that answer the question **wohin?** *whereto, to what place?* and those that answer the question **wo?** *where, at what place?*

All **wohin**-phrases are directives, and are therefore position-fixed in the second prong.

>   **Ich fahre morgen mit meinem Mann nach Frankfurt.**

The position of **wo**-phrases is determined by news value, unless they are verbal complements as in **zu Hause sein** or **in Berlin wohnen.**

>   **Ich will morgen in Frankfurt eine *Kamera* kaufen.**
>   **Ich will die Kamera morgen in *Frank*furt kaufen.**

Place phrases normally follow time phrases and phrases answering *how?, with what?, with whom?* (manner-phrases).

>   **Ich will**   **morgen**   **mit der Kamera**   **im Zoo**   **Tiere photografieren.**
>   (*time*)   (*manner*)   (*place*)

Summary: The following variations show some of the possible positions of elements in the inner field. Note particularly how pronouns (no news value) are position-fixed at the beginning of the inner field and **ein**-nouns (always news value) are position-fixed at the end of the inner field. The elements in between are interchangeable; their sequence depends largely on increasing news value. Continue the table below by adding other possible arrangements of the same basic sentence.

FRONT FIELD	1ST PRONG			INNER FIELD		NICHT	2ND PRONG
		Subject	Pos.-Fixed Pronouns	Interchangeable Elements	Pos.-Fixed ein-Nouns		
Hans	will			seinem Freund das Buch morgen			geben.
Hans	will			morgen seinem Freund das Buch			geben.
Er	will			das Buch seinem Freund morgen		nicht	geben.
Er	will		es	seinem Freund morgen			geben.
Er	will		es	morgen seinem Freund			geben.
Er	will		ihm	morgen das Buch		nicht	geben.
Morgen	will	Hans		seinem Freund in der Schule	ein Buch		geben.
Er	will		ihm	morgen in der Schule das Buch			geben.
Hans	will		es ihm	morgen		nicht	geben.
Seinem Freund	will	Hans		morgen in der Schule	ein Buch		geben.
Er	will			morgen das Buch	einem Freund		geben.
Morgen	will	er	es	in der Schule seinem Freund			geben.
Morgen	will	er	es ihm				geben.

62 Replacement of er, sie, es by der, die, das

In informal but perfectly acceptable German, nouns and names are frequently replaced by der, die, das instead of by er, sie, es. When used in this function, der, die, and das are not articles, but demonstrative pronouns, and the dative plural is denen, not den. These demonstrative pronouns may be stressed or unstressed.

Wem gehört denn der *Wagen*?	Der Wagen gehört *mir*.
	Er gehört *mir*.
	Der gehört *mir*.
Kennen Sie Frau Dr. Walter?	Ja, die kenne ich sehr *gut*.
	Ja, mit *der* gehe ich heute abend ins Theater.
Was hörst du denn von Schmidts?	Oh, denen geht's *gut*.

For the time being, do not use either the personal pronouns or the demonstrative pronouns after a preposition unless they refer to persons.

63 es and das, Followed by Plural Verb Forms

A daughter recognizing that a woman on the TV screen is her mother can say:

That's my mother!

This impersonal *that* is used in sentences identifying somebody or something for the first time. *She is my mother*, on the other hand, is used when *she* has already been talked about and a further statement is being made about her. German makes the same distinction.

Das ist meine Mutter!

But

Kennen Sie Frau Bertram?
Natürlich! Sie ist meine Mutter!

In contrast to English *that*, German es and das are followed by plural verb forms when the identifying nouns are in the plural.

Es sind die Kinder.	It's the children.
Das sind die Kinder.	That's the children.

Conversations

I

MÜLLER: Sind Sie morgen noch hier in Frankfurt?

SCHMIDT: Nein, ich muß morgen nach Bonn.

MÜLLER: Fahren Sie mit dem Wagen?

SCHMIDT: Nein, mit dem Zug. Auf der Autobahn ist mir zu viel Verkehr, besonders am Wochenende. Außerdem kann ich im Zug arbeiten.

MULLER: Da haben Sie recht. Ich fahre auch lieber mit dem Zug. Wann kommen Sie denn
          zurück?

SCHMIDT: Ich bleibe nur fünf Tage; Freitag abend bin ich wieder hier.

MULLER: Dann müssen Sie uns aber Samstag oder Sonntag besuchen.

SCHMIDT: Ja, gerne.

II

The student and the man in the restaurant (see Unit 4, p. 101) continue to talk while waiting for their
meals:

STUDENT: Übrigens, ich heiße Ray, John Ray.

MANN: Jürgens. (Der Mann gibt dem Studenten die Hand.) Sie sind Ausländer, nicht
          wahr? Amerikaner?

STUDENT: Ja, aber wie wissen Sie, . . . ?

MANN: Man hört es an Ihrem Akzent.

STUDENT: Oh? —Aber Sie haben recht. Ich bin noch nicht lange in Deutschland.

MANN: Sie sprechen aber sehr gut Deutsch.

> STUDENT: By the way, my name is Ray, John Ray.
> MAN: Jürgens. (They shake hands.) You are a foreigner, aren't you? American?
> STUDENT: Yes, but how do you know . . . ?
> MAN: One can tell by your accent.
> STUDENT: Oh? But you are right. I haven't been in Germany very long.
> MAN: But you speak German very well.

MANN: Und was machen Sie in Deutschland, Herr Ray?

STUDENT: Ich studiere hier an der Universität. Ich habe ein Stipendium für ein Jahr, vom
          DAAD.

MANN: DAAD?

STUDENT: Der Deutsche Akademische Austauschdienst. —Ich möchte natürlich auch reisen
          und Deutschland wirklich gut kennenlernen, aber nicht als Tourist.

MANN: Sie müssen aber auch mal nach Österreich fahren, oder in die Schweiz.

STUDENT: Das tue ich bestimmt. Ich habe eine Freundin in Wien. Sie studiert dort.

> MAN: And what are you doing in Germany, Mr. Ray?
> STUDENT: I am studying at the university here. I have a fellowship for a year, from the DAAD.
> MAN: DAAD?
> STUDENT: The German Academic Exchange Service. —But I'd like to travel, too, of course, and
>   really get to know Germany well, but not as a tourist.
> MAN: Then you should go to Austria, too, some time, or to Switzerland.
> STUDENT: I'll certainly do that. I have a girlfriend in Vienna. She goes to the university there.

STUDENT: Und Sie, Herr Jürgens, was sind Sie von Beruf?

MANN: Ich bin Flugkapitän bei der Lufthansa.

STUDENT: Wirklich? Das muß sehr interessant sein.

MANN: Ja, interessant ist es, aber auch anstrengend.

STUDENT: Fliegen Sie auch manchmal nach Amerika?

MANN: Nein, hauptsächlich fliege ich in Europa, —Rom, Athen, Wien, Budapest, Belgrad.

> STUDENT: And you, Mr. Jürgens, what is your profession?
> MAN: I'm a pilot with Lufthansa.
> STUDENT: Really? That must be very interesting.
> MAN: Yes, it's interesting all right, but also strenuous.
> STUDENT: Do you fly to America sometimes?
> MAN: No, I mainly fly in Europe—Rome, Athens, Vienna, Budapest, Belgrade.

Ungarn Hungary Hungría		MA 521 TU154 F/Y ①②③ ⑤⑦	LH 356 B 727 F/Y ①④ ⑥⑦	LH 358 B 737 Y ①⑤
Frankfurt	ab/dp	13.30	16.15	—
Düsseldorf	an/ar ab/dp	— —	— —	— 13.20
München	an/ar ab/dp	— —	— —	14.25 15.10
Budapest	an/ar	15.00	17.45	16.20

"Bitte, wann fliegt die Maschine nach Budapest?"

OBER: So, die Herren, hier ist erst mal die Suppe. Vorsicht, sehr heiß. Und das Bier. Ich
          wünsche Ihnen guten Appetit.
MANN: (hebt sein Glas) Auf Ihr Wohl, Herr Ray, und ein gutes Studienjahr. (Sie trinken.)
          Also, guten Appetit.
STUDENT: Danke, ebenfalls. —Die Suppe ist wirklich heiß.
WAITER: There, gentlemen, here's your soup for a starter. Careful, very hot. And the beer. I
          wish you good appetite.
MAN: (raises his glass) Here's to you, Mr. Ray, and to a good year of studies. (They drink.)
          Now then, good appetite.
STUDENT: Thanks, same to you. —This soup is really hot.

Fragen an Sie persönlich

1. Was möchten Sie werden, wenn Sie Ihr Studium beendet haben?
2. Photografieren Sie gern?
   Was für eine Kamera (Filmkamera) haben Sie?   **Was für**   What kind of
   Was photografieren Sie?
      Menschen, Landschaften, Sport, Blumen?
3. Machen Sie oft Reisen?
   (Reisen Sie oft, viel, wenig, selten, nie, gern?)
   Mit dem Flugzeug? dem Wagen?
   Wandern Sie gern?   **wandern**   to hike
   Gehen Sie campen?
      das Zelt tent
      der Rucksack backpack

Reading

HORST BIENEK

Horst Bienek was born in Gleiwitz in 1930. The following poem is from the
same collection as the poem on p. 105.

Klatsch am Sonntagmorgen

Klatsch   gossip

Wer mit wem?
Die mit dem!
Der mit der?
(Ohne Gewähr)

ohne Gewähr   without guarantee

Sie und er?   5
Der und er??
Wer ist wer?

Wir mit ihr?
Sie mit dir!
(Am Klavier)   10

am Klavier   at the piano

Du mit ihm!
Sie mit him!
Ich und du?
Who is who?

Noch einmal Mitteleuropa

Mitteleuropa, wie wir es definieren, ist das Gebiet, in dem man Deutsch spricht, eine kulturell homogene Einheit mit gemeinsamer Tradition, mit gemeinsamen Sitten, sogar mit gemeinsamer Denkweise. Und 5 doch ist dieses Mitteleuropa ein sehr komplexes Gebilde; es ist trotz seiner Homogeneität auch heterogen, gegliedert in eine Reihe von Subkulturen, die man nur sehr schwierig begrenzen und definieren kann, und die 10 zwischen Norden und Süden, zwischen Osten und Westen große Unterschiede aufweisen.

Diese Subkulturen sind nicht überall identisch mit den politischen Grenzen der Staaten 15 Mitteleuropas, obwohl jeder dieser Staaten eine klare *politische* Identität hat. Ein Österreicher oder ein Schweizer ist *kein* Deutscher, auch wenn er Deutsch spricht, und die BRD und die DDR sind juristisch und politisch 20 zwei separate Staaten.

Dennoch sind zum Beispiel die Menschen in Schleswig-Holstein (im Norden der Bundesrepublik) den Menschen in Mecklenburg (im Norden der DDR) ähnlicher als den Bundes- 25

Central Europe Once Again

Central Europe, as we define it, is the area in which German is spoken, a culturally homogeneous unity with a common tradition, common customs, and even a common way of thinking. And yet this Central Europe is a very complex structure; in spite of its homogeneity it is heterogeneous, too, divided into a series of subcultures which are hard to delineate and to define, and which show great differences between north and south, east and west.

These subcultures are not everywhere identical with the political borders of the countries of Central Europe, although each of these countries has a clear *political* identity. An Austrian or a Swiss is *not* a German, even though he speaks German; and the FRG and the GDR are legally and politically two separate states.

Nevertheless, for example, the people in Schleswig-Holstein (in the north of the Federal Republic) are much more similar to the people in Mecklenburg (in the north of the

bürgern in Baden-Württemberg (im Süden der BRD). Die Württemberger dagegen haben vieles gemeinsam mit den Schweizern, mit den Liechtensteinern und mit den Österreichern im österreichischen Bundesland Vorarlberg. Kompliziert? —Gewiß; aber so sieht die Wirklichkeit der „einheitlichen" Kultur Mitteleuropas aus.

Das Gebiet um den Bodensee, den größten See Mitteleuropas, ist ein gutes Beispiel für eine solche regionale, aber trans-nationale Subkultur. Ob Schweizer, Österreicher, Bayern oder Württemberger, die Menschen am Bodensee sprechen alle den gleichen Dialekt, Alemannisch, und haben eine ähnliche Mentalität. Die Architektur des Bodenseegebiets ist einheitlich; die Landschaft ist die gleiche, dominiert vom See; landwirtschaftliche Methoden, soziale Struktur, religiöse Gebräuche zeigen kaum Unterschiede.

GDR) than to the federal citizens in Baden-Württemberg (in the south of the FRG). The Württemberg people, on the other hand, have much in common with the Swiss, the Liechtensteiner, and the Austrians in the Austrian federal state of Vorarlberg. Complicated? —Certainly; but that's what the reality of the "unified" culture of Central Europe looks like.

The area around Lake Constance, the largest lake of Central Europe, is a good example for such a regional, but trans-national subculture. Whether Swiss, Austrians, Bavarians, or Württemberger, the people around Lake Constance all speak the same dialect, Alamannic, and have a similar mentality. The architecture of the Lake Constance area is unified; the landscape is the same, dominated by the Lake; agricultural methods, social structure, religious customs hardly show any differences.

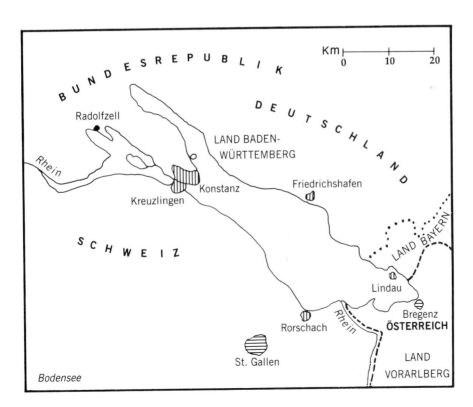

Von Rorschach in der Schweiz kann man in einer Viertelstunde bis zur Grenze von Österreich fahren. Fünfzehn Minuten später fährt man* durch die Stadt Bregenz, die Hauptstadt von Vorarlberg, und schon ist man an der deutschen Grenze. Dort steht neben dem Schild „Bundesrepublik Deutschland" ein zweites Schild mit „Freistaat Bayern". Aber schon nach zehn Minuten heißt es „Land Baden-Württemberg", und man ist fast in Friedrichshafen. Kaum 60 Kilometer von Rorschach nach Friedrichshafen, und doch drei Staaten, zwei Grenzübergänge. Aber wenn die Grenzpolizei und die Paßkontrolle nicht wären,† wüßte man nicht, daß man von einem Land ins andere fährt, so ähnlich ist die Landschaft, so ähnlich die Architektur, so ähnlich die Menschen.

Für europäische Begriffe ist der Bodensee groß, aber im Vergleich zu den großen amerikanischen Seen ist er kaum bemerkenswert. Der Bodensee ist von Radolfzell im Westen bis Bregenz im Osten etwa 65 km lang; der Lake Michigan ist von Süden nach Norden etwa 500 km lang, das ist so weit wie von München nach Hannover.

Für Amerikaner ist es immer überraschend, wie klein Europa ist im Vergleich zu den Vereinigten Staaten, wie kurz die Entfernungen von Land zu Land. Wenn man in Europa so weit fliegen will wie von Los Angeles nach New York, muß man zum Beispiel von Gibraltar nach Leningrad fliegen, oder von Oslo nach Kairo, oder von London nach Teheran. Die Bundesrepublik, der größte Staat Mitteleuropas, ist genau so groß wie Oregon, und das Fürstentum Liechtenstein ist nicht ganz so groß wie der District of Columbia. Der Rhein ist 1320 km lang, die Ruhr—so wichtig für die deutsche Industrie—nur 235 km. Der Missouri-Mississippi ist dagegen ein Gigant von 6200 km.

From Rorschach in Switzerland you can drive to the border of Austria in a quarter of an hour. Fifteen minutes later, you drive through the city of Bregenz, the capital of Vorarlberg, and already you are at the German border. There, next to the sign "Federal Republic of Germany," is another sign, "Free State of Bavaria." But only ten minutes later, it says "State of Baden-Württemberg," and you are almost in Friedrichshafen. Hardly sixty kilometers from Rorschach to Friedrichshafen, and yet three countries, two border crossings. But if it were not for the border police and the passport control, you wouldn't know that you were driving from one country into the next, so similar is the landscape, so similar the architecture, so similar the people.

In European terms, Lake Constance is large, but in comparison to the great American lakes it is hardly remarkable. From Radolfzell in the west to Bregenz in the east, Lake Constance is about 65 km. long; Lake Michigan, from south to north, extends over approximately 500 km., which is as far as from Munich to Hanover.

For Americans it is always surprising how small Europe is in comparison to the United States, how short the distances from country to country. If in Europe you want to fly as far as from Los Angeles to New York, you have to fly, for example, from Gibraltar to Leningrad, or from Oslo to Cairo, or from London to Tehran. The Federal Republic, the largest country of Central Europe, is exactly the size of Oregon, and the principality of Liechtenstein is not quite as large as the District of Columbia. The Rhine is 1,320 km. long, the Ruhr—so important for German industry—only 235 km. The Missouri-Mississippi, on the other hand, is a giant of 6,200 km.

---

*Note that the third-person pronoun **man** is often rendered in English by an impersonal *you*.
†These verb forms are in the subjunctive mood, which will be introduced in Unit 9.

Nicht viele Amerikaner wissen, wie weit im Norden Mitteleuropa liegt. Die Grenze zwischen den USA und Kanada ist 49°N(neunundvierzig Grad Nord), das ist genau die Breite von Stuttgart. New York 5 liegt auf der Breite von Neapel, und Los Angeles ist so weit südlich wie Nordafrika. Die deutsch-dänische Grenze ist 55°N, das ist Labrador, Hudson Bay und fast so weit nördlich wie Juneau in Alaska. Dennoch ist 10 Deutschland relativ warm, weil der Golfstrom die Westküste Europas erwärmt.

Not many Americans know how far north Central Europe is located. The border between the U.S. and Canada is the 49th parallel; that is exactly the latitude of Stuttgart. New York lies on the latitude of Naples, and Los Angeles is as far south as North Africa. The German-Danish border is 55° N, that is Labrador, Hudson Bay, and almost as far north as Juneau, Alaska. Nevertheless, Germany is relatively warm, because the Gulf Stream warms the west coast of Europe.

EINIGE STATISTISCHE DATEN ZUM VERGLEICH

SOME STATISTICAL DATA FOR COMPARISON

1 km (**der Kilometer,-**)	= 0,621 mi. (**die Meile,-n**)
1 mi.	= 1,609 km
1 km² (**der Quadratkilometer**)	= 0,386 sq.mi. (**die Quadratmeile**)
1 sq. mi.	= 2,590 km²

FLÜSSE			der Fluß,-̈e river
Ruhr	235 km	146 mi.	
Rhein	1320 km	820 mi.	
Donau	2850 km	1767 mi.	
Missouri-Mississippi	6207 km	3860 mi.	

FLÄCHEN			die Fläche,-n area
Bodensee	539 km²	208 sq.mi.	
New York City	932 km²	360 sq.mi.	
Los Angeles	1178 km²	455 sq.mi.	
Lake Michigan	58016 km²	22400 sq.mi.	

BRD	248 461 km²	95 931 sq.mi.	Oregon	96 315 sq.mi.
DDR	107 860 km²	41 645 sq.mi.	Ohio	41 000 sq.mi.
Österreich	83 848 km²	32 374 sq.mi.	Maine	31 040 sq.mi.
Schweiz	41 294 km²	15 944 sq.mi.	Mass. + N.H.	16 884 sq.mi.
Liechtenstein	157 km²	61 sq.mi.	D.C.	69 sq.mi.
Mitteleuropa	481 620 km²	185 955 sq.mi.	California	156 740 sq.mi.
			Texas	263 513 sq.mi.
			Alaska	571 065 sq.mi.
			USA	3,615 210 sq.mi.

Exercises

SEE
ANALYSIS
34–38
(pp. 67–70)

A. Give negative answers to the following questions.

1. Bist du glücklich mit ihm?
2. Wohnt ihr noch in Freiburg?
3. Mußt du denn morgen nach Augsburg fahren?
4. Hast du noch Geld?
5. Redet Frau Müller noch immer soviel?
6. Ist Erika intelligent?
7. Geht Fritz schon in die Schule?
8. Lebt Meyer noch?
9. Brauchst du *auch* einen Hut? (Use contrast intonation.)
10. Brauchst du auch einen *Hut*? (Use contrast intonation.)

SEE
ANALYSIS
55–57
(pp. 118–121)

B. Replace the dative or accusative pronouns in italics by the proper form of the nouns in parentheses.

1. Ich will *es* nicht lesen. (Buch)
2. Kennst du *ihn?* (mein Vater)
3. Ich kann *ihn* schon sehen. (Zug)
4. Kennt er *sie?* (deine Frau)
5. Tante Amalie will mit *ihr* nach Spanien fahren. (unsere Tochter)
6. Die Uhr gehört *ihr.* (meine Frau)
7. Liebt sie *ihn* denn nicht? (ihr Mann)
8. Liebt er *sie* denn nicht? (seine Frau)
9. Ich will nicht für *ihn* arbeiten (Herr Meyer)
10. Bei *der* möchte ich nicht wohnen. (deine Tante)

SEE
ANALYSIS
57
(p. 121)

C. Express in German.

1. That is my house.
2. It (the house) belongs to me.
3. It (the house) belongs to you?
4. Yes, to me.
5. This house belongs to Hans.
6. It (the house) belongs to him.
7. It (the house) belongs to her.
8. The car belongs to her.
9. It (the car) belongs to her.
10. It is her car.

D. Replace nouns and names by personal pronouns.

Ich fahre mit meinem Freund Fritz.
Ich fahre mit ihm.

SEE
ANALYSIS
57, 59, 60
(pp. 121, 122,
123)

1. Er wohnt bei seiner Tante.
2. Er will zu seinem Vater.
3. Er hilft seiner Mutter.
4. Er hilft seiner Freundin.
5. Er hilft seinem Freund.
6. Er kommt von seinem Freund Hans.
7. Er arbeitet für seinen Bruder.
8. Er arbeitet heute ohne seinen Freund.
9. Außer Erika sind wir alle hier.
10. Bei meiner Tante bin ich gern.

SEE
ANALYSIS
59–60
(pp. 122–123)

E. Complete the following sentences by using either **nach, zu,** or **bei.**

1. Ich gehe _____ Bahnhof.
2. Er wohnt _____ seiner Tante.
3. Wir gehen _____ Meyers.
4. Sie sind _____ Hans.
5. Wir fahren _____ Europa.
6. Wir fahren _____ Universität.
7. Wir fahren _____ Hotel.
8. Wir fahren _____ Wien.
9. Man spricht nicht _____ Essen.
10. Oskar wohnt _____ Schmidts.

SEE
ANALYSIS
61
(p. 124)

F. In the following sentences, the inner field is left empty. Fill the inner field with each of the several series of words by rearranging them in the correct word order.

1. Ich will _____ schenken.
   (a) es, morgen, ihm
   (b) das Buch, morgen, ihm
   (c) ein Buch, morgen, meinem Vater
   (d) es, morgen, meinem Vater

2. Willst du _____ schenken?

    (a) einen Hund, deiner Freundin

    (b) den Hund, deiner Freundin

    (c) deiner Freundin, ihn

    (d) einen Hund, ihr

    (e) ihn, ihr

3. Wollen Sie _____ schicken?

    (a) Ihrem Vater, das Buch

    (b) ein Buch, ihm (Ihrem Vater)

    (c) es, ihm

    (d) Ihrem Vater, es

    (e) das Buch, ihm

4. Ich will _____ mitbringen.

    (a) ein Buch, meiner Freundin, aus Berlin

    (b) aus Berlin, ein Buch, ihr

    (c) das Buch, ihr, aus Berlin

    (d) ihr, es, aus Berlin

5. Darf ich _____ ins Haus schicken, Herr Doktor?

    (a) morgen, Ihnen, den Wein

    (b) die Blumen, morgen, Ihrer Frau

    (c) sie (die Blumen), ihr (Ihrer Frau), morgen

    (d) sie (die Blumen), morgen, Ihrer Frau

    (e) Blumen, Ihrer Frau, morgen

    (f) Blumen, ihr, morgen

    (g) die Blumen, ihr, morgen

G. Form sentences from the following elements.

1. Hans / sein Vater / helfen.
2. Herr Müller / sein Sohn / Kamera / kaufen / wollen.
3. Erika / ein Roman / von Schmidt-Ingelheim / lesen.
4. Ich / sie (2 forms) / nicht glauben.
5. Buch / ich / nicht gehören // es / Freundin / gehören.
6. Wer / dieses Haus / gehören?
7. Wie / du / gehen? // Danke // gut / gehen.
8. Ich / Uhr / nicht kaufen // zu teuer.
9. Kurt / aus Stadt / kommen / und / Universität / gehen.
10. Wir / durch Stadt / fahren / müssen.

H. Construct sentences as indicated.

1. Mr. Meyer is not well today.

    (a) He is well. (Start with **Es;** use **gehen.**)

    (b) Start with *Mr. Meyer* (Watch dative; move **es.**)

    (c) add: *not*

    (d) add: *today*

2. Mr. Hansen always seems to recommend novels to his customers.

    (a) Mr. Hansen recommends novels.

    (b) add: *seems to*

    (c) add: *to his customers* (word order!)

    (d) insert *always* between objects

3. Mrs. Müller would like to give (as a present) her husband 12 bottles of wine for his birthday.

    (a) *to give as a present* (not: **geben**)

    (b) Mrs. Müller gives her husband 12 bottles (of) wine.

    (c) add: *would like to*

    (d) add: *for his birthday* (second prong, first box)

    (e) add: *This year* (Move subject!)

I. Express in German.

1. How are you? (3 sentences)
2. I give her the book.
3. He gives it to his father.
4. We give it to them.
5. He is coming from the movies.
6. Inge is with us.
7. I'm going to the railroad station.
8. He went around the corner and then always straight ahead.
9. Do you work for him?
10. You have to go without me.
11. That's news to me.
12. Does this book belong to you, Hans?
13. Can you help him?
14. Please believe me.
15. Must you have it (the book) today?

Vocabulary

ähnlich	similar
anbieten	to offer
anstrengend	strenuous
der Apparat', -e	apparatus, instrument
der Photoapparat	camera
am Apparat	speaking (on the telephone)
der Appetit' (*no pl.*)	appetite
aussehen (siehst aus, sieht aus)	to appear; to look
außer (*with dat.*)	besides, except for
außerdem	moreover
begrenzen	to border; to limit
der Begriff, -e	idea, notion; term
das Beispiel, -e	example
zum Beispiel	for example
der Beruf, -e	job, profession
die Blume, -n	flower
die Breite, -n	latitude; breadth
dagegen	in comparison with; on the other hand
dennoch	yet; though, nevertheless
durch (*with acc.*)	through
ebenfalls	likewise, too
einheitlich	uniform, homogeneous
einige	some, any, a few
die Entfernung, -en	distance
die Erde, -n	earth
die Fläche, -n	area
der Fluß, *pl.* die Flüsse	river
für (*with acc.*)	for
gar	fully, even; quite, very
gar nicht	not at all
der Gebrauch, -̈e	use; custom, habit
der Geburtstag, -e	birthday
gegen (*with acc.*)	against; around
gegen neun	around nine o'clock
gehören (*with dat.*)	to belong to
gemeinsam	common, mutual
genau	exact (ly)
gerade	straight; just
gewiß	certain (ly)
der Grad, -e	degree
die Grenze, -n	border
die Grenzpolizei	border police
der Grenzüber-gang, -̈e	border crossing
groß	large, big
die Großmutter, -̈	grandmother
der Großvater, -̈	grandfather
hauptsächlich	mainly, primarily
die Hauptstadt, -̈e	capital (city)
heben	to lift, to raise
helfen (hilfst, hilft) (*with dat.*)	to give help to, to help
der Hund, -e	dog
der Hut, -̈e	hat
die Industrie', die Industri'en	industry
die Kamera, -s	camera
die Kasse, -n	cash register, cash box
der Kilometer, -	kilometer
der Quadratkilo-meter, -	square kilometer
klar	clear
klein	small
kompliziert	complicated
der Kopf, -̈e	head
die Kultur', -en	culture
die Subkultur, -en	subculture
kurz	short

die Landschaft, -en	landscape	sozial	social
landwirtschaftlich	agricultural	der Sport (*no pl.*)	sport
leihen	to lend	die Struktur', -en	structure
manchmal	sometimes	das Studium, die	study, studies (at a
der Mantel, ⸚	coat	Studien	university
die Meile, -n	mile	der Süden	south
die Quadrat-	square mile	tragen (du trägst, er	to carry; to wear
meile, -n		trägt)	(clothes)
die Methode, -n	method	trotz	despite, in spite of
der Mond, -e	moon	überall	everywhere
neben	beside, next to	der Unterschied, -e	difference
der Norden	north	vereinigen	to unify
nördlich	northern	die Vereinigten	the United States
obwohl	even though, although	Staaten	
der Osten	east	der Vergleich, -e	comparison
photographie'ren	to photograph	der Verkäufer, -	salesman
also: fotografieren		die Verkäuferin,	saleswoman
die Reihe, -n	row; series	-nen	
reisen	to travel	der Verkehr	traffic
relativ	relative(ly)	versprechen (du ver-	to promise
religiös	religious	sprichst, er	
schenken	to give (as a present)	verspricht)	
schicken	to send	die Vorsicht (*no pl.*)	caution
das Schild, -er	sign	Vorsicht!	Careful! Watch out!
der Schmerz, -en	pain	wandern	to hike
die Kopfschmerzen	headache	(die) Weihnachten	Christmas
schwierig	difficult, hard	(*pl.*)	
der See, -n	lake	wenig	little
selten	rare(ly)	wichtig	important
sofort	right away, immediately	die Wirklichkeit, -en	reality
solch-	such	zeigen	to show
sonst	otherwise	das Zelt, -e	tent
sonst nichts	nothing else		

Additional Vocabulary

der Akzent', -e	accent	homogen'	homogeneous
die Architektur', -en	architecture	die Homogenität'	homogeneity
aufweisen	to show, to present	die Identität', -en	identity
ausprobieren	to try out	juris'tisch	legal
bemerkenswert	noteworthy, remarkable	komplex'	complex
die Denkweise, -n	way of thinking	kreisen	to revolve; to circle
dominieren	to dominate	die Mentalität', -en	mentality
erwärmen	to warm (up)	die Paßkontrolle, -n	passport control
der Flugkapitän, -e	flight captain	der Sack, ⸚e	sack; bag
das Fürstentum, ⸚er	principality	der Rucksack	backpack, knapsack
das Gebilde, -	structure	die Sitte, -n	custom
der Gigant', -en	giant	das Stipen'dium, die	scholarship, fellow-
gliedern	to arrange, to divide	Stipendien	ship, stipend
heterogen'	heterogeneous	überraschend	surprising(ly)

BURG GASTHOF STAUFEN ECK

Speisenkarte

WILD- UND FISCHGERICHTE

*Rehbraten mit handgem. Spätzle, Preiselbeeren und Salate		8.20
Lebendfrische Forelle blau mit Salzkartoffeln und zerlassener Butter	ab	6.80
Lebendfrische Forelle „Müllerin Art", Salzkartoffeln und Kopfsalat	ab	6.80

VOM SCHWEIN

1 Paar Bratwürste mit Salate	3.20
Warmes Ripple mit Sauerkraut und Kartoffeln	5.—
Schweinebraten mit handgem. Spätzle und Salate	5.—
Kotelette paniert mit Salatplatte	6.—

VOM KALB

Kalbsgulasch mit handgem. Spätzle und Salate	6.—
Wiener Schnitzel mit Salatplatte	6.80
Rahmschnitzel mit pommes frites und Buttererbsen	7.50
Kalbsleber „Hawaii" mit Bratkartoffeln und Salate	7.50
Schnitzel natur mit Butterreis, Champignon u. Salate	8.—
Kalbsteak „Princess" mit Spargel, Sauce Hollandaise, pommes frites und Salate	9.50
Kalbsmedaillon vom Grill mit Curryreis, Champignon und feiner Gemüsegarnitur	9.20

VOM RIND

Kleines Filetsteak auf Toast mit Spiegelei	6.20
Rindsgulasch mit Weckknödel und Salate	6.50
Wiener Zwiebelrostbraten mit Bratkartoffeln und Salate	7.20
Mixed Grill mit Kräuterbutter, pommes frites und Salate	7.80
Rumpsteak „Haushofmeister" mit Kräuterbutter, pommes frites und feinem Gemüse	8.50
Filetsteak „Gärtnerin Art" mit pommes frites, Gemüsegarnitur und Kräuterbutter	9.50

Stuttgarter Hofbräu

Burggasthof
Staufeneck
Ernst Wörner
Post Salach/Württ.
Telefon Süßen
(0 71 62) 73 12

UNIT 6 The Perfect Tense—Time Phrases—
Cardinal Numbers

Until now you have been able, as it were, to live only for the moment because you had only the present tense of verbs at your disposal. From Unit 6 on, you will be able to talk about what happened yesterday or a hundred years ago, but there are some major differences between German and English, and you will have to make a conscious effort to overcome your own ingrained linguistic behavior. You may have noticed that Germans in America are often recognizable not only by their German accent in English, but also by certain "odd" ways of expressing themselves, ways which, of course, are not odd at all, but simply represent a transfer of German syntactic patterns to English. A recently arrived German is apt to say, "*I have gone to the movies last night*," clearly a wrong construction in English, but a literal translation of **Ich bin gestern abend ins Kino gegangen.**

It is often said that mastery of a foreign language has been achieved when one can do everyday arithmetic in the foreign language without hesitation. Trying to give answers to "What time is it?" "How far is it to Rottenegg?" or "What does it cost?" is apt to make you feel absolutely tongue-tied at first. Having all cardinal numbers available from Unit 6 on will enable you to start practicing such answers. A number of exercises as well as the reading selections of this unit will give you ample opportunity to use numbers in German.

It takes a while to get used to the different monetary systems of European countries, none of which have a 1:1 parity. West Germans use deutsche mark (DM) and pfennigs (pennies), East Germans also use marks but without the "D" and they put the "M" behind the figure rather than in front. Thus, you can easily tell the difference between DM5 and 5M. Theoretically, West and East marks have the same value, but they are not freely and easily convertible. It is illegal, for example, to take any East marks out of the DDR. The Swiss use francs, like the French and the Belgians, but the schweizer franken (sFr) is worth considerably more than either of the other two. The German pfennig corresponds to the Swiss rappen. The Austrian schilling (1öS = 100 groschen) is worth about one-sixth of the DM; thus, if you have to pay DM10 for a German meal, or about sFr10 for a Swiss meal, you will have to expect a bill for about öS60. And then try to convert all that into what some tourists still like to refer to as "real money," namely U.S. dollars!

Patterns

[1] The Perfect Tense

Read these sentences aloud to get used to this pattern, in which the participle appears at the end of the sentence.

SEE ANALYSIS 64–66 (pp. 146–148)

FRONT FIELD	1ST PRONG	INNER FIELD	NICHT	2ND PRONG 1ST BOX	2ND BOX

A. Auxiliary: haben

WEAK VERBS

Er	hat	lange		in Berlin	gewohnt.
Wir	haben	ihn leider	nicht		gekannt.
Wo	hast	du ihn		kennen-	gelernt?
Ich	habe	Tante Amalie			besucht.
Karl	hat	in Berlin		Medizin	studiert.

STRONG VERBS

Wir	haben	sie leider	nicht		gesehen.
Was	habt	ihr denn			getrunken?
Wir	haben	schon		zu Mittag	gegessen.
	Haben	Sie mich	nicht		verstanden?

MODALS

Ich	habe	gestern			arbeiten müssen.
Ich	habe	gestern	nicht		zu arbeiten brauchen.
Er	hat	gestern	nicht	zu Hause	bleiben wollen.
Ich	habe	leider	nicht		mitgehen können.
Ich	habe	leider	nicht		gekonnt.
Er	hat	es	nicht		tun wollen.
Er	hat	es	nicht		gewollt.

B. Auxiliary: sein

WEAK VERBS

Sie	sind	schnell		nach Hause	geeilt.
Er	ist	mir			gefolgt.
Wir	sind	damals oft		nach Italien	gereist.
Sie	ist	gestern			verreist.

				2ND PRONG	
FRONT FIELD	1ST PRONG	INNER FIELD	NICHT	1ST BOX	2ND BOX

STRONG VERBS

	Ist	Hans schon			**gekommen?**
Der Zug	**ist**	gerade		an-	**gekommen.**
Warum	**seid**	ihr denn	nicht	zu Hause	**geblieben?**
Inge	**ist**	schon oft		hier	**gewesen.**
Er	**ist**	erst um elf		auf-	**gestanden.**
	Ist	Hans jetzt endlich			**erschienen?**
Dann	**ist**	er plötzlich			**verschwunden.**

[2] The Perfect as Conversational Tense

The following sentences, although they are a continuous text of sorts, are not a "story"; being in the perfect tense, they have the flavor of spoken, conversational German as if the young woman were telling a friend about her trip. Note that the English translations all use the past tense.

SEE ANALYSIS 68 (p. 149)

Ich habe Frau Enderle letztes Jahr in Stuttgart kennengelernt.

I met Mrs. Enderle in Stuttgart last year.

Vor drei Wochen habe ich ihr von Wien aus* einen Brief geschrieben.

Three weeks ago I wrote her a letter from Vienna.

Sie hat mich zu einem Besuch in Burgbach eingeladen.

She invited me to visit her in Burgbach.

Gestern habe ich sie und ihre Familie besucht.

Yesterday I visited her and her family.

Ich habe den Nachtzug von Wien nach Stuttgart genommen.

I took the night train from Vienna to Stuttgart.

Dann bin ich gestern morgen mit dem Personenzug nach Burgbach gefahren.

Then I took a local train to Burgbach yesterday morning.

Frau Enderle hat mich mit dem Wagen am Bahnhof abgeholt.

Mrs. Enderle picked me up at the station with her car.

Auf dem Weg zu ihrem Haus haben wir eingekauft.

On the way to her house we went shopping.

Das Haus haben Enderles erst vor vier Jahren gebaut.

The Enderles built the house only four years ago.

Vorher haben sie zwölf Jahre lang bei den Eltern von Herrn Enderle gewohnt.

Before that they lived with Mr. Enderle's parents for twelve years.

Frau Enderle hat mir das Haus gezeigt, und ich habe ihren Garten bewundert.

Mrs. Enderle showed me the house, and I admired her garden.

Dann habe ich ihr in der Küche geholfen.

Then I helped her in the kitchen.

*Note that **von Wien aus** is one syntactical unit, meaning *from Vienna*.

Um ein Uhr sind die Kinder aus der Schule gekommen, und wir haben zu Mittag gegessen.	At one o'clock the children came home from school, and we ate dinner.
Nach dem Mittagessen haben wir lange im Wohnzimmer gesessen und haben geplaudert.	After dinner we sat in the living room for a long time and talked.
Die Kinder sind schwimmen gegangen.	The children went swimming.
Um halb fünf haben wir eine Tasse Kaffee getrunken und ein Stück Kuchen gegessen.	At 4:30 we had a cup of coffee and a piece of cake.
Herr Enderle ist erst um viertel nach sechs nach Hause gekommen, und um dreiviertel sieben haben wir zu Abend gegessen.	Mr. Enderle did not get home until 6:15, and at 6:45 we ate supper.
Nach dem Abendessen sind wir spazierengegangen.	After supper we went for a walk.
Auf einem Hügel über dem Dorf haben wir lange auf einer Bank gesessen, und Herr und Frau Enderle haben mir viel über das Leben in Burgbach erzählt.	On a hill above the village we sat on a bench for a long time, and Mr. and Mrs. Enderle told me a lot about life in Burgbach.

[3] Point-in-Time Phrases

SEE
ANALYSIS
69–70
(pp. 150–151)

Wann kommt Karl denn?—Morgen früh.	When is Karl coming?—Tomorrow morning.
Wann gehst du ins Theater?—Heute abend.	When are you going to the theater?—Tonight.
Wann fahrt ihr denn in den Schwarzwald?—Nächsten Sonntag.	When are you going to the Black Forest?—Next Sunday.
Wann sehe ich dich wieder?—In drei Wochen.	When will I see you again?—In three weeks.
Frau Enderle habe ich vor einem Jahr in Stuttgart kennengelernt.	I met Mrs. Enderle a year ago in Stuttgart.
Meyer ist gestern nach München gefahren.	Meyer went to Munich yesterday.
Wann fährt denn der Zug nach Bonn?—Der Zug ist schon vor zehn Minuten abgefahren.	When does the train to Bonn leave?—The train left ten minutes ago.

[4] Frequency Phrases

SEE
ANALYSIS
71
(p. 151)

Wie oft müssen Sie denn nach Wien fliegen, Herr Jürgens?—Dreimal im Monat.	How often do you have to fly to Vienna, Mr. Jürgens?—Three times a month.
Fliegen Sie auch manchmal nach Amerika?—Nein, nie.	Do you sometimes fly to America, too?—No, never.
Essen Sie oft Sauerkraut, Frau Enderle?—Nein, nur sehr selten.	Do you often eat sauerkraut, Mrs. Enderle?—No, only very rarely.
Meyers wohnen jetzt auch hier in München, aber sie besuchen uns nie.	The Meyers live in Munich, too, now, but they never visit us.

Wie heißt denn der Film?—Er heißt *Sonntags nie.*

What's the name of the movie?—It's called *Never on Sunday.*

Wie oft seid ihr denn in den Ferien schwimmen gegangen?—Leider nur zweimal.

How often did you go swimming during vacation?—Unfortunately only twice.

Wie oft seid ihr denn diesen Sommer schon schwimmen gegangen? — Mindestens schon zehnmal.—Leider erst zweimal.

How often have you been swimming this summer?—At least ten times.—Unfortunately only twice.

Sind Sie schon einmal in Paris gewesen?—Nein, noch nicht.

Have you been in Paris yet?—No, not yet.

Ich bin auch noch nie in Rom gewesen.

I have not yet (never) been in Rome either.

So, Sie haben zehn Jahre in Europa gelebt. Sind Sie auch einmal in Paris gewesen?—Ja, sehr oft.

So you lived in Europe for ten years. Did you ever go to Paris?—Yes, quite often.

Haben Sie in Deutschland je Leberknödelsuppe gegessen?—In München sehr oft, aber in Hamburg nie.

Did you ever eat liver dumpling soup in Germany?—In Munich very frequently, but in Hamburg never.

Fritz studiert jetzt Mathematik? Aber er hat doch immer Arzt werden wollen.

Fritz is studying mathematics now? But he always wanted to be a doctor.

Natürlich studiert Brigitte Medizin; sie hat doch schon immer Ärztin werden wollen.

Of course Bridget is studying medicine; she has always wanted to be a doctor.

[5] Stretch-of-Time Phrases

Ich habe zehn Jahre in Bern gewohnt.

I lived in Berne for ten years.

Müller hat jahrelang bei Mercedes-Benz gearbeitet.

Müller worked for Mercedes-Benz for years.

SEE ANALYSIS 72 (p. 153)

Diesen Sommer hat es wochenlang geregnet.

This summer it rained for weeks.

Wir haben lange im Garten auf einer Bank gesessen.

For a long time we sat on a bench in the garden.

An dem Abend habe ich noch lange wach gelegen.

That evening I lay awake for a long time.

Tante Amalie bleibt sicher noch lange hier.—Ja, sie hat gesagt, sie will drei Wochen hierbleiben.

I'm sure Aunt Amalie is going to stay here for a long time.—Yes, she said she wants to stay for three weeks.

Wie lange bleibt Ihr Mann denn in Bremen, Frau König?—Drei Wochen.

How long is your husband going to stay in Bremen, Mrs. König?—For three weeks.

Er ist krank gewesen, und der Arzt hat ihm gesagt, er darf vier Wochen lang nicht schilaufen.

He has been ill, and the doctor told him not to go skiing for four weeks.

Schmitz wohnt schon drei Jahre (seit drei Jahren, schon seit drei Jahren) in Düsseldorf.

Schmitz has been living in Düsseldorf for three years.

Ich warte seit fünf Uhr auf meinen Mann, aber das Flugzeug hat Verspätung, und er ist immer noch nicht hier.

I have been waiting for my husband since five o'clock, but his plane is late, and he still isn't here.

Jetzt stehe ich schon über eine Stunde hier, und Hans ist immer noch nicht gekommen.	I've been standing here for over an hour now, and Hans still hasn't come.
So gut habe ich schon lange nicht gegessen, Frau Enderle.	I haven't eaten this well for a long time, Mrs. Enderle.
Gut, daß du endlich hier bist; ich habe seit zwei Stunden auf dich gewartet.	Good that you're here at last; I've been waiting for you for two hours.
Vielen Dank für die Kamera, Vater; du weißt ja, die habe ich mir schon lange gewünscht.	Thanks for the camera, Dad; you know I've wanted it for a long time.

[6] Cardinal Numbers

Learn the numbers; then go through the drills as indicated.

SEE
ANALYSIS
73
(p. 156)

Null, eins, zwei, drei, vier, fünf, sechs, sieben, acht, neun, zehn, elf, zwölf, dreizehn, vierzehn, fünfzehn, sechzehn, siebzehn, achtzehn, neunzehn, zwanzig.

eins und eins ist zwei	eins plus eins ist zwei
eins und zwei ist . . .	eins plus zwei ist . . .
eins . . .	eins . . .
zwanzig weniger eins ist neunzehn	zwanzig minus eins ist neunzehn
neunzehn weniger eins . . .	zwanzig minus zwei ist . . .
achtzehn . . .	zwanzig . . .
Wieviel Uhr ist es?	Es ist zehn Uhr dreizehn.
Wie spät ist es?*	Es ist zehn Uhr dreizehn.
Wann kommt der Zug an?	Um sechs Uhr siebzehn.
Um wieviel Uhr kommt der Zug an?	Um sechs Uhr siebzehn.

*This does not normally mean "How late is it?" but "What time is it?"

Wann fährt der Zug ab?   Um sieben Uhr sechzehn.
Um wieviel Uhr fährt der Zug ab?   Um sieben Uhr sechzehn.

Wann fängt das Theater an?   Um acht Uhr fünfzehn.

zwanzig, einundzwanzig, zweiundzwanzig, dreiundzwanzig, vierundzwan-
zig, fünfundzwanzig, sechsundzwanzig, siebenundzwanzig, achtundzwanzig,
neunundzwanzig, dreißig, einunddreißig, zweiunddreißig, vierzig, dreiund-
vierzig, vierundvierzig, fünfundvierzig, fünfzig, fünfundfünfzig, sechsund-
fünfzig, sechzig, sechsundsechzig, siebenundsechzig, siebzig, siebenundsieb-
zig, achtundsiebzig, achtzig, achtundachtzig, neunundachtzig, neunzig,
hundert (einhundert)

ein mal zwei ist zwei   hundert (geteilt) durch zehn ist zehn
zwei mal zwei ist vier   neunzig (geteilt) durch zehn ist neun
drei mal zwei ist sechs   achtzig (geteilt) durch zehn ist acht
vier mal zwei ist acht   siebzig (geteilt) durch zehn ist sieben
fünf mal zwei ist zehn   sechzig (geteilt) durch zehn ist sechs

100 *hund*ert   100 *ein*hundert
101 hundert*eins*   200 *zwei*hundert
102 hundert*zwei*   300 *drei*hundert
110 hundert*zehn*   900 *neun*hundert
120 hundert*zwan*zig   1.000 *tausend*
121 hundert*einund*zwanzig
122 hundert*zweiund*zwanzig   7.839 *siebentausendacht*hundert*neunund*dreißig
198 hundert*achtundneun*zig   1.000.000 eine Milli*on*
199 hundert*neunundneun*zig   2.000.000 zwei Milli*on*en
200 *zweihun*dert   1.000.000.000 eine Milli*arde* (one billion)

Ich brauche zweihundert*ein*undvierzig *Mark*.
In unserer Stadt wohnen jetzt über *drei*hunderttausend *Menschen*.
Unsere Bibliothek hat drei Millionen *Mark* gekostet.

0, 7   *null* komma *sieben*
0,17   *null* komma *siebzehn* (*null* komma *eins sieben*)
3,14159 *drei* komma *eins vier eins fünf neun*

Read the following numbers.

        758   75,8   7,58   2,718282   232.493,00   232,493

DM   4,20   vier Mark zwanzig (West) —   4,20 M   vier Mark zwanzig (Ost)
öS 121,00   hunderteinundzwanzig Schilling
sFr 100,21   hundert Franken einundzwanzig
DM   0,75   fünfundsiebzig Pfennig
$ 1.477,00 vierzehnhundertsiebenundsiebzig Dollar
             eintausendvierhundertsiebenundsiebzig Dollar
$ 18,37 achtzehn Dollar siebenunddreißig

[7] Time

SEE
ANALYSIS
74
(p. 157)

11.00 Uhr	elf Uhr	11.35 Uhr	fünf nach halb zwölf
11.05 Uhr	fünf (Minuten) nach elf	11.40 Uhr	zehn nach halb zwölf
11.10 Uhr	zehn nach elf	11.45 Uhr	dreiviertel zwölf; viertel vor zwölf
11.15 Uhr	viertel nach elf; viertel zwölf	11.50 Uhr	zehn vor zwölf
11.20 Uhr	zwanzig nach elf	11.55 Uhr	fünf vor zwölf
11.25 Uhr	fünf vor halb zwölf	12.00 Uhr	zwölf Uhr
11.30 Uhr	halb zwölf		

Read aloud and, where possible, in several ways:

9.05 (Uhr)	4.25 (Uhr)	12.45 (Uhr)
9.15	7.45	1.30
10.30	7.57	21.45

What are the equivalents?

18.45 Uhr   (achtzehn Uhr fünfundvierzig) = sechs Uhr fünfundvierzig
                                                                        dreiviertel sieben
                                                                        viertel vor sieben

15.10 Uhr =
21.30 Uhr =
13.55 Uhr =

Analysis

64 The German Perfect

By now you have become accustomed to the fact that German does not have as many verb forms as English. English *I see*, *I am seeing*, and *I do see* are all expressed in German by **ich sehe**.

This is also true in regard to the past tenses. While English has the forms

PAST	I saw	PRESENT PERFECT	I have seen
	I was seeing		I have been seeing

German must get along with

PAST	**Ich sah**	PERFECT	**Ich habe gesehen**

In Unit 6, only the German perfect is introduced. The past tense follows in Unit 7.

65 Formation of the German Participle

The English present perfect (*I have seen*) consists of an auxiliary verb plus a participle; the perfect in German is formed in the same manner. German participles are formed in one of two ways which are traditionally referred to as *weak* and *strong*.

Weak Verbs

All weak verbs place the unchanged stem into the frame **ge**_____**t.**

INFINITIVE	STEM	AUXILIARY	PARTICIPLE
machen	**mach-**	**hat**	**gemacht**
sagen	**sag-**	**hat**	**gesagt**
regnen	**regn-**	**hat**	**geregnet**

The **ge-** prefix is never stressed. Since the **-t** of the frame must be audible, stems ending in **-t** or **-d** insert **-e** before the **-t.**

INFINITIVE	STEM	AUXILIARY	PARTICIPLE
arbeiten	**arbeit-**	**hat**	**gearbeitet**
baden	**bad-**	**hat**	**gebadet**

A participle cannot have more than one unstressed prefix. Therefore all verbs formed with the unstressed prefixes **be-, emp-, ent-, er-, ge-, ver-,** and **zer-** form their participle without the **ge-** prefix. Verbs ending in **-ieren,** like **studieren,** which always begin with at least one unstressed syllable, also form their participles without **ge-.**

INFINITIVE	PARTICIPLE
besuchen	**besucht**
telefonieren	**telefoniert**

Irregular Weak Verbs

A few weak verbs use a different stem in the participle, for example:

bringen — gebracht
denken — gedacht
kennen — gekannt
wissen — gewußt

Note that the participles of English *to bring* and *to think* are irregular in the same fashion: *brought, thought.*

Strong Verbs

All strong verbs place either the unchanged stem, or a changed form of the stem, or even an entirely different stem into the frame **ge**_____**en.**

INFINITIVE	STEM	AUXILIARY	PARTICIPLE
beginnen	**beginn-**	**hat**	**begonnen**
bekommen	**bekomm-**	**hat**	**bekommen**
bleiben	**bleib-**	**ist**	**geblieben**

Since the type of change in these strong verbs is as unpredictable as English *sing, sang, sung* versus *sting, stung, stung*, we will list all strong verbs together with the irregular weak verbs in the tables of "Strong and Irregular Verbs" at the end of all subsequent units.

Strong verbs are used with such great frequency that you must memorize the participles together with their auxiliaries. The participles of strong verbs introduced in Units 1–5 are listed at the end of this unit.

NOTE: All verbs, weak or strong, with stressed complements like **ein-** or **auf-** place the complement in front of the participle and form one word with it.

> **einkaufen — eingekauft**
> **aufstehen — aufgestanden**

Modal Auxiliaries

Whenever the modal auxiliaries and **brauchen** are used with a dependent infinitive, their participles are identical with their infinitives. These forms are often referred to as "double infinitives."

Er	hat	gestern	arbeiten müssen.
Er	hat	gestern nicht	zu arbeiten brauchen.

If the modals are used without a dependent infinitive, their participles are "normal"; that is, **gemußt, gewollt, gekonnt, gesollt, gedurft.**

> **Das habe ich nicht gewollt.**   This is not what I intended.
> **Ich habe nicht arbeiten wollen, aber ich**   I didn't want to work, but I had to.
> **habe gemußt.**

66 The Use of **sein** and **haben** as Auxiliaries

Certain English verbs used to form their compound tenses with *to be*. The line from the thirteenth-century Cuckoo Song "sumer is icumen in" is still widely known and easily recognized; older editions of the King James Version of the Bible, translated in the seventeenth century, still had *Christ is risen*. But now even the Bible translations have changed to *Christ has risen*, so that *to have* is today the only auxiliary used. In contrast, the use of **sein** as an auxiliary is still very common in German.

The German verbs using **sein** instead of **haben** are all intransitive; that is, they do not govern an accusative object. Usually, though not in the case of **sein** and **bleiben,** they indicate a change in the position or the condition of the grammatical subject. If no such change is involved, even intransitive verbs use **haben.**

> **Er hat gelogen.**   He has lied.

The choice between **haben** and **sein** has nothing to do with the difference between weak and strong verbs. Even weak verbs like **verreisen** take **sein** because a change in the location of the subject is involved.

Er ist gestern verreist.	He went on a trip yesterday.
Er ist mir gefolgt.	He followed me.

67 Position of the Participle

The participle has a reserved "slot": the second box of the second prong. This means that it is preceded by **nicht** and by the verbal complements (if any) in the first box.

				2ND PRONG	
FRONT FIELD	1ST PRONG	INNER FIELD	NICHT	1ST BOX	2ND BOX
Er	kommt	heute.			
Er	ist	gestern			gekommen.
Der Zug	fährt		noch nicht	ab.	
Der Zug	ist		noch nicht	ab-	gefahren.
Ich	bleibe	natürlich	nicht	zu Hause.	
Ich	bin	natürlich	nicht	zu Hause	geblieben.

NOTE: Verb complements like **aus, ab,** and **wieder** are written with the participle as one word: **abgefahren, ausgemacht, wiedergekommen.**

When a modal is used with an infinitive, the participle of the modal (which looks like an infinitive) goes into the second box behind the dependent infinitive.

FRONT FIELD	1ST PRONG	INNER FIELD	NICHT	1ST BOX	2ND BOX
Ich	muß	morgen		nach Köln	fahren.
Ich	habe	gestern	nicht	nach Köln	fahren können.
Ich	habe	gestern	nicht	nach Köln	zu fahren brauchen.

68 The Use of the German Perfect

Take a look at the following English and German sentences and compare the verb tenses:

1. **Ich glaube, er wohnt in Berlin.** (present)	I think he lives in Berlin. (present)
2. **Nein, er wohnt jetzt in Berlin.** (present)	No, he is now living in Berlin. (present progressive)
3. **Mein Vater hat nie in Berlin gewohnt.** (perfect)	My (late) father never lived in Berlin. (past)

4. **Vor drei Jahren habe ich noch in Berlin gewohnt.** (perfect)

Three years ago I was still living in Berlin. (past progressive)

5. **Haben Sie schon einmal in Berlin gewohnt?** (perfect)

Have you ever lived in Berlin? (present perfect)

6. **Wir wohnen seit Jahren in Berlin.** (present)

We have been living in Berlin for years. (perfect progressive)

You can see that in conversational sentences of this type English uses six different tenses where German can get along with two, the present and the perfect.

Leaving out the German future (which will be introduced later), it can be stated that German, which has no progressive forms at all, has only four major tenses: the present, the perfect, the past, and the pluperfect. The past and the pluperfect are the major tenses for story telling. The present and the perfect are the set used for conversation.

In conversational situations the present is used to refer to what is happening at the moment of speaking or what will happen later. The perfect is used to refer to what happened prior to the moment of speaking. This is why **er wohnt** and **wir wohnen,** in sentences 1, 2, and 6 above, mean *he lives, he is living,* and *we have been living.* The wording of 6 is most alien to native speakers of English. However, the sentence *Fritz has been living in Berlin since 1970* implies that Fritz is living in Berlin at the moment of speaking. So German, which uses the present to refer to everything that is happening at the moment of speaking or later, remains consistent by using the present tense: **Fritz wohnt seit 1970 in Berlin.** Similarly, **hat gewohnt,** in sentences 3, 4, and 5 above, means *lived, was living,* and *has lived,* for in all these cases the verbs refer to something that happened prior to the moment of speaking. You should acquire the habit of expressing *all* actions which happened before the moment of speaking by using the perfect.

This means that the important difference in English between

Last winter we went to the opera three times

and

This winter we have gone to the opera three times

cannot be expressed in German by changing tenses, because in German both sentences have to use the frame

Wir sind . . . in die Oper gegangen.

69 Time Phrases

Both German and English use three types of time phrases:

1. Point-in-time phrases (**jetzt,** *now;* **morgen,** *tomorrow;* **vor einem Jahr,** *a year ago;* etc.)
2. Frequency phrases (**oft,** *often;* **nie,** *never, not once;* **dreimal,** *three times;* etc.)

3. Stretch-of-time phrases (**drei Jahre**, *for three years*; **seit 1970**, *since 1970*; etc.)

These three types of time phrases are easy to distinguish by the question to which they are—or could be—the answers:

1. Point-in-time: **Wann** (*when?*)—**Um drei Uhr** (*at three o'clock*)
2. Frequency: **Wie oft** (*how often?*)—**Dreimal** (*three times*)
3. Stretch-of-time: **Wie lange** (*how long?*)—**Drei Jahre** (*for three years*)

70 Point-in-Time Phrases

Point-in-time phrases always answer the question **Wann?** *When?*

> **Wir wollen nächsten Sommer nach Italien fahren.**
> We want to go to Italy next summer.

This sentence is most likely an unsolicited statement, but it could, of course, be preceded by a question; if so, the question could only be **Wann wollt ihr nach Italien fahren?** and not **Wie lange wollt ihr nach Italien fahren?** As long as the time phrase answers the question **Wann?**, it is a point-in-time phrase, even if the phrase itself looks like a time stretch. Thus, **nächsten Sommer** here means "at some point during the coming summer."

SOME COMMONLY USED POINT-IN-TIME PHRASES

ADVERBS: **gestern, heute, morgen, heute abend, jetzt, Sonntag**
NOUNS (in the accusative case): **nächsten Sonntag, nächste Woche, nächstes Jahr**
PREPOSITIONAL PHRASES: **um drei Uhr, in drei Wochen, vor einem Jahr**

NOTE: In time phrases, **vor** (plus dative) corresponds to English *ago*, but unlike *ago*, it precedes the noun: **vor einem Jahr**, *a year ago*.

71 Frequency Phrases

Frequency phrases always answer the question **Wie oft?**—*How often?* Consider the following two sentences:

1. Last year I went to three football games.
2. This year I have gone to three football games.

In sentence 1, you are speaking of a period of time that is all over. You are talking about *last year*, a period of time that had a beginning and a definite end. The season has ended, and you are now looking back and saying that during that period, *last year*, you went to three football games. Such a period of time we shall call a "closed-ended" period of time.

In the second sentence you are reporting not on last year but on what is happening this year. The season is still going and has not yet ended. Within this season you have already attended three games, and the implication is that you may well attend a few more before the season is over. Such a situation we shall call an "open-ended" situation as the season has not yet come to a close.

Notice that in sentence 1, the closed-ended situation, you used the past tense, *I went*. English normally distinguishes between closed-ended and open-ended situations by using the past tense and the perfect tense, respectively. Thus you would say (closed-ended situation, past tense): *Yesterday I tried three times to reach her on the phone, but she was not in*. But if you are talking about an ongoing situation today, you would say (open-ended situation, perfect tense): *I have tried three times to reach her today, but she still isn't in*; the implication being that you are going to keep on trying until she is in.

We now encounter one of the major differences between the way in which German and English express time. English differentiates between closed-ended situations and open-ended situations by using different tenses; German differentiates between closed-ended and open-ended situations by using different types of time phrases. Thus, if you want to say in German, *Last year I went to the opera three times*, you say: **Letztes Jahr bin ich *dreimal* in die Oper gegangen.** But if you want to say *This year I have gone to the opera three times*, you say: **Dieses Jahr bin ich *schon dreimal* in die Oper gegangen.** Notice that in both cases German uses the same tense, the perfect tense (which is, as you have learned, the tense normally used for talking about events in the past), and note also that the time phrase for the closed-ended situation, **dreimal,** is different from that used in the open-ended situation, **schon dreimal.**

Listed below are German time phrases used to express frequency, that is, time phrases which answer the question **Wie oft?** (*How often?*). Whenever you are reporting on a closed-ended situation, you must use one of the phrases from the left-hand column. Whenever you are reporting on an open-ended situation, you must use one of the phrases from the right-hand column. In both cases you will be using a verb in the perfect tense.

SOME COMMONLY USED FREQUENCY PHRASES

CLOSED-END TERMS (GERMAN PERFECT, ENGLISH PAST)		OPEN-END TERMS (GERMAN PERFECT, ENGLISH PRESENT PERFECT)	
not once			
nicht *ein*mal	not a single time	**noch nicht *ein*mal**	not once
nie	never, not once	**noch nie**	never yet
gar nicht	not at all	**noch gar nicht**	not at all
once			
je?	ever?		
mal, einmal	once	**schon einmal**	once (so far)
nur *ein*mal	just once	***schon* einmal**	once before
		erst *ein*mal	only once so far

often

oft	often	**schon oft**	often
dreimal	three times	**schon dreimal**	three times so far
nur dreimal	only three times	**erst dreimal**	only three times so far
selten	seldom, rarely		

at all times

immer	always	**schon immer**	always

NOTE: There is a neat difference between **nur dreimal, schon dreimal,** and **erst dreimal.** The **nur** adds to the simple **dreimal** the flavor "and that was all." The **schon** adds not only the open-end meaning but sometimes the notion "and that is more than expected." The **erst** adds the expectation "I hope that was merely the first three times."

If the events reported belong to the present time (or are timeless), both German and English use the present tense:

Ich gehe jede Woche dreimal schwimmen.
I go swimming three times every week.

If the events reported belong to the future, German uses the present, English the future tense:

Ich gehe nie wieder in die Oper.
I'll never go to the opera again.

72 Stretch-of-Time Phrases

In **71,** we explained how to deal with sentences that are answers to the question **Wie oft?**—*How often?* We shall now deal with sentences that answer the question **Wie lange?**—*(For) how long?* Such sentences contain a phrase which we shall call a stretch-of-time phrase. We are dealing now with duration (three hours) rather than frequency (three times).

Let us assume that you want to tell somebody that you used to live in Berlin and that you lived there for three years. You will say in English, *I lived in Berlin (for) three years.* Notice that you are reporting on a situation that is all past, that you are using the past tense *I lived,* and that you have the option of expressing the period of duration with or without the preposition *for.* In the German equivalent of this sentence, however, you must, as in all conversation referring to the past, use the perfect tense. Hence, you will say, **Ich habe drei Jahre in Berlin gewohnt.** Notice, too, that in German the period of duration is expressed with a time phrase in the accusative case and *without a preposition.*

Now let us assume that you are living in Berlin right now and that somebody asks you, *How long have you been living in Berlin?* You could reply, for example, *I have been living in Berlin (for) three years.* Notice that you used the *perfect* tense (*I have been living*) to talk about a *present* situation (you are, you admit, living in Berlin right now), and that you again expressed the period of duration with an optional *for.*

A German does things quite differently. As he is dealing with a *present* situation, he uses what is to him very logical, the *present* tense. Thus, if somebody says, **Ich wohne in Berlin** and somebody wants to find out since when (**seit wann?**), the reply is, **Ich wohne seit drei Jahren in Berlin**, which is the equivalent of the English sentence above, *I have been living in Berlin (for) three years*. Notice that in this situation, in which English uses the *perfect* tense, German uses the *present* tense. Furthermore, in the two English sentences

1. I lived in Berlin *(for) three years*
2. I have been living in Berlin *(for) three years*

the time phrases are identical. In German they are not. The German says

1. **Ich habe *drei Jahre* in Berlin gewohnt**

but, to express *(for) three years* as in (2), the German says

2. **Ich wohne *seit drei Jahren* in Berlin.**

German stretch-of-time phrases, that is, phrases used to report on duration (**Wie lange?**—*(For) how long?*), divide into two groups: those used in sentences of type (1) and those used in sentences of type (2).

Sentences of type (1) report on closed periods of time. This closed period of time may be either in the past, as in the sentence **Ich habe *drei Jahre* in Berlin gewohnt**, or in the future, as in the sentence **Ich bleibe *drei Jahre* in Berlin**, the equivalent of the English "I'll stay in Berlin *(for) three years.*"

Sentences of type (2) report on periods of time that began in the past and are still continuing. These phrases are introduced by **seit, schon,** or **schon seit**. A phrase introduced by **seit** or **schon seit** is followed by a dative; a phrase introduced by **schon** is, however, followed by an accusative. Hence, **seit drei Jahren** (dative) and **schon seit drei Jahren** (dative), but **schon drei Jahre** (accusative).

Listed here are some commonly used stretch-of-time phrases. Closed-end phrases, for use in sentences of type (1) are listed on the left. Open-end phrases, for use in sentences of type (2) are listed on the right.

SOME COMMONLY USED STRETCH-OF-TIME PHRASES

CLOSED-END	OPEN-END	
lange	schon lange	for a long time
	seit langem	
	schon seit langem	
noch lange		for a long time thereafter
	seitdem	ever since
drei Jahre	schon drei Jahre	for three years
	seit drei Jahren	
	schon seit drei Jahren	
tagelang	schon tagelang	for days
wochenlang	schon wochenlang	for weeks
jahrelang	schon jahrelang	for years

There is one type of situation in which German does use the perfect tense with open-end time phrases, namely when the activity described comes to an end *at the moment of speaking*:

So gut wie heute abend habe ich schon lange nicht gegessen.
For a long time, I have not eaten as well as I am eating this evening.

Darauf haben Sie schon lange gewartet:
Eine Suppe für den großen Hunger.

Auf diese Suppe haben Sie schon lange gewartet.—You have been waiting for this soup a long time. (Now it is on the shelves.)

STRETCH-OF-TIME: SUMMARY

	ENGLISH	GERMAN
A. Closed-end past	PAST TENSE	PERFECT WITHOUT **schon/seit**
	I lived in Berlin (for) three years.	**Ich habe drei Jahre (lang) in Berlin gelebt.**
B. Closed-end present or future	PRESENT TENSE	PRESENT WITHOUT **schon/seit**
	I am living in Berlin (for) three years. I'll be living in Berlin (for) three years.	**Ich wohne drei Jahre (lang) in Berlin.**
C. Open-end past	PERFECT TENSE	PRESENT PLUS **schon/seit**
	I've been living in Berlin (for) three years.	**Ich wohne schon drei Jahre in Berlin.** **seit drei Jahren** **schon seit drei Jahren**
D. Ending at moment of speaking	PERFECT TENSE	PERFECT PLUS **schon/seit**
	I've been waiting (for) three hours.	**Ich habe seit drei Stunden gewartet.**

From the English point of view, C presents the greatest difficulty because it is very hard to overcome a life-long habit of using the perfect when in German you must use the present tense.

73 Cardinal Numbers

The German system is quite similar to English. From 0 to 12, each number has its own name; from 13 on, and with the exception of 100, the numbers are either compounded or are derived from the basic set 1–9. Note that from 21 to 29, 31 to 39, and so on, German reverses the English pattern: *twenty-one* becomes **einundzwanzig.**

null	zehn	zwanzig	
eins	elf	einundzwanzig	
zwei	zwölf	zweiundzwanzig	*zwanzig*
drei	dreizehn	dreiundzwanzig	*dreißig*
vier	vierzehn	vierundzwanzig	vierzig
fünf	fünfzehn	fünfundzwanzig	fünfzig
sechs	*sechzehn*	sechsundzwanzig	*sechzig*
sieben	*siebzehn*	siebenundzwanzig	*siebzig*
acht	achtzehn	achtundzwanzig	achtzig
neun	neunzehn	neunundzwanzig	neunzig
			(ein) hundert

Particular attention must be paid to the spelling and pronunciation of the italicized numbers in the table.

100 **hundert (einhundert)**	600 **sechshundert**
101 **hunderteins**	1.000 **tausend (eintausend)**
102 **hundertzwei**	7.625 **siebentausendsechshundertfünfundzwanzig**
110 **hundertzehn**	1.000.000 **eine Million**
121 **hunderteinundzwanzig**	2.000.000 **zwei Millionen**
200 **zweihundert**	1.000.000.000 **eine Milliarde** (*one billion*)

Note that German uses periods where English uses commas: 2.325.641. Conversely, in *decimal numbers*, German uses commas where English uses periods.

0,3	**null komma drei**
12,17	**zwölf komma siebzehn**
6,5342	**sechs komma fünf drei vier zwei**
2.051,23	**zweitausend einundfünfzig komma dreiundzwanzig**

One can say either

    zwei und zwei ist vier or **zwei plus zwei ist vier**

and

    vier weniger zwei ist zwei or **vier minus zwei ist zwei**

Plus and **minus** are mathematical terms; **und** and **weniger** are used in nonmathematical everyday language.

Multiplication and division are expressed as follows:

> **zwei mal zwei ist vier**
> **vier (geteilt) durch zwei ist zwei**

74 Time

In *colloquial* German, the following terms are used to tell time:

8.00 Uhr	acht Uhr	8.30 Uhr	halb neun
8.05 Uhr	fünf nach acht	8.35 Uhr	fünf nach halb neun
8.10 Uhr	zehn nach acht	8.40 Uhr	zehn nach halb neun
8.15 Uhr	viertel nach acht	8.45 Uhr	dreiviertel neun; viertel vor neun
8.20 Uhr	zwanzig nach acht	8.50 Uhr	zehn vor neun
8.25 Uhr	fünf vor halb neun	8.55 Uhr	fünf vor neun

For official purposes (transportation, radio, etc.), the following pattern is used:

0.10 Uhr	null Uhr zehn (12:10 A.M.)	20.05 Uhr	zwanzig Uhr fünf (8:05 P.M.)
8.05 Uhr	acht Uhr fünf (8:05 A.M.)	24.00 Uhr	vierundzwanzig Uhr (midnight)

Conversations

I

HERR LORENZ:	So, jetzt muß ich aber *wirk*lich gehen, Herr Kunz.
HERR KUNZ:	Aber wa*rum* denn? Es ist doch erst fünf *Uhr*.
HERR LORENZ:	*Ja*, aber ich will nach dem Essen noch mit meiner Frau ins *Ki*no.
HERR KUNZ:	Mit dem *Wa*gen sind Sie doch in zehn Mi*nu*ten zu Hause.
HERR LORENZ:	Mit dem *Wa*gen, *ja*. Ich *ha*be aber heute keinen Wagen.
HERR KUNZ:	Sie haben keinen *Wa*gen? Bei *dem* *Re*gen?
HERR LORENZ:	Nein, den *Wa*gen hat heute meine *Frau*. Bei dem Regen hat sie nicht mit dem *Zug* in die Stadt fahren wollen.
HERR KUNZ:	Aha, also sind *Sie* mit dem Zug gefahren.

II

FRAU KUNZ:	Herr Lorenz, glauben Sie, Ihre Frau ist schon aus der Stadt zu*rück*?
HERR LORENZ:	Na*tür*lich, Sie hat doch den *Wa*gen.
FRAU KUNZ:	Dann rufen Sie sie doch *an*; sie soll mit dem Wagen zu *uns* kommen. Ich habe Ihre Frau schon *so* lange nicht ge*se*hen.
HERR LORENZ:	Das ist eine I*dee*.
FRAU KUNZ:	Na*tür*lich, und *Sie* können mit meinem Mann noch ein Glas *Bier* trinken.
HERR LORENZ:	Vielen *Dank*, Frau Kunz. Und meine *Frau* rufe ich so*fort an*.
FRAU KUNZ:	Darf *ich* mit Ihrer Frau sprechen, Herr Lorenz?
HERR LORENZ:	Aber na*tür*lich.

III

FRAU KUNZ: Frau *Lorenz*? Guten Abend, hier ist Gertrud *Kunz*.

FRAU LORENZ: Ah, Frau *Kunz*, guten Abend. Wie *geht's* Ihnen denn?

FRAU KUNZ: *Danke*, mir geht's *gut*, *Ihnen* hoffentlich *auch*.

FRAU LORENZ: *Danke, ja*. Ich komme gerade aus der *Stadt*,—es hat ja *so* geregnet.

FRAU KUNZ: Ja, *hier* regnet es *im*mer noch.

FRAU LORENZ: Gottseidank bin ich heute mit dem *Wagen* gefahren, und mein Mann ist mit dem *Zug* in die Stadt gefahren.

FRAU KUNZ: Ich *weiß*. Ihr Mann ist *hier* bei *uns*. Er hat seit zwei Uhr mit meinem Mann hier gearbeitet. Aber *jetzt* sind sie *fer*tig.

FRAU LORENZ: Das ist *gut*. Dann kann ich doch mit dem Wagen kommen und ihn *ab*holen.

FRAU KUNZ: Ich *höre*, Sie wollen heute abend noch ins *Kino*.

FRAU LORENZ: *Ja*, nach dem *Essen*.

FRAU KUNZ: *Hören* Sie, Frau Lorenz, können Sie nicht zum Essen zu *uns* kommen?

FRAU LORENZ: Aber *gerne*, vielen *Dank*, Frau Kunz. Ich habe Sie ja schon *so* lange nicht gesehen.

FRAU KUNZ: *Ja*, und wenn es Ihnen *recht* ist, können wir nach dem Essen alle *vier* ins Kino gehen.

IV

Using the following two restaurant menus, construct and memorize some mini-conversations as in Unit 4, pp. 101–102 and Unit 5, pp. 127–129. The first menu is Bavarian, and prices are in German marks; the second is Austrian (note the term **Fleischhauerei**), and you will have to pay in Austrian schillings.

When you want to pay your bill, the following exchange might take place:

Herr Ober (or: Fräulein), ich möchte zahlen.

Bitte, die Damen. Zweimal Menü eins, ein Rotwein, ein Bier, zwei Kaffee,—hundertvierzig Schilling, bitte.

V

Since there are lots of dishes on these menus whose names you can't figure out—which is, of course, exactly what happens when you first look at the menu, **die Speisenkarte**, in a German restaurant—get your teacher into the act. You be the guest, and let your teacher be the waiter or waitress. Ask questions like the following:

Bitte, was ist ein "Bauernschmaus"?
Was bekommt man auf der "Ederplatte"?
Ist das Schnitzel vom Schwein oder vom Kalb?

VI

Find out from the newspaper or from a local bank what the current exchange rate is, and determine how much your meal costs you in American dollars. You can also figure out how much an Austrian meal would cost in marks, and a German meal in schillings.

HOTEL WASTLSÄGE — Menükarte

HERZLICH WILLKOMMEN ZU UNSEREM BAYERISCHEN ABEND !

	DM
Leberknödelsuppe	1.95
Original Bauerngeräuchertes mit Brot und Butter	7.20
Ripperl mit Sauerkraut und Salzkartoffeln	8.--
Saftiger Schweinebraten mit Kraut und Semmelknödel	8.50
Kalbsschnitzel "Münchner Art" mit Röstkartoffeln und gemischtem Salat	9.50
Rumpsteak mit grünen Bohnen und Pommes frites	10.20

Frischer Radi mit Butterbrot	1.50
Münchner Weisswurst, süsser Senf, Brot	3.50
Weisser und schwarzer Pressack mit Zwiebeln, Essig und Öl	3.80
Warmer Leberkäs, Speckkartoffelnsalat	5.--

Alle unsere Preise sind Endpreise und enthalten
15% Bedienung, sowie 11% Mehrwertsteuer

GASTHOF EDER
MIT EIGENER FLEISCHHAUEREI
SALZBURG-PARSCH, GAISBERGSTRASSE 20, TELEFON 20170

MITTAGKARTE

am 27. Juli

MENÜ:	MENÜ:	MENÜ:
S. 51.-	S. 44.-	S. 40.-
Schöberl - Suppe	Geflügelpürree - Suppe	Geflügelpürree Suppe
Pikantes Ei	Selchkarree m. Sauerkraut	Ochsenfleisch m.
Schweinskotelette natur	u. Semmel-Knödel	Eingebrannte Kart.
m. Kart. u. Salat		
Ringlotten - Kompott	Obst - Schnitte	Moccacrem - Schnitte

SUPPEN	SCHILLING	FERTIGE SPEISEN	SCHILLING
Bouillon m. Ei	7.-	Kalbs-Nierenbraten m. Reis u.	43.-
Nudel - Suppe	6.50	Häuptelsalat	
		1/2 Brathuhn m. Reis u. Kompott	41.-
VORSPEISEN		Mastochsenfleisch m. Kohlrüben	35.-
Omelette fines herbes	22.-	u. geröstete Kartoffel	
Rühreier m. Schinken	24.-	Kalbsbraten m. Reis u. Salat	41.-
Thunfisch in Gemüse	12.-	Schweinsbrüstl m. Kart. u. Salat	28.-
KALTE SPEISEN		SPEISEN AUF BESTELLUNG	
Ederplatte (f. 2 Pers.)	44.-		
Feiner Aufschnitt	34.-	20 MINUTEN	
Ederschinken m. Kren	28.-		
Gemischter Aufschnitt	27.-	Ham and eggs	29.-
Russisches Ei	18.-	Wiener-Schnitzl m. Kart. u. Salat	46.-
1 Port. Salami	24.-	Natur-Schnitzl m. Reis u. Salat	48.-
Beefsteak-tartar m. Ei	41.-	Schweinskotelette natur m. Kart.	40.-
		u. Salat	
SALATE		Kalbsteak m. Ei garniert	54.-
Tomaten	8.-	Schweinsschnitz geb. m. Kart.	40.-
Gurken	8.-	u. Salat	
Häuptel	7.-		
Gemischter	6.-	MEHLSPEISEN UND TORTEN	
Kartoffel	6.-	Salzburger Nockerl	34.-
		Omelette gefüllt m. Marmelade	24.-
FISCHE		Kaiserschmarrn	24.-
Fisch Filet gebacken m. Kartoffel	24.-	Gef. Palatschinken	19.-
u. Salat		Erdbeer m. Schlag	14.-
		Linzer - Torte	8.-

Preise incl. Bedienungszuschlag!

Fragen an Sie persönlich

1. Sind Sie schon einmal in Europa gewesen?
                   in Deutschland
                   in Österreich
                   in der Schweiz
          Wenn ja, wann?—Letzten Sommer?
                   Letztes Jahr?
                   1975?
2. Möchten Sie einmal nach Europa fahren, und warum?
                   noch einmal
3. Sind Sie in Amerika (in den Vereinigten Staaten) schon viel gereist?
          Wann, und wohin?
          Mit wem?—Allein?
                   Mit den Eltern?
                   Mit Freunden?
4. Wie haben Sie den letzten Sommer verbracht?
5. Was haben Sie in den Ferien gemacht?
                   letztes Wochenende
                   gestern abend

verbringen to spend
die Ferien (*pl.*)
  vacation

Reading

Maße, Gewichte und das Dezimalsystem

Überall in Europa gebraucht man das Dezimalsystem, es gibt keine Anachronismen wie *inches, feet* und *yards,* oder *quarts* und *gallons,* und man mißt die Temperatur nach Celsius und nicht nach Fahrenheit. Das System ist sehr einfach und leicht zu verstehen, aber Amerikaner können es oft erst nach viel Übung benutzen, Wenn man Sie fragt:,,Wie groß sind Sie?", dann denken Sie instinktiv ,,Fünf Fuß vier" oder ,,Sechs Fuß", aber der Deutsche erwartet ,,Ein Meter zweiundsechzig" oder ,,Eins dreiundachtzig". An einer Straße sehen Sie ein Schild ,,Höchstgeschwindigkeit 80", und Sie denken vielleicht: ,,So schnell fahre ich nie", aber 80 Kilometer sind nur 50 Meilen.

Beim Einkaufen verlangen Sie zum Beispiel ein Kilo Ochsenfleisch (1 Kilogramm =

Measures, Weights, and the Decimal System

Everywhere in Europe the decimal system is used; there are no anachronisms such as inches, feet, and yards, or quarts and gallons, and temperature is measured in centigrade and not in fahrenheit. The system is very simple and easy to comprehend, but Americans often can use it only after much practice. When someone asks you, "How tall are you?" you instinctively think "five foot four" or "six feet," but the German expects "one meter sixty-two" or "one eighty-three." By a road, you see a sign "maximum speed 80," and perhaps you think, "I never drive that fast," but 80 kilometers are only 50 miles.

When shopping, you ask, for example, for a kilo of beef (1 kilogram = 1,000 grams) or a

Was kostet das?

1000 Gramm) oder ein Pfund Butter. Ein Pfund hat 500 Gramm (das amerikanische Pfund hat nur 454 Gramm), und Sie können auch zum Beispiel 200 Gramm Leberwurst verlangen, oder in Österreich 20 Deka (1 Deka = 10 Gramm). Getränke wie Wein, Bier und Milch kauft man in Literflaschen (1 l) oder Halbliterflaschen (0.5 l) oder Viertelliterflaschen (0.25 l).

„Wie kalt ist es denn?" fragt jemand. „Fünf Grad unter Null." Minnesota im Januar? Nein, so kalt ist es nicht; fünf Grad unter Null ist 23 Grad Fahrenheit, denn Null Grad Celsius ist ja 32 Grad Fahrenheit. Wie rechnet man das um? Nehmen wir ein Beispiel: Wasser kocht bei 100°C oder 212°F.

pound of butter. A pound has 500 grams (the American pound has only 454 grams), and you can also, for example, ask for 200 grams of liverwurst, or in Austria for 20 decagrams (1 deca = 10 grams). Beverages like wine, beer, and milk you buy in liter bottles (1 l.) or half-liter bottles (.5 l.) or quarter-liter bottles (.25 l.).

"How cold is it?" someone asks. "Five degrees below zero." Minnesota in January? No, it's not that cold; five degrees below zero degrees centigrade is 23 degrees fahrenheit, because zero degrees centigrade is 32 degrees fahrenheit. How do you convert that? Let's take an example: Water boils at 100°C. or 212°F.

```
212 – 32 = 180
180 :  9 =  20
 20 ×  5 = 100
```

Oder umgekehrt:

```
100 :  5 =  20
 20 ×  9 = 180
180 + 32 = 212
```

Hier sind die Formeln:

°F → °C: minus 32, geteilt durch 9, mal fünf

```
212 – 32 = 180
180 :  9 =  20
 20 ×  5 = 100
```

Or the other way around:

```
100 :  5 =  20
 20 ×  9 = 180
180 + 32 = 212
```

Here are the formulas:

°F → °C: minus 32, divided by 9, times 5

°C → °F: geteilt durch 5, mal neun, plus 32   °C → °F: divided by 5, times 9, plus 32

$$(°F - 32) \times \frac{5}{9} = °C$$

$$(°C \times \frac{9}{5}) + 32 = °F$$

Nummernschilder und das deutsche Alphabet

License Plates and the German Alphabet

Das Alphabet hat 26 Buchstaben. Man spricht sie aus wie folgt:*

The alphabet has 26 letters. They are pronounced as follows:

A (ah)	J (jott)	S (ess)
B (beh)	K (kah)	T (teh)
C (zeh)	L (ell)	U (uh)
D (deh)	M (emm)	V (fau)
E (eh)	N (enn)	W (weh)
F (eff)	O (oh)	X (iks)
G (geh)	P (peh)	Y (üpsilon)
H (hah)	Q (kuh)	Z (zett)
I (ih)	R (err)	

Jedes Auto hat ein Nummernschild (oder Kraftfahrzeugkennzeichen); diese Schilder sind rechteckig. Außerdem sieht man in Europa viele internationale Kennzeichen. Diese internationalen Schilder sind oval und zeigen die Abkürzung für das Land, aus dem sie kommen; also

Each car has a "number plate" (or "motor vehicle identification sign"); these plates are rectangular. In addition, you see many international plates in Europe. These international plates are oval and show the abbreviation for the country from which they come; thus

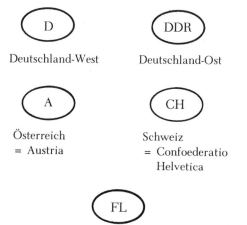

D
Deutschland-West

DDR
Deutschland-Ost

A
Österreich
= Austria

CH
Schweiz
= Confoederatio
  Helvetica

FL
Fürstentum Liechtenstein

*To pronounce the German letters, read the transcriptions in parentheses as *German* words with *German* pronunciation.

Die Buchstaben auf den BRD-Nummern-schildern sind Abkürzungen für die Stadt oder für den Kreis. Großstädte haben einen Buchstaben, Kleinstädte oder Landkreise haben zwei oder drei Buchstaben; dann kommen noch zwei Buchstaben und zwei oder drei Zahlen; zum Beispiel: M = München, MZ = Mainz, MOS = Mosbach/Baden. BD steht für „Bundestag, Bundesrat oder Bundesregierung", BP für „Bundespost", O für „Diplomatisches Corps" und Y für „Bundeswehr". Ausländer, die ihre Wagen exportieren wollen, bekommen in der BRD eine ovale Zollnummer.

Die DDR benutzt für jeden Verwaltungsbezirk einen oder zwei Buchstaben, z.B. I für Berlin (Ost), T oder X für Karl-Marx-Stadt (früher Chemnitz). In Österreich erkennt man die Bundesländer, z.B. OÖ = Oberösterreich, K = Kärnten, oder die Großstädte: W = Wien, L = Linz. Die Schweizer Schilder zeigen Abkürzungen für den Kanton, z.B. ZH für Zürich.

Lesen Sie die folgenden Kennzeichen als Ausspracheübung für Buchstaben und Zahlen:

The letters on the FRG license plates are abbreviations for the city or for the county. Large cities have one letter, small towns or rural counties have two or three letters; then come two more letters and two or three numbers; for example: M = Munich, MZ = Mainz, MOS = Mosbach/Baden. BD stands for "Federal Parliament, Federal Council, or Federal Government," BP for "Federal Post Office," O for "the Diplomatic Corps," and Y for "Federal Army." Foreigners who want to export their cars, get an oval customs plate in the FRG.

The GDR uses one or two letters for each administrative district, e.g., I for Berlin (East), T or X for Karl-Marx-Stadt (formerly Chemnitz). In Austria, you recognize the federal states, e.g., OÖ = Upper Austria, K = Carinthia, or the large cities: W = Vienna, L = Linz. The Swiss plates show abbreviations for the canton, e.g., ZH for Zürich.

Read the following license plates as a pronunciation exercise for letters and numbers:

D:	B - CV 593	(Berlin)	
	F - DA 13	(Frankfurt)	
	K - RS 259	(Köln)	
	HX - WP 517	(Höxter)	
	JEV - HD 67	(Jever)	5
DDR:	IA 08 93	(Berlin)	
	RE 97 13	(Dresden)	
	AO 04 59	(Greifswald)	
	SM 43 59	(Leipzig)	
A:	W 352.751	(Wien)	10
	T 64.321	(Tirol)	
	NÖ 610.389	(Niederösterreich)	
CH:	ZH 182 369	(Zürich)	
	LU 98 054	(Luzern)	
	VD 651 317	(Vaud)	15

Peter Otto Chotjewitz

Peter Otto Chotjewitz (born 1934 in Berlin) is another contemporary writer who joined Günter Bruno Fuchs in playing the "titmouse fiddle."

Reisen

ich
bin mit dem Zug nach Ulm gefahren
ich bin
mit dem Zug nach Ulm gefahren
ich bin mit   5
dem Zug nach Ulm gefahren
ich bin mit dem
Zug nach Ulm gefahren
ich bin mit dem Zug
nach Ulm gefahren   10
ich bin mit dem Zug nach Ulm
gefahren
ich bin mit dem Zug nach Ulm gefahren

nun bin ich in Ulm:
was soll ich hier?   15

From: G. B. Fuchs, *Die Meisengeige: Zeitgenössische Nonsensverse* (Munich: Carl Hanser Verlag, 1964).

In 39 Staaten gelten die Eurocheques.
Inzwischen auch in Albanien und der
UdSSR.

Exercises

A. Restate the following sentences in the perfect tense.

> **Karin schläft heute nicht lange.**
> **Karin hat heute nicht lange geschlafen.**

> **Karin steht um sieben Uhr auf.**
> **Karin ist um sieben Uhr aufgestanden.**

1. Sie trinkt eine Tasse Kaffee.
2. Sie ißt zwei Brötchen.
3. Dann geht sie einkaufen.
4. Um neun Uhr telefoniert* sie mit ihrem Freund Rolf.
5. Sie fährt mit dem Fahrrad zum Bahnhof.
6. Dort trifft sie ihren Freund.
7. Sie nehmen den 11-Uhr-Zug in die Stadt.
8. Der Zug fährt pünktlich ab.
9. Um elf Uhr dreißig kommen sie in der Stadt an.
10. Sie essen im Ratskeller zu Mittag.

SEE
ANALYSIS
64–68
(pp. 146–149)

*telefonieren mit to talk on the telephone with somebody = to call somebody.

11. Das Essen schmeckt gut.
12. Nach dem Mittagessen besuchen sie Freunde.
13. Sie gehen mit ihren Freunden ins Kino.
14. Der Film fängt um drei Uhr an.
15. Sie müssen fünfzehn Minuten warten.
16. Der Film dauert zwei Stunden.
17. Er gefällt ihnen gut.
18. Um fünf Uhr kommen sie aus dem Kino.
19. Es regnet.
20. Im Regen wandern sie durch die Stadt.
21. Und dann suchen sie ein Weinrestaurant.
22. Nach dem Abendessen sitzen sie noch lange zusammen.
23. Sie bleiben bis zehn Uhr in der Stadt.
24. Dann fahren sie nach Burgbach zurück.
25. Rolf bringt Karin noch nach Hause.

B. Reread Patterns [2]; then, without looking at the original sentences, use the following elements to reconstruct the text. Use the perfect tense whenever appropriate, and use the third person. Supply the subject (**Karin** or **sie**) when necessary.

> **Frau Enderle / letztes Jahr / kennenlernen.**
> **Karin hat Frau Enderle letztes Jahr kennengelernt.**

SEE
ANALYSIS
65-67
(pp. 146-148)

1. Vor drei Wochen / Brief schreiben.
2. Frau Enderle / Karin / einladen.
3. Gestern / Familie Enderle / besuchen.
4. Nachtzug / von Wien nach Stuttgart / nehmen.
5. Dann / mit Personenzug / nach Burgbach fahren.
6. Frau Enderle / am Bahnhof / abholen.
7. Karin und Frau Enderle / einkaufen gehen.
8. Enderles / Haus / vor einem Jahr / bauen.
9. Vorher / bei Eltern von Herrn Enderle / wohnen.
10. Frau Enderle / Haus und Garten / zeigen.
11. Karin / Frau Enderle / in Küche / helfen.
12. Ein Uhr / Kinder / aus der Schule kommen.
13. Nach Mittagessen / lange / Wohnzimmer / sitzen.
14. Kinder / schwimmen gehen.
15. Sieben Uhr / zu Abend essen.

C. Express in German. Be sure you use the correct tenses and time phrases.

> Ask somebody how long he has been living here.
> **Wie lange wohnen Sie schon hier?**

Ask somebody:

1. how often he has been in Berlin this year.
2. how often he was in Berlin last year.
3. since when he has had his Leica.
4. whether he went to the movies last night.
5. whether he has never been in Austria yet.

6. whether he has ever been in Zurich.
7. how long he has already been waiting for his friend.
8. how long he waited for his friend.

Tell somebody that you've been sick for a long time.
  Ich bin schon lange krank.

Tell somebody:

1. that you were sick for a long time.
2. that you were not able to drive for two months.
3. that you won't be able to drive for two months.
4. that you haven't been able to drive since October.
5. that you've had that camera for five years.
6. that you want to stay with Aunt Amalie for four weeks.
7. that you've wanted that novel for a long time.

D. In order to test your understanding of time phrases, place each of the sentences below into one of the following categories:

a. having come to an end in the past
b. reaching from the past into the moment of speaking
c. ending at the moment of speaking
d. definitely ending in the future

1. Wir bleiben *noch ein Jahr* in Köln.
2. Wir sind *noch ein Jahr* in Deutschland geblieben.
3. Sie hat *zwei Jahre* auf Hans gewartet.
4. Sie wartet *seit zwei Jahren* auf Hans.
5. Meine Mutter hat uns *nur zweimal* besucht.
6. Ich habe ihn *oft* besucht.
7. *Wie lange* wartest du denn *schon?*
8. *Wie lange* hast du denn *schon* gewartet?
9. Ich warte *eine Stunde.*
10. *Wie lange* hast du denn gewartet?
11. Wir wollen ihn *schon lange* besuchen.
12. Wir haben uns *lange* einen Sohn gewünscht.
13. Das habe ich dir *schon lange* sagen wollen.
14. Er hat doch *immer* Arzt werden wollen.
15. Er hat doch *schon immer* Arzt werden wollen.
16. Ich kann *nur zwei Stunden* bleiben.
17. George Washington hat *nie* gelogen?
18. So einen Mantel habe ich mir *schon lange* gewünscht.

SEE ANALYSIS 69–72 (pp. 150–153)

E. Read the following problems.

2 + 4 = 6	1 + 14 = 15	19 − 12 = 7
12 + 4 = 16	9 + 11 = 20	16 − 10 = 6
7 + 3 = 10	18 + 1 = 19	8 − 5 = 3
7 + 10 = 17	16 + 2 = 18	20 − 3 = 17
5 + 8 = 13	17 + 2 = 19	11 − 11 = 0

SEE ANALYSIS 73 (p. 156)

F. The following is an excerpt from a railroad timetable. Form questions and statements using the information given.

Wann fährt der Zug nach München in Köln ab?—Um 2 Uhr.
Der Zug kommt um 8 Uhr 16 in Ulm an.
Wie lange hält der Zug in Frankfurt?—12 Minuten.

SEE
ANALYSIS
74
(p. 157)

Köln	ab	2.00		München	ab	1.20
Bonn	an	2.18		Ulm	an	4.04
	ab	2.20			ab	4.05
Frankfurt	an	4.15		Stuttgart	an	5.08
	ab	4.20			ab	5.14
Heidelberg	an	5.12		Heidelberg	an	8.02
	ab	5.17			ab	8.06
Stuttgart	an	7.01		Frankfurt	an	9.08
	ab	7.06			ab	9.20
Ulm	an	8.16		Bonn	an	11.17
	ab	8.17			ab	11.20
München	an	10.03		Köln	an	12.00

G. Solve the following problems.

SEE
ANALYSIS
73
(p. 156)

$10 \times 6 =$ $212 - 32 =$

$77 : 7 =$ $180 : 9 =$

$6 \times 9 =$ $20 \times 5 =$

$144 : 12 =$ $0,9 + 1,8 =$

H. Read aloud.

SEE
ANALYSIS
73
(p. 156)

21   32   34   54   65   76   87   98   109   120   213   324   435   546   657   768   879   987
1.003   1.011   1.248   1.376   1.492   2.549   14.395   27.603   849.527   3.492.716   0,3
7,45   421,7   3.054,25
DM 10,25   7,50 M   öS 300,00   sFr 16.500,00   DM 0,75   öS 0,50   sFr 0,60

I. Following the model of Exercise **A** above, write 15–20 sentences describing a day's activities from either your own life or that of an invented character. Use only the perfect tense. You might start with:

1. Herr Meyer ist schon um fünf Uhr aufgestanden.
2. . . .

J. Express in German.

SEE
ANALYSIS
64-68
(pp. 146–149)

1. I met him in Graz.
2. We had to work last Sunday.
3. He never wanted to stay at home.
4. Unfortunately, Mr. Schmidt went on a trip yesterday. (Use **verreisen.**)
5. We got up at six o'clock.
6. Monika has not come yet.
7. Why didn't you follow me?
8. Please visit us next summer.
9. I helped her in the kitchen.
10. At four o'clock we went swimming.

Vocabulary

achtzehn	eighteen
achtzig	eighty
anfangen (fängst an, fängt an)	to begin, start
ankommen	to arrive
bauen	to build
benutzen	to use
der Besuch, -	visit
damals	at that time
das Dorf, ̈er	village
dreißig	thirty
dreizehn	thirteen
einfach	easy, simple
einladen (lädst ein, läd ein)	to invite
einmal	once; at some time
zweimal	twice
dreimal	three times
viermal	four times
nicht einmal	not once
noch einmal	once more
nur einmal	just once
erkennen	to recognize
erscheinen	to appear
erzählen	to tell (story)
die Fami'lie, -n	family
die Ferien (pl.)	vacation
fertig	ready, complete, finished
der Film, -e	film
folgen	to follow
fünfzehn	fifteen
fünfzig	fifty
der Garten, ̈	garden
gebrauchen	to use
gefallen (gefällst, gefällt)	to be pleasing to
das gefällt mir	I like that
gelten (giltst, gilt)	to be valid
gestern	yesterday
gestern abend	last night
gestern morgen	yesterday morning
das Gewicht, -e	weight
halb	half
halb zehn	9:30, half past nine
die Idee', die Ide'en	idea
inzwischen	meanwhile, in the meantime
der Januar	January
je	ever
kochen	to boil; to cook
krank	sick
der Kreis, -e	circle; county
der Landkreis, -e	rural county
die Küche, -n	kitchen
leicht	easy; light
letzt-	last
letzten Sommer	last summer
letztes Jahr	last year
letzte Woche	last week
das Liter, -	liter
lügen	to tell a lie
das Maß, -e	measure, measurement
messen (mißt, mißt)	to measure
die Milliar'de, -n	billion
die Million', -en	million
der Mittag, -e	noon
der Nachmittag	afternoon
die Nacht, ̈e	night
nachts	at night
der Nachtzug, ̈e	night train
neunzehn	nineteen
neunzig	ninety
die Null, -en	zero
die Person, -en	person
der Personenzug, ̈e	local train
der Pfennig, -e	penny
rechnen	to figure, to calculate
die Schule, -n	school
schwarz	black
der Schwarzwald	Black Forest
sechzehn	sixteen
sechzig	sixty
siebzehn	seventeen
siebzig	seventy
spazierengehen	to go for a walk
das Stück, -e	piece
ein Stück Kuchen	a piece of cake
tausend	thousand
teilen	to divide
geteilt durch	divided by
die Temperatur', -en	temperature
treffen (triffst, trifft)	to meet; to hit
verbringen	to spend (time)
verlangen	to demand
vierzehn	fourteen

vierzig	forty	die Zahl, -en	number
vorher	before	zahlen	to pay
wieviel	how much	das Zimmer, -	room
wieviel Uhr	what time	das Wohnzimmer, -	living room
wünschen	to wish		

Additional Vocabulary

abholen	to pick up (at station, airport, etc.)	jahrelang	for years
		das Kennzeichen, -	identification symbol
die Abkürzung, -en	abbreviation	das Kraftfahrzeug, -e	motor vehicle
anrufen	to call (on the telephone)	das Kraftfahrzeug-kennzeichen	license plate
aussprechen	to pronounce	das Nummernschild, -er	number plate, license plate
die Ausspracheübung, -en	pronunciation exercise		
		plaudern	to chat
bewundern	to admire	rechteckig	rectangular
der Bezirk, -e	district	der Schilling, -e	schilling (Austrian)
die Bibliothek', -en	library	telefonie'ren	to talk on the phone, to make a phone call
der Buchstabe, -n	letter (of alphabet)		
das Bundesland, ̈er	federal state		
die Bundespost	federal post office	die Übung, -en	practice
der Bundesrat	federal council	umgekehrt	vice versa, conversely
die Bundesregierung	federal government	verschwinden	to disappear
der Bundestag	federal parliament	die Verspätung, -en	delay
die Bundeswehr	federal army	verwalten	to administer
dreiviertel sieben	6:45, a quarter of seven	die Verwaltung, -en	administration
eilen	to hurry	der Verwaltungs-bezirk	administrative district
das Einkaufen	shopping	von . . . aus	from
die Formel, -n	formula	von Wien aus	from Vienna
der Franken, -	franc (Swiss)	wach	awake
die Geschwindigkeit, -en	speed	weniger	minus; less
die Höchstge-schwindigkeit, -en	speed limit, maximum speed	wochenlang	for weeks
		der Zoll (no pl.)	customs (airport, etc.)
das Getränk, -e	beverage	der Zoll, ̈e	duty
der Hügel, -	hill	die Zollnummer, -n	customs plate (for car)

Strong Verbs and Irregular Weak Verbs, Units 1–6

INFINITIVE	PERFECT	
abfahren	ist abgefahren	to depart
anfangen	hat angefangen	to begin, start
aufweisen	hat aufgewiesen	to show
beginnen	hat begonnen	to begin, start
bekommen	hat bekommen	to get, receive
bleiben	ist geblieben	to stay, remain
braten	hat gebraten	to roast; to fry

INFINITIVE	PERFECT	
bringen	hat gebracht	to bring
denken	hat gedacht	to think
dürfen	hat gedurft	to be allowed to
empfehlen	hat empfohlen	to recommend
erkennen	hat erkannt	to recognize
essen	hat gegessen	to eat
fahren	ist gefahren	to drive; go (by train, boat, plane, car)
finden	hat gefunden	to find
fliegen	ist geflogen	to fly
geben	hat gegeben	to give
gefallen	hat gefallen	to please
gehen	ist gegangen	to go; walk
heben	hat gehoben	to lift
heißen	hat geheißen	to be called; to mean
helfen	hat geholfen	to help
kennen	hat gekannt	to know, be acquainted with
klingen	hat geklungen	to sound
kommen	ist gekommen	to come
können	hat gekonnt	to be able to
lassen	hat gelassen	to let; to leave
laufen	ist gelaufen	to run
leihen	hat geliehen	to lend, to loan; to borrow
lesen	hat gelesen	to read
liegen	hat gelegen	to lie (flat); to be situated
lügen	hat gelogen	to tell a lie
mögen	hat gemocht	would like to
müssen	hat gemußt	to have to
nehmen	hat genommen	to take
nennen	hat genannt	to name, call
scheinen	hat geschienen	to seem; to shine
schlafen	hat geschlafen	to sleep
schreiben	hat geschrieben	to write
schwimmen	ist geschwommen	to swim
sehen	hat gesehen	to see
sein	ist gewesen	to be
sitzen	hat gesessen	to sit
sprechen	hat gesprochen	to speak, talk
stehen	hat gestanden	to stand
tragen	hat getragen	to carry
treffen	hat getroffen	to meet; to hit
trinken	hat getrunken	to drink
tun	hat getan	to do
verbieten	hat verboten	to forbid
versprechen	hat versprochen	to promise
verstehen	hat verstanden	to understand
werden	ist geworden	to become
wissen	hat gewußt	to know (as a fact)
zwingen	hat gezwungen	to force

Bit im Februar ⁷⁵

"Früher" die Zeit vor dem großen Fasten.
Auch heute noch : die Zeit der Narren.
Die Zeit der lustigen Typen.
Die fröhliche Zeit für jeden Bit-Typ.
Helau! Alaaf !!
– was ist schon dabei !
...und immer wieder Bit,
das unverwechselbare,
bekömmliche Bitburger Pils.
Gebraut in Bitburg.
Mit dem reinen Wasser der Eifel.

Bitte ein Bit !

Immer und überall - ein Bit ist ein Erlebnis

UNIT 7   The Past—The Pluperfect—Word Formation

Unit 7 introduces two more German verb tenses, the past and the pluperfect. The pluperfect is easy to master: you use it as you would the English pluperfect, and *I had lived* becomes **ich hatte gewohnt.** But it will take a while to get used to the different ways German uses the past tense as compared to the perfect. The difference is mainly one of perspective: the perfect relates past events to the present time, whereas the past tense fixes its point of reference somewhere else in time. Hence the past is used in "story telling" in the broadest sense; that is, in any report about a string of events, often imaginary or imagined events, told without reference to the chronological present. The learning problem here is that English uses the past and perfect tenses quite differently. By now you should have become used to using the German perfect where your English instinct wants you to use the past. Now that you will be learning the German past, watch out that you don't lose your "perfect" habits.

Unit 7 also adds to your store of knowledge of German culture, both of the contemporary scene and its historical background. What is happening, for example, in those quaint villages of tourist poster fame that adorn the walls of many a classroom? Is Germany, or Austria, or Switzerland really still as romantic as all that? Our fictitious village, Burgbach, has been caught in the process of urbanization which is rapidly transforming large parts of Central Europe; yet history and tradition exert a powerful and tenacious hold on villages like this and may yet produce a blend of the old and the new that people will be able to live with.

Another bit of culture, though decidedly tongue-in-cheek, is introduced in patterns [8], namely the inebriant effect of celebrating **Karneval,** the German equivalent of Mardi Gras. In this section, you will also find a few examples of what happens when German is spoken colloquially and casually in everyday informal conversation. Very few Germans speak as slowly and deliberately as the speakers on our tapes. In real situations, speech is compressed and often slurred. **Wo ist er denn?** will sound like **Wo isser denn?**, **Willst du . . . ?** becomes **Willste?**, and a question starting with **Haben wir . . .** with increasingly casual intonation turns into **Hab'm wer, Ham wer,** and **Hammer.** This kind of abbreviation is by no means substandard, but an accepted part of everyday speech.

Patterns

[1] Past Tense of Weak Verbs

Note the narrative character of these sentences.

SEE
ANALYSIS
75
(p. 179)

Ich lebte* damals noch zu Hause und studierte in Stuttgart.	I was still living at home at that time and was studying in Stuttgart.
Meine Frau wohnte* seit 1958 in Hamburg und studierte dort an der Universität.	My wife had been living in Hamburg since 1958 and was studying at the university there.
In den Sommerferien arbeitete sie an der Ostsee, in einem Sportgeschäft in Travemünde.	During summer vacation, she worked at the Baltic Sea, in a sports shop in Travemünde.
Dort lernte ich sie kennen.	That's where I met her.
Jede Woche kaufte ich mindestens ein Paar Tennisschuhe.	Every week I bought at least one pair of tennis shoes.
Ich glaube, sie wußte, daß ich die Tennisschuhe nicht kaufte, weil ich sie brauchte.	I think she knew that I didn't buy the tennis shoes because I needed them.
Aber sie sagte nichts; sie lachte nur.	But she didn't say anything; she only laughed.
Eines Tages brachte ich ihr eine Rose.	One day I took† a rose to her.
Ich dachte immer an sie.	I always thought of her.
Im Winter besuchte sie mich in Burgbach.	In the winter she visited me in Burgbach.
Wir heirateten ein Jahr später.	We got married a year later.

[2] Past Tense of the Modals

With modals, the past tense is used even in conversational situations where other verbs demand the perfect; note the shift to the perfect in the last sentence.

SEE
ANALYSIS
76
(p. 180)

Konntest du nicht ein bißchen früher nach Hause kommen?	Couldn't you come home a little earlier?
Ich wollte ja schon um zwei Uhr zu Hause sein.	Well, I wanted to be home at two o'clock.
Aber ich mußte noch einen Bericht schreiben. Der sollte schon gestern fertig sein und durfte auf keinen Fall bis morgen liegen bleiben.	But I still had to write a report. It was supposed to be finished by yesterday and couldn't under any circumstances wait (remain lying) until tomorrow.
Wir mußten sogar über die Mittagszeit im Büro bleiben, denn wir wollten um fünf Uhr fertig sein.	We even had to stay in the office over the noon hour, because we wanted to be finished by five o'clock.

*English *to live* can be expressed by either **leben** or **wohnen**; **leben** is the more inclusive term in the sense of *to spend one's life*; **wohnen** means *to reside, to have a residence.*
†Note that **bringen** can mean both *to bring* and *to take.*

Konntet ihr denn wenigstens im Büro etwas   Could you at least get something to eat at the
    zu essen kriegen?   office?
Aber natürlich. Wir haben Wurst- und Käse-   But of course. We ate meat and cheese sand-
    brote gegessen.   wiches.

[3] Past Tense of **haben**

The verb **haben** is frequently used in the past tense rather than in the perfect, though
not as regularly as the modals.

Ich fahre *heute* nach Berchtesgaden; *gestern*   I am going to Berchtesgaden today; yester-   **SEE**
    hatte ich keine *Zeit*.   day I didn't have time.   **ANALYSIS**
Warum *hat*test du denn keine Zeit?   Why didn't you have any time?   **76**
Herr Lenz hatte *auch* keine Zeit. Wir hatten   Mr. Lenz had no time either. We all had too   (p. 180)
    alle zu viel zu tun.   much to do.
Was, ihr hattet keine *Zeit?*   What, you had no time?
Sie hatten *alle* zu viel zu tun.   They all had too much to do.
Hatten Sie gestern *auch* so viel zu tun, Herr   Did you also have so much to do yesterday,
    Lohmann?   Mr. Lohmann?

[4] Past Tense of **sein**

Like the modals, **sein** is routinely used in the past tense where other verbs require the
perfect. Again, note the shift to the perfect in the last sentence.

Herr Lenz ist heute in Saar*brücken.*—*Gestern*   Mr. Lenz is in Saarbrücken today.—Yester-   **SEE**
    war er in *Trier*.   day he was in Trier.   **ANALYSIS**
Wo warst *du* gestern, Inge?—*Ich* war in   Where were you yesterday, Inge?—I was in   **77**
    *Frank*furt.   Frankfurt.   (p. 181)
Ist Fritz heute *auch* hier?—Nein, er war *ges*-   Is Fritz here too today?—No, he was here
    tern hier; *heute* ist er in *Frank*furt.   yesterday; today he is in Frankfurt.
Wir waren gestern *auch* in Frankfurt.—Wo   We were in Frankfurt, too, yesterday.—
    wart *ihr* gestern?   Where were you yesterday?
Wo waren *Sie* denn, Herr Lenz?   Where were you, Mr. Lenz?
Ich war gestern krank und bin zu Hause   I was sick yesterday and stayed home.
    geblieben.

[5] Past Tense of Strong Verbs

Again, note the narrative character of these sentences.

Es begann 1959 in Travemünde.   It began in Travemünde in 1959.   **SEE**
Er kam jeden Tag ins Sportgeschäft.   He came to the sports shop every day.   **ANALYSIS**
Zuerst fand ich ihn einfach sehr nett.   At first I just thought he was very nice.   **77**
Dann gefiel er mir immer besser.   Then I liked him better and better.*   (p. 181)
Ich bekam Herzklopfen, wenn ich ihn sah.   My heart started thumping when I saw him.

*The English double comparative (*better and better*) is expressed in German by **immer** plus comparative (**immer
besser**).

Er schien Student zu sein, aber ich wußte zuerst nicht, wie er hieß.	He seemed to be a student, but at first I didn't know his name.
Er sprach mit einem Akzent,—Schwäbisch, fand ich später heraus—, und seine Stimme klang sehr sympathisch.	He talked with an accent—Swabian, I found out later—and his voice sounded very attractive.
An einem Samstag bat er mich, mit ihm auszugehen.	On a Saturday he asked me to go out with him.
In einem Fischlokal saß er mir gegenüber.	In a fish restaurant he sat across from me.
Wir aßen Flundern und tranken Moselwein, und er sprach von Burgbach und von seiner Familie.	We ate flounders and drank Moselle wine, and he talked about Burgbach and his family.
Er lud mich ein, ihn dort zu besuchen.	He invited me to visit him there.
Wir blieben beide bis Ende September in Travemünde.	We both stayed in Travemünde until the end of September.
Dann ging ich nach Hamburg zurück und er fuhr nach Hause.	Then I went back to Hamburg and he went home.
Ich versprach, ihm oft zu schreiben.	I promised to write him often.
Er schrieb mir jede Woche einen Brief und rief mich auch manchmal an.	He wrote me a letter every week, and sometimes called me too.
Weihnachten sah ich ihn wieder.	At Christmas I saw him again.
Später wurde er Ingenieur, und ich wurde Studienrätin.	Later he became an engineer and I became a teacher.

[6] The Pluperfect

SEE
ANALYSIS
81
(p. 184)

Als ich ihn kennenlernte, war er gerade aus Hamburg gekommen.*	When I met him, he had just come from Hamburg.
Wir wußten nicht, daß er Arzt geworden war.	We didn't know that he had become a doctor.
Er war zwei Jahre lang in Berlin gewesen, bevor er nach Stuttgart zurückkam.	He had been in Berlin for two years before he returned to Stuttgart.
Ich hatte Hunger, denn ich hatte lange nichts gegessen.	I was hungry for I hadn't eaten anything for a long time.
Er war den ganzen Tag müde, denn er hatte schlecht geschlafen.	He was tired all day, for he had slept badly.

VARIATIONS

Add the correct past-tense form of **sein** or **haben**; then express in English.

Als er gerade eingeschlafen _____, klingelte das Telefon.

Er _____ in Göttingen studiert und wurde dann Arzt in München.

Weil es die ganze Nacht geregnet _____, blieben wir zu Hause.

Er _____ nach Wien gefahren, weil er Karin wiedersehen wollte.

---

*Note that in dependent clauses starting with **als, weil, daß**, etc., the finite verb (the first prong) appears at the end of the clause. This pattern will be explained in Unit 8.

[7] um . . . zu

Inge fuhr nach Salzburg, um ins Theater zu gehen.
Er fuhr nach Rom, um dort einen Roman zu schreiben.
Sie ging ins Theater, um *Hamlet* zu sehen.
Er studiert Englisch, um Shakespeare lesen zu können.
Herr Lenz ging in die Stadt, um seiner Frau ein Buch zu kaufen.

SEE
ANALYSIS
82
(p. 184)

[8] Review: Dative and Accusative Forms in Context

Identify the case (nom., acc., dat.) of each noun and pronoun and give the reason for the
use of each given case.

Beim Kölner Karneval*

Es regnet.	It is raining.
An der Ecke, beim Wirtshaus „Zum Löwen", steht ein Wagen.	At the corner by the "Lion's Inn" stands a car.
Bei dem Wagen steht mein Freund Fridolin Pechhammer mit seiner Freundin Brunhilde.	By the car stands my friend Fridolin Pechhammer with his friend Brunhilde.
Er scheint traurig zu sein.	He seems to be sad.
Wo kommen die beiden her? Aus dem Kino? Aus der Kirche? Aus dem Wirtshaus?	Where are the two coming from? From the movies? From church? From the pub?

SEE
ANALYSIS
55–61
(pp. 118–124)

*Karneval is the season before Lent. It is celebrated mainly in the Catholic regions of Germany—the Rhineland and Bavaria—and is a period of public merriment, of costume parties, and of considerable imbibing.

Salzburg Hauptbahnhof.

Ich gehe zu ihnen und sage „Guten Tag"
und ich sage zu meinem Freund: „Frido,
was ist mit dir los? Geht es dir nicht gut?
Bist du krank?"

Aber Fridolin antwortet mir nicht. Er schüttelt nur den Kopf.

„Frido", sage ich, „was kann ich für euch
tun? Kann ich euch helfen?"

„Nein", sagt er, „ja, —doch, vielleicht. Das
Auto ist nämlich kaputt; es läuft nicht
mehr."

„Sei mir nicht böse, Frido, aber das glaube
ich dir nicht. Ich glaube, du hast zu viel
getrunken. Ihr kommt doch gerade aus
dem Wirtshaus."

„Na ja", sagt Frido, „wir sitzen seit dem
Mittagessen hier im Löwen und trinken
Bier. Bei dem Wetter kann man doch
sonst nichts machen. Und jetzt kommen
wir gerade aus dem Löwen und wollen
mit dem Wagen nach Hause fahren
und . . ."

I walk up to them and say "Hello," and I say
to my friend, "Frido, what's the matter
with you? Are you not well? Are you
sick?"

But Fridolin doesn't answer me. He only
shakes his head.

"Frido," I say, "what can I do for you two?
Can I help you?"

"No," he says, "yes—yes, perhaps. You see,
the car is busted; it won't run anymore."

"Don't get mad at me, Frido, but I don't believe you. I think you've had too much to
drink. You're just coming from the pub,
aren't you?"

"Well, OK," says Frido, "we've been sitting
here at the Lion since lunch drinking
beer. In this weather, what else is there to
do? And now we've just come out of there
and want to drive home, and . . ."

„Und was, Frido?"

„Pechhammer", sagt er.

„Natürlich", sage ich, „ich weiß, wie du heißt."

„Nein", sagt er, „mit dem Wagen hammer* Pech. Und dabei ist es nicht einmal mein Wagen. Der gehört meinem Bruder. Aber der Schlüssel funktioniert nicht. Hier, willste† mal sehen?"

Jetzt verstehe ich: „Pech haben wir." Und Frido gibt mir den Schlüssel, und ich muß lachen.

„Natürlich kannst du mit dem Schlüssel den Wagen nicht starten. Das ist doch dein Hausschlüssel."

„Ja so was", sagt Frido, und schüttelt wieder den Kopf. Brunhilde kichert.

„Frido, mein Freund, am besten fahrt ihr mit mir nach Hause zum Abendessen. Bratwurst, Sauerkraut und Kartoffel- püree. Wie klingt das?"

„Das klingt gut", sagt Brunhilde. „Natürlich kommen wir. Und für den Fridolin hast du doch sicher einen sauren Hering."

„O.K.", sagt Fridolin, „du fährst mit deinem Auto voraus, und ich folge dir mit meinem Auto."

„Nein, Frido, du folgst mir nicht, sonst folgt uns nämlich bald die Polizei. Ihr fahrt beide mit mir; ich habe Platz für uns alle."

"And what, Frido?"

"Pechhammer," he says.

"Of course," I say, "I know what your name is."

"No," he says, "we're having bad luck with this car. And it isn't even my car. It be- longs to my brother. But the key doesn't work. Here, you want to see?"

Now I understand: "We are having bad luck." And Frido gives me the key, and I have to laugh.

"Of course you can't start the car with this key. That's your house key."

"What do you know," says Frido and shakes his head again. Brunhilde giggles.

"Frido, my friend, the best thing to do is for you to come home with me for supper. Bratwurst, sauerkraut, and mashed pota- toes. How does that sound?"

"That sounds good," says Brunhilde. "Of course we'll come. And for Fridolin you'll have a sour herring, I hope."

"OK," says Fridolin, "you go ahead with your car, and I'll follow you with my car."

"No, Frido, you won't follow me, or else we'll soon be followed by the police. You'll both come with me; I have room for all of us."

Analysis

75 The Past Tense of Weak Verbs

Just as the present-tense form **ich gehe** may mean both *I go* and *I am going*, the past-tense form **ich ging** may mean both *I went* and *I was going*; in other words, German does not have progressive forms in any tense.

*hammer = haben wir.
†willste = willst du.

It was pointed out in Unit 6 that weak verbs form their participles by prefixing
ge- and adding **-t** to the stem, whereas strong verbs form their participles by
prefixing **ge-** and adding **-en** to the stem.

WEAK	STRONG
lieben, geliebt	bleiben, geblieben
lachen, gelacht	lesen, gelesen
kennen, gekannt	sein, gewesen

There is also a difference in the way weak and strong verbs form the past
tense. Weak verbs form the past tense by adding a personal ending starting
with **-t-** to the unchanged (or only slightly changed) stem.

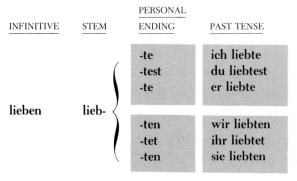

INFINITIVE	STEM	PERSONAL ENDING	PAST TENSE
		-te	ich liebte
		-test	du liebtest
		-te	er liebte
lieben	lieb-	-ten	wir liebten
		-tet	ihr liebtet
		-ten	sie liebten

Thousands of verbs follow the pattern of **lieben** without any deviation. Some
deviations are regular and will be discussed in the next paragraph. The few irregular deviations will be found in the tables of irregular verbs which, from
now on, will follow the vocabulary of each unit.

76 Deviations in the Past Tense of Weak Verbs

Modals

The modals lose the umlaut found in the infinitive.

dürfen	ich durfte	sollen	ich sollte
können	ich konnte	wollen	ich wollte
müssen	ich mußte		

We will not use, for a while, the past-tense forms belonging to **ich möchte**. Note
the difference between **ich konnte** (*I was able to*) and **ich kannte** (*I knew*).

Verbs with an -e- before the Ending -te

The endings **-te, -test, -te, -ten, -tet,** and **-ten** must be clearly audible. Therefore,
verbs with a stem ending in **-d** or **-t**, like **arbeiten** and **reden**, insert an **-e-** be-

tween the stem and the ending to make the ending clearly audible.

ich arbeitete	ich redete
du arbeitetest	du redetest
er arbeitete	er redete
wir arbeiteten	wir redeten
ihr arbeitetet	ihr redetet
sie arbeiteten	sie redeten

In order to make sure that the second syllable starts with the same consonant as it does in the infinitive, an **-e-** before the ending **-t** is also found in the past forms of verbs like **regnen, atmen** (*to breathe*), and **rechnen** (*to figure, to calculate*).

es regnete   **er atmete**   **er rechnete**

The Verb **haben**

ich hatte	wir hatten
du hattest	ihr hattet
er hatte	sie hatten

Irregular Weak Verbs

INFINITIVE	PAST TENSE
bringen	ich brachte
denken	ich dachte
nennen	ich nannte
kennen	ich kannte
werden	ich wurde
wissen	ich wußte

NOTE: In the past tense, the third person singular of a weak verb *never* ends in **-t.**

77 Past Tense of Strong Verbs

To form the past, strong verbs add the following endings to the changed stem:

ich:	—		wir:	-en
du:	-st		ihr:	-t
er:	—		sie:	-en

The change in the stem is unpredictable, and the best way to master these forms is to memorize them as they appear in the tables of irregular verbs.

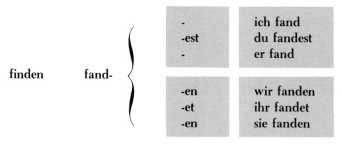

| | | PERSONAL | |
| INFINITIVE | CHANGED STEM | ENDING | PAST TENSE |

Like the weak verbs whose stems end in **-d** or **-t**, strong verbs ending in **-d** or **-t** insert an **-e-** between the stem and the ending in the **du**-form and the **ihr**-form.

NOTE: In the past tense, the first and third persons singular of a strong verb *never* have an ending. The past tense stem of the irregular verb **sein** is **war**.

78 The Principal Parts of Strong Verbs and Irregular Weak Verbs

One can form all the tenses of an English verb like *to sing* if one knows the three forms

    sing   sang   sung

These three forms are called the *principal parts* of *to sing*.

In learning German you must learn two additional forms:

1. The **er**-form of verbs like **fahren**—that is, of strong verbs with a vowel change in the second and third persons singular. (Weak verbs never change their stem vowel in the present tense.)

2. The auxiliary (**haben** or **sein**) used to form the perfect.

Thus the principal parts of **kennen, schreiben,** and **fahren** are:

kennen	**kennt**	**kannte**	**hat gekannt**
schreiben	**schreibt**	**schrieb**	**hat geschrieben**
fahren	**fährt**	**fuhr**	**ist gefahren**

The verb **kennen** is a weak verb. However, it changes the vowel in the past and in the perfect in an unpredictable way and therefore appears in the table of irregular verbs at the end of this unit.

By looking at the infinitive form of a verb, you can never tell whether it is weak or strong: **leben** is weak, but **geben** is strong. There is only one "rule": if a verb is not listed under the strong verbs, it must be weak.

79 The Difference in the Use of the Past and the Perfect

In conversational situations, German uses only the perfect to refer to actions that were completed before the moment of speaking. Now that you will start memorizing

schlafen   **schläft**   **schlief**   **hat geschlafen**

you will be tempted to use **er schlief** when you should use **er hat geschlafen**.

Thus, when Aunt Amalie shows up for breakfast in the morning, you should not ask her:

[**Schliefst du heute nacht gut, Tante Amalie?**]

You can only ask her:

Hast du heute nacht gut geschlafen, Tante Amalie?

She, too, will use the perfect and answer:

Nein, heute nacht habe ich nicht gut geschlafen.

As long as you are having a two-way conversation with someone, you must refer to all things which preceded the moment of speaking by using the perfect. However, if two-way conversation is suspended while you start retelling the events of the past as you see them, then conversation changes to narration, and you must use the simple past to enumerate, step by step, those events, and *only* those events, which are part of the progressing story.

> **Wir wohnten damals in Bonn, in der Beethovenstraße. Uns gegenüber wohnte ein Arzt, ein Dr. Müller, mit seiner Familie. Eines Tages hörten wir, daß Dr. Müller mit Hepatitis im Krankenhaus lag. Er starb kurz vor Weihnachten, und seine Frau zog im Januar mit den Kindern nach München. Seitdem haben wir nichts mehr von Frau Dr. Müller gehört.**

80 The Use of the Past Tense of **haben, sein,** and the Modals

What has been said about the difference between the past and the perfect is not applicable to the modals, to **sein,** and sometimes to **haben.** They are normally used in the past, even when other verbs are used in the perfect. Thus **ich war** rather than **ich bin gewesen,** and **er sollte kommen** rather than **er hat kommen sollen.**

It is not exactly wrong to use the perfect. One *does* hear it, especially in connection with such open-end phrases as **noch nie, schon oft,** or **erst zweimal.**

> **Ich bin noch nie in Paris gewesen.**
> **Ich bin erst zweimal in Paris gewesen.**
> **Wir haben sonntags immer arbeiten müssen.**

But one also hears:

> **Ich war noch nie in Paris.**
> **Ich war erst zweimal in Paris.**
> **Wir mußten sonntags immer arbeiten.**

81 Formation and Use of the Pluperfect

The German pluperfect is formed by combining the simple past of **haben** or **sein** with the participle of the main verb. Verbs which use **sein** for the perfect, like **bleiben,** also form their pluperfect with **sein: ich war geblieben** (*I had stayed*). Verbs which, like **schreiben,** use **haben** for the perfect, also use **haben** for the pluperfect: **ich hatte geschrieben** (*I had written*).

Like the English past perfect, the German pluperfect is the tense used to describe events or situations which precede events or situations that occurred in the past.

> **Er war den ganzen Tag müde, denn er**   He was tired all day, for he had slept badly.
> **hatte schlecht geschlafen.**
>
> **Es war Abend geworden, und es regnete.**   Night had come and it was raining.

When the sentence

> **Erich wohnt jetzt schon drei Jahre in München, ist aber noch nie ins Theater**
> **gegangen**

becomes part of a narrative, it will appear as

> **Erich wohnte damals schon drei Jahre in München, war aber noch nie ins**
> **Theater gegangen.**

The up-to-now situation of the first sentence has become an up-to-then situation in the second sentence.

82 um . . . zu

We have introduced a number of situations in which an infinitive must be used with the preposition **zu.**

> **Er braucht heute nicht zu arbeiten.**

There is another type of infinitive construction, as, for example, in the English sentence *We eat to stay alive,* which can be expanded into *We eat in order to stay alive.* Whenever this English expansion is possible, German *must* introduce the infinitive phrase with the preposition **um:**

> **Wir essen, um zu leben.**

This construction with **um . . . zu** must be separated from the main clause by a comma. When it is expanded by other syntactical units, **um** stands at the beginning and the infinitive, with **zu,** stands at the end of the phrase.

83 mit as a Verbal Complement

The preposition **mit** is frequently used as a verbal complement, meaning *along.* It forms the second prong of the predicate.

> **Rosemarie geht *auch* mit.**   Rosemarie is coming along too.

If the sentence is negated, **mit** is preceded by **nicht.**

> **Rosemarie geht diesmal leider nicht mit.**

Mit is often used with, and always precedes, directives.

> **Sie geht wieder mit nach Deutschland.**

Mit alone can never occupy the front field.

> IMPOSSIBLE: **[Mit geht sie diesmal nicht.]**

If used with an infinitive, **mit** and the infinitive are written as one word.

> **Sie möchte wieder mitgehen.**

If the sentence contains a prepositional phrase with **mit,** the verbal complement **mit** is not used.

> **Ich gehe mit ihr nach Deutschland.**

84 Word Formation

The native speaker of any language not only has an active and a passive vocabulary at his disposal, but also knows how to construct new words from known stems. Thus, by adding the suffix *-ing* to the stem of *love,* English derives the form *loving;* by adding the suffix *-er,* English forms the agent noun *lover,* and by adding the prefix *be-* plus the suffix *-ed,* the adjective *beloved* is formed. The suffix *-er* can not only be added to the stem *lov-;* it also appears in *worker, reader, listener, drinker, driver,* and many other agent nouns. The suffix *-er* is a very important part of our active vocabulary. We know how to use it, we know its semantic function, and anyone who doesn't know how to use the suffix *-er* cannot use English properly.

In German, even more frequently than in English, prefixes and suffixes are used to form derivatives. It is therefore important to learn when and how to apply the German prefixes and suffixes. From now on we shall present a section on word formation in most units.

85 The Suffixes -chen and -lein

The suffix **-chen** is normally used to form diminutive nouns, all of which are neuter. Most diminutives have an umlaut, and unstressed endings are dropped.

das Glas	das Gläschen
der Hund	das Hündchen
die Katze	das Kätzchen
die Tasse	das Täßchen
der Garten	das Gärtchen

The noun **das Mädchen** is derived from the obsolete **die Maid** and is no longer a diminutive.

The suffix **-lein** is used infrequently. It still occurs in **das Fräulein**, also no longer a diminutive, and with nouns ending in **-ch: der Bach, das Bächlein.**

In southern Germany, **-lein** has become **-le** or **-el** and is preferred over **-chen: das Haus, das Häusle, das Häusel.** The Swiss use **-li, das Häusli,** and the Viennese use **-erl, das Häuserl.**

86 The Suffix -er

The German suffix **-er** corresponds to the English suffixes *-er* and *-or*. It is added to verb stems to form agent nouns, which denote the person or instrument that performs the action implied.

denken	der Denker	the thinker
lesen	der Leser	the reader
starten	der Starter	the starter

In some cases, the agent noun shows a vowel change from **a** to **ä.**

schlafen	der Schläfer	the sleeper (sleeping person)

If agent nouns refer to human beings, the suffix **-in** is added to the suffix **-er** to form feminine agent nouns.

lesen	der Leser,-	die Leserin,-nen

NOTE: The suffix **-in** may also be added to other nouns.

der Student,-en	die Studentin,-nen
der Freund,-e	die Freundin,-nen

87 Infinitives as Neuter Nouns

German infinitives can be used as neuter nouns.

mit einem Lachen	with a laugh
Das Leben ist schön.	Life is beautiful.

These neuter nouns denote the activity expressed by the verb. **Beim (bei dem)**, followed by such a verbal noun, always means "in the process (or act) of" or "while."

beim Fahren	in the act of driving
beim Essen	while eating
beim Trinken	while drinking

88 Compound Nouns

Both in English and in German two nouns can be combined to form a compound noun. For example, *house* and *dog* can form two combinations—*house dog* and *doghouse*, a house dog being a kind of dog and a doghouse being a kind of house. The second part of the compound is always the basic form, which is modified by the first part. For this reason, German compounds derive their gender from the second part. Thus:

das Haus	**der Hund**	**der Haushund**
der Hund	**das Haus**	**das Hundehaus**

Other examples:

der Sport	**das Geschäft**	**das Sportgeschäft**
der Sommer	**die Ferien**	**die Sommerferien**
(das) Tennis	**die Schuhe**	**die Tennisschuhe**
der Käse	**das Brot**	**das Käsebrot**
der Abend	**das Essen**	**das Abendessen**

NOTE: In many such compounds, a letter is inserted between the two parts— for example, **Mittagszeit, Damenhut, Liebesbrief.** Since there are no general rules, it is best to memorize these compounds as they occur.

Conversations

I

ULRICH M.:	Darf ich mich zu dir setzen?
LIESELOTTE A.:	Aber gerne; hier ist ja Platz.
ULRICH:	Übrigens, ich heiße Markwardt, Ulrich Markwardt, aber man nennt mich Uli.
LIESELOTTE:	Ich bin Lieselotte Aumüller, aber du darfst mich ruhig Lilo nennen.
ULRICH M.:	May I sit down by you?
LIESELOTTE A.:	Sure; there's enough room.
ULRICH:	Incidentally, my name is Markwardt, Ulrich Markwardt, but they call me Uli.
LIESELOTTE:	I am Lieselotte Aumüller, but you might just as well call me Lilo.

II

LIESELOTTE:	Wie lange bist du schon hier an der Uni?
ULRICH:	Zwei Semester. Vorher war ich drei Semester in Tübingen, und im letzten Sommersemester habe ich gearbeitet. Mir war nämlich das Geld ausgegangen.
LIESELOTTE:	Das kann ich gut verstehen. Ich bin auch immer knapp bei Kasse. Aber ich arbeite jetzt an den Wochenenden als Kellnerin. Kennst du den „Grünen Baum"?
ULRICH:	Das ist doch das Lokal in der Hohen Straße, nicht wahr? Da komme ich nächsten Sonntag hin;—dann kannst du mich bedienen.
LIESELOTTE:	How long have you been here at the university?
ULRICH:	Two semesters. Before that I was in Tübingen for three semesters, and during the last summer semester I worked. I'd run out of money.
LIESELOTTE:	I can understand that very well. I too am always short of cash. But I work on weekends now, as a waitress. Do you know the "Green Tree"?
ULRICH:	That's the restaurant on High Street, isn't it? I'll be going there next Sunday—then you can wait on me.

III

LIESELOTTE: Im Wintersemester gehe ich nach Paris. Ich bin nämlich Romanistin, aber ich war bis jetzt nur in den Ferien ein paar Mal in Frankreich.

ULRICH: Ja, jeder sollte eigentlich ein oder zwei Semester im Ausland studieren; sonst bleibt man ewig provinziell.

LIESELOTTE: Warst du schon mal im Ausland an einer Uni?

ULRICH: Ja. Ich wollte eigentlich Germanist werden. Aber dann war ich ein Jahr in den USA und jetzt mache ich Anglistik und Amerikanistik.

LIESELOTTE: In the winter semester I'll be going to Paris. I'm a Romanist, you see, but so far I've only been in France a few times during vacations.

ULRICH: Yes, everybody really ought to study abroad for a semester or two; otherwise you stay provincial forever.

LIESELOTTE: Have you ever studied at a foreign university?

ULRICH: Yes. Actually, I wanted to study German. But then I was in America for a year, and now I'm in English and American studies.

IV

ULRICH: Warst du schon mal in der Diskothek am Alten Markt?

LIESELOTTE: Meinst du den „Hot Spot"? Ja, die kenne ich; da ist immer was* los.

ULRICH: Ich kenne ein paar Amerikaner. Die treffe ich heute abend dort. Möchtest du nicht mit?

LIESELOTTE: Gern. Aber ich muß nach dem Abendessen noch einen Brief an meine Eltern schreiben. Meine Mutter hat nämlich am Sonntag Geburtstag.

ULRICH: Have you ever been in the discotheque at the Old Market Square?

LIESELOTTE: You mean the "Hot Spot"? Yes, I know it; there is always something going on there.

ULRICH: I know some Americans whom I'm going to meet there tonight. Wouldn't you like to come along?

LIESELOTTE: I'd be glad to. But first I have to write a letter to my parents after dinner. My mother's birthday is next Sunday.

*was = etwas.

Im „Grünen Baum" trinkt man viel Bier.

Fragen an Sie persönlich

1. Erzählen Sie, wie Sie einen Freund (eine Freundin) kennengelernt haben. (Watch your use of tenses: use either the past or the perfect, but don't mix the two; remember **haben, sein,** and the modals.)

2. Erzählen Sie, wie Sie einen Tag verbracht haben.   **verbringen**   to spend

   > gestern
   > letzten Sonntag
   > einen Tag im Sommer
   > Ihren Geburtstag

3. Wie lange leben Sie (lebt Ihre Familie) schon im gleichen Ort (in the same place)? Erzählen Sie, wo Sie und Ihre Eltern früher gewohnt haben.

Reading

Familiengeschichten

Herr und Frau Enderle sitzen mit der Studentin Karin, ihrer amerikanischen Besucherin aus Wien, auf einer Bank. Die Bank steht mitten in den Weinbergen, hoch über dem Ort Burgbach. Es ist neun Uhr abends 5 an einem warmen Juliabend. Herr Enderle erzählt von seiner Familie.

„Sehen Sie, das Haus dort rechts von der Kirche gehört schon seit Generationen meiner Familie. Enderles hat es hier schon 10 vor dem 30-jährigen Krieg* gegeben, —und sie haben alle Wein gemacht. Mein Bruder wohnt immer noch dort, bei meinen Eltern."

*1618–1648.

Family Stories

Mr. and Mrs. Enderle are sitting on a bench with the student, Karin, their American visitor from Vienna. The bench stands in the middle of the vineyards, high above the town of Burgbach. It is nine o'clock on a warm July evening. Mr. Enderle is talking about his family.

"You see, the house over there to the right of the church has belonged to my family for generations. There were Enderles here even before the Thirty Years' War—and they all made wine. My brother still lives there with my parents."

Stuttgart
Großstadt
zwischen Wald und Reben

„Aber er macht sicher keinen Wein mehr", meint Karin. „Sie haben doch gesagt, daß er Apotheker ist."

„Die Apotheke, das ist sein Beruf, aber seine heimliche Liebe ist immer noch der Wein- 5 bau. Dort drüben, sehen Sie, unter der Burgruine, dort ist unser Weinberg, —Burghalde heißt die Lage—, und wir machen einen prima Trollinger. Wenn es da viel Arbeit gibt, helfen wir immer noch alle mit. 10

„Seit dem 30-jährigen Krieg", sagt Karin, „das sind mindestens zehn oder zwölf Generationen, die alle in einem Haus gewohnt haben, —und *wir* wohnen erst seit fünf Jahren in Seattle, und mein Vater ist in New 15 York geboren, und meine Mutter in Ohio."

„Ja, sehen Sie, wir wohnen ja auch nicht mehr alle zusammen. Früher haben ganze Familien immer zusammen gewohnt, —Großeltern, Eltern, Kinder und Enkelkin- 20 der, und vielleicht noch ein unverheirateter Onkel oder eine unverheiratete Tante; Großfamilien nennen die Anthropologen das, manchmal fünfzehn oder zwanzig Menschen unter einem Dach. Aber nun haben wir das 25 neue Haus gebaut und sind vor vier Jahren ausgezogen. Meine Schwester wohnt seit acht Jahren in Schwäbisch-Gmünd; sie hat dort einen Geschäftsmann geheiratet."

Frau Enderle lacht. „Und ich bin noch nicht 30 einmal eine Schwäbin."

„Ja", sagt Karin, „ich wollte gerade fragen: Sie sind doch nicht von hier; man hört es an Ihrer Sprache."

„Nein, ich bin in Ostpreußen geboren, in 35 einem Dorf in der Nähe von Königsberg. 1945 sind wir dann nach Berlin geflüchtet; meine Eltern wohnen noch dort."

„Und wie haben Sie Ihren Mann kennengelernt?" 40

"But I'm sure he doesn't make wine anymore," Karin says. "You told me, didn't you, that he is a pharmacist."

"The pharmacy, that's his profession, but his secret love is still wine-making. Over there, you see, below the castle ruin, that's where our vineyard is—the site is called Burghalde (castle slope)—and we make a top Trollinger (type of red wine). Whenever there's a lot of work, we all still help.

"Since the Thirty Years' War," says Karin, "that's at least ten or twelve generations that have all lived in one house—and we've been living in Seattle for only five years, and my father was born in New York, and my mother in Ohio."

"Well, you see, we don't all live together anymore either. It used to be that entire families would always live together—grandparents, parents, children, and grandchildren, and perhaps even an unmarried uncle or an unmarried aunt; the anthropologists call that extended families, sometimes fifteen or twenty people under one roof. But now we've built the new house and moved out four years ago. My sister has been living in Schwäbisch-Gmünd for eight years; she married a businessman there."

Mrs. Enderle laughs. "And I am not even a Swabian."

"Yes," says Karin, "I was just about to ask: You are not from here, are you; I can hear it by your language."

"No, I was born in East Prussia,* in a village near Königsberg. In 1945 we fled to Berlin; my parents are still living there."

"And how did you meet your husband?"

*The northern half of East Prussia is now part of the Soviet Union; the southern half is part of Poland. Königsberg has been renamed Kaliningrad.

„Ach, das war '59, in den Ferien an der Ostsee. Wir waren beide Studenten, er an der T.H. in Stuttgart, und ich in Hamburg."

"Well, that was in '59, during vacation at the Baltic Sea. We were both students, he at the T.H. in Stuttgart, and I in Hamburg."

„T.H.?" fragt Karin, „was heißt das?"

"T.H.?" Karin asks, "what does that mean?"

„Technische Hochschule", sagt Herr En-5 derle, „das ist so etwas wie bei Ihnen zum Beispiel M.I.T. Sie wissen ja, ich bin Techniker; ich habe schon als Schüler auf dem Gymnasium Ingenieur werden wollen, —und der Weinbau schien damals keine Zukunft 10 zu haben."

"Technische Hochschule," Mr. Enderle replies, "that is something like, for example, M.I.T. in your country. You know, I'm a technician; I wanted to be an engineer even when I was a student in secondary school—and wine-making didn't seem to have a future then."

„So!" Frau Enderle steht auf. „Jetzt gehen wir aber nach Hause. Die Kinder müssen ins Bett, und morgen müssen wir alle früh aufstehen."

"All right!" Mrs. Enderle gets up. "Now we'd better go home. The children have to go to bed, and tomorrow we all have to get 15 up early."

„Aber zuerst trinken wir noch eine Flasche Wein", sagt Herr Enderle.

"But before that we'll have a bottle of wine," says Mr. Enderle.

„Einen Trollinger von der Burghalde?" möchte Karin wissen.

"A Trollinger from the Burghalde?" Karin wants to know.

„Genau. Und Sie werden sehen: Der Wein ist 20 wirklich gut hier in Burgbach."

"Exactly. And you'll see: The wine is really good here in Burgbach."

Additional Reading

Viel Lärm um nichts?

I. A News Item

New York Star. International Edition. Paris, April 30—According to a report from Konstanz, Germany, the famous German novelist Johannes Schmidt-Ingelheim has been missing since April 8. Schmidt-Ingelheim had gone to Africa to collect material for a new novel which is to deal with the fate of General Rommel, the famous com-5 mander of the German Afrika Korps in World War II. In a letter from Cairo, dated April 8, Schmidt-Ingelheim promised to call his wife on April 12, her birthday, from Casablanca. Since then he has not been heard from. Schmidt-Ingelheim's novel *Wie das Gesetz es befahl (As the Law Demanded)* is the literary sensation of the year. Even here in 10 Paris, critics praise his objectivity and the penetrating realism of the scenes dealing with the battle on the Normandy beaches. Everybody here feels that this book was written by a man who, "as the law demanded," did his best as a soldier, but who nevertheless remained a human being. Just a few weeks ago Schmidt-Ingelheim was awarded 15 the *Grand Prix Littéraire de l'Europe.*

Viel Lärm um nichts
the German translation of *Much Ado about Nothing*

II. Frau Schmidt-Ingelheim am Telefon

Hier Frau Schmidt-*In*gelheim! . . .
*Mehr*ens?—*Bit*te, ich kann Sie nicht ver*ste*hen. . . .

Ach *so*, Behrens, B wie *Ber*ta. . . .
Und Sie sind ein Freund von meinem *Mann*, Herr Behrens? . . .

Ach *so*, Sie haben den Artikel im *New York Star* gelesen. Und *Sie* sind 5
von der *Bild*-Zeitung? . . .

Nein, nein, ich bin *nicht* mit meinem Mann nach *Kairo* gefahren. Er
hat mir nur aus Kairo ge*schrie*ben! „Ich fahre morgen nach Casa-
*blan*ca", hat er geschrieben. . . .

Nein, nein, *nicht* mit einer *Jacht!* Mit der *Luft*hansa! . . . 10

So, Sie kennen Herrn Thistlethwaite? Ja, Herr Thistlethwaite ist ein
Freund von meinem Mann. . . .

Und Sie sagen, Herr Thistlethwaite hat am 9. April [am *neun*ten
April] auf seiner Jacht in Alexandria von *den* Ingelheims geredet? . . .

„Die *In*gelheims sind auf meiner Jacht", hat er gesagt? . . . 15

Nein, da haben Sie Herrn Thistlethwaite nicht richtig ver*stan*den. Ich
*sa*ge Ihnen doch, ich bin *nicht* mit meinem Mann nach Ägypten
gefahren. Ich bin zu *Hau*se geblieben. . . .

Nein, unsere Tochter ist es *auch* nicht ge*we*sen. Unsere *Toch*ter ist
doch erst *acht*. Wir haben ja erst vor *neun* Jahren ge*hei*ratet, in 20
Berlin! . . .

Bin ich *glück*lich mit Johannes? Aber na*tür*lich bin ich *glück*lich! . . .

Warum *Kä*the nicht glücklich mit ihm gewesen ist? Aber wo haben
Sie denn von *Kä*the gehört? . . .

So, so, die *Zei*tung weiß alles! *Ja*, mein Mann hat von seiner ersten 25
Frau eine *Toch*ter. Erika heißt sie. . . .

Nein, sie muß jetzt *zwan*zig sein. Ich *ken*ne sie nicht. Ich habe sie
noch *nie* gesehen. . . .

Ja, mein Mann redet *viel* von seiner *Toch*ter. Aber be*sucht* hat sie uns
noch *nie*. . . . 30

Na*tür*lich möchte ich die Erika *ken*nenlernen. Aber sie *darf* uns nicht
besuchen, die Mutter *will* das nicht. . . .

Nein, die Tochter ist *nicht* mit ihrem Vater nach Alexandria gefahren. . . .

Was die Tochter *tut?* Ich *glau*be, sie studiert Archäo*lo*gie.—Aber hier 35
kommt der *Brief*träger. Vielleicht bringt er einen Brief von meinem
Mann. . . .

Gut, Sie rufen mich später wieder *an*.

III. Ein Interview mit Schmidt-Ingelheim

REPORTER: Wie lange sind Sie schon in Kairo, Herr Schmidt-Ingelheim?

SCHMIDT-INGELHEIM: Seit vierzehn Tagen*—seit Anfang April.

REPORTER: Und wie lange wollen Sie noch hierbleiben?

SCHMIDT-INGELHEIM: Das kann ich Ihnen noch nicht sagen; ich wollte noch zwei, drei Wochen hier arbeiten, aber gerade hat mich ein Freund angerufen und wollte 5 wissen, ob ich mit nach Casablanca fahren will. Er hat eine Jacht, wissen Sie, und weil ich schon lange nicht mehr auf einem Schiff gewesen bin, dachte ich, ich fahre vielleicht mit.

REPORTER: Das kann nur Mr. Thistlethwaite gewesen sein, oder?

SCHMIDT-INGELHEIM: Sie haben recht—aber wie wußten Sie denn, . . . ?   10

REPORTER: Ich habe ihn vor drei oder vier Wochen zufällig kennengelernt und habe ihn seitdem zwei- oder dreimal besucht. Von ihm weiß ich auch, daß Sie hier sind. Er hat viel von Ihnen und von Ihrer Frau gesprochen—wie schön Ihre Frau ist, und wie intelligent—und er hat mir auch erzählt, daß Sie wieder an einem Roman arbeiten.   15

SCHMIDT-INGELHEIM: Ja, mein Roman! Um diesen Roman zu schreiben, bin ich nach Kairo gekommen, wissen Sie—ich mußte ein paar† Wochen allein sein, um arbeiten zu können. Und außerdem wollte ich Afrika wiedersehen,—der Roman hat viel mit Afrika zu tun.

REPORTER: Es ist also wieder ein Kriegsroman, Herr Schmidt-Ingelheim?   20

SCHMIDT-INGELHEIM: Ja, ja,—*Ende bei Karthago* heißt er. Ich arbeite jetzt schon seit zwei Jahren an diesem Roman, aber wissen Sie, wenn man immer so zu Hause sitzt, dann . . .

REPORTER: Das kann ich gut verstehen, Herr Schmidt-Ingelheim.—Sie mußten eine Reise machen; Sie mußten nach Afrika kommen, um über Ihren Roman 25 nachdenken zu können; Sie mußten einmal verschwinden . . .

SCHMIDT-INGELHEIM: Richtig! Kein Telefon, kein Briefträger, keine Reporter—verstehen Sie, ich möchte wirklich einmal verschwinden, spurlos verschwinden. Nur so für vierzehn Tage oder drei Wochen. Aber so ist das Leben leider nicht. Und der Briefträger kommt auch; heute morgen zum Beispiel 30 habe ich einen Brief von meiner Tochter bekommen—sie schreibt, daß sie seit drei Wochen mit einer Gruppe von Archäologen in Ägypten ist und zufällig in der Zeitung gelesen hat, daß ich in Kairo bin.

REPORTER: Ihre Tochter? Das habe ich nicht gewußt, daß Sie eine Tochter haben.

SCHMIDT-INGELHEIM: Oh, doch,—von meiner ersten‡ Frau; sie wird Ende Mai zwanzig und 35 studiert in Mainz Archäologie. Ich habe sie seit zehn Jahren nicht gesehen.

---

*vierzehn Tage in German, the usual way of expressing *two weeks*.
†ein paar a few.
‡ersten first

REPORTER: Das ist ja interessant.—Aber ich möchte Sie noch etwas fragen, Herr Ingelheim. Ihr Roman—können Sie mir nicht noch etwas von Ihrem Roman erzählen?

SCHMIDT-INGELHEIM: Möchte ich ja gern, aber ich muß jetzt wirklich gehen. Meine Tochter erwartet mich zum Frühstück. Ich bin neugierig, ob wir uns wiederer-5 kennen.

IV. Ein Brief an Frau Schmidt-Ingelheim

KATHARINA SCHMIDT   *Riedbachstraße 4*
                                        65   Mainz/Rhein
                                        den 12. Mai

Sehr geehrte Frau Schmidt-Ingelheim!

Gerade habe ich in der Zeitung gelesen, daß Ihr Mann seit drei Wochen in Afrika spurlos verschwunden ist.

Ich weiß, was Sie durchmachen. Mein Mann war auch einmal drei Wochen spurlos verschwunden. Aber wenn Sie diesen Brief bekom-5 men, ist Hans vielleicht schon wieder zu Hause und sagt Ihnen beim Frühstück: „Ohne deinen Kaffee, Ingrid, wäre das Leben nur halb so schön."

Woher ich weiß, daß er das sagt? Ich bin Frau Schmidt Nummer eins, und ich glaube, Sie sind Frau Schmidt Nummer zwei oder drei. Ich 10 weiß nicht, wie oft Hans geheiratet hat, und ich möchte es auch nicht wissen. Ich möchte aber, daß Sie warten, bis Hans wiederkommt, und daß er nicht mehr in die Zeitung kommt. Sie brauchen nicht zu fürchten, daß ihm etwas passiert ist. Ihrem Hans passiert nie etwas; ich kenne ihn. Ich habe ihn einmal geliebt, wissen Sie; und oft, wenn ich 15 sehe, wie seine Tochter mit einem Lachen in den Augen zum Frühstück kommt, gerade wie früher ihr Vater, dann frage ich mich, ob ich ihn nicht vielleicht doch noch liebe.

Sehr geehrte standard form of address: literally "very honored Mrs. Schmidt-Ingelheim"

wäre would be

Nein, passiert ist ihm nichts. Wie habe ich Angst gehabt, als er 1939
Soldat wurde. Damals wußte ich noch nicht, daß ich keine Angst zu
haben brauchte. Man schickte ihn in ein Städtchen hinter der Westfront, und da hat er ein Jahr lang Brieftauben gefüttert. Gerade als es
1940 im Westen gefährlich wurde, schickte man ihn nach Hause, weil ₅
er Hepatitis bekam.

Wir heirateten.

Hans hatte aber keine Hepatitis. Er hatte nur Gelbsucht, weil er zu   **die Gelbsucht** jaundice
gut gegessen und zu viel getrunken hatte; und so wurde er 1941 wieder
Soldat. Man schickte ihn, wieder mit Brieftauben, nach Norwegen. ₁₀
Seine Briefe sprachen im Sommer vom Fischen, und im Winter vom
Schilaufen. Bei Kriegsende war er zufällig in Ingelheim, und die
Amerikaner nahmen ihn gefangen. Jetzt bekam er wirklich Hepatitis,
und man schickte ihn nach Hause. Dreiundzwanzig Schüler haben
1931 mit ihm das Abitur gemacht. Von den dreiundzwanzig leben ₁₅ **Abitur** comprehensive
heute noch sechs, und ihm allein ist im Krieg nichts passiert.   examination at the
                                                                           end of German sec-
                                                                           ondary school

Hans wurde Schriftsteller. Seinen Kriegsroman *Wie das Gesetz es
befahl* habe ich auf der Maschine geschrieben. Er machte damals oft
Reisen, ohne mich, und wohin, weiß ich nicht. Ich habe ihn auch nie
gefragt. Er mußte, so sagte er, zwei oder drei Wochen allein sein, um ₂₀
seine Romane schreiben zu können. Aber er kam immer wieder, mit
seinem Lachen in den Augen, und trank seinen Kaffee, wie man Rheinwein trinkt. Aber dann passierte ihm doch etwas. Als er von einer
Reise zurückkam, sagte er beim Frühstück: ,,Ohne deinen Kaffee,
Gisela, wäre das Leben nur halb so schön.'' Ich weiß nicht, wer Gisela ₂₅
war, aber ich fuhr mit meiner Tochter zu meiner Mutter.

Noch einmal, sehr geehrte Frau Schmidt, Ihrem Hans ist nichts
passiert. Ich weiß, er lebt und ist gesund. Seit Sie geheiratet haben,
war er wohl noch nie so lange ,,spurlos verschwunden''. Ich gratuliere
Ihnen; Sie müssen interessant sein, interessanter als ich. Aber wenn er ₃₀
wieder zu Hause ist, dann fragen Sie ihn doch beim Frühstück: ,,Wie
war Giselas Kaffee? Oder hieß sie diesmal nicht Gisela?'' Vielleicht
verschwindet er dann drei Wochen mit Ihnen. Auf keinen Fall aber   **Auf . . . Fall** under no
dürfen Sie mit Ihren Kindern zu Ihrer Mutter fahren. Ich habe damals   circumstances
einen Fehler gemacht; ich hoffe, Sie machen diesen Fehler nicht. ₃₅

Ihre
Katharina Schmidt

P.S.   Meine Tochter ist übrigens seit drei Wochen mit einer Gruppe
von Archäologen in Ägypten. Ich hoffe, sie erfährt nicht, daß ihr
Vater in Kairo ist. ₄₀

V. Frau Schmidt-Ingelheim wieder am Telefon

Ah, Herr Behrens; gut, daß Sie wieder anrufen. Wissen Sie was? Der
Briefträger hatte wirklich zwei Briefe von meinem Mann. Und seine
Tochter, die Erika, war *doch* in Kairo. . . .

Nein, Johannes wußte es auch nicht. Sie studiert doch Archäologie und war gerade in Ägypten, und zufällig war sie in Kairo, als mein Mann in Kairo war. Die Welt ist doch wirklich klein, nicht? . . .

Und diese Männer! Er hatte mir geschrieben, daß er nicht mit der Lufthansa nach Casablanca wollte. Thistlethwaite hatte ihn und seine 5 Tochter eingeladen, mit ihm auf seiner Jacht nach Casablanca zu fahren. Und dann nimmt der Mann den Brief mit aufs Schiff, und gefunden hat er ihn erst in Casablanca im Hotel. . . .

Nein, nein, alles ist O.K.; ich fahre morgen nach Zürich und hole ihn ab. . . . 10

Ja, so sind die Männer, aber ich bin ja so glücklich, daß er gesund ist. . . .

Ja, mit dem Nekrolog müssen Sie jetzt natürlich noch warten. . . .

Natürlich, ich sage ihm morgen, daß Sie angerufen haben. Ich danke 15 Ihnen, Herr Behrens. Auf Wiederhören!

Exercises

A. Form the present, past, and perfect. This exercise is meant as a quick oral drill of the forms of weak verbs.

antworten — er antwortet, er antwortete, er hat geantwortet

arbeiten	— ich	heiraten	— wir	
brauchen	— wir	hoffen	— ich	
danken	— er	kochen	— sie	
fragen	— sie	lachen	— er	
gehören	— es	leben	— wir	
glauben	— du	lernen	— wir	
hassen	— er	lieben	— ich	

SEE
ANALYSIS
64–68, 75–80
(pp. 146– 149,
179–183)

B. Restate the following sentences in the past tense. In each sentence, add **damals.**

Erika studiert in München.
Erika studierte damals in München.

1. Hans hat nie Hunger.
2. Er besucht seinen Vater in Nürnberg.
3. Wir wohnen in Bayreuth.
4. Dieses Haus gehört meinem Vater.
5. Er antwortet mir nicht.
6. Ist deine Mutter nicht in Dortmund?
7. Wir können leider nicht kommen.
8. Ich will ihm die Stadt zeigen.
9. Er soll zu Hause bleiben.
10. Ich darf es ihm nicht sagen.
11. Wir müssen leider nach Hause fahren.
12. Er braucht nicht zu arbeiten.

SEE
ANALYSIS
75-76
(pp. 179-180)

C. Form the present, past, and perfect. All verbs in this oral exercise are strong or irregular weak verbs.

> bleiben   —   wir bleiben, wir blieben, wir sind geblieben

SEE
ANALYSIS
64–66, 77–78
(pp. 146–148,
181–182)

anfangen	—	ich	kennen	—	ich	sitzen	—	wir
anrufen	—	er	kommen	—	wir	sprechen	—	ich
bringen	—	er	lassen	—	er	sterben	—	er
essen	—	er	lesen	—	er	trinken	—	wir
fahren	—	du	scheinen	—	es	tun	—	ich
geben	—	er	schlafen	—	er	verstehen	—	er
gehen	—	wir	schreiben	—	ich	werden	—	er
helfen	—	er	sehen	—	er	wissen	—	du
heißen	—	sie	sein	—	ihr			

D. Restate the following sentences in the past tense.

SEE
ANALYSIS
75–80
(pp. 179–183)

1. Kurt geht zum Bahnhof.
2. Er versteht Professor Hansen sehr gut.
3. Georg hört mich nicht.
4. Jutta hilft mir bei der Arbeit.
5. Ingelheim antwortet nicht.
6. Herr Bergmann kommt um 9 Uhr aus dem Kino.
7. Herr Lenz fährt mit seinem Freund durch die Stadt.
8. Ich sehe meine Mutter in Freiburg.
9. Er trinkt keinen Wein.
10. Ich hole ihn in Tübingen ab.
11. Er bekommt jeden Tag einen Brief von seiner Freundin.
12. Hans lädt mich oft zum Essen ein.
13. Er denkt lange nach.
14. So etwas passiert nicht oft.
15. Hans und Inge stehen vor dem Theater.

E. Form sentences from the elements given. In each case, the clause in italics should be in the past tense and the other in the pluperfect.

> *Ich / müde / sein //* denn / ganze Nacht / nicht schlafen.
> Ich war müde, denn ich hatte die ganze Nacht nicht geschlafen.

1. *Herr Enderle / Hamburg / gut kennen //* denn / dort / studieren.
2. Ich / 10 Stunden / fahren // *und / um 8 Uhr abends / in Köln / ankommen.*
3. Dr. Schmidt / in Wien / studieren // *und / dann / Arzt / in Salzburg / werden.*
4. *Herr Müller / uns / nicht anrufen //* denn / unsere Telefonnummer / verlieren.
5. *Inge / sofort / nach Hause / fahren //* denn / Großvater / sterben.

F. Of the following pairs of sentences, change the second to an infinitive with **um . . . zu.** Note that in the second sentence of each pair both the subject (**Er** or **Sie**) and the modal (**wollte**) must be dropped.

> **Inge fuhr nach Frankfurt. Sie wollte ins Theater gehen.**
> **Inge fuhr nach Frankfurt, um ins Theater zu gehen.**

1. Ingelheim fuhr nach Afrika. Er wollte einen Roman schreiben.
2. Er kam nach Frankfurt. Er wollte seinen Vater besuchen.
3. Seine Tochter ging nach Mainz. Sie wollte Archäologie studieren.
4. John fuhr nach Deutschland. Er wollte Deutsch lernen.
5. Hans ging zum Telefon. Er wollte Inge anrufen.

SEE
ANALYSIS
82
(p. 184)

G. Form diminutives with **-chen** with the following nouns.

1. das Rad	5. das Tier	9. die Stadt
2. das Glas	6. das Bild	10. der Garten
3. der Hund	7. der Brief	11. der Kopf
4. die Tasse	8. der Hut	12. die Katze

SEE
ANALYSIS
85
(p. 186)

H. Try to guess the meaning of the following nouns in **-er.**

1. der Fahrer	6. der Läufer	11. der Lügner
2. der Erzähler	7. der Arbeiter	12. der Hörer
3. der Weinkenner	8. der Anfänger	13. der Nichtraucher
4. der Käufer	9. der Korkzieher	14. der Fernsprecher
5. der Uhrmacher	10. der Redner	15. der Fernseher

SEE
ANALYSIS
86
(p. 186)

I. Composition. Write a short conversation between two students, based on the conversations in this and previous units. Use the following outline:

A says hello to B, but B is in a hurry because he/she is going to work and has no time. A is surprised and wonders if B is still at the university. The answer is yes, but B is short of cash. He/She needs money because he/she wants to go to London for a semester. He/She is an Anglicist and feels that one must go to England in order to really learn English.

J. Construct sentences as indicated.

1. Unfortunately, Mr. Schmidt had been in Berlin with his wife at that time.
   (a) Mr. Schmidt is in Berlin.
   (b) change to pluperfect (Use correct auxiliary!)
   (c) add: *at that time*
   (d) add: *with his wife* (sequence of adverbs!)
   (e) start with *Unfortunately* (Move subject!)
2. I simply haven't wanted to drive home in this rain.
   (a) *I drive home.*
   (b) *I want to drive home.*
   (c) *I have wanted to drive home.* ("double infinitive")
   (d) negate
   (e) add: *simply*
   (f) add: *in this rain* (end field!)

K. Express in German.

1. He gave his girlfriend a watch.
2. He gave the watch to his girlfriend.
3. He gave it (the watch) to her.
4. He was coming from the movies.
5. Were you living with your aunt at that time?
6. Why did you come home so late?
7. Meyer bought a car in Stuttgart.
8. For a long time I did not know that.
9. I did not smoke for two years.
10. Two years ago I smoked too much.
11. You are still smoking too much.
12. Meyer died three years ago.

Vocabulary

das Abendessen, -	supper
der Anfang, ⸚e	beginning
der Anfänger, -	beginner
die Angst, ⸚e	fear, anxiety
der April'	April
die Arbeit, -en	work
der Arbeiter, -	worker
der Artikel, -	article
ausgehen	to go out
mir war das Geld	I had spent all my
ausgegangen	money
das Ausland	foreign countries
im Ausland	abroad
ausziehen	to move out
der Baum, ⸚e	tree
bedienen	to wait on, to serve
der Bericht, -e	report
das Bett, -en	bed
bißchen	bit, a little, little bit
bitten	to beg, to request
böse	evil; angry, mad at
jemandem böse sein	to be mad, angry
	at somebody
der Briefträger, -	mailman
das Dach, ⸚er	roof
eigentlich	actually
erfahren	to find out, learn;
	experience
der Fahrer, -	driver
der Fall, ⸚e	case
auf jeden Fall	in any case
auf keinen Fall	in no case
der Fehler, -	mistake
das Frühstück, -e	breakfast
fürchten	to fear
gefährlich	dangerous
die Geschichte, -n	story; history
das Gesetz, -e	law
gesund	healthy
das Gymna'sium, die	German secondary
Gymna'sien	school, grades 5–13
herausfinden	to find out
das Herz (des Herzens,	heart
-en)	
das Herzklopfen	palpitation of the
	heart
hin	away from the speaker

hoch, (hoh- before	high
ending)	
der Hunger	hunger
der Ju'li	July
kaputt'	busted, broken
der Kellner, -	waiter
die Kellnerin, -nen	waitress
die Kirche, -n	church
klingeln	to ring (the bell)
klopfen	to knock, to pound; to
	beat
lachen	to laugh
das Lachen	laughter
die Lage	site
der Lärm (no pl.)	noise; din
das Leben (no pl.)	life
los	loose; going on
was ist hier los?	what's going on here?
was ist mit dir los?	what's the matter
	with you?
die Maschi'ne, -n	machine; typewriter
mindestens	at least
mitfahren	to ride with
nah	near, close by
die Nähe	proximity, close-
	ness, nearness
nämlich	namely; to be specific,
	you see
nett	nice
nichts	nothing
die Nummer, -n	number
ob	whether; if
das Paar, -e	pair
ein Paar Schuhe	pair of shoes
passieren	to happen
die Polizei' (no pl.)	police
reden	to talk
der Redner, -	speaker
ruhig	quiet, restful; (sent.
	adv.) it won't
	bother me, I'll
	stay calm about it
das Schiff, -e	ship
der Schlüssel, -	key
der Hausschlüssel, -	house key
der Schriftsteller, -	writer, author
der Schüler, -	pupil, (Gymnasium) student

setzen	to set; to seat
der Soldat', -en	soldier
sterben	to die
die technische Hoch- schule, -n	institute of technology
das Telefon, -e	telephone
traurig	sad
vielleicht	perhaps
voraus	ahead
vorausfahren	to drive ahead
die Welt, -en	world
wiederhören	to hear again
Auf Wiederhören	good-bye (tele- phone)

ziehen	to pull; to move (from one place to an- other)
nach München ziehen	to move to Munich
die Zeit, -en	time
keine Zeit	no time
zuerst'	at first
zufällig	by coincidence, by chance, acci- dentally
die Zukunft (no pl.)	future
zusammen	together

Additional Vocabulary

das Abitur'	final examination in secondary school
die Amerikani'stik	American studies
die Angli'stik	English studies
der Anthropolo'ge, -n	anthropologist
die Archäologie'	archaeology
befehlen	to command, order
die Brieftaube, -n	carrier pigeon
die Diskothek', -en	discotheque
durchmachen	to go through, suffer
ehren	to honor
Sehr geehrter Herr Meyer	very honored Mr. Meyer (standard form of address)
das Enkelkind, -er	grandchild
der Erzähler, -	narrator
ewig	eternal, forever
der Fernseher, -	television
der Fernsprecher, -	telephone
flüchten	to flee
die Flunder, -n	flounder
funktionieren	to function
füttern	to feed
gefangennehmen	to capture, take prisoner
die Gelbsucht	jaundice
die Generation, -en	generation
der Germanist', -en	Germanist
der Geschäftsmann, pl. die Geschäftsleute	business man
gratulieren	to congratulate

die Großeltern (pl.)	grandparents
die Großfamilie, -n	extended family
die Halde, -n	slope
heimlich	secret, hidden
die Hepatitis	hepatitis
der Hering, -e	herring
der Hörer, -	telephone receiver; listener
die Jacht, -en	yacht
der Karneval	carnival, season before Lent
der Käufer, -	buyer, purchaser
kichern	to giggle
klingen	to sound
knapp	scarce, tight
knapp bei Kasse	low on cash
der Korkzieher, -	corkscrew
der Läufer, -	runner
das Lokal, -e	restaurant, place
der Löwe, -n	lion
der Lügner, -	liar
der Moselwein, -e	Moselle wine
der Nekrolog, -e	necrology, obituary notice
neugierig	curious
der Nichtraucher, -	nonsmoker
das Pech	bad luck
prima	top, excellent
der Profes'sor, die Professo'ren	professor
provinziell	provincial
das Püree	puree

Kartoffelpüree	mashed potatoes	sympa'thisch	likeable
der Romanist, -en	Romanist	der Techniker, -	engineer, technician
das Sauerkraut	sauerkraut	das Tennis	tennis
schütteln	to shake	der Tennisschuh, -e	tennis shoe
den Kopf schütteln	to shake one's head	der Uhrmacher, -	watchmaker
seitdem	since then, since that time	unverheiratet	unmarried
		der Weinbau	wine-growing
spurlos	without a trace	der Weinberg, -e	vineyard
die Stimme, -n	voice	der Weinkenner, -	judge of wines
der Studienrat	*Gymnasium* teacher (male)	wenigstens	at least
		die Westfront	western front
die Studienrätin	*Gymnasium* teacher (female)	das Wirtshaus, ̈er	inn

Strong Verbs and Irregular Weak Verbs

The following verbs have occurred in Units 1–7.

INFINITIVE	PRESENT	PAST TENSE	PERFECT	
anfangen	fängt an	fing an	angefangen	to begin, start
aufweisen		wies auf	aufgewiesen	to show
ausgehen		ging aus	ist ausgegangen	to go out
ausziehen		zog aus	ist ausgezogen	to move out
befehlen	befiehlt	befahl	befohlen	to order, command
beginnen		begann	begonnen	to begin, start
bekommen		bekam	bekommen	to receive
bitten		bat	gebeten	to request
bleiben		blieb	ist geblieben	to stay, remain
braten	brät	briet	gebraten	to roast
bringen		brachte	gebracht	to bring
denken		dachte	gedacht	to think
dürfen	darf	durfte	gedurft	to be allowed to
empfehlen	empfiehlt	empfahl	empfohlen	to recommend
erfahren	erfährt	erfuhr	erfahren	to find out, to learn
erkennen		erkannte	erkannt	to recognize
essen	ißt	aß	gegessen	to eat
fahren	fährt	fuhr	ist gefahren	to drive
finden		fand	gefunden	to find
fliegen		flog	ist geflogen	to fly
geben	gibt	gab	gegeben	to give
gefallen	gefällt	gefiel	gefallen	to please
gefangennehmen	nimmt gefangen	nahm gefangen	gefangengenommen	to capture, to take prisoner
gehen		ging	ist gegangen	to go
heben		hob	gehoben	to lift

INFINITIVE	PRESENT	PAST TENSE	PERFECT	
heißen		hieß	geheißen	to be called, to mean
helfen	hilft	half	geholfen	to help
kennen		kannte	gekannt	to know, to be acquainted with
klingen		klang	geklungen	to sound
kommen		kam	ist gekommen	to come
können	kann	konnte	gekonnt	to be able to
lassen	läßt	ließ	gelassen	to leave
laufen	läuft	lief	ist gelaufen	to run
leihen		lieh	geliehen	to lend, loan; to borrow
lesen	liest	las	gelesen	to read
liegen		lag	gelegen	to lie (flat), to be situated
lügen		log	gelogen	to tell a lie
mitfahren	fährt mit	fuhr mit	ist mitgefahren	to drive with, come along
mögen	mag	mochte	gemocht	to like to
müssen	muß	mußte	gemußt	to have to
nehmen	nimmt	nahm	genommen	to take
nennen		nannte	genannt	to name
scheinen		schien	geschienen	to seem; to shine
schlafen	schläft	schlief	geschlafen	to sleep
schreiben		schrieb	geschrieben	to write
schwimmen		schwamm	ist geschwommen	to swim
sehen	sieht	sah	gesehen	to see
sein	ist	war	ist gewesen	to be
sitzen		saß	gesessen	to sit
sprechen	spricht	sprach	gesprochen	to speak
stehen		stand	gestanden	to stand
sterben	stirbt	starb	ist gestorben	to die
tragen	trägt	trug	getragen	to carry
treffen	trifft	traf	getroffen	to meet; to hit
trinken		trank	getrunken	to drink
tun		tat	getan	to do
verbieten		verbot	verboten	to forbid
versprechen	verspricht	versprach	versprochen	to promise
verstehen		verstand	verstanden	to understand
werden	wird	wurde	ist geworden	to become
wissen	weiß	wußte	gewußt	to know
ziehen		zog	gezogen	to pull
zwingen		zwang	gezwungen	to force

Wein- und Ausflugsort

BEUTELSBACH

UNIT 8 Dependent Clauses—Open Conditions—The Imperative

Unit 8 introduces several new grammar topics, none of which, however, present major difficulties. We have already used a number of dependent clauses in which the finite verb, that is, the first prong, must appear in verb-last position behind the second prong. Open conditions ("If the weather is nice, we'll have a picnic") and the future tense pave the way for the subjunctive mood, the only grammar topic of Unit 9.

You are used to the **Sie**-forms of the imperative. In this unit, the remaining imperative forms are introduced, and henceforth you'll be able to order around those you call **du.** But imperative forms are used in a wide variety of other ways, for example, in recipes, and particularly in advertising (*Buy! Buy! Buy!*). If you have access to German newspapers and magazines, find other examples of imperatives in advertisements. In fact, papers and magazines are good sources for many illustrations similar to the ones in this book, and you might well start your own collection.

Three recipes, taken from three different cookbooks, not only demonstrate the use of the impersonal imperative, but they again show that there is still a great deal of regionalism in Central Europe. In this connection, take another look at the two restaurant menus in Unit 7, and while you are at it, reread *Familiengeschichten*, the reading selection in Unit 7, which shows another aspect of regionalism. The reading of Unit 8, *Burgbach, zum Beispiel*, deals with the same fictitious village—which is very real nevertheless. It provides more background, historical and contemporary, to a situation that is both specific and general.

The analysis of Unit 8 again contains a section on word formation. Although there are no pattern sections and only a few exercises that deal with word formation, you should pay close attention to the ways in which German derives new meanings from common stems. If you understand the principles of word formation, your ability to recognize new words will increase considerably.

Patterns

[1] Unintroduced and Introduced Dependent Clauses

Note the shift of the finite verb from verb-second or verb-first position to verb-last position.

SEE
ANALYSIS
89–96
(pp. 214–221)

	Er	kommt heute erst spät nach Hause.		
Ich glaube,	er	kommt heute erst spät nach Hause.		

Ich glaube,	**daß**	er	heute erst spät nach Hause	**kommt.**
Ich glaube nicht,	**daß**	er	heute erst spät nach Hause	**kommt.**

	Hat Frau Enderle den Brief schon bekommen?	
Meinst du,	Frau Enderle hat den Brief schon bekommen?	

Meinst du,	**daß**	Frau Enderle	den Brief schon bekommen	**hat?**
Meinst du nicht,	**daß**	Frau Enderle	den Brief schon bekommen	**hat?**

VARIATIONS

Complete as indicated:

Sie hat dich nach Burgbach eingeladen.
Ich höre, _____.
Ich höre, daß _____.

Er hatte noch lange bei seinen Eltern gewohnt.
Ich wußte, _____.
Ich wußte, daß _____.
Ich wußte nicht, daß _____.

[2] Verb-Last Position in Dependent Clauses

By leaving out the introductory clauses, change the dependent clauses into assertions or questions.

SEE
ANALYSIS
89–96
(pp. 214–221)

Ich weiß, daß er Geld	**hat.**
Ich weiß, daß er Geld	**hatte.**
Ich weiß, daß er Geld	**gehabt hat.**

Ich weiß nicht, ob Fritz mit dem Auto zum Bahnhof	**fährt.**
Ich wußte, daß er immer mit dem Auto zur Arbeit	**fuhr.**
Ich glaube nicht, daß er mit dem Auto zum Bahnhof	**gefahren ist.**

Ich möchte, daß du morgen vernünftig	**bist.**
Ich hoffe, daß du gestern vernünftig	**warst.**
Ich weiß, daß du immer vernünftig	**gewesen bist.**

Wissen Sie, ob Meyers hier   **wohnen?**
Wir wußten, daß Meyers da   **wohnten.**
Wie soll ich wissen, wo Meyers   **gewohnt haben?**

Weiß er, daß er dir helfen   **soll?**
Er wußte, daß er mir helfen   **sollte.**

[3] Word Order in Sentences with Dependent Clauses

Ich war müde. Ich ging ins Bett. | I was tired. I went to bed.
Ich ging ins Bett, weil ich müde war. | I went to bed because I was tired.
Weil ich müde war, ging ich ins Bett. | Because I was tired, I went to bed.

Wenn er kommt, gehen wir sofort. | When he comes, we'll leave immediately.
Wir gehen sofort, wenn er kommt. | We'll leave immediately when he comes.
Wenn er bis sieben Uhr nicht hier ist, dann gehen wir ohne ihn. | If he isn't here by seven o'clock, we'll leave without him.

Er fuhr, als er die Stadt erreichte, sofort zu seinem Bruder. | When he reached the city, he drove immediately to his brother ('s house).
In Köln, wo seine Mutter damals noch lebte, blieb er nicht lange. | In Cologne, where his mother was then still living, he didn't stay long.

[4] Subordinating Conjunctions

Als ich meinen Mann kennenlernte, waren wir noch Studenten. | When I met my husband, we were still students.

SEE ANALYSIS 91 (p. 218)

Bevor Frau Enderle nach Burgbach kam, hatte sie lange in Berlin gelebt. | Before Mrs. Enderle came to Burgbach, she had lived in Berlin for a long time.

Wir saßen im Wohnzimmer und plauderten, bis Herr Enderle aus Stuttgart zurückkam. | We sat in the living room and talked until Mr. Enderle returned from Stuttgart.

Da das Haus zu klein für uns alle geworden war, bin ich vor drei Jahren mit meiner Familie ausgezogen. | Since the house had become too small for all of us, I moved out three years ago with my family.

Nachdem er weggegangen war, schrieb er mir jede Woche einen Brief. | After he had left, he wrote me a letter every week.

Obwohl mein Betrieb in Stuttgart ist, sind wir doch in Burgbach geblieben. | Although my place of work is in Stuttgart, we continued to live in Burgbach.

Meine Schwester kommt nur noch selten nach Hause, seit sie geheiratet hat. | My sister rarely comes home anymore since she got married.

Während die Kinder schwimmen gingen, saßen wir im Garten. | While the children went swimming, we sat in the garden.

Wir rannten den ganzen Weg ins Dorf hinunter, weil wir nicht zu spät zum Essen kommen wollten.

We ran all the way down to the village because we didn't want to be late for dinner.

Wenn wir gegessen haben, gehen wir ins Wohnzimmer und sehen fern.

When we have eaten, we'll go into the living room and watch TV.

Daß ihr noch zwei Tage hierbleiben wollt, ist großartig.
Es ist großartig, daß ihr noch zwei Tage hierbleiben wollt.

It's marvelous that you want to stay another two days.

Ich wußte nicht, daß ihr noch zwei Tage bleiben wollt.
Daß ihr noch zwei Tage bleiben wollt, habe ich nicht gewußt.

I didn't know that you want to stay two more days.

[5] Direct and Indirect Questions

SEE
ANALYSIS
92
(p. 219)

Denkt er noch an dich?
Ich möchte wissen, ob er noch an dich denkt.

Ruft er sie denn immer noch jede Woche an?
Sie wollte mir nicht sagen, ob er sie immer noch jede Woche anruft.

Möchtest du denn lieber hierbleiben, Fritz?
Ich habe Fritz gefragt, ob er lieber hierbleiben möchte.

Wer ist das denn?
Weißt du, wer das ist?

Wen haben Sie denn in der Stadt getroffen?
Können Sie mir bitte sagen, wen Sie in der Stadt getroffen haben?

Wie heißen Sie denn?
Darf ich Sie fragen, wie Sie heißen?

VARIATIONS

Change the following direct questions to indirect questions, starting with **Weißt du,** . . .
Be sure to leave out **denn** in the indirect questions.

Wie weit sind wir denn heute gefahren?
Was kostet ein Pfund Kalbfleisch?
Wieviel Gramm hat ein amerikanisches Pfund?
Wo ist Frau Enderle denn geboren?
Wie rechnet man Fahrenheit in Celsius um?
Wem gehört der Wagen mit der Zollnummer?
Wann fährt unser Zug denn ab?
Wie lange dauert der Film denn?

[6] Open Conditions

Reverse the order of conditions and conclusions.

> **Wenn es morgen nicht regnet, können wir arbeiten.**
> **Wir können morgen nur arbeiten, wenn es nicht regnet.**

Wenn ich kann, komme ich.

Ich _____, wenn _____.

Ich fahre nach Zürich, wenn du auch fährst.

Wenn du _____, _____ auch.

Wenn Herr Büttner schon hier ist, schicken Sie ihn zu mir.

Schicken Sie _____, wenn er _____.

Wenn du kein Geld hast, helfe ich dir gerne.

Ich helfe _____, _____.

SEE
ANALYSIS
97
(p. 221)

[7] Imperative, **du**-Form

Ruf mich bitte *nicht* vor *acht* an!
Bitte ruf mich *nicht* vor *acht* an!
Aber ruf mich *nicht* vor *acht* an, bitte!

SEE
ANALYSIS
98–102
(pp. 222–226)

Ruf sie doch noch einmal *an*. Vielleicht ist sie jetzt zu *Hause*.
Bitte ruf sie doch noch einmal *an!*
Ruf sie doch noch mal *an*, bitte!
Bitte sei doch so gut und fahr mich mal eben in die Stadt.

Fahr doch mit uns in den *Schwarz*wald!
Sei mir nicht böse, aber ich muß jetzt gehen.
Sei doch nicht so nervös!

Steh *du* doch mal zuerst auf.
Rede *du* mal mit Meyer, du kennst ihn doch besser als ich.
Bleib *du* doch wenigstens vernünftig.

Ruf doch mal zu Hause an...

VARIATIONS

Change the following sentences into **du**-form imperatives; use **doch**, **doch mal**, or **mal** where appropriate.

Ich bringe dir ein Glas Wasser.
Ich gehe in den Garten.
Ich besuche euch in München.

Ich gebe dir das Buch morgen.
Ich nehme mir eine Taxe.
Ich sehe mal nach, ob Meyer schon da ist.

[8] Imperative, **ihr**-Form

SEE
ANALYSIS
99-102
(pp. 222–226)

Kinder, vergeßt nicht, euch die Hände zu waschen.

Es war schön, daß ihr kommen konntet; besucht uns bald mal wieder.
Seid mir nicht böse. Aber ich muß jetzt wirklich nach Hause.
Also auf Wiedersehen. Und ruft uns an, wenn ihr nach Hause kommt.

Geht *ihr* ruhig ins Theater. Ich muß noch arbeiten.
Warum ich sonntags immer zu Hause bleibe? Arbeitet *ihr* einmal jeden Tag zehn Stunden, dann wißt ihr warum.

VARIATIONS

Change to **ihr**-form imperatives.

Wir kommen bald wieder.   Wir bringen euch ein paar Blumen mit.
Wir trinken doch nicht so viel Kaffee.   Wir bleiben noch ein bißchen hier.
Wir sind euch nicht böse.   Wir nehmen den Bus.

[9] Imperative, **wir**-Form

Wo sollen wir denn essen, Rosemarie?—Gehen wir doch mal ins Regina, Klaus, da waren
    wir schon so lange nicht mehr.
Müssen wir denn heute schon wieder zu Müllers?—Natürlich müssen wir.—Also schön,
    fahren wir wieder zu Müllers.

SEE
ANALYSIS
99–102
(pp. 222–226)

VARIATIONS

Change to the **wir**-form, starting with **Schön**, . . .

> **Ich möchte nach München fahren.**
> **Schön, fahren wir doch nach München.**

Ich möchte zu Hause bleiben.
Ich möchte heute im Hotel Berlin essen.
Ich möchte heute schwimmen gehen.

[10] Imperative, **Sie**-Form

Bitte, Fräulein, geben Sie mir Zimmer 641.
Seien Sie herzlich gegrüßt von Ihrem Hans Meyer.
Entschuldigen Sie bitte, gnädige Frau; Ihr Ferngespräch nach Hamburg ist da.
Es gibt keine bessere Kamera. Fragen Sie Ihren Fotohändler.
Lassen Sie Ihren Wagen doch mal zu Hause: Fahren Sie mit der U-Bahn.

SEE
ANALYSIS
99–102
(pp. 222–226)

[11] Impersonal Imperative

SEE
ANALYSIS
99–102
(pp. 222–226)

Alles aussteigen.
Einsteigen bitte.
Bitte einsteigen.
Nicht öffnen, bevor der Zug hält.
Langsam fahren.
Nicht rauchen.
Nicht benutzen, während der Zug hält.

Bitte anschnallen.
Nicht mit dem Fahrer sprechen.
Eintreten ohne zu klingeln.
Nicht stören.
Bitte an der Kasse zahlen.
Nach rechts einordnen.

Selbständig denken, planen, handeln!
Immer mehr Frauen haben ihre eigene
Lebensversicherung.

Think, plan, act independently! More and more women have their own life
insurance.

[12] The Future Tense

SEE
ANALYSIS
103
(p. 226)

Ich glaube, ich werde sie nie wiedersehen.

I believe I will never see them (her) again.

Diesen Sonntag werde ich nie vergessen.

I shall never forget this Sunday.

Diesen Sonntag werde ich leider nie vergessen können.

Unfortunately, I shall never be able to forget this Sunday.

Nein, Herr Harms, ich werde es nicht vergessen. Ich werde Sie morgen um 9 Uhr 10 anrufen.

No, Mr. Harms, I shall not forget it. I'll give you a ring at 9:10 tomorrow.

Gertrud ist schon vor einer Stunde abgefahren, also wird sie jetzt schon lange zu Hause sein.

Gertrude left an hour ago, so she has probably been home for a long time now.

Ich möchte wissen, warum Peter mich immer noch nicht angerufen hat; ob er mir böse ist?—Warum soll er dir böse sein? Er wird (wohl) noch schlafen.

I'd like to know why Peter hasn't called me up yet. I wonder whether he's mad at me. —Why would he be mad at you? He's probably still asleep.

Den Helmut habe ich schon wochenlang nicht gesehen. Wo kann der denn nur sein?—Er wird wieder in Essen arbeiten müssen.

I haven't seen Helmut in weeks. Where could he be?—He probably has to work in Essen again.

[13] Vocabulary Review: Adjectival Antonyms

Ist dein Mantel neu, Ilse?
Nein, er ist ganz alt.

Is your coat new, Ilse?
No, it's quite old.

Zwei und zwei ist fünf,—richtig?
Nein, das ist falsch.

Two and two is five—right?
No, that's wrong.

Wie hoch ist der Berg?
Wie tief ist das Wasser?

How high is this mountain?
How deep is the water?

Ist das Hotel weit von hier?
Nein, ganz nahe beim Bahnhof.

Is the hotel far from here?
No, quite near the station.

Ist das Buch sehr teuer?
Nein, als Paperback ist es billig.

Is the book very expensive?
No, as a paperback it's cheap.

Fahren Sie bitte langsam.
Bei dem Wetter können Sie doch nicht so schnell fahren.

Please drive slowly.
In this weather you can't drive so fast.

Im Sommer ist es in Berlin um zehn Uhr noch hell.
Im Winter ist es in Berlin um vier Uhr schon dunkel.

In the summer, it is still light at ten o'clock in Berlin.
In the winter, it is already dark at four o'clock in Berlin.

[14] Vocabulary Review: Nominal Antonyms

Von der Burgruine hoch oben auf dem Berg konnte man unten im Tal das Dorf sehen.

From the castle ruin high up on the mountain one could see the village down in the valley.

Früh am Morgen fuhr er in die Stadt und kam erst spät am Abend wieder zurück.

Early in the morning he went to the city and didn't return until late at night.

Heute ist doch Sonntag. Der Zug fährt heute nicht; er fährt nur an Werktagen.

Today is Sunday. The train doesn't run today; it only runs on workdays (weekdays).

Auf diese Frage konnte er mir keine Antwort geben.

To this question he couldn't give me an answer.

Eusebius hatte überall Freunde; ich glaube nicht, daß er je einen Feind gehabt hat.

Eusebius had friends everywhere; I don't think he ever had an enemy.

Er lebte ein schönes Leben, und nach seinem Tod vermißten wir ihn sehr.

He lived a good life, and after his death we missed him very much.

Am Anfang war ja alles gut gegangen, aber am Ende hatte er dann doch Pech.

At the beginning, everything had gone well, but in the end he had bad luck after all.

Wir mußten drei Tage und zwei Nächte fahren, um rechtzeitig nach New York zu kommen.

We had to drive for three days and two nights in order to get to New York on time.

Analysis

89 Dependent Clauses: Definition

Consider the following sentences:

1. **Ich gehe ins Bett. Ich bin müde.**
   I am going to bed. I am tired.
2. **Ich gehe ins Bett, weil ich müde bin.**
   I am going to bed, because I am tired.
3. **Weil ich müde bin, gehe ich ins Bett.**
   Because I am tired, I am going to bed.

Sentence 1 contains two independent (main) clauses. In (2), the second clause is joined to the first with the conjunction **weil** (*because*) and the finite verb **bin** appears at the end of the clause. In (3), the two clauses are reversed, and the subject of the second clause, **ich**, now appears after the finite verb **gehe** because the preceding dependent clause constitutes the front field.

All clauses introduced by subordinating conjunctions like **weil** (see **91** below) are called dependent (or subordinate) clauses. They do not convey a complete message unless accompanied by a "main" clause: *although he was tired* does not make sense without a statement like *he didn't go to bed* preceding or following:

> **Obwohl er müde war, ging er nicht ins Bett.**
> **Er ging nicht ins Bett, obwohl er müde war.**

The term "main clause," however, does not imply that such clauses can always stand alone and retain their original meaning when separated from their dependent clauses (though this is certainly the case with the above **Ich bin müde** and **Ich gehe ins Bett**). But a clause like **Sie haben das große Haus nicht gekauft** (*They didn't buy that big house*) doesn't mean that they did *not* buy the house if it is followed by **weil sie sehr viel Geld hatten, sondern weil sie fünf Schlafzimmer brauchten** (*because they had lots of money, but because they needed five bedrooms*). Thus, in this case, the main clause and the two dependent clauses form a single meaningful utterance from which the dependent clauses cannot be amputated without impairing the meaning of the main clause.

Every dependent clause, including its verb, functions as one single syntactical unit of the main clause. For example, dependent clauses can function as:

SUBJECT	*The winner* gets the prize.
	Whoever wins gets the prize.
PREDICATE NOUN	This is not *the expected result.*
	This is not *what I had expected.*
OBJECT	I'll never know *your thoughts.*
	I'll never know *what you think.*
ADVERB	He met John *during his stay in New York.*
	He met John *while he stayed in New York.*

90 Word Order in Introduced and Unintroduced Dependent Clauses

Most dependent clauses are introduced by such connecting words as *that, because, although,* but in both English and German there is a type of dependent clause that does not require such a connecting word and is thus "unintroduced." English phrases of the type *I believe* and *I don't believe* can be followed by either kind of dependent clause.

> I believe (don't believe) he is in Cologne.
> that he is in Cologne.

In German, *only positive introductory statements* using verbs like **denken, glauben, wissen** can be followed by both.

> **Ich glaube, er ist in Köln.**
> **daß er in Köln ist.**

Negative introductory statements *must* be followed by introduced dependent clauses:

> **Ich glaube nicht, daß er in Köln ist.**

We have used many unintroduced dependent clauses in the preceding units; they have posed no problems because their word order is the same as that of main clauses. Introduced dependent clauses, however, show a new syntactic principle: *In all introduced dependent clauses, the finite verb (i.e., the first prong) appears behind the second prong at the very end of the clause.* This is referred to as "verb-last position."

	FRONT FIELD	1ST PRONG	INNER FIELD	2ND PRONG	
MAIN CLAUSE	**Er**	ist	heute	hier.	
UNINTRODUCED DEPENDENT CLAUSE	**Ich glaube, er**	ist	heute	hier.	
INTRODUCED DEPENDENT CLAUSE	**Ich glaube, daß er**		heute	hier	ist.

The sequence of elements following the subject **er** is a mirror image of the sequence of elements in the corresponding English sentence; that is, if the German sequence is 1–2–3, the English sequence will be 3–2–1.

	1	2	3
, daß er	heute	hier	ist
that he	is	here	today

                                    3   2   1

Here are some further examples of this mirror image principle, which holds for a great many English and German sentences and explains, for example, why the German sequence of time-place corresponds to the English sequence of place-time.

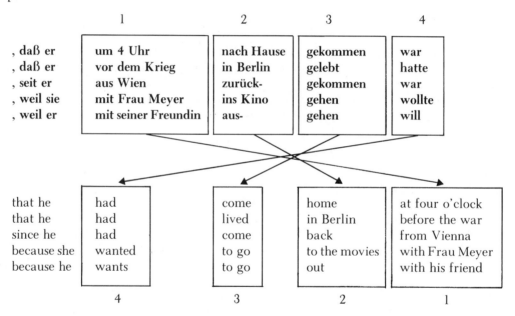

	1
, daß er	um 4 Uhr
, daß er	vor dem Krieg
, seit er	aus Wien
, weil sie	mit Frau Meyer
, weil er	mit seiner Freundin

Find other examples for this mirror image principle in the patterns and exercises.

In example 3 in **89** above,

   Weil ich müde bin, gehe ich jetzt ins Bett

the dependent clause precedes the main clause. Since each dependent clause represents one syntactic element of the main clause, it follows that the first prong of the main clause, **gehe**, must come immediately after the dependent clause, according to the principle of verb-second position. Thus, if a dependent clause precedes a main clause, their two finite verb forms always stand next to one another, and are *always* separated by a comma: . . . **bin, gehe** . . .

| In Hamburg | bin | ich jeden Abend | ins Kino | gegangen. |

| Als ich in Hamburg | war, | bin | ich jeden Abend | ins Kino | gegangen. |

Frequently, especially after **wenn**-clauses, the dependent clause—that is, the first element of the main clause—is repeated and summed up at the beginning of the main clause by either **dann** or **so.** This **dann** or **so** immediately precedes the first prong—that is, the second element of the main clause.

Wenn er nicht bald kommt,
    1

         dann | *müssen* wir halt ohne ihn gehen.
        1a | 2

If he doesn't come soon, then we'll just have to go without him.

In both English and German, dependent clauses are occasionally inserted into main clauses, but the English pattern

Karl, though he was very tired, did not go to bed yet

in which the dependent clause follows the subject in the front field, cannot be imitated in German. German has the following two possibilities:

Karl ging, obwohl er sehr müde war, noch nicht ins Bett.
Obwohl Karl sehr müde war, ging er noch nicht ins Bett.

This means that a German sentence with the subject in the front field can be interrupted by a dependent clause introduced by a subordinating conjunction only after the first prong.

Another English pattern that cannot be imitated in German anticipates the noun subject in the main clause by a pronoun subject in the preceding dependent clause:

When *he* came to visit us, *John* had just bought the house on Main Street.

The normal implication is that *he* and *John* are the same person. The German equivalent of this sentence, however,

Als *er* uns besuchte, hatte *Hans* gerade das Haus in der Hauptstraße gekauft

implies that *he* is not *Hans.* In sentences of this type, German *must* mention the noun subject first to avoid ambiguity:

Als *Hans* uns besuchte, hatte *er* gerade das Haus in der Hauptstraße gekauft.

Verbal complements like **an-, aus-, ab-,** and any others that are written as one word with an infinitive, must also be connected in verb-last position.

Die Laternen gehen an.—Wenn die Laternen angehen, . . .
Er macht das Licht aus.—Daß er das Licht ausmacht, . . .
Er lernte sie in Bonn kennen.—Als er sie in Bonn kennenlernte, . . .

"Double Infinitives" in Dependent Clauses

It was pointed out in Analysis **65**, p. 146, that when modals and **brauchen** are used with a dependent infinitive, their participles look like infinitives.

Ich habe Sie noch nicht besuchen können.

As a result, **besuchen können** looks like a double infinitive. If such double infinitives occur in dependent clauses, they are *preceded* by the finite verb; that is, in this one case the principle of verb-last position does not apply.

Es tut mir leid, daß ich Sie noch nicht habe besuchen können.
I am sorry that I haven't been able to visit you yet.

However, as a rule, the past tense of the modals is used rather than the perfect, and the double infinitive construction is avoided.

Es tut mir leid, daß ich Sie noch nicht besuchen konnte.

91 Coordinating and Subordinating Conjunctions

Coordinating conjunctions always join two main clauses or two dependent clauses; they do not have any influence on the word order of either:

Hans wollte schon gehen, und Otto wollte noch hierbleiben.
Ich gehe ins Bett, weil ich müde bin und weil ich Kopfschmerzen habe.

The most important coordinating conjunctions are: **und, aber, oder, denn** (see **45**).

Subordinating conjunctions always introduce dependent clauses and require verb-last position. Other connecting words for dependent clauses are question words and relative pronouns. The most important subordinating conjunctions are:

als	when (refers to a single event in the past)
bevor	before
bis	until
da	since (causal)
nachdem	after
obwohl	although
seit	since (temporal)
während	while
weil	because
wenn	when; if

The conjunction **daß** introduces subject and object clauses:

SUBJECT **Daß du das für mich getan hast, war sehr nett von dir.**
OBJECT **Ich wußte nicht, daß er damals in Freiburg wohnte.**

If a subject clause follows the main clause, the "dummy subject" **es** occupies the front field to anticipate the subject clause:

Es war sehr nett von dir, daß du das für mich getan hast.

92 Indirect Questions

If the questions

Does he live in Berlin?	**Wohnt er in Berlin?**
Where does he live in Berlin?	**Wo wohnt er denn in Berlin?**

are preceded by clauses like *Do you know*, **Wissen Sie** or *Ask him*, **Fragen Sie ihn**, they become indirect questions. Such indirect questions are always dependent clauses and, in German, show verb-last position and cannot contain **denn**.

Indirect yes-or-no questions are introduced by *whether* or *if* in English and by **ob** in German. English *if* is the equivalent of **ob** only if it can be replaced by *whether*.

Do you know if he lives in Berlin?	**Wissen Sie, ob er in Berlin wohnt?**
whether he lives in Berlin?	

Indirect word questions retain their question word. The sentence adverb **denn** must be dropped in indirect questions.

Do you know where he lives in Berlin?	**Wissen Sie, wo er in Berlin wohnt?**

93 The Use of the Past in Dependent Clauses

Frequently a perfect form in the main clause is accompanied by a past form in the dependent clause. This is virtually obligatory in **als**-clauses and in all other clauses which fix the time of an event or describe the circumstances that brought the event about.

Ich habe bis elf gewartet. Aber als er dann immer noch nicht kam, bin ich ins Bett gegangen.	I waited until eleven. But when he still did not come, I went to bed.

NOTE: If the action of the dependent clause occurs while the action of the main clause is in progress, the past tense may be used in both clauses.

Als ich meine Frau kennenlernte, wohnte sie in München.

94 Position of the Subject in Dependent Clauses

In most dependent clauses, the subject follows the connecting word. However, a noun subject may be preceded by pronoun objects.

Ich weiß, daß *Herr Meyer seiner Frau* einen Sportwagen geschenkt hat.
Ich weiß, daß *Herr Meyer ihr* einen Sportwagen geschenkt hat.
Ich weiß, daß *ihr Herr Meyer* einen Sportwagen geschenkt hat.

In order to increase the news value of a noun subject, it may be moved toward the end of the inner field. Thus, in the following sentences, the news value is shifted from the time element to the subject:

Ich kann nicht glauben, daß *der Winter* hier schon im Oktober beginnt.
Ich kann nicht glauben, daß hier schon im Oktober *der Winter* beginnt.

95 Intonation of Dependent Clauses

It was pointed out in Unit 1 that when a German assertion sinks down at the end to level 1 of the three intonation levels, as it does in

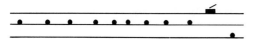

Wir blei·ben heu·te na·tür·lich zu Hau·se

the fall to level 1 means "this is the end of the sentence."

Whenever an assertion is followed by a dependent clause, the speaker has several possibilities.

1. He may want to indicate that everything important has already been said in the main clause. In that case the entire dependent clause may have level-1 intonation, and the preceding main clause shows the usual 2-3-1 intonation pattern.

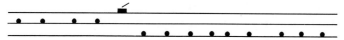

Ich war schon ins Bett ge·gang·en, als er nach Hau·se kam

2. He may pack *all* the news value into the dependent clause and speak the preceding main clause entirely on level 2.

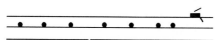

Ich war doch schon hier, als er kam

3. He may want to distribute the news value over the main clause and the dependent clause by placing (at least) *one* stressed syllable in the main clause and (at least) *one* stressed syllable in the dependent clause.

Er will war·ten   , bis du kommst

The intonation patterns in (1) and (2) contain nothing new (they simply represent a "long-breath" variation of **Es regnet**), but the intonation pattern under (3) illustrates a new principle:

The main clause and the dependent clause are usually separated by a slight pause; and at the end of the main clause the pitch of the unstressed syllables does not sink to level 1 (which would signal the end of the sentence), but is spoken on level 3. This lack of a drop in pitch is a signal meaning: "This is not the end of the sentence; wait for the next clause."

The high-pitch last-syllable intonation is also characteristic for dependent clauses which precede a main clause.

Wenn es mor-gen reg-net , blei-ben wir zu Hau-se

96 wenn and wann

**So viel wie gestern abend redet Meyer nur, wenn er zuviel getrunken hat.
Weißt du, wann Meyer gestern nach Hause gegangen ist?**

Both **wenn** and **wann** frequently correspond to English *when*. But German **wann** *is an interrogative and means only "at what time,"* that is, only an English *when* which can be replaced by *at what time* can be expressed by German **wann.**

97 Open Conditions

A condition is an event or a situation without which another event or situation cannot take place. Thus, in the statement *If the weather is good tomorrow, we can go to the beach*, good weather is the prerequisite for the trip to the beach. The *if*-clause (the grammatical "condition") does not indicate whether or not the weather will be good; it simply states that unless the weather is good, the second part of the statement (the grammatical "conclusion") will not become a reality.

If someone says, *I haven't seen my old teacher for years. If he is still alive, he was eighty years old last Monday*, this means that the speaker does not know whether the teacher is still alive, and that consequently he doesn't know whether the teacher was able to celebrate his eightieth birthday. *The question as to the reality of the facts is left open.* However, this question *is not left open* if someone says, *If my teacher were still alive, he would have turned eighty last Monday*. The speaker now implies that the teacher is dead. In other words: The situation described in the condition is known to be unreal and to exist only in the speaker's thought and imagination.

The difference in meaning between *if he is alive* and *if he were alive* depends entirely on verb forms. The *is* leaves the question of the actual facts open; the *were* expresses the unreality of the situation imagined.

We use the term "open condition" to indicate that the question of the facts is open, and we use the term "irreal condition" or "contrary-to-fact condition" to indicate that these facts are contrary to reality and merely assumed in imagination.

In Unit 8, only open conditions are introduced. Irreal conditions, which require the use of the subjunctive, will be discussed in Unit 9. German *if*-clauses are introduced by the subordinating conjunction **wenn.** As dependent clauses, they require verb-last position.

> **Wenn Else kommen kann, gehe ich mit ihr ins Museum.**
> **Wenn ihm nichts passiert ist, muß er schon zu Hause sein.**
> **Ich schenke dir den Roman gern, wenn du ihn haben möchtest.**
> **Wenn Sie diesen Brief bekommen, müssen Sie mir sofort antworten.**
> **Ich habe keine Angst, wenn mein Mann nach Afrika fährt.**

Without context, some of these sentences, especially the last two, are ambiguous, since **wenn** means both *when* and *if*. Thus the last sentence may mean

> I won't be afraid if my husband goes to Africa

or

> I am not afraid when my husband goes to Africa.

NOTE: If an **um . . . zu** clause precedes the main clause, it can be replaced by an open condition.

> **Um nach Berlin fahren zu können, braucht man Geld.**
> **Wenn man nach Berlin fahren will, braucht man Geld.**

98 The Imperative: Definition

Imperative forms are used to ask someone to do, or not to do, something. This can take the form of a polite request (*Hand me that corkscrew, dear, would you, please?*), of a cookbook instruction (*Sift the flour*), of an impatient shout (*Shut up! Get out!*), or of an order or command (*Stop! Drop that gun!*). Imperatives are used in the most varied situations, from religious services (*Let us pray*) to advertising (*Be a needlepointer!*), from child rearing (*Eat your spinach!*) to language instruction (*Change the following statements to imperatives*).

In German, you must use the form of the imperative that corresponds to the pronoun of address used in a given situation: **du, ihr, wir,** or **Sie.** There is also a widely used impersonal form of the imperative which is identical with the infinitive.

99 Forms of the Imperative

The **Sie**-form was introduced in Unit 4. Of the personal forms, only the **du**-form is not identical with the corresponding forms of the present indicative.

In principle, the ending **-e** of the **du**-form is optional. However, verbs whose stems end in **-d** (**reden**) or **-t** (**antworten**) or in the suffix **-ig** (**entschuldigen**) are usually not used without the **-e** ending.

Weak Verbs

du-FORM	sag(e)	rede	antworte	entschuldige
ihr-FORM	sagt	redet	antwortet	entschuldigt
wir-FORM	sagen wir	reden wir	antworten wir	entschuldigen wir
Sie-FORM	sagen Sie	reden Sie	antworten Sie	entschuldigen Sie

Strong Verbs

du-FORM	geh(e)	fang(e) an	finde	gib	lauf
ihr-FORM	geht	fangt an	findet	gebt	lauft
wir-FORM	gehen wir	fangen wir an	finden wir	geben wir	laufen wir
Sie-FORM	gehen Sie	fangen Sie an	finden Sie	geben Sie	laufen Sie
du-FORM	nimm	sieh	sei	fahre	werde
ihr-FORM	nehmt	seht	seid	fahrt	werdet
wir-FORM	nehmen wir	sehen wir	seien wir	fahren wir	werden wir
Sie-FORM	nehmen Sie	sehen Sie	seien Sie	fahren Sie	werden Sie

Again, only the **du**-form is not identical with the present indicative. The change of vowel from **a** to **ä** (**ich fahre, du fährst**), from **au** to **äu** (**ich laufe, du läufst**), and from **o** to **ö** (**stoßen, du stößt**) does not occur in the imperative. However, the change from **e** to **ie** or **i** (**ich gebe, du gibst; ich sehe, du siehst**) must be observed. These changed-vowel forms never show the ending **-e** in the **du**-form. The **du**-form **werde** is irregular, as are the forms of **sein.** In principle, the ending **-e** of the **du**-form is again optional.

Impersonal Imperatives

With some verbs, both weak and strong, the infinitive can be used as an impersonal imperative, for example, **Nicht öffnen, Bitte weitergehen.**

100 The Use of the Imperative

1. The **du**-form is used when the persons involved say **du** to each other. It may also be used in advertisements.

Bring mir bitte Zigaretten mit,
Bring mir doch bitte Zigaretten mit, } **wenn du in die Stadt fährst!**
Bitte bring mir Zigaretten mit,

Mach mal Pause, trink Coca-Cola!

This form can be used with a strongly stressed **du** immediately following the imperative. This **du** always establishes a contrast between the person addressed and someone else.

Rede *du* mal mit Meyer!   (Implication: I have talked with Meyer already.)

This pattern is sometimes expressed in English by "Why don't *you* . . ."

2. Like the **du**-form, the **ihr**-form is used between persons who say **du** to each other.

> **Kinder, vergeßt nicht,**
> **Kinder, bitte vergeßt nicht,** } **daß ihr um zehn zu Hause sein sollt.**
> **Kinder, vergeßt bitte nicht,**

The use of a stressed **ihr** is parallel to the use of a stressed **du** with the **du**-form.

> **Versucht *ihr* doch mal, mit Meyer zu reden. *Mir glaubt* er nicht.**

3. The **wir**-form can only be used if the speaker includes himself among the persons addressed; the pronoun **wir** is always used.

> **Wo sollen wir denn essen? Im Grünen Baum? Gut, fahren wir in den Grünen Baum!**

The English equivalent is *Let's* (*go*).

4. The **Sie**-form is used (with or without **bitte**) between persons who say **Sie** to each other.

> **(Bitte) bringen Sie mir noch ein Glas Wein.**

In advertising it is used without **bitte**.

> **Versuchen Sie SUNIL.**
> **Kommen Sie zu uns, wenn Sie Geld brauchen.**

5. The impersonal form is the infinitive used to express a request. It is used to give instructions to the public, and is found on traffic signs, at airports, in planes, in railroad stations, and so on. It is also used in advertising and in cookbooks, without exclamation marks.

> Aussteigen bitte.
> Nicht öffnen, bevor der Zug hält.
> Nicht rauchen.
> Karotten, Sellerie und Bohnen in Salzwasser
>   weich kochen, Parmesan daruntermischen.

101 The Intonation of Imperatives

The imperative as a command is distinguished from the imperative as a polite request by level of intonation.

The imperative expressing a command follows the usual 2-3-1 assertion pattern; that is, the intonation curve goes up to level 3 and then sinks to level 1.

Rede nicht so viel!

Bringen Sie mir doch mal die *Spei*sekarte.
(Implication: don't be so inattentive.)

In a polite request using imperative forms, the unstressed syllables preceding the stress point are usually arranged in a downward trend toward level 1, and then the first stressed syllable is raised only to level 2, not to level 3.

Sei mir nicht *böse*!

Bitte bring mir etwas zu *lesen* mit!

Bringen Sie mir doch mal die *Speise*karte.
(Would you be so kind as to bring me the menu?)

102 The Syntax of the Imperative

The personal forms of the imperative normally begin the sentence, but they are frequently preceded by **bitte**.

Bring mir etwas zu lesen mit!
Bitte bring mir etwas zu lesen mit!

Since the impersonal imperatives are infinitives, they stand at the end of the imperative phrase.

Langsam fahren!
Bitte die Türen schließen!

When imperatives are negated, **nicht** stands, as usual, at the end of the inner field and precedes the second prong.

Bitte fahr morgen nicht nach Berlin!
Sei doch nicht so ungeduldig!

103 The Future Tense

Formation

The German future is formed by using **werden** as an auxiliary in the first prong and any infinitive in the second prong.

ich werde . . . fahren	wir werden . . . fahren
du wirst . . . fahren	ihr werdet . . . fahren
er wird . . . fahren	sie werden . . . fahren

Use

Since the present tense can refer to future time, the future tense is comparatively rare. One usually hears

Ich fahre morgen nach Berlin

but it is also perfectly normal to say

Ich werde morgen nach Berlin fahren.

If a sentence contains no time phrase, the future is used more frequently in order to avoid ambiguity.

Ihr werdet ja sehen, wie es ist.   You'll see how it is.

Very frequently, future forms express not futurity, but present probability. Such a probability statement often contains adverbs such as **wohl** (*probably*), **sicher** (*certainly*), **vielleicht** (*perhaps*), and **wahrscheinlich** (*probably*).

Es ist jetzt sieben. Inge wird wohl (sicher,   It's seven o'clock now. Inge is probably at
wahrscheinlich) schon zu Hause sein.   home by now.

104 einmal, mal

When **einmal** or the shorter **mal** is used in assertions and requests, it may mean *once*, *for once*, or *for a change*.

Ich will dieses Jahr nicht an die Nordsee. Ich möchte mal in die Berge
fahren.
I don't want to go to the North Sea this year. I'd like to go to the mountains
for a change.

Very often, however, the short **mal** loses its literal meaning and expresses simply a note of casualness.

Ich geh' mal in die Stadt.
Ich muß mal telefonieren.

In requests, this casual **mal** is usually preceded by an unstressed **doch.**

Mach uns doch mal eine Tasse Kaffee.   How about fixing us a cup of coffee?

Noch (ein)mal and **doch noch (ein)mal** always mean *once more* or *again*.

Ruf sie doch noch mal an.   (Why don't you) call her up again.

105 Word Formation: Groups of Derivatives

As was pointed out in **84**, both English and German use prefixes and suffixes to create new words based on a common stem (or root). Note, however, that German derivatives often do not have an exact English equivalent, and that it is not always possible to guess the meaning of the derived word. Also, in some cases the stem vowel is changed in some derivatives.

Here are some groups of words based on the same stem, to which you can add others as they occur. In addition to derivatives, some compound nouns are given.

arbeiten	to work	kaufen	to buy, purchase
die Arbeit,-en	work, task	der Kauf,⸚e	purchase
der Arbeiter,-	workman, (blue-collar) worker	der Käufer,-	buyer
		das Kaufhaus,⸚er	department store
arbeitslos	unemployed		
verarbeiten	to process	verkaufen	to sell
die Verarbeitung	processing	der Verkauf,⸚e	sale
die Datenverarbeitung	data processing	der Verkäufer,-	salesman
		die Verkäuferin,-nen	saleswoman
die Bahn,-en	track; railroad; streetcar	kochen	to cook, to boil
die Autobahn,-en	superhighway, freeway	der Koch,⸚e	cook
		die Köchin,-nen	cook
die Eisenbahn,-en	railroad	die Küche,-n	kitchen
die Straßenbahn,-en	streetcar	lehren	to teach
der Bahnhof,⸚e	railroad station	der Lehrer,-	teacher
		die Lehrerin,-nen	teacher
fahren	to drive	der Lehrling,-e	apprentice
der Fahrer,-	driver		
die Fahrt,-en	drive; trip	reisen	to travel
der Fahrgast,⸚e	passenger	die Reise,-n	trip
abfahren	to leave, depart	abreisen	to leave (for a trip), depart
die Abfahrt,-en	departure		
die Einfahrt,-en	entrance (for vehicles)	verreisen	to go on a trip, travel
die Ausfahrt,-en	exit (for vehicles)	verreist sein	to be on a trip
fliegen	to fly	zahlen	to pay
der Flieger,-	flier, pilot	bezahlen	to pay
der Flug,⸚e	flight	die Zahl,-en	number, figure
der Fluggast,⸚e	(airline) passenger	zählen	to count
das Flugzeug,-e	airplane		

Conversations

Zwei Studentinnen sprechen nach einer Vorlesung miteinander:

I

GERDA WOLLNER: Sag mal, wo wohnst du eigentlich dieses Semester? Immer noch im Studentenheim?

LOTTE VOGT: Nein, ich wohne jetzt privat. Ich habe ein möbliertes Zimmer gefunden, ganz prima, in einem Einfamilienhaus direkt am Fluß.

G.W.: Na, da mußt du aber sicher ganz schön bezahlen.

CONVERSATIONS

Mieterkarte

Studentenwerk Bonn AöR

Name: Hyams
Vorname: Barbara
Mieter-Nr.: 23 o64 4
Miete DM: 1o5,--
Mietkonto: Bank für Gemeinwirtschaft Bonn
Konto-Nr.: 10156505/23

Ihr Überweisungsträger muß die vorstehenden Angaben sowie den Bezugsmonat enthalten.
Spätester Zahltermin ist der 7. des lfd. Monats.

L.V.: Nein, gar nicht. Die Leute sind viel weg und sind froh, wenn sie jemand im Hause haben.

G.W.: Say, where are you living this semester? Still in the dorm?

L.V.: No, I live in town now. I've found a furnished room, really first-class, in a one-family house right by the river.

G.W.: Well, I guess you have to pay a steep price for it.

L.V.: No, not at all. The people are away a lot and are glad if they have someone in the house.

II

LOTTE VOGT: Und du, Gerda?

GERDA WOLLNER: Ich wohne jetzt auch möbliert, in der Altstadt, in der Nähe vom Dom.

L.V.: Wirklich? Stören dich denn da die Domglocken nicht?

G.W.: Zuerst ja, aber jetzt gar nicht mehr. Außerdem bin ich sowieso fast immer in der Bibliothek.

L.V.: Richtig, du hast ja dieses Semester Examen. Und wie ist dein Zimmer sonst?

G.W.: Klein, aber sehr gemütlich, direkt unterm Dach. Du mußt mich bald mal besuchen.

L.V.: And you, Gerda?

G.W.: I'm renting a room too, now (I live in a furnished room), in the old city, near the cathedral.

L.V.: Really? Don't the cathedral bells bother you?

G.W.: At first they did, but now not at all anymore. Besides, I'm almost always in the library anyway.

L.V.: That's right, you have your exams this semester. And how's your room otherwise?

G.W.: Small, but very cosy and comfortable, right under the roof. You've got to come see me soon.

III

GERDA WOLLNER: Übrigens macht der Karlheinz am Samstag wieder 'ne Party.

LOTTE VOGT: Ja, ich weiß; er hat mich auch eingeladen. Gehst du hin?

G.W.: Klar. Ich habe zwar ziemlich wenig Zeit, aber die Partys bei Karlheinz sind ja immer toll.

L.V.: Er hat mir gesagt, daß er eine Menge neue Schallplatten hat, und seine Eltern haben ihm zu Weihnachten einen neuen Plattenspieler geschenkt.

G.W.: Incidentally, Karlheinz is going to have another party on Saturday.

L.V.: Yes, I know; he's invited me too. Are you going?

G.W.: Sure. I haven't got much time, but those parties at Karlheinz's are always great.

L.V.: He told me that he has a lot of new records, and his parents gave him a new record player for Christmas.

IV

LOTTE VOGT: Am Sonntag wollen wir alle eine Wanderung machen.

GERDA WOLLNER: Wo wollt ihr denn hin?

L.V.: Wir fahren mit dem Wagen in den Auwald, und dann wollen wir auf den Donnersberg.

G.W.: Das ist aber ganz schön weit. —Und der Willi bringt seine Gitarre mit?

L.V.: Aber sicher. Und der Werner will das Bier mitbringen.

G.W.: Das klingt ja sehr romantisch, —wie bei den Wandervögeln.*

L.V.: Sei nicht so sarkastisch. Das macht doch Spaß bei dem Wetter.

L.V.: On Sunday we all want to go for a hike.

G.W.: Where do you want to go?

L.V.: We'll drive to the Au Forest, and then we want to hike up Thunder Mountain.

G.W.: That's quite a distance. —And Willi is going to bring his guitar?

L.V.: Sure. And Werner wants to bring the beer.

G.W.: Sounds very romantic—just like the *Wandervögel.*

L.V.: Don't be so sarcastic. It's fun in weather like this.

V

Eine deutsche "Shaggy Dog Story"

Die Domglocken

Zwei Männer gehen über den Platz am Dom. Die Domglocken läuten. „Läuten die Glocken nicht wunderschön?" fragt der eine. „Was?" sagt der andere. Der eine brüllt: „Ich habe gesagt, läuten die Glocken nicht wunderschön?" „Ich kann dich nicht verstehen", brüllt der andere zurück, „die Glocken sind so verdammt laut."

Diese Geschichte hat viele Varianten, zum Beispiel:
Zwei Jungen fahren mit dem Fahrrad hintereinander her. Der eine ruft: „He, Fritz, dein Schutzblech klappert." (Your mud guard is rattling.)
Erzählen Sie diese Version zu Ende.

Oder: Ein Mann kommt in eine Bar mit einer Banane im Ohr. Jemand fragt ihn: „Warum haben Sie denn eine Banane im Ohr?"
Was sagt der Mann jetzt?

Variante zur Variante: Er sagt: „Weil ich heute meine Karotte vergessen habe."

VI

Invent appropriate statements for Person B:

A.: Karl macht am Freitag eine Party. Kannst du kommen?

B.: _____

*__Wandervögel__, literally, *migratory birds,* a reference to the nationalistic youth movement of the early twentieth century.

A.: Das ist aber schade. Warum denn nicht?

B.: _____

A.: Aber das kannst du doch auch am Samstag machen.

B.: _____

A.: Na, dann vielleicht das nächste Mal.

B.: _____

VII

Construct mini-conversations, starting with the following elements:

1. A.: Wo ist denn dein neues Zimmer?

   B.: _____

2. A.: Warum hast du denn dieses Semester so wenig Zeit?

   B.: _____

3. A.: Wanderungen sind mir zu romantisch!

   B.: _____

4. A.: Mußt du wirklich schon gehen, Lotte?

   B.: _____

Fragen an Sie persönlich

1. Wohen Sie in einem Studentenheim oder privat?
                                    bei einer Familie?
                                    in einem möblierten Zimmer?

2. Wohnen Sie allein oder mit anderen Studenten zusammen?
      Warum in einem Studentenheim? Weil . . .
      Warum allein? Weil . . .

3. Gehen Sie früh ins Bett oder bleiben Sie gern lange auf? Bis wann?
      Werktags? Am Wochenende? Sonntags?

4. Arbeiten Sie (do you study) lieber am Tag oder abends?

5. Gehen Sie oft auf Partys?

6. Gehen Sie gern zu Fuß, oder fahren Sie lieber
                                    mit dem Rad?
                                    mit dem Auto?

7. Wandern Sie gern? (**wandern** to go for a hike)
8. Warum, glauben Sie, kann man in Amerika nicht so gut wandern wie in Deutschland?

Reading

Die deutsche Küche

die Küche cuisine; kitchen

This reading selection on the German cuisine contains three recipes from a Viennese, a Bavarian, and a Berlin cookbook. They have been included here to demonstrate the use of the impersonal imperative (that is, the infinitive form) in cooking instructions.

Die deutsche Küche, die österreichische Küche und die Schweizer Küche sind nicht so weltbekannt wie etwa die französische oder die chinesische. Aber trotzdem hat man in Mitteleuropa schon immer gut gekocht, und nicht nur Sauerkraut und Kartoffeln. Bis zum zweiten Weltkrieg waren die deutschen Hausfrauen vielleicht ein bißchen 5 provinziell in ihrem Geschmack, —man aß zum Beispiel kaum Reis, und viele Gemüse, wie Zucchini oder Auberginen, waren fast unbekannt. Aber heute kaufen die deutschen Frauen im Supermarkt Schafskäse aus Bulgarien, Spaghetti aus Italien, Aprikosen aus Griechenland, Orangen aus Israel und Ananas aus China, und ihre 10 Männer kochen ungarische Gulaschsuppe und serbische Bohnensuppe, sie grillen jugoslawischen Schaschlik im Garten hinter dem Haus und machen um Mitternacht schnell noch einen „Toast Hawaii."

weltbekannt world famous
trotzdem nevertheless
die Welt world
der Geschmack taste
das Gemüse vegetable
die Aubergine,-n eggplant
bekannt known
das Schaf sheep
die Ananas pineapple

Obwohl die deutsche Küche ziemlich international geworden ist, ißt 15 man doch noch viele traditionelle Gerichte. Diese Gerichte sind oft von Gebiet zu Gebiet verschieden: die Österreicher haben ihre Mehlspeisen* und die Schwaben ihre Spätzle; die Hessen, und besonders die Frankfurter, essen Rippchen mit Sauerkraut, und an der Nordseeküste ißt man Fisch, gekocht, gebraten, gebacken, gegrillt, geräuchert. 20

Es folgen drei typische Rezepte:

ziemlich rather
das Gericht dish
verschieden different
Spätzle a kind of noodle
das Rippchen cured and smoked pork chop
räuchern to smoke

Wiener Tafelspitz

1,5 kg Rindfleisch und 0,5 kg Kalbsknochen mit Karotten, Petersilie, Sellerie† und Zwie-

Viennese Boiled Beef

Brown 3 lbs. beef and 1 lb. veal bones with carrots, parsley, celery, and onions. Salt and

---

*Mehlspeise, literally "a dish made with flour," Austrian term for desserts made with flour, such as pancakes, but also for desserts and sweets in a more general sense. (See the menu from Salzburg in Unit 6, p. 159.)
†Sellerie, though translated as celery, in Central Europe always means celery root (celeriac); the celery-stalks you are used to are virtually unknown.

Der Tip in **BERLIN**

beln anbraten. Das Fleisch gut salzen und pfeffern. Wasser zugießen, Tomaten, Pfefferkörner und ein Lorbeerblatt dazugeben, sowie etwas Madeirawein. Gut zudecken und weich dünsten.

pepper the meat well. Cover with water, add tomatoes, pepper corns, and a bay leaf, as well as some Madeira wine. Cover tightly and simmer until soft.

5

Bayerische Leberknödel

5 alte Semmeln klein schneiden, salzen und mit 1/2 l lauwarmer Milch übergiessen. 500 g Rindsleber mit einer Zwiebel durch die Fleischmaschine geben, dann mit den Semmeln und mit drei Eiern und Majoran zu einem Teig verarbeiten. Knödel formen und in kochendem Salzwasser 1/2 Stunde leise kochen.

Bavarian Liver Dumplings

Cut 5 day-old hard rolls in small pieces, salt them, and cover with 1/2 liter lukewarm milk. Run 1 lb. beef liver and an onion through the meat grinder, then make into a dough together with the rolls, three eggs, and marjoram. Form dumplings and simmer (cook softly) in boiling salted water for half an hour.

Berliner Buletten*

2 Schrippen† von vorgestern in Wasser aufweichen. Dann mit 500 g Gehacktem vom Schwein gut durchkneten, ein Ei und eine feingeschnittene Zwiebel untermischen und mit Salz und Pfeffer würzen. Die Fleischmasse zu mehreren Buletten formen und in heißem Schmalz in der Pfanne knusprig braten.

Berlin Meat Patties

Soften two old rolls. Knead together well with 500 g. of ground pork, mix with an egg and a finely chopped onion, and season with salt and pepper. Form the meat-mass into several patties and fry in hot lard in a pan until crisp.

*The standard term for **Bulette** is **Frikadelle.**
†The standard term **das Brötchen,** (hard) roll, has several regional variants: in Bavaria and Austria, **die Semmel** is used (cf. the **Leberknödel** recipe above); in Berlin, it is **die Schrippe,** and in Southwest Germany, the term **der Weck** (also **die Wecke**) is commonly used.

The following reading selection and others in subsequent units appear without an English translation. Instead, some vocabulary and some grammatical constructions are glossed in the margin, following the symbol °. Glossed words, most of which are used relatively infrequently, do not appear in the vocabulary lists; others, that appear with greater frequency, will be found in the end-of-unit vocabularies. The meaning of some words you will be able to guess from their context. Given these aids, you should have no difficulty comprehending the German text.

Burgbach, zum Beispiel*

Instead of a translation, we have provided marginal glosses for this text; the glossed word or group of words, followed by the symbol °, is translated as it occurs in the text, not necessarily in basic form or with basic meaning.

Ein Samstagvormittag im Juni. Die Glocken läuten. Eine Taufe° in — baptism
der katholischen Kirche. Die Eltern sind jugoslawische Gastarbeiter,
oder „ausländische Arbeitnehmer",° wie man sie offiziell nennt; der — foreign employees
Vater arbeitet in einer Fabrik im „Industriegebiet" von Burgbach, die
Mutter war bis vor ein paar Wochen Kellnerin in einem Restaurant in 5
Stuttgart. Er ist seit fünf Jahren in Deutschland, sie seit drei Jahren; er
hat sie in Stuttgart kennengelernt, aber geheiratet haben sie zu Hause,
in Jugoslawien. Nun lassen° sie ihr Kind hier in Burgbach taufen,° — have . . . baptized
denn hier sind sie ja nun sozusagen auch zu Hause, obwohl sie in ein
paar Jahren nach Jugoslawien zurückwollen. Nach der Taufe feiern° 10 — celebrate
sie mit ihren jugoslawischen Freunden, die,† wie sie, in einem alten
Fachwerkhaus° wohnen. Das Haus gehört einem Burgbacher Bauer, — half-timbered house
der plötzlich reich geworden ist, weil er einen Teil seines Landes an
eine Baufirma° verkauft hat, die dort ein achtstöckiges Apartment- — construction firm
haus gebaut hat. Mit dem Geld hat er ein modernes Einfamilienhaus 15
gekauft, oben am Hang° über dem Dorf, weil ihm das 300 Jahre alte — slope
Fachwerkhaus auf einmal zu primitiv geworden war.

Eine Stunde später. Die Glocken läuten wieder, aber diesmal in der
alten protestantischen Kirche; sie läuten zur Hochzeit° von zwei — wedding
jungen Burgbachern. Der Bräutigam ist Lehrer an der Grundschule°, 20 — elementary school
gleich hinter der Kirche und gegenüber vom Friedhof°; er stammt aus — cemetery, graveyard
einer alten Weinbauernfamilie, die seit Generationen in einem großen
Haus am Markt wohnt. Sein älterer Bruder macht jetzt, zusammen
mit dem Vater, den Weinbau°; er selbst hat an der Pädagogischen — grows the wine
Hochschule° studiert, —er ist der erste Akademiker° in seiner Fami- 25 — teacher training
lie—, und ist Lehrer geworden. Bis jetzt hat auch er im alten Haus — institution
gewohnt, aber nun zieht er mit seiner jungen Frau in eine Zweizim- — university graduate

*For some details in this reading selection, we are indebted to our colleague George D. Spindler and his book *Burgbach: Urbanization and Identity in a German Village* (with Stanford student collaborators) (New York: Holt, Rinehart and Winston, 1973).
†This text contains a number of relative clauses. All relative clauses are dependent clauses and therefore have verb-last position. They will be introduced systematically in Unit 12.

merwohnung in der neuen Siedlung° am Ortsrand.° Die Braut° ist auch in Burgbach geboren und spricht Schwäbisch wie er, aber ihre Eltern waren als Flüchtlinge 1945 aus Schlesien° ins Dorf gekommen. Ihr Vater war Beamter° in Breslau* gewesen und arbeitet jetzt in der Stadtverwaltung° in Stuttgart.

Nach der Trauung° geht die ganze Hochzeitsgesellschaft° über den Marktplatz und die Marktstraße hinunter zum Gasthof „Krone". Während man dort Rehrücken° und Spätzle ißt, läuten die Glocken noch einmal. Viele Leute, vor allem ältere, bäuerlich gekleidete Leute, die alten Frauen mit langen schwarzen Röcken und schwarzen Kopf-tüchern°, gehen an der Kirche vorbei° zum Friedhof, wo um ein Uhr eine Beerdigung° stattfindet. Die Tote, eine 86-jährige ungarn-deutsche Bäuerin aus Siebenbürgen°, war am Ende des Krieges mit ihrer Familie nach Burgbach gekommen, Flüchtlinge wie so viele, und hatte hier eine neue Heimat° gefunden. Ihre letzten Jahre hatte sie in einem Altenheim° verbracht, wo sie sehr beliebt° gewesen war. Kaum jemand ist mit dem Auto zur Beerdigung gekommen, während am Samstag vorher°, als ein junger Mann beerdigt wurde, der bei einem Autounfall ums Leben gekommen° war, auf der Straße am Friedhof ein Mercedes hinter dem anderen stand.

Während der Pfarrer spricht, donnert eine Boeing 727 der Pan Am über das Dorf, auf dem Weg vom 15 km entfernten Stuttgarter Flug-hafen nach Berlin, und ab und zu hört man Schallplattenmusik aus dem nahen Jugendzentrum°, dem Treffpunkt° für die Burgbacher Teenager. Sie kommen fast alle mit dem Motorrad, sie sind laut, und am liebsten hören sie amerikanische Rockmusik.

Die Zeit ist etwa 1975. Vierzig Jahre vorher, in der Zeit vor dem zweiten Weltkrieg, hätten zwar auch die Glocken geläutet°, aber nicht in der katholischen Kirche, denn die gab es damals noch nicht.

*The city of Breslau, former capital of Silesia, is now known as Wroclaw.

Margin glosses: development / edge of town   bride / Silesia (now part of Poland) / 5 civil servant / city administration / marriage ceremony / wedding party / saddle of venison / 10 kerchief / past the church / funeral / (part of Romania) / 15 home / old-age home / well-liked / on the Saturday before / had lost his life / 20 / youth center / 25 meeting place / would have rung

Gastarbeiterkinder wären in Burgbach nicht getauft worden°, Töch- *would not have been baptized*
ter von schlesischen Beamten hätten nicht in Burgbach geheiratet,
und ungarische Bäuerinnen wären nicht einmal bis an die österreichische Grenze gekommen, geschweige denn° in ein schwäbisches Dorf. *let alone*

1935 lebten in Burgbach 1600 Menschen, unter ihnen nur 16 Katholi- 5
ken, alle anderen waren Protestanten. Die Bevölkerung° war homo- *population*
gen und konservativ; das Leben in Burgbach orientierte sich° am *itself (reflexive)*
Land; Weinberge, Getreidefelder°, Obst- und Gemüsegärten waren *grain fields*
der wichtigste Lebensinhalt°, und in den großen Bauernhäusern hielt *content of life*
man Kühe, Schweine, Gänse und Hühner. An Politik hatte man nicht 10
viel Interesse.

Dann kam der Krieg, und 1945 war das Jahr Null. Von den Burgbachern, die Soldaten geworden waren, kamen über 100 nicht zurück.
Und mit dem Krieg ging auch ein Zeitalter° zu Ende. Burgbach *epoch, age*
konnte nie mehr werden, was es einmal gewesen war. Es begann 15
damals eine Entwicklung, die bis heute nicht abgeschlossen ist:
rapider Bevölkerungszuwachs°, Veränderung° der sozialen Struktur, *population increase / changing*
immer schnellere Urbanisierung.

Heute hat Burgbach eine Bevölkerung von fast 7000 Menschen, von
denen° nur etwas mehr als die Hälfte in Burgbach und Umgebung 20 *of whom*
geboren sind. Fast ein Viertel sind Flüchtlinge und Vertriebene° aus *refugees and expellees*
dem Osten. Schon 1945 schickte die amerikanische Militärregierung° *military government*
die ersten 500 Flüchtlinge, und die Burgbacher mußten ihre Häuser
und ihre Lebensmittel mit ihnen teilen.° Sie kamen aus Pommern°, *share Pomerania (now in Poland)*
aus Schlesien, aus Ostpreußen°; andere aus Polen, aus der Tschecho- 25 *East Prussia (now divided between the Soviet Union and Poland)*
slowakei, aus Ungarn, aus Rumänien, ja sogar aus der Ukraine. Später
kamen Flüchtlinge aus der von Rußland besetzten° Zone, das heißt,
aus dem Teil Deutschlands, der heute die Deutsche Demokratische

Republik, die DDR, ist. Dieser Zustrom° hörte allerdings mit dem Bau   occupied   influx
der Berliner Mauer° im Jahre 1961 auf.   wall

Das „Wirtschaftswunder"° der fünfziger und sechziger Jahre brachte   economic miracle
neuen Wohlstand° nach Burgbach. In fast jedem Dorf entstand° ein   wealth, affluence
Industriegebiet, und mit zunehmender° Industrialisierung nahm auch 5   originated, developed
die Bevölkerung weiter zu. Fast 1000 der 6000 Burgbacher stammen   increasing
aus anderen Teilen der Bundesrepublik, aber auch viele Stuttgarter
haben hier draußen „auf dem Lande" Häuser gebaut, so daß Burgbach heute schon fast ein Vorort° von Stuttgart ist, oder das, was man   suburb
in Amerika eine Schlafzimmer-Gemeinde° nennt.   10 bedroom community

Zuletzt kamen die Gastarbeiter, die heute etwa 10% (zehn Prozent)
der Bevölkerung von Burgbach ausmachen. In den ersten zehn oder
fünfzehn Jahren nach dem zweiten Weltkrieg mußte man in der
Bundesrepublik Arbeitsplätze für die Ostflüchtlinge° schaffen, aber   refugees from the East
dann gab es jahrelang mehr Arbeitsplätze als Arbeitsuchende, und so 15   (i.e., from the former
fing man an, ausländische Arbeiter zu beschäftigen°, zuerst meist   German territories
Italiener, dann Jugoslawen, Spanier, Griechen, Türken. Viele von   and from Eastern
diesen Ausländern leben nun schon jahrelang in Burgbach, und ihre   Europe)
Kinder sprechen nicht nur Türkisch oder Griechisch, sondern auch   employ
fließend Schwäbisch. Es ist ein interessantes Phänomen, daß auch die 20
Kinder der aus Ost- und Norddeutschland Zugewanderten° neben   immigrants
dem Hochdeutschen auch den Dialekt lernen, der ihren Eltern für immer unzugänglich° bleibt.   impenetrable

Für die alten Weinbauern sind die „Neuen" immer noch „Fremde",
auch nach dreißig Jahren noch. Die mittlere Generation hat die neue 25
Zeit akzeptiert, und für die jungen Leute ist es ganz selbstverständ-

Es gibt Weinorte
und es gibt Bierstädte.

lich°, daß Burgbach kein Dorf mehr ist, sondern Teil eines städtischen   self-understood, a
Großraumes°, heterogen, zentrifugal und mit einer sehr komplexen   matter of course
Sozialstruktur. Burgbach ist immer noch ein „beliebter Weinort", wie   metropolitan urban area
es in den Broschüren für den Fremdenverkehr heißt; zugleich aber ist
es ein moderner Industrieort, der ebensogut in der Nähe von jeder 5
anderen Großstadt liegen könnte.

Dennoch lebt die Vergangenheit°. Auch die rapide Urbanisierung   past
kann eine Tradition von vielen hundert Jahren nicht einfach aus-
wischen°. Alte Sitten und Gebräuche° leben fort; die alten Bauwerke°   wipe out   ways and
erinnern an die Geschichte, und der Zement, sozusagen, ist der 10   customs   buildings
schwäbische Dialekt.

(Fortsetzung folgt—continued in Unit 9)

Exercises

A. Transform the ten sentences of this exercise according to the following pattern.

> **Er wohnt in Berlin.**
> **a. Ich glaube, er wohnt in Berlin.**
> **b. Ich glaube nicht, daß er in Berlin wohnt.**
> **c. Ich möchte wissen, ob er in Berlin wohnt.**

SEE
ANALYSIS
89-90
(pp. 214-215)

1. Ernst Wagner studiert Mathematik.
2. Der Wagen gehört Frau Körner.
3. Sie kann sie sehen.
4. Er will mir die Stadt zeigen.
5. Frau Lenz geht mit Frau Hoffmann ins Kino.
6. Er muß heute nach Düsseldorf.
7. Hans will ohne Inge ins Theater gehen.
8. Herr Meyer hat zu viel Wein getrunken.
9. Sie sind gestern in Berlin gewesen.
10. Er hat in Innsbruck einen Freund besucht.

B. Ask correct questions for the following answers. Your questions should ask for the italicized parts of the answers.

> **Er geht *heute abend* ins Kino.**
> **Wann geht er ins Kino?**

Then restate the question, starting with **Ich möchte wissen.**

> **Ich möchte wissen, wann er ins Kino geht.**

SEE
ANALYSIS
92
(p. 219)

1. Ihr Mann ist *gestern* nach Wien gefahren.
2. Erika war gestern *in Berlin*.
3. Es (das Buch) gehört *meinem Vater*.
4. Er hat ihr *ein Buch* geschenkt.
5. Er heißt *Fritz*.
6. *Mein Vater* hat das gesagt.
7. Er geht *mit Inge* ins Kino.
8. Karin war *vierzehn Tage* in Burgbach.

C. Join the following pairs of sentences to form open conditions. The first sentence should always become the **wenn**-clause.

> **Es regnet morgen. Wir gehen ins Kino.**
> **Wenn es morgen regnet, gehen wir ins Kino.**

1. Du hast Geld. Du kannst ein Haus kaufen.
2. Du hast kein Geld. Du kannst das Haus nicht kaufen.
3. Er studiert Mathematik. Er muß intelligent sein.
4. Morgen regnet es nicht. Wir besuchen euch.
5. Ihr wollt ins Kino gehen. Wir gehen mit.
6. Herr Meyer wohnt in Berlin. Ich kann ihn besuchen.
7. Er ist dein Freund. Er hilft dir bestimmt.

SEE
ANALYSIS
97
(p. 221)

D. Change the following sentences to dependent clauses as indicated. Note that in each case you will have to rearrange the subject, and, in some cases, other elements as well.

> **Gestern abend ist er sehr früh ins Bett gegangen.**
> **Ich hoffe, daß er gestern abend sehr früh ins Bett gegangen ist.**

1. Seit ihrem Besuch in München hatte ich Charlotte nicht mehr gesehen.
   Ich war unglücklich, weil _____.

2. Von Wien aus habe ich Charlotte einen Brief geschrieben.
   Ich habe nichts von Charlotte gehört, obwohl _____.

3. Leider war sie schon nach Graz gefahren.
   Sie hat nicht geschrieben, da _____.

4. In Graz hat sie unser Freund Gerhard am Bahnhof abgeholt.
   Heute weiß ich, daß _____.

SEE
ANALYSIS
91
(p. 218)

E. In the following sentences, change the **wenn**- and **weil**-clauses to **um . . . zu**-clauses.

1. Wenn Gudrun ins Theater gehen wollte, mußte sie immer nach Salzburg fahren.
   Um _____ zu können, mußte _____.

2. Wenn man in Baden-Baden wohnen will, muß man viel Geld haben.
   Um _____ zu können, muß _____.

3. Er lernt Deutsch, weil er Nietzsche lesen will.
   Er lernt Deutsch, um _____ zu können.

4. Herr Köhler ist in die Stadt gefahren, weil er seiner Frau ein Buch kaufen will.
   Herr Köhler ist in die Stadt gefahren, um _____ zu kaufen.

SEE
ANALYSIS
82
(p. 184)

F. Repeat the following sentences three times, with **bitte** in the front field, the inner field, and the end field.

> **Seien Sie vorsichtig.**   **Bitte, seien Sie vorsichtig.**
> **Seien Sie bitte vorsichtig.**
> **Seien Sie vorsichtig, bitte.**

SEE
ANALYSIS
98–102
(pp. 222–226)

1. Schreib ihr doch einen Brief.
2. Laden Sie ihn doch auch ein.
3. Bleibt noch ein bißchen hier.

4. Geh ins Bett.
5. Kommt nicht zu spät zum Essen.

G. Change the following questions to imperatives; use **doch mal** in the inner field.

SEE
ANALYSIS
98–102
(pp. 222–226)

1. Kannst du uns eine Tasse Kaffee machen?
2. Könnt ihr uns in Basel besuchen?
3. Kannst du mir ein bißchen in der Küche helfen?
4. Kannst du einen Moment ruhig sein, bitte?
5. Können Sie mit uns in die Berge fahren?

H. Change the following imperatives to the **du**-form and the **ihr**-form. Use **du** and **ihr** only when **Sie** is italicized.

SEE
ANALYSIS
99
(p. 222)

1. Seien Sie doch nicht so aufgeregt!
2. Stehen Sie doch morgen etwas früher auf!
3. Bringen Sie mir ruhig noch eine Tasse Kaffee!
4. Gehen *Sie* doch mal mit Tante Amalie ins Museum!
5. Sprechen Sie ruhig lauter!
6. Gute Nacht, schlafen Sie gut.
7. Denken Sie mal, wen ich gestern getroffen habe!
8. Fahren Sie doch mal eben zur Post.
9. Bringen Sie die Bücher bitte in die Bibliothek zurück.
10. Nehmen Sie uns doch bitte mit.
11. Schreien Sie doch nicht so laut!
12. Schwimmen *Sie* doch mal über den Rhein!

I. Change the following complaints into imperatives. Use **doch bitte** in the inner field.

SEE
ANALYSIS
100
(p. 223)

1. Du rauchst zuviel.
2. Du gibst zuviel Geld aus.
3. Du bist immer so unfreundlich.

4. Können Sie mir kein Zimmer mit Bad geben?
5. Kannst du nicht mal vernünftig sein?

J. Express in German. All German sentences should be imperatives; use the imperative form indicated by the pronoun following the English sentence.

SEE
ANALYSIS
99–102
(pp. 222–226)

1. Be good to him. (Sie)
2. Don't be so nervous. (du)
3. Please be here at nine o'clock. (ihr)
4. Take me along, please. (du)
5. Why don't *you* talk to him for a change? (du)
6. Sleep well. (Sie)
7. Stay well. (Sie)
8. Don't always read the *Spiegel*. (du)
9. Don't talk with the driver. (impersonal)
10. Wash and cut (**klein schneiden**) the vegetables and cook with the meat for 2 hours. (impersonal)

K. Rewrite the following sentences in the future tense. Leave out the time phrases.

SEE
ANALYSIS
103
(p. 226)

1. Wir gehen morgen ins Theater.
2. Ich besuche Sie nächste Woche, Herr Schulte.
3. Für die Reise nächsten Sommer brauchen wir viel Geld.

4. Hilfst du mir morgen bei der Arbeit?

5. Das Wetter ist morgen bestimmt gut.

L. Rewrite the following sentences, using the future tense to express present probability.

> Ich glaube, er ist noch hier.
> Er wird (wohl) noch hier sein.

1. Ich glaube, Kurt arbeitet noch.

2. Ich glaube, er will ihn nicht einladen.

3. Ich glaube, es ist zu warm zum Schilaufen.

4. Ich glaube, Katharina wartet schon auf uns.

5. Ich glaube, er muß wieder nach Zürich fahren.

SEE ANALYSIS 103 (p. 226)

M. List the antonyms of the following adjectives. Then form short sentences with all of them.

> jung — alt
> Das Kind ist jung.
> Der Großvater ist alt.

neu	— _____		hoch	— _____
groß	— _____		weit	— _____
viel	— _____		billig	— _____
lang	— _____		kalt	— _____
gut	— _____		schnell	— _____
wahr	— _____		süß	— _____
richtig	— _____			

Vocabulary

abschließen	to close
allerdings	however
amerikanisch	American
der Arbeitnehmer, -	employee, worker
aufgeregt	excited
aufhören	to stop, to cease
ausgeben	to give out, to spend
ausländisch	foreign
backen	to bake
das Bad, ̈er	bath(room)
der Bahnsteig, -e	platform (in a station)
die Banane, -n	banana
der Bau	construction
das Bauwerk, -e	building
die Baufirma, *pl.*	construction firm
die Baufirmen	
der Bauer, -n	farmer
die Bäuerin, -nen	farmer's wife
der Beamte, -n	civil servant

bekannt	(well-) known
unbekannt	unknown
beliebt	well-liked
beschäftigen	to employ
besetzt	busy, occupied
der Betrieb, -e	place of work; plant, factory
die Bevölkerung	population
der Bevölkerungs-zuwachs	population increase
bevor	before
das Blatt, ̈er	leaf
das Lorbeerblatt, ̈er	laurel leaf, bay leaf
brüllen	to yell
daß	that (*conj.*)
direkt	direct(ly)
der Donner, -	thunder
donnern	to thunder

eben	just (*adv.* expressing casualness)	die Krone, -n	crown
		die Kuh, ⁅e	cow
ebensogut	just as well	die Küste, -n	coast
eintreten	to enter	die Nordseeküste	North Sea coast
einziehen	to move in	laut	loud
entstehen	to originate	läuten	to ring
die Entwicklung, -en	development	leise	quiet(ly)
erinnern	to remind	die Mauer, -n	wall
erreichen	to reach (destination)	das Mehl	flour
etwa	about; by any chance	die Mehlspeise, -n	dish made with flour
die Fabrik', -en	factory		
falsch	false, wrong	meinen	to think, express an opinion
fast	almost		
feiern	to celebrate	die Menge, -n	quantity, lot
der Feind, -e	enemy	mitbringen	to bring (along)
das Ferngespräch, -e	long-distance call	möblieren	to furnish (a room)
fernsehen	to watch TV	möbliert	furnished
fließend	fluent; flowing	modern'	modern
formen	to form, mold	nachdem	after
freundlich	friendly	nervös	nervous
unfreundlich	unfriendly	oben (*adv.*)	up, above
froh	happy	offiziell'	official
die Gans, ⁅e	goose	öffnen	to open
geboren	born	das Ohr, -en	ear
das Gemüse	vegetables	parken	to park
gemütlich	cozy	die Party, -s	party
das Gericht, -e	dish (on menu)	das Phänomen'	phenomenon
der Geschmack	taste	die Platte, -n	music record
die Glocke, -n	bell	der Plattenspieler, -	record player
hacken	to chop.	die Politik'	politics
das Gehackte	ground meat	die Post	mail; post office
halten	to hold	primitiv'	primitive
halt	just	privat'	private
die Hand, ⁅e	hand	reich	rich
die Heimat	home, native land	das Restaurant', -s	restaurant
herzlich	cordial	das Rezept', -e	recipe
hinter	behind	richtig	correct, right
hintereinander her	one behind the other	der Rock, ⁅e	skirt
		schaden	to damage
die Hochzeit, -en	wedding	schade	too bad, what a shame
die Hochzeitsgesell- schaft, -en	wedding party		
		das Schaf, -e	sheep
das Hotel', -s	hotel	der Schafskäse	sheep cheese
das Huhn, ⁅er	chicken	schaffen	to create, to make
das Interes'se, -n	interest	der Schall	sound, ring
jemand	somebody, someone	die Schallplatte, -n	record
katho'lisch	Catholic	die Schallplatten- musik	record music
der Knochen, -	bone		
der Kalbsknochen, -	calf's bone	schneiden	to cut
konservativ	conservative	schön	pretty, beautiful

selbständig	independent	unter	under
selbstverständlich	self-evident, obvious;	untermischen	to mix
	of course	die Veränderung, -en	change
sich	himself, herself	die Vergangenheit	past
	(*reflexive*)	vergessen	to forget
die Siedlung, -en	development, settlement	vernünftig	reasonable
sowieso	anyhow, in any case	verschieden	different
sozusagen	so to say, as it were	die Versicherung, -en	insurance; assurance
das Spaß, ⸚e	fun; joke	vorgestern	the day before yester-
Spaß haben	to have fun		day
Spaß machen	to joke	der Vorort, -e	suburb
stammen	to come from	vorsichtig	careful
stattfinden	to take place	während	during, while
steigen	to climb	die Wanderung, -en	hike
einsteigen	to get in/on (train,	waschen	to wash
	car)	der Weg, -e	way
aussteigen	to get out/off	weg	away
	(train, car)	weggehen	to go away
der Stock, ⸚e	stick; floor (of a building)	weich	soft
stören	to disturb	weil (*subord. conj.*)	because
Nicht stören!	Do not disturb!	der Weltkrieg, -e	world war
das Tal, ⸚er	valley	die Wohnung, -en	apartment
die Tat, -en	action, deed	wunderschön	wonderful; very
die Taxe, -n	taxi		beautiful
das Taxi, -s		das Zeitalter, -	age, epoch
der Teil, -e	piece, part	ziemlich	rather
der Tod	death	zugleich	at the same time
tot	dead	zuletzt	last, lastly, finally
trotzdem	nevertheless	zunehmen	to increase
typisch	typical	zunehmend	increasing
die Umgebung	surroundings	zwar	indeed, to be sure
unten	down, down below,	die Zwiebel, -n	onion
	downstairs		

Additional Vocabulary

ab und zu	now and then	aufbleiben	to stay awake
der Akademiker, -	university graduate	aufweichen	to soften
akzeptieren	to accept	auswischen	to wipe out
das Altenheim, -e	old-age home	der Autounfall, ⸚e	car accident
die Altstadt, ⸚e	old city	die Bar	bar, tavern
die Ananas	pineapple	bäuerlich	rural
anschnallen	to fasten, to buckle on	die Beerdigung, -en	funeral
die Aprikose, -n	apricot	beerdigen	to bury
der Arbeitsplatz, ⸚e	place of work	die Bohne, -n	bean
die Aubergine, -n	eggplant	die Bohnensuppe	bean soup

die Braut, -e	bride	das Pfefferkorn	peppercorn
der Bräutigam, -e	groom	rapid'	rapid
der Dom, -e	cathedral	räuchern	to smoke (meat)
die Domglocke, -n	cathedral bell	rechtzeitig	on time
dünsten	to simmer; to steam	der Rehrücken, -	saddle of venison
einordnen	(traffic) to get into the correct lane; to merge	das Rind, -er	cattle
		das Rindfleisch	beef
		die Rindsleber	beef liver
entfernt	distant	das Rippchen, -	cured and smoked pork chop
das Examen, -	examination		
das Fachwerkhaus, ⸚er	half-timbered house	roman'tisch	romantic
feingeschnitten	finely sliced, chopped	salzen	to salt
der Flüchtling, -e	refugee	sarka'stisch	sarcastic
fortleben	to survive	die Sellerie	celery
die Fortsetzung, -en	continuation	die Stadtverwaltung, -en	city administration
der Fotohändler, -	photo-dealer	das Studentenheim, -e	dormitory
der Fremdenverkehr	foreign visitors, tourist traffic	die Taufe, -n	baptism
		der Teig	dough
der Friedhof, ⸚e	cemetery, graveyard	toll	crazy; great
der Gastarbeiter, -	foreign worker	die Toma'te, -n	tomato
der Gasthof, ⸚e	inn, restaurant	traditionell'	traditional
geschweige	not to mention	die Trauung, -en	marriage ceremony, wedding
das Getreidefeld, -er	grain field		
die Gitar're, -n	guitar	der Treffpunkt, -e	meeting place
grillen	to grill, to barbeque	die U-Bahn	subway
großartig	wonderful, magnificent	übergießen	to pour over
		umrechnen	to convert
die Grundschule, -n	elementary school	unzulänglich	insufficient
das Gulasch	goulash	die Urbanisierung	urbanization
die Gulaschsuppe	goulash soup	die Variante, -n	variation
der Hang, ⸚e	slope	verarbeiten	to process
hinunterrennen	to run down (a street)	die Verarbeitung	processing
das Industriegebiet, -e	industrial area	verdammt	damned
die Industrialisierung	industrialization	verdammt noch mal!	damn it!
das Jugendzentrum	youth center		
die Karot'te, -n	carrot	vermissen	to miss
klappern	to rattle	der Vertriebene, -n	expellee
kleiden	to dress	vorbeigehen	to pass by
kneten	to knead	weltbekannt	world-famous
knusprig	crispy	werktags	weekdays
kochend	boiling	der Wohlstand	wealth, affluence
lauwarm	lukewarm	das Wunder, -	miracle
der Lebensinhalt	content of life	das Wirtschaftswunder	economic miracle
die Militärregierung	military government		
nachsehen	to check	würzen	to spice
orientieren	to orient	zudecken	to cover
der Ortsrand, -er	edge of town	der Zugewanderte, -n	immigrant
die Petersilie	parsley	zugießen	to pour
pfeffern	to pepper	der Zustrom, ⸚e	influx

Strong Verbs and Irregular Weak Verbs

abschließen		schloß ab	abgeschloßen	to close
aufbleiben		blieb auf	ist aufgeblieben	to stay awake
ausgeben	gibt aus	gab aus	ausgegeben	to give out, spend
backen	bäckt	buk (backte)	gebacken	to bake
eintreten	tritt ein	trat ein	ist eingetreten	to enter
einziehen		zog ein	ist eingezogen	to move in
entstehen		entstand	ist entstanden	to originate
fernsehen	sieht fern	sah fern	ferngesehen	to watch TV
halten	hält	hielt	gehalten	to hold
hinunterrennen		rannte hinunter	hinuntergerannt	to run down
mitbringen		brachte mit	mitgebracht	to bring (along)
nachsehen	sieht nach	sah nach	nachgesehen	to check
schaffen		schuf	geschaffen	to create
schneiden		schnitt	geschnitten	to cut
stattfinden		fand statt	stattgefunden	to take place
steigen		stieg	ist gestiegen	to climb
übergießen		goß über	übergossen	to pour over
vergessen	vergißt	vergaß	vergessen	to forget
vorbeigehen		ging vorbei	ist vorbeigegangen	to pass by
waschen	wäscht	wusch	gewaschen	to wash
zugießen		goß zu	zugegossen	to pour
zunehmen	nimmt zu	nahm zu	zugenommen	to increase

Die wichtigsten Verkehrszeichen
aus der neuen Straßenverkehrsordnung
Kreuzung Vorfahrt von rechts
Kurve (rechts)
Gefahrstelle
Doppelkurve (zunächst rechts)
Unebene Fahrbahn
Zusatzschild schlechter Fahrbahnrand
10%
Gefälle
12%
Steigung
Zusatzschild Wintersport
Steinschlag
Seitenwind
Verengte Fahrbahn
Einseitig (rechts)
Schleudergefahr bei Nässe oder Schmutz
Baustelle
Gegenverkehr
Bewegliche Brücke
Ufer
Zusatzschild unerwartete Glatteisbildung
Lichtzeichen-anlage
Radfahrer kreuzen
Kinder
Fußgänger-überweg
Treiben von Großtieren
Flugbetrieb
Wildwechsel
Zusatztafel: Abknickende Vorfahrt
Vorfahrt gewähren!
STOP
Ankündigung des Stop-Zeichens
STOP
Halt! Vorfahrt gewähren!
Dem Gegenverkehr Vorrang gewähren!
Verbot für Kraftwagen
Verbot für Lkw über 2,8 t zul. Gesamtgewicht u. Zugmasch.
Gleiche Zeichen mit Symbolen Krafträder, Lastzüge, Radfahrer, Fußgänger, Reiter usw.
Verbot für Fahrzeuge aller Art
Schnee-ketten sind vor-geschrieben
Verbot einer Fahrtrichtung oder Einfahrt
5,5t
8t
2m
3m
Verbot für Fahrzeuge, deren tatsächliches Gewicht, tatsächliche Achslast, Breite, Höhe oder Länge ein bestimmtes Maß überschreitet
60
Zulässige Höchstgeschwindigkeit Ende
Verbot für Kfz aller Art, mehrspurige Kfz zu überholen Ende
Überholverbot für Lkw mit zul. Gesamtgew. über 2,8 t sowie Lkw und Zugmasch. m. Anh. Ende
30
Vorgeschriebene Mindestgeschwindigkeit Ende
Ende aller Streckenverbote
Haltverbot
Eingeschränktes Haltverbot
70-110 km
Richtgeschwindigkeit
Vorfahrt
3 Stunden
Zonenhalteverbot für einen Stadtbezirk Ende
H
H
Haltestelle Kraftfahrlinien Straßenbahnen
Vorfahrtstraße Ende
Zusatzschild Halteverbot auch auf dem Seitenstreifen
Kennzeichen für Bahnübergänge in Schienenhöhe
Warnkreuz für Bahnübergänge
Dreistreifige Bake 240 m vor beschranktem Bahnübergang
Einstreifige Bake 80 m vor Bahnübergang
Zweistreifige Bake 160 m vor Bahnübergang
Dreistreifige Bake 240 m vor unbeschranktem Bahnübergang
Vorgeschriebene Fahrtrichtung:
Geradeaus
Hier rechts
Rechts
Links vorbeifahren
Rechts oder Geradeaus
Einbahnstraße
Einbahn-straße
Sonderwege
Autobahn
Ende der Autobahn
Radfahrer
Reiter
Fußgänger
Kraftfahrstraße Ende
P
P
Parkplatz (auf Gehweg)
Schülerlotsen
Schülerlotsen
Wasser Schutzgebiet
Wasser-schutzgebiet
Sackgasse
TAXI
Taxistand
Laternen, die nicht die ganze Nacht brennen
Vorrang vor Gegenverkehr
Fußgänger-überweg
35
Bundes-straße
E36
Europa-straße
Diese Schilder geben keine Vorfahrt
1000 m
Baustellen-lenkungstafel
Wilster Kreis Steinburg
Wilster Kreis Steinburg
Anfang und Ende einer geschlossenen Ortschaft und der für diese geltenden Verkehrsvorschriften
U22
Bedarfsumleitung für Autobahn
Hilfsposten
Fußgänger-unter- oder -überführung
Zusatzschild: Kindern ist erlaubt auf der Fahrbahn zu spielen
200 m
Zusatzschild: Länge der Verbots- oder Gefahrenstrecke
Gleiches Schild mit anderen Symbolen für Autobahnhotel, Autobahngasthaus, Autobahnkiosk
Pannenhilfe
Neben den in diesen Zeichen gezeigten Symbolen sind die nachfolgenden weiteren Symbole zugelassen
Kraftfahrzeuge, die nicht schneller als 20 km/h fahren können oder dürfen
Kennzeichnungspflichtige Kraftfahrzeuge mit explosionsgefährlichen Stoffen
Straßenbahn
Kraftomnibus
Personenkraftwagen mit Anhänger
Lastkraftwagen mit Anhänger
Krafträder auch mit Beiwagen
Kleinkrafträder und Fahrräder mit Hilfsmotor
Gespannfuhrwerke
Fußgänger mit Hand-fahrzeugen oder sperrigen Gegenständen
Wichtige Verkehrszeichen europäischer Länder
Hupverbot
Bergpoststr. Schweiz
Bergpoststr. Italien
Überholen verboten
Verbot des Abbiegens

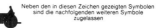

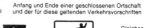

UNIT 9 The Subjunctive

Wherever you go in Central Europe, you will be reminded of the past. You will constantly experience flashbacks into history—through talking to local people, looking at the architecture, visiting museums, and studying place names. The central square in the old city of Frankfurt is called the *Römerberg*, Hill of the Romans, because a Roman settlement was located there to protect the ford across the Main River which later gave the town its name: Frankfurt means "the ford of the Franks." You will encounter history if you listen to Bach in the Thomaskirche in Leipzig or to Mozart in the palace at Brühl, once the summer residence of the archbishops of Cologne, or if you watch *Jedermann*, Hugo von Hofmannsthal's 1911 re-creation of the fifteenth-century *Everyman* play, during the summer festival in Salzburg. High culture and low culture feed on the same tradition.

The conversations in this unit, on the other hand, deal with one of the nuisances of a modern affluent society, traffic and traffic jams. You can create additional conversations by using the "traffic vocabulary" that precedes the conversations, and you are encouraged to make lists of words on other topics, such as school and university, shopping, eating out.

The traffic conversations are anticipated in the pattern sections, where the same vocabulary is used to express such sentiments as "I wish I could find a parking space" and "If only I had taken the bus." In sentences such as these, since they express what might be but is not, German must use the subjunctive mood. English, with but few exceptions, no longer has a subjunctive, and you will again have to do quite a bit of drilling before you get used to a new set of verb forms and before you will be able to use these forms correctly and spontaneously.

Patterns

[1] The Future Subjunctive: the **würde**-Forms

Ich wollte, du würdest mitgehen.	I wish you would come along.	**SEE ANALYSIS 106–107**
Ich wünschte, du würdest mitgehen.	I wish you would come along.	(pp. 253–255)
Es wäre schön, wenn du mitfahren würdest.	It would be nice if you came along.	
Wie wäre es, wenn er mitfahren würde?	How would it be if he came along?	
Wenn er doch nur mitfahren würde.	If only he would come along.	

247

Es wäre gut, wenn wir einmal früher in die Stadt fahren würden. Dann würden wir bestimmt noch einen Parkplatz finden.

It would be good if we drove to town earlier for a change. Then we would still find a place to park, I'm sure.

Wenn wir vor dem Berufsverkehr fahren würden, würden wir im Parkhaus am Markt noch Platz finden.

If we went before the commuter traffic, we would still find a space in the parking garage at the Market Square.

Wir würden schneller hinkommen, wenn wir die Autobahn* nehmen würden.

We would get there faster if we took the Autobahn.

Ich würde gern mitten in der Stadt wohnen. Dann würde ich nur noch zu Fuß gehen.

I would like to live in the middle of the city. Then I would only walk.

An deiner Stelle würde ich die Bundesstraße† nehmen. Auf der Autobahn sind um diese Zeit doch immer Stauungen.

If I were you (in your place) I would take the Bundesstraße. There are always slow-downs on the Autobahn at this hour.

Ich würde lieber hier draußen einkaufen gehen. Dann würden wir viel Zeit sparen.

I would rather go shopping out here. Then we would save a lot of time.

Am liebsten würde ich heute zu Hause bleiben.

I would like best to stay at home today.

Bundesstraße 14 in der Nähe von Stuttgart.

[2] The Present Subjunctive of Weak and Strong Verbs

SEE
ANALYSIS
108
(p. 257)

Ich wünschte, wir wohnten nicht so weit draußen vor der Stadt.

I wish we didn't live so far outside the city.

Ich wünschte, wir würden nicht so weit draußen wohnen.

I wish we wouldn't live so far out.

---

*The **Autobahn** (cf. **Eisenbahn**) is the system of four- or six-lane superhighways that crisscrosses all of Central Europe.
†A **Bundesstraße** is a federal highway. These are usually well-improved roads that bypass villages and small towns, though many are still only two-lane roads. They are referred to by their numbers, e.g., B 14.

Wie wäre es, wenn wir zum Mittagessen in der Stadt blieben (bleiben würden)?

How would it be if we stayed in town for lunch? (How about staying in town for lunch?)

Ich ginge eigentlich gern mal wieder in den Ratskeller.

I would like to go to the Ratskeller again for a change.

Wenn er den Wagen in einer Seitenstraße parken würde, brauchte er nicht ins Parkhaus zu fahren.

If he parked the car in a side street, he wouldn't have to go to the parking garage.

Wenn er sehr früh führe, bekäme er auch direkt am Dom noch einen Platz zum Parken.

If he went very early, he would of course find a place to park, even right by the cathedral.

Wenn es doch nur nicht schon wieder regnete (regnen würde). Ich wollte, die Sonne schiene endlich wieder.

If only it weren't raining again. I wish the sun would shine again at last.

Ja, wenn die Sonne wieder schiene, gäbe es auch nicht mehr so viele Unfälle auf der Autobahn.

Yes, if the sun were out again, there also wouldn't be so many accidents on the Autobahn anymore.

Und wenn die Leute vernünftiger führen, würde auch nicht so viel passieren.

And if people drove more reasonably, not as much would happen either (there wouldn't be so many accidents).

VARIATIONS

Complete the following sentences with the correct subjunctive form of the verb in parentheses; then repeat the sentence, replacing the subjunctive with a **würde**-form.

> **Ich wollte, er _____ nicht immer mit dem Wagen. (fahren)**
> **Ich wollte, er führe nicht immer mit dem Wagen.**
> **Ich wollte, er würde nicht immer mit dem Wagen fahren.**

Ich wollte, er _____ bald aus der Stadt zurück. (kommen)

Ich wollte, der Wagen _____ mir. (gehören)

Ich wollte, es _____ nicht so lange, einen Parkplatz zu finden. (dauern)

Wenn er nur nicht immer so lange in der Stadt _____. (bleiben)

An deiner Stelle _____ ich den Wagen zu Hause (lassen) und _____ mit der Bahn. (fahren)

Den Wagen zu Hause lassen? Das _____ ich nie. (tun)

[3] The Present Subjunctive of **haben**, **sein**, and the Modals

Ich wollte, wir hätten in Amerika so viele Fußgängerzonen* wie in Deutschland.

I wish we had as many pedestrian zones in America as (they have) in Germany.

SEE ANALYSIS 109 (p. 258)

*In recent years, more and more cities have removed all vehicular traffic from large parts of their downtown areas, particularly where the core of medieval towns is still intact. Usually, this includes the area around the city hall and the cathedral.

Dann wäre es ein Vergnügen, in der Innenstadt einkaufen zu gehen.	Then it would be a pleasure to go shopping in the inner city (downtown).
Wenn die Straßen um den Dom herum nicht so eng wären, hätten wir sicher keine Fußgängerzone.	If the streets around the cathedral weren't so narrow, we probably wouldn't have a pedestrian zone.
Der Verkehr wäre noch viel schlimmer, wenn es keine U-Bahn gäbe.	The traffic would be much worse if there were no subway.
Ich wollte, ich könnte mit der Straßenbahn fahren; aber da müßte ich dreimal umsteigen, und das dauert mir zu lange.	I wish I could take the streetcar; but then I would have to change three times, and that takes too long for me.
Wenn du doch nur nicht immer mit dem Wagen fahren wolltest.	If only you didn't always want to take the car.
Wir sollten eigentlich mal versuchen, die U-Bahn zu nehmen.	We really ought to try taking the subway sometime.
U-Bahn? Das wäre eine Idee. Wir könnten am Markt aussteigen und dann zu Fuß	Subway? That would be an idea. We could get out at the Market Square and then

B: Was würdest Du als erstes tun, wenn Du ein Mensch wärst?

W: Endlich mal ein Glas von unserem Whisky trinken.

gehen. Dann wären wir in fünf Minuten im Kaufhof.* Das würde Benzin, Zeit und Nerven sparen.

walk. We'd be at the Kaufhof in five minutes. That would save gasoline, time, and nerves.

VARIATIONS

Complete the following sentences with proper subjunctive forms. In several sentences, more than one verb is possible.

Ich wollte, das Benzin _____ nicht so teuer.

Wie _____ es, wenn du mal mit der Straßenbahn fahren _____.

Du _____ auch mal mit der U-Bahn fahren.

Dann _____ du aber ein bißchen früher aufstehen.

Wenn ich genug Geld _____, _____ ich mir einen neuen Diesel kaufen.

Ja, wenn das Wörtchen „wenn" nicht wäre, dann _____ du schon lange ein Millionär.

[4] The Past Subjunctive

Ich wollte, wir wären nicht am Wochenende in die Berge gefahren. Der Wochenendverkehr war wieder mal unmöglich.

I wish we hadn't gone to the mountains over the weekend. The weekend traffic on the Autobahn was impossible again.

SEE ANALYSIS 110 (p. 259)

Ich wollte, die† hätten nicht überall Stopschilder hingestellt; dann käme man viel schneller vorwärts.

I wish they hadn't put up stop signs everywhere; then you could get ahead much faster.

Wenn nur das Benzin nicht so teuer geworden wäre.

If only gasoline hadn't become so expensive.

Ja, wir hätten einen Diesel kaufen sollen; dann könnten wir heute viel billiger fahren.

Yes, we should have bought a diesel; then we could drive much more cheaply today.

Wenn nicht alle Ampeln rot gewesen wären, wäre ich bestimmt rechtzeitig hier gewesen.

If all traffic lights hadn't been red, I'm sure I would have gotten here on time.

Wenn du nicht so schnell gefahren wärst, hättest du keinen Strafzettel bekommen. Aber du mußt ja immer rasen wie ein Irrer.

If you hadn't driven so fast you wouldn't have gotten a ticket. But you've always got to race like an idiot.

Wenn das Wetter besser gewesen wäre, hätte es auf der Autobahn nicht so viele Unfälle gegeben.

If the weather had been better, there wouldn't have been so many accidents on the Autobahn.

Aber wenn es nicht geschneit hätte, hätten wir nicht schilaufen können.

But if it hadn't snowed, we could not have gone skiing.

* Name of a department store chain.

† In colloquial German, **die** is used as the plural of the impersonal **man** and corresponds to *they* as used above.

Lotti wäre letztes Wochenende gern mitge-
fahren, aber sie hatte zu viel zu tun.

Lotti would have liked to come along last
weekend, but she had too much to do.

Ich wäre lieber zu Hause geblieben. Dann
wäre ich am Montag nicht so müde
gewesen.

I would rather have stayed at home. Then I
wouldn't have been so tired on Monday.

Der Verkehr war so stark, daß mein Mann
am liebsten den Wagen verkauft hätte
und mit der Bahn nach Hause gefahren
wäre.

The traffic was so heavy that my husband
would have liked to sell the car and take
the train home.

VARIATIONS

Change the following pairs of sentences into irreal **wenn**-clauses with irreal
conclusions.

Es war neblig, und wir konnten die Berge nicht sehen. Wenn es nicht so neblig _____,
_____ wir die Berge _____ .

Erika studierte *auch* Germanistik, und so haben wir uns kennengelernt. Wenn Erika nicht
auch Germanistik _____, _____ wir uns nicht _____ .

Ich hatte kein Geld. Ich konnte nicht nach Österreich fahren. Wenn ich Geld _____
_____, _____ ich nach Österreich _____ .

[5] **hätte** in Dependent Clauses with "Double Infinitive"

SEE
ANALYSIS
111
(p. 260)

Wenn Dora nicht hätte nach München
fahren müssen, hätte Schulz sie nie kennengelernt.*

If Dora hadn't had to go to Munich, Schulz
would never have met her.

Wenn du nicht hättest kommen können,
wäre ich sehr unglücklich gewesen.

If you had not been able to come, I would
have been very unhappy.

Wenn er gestern abend nicht hätte zu Hause
bleiben müssen, hätte er mit uns ins
Kino gehen können.

If he had not had to stay home last night, he
could have gone to the movies with us.

VARIATIONS

Wolfgang konnte nicht kommen. Es wäre nett gewesen, wenn _____ .
Andrea durfte nicht mitgehen. Es wäre nett gewesen, wenn _____ .
Bernhard mußte zu Hause bleiben. Es wäre nett gewesen, wenn _____ .
Sie hat nie zu kochen brauchen. Es wäre nett gewesen, wenn sie auch einmal _____ .

[6] Polite Requests

SEE
ANALYSIS
112
(p. 261)

Guten Abend. Hätten Sie vielleicht noch
ein Zimmer frei?

Good evening. Would you by any chance
still have a room available?

Ich hätte gern ein Zimmer mit Bad oder
Dusche, —und mit WC.

I'd like a room with bath or shower—and
with a toilet.

*In irreal **wenn**-clauses, **nicht müssen** is used rather than **nicht brauchen zu**.

Könnten (Würden) Sie mich bitte um sieben Uhr wecken? — Could (Would) you please wake me at seven o'clock?

Dürfte ich um das Telefonbuch bitten? — Could I ask you for the telephone book?

Ich hätte gerne Weinstadt bei Stuttgart, —Vorwahl 07151, und die Nummer ist 6 38 20. — I'd like to have Weinstadt near Stuttgart —area code 07151, and the number is 6 38 20.

Analysis

106 The Subjunctive Mood: Definition

All verb forms used in Units 1 to 8 refer to facts and real events or, occasionally, to open conditions which may turn out to be real events. All these forms belong to the *indicative* (reality) *mood*. In contrast, all verb forms which refer in some recognizable way to situations which do not actually exist or to events which are only hypothetical, imaginative, or prospective, belong to the *subjunctive* (irreality) *mood*.

In English, only a few constructions are left where subjunctive forms still *must* be used; in German, on the other hand, the subjunctive is very common, and you will have to get used to using a new set of forms that is distinctly different from indicative forms.

Some English subjunctive forms still occur in stereotype phrases such as *God bless you* (not "*blesses*") and in biblical quotations such as *The Lord be gracious unto you and give you peace* (not "*is*" and "*gives*"). Subjunctives are also found in legal language, *Judge Brown ruled that bail be lowered* (not "*is*") and in formal motions, *I move that the President appoint an ad hoc committee* (not "*appoints*").

But, leaving these archaic subjunctive forms aside, there is indeed a normal way of expressing by verb forms alone that a situation does not (or did not) actually exist. Consider the following four sentences:

1. I wish I had his aptitude for math (but I don't).
2. I wish you were here now (but you aren't).
3. If only she had listened to me (but she didn't).
4. If I were rich, I'd live in Acapulco (but I'm not rich).

There is nothing archaic in *I had* and *you were* (sentences 1 and 2); in a different context, *I had* and *you were* are the past indicative forms of *I have* and *you are:*

> Fortunately, *I had* my mother's aptitude for math.
> I know *you were* here yesterday.

Also, *she had listened* (sentence 3), in a different context, is the pluperfect.

Fortunately, *she had listened* to me and had not sold the house.

However, these same past and pluperfect indicative forms in sentences 1, 2, and 3 above, do not refer to reality but to irreality. Thus:

(a) Every past indicative (reality) form can also serve as a present subjunctive (irreality) form, and
(b) Every pluperfect indicative (reality) form can also serve as a past subjunctive (irreality) form.

In sentence 4, the form *I were* is the only one that can never refer to past reality and is thus the only genuine subjunctive form in these sentences. However, contemporary English grammars recognize this form as obsolescent and accept *I was* as a substitute, even though, especially in formal situations, *I were* is still preferred. *I was*, then, functions exactly as the verb form in sentences 1, 2, and 3:

PAST REALITY   I was rich once upon a time and could afford to live in Acapulco.

PRESENT IRREALITY I wish I was still rich enough to live in Acapulco (but I haven't got that kind of money anymore).

Preferred   I wish that he were here now.
Informal   I wish that he was here now.

However, this does not mean that the formal *subjunctive, were,* is being replaced by an informal *indicative, was,* because *was* is still *subjunctive.* To be sure, the *was* in *I wish he was here now* looks exactly like the *was* in *He was here yesterday,* where it clearly refers to a past fact and is thus by definition in the indicative mood. However, in modern English, this past indicative *was* can also function as a present subjunctive *but not without a change in the time reference.* In *I wish that he was here now, was* no longer refers to the past, but to the Now of the moment of speaking. It no longer refers to a fact, but to an imaginary situation; *was* is therefore the *present tense subjunctive* form of *to be.*

	INDICATIVE	SUBJUNCTIVE
PAST	He **was** here yesterday.	
PRESENT	He **is** here today.	I wish he **was** here today.

In principle, all English past indicatives can also be used as present tense subjunctives. Only *to be* can distinguish between the two with the *was/were* forms in the first and third person singular. Compare the following pairs of sentences:

In 1972 we *lived* in Vienna, and we *could* go to the opera every night.

If we *lived* in Vienna now, we *could* still go to the opera every night.

By then he *had* his driver's license, and we *could* hire him as a truck driver.

If he already *had* his driver's license, we *could* hire him as a truck driver right now.

Too bad the Giants *lost* the game last night.

Wouldn't it be terrible if they *lost* next week's game too?

In the same fashion, all English pluperfect indicative forms, like *had been*, can be used as past subjunctives to refer to events that actually did not happen in the past.

When we arrived in Bonn yesterday, we heard that John *had been* there for a week and *had left* only an hour before we came.

If John *had left* an hour later and *had been* there when we arrived, we *could* still *have talked* to him.

As long as you remember that English past indicatives can double up as present subjunctives, and pluperfect indicatives as past subjunctives, you will find the German subjunctive quite easy.

	INDICATIVE	SUBJUNCTIVE
PRE-PAST (= PLUPERFECT)	He had been here day before yesterday.	
PAST	He was here yesterday.	I wish he had been here yesterday.
PRESENT	He is here today.	I wish he was/were here today.

107 The Future Subjunctive: the **würde**-Forms

The future subjunctive, **würde** plus infinitive, corresponds to English *would* plus infinitive.

Er *würde* bestimmt *mitgehen.*
He *would come along*, I'm sure.

These **würde**-forms also serve as the "conditional" and are rapidly gaining ground in contemporary German. Though originally implying a time reference to the future, they are also used now, especially in irreal conclusions, with a clear reference to the moment of speaking:

Wenn es nicht so neblig wäre, würden wir von hier aus die Berge sehen können.

If it weren't so foggy, we would be able to see the mountains from here.

FUTURE INDICATIVE   FUTURE SUBJUNCTIVE

ich	werde	gehen	
du	wirst	gehen	
er	wird	gehen	
wir	werden	gehen	
ihr	werdet	gehen	
sie	werden	gehen	

ich	würde	gehen
du	würdest	gehen
er	würde	gehen
wir	würden	gehen
ihr	würdet	gehen
sie	würden	gehen

The future subjunctive, like all other subjunctives introduced below, appears primarily in three constructions:

CONSTRUCTION 1   Unfulfilled wishes starting with

ich wollte, ich wünschte, . . .	I wish . . .
es wäre nett (schön, gut, besser), wenn . . .	it would be nice (good, better) if . . .
wie wäre es, wenn . . .	how would it be if . . .
wenn ich doch nur . . .	if only I . . .

Ich wollte, du würdest mitgehen.
Es wäre nett, wenn du mitgehen würdest.
Wie wäre es, wenn du mitgehen würdest?
Wenn du doch nur mitgehen würdest.

These are all stereotype constructions which have such a strong flavor of irreality that even ambiguous forms like **wir wohnten** (which could be a past tense indicative) automatically are considered to be subjunctives (see **108** below).

Ich wünschte, wir wohnten in München.
I wish we lived in Munich.

CONSTRUCTION 2   Irreal **wenn**-clauses followed or preceded by irreal conclusions (contrary-to-fact conditional sentences). For a discussion of the distinction between contrary-to-fact conditions and open conditions, see Analysis **97**, p. 221.

Natürlich würde ich gerne mitgehen, wenn er mich bitten würde.
Wenn er mich bitten würde, würde ich natürlich gerne mitgehen.
Of course I'd like to go along if he would ask me.

CONSTRUCTION 3   Irreal speculations often using **gern, lieber, am liebsten.**

Natürlich würde ich gern in München wohnen.
Of course I'd like to live in Munich.

Ich würde lieber in Salzburg wohnen.
I would prefer to live (would rather live) in Salzburg.

Aber am liebsten würde ich in Wien wohnen.
But I would like best to live in Vienna.

108 The Present Subjunctive of Weak and Strong Verbs

The present subjunctive forms of weak verbs are identical with the past indicative forms.

PAST INDICATIVE		PRESENT SUBJUNCTIVE	
ich **wohn-te**	I was living	wenn ich **wohn-te**	if I were living
du **wohn-test**		wenn du **wohn-test**	
er **wohn-te**		wenn er **wohn-te**	
wir **wohn-ten**		wenn wir **wohn-ten**	
ihr **wohn-tet**		wenn ihr **wohn-tet**	
sie **wohn-ten**		wenn sie **wohn-ten**	

Strong verbs form the present subjunctive by adding the same set of endings as the weak verbs, but minus the **-t-**, to the stem of the past, which receives an umlaut whenever possible. The endings **-est** and **-et** are often shortened to **-st** and **-t**, especially when spoken.

PAST INDICATIVE		PRESENT SUBJUNCTIVE	
ich **ging**	I went	wenn ich **ging-e**	if I went
du **ging-st**		wenn du **ging-est, ging-st**	
er **ging**		wenn er **ging-e**	
wir **ging-en**		wenn wir **ging-en**	
ihr **ging-t**		wenn ihr **ging-et, ging-t**	
sie **ging-en**		wenn sie **ging-en**	
ich **fuhr**	I went	wenn ich **führ-e**	if I went
du **fuhr-st**		wenn du **führ-est, führ-st**	
er **fuhr**		wenn er **führ-e**	
wir **fuhr-en**		wenn wir **führ-en**	
ihr **fuhr-t**		wenn ihr **führ-et, führ-t**	
sie **fuhr-en**		wenn sie **führ-en**	

The ambiguity of weak forms like **wir wohnten** and of strong forms like **wir gingen** is not disturbing at all, as long as they are used in the three constructions described in **107**.

CONSTRUCTION 1   **Ich wollte, ich wohnte noch in München.**
Ich wünschte, du kämst (kämest) schon morgen wieder.

CONSTRUCTION 2   **Wenn wir noch in der Stadt** *wohnten,* *brauchten* **wir nur einen Wagen.**
Wenn Hans *käme,* *führen* **wir sofort nach München.**

In contrary-to-fact statements, German and English are only partly parallel: of the four verb forms above (**wohnten, brauchten, käme, führen**), only **wohnten** is expressed by an English present tense subjunctive while the other three are expressed by *would*-forms:

If we still *lived* in town, we *would need* only one car.
If Hans *would come* now, we *would* immediately *drive* to Munich.

CONSTRUCTION 3 **Wir wohnten natürlich lieber in Wien.**
Ich bliebe gerne noch zwei Wochen hier.

Here again, English uses *would* rather than the present subjunctive: We *would* rather *live* in Vienna.

Present Subjunctive or **würde**-Form?
_____

It is in sentences with the present subjunctive that **würde**-forms are making the greatest inroads in contemporary German. The sentence

Wir wohnten natürlich lieber in Wien

is ambiguous without a context; it could be part of a narrative and would then, of course, have a past indicative meaning.

We preferred living in Vienna, of course.

Given the right context, the present subjunctive meaning is clear.

Leider wohnen wir in Linz; wir wohnten natürlich lieber in Wien.
Unfortunately, we live in Linz; we would rather live in Vienna, of course.

But even if the context makes it clear that it is an irreal present time statement, many Germans would say:

Wir würden natürlich lieber in Wien wohnen.
We would rather live in Vienna, of course.

In contrary-to-fact statements, the conclusions more often than not contain **würde**-forms, and in many cases, especially in spoken German, **würde**-forms are used in the **wenn**-clause (the condition) as well. Unfortunately, there is no hard and fast rule for when to use the present subjunctive and when to use **würde**-forms.

109 The Present Subjunctive of **haben, sein,** and the Modals

	INDICATIVE	SUBJUNCTIVE	INDICATIVE	SUBJUNCTIVE	INDICATIVE	SUBJUNCTIVE
ich	war	wäre	hatte	hätte	konnte	könnte
du	warst	wär(e)st	hattest	hättest	konntest	könntest
er	war	wäre	hatte	hätte	konnte	könnte
wir	waren	wären	hatten	hätten	konnten	könnten
ihr	wart	wär(e)t	hattet	hättet	konntet	könntet
sie	waren	wären	hatten	hätten	konnten	könnten

	INDICATIVE	SUBJUNCTIVE	INDICATIVE	SUBJUNCTIVE	INDICATIVE	SUBJUNCTIVE
ich	wollte	wollte	durfte	dürfte	sollte	sollte
du	wolltest	wolltest	durftest	dürftest	solltest	solltest
er	wollte	wollte	durfte	dürfte	sollte	sollte
wir	wollten	wollten	durften	dürften	sollten	sollten
ihr	wolltet	wolltet	durftet	dürftet	solltet	solltet
sie	wollten	wollten	durften	dürften	sollten	sollten

	INDICATIVE	SUBJUNCTIVE
ich	mußte	müßte
du	mußtest	müßtest
er	mußte	müßte
wir	mußten	müßten
ihr	mußtet	müßtet
sie	mußten	müßten

With the exception of **wollen** and **sollen**, all these verbs make a sharp distinction between the past indicative and the present subjunctive. The corresponding English forms (*was, had, could, had to, had the permission to, would, should*) make no such distinctions: the English past indicatives are also used as present subjunctives, the only exception being the possible *was/were* distinction discussed above.

The forms in the table above are the most frequently used of all German subjunctives. They appear in the usual three constructions.

CONSTRUCTION 1   **Wenn es nur nicht so kalt wäre.**
                    Es wäre schön, wenn du morgen kommen könntest.

CONSTRUCTION 2   **Ich wäre sehr froh, wenn er jetzt hier wäre.**
                    Wenn ich nicht so viel arbeiten müßte, könnte ich auch
                             öfter in die Oper gehen.

CONSTRUCTION 3   **Das Essen hier könnte aber wirklich besser sein.**
                    Ich hätte natürlich viel lieber einen Mercedes.

110   The Past Subjunctive

The past subjunctive is derived from the pluperfect. If the auxiliary in the indicative is **hatte** in the pluperfect, it is **hätte** in the past subjunctive, and the indicative **war** is changed to **wäre**; thus there are never any ambiguous forms.

PLUPERFECT INDICATIVE	PAST SUBJUNCTIVE	PLUPERFECT INDICATIVE	PAST SUBJUNCTIVE
ich hatte gekauft	ich hätte gekauft	ich war gegangen	ich wäre gegangen
du hattest gekauft	du hättest gekauft	du warst gegangen	du wär(e)st gegangen
er hatte gekauft	er hätte gekauft	er war gegangen	er wäre gegangen
wir hatten gekauft	wir hätten gekauft	wir waren gegangen	wir wären gegangen
ihr hattet gekauft	ihr hättet gekauft	ihr wart gegangen	ihr wär(e)t gegangen
sie hatten gekauft	sie hätten gekauft	sie waren gegangen	sie wären gegangen

PAST SUBJUNCTIVE OF MODALS

ich hätte arbeiten müssen	I would have had to work
du hättest arbeiten müssen	you would have had to work
er hätte arbeiten müssen	he would have had to work
wir hätten nicht zu arbeiten brauchen	we would not have had to work
ihr hättet nicht zu arbeiten brauchen	you would not have had to work
sie hätten nicht zu arbeiten brauchen	they would not have had to work

NOTE: Forms like **hätte können, hätte müssen,** or **hätte brauchen** are structured like **hätte gekauft.** The participles of the modals look like infinitives as long as they follow another infinitive; hence the term "double infinitive," which, strictly speaking, is incorrect because the second infinitive is really a past participle. As with indicative forms, the subjunctive double infinitive is preceded by the finite verb in dependent clauses (see 111). Observe that the English forms *could have, should have, would have* always start with **hätte** in German.

Like all other forms of the subjunctive, the past subjunctive is used with great frequency in the usual three constructions.

CONSTRUCTION 1

Ich wollte, mein Vater hätte das Haus nicht verkauft.
Es wäre schön gewesen, wenn du hättest kommen können.

CONSTRUCTION 2

Wenn er nicht gekommen wäre, hätte ich ohne ihn fahren müssen.
Ich wäre natürlich sofort gekommen, wenn du mich angerufen hättest.

CONSTRUCTION 3

Am liebsten wäre ich heute gar nicht aufgestanden.
Ich hätte natürlich auch zu Hause arbeiten können.

Note that in the English equivalents of these sentences, the past subjunctive is normally used in the *if*-clauses, and *would have* in all others.

I would have come immediately if you had called me.

111 Position of **hätte** in Connection with "Double Infinitives"

If subjunctive sentences like

Er hätte zu Hause bleiben können

or

Er hätte nicht zu Hause bleiben sollen

are changed into dependent clauses which should show verb-last position, the **hätte** does not go to the end, but follows **nicht** and precedes the second prong.

Wenn ich doch nur hätte zu Hause bleiben können.
Es wäre nett gewesen, wenn ich gestern nicht hätte zurückfahren müssen.

112 Polite Requests

In social gatherings, in hotels, stores, and so forth, the **würde**-forms and the present subjunctives are used to express polite requests.

Hätten Sie vielleicht noch ein Zimmer frei?
Ich hätte gerne ein Zimmer mit Bad.
Könnte ich noch eine Tasse Kaffee haben?
Würden Sie mir vielleicht noch eine Tasse Kaffee bringen?

113 Irregular Subjunctive Forms

A few verbs form the present subjunctive in an irregular way.

PAST INDICATIVE	PRESENT INDICATIVE
ich brachte	ich brächte
ich kannte	ich kennte
ich half	ich hülfe
ich starb	ich stürbe

114 sollte

German **sollte** is one of the ambiguous forms which can be used either as a past indicative or as a present subjunctive.

Past Indicative

Jedesmal, wenn du mit mir ins Theater gehen solltest, hattest du Kopfschmerzen.

Every time you were supposed (Every time I wanted you) to go to the theater with me, you had a headache.

Wir sollten schon um acht in Köln sein. Jetzt ist es neun, und wir sind immer noch in Bonn.

We were supposed to be in Cologne at eight. Now it is nine, and we are still in Bonn.

Present Subjunctive

In the *if*-clause, the present subjunctive denotes a future possibility which the speaker does not expect to materialize. The conclusion shows the indicative.

Wenn es morgen regnen sollte, bleiben wir zu Hause.

If it should rain tomorrow, we'll stay at home.

In the conclusion, the present subjunctive denotes an as yet unfulfilled obligation. The *if*-clause shows the indicative.

Wenn du kannst, solltest du ihm helfen.
Du solltest nicht soviel essen.

If you can, you should (ought to) help him.
You should not (ought not to) eat so much.

115 eigentlich

Eigentlich is a frequently used sentence adverb which has no equivalent in English. To questions, it gives the flavor of "to come right down to it."

Warum sind wir eigentlich in die Schweiz gefahren?

In assertions, usually containing subjunctives like **sollte, wollte, müßte,** and **dürfte, eigentlich** adds the flavor "but I guess that's out."

Eigentlich sollten wir morgen nach Berlin fahren.

We were supposed to go to Berlin tomorrow. (But I guess we won't.)

116 The Position of **nicht** Again

Irreal wishes and irreal **wenn**-clauses frequently follow the pattern: I wish "the whole thing" hadn't happened. One such "whole thing" is described within the brackets of the factual statement.

Gestern abend hat Ingelheim [wieder drei Stunden lang nur von seinem Hobby geredet].

Last night, Ingelheim [talked again for three hours about nothing but his hobby].

The "whole thing" was unpleasant. It should not have happened. But it did happen, and nobody can change it. But one can, at least in thought, erase it from the realm of reality. This is done by using a contrary-to-fact subjunctive and by placing a condemning **nicht** right in front of the "whole thing."

Ich wollte, Ingelheim hätte gestern abend nicht [wieder drei Stunden lang nur von seinem Hobby geredet].

The **nicht**, in such cases, does not precede the second prong (**geredet**), but the complete description of whatever the speaker considers the "whole thing."

117 Word Formation

The Prefix **un-**

The prefix **un-** is added to many adjectives and a few nouns to form antonyms.

glücklich	unglücklich
interessant	uninteressant
vernünftig	unvernünftig
das Wissen (knowledge)	das Unwissen (ignorance)
das Glück (happiness, good luck)	das Unglück (misfortune, accident)

The Suffix **-lich** Added to Nouns

Like the English suffix -ly, the German suffix **-lich** is added to nouns. It forms adjectives with the meaning of "having the qualities one associates with things

or people of such a nature." The stem vowel of the noun is usually umlauted.

der Freund	friend	**freundlich**	friendly
die Mutter	mother	**mütterlich**	motherly
das Kind	child	**kindlich**	childlike
die Welt	world	**weltlich**	worldly, secular
die Natur	nature	**natürlich**	naturally

The Suffixes -bar and -lich Added to Verb Stems

Added to verb stems, **-bar** and **-lich** form passive adjectives corresponding to English adjectives in *-able* and *-ible*.

glauben	to believe	**unglaublich**	unbelievable
brauchen	to use	**brauchbar**	usable
vergessen	to forget	**unvergeßlich**	unforgettable

Some of the adjectives formed by **-lich** have an active meaning. (Compare English *durable*.)

sterben	to die	**sterblich**	mortal, apt to die
vergessen	to forget	**vergeßlich**	forgetful

Conversations

In the pattern sections of this unit, we have used a number of words pertaining to traffic. Since many of these words recur in the conversations below, we have listed them together. This should enable you to use them more readily in free conversation.

der Verkehr (*no pl.*)	traffic	die Hauptstraße	main street, artery, through street
der Berufsverkehr	commuter traffic		
der Beruf, -e	vocation, profession	die Seitenstraße	side street
der Wochenend-verkehr	weekend traffic	die Bundesstraße	federal road
		die B 14	federal road number 14
gehen	to go, walk		
zu Fuß gehen	to walk, go on foot	parken	to park
einkaufen gehen	to go shopping	der Parkplatz, ⁝e	place to park, parking space; parking lot
einkaufen	to shop		
das Einkaufszen-trum (*pl. die -zentren*)	shopping center	das Parkhaus, ⁝er	parking garage
das Kaufhaus, ⁝er	department store	der Unfall, ⁝e	accident
		der Autounfall	automobile accident
mitgehen, mitfahren	to come along, go along, drive along	passieren	to happen
		es ist etwas passiert	there's been an accident
in die Stadt fahren	to go (drive) to town, to the city	die Innenstadt	downtown, inner city
		der Dom, -e	cathedral
das Land (*no pl.*)	country(side)	der Fußgänger, -	pedestrian
auf dem Land	in the country	die Fußgänger-zone, -n	pedestrian area
draußen	outside (the city)		
draußen auf dem Land	out in the country	umsteigen	to change (trains, streetcars, buses)
die Bahn, -en	way, path; course; track	das Benzin (*no pl.*)	gasoline
die Eisenbahn = die Bahn	railroad	das Diesel(öl)	diesel (oil)
die Straßenbahn	streetcar	der Diesel, -	diesel car
die U-Bahn = die Untergrundbahn	subway	die (Verkehrs)ampel, -n	traffic light
die Autobahn	superhighway	das Schild, -er	sign
		das Stopschild	stop sign
die Straße, -n	street	der Strafzettel, -	traffic ticket

I

Am Telefon:

KARLA B.: Ich muß heute nachmittag in die Stadt. Wie wäre es, wenn du mitfahren würdest?

ELISABETH R.: Gerne. Ich hätte zwar zu Hause viel zu tun, aber ich muß auch unbedingt in der Stadt ein paar Dinge erledigen. Nimmst du den Wagen?

K.B.: Nein, ich wollte eigentlich mit der Bahn fahren. Mit dem Wagen kämen wir auf der Heimfahrt mitten in den Berufsverkehr.

E.R.: Da hast du recht. Das letzte Mal habe ich vom Parkhaus am Dom bis zur Autobahn über eine halbe Stunde gebraucht.

CONVERSATIONS

Wieviel Zeit haben wir noch?

II

Beim Verlassen des Hauptbahnhofs:

K.B.: So, da sind wir.

E.R.: Ja, und ich bin froh, daß wir den Wagen zu Hause gelassen haben.

K.B.: Genau. Mit dem Wagen wären wir noch gar nicht hier.

E.R.: Der Verkehr ist wieder mal unmöglich. Heute hätten wir bestimmt keinen Platz zum Parken gefunden.

III

Vor dem Kaufhof:

E.R.: Gottseidank für die Fußgängerzone. Da braucht man wenigstens nicht immer Angst vor den Autos zu haben.

K.B.: Hier in der Altstadt wäre es heute ja gar nicht mehr möglich, noch Autos reinzulassen. Da käme keiner mehr vorwärts, bei den engen Straßen.

E.R.: Natürlich; wenn die Straßen nicht so eng wären, hätten wir sicher auch keine Fußgängerzone.

K.B.: Genau. Dann hätte man mit dem Geld noch mehr Straßen gebaut, und der Verkehr wäre noch viel schlimmer.

In **IV**, **V**, and **VI**, construct a few exchanges according to the English outline. Use subjunctive constructions where possible.

IV

Nach dem Einkaufen:

K.B.: How about a cup of coffee? (Wie wäre es, . . .)

E.R.: That would be fine, but where?

K.B.: We could go to the Dom Café.

E.R.: I would rather go to the Café Schneider. OK with you?

V

Im Hauptbahnhof:

E. tells K. that they still have twenty minutes before their train leaves; it is now 5:20 P.M. K. wishes they had a shopping center out where they live. E. agrees that that would be very good. They could then do all their shopping out there and wouldn't have to come into town so often.

VI

Im Zug, kurz nach der Abfahrt:

From the train, they can see the *Bundesstraße*. Lots of cars, motorcycles, buses, even streetcars. K. wonders if something has happened, but E. doesn't think there has been an accident; just the many traffic lights—and they all seem to be always red. If there weren't so many people living in the suburbs and working in the city, it wouldn't be so bad. And if more people would take the bus or the train, that would help too.

VII

Construct similar short exchanges, using the traffic vocabulary. Make your sentences simple and straightforward, but try to use as many subjunctive forms as you can.

Fragen an Sie persönlich
_____

1. Wie ist der Verkehr in Ihrer Heimatstadt?*
2. Wie wäre es, wenn es in der Innenstadt keine Autos mehr gäbe? (Fußgängerzonen!)
3. Gibt es in Ihrem Heimatstaat* noch Personenzüge (passenger trains)?
4. Sind Sie schon einmal mit der Eisenbahn gefahren?
5. Gibt es eine U-Bahn in Ihrer Heimatstadt? Straßenbahn? Busse? andere öffentliche Verkehrsmittel (public means of transportation)?
6. Was würden Sie machen, wenn Sie der Verkehrsplaner in einer Großstadt wären? Was würden Sie zum Beispiel für den Berufsverkehr tun?
7. Welchen Einfluß, glauben Sie, wird die Energiekrise auf den Verkehr haben?

Reading

Burgbach, zum Beispiel (Fortsetzung°)   continuation

Otto Schmid, etwa 50 Jahre alt und gebürtiger° Burgbacher, ist   native
Lehrer. Er unterrichtet° seit vielen Jahren an der Grundschule° in   teaches primary school
Burgbach und hat die Veränderungen im Ort an immer neuen Gen-
erationen von Schülern erlebt°. Im Grundschulunterricht, vor allem   experienced
in Deutsch, Geographie und Heimatkunde°, sieht er den Grund dafür, 5 study of the local area

_____
*Note the difference between **die Stadt** *town, city* and **der Staat** *state.*

daß° trotz der Urbanisierung die Tradition immer noch eine große   the reason for the fact
Rolle spielt. „Sehen Sie", sagt er, auf Hochdeutsch, aber mit starkem   that
schwäbischem Akzent, „die Kinder kommen mit sechs Jahren zu uns,
—Kinder von Weingärtnern°, von Industriearbeitern, von Beamten°,   vintners   civil servants
auch Kinder von Ausländern, und dann lernen sie in den unteren 5
Klassen zuerst einmal sehr viel über unsere Gegend° hier, über den   area
Ort, über die Landwirtschaft°, über den Weinbau und so weiter."   agriculture

Herr Schmid geht mit den Kindern durchs Dorf; er zeigt ihnen die
Kirche, das alte und das neue Rathaus, er erklärt ihnen, wie man ein
Fachwerkhaus° baut, und warum heute nur noch ganz wenige 10   half-timbered house
Bauern Kühe und Schweine im Stall haben. Vor allem aber erzählt er
ihnen aus der Geschichte von Burgbach, und bei Schulausflügen° führt   school excursions
er die Kinder dorthin, wo man die Spuren° dieser Geschichte heute   traces
noch sehen kann.

Im Nachbardorf zum Beispiel hat man vor ein paar Jahren das 15
Fundament einer römischen Villa entdeckt°, und Herr Schmid hat   discovered
diese Entdeckung benutzt°, um den Kindern zu beweisen°, daß   used   to prove
tatsächlich° einmal Römer hier gewohnt haben. Wenn er mit einer   in fact, indeed
Klasse nach Lorch fährt,— etwa 15 km von Burgbach entfernt—, um
das mittelalterliche Kloster° mit seiner romanischen° Kirche zu 20   medieval monastery
betrachten°, dann zeigt er den Kindern auch, daß man dort noch sehr   Romanesque
gut den römischen Limes sehen kann, die 548 km lange römische   to look at
Grenzbefestigung°, die von der Donau bis zum Rhein führte. Die   border fortification
gotische Stadtkirche von Lorch steht an der Stelle° eines römischen   in place of
Limeskastells.   25

Bis vor etwa 2000 Jahren hatten Kelten° in der Gegend gesiedelt.   Celts
Dann kamen, um Christi Geburt, die Römer, die am Ende der
römischen Expansionsperiode den Limes bauten, zur Verteidigung°   defense
gegen die Barbaren aus dem Norden, die Germanen. Mit der
römischen Kultur kam auch der Wein ins Land, und die Nordgrenze° 30   northern border
des römischen Reiches ist heute noch die Nordgrenze des Weinbaus in
Mitteleuropa, vom Burgenland und der Wachau in Österreich bis
nach Schwaben, nach Franken, zum Rhein und zur Mosel. Nach den
Römern kamen, im zweiten und dritten Jahrhundert n. Chr., die   the Germanic
germanischen Alemannen°; und ein Alemanne namens° Butilo 35   Alemannians
gründete°, der Sage nach°, eine Siedlung dort, wo heute der Markt-   by the name of
platz von Burgbach ist. Dann kamen christliche Missionare, vor allem   founded
aus Irland, und es heißt°, daß schon um 700 ein Missionar die erste   according to local
Kirche gebaut hat. Den Namen „Burgbach" erwähnt° zum ersten   legend (*see footnote*)
Mal eine Urkunde° aus dem Jahr 1092, als eine Tochter der Herren° 40   it is said
von Burgbach den Grafen von Wirtenberg (heute Württemberg)   mentions
heiratete.   document   lords

If the preposition **nach** follows a noun, it corresponds to English *according to*.

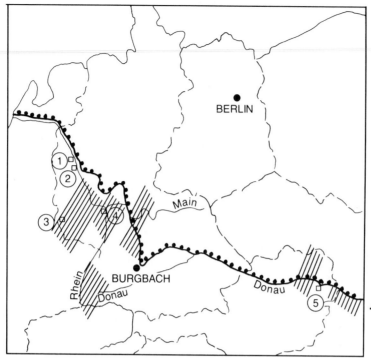

DIE RÖMER IN MITTELEUROPA
1 Colonia Agrippina = Köln
2 Bonna = Bonn
3 Augusta Treverorum = Trier
4 Mogontiacum = Mainz
5 Vindibona = Wien
ııı Weinbaugebiete
▪▪▪▪ Limes

Auch die „Burg" hat man wiedergefunden, und Herr Schmid steigt°   climbs
jedes Jahr mit seinen Schülern auf den Berg, wo man die alte Ruine
ausgegraben° hat. Um den Weinbau zu rationalisieren, hat man in   dug out
den sechziger Jahren° die vielen alten kleinen Weingärten mit ihren   in the sixties
horizontalen Terrassen in neue große vertikale Weinberge 5
umgewandelt.° Dabei° mußte man ganze Berghänge neu profilieren,   transformed
und so fand man dann die Burg. Von hier oben kann man fast bis nach   in the process
Stuttgart sehen, und Herr Schmid kann den Kindern zeigen, wie die
revoltierenden Bauern am Anfang des 16. Jahrhunderts von Ort zu
Ort zogen°, und wie die Armee des Herzogs° von Württemberg sie dann 10   roamed   duke
schließlich besiegte°. 300 Jahre später, zur Zeit Napoleons, kamen   defeated
dann die Franzosen durch das Tal, auf dem Weg nach Rußland; und
wieder 150 Jahre später kamen am Ende des Zweiten Weltkriegs die
Amerikaner.

„Wenn die Geschichte eines Dorfes auf beinahe 1000 Jahre doku- 15
mentierbar° ist", meint Herr Schmid, „dann soll man diese Tradi-   documentable
tion nicht aussterben lassen." Sicher hat er recht, denn die
Sozialstruktur und die Identität des alten Burgbach waren durch die
Geschichte geprägt°, und die gemeinsame Vergangenheit° führte zu   formed   common past
einem Gefühl des Zusammengehörens. Wer° Schwäbisch sprach und 20   whoever
dazu noch einen Namen mit -le hatte, gehörte schon fast automatisch
zu den Einheimischen°. Die neuen Burgbacher aus dem Osten und   natives
aus dem Norden Deutschlands hatten es oft schwer, diesen Stolz° auf   pride
die lokale Vergangenheit zu verstehen, aber ihre Kinder lernten dann
eben° doch Schwäbisch, —und hatten Herrn Schmid als Lehrer.   25 anyway

Dennoch hat das Dorf seine neue Rolle überraschend° gut akzeptiert; surprisingly
nach der Katastrophe von 1945 mußte man positiv denken, um zu
überleben°, und seitdem ist die Entwicklung° so schnell gegangen, survive development
daß ein Dorf wie Burgbach, selbst wenn° es wollte, einfach nicht even if
dagegen ankommen könnte. Vor dem Krieg zum Beispiel war es fast 5
undenkbar, daß ein Burgbacher eine Katholikin geheiratet hätte. In
den Dörfern gab es starke religiöse Vorurteile°; Württemberg war prejudices
protestantisch, und man mußte schon 40 km talaufwärts° gehen, up the valley
bevor man eine katholische Gemeinde° fand: Schwäbisch-Gmünd, community, parish
das trotz der Reformation katholisch geblieben war, denn es war eine 10
Freie Reichsstadt° und gehörte nicht zu Württemberg. Nach dem free imperial city
Krieg, als die ersten katholischen Flüchtlinge ins Dorf gekommen
waren, half die protestantische Gemeinde den Katholiken beim Bau° with the construction
ihrer eigenen° Kirche, und heute ist jede fünfte Ehe° in Burgbach eine own marriage
Ehe zwischen Protestanten und Katholiken. Wenn Lehrer Schmid 15
seinen Schülern die alte Kirche erklärt, dann beschreibt er sie nicht als
religiöses, sondern als historisches Objekt: 1522 vollendet°, über completed
den Resten einer noch viel älteren Kirche, diente° sie als Zentrum served
einer lebhaften° Marktgemeinde, die zweimal im Jahr zum lively
„Jahrmarkt" Bauern und Händler° aus der ganzen Gegend nach 20 tradesmen
Burgbach brachte. Noch heute hält man einmal in der Woche offenen
Markt. Metzger, Bäcker, Gemüse- und Blumenhändler und manche
andere stellen° dann auf dem Marktplatz vor der Kirche ihre
Waren aus°. exhibit
So existiert in Burgbach das Neue relativ harmonisch neben dem 25
Alten. Kirche, Marktplatz, Friedhof, die alten Gasthöfe° sind immer inns
noch das Zentrum inmitten des alten Dorfes mit seinen Fachwerk-
häusern und engen, krummen° Straßen. Den Bach°, der mitten durch crooked brook
das Dorf fließt, hat ·man mit Beton° überdeckt°, um Parkmöglich- concrete covered
keiten für die vielen Autos zu schaffen°. Um den Kern° liegt in 30 create core
konzentrischen Kreisen das neue Burgbach: Reihenhäuser° und row houses
Einfamilienhäuser, die in den ersten 25 Jahren nach dem Krieg (condominiums)
entstanden°, und am Ortsrand° die neue Industrie, ein kleines were built
Einkaufszentrum°, und ein halbes Dutzend° acht- bis zwölfstöckige edge of town
Apartmenthäuser. Mit der Eisenbahn und vor allem auf der neuen 35 shopping center dozen
Autobahn ist man in weniger als einer halben Stunde in Stuttgart.

Siegle Anna Bei... ...9		
Siegle Berta (Rem) Burgstallweg 11		Siegle Helmut ...enhäldle 27	
Siegle Dora (Wei) Am Sonnenhang 13	6 38 1...	Siegle Helmut (Rem) Gaisgasse 1	7 1...
Siegle Eduard Metzgerei (Rem) Untere		Siegle Hermann (Wei) Weinsteige 23	6 58 96
Hauptstr. 13	77 89	**Siegle Hermann**	
Siegle Elise (Rem) Amselweg 23	76 83	**Zentralheizungen**	
Siegle Emilie (Rem) Ziegelweg 2	7 94 76	**Ölfeuerungsanlagen**	
Siegle Erich Korb Wiesenstr. 2	6 83 73	Remshalden-Geradstetten	
Siegle Eugen (Wei) Annastr. 16	6 36 43	Wilhelm-Enßle-Str. 51	9 77 41
Siegle Friedrich (Rem) Winnender Str. 18		Siegle K. Jürgen Versich.-Kfm. (Wei)	
	7 21 87	Aichwaldstr. 18	6 55 29
Siegle Friedrich Richard-Wagner-Str. 25	5 96 55	Siegle Karl Salierstr. 33	2 19 92

Viele heißen Siegle.

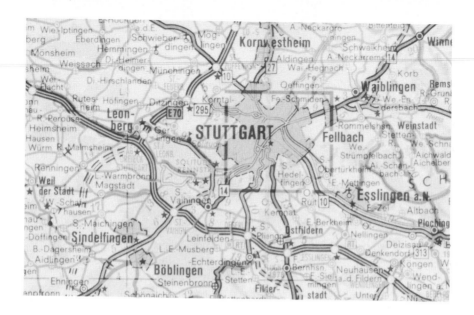

Zwischen Burgbach und den Nachbargemeinden ist immer noch überraschend viel offenes Land: Felder, Wiesen°, Obstgärten°, Weinberge und, oben auf der Höhe, ausgedehnte Wälder°. Die Hochhäuser sind zwar oft häßlich°, aber sie erhalten° wertvolles Ackerland.

      meadows orchards

      extensive forests

      ugly preserve

      5

Am ersten Januar 1975 verlor Burgbach seine Selbständigkeit° und bildet° jetzt mit vier anderen Dörfern zusammen eine neue „Stadt". Damit scheint der Prozeß der Urbanisierung abgeschlossen° zu sein. Burgbach wird wohl seinen eigenen Charakter verlieren, und was aus den offenen Grünflächen° zwischen den „Ortsteilen" werden wird, kann erst die Zukunft° zeigen. Für Otto Schmid wird es auf jeden Fall° schwer werden, seine jungen Schüler im Sinne° der Burgbacher Tradition zu erziehen.

      independence

      forms

      completed

      10 green areas

      future

      in any case spirit

Exercises

A. Change the following factual statements to irreal wishes, starting with **ich wollte (wünschte),** . . . , **es wäre nett, wenn** . . . , **wie wäre es, wenn** . . . , or **wenn** . . . **doch nur** . . . . Be sure to change from affirmative to negative and vice versa. Use only **würde**-forms.

> **Du gehst nicht mit.**
> **Es wäre nett, wenn du mitgehen würdest.**

SEE
ANALYSIS
107
(p. 255)

1. Du redest zu oft von deinem Hobby. (Change **zu** to **nicht so.**)
2. Wir fahren dieses Wochenende nicht in die Berge.
3. Wir fahren heute in die Stadt.
4. Du gehst nie zu Fuß. (Change **nie** to **einmal.**)
5. Du bleibst heute nicht zu Hause.

B. Replacing **leider** by **gerne, lieber,** or **am liebsten,** change the following factual statements to preferential statements using only **würde**-forms. Change from negative to affirmative.

> Wir fahren leider nicht nach Deutschland.
> Wir würden am liebsten nach Deutschland fahren.

1. Ich gehe heute abend leider nicht ins Kino.
2. Wir wohnen ja leider nicht im Vienna-Hilton.
3. Er kauft leider keinen Mercedes.
4. Er nimmt leider nie die Bundesstraße.
5. Wir bleiben dieses Wochenende leider nicht zu Hause.

SEE ANALYSIS 107 (p. 255)

C. Using both the short forms, like **führen,** and the long forms, like **würden fahren,** change the following factual statements into irreal wishes, starting first with **ich wollte** or **ich wünschte,** then with **es wäre nett, wenn . . . ,** and finally with **wenn** (subject) **doch nur . . . .**

> Sie wohnen leider nicht mehr hier in Köln.
> Wenn sie doch nur noch hier in Köln wohnten.
> Wenn sie doch nur noch hier in Köln wohnen würden.

1. Du fährst leider morgen schon wieder nach Hause. (Place **nicht** in front of **schon.**)
2. Ernst ruft mich heute abend nicht an.
3. Unser Sohn telefoniert jeden Abend zwei Stunden mit seiner Freundin. (Place **nicht** in front of **jeden Abend.**)

SEE ANALYSIS 108 (p. 257)

D. Formulate irreal preferential statements using only **am liebsten** this time. Place this **am liebsten** in the front field. Change from negative to affirmative and vice versa. Use both the short forms and the **würde**-forms.

> Wir fahren dieses Wochenende leider nicht in die Berge.
> Am liebsten führen wir dieses Wochenende in die Berge.
> Am liebsten würden wir dieses Wochenende in die Berge fahren.

1. Ich sitze jetzt leider nicht im Hofbräuhaus.
2. Ich studiere leider nicht Medizin.
3. Ich bleibe nicht jeden Tag bis neun im Bett.
4. Wir wohnen leider nicht in München.
5. Wir gehen leider nicht zum Essen in den Ratskeller.

SEE ANALYSIS 108 (p. 257)

E. The following sentences contain a dependent clause introduced by **weil.** Changing the **weil**-clause into a **wenn**-clause, transform the sentences into irreal conditions. Use both short forms and **würde**-forms as appropriate.

> Wir wohnen in der Stadt, weil wir keine Kinder haben.
> Wenn wir Kinder hätten, wohnten wir nicht in der Stadt.
> Wenn wir Kinder hätten, würden wir nicht in der Stadt wohnen.

1. Weil ich nicht in München wohne, gehe ich nicht jeden Tag ins Theater.
2. Weil Meyer nicht Auto fahren will, fährt er immer mit dem Zug in die Stadt. (Place **nicht** in front of **immer.**)
3. Weil wir einen Hund haben, finden wir keine Wohnung.
4. Weil er nicht früh in die Stadt fährt, findet er bestimmt keinen Parkplatz.
5. Weil es jeden Tag regnet, fahren wir schon wieder nach Hause.

SEE ANALYSIS 108-109 (pp. 257-258)

F. Change the following factual statements to irreal wishes starting first with **ich wollte**, then with **ich wünschte**, then with **es wäre gut, wenn** . . . , and finally with **wenn wir (er) doch nur** . . . . Change from affirmative to negative and vice versa.

> **Mein Mann muß zu schwer arbeiten.**
> **Ich wollte, mein Mann brauchte nicht so schwer zu arbeiten.**
> **Ich wünschte, mein Mann brauchte nicht so schwer zu arbeiten.**
> **Es wäre gut, wenn mein Mann nicht so schwer zu arbeiten brauchte.**
> **Wenn mein Mann doch nur nicht so schwer zu arbeiten brauchte.**

SEE
ANALYSIS
108–109
(pp. 257–258)

1. Ich habe leider keinen Bruder.
2. Wir sind noch nicht zu Hause. (Replace **noch nicht** by **schon**.)
3. Du bist immer so pessimistisch. (Place **nicht** in front of **immer**.)
4. Wir dürfen ihn heute noch nicht besuchen. (Change **heute noch nicht** to **schon heute**.)
5. Wir können nicht jedes Wochenende in die Berge fahren.

G. Change the following factual statements to irreal statements about what should or could be, but is not. Use the verb in parentheses.

> **Ich trinke zu viel. (sollen)**
> **Ich sollte nicht so viel trinken.**

SEE
ANALYSIS
109
(p. 258)

1. Wir haben kein Auto. (müssen)
2. Wir fahren Sonntag nicht in die Berge. (können)
3. Wir schwimmen nicht jeden Tag eine halbe Stunde. (sollen)
4. Morgen abend gehen wir nicht ins Theater. (können)

H. Combine the following pairs of sentences to irreal **wenn**-clauses followed or preceded by an irreal conclusion.

> **Wir können nicht nach Italien fahren. Mein Mann ist nicht gesund.**
> **Wenn mein Mann gesund wäre, könnten wir nach Italien fahren.**

SEE
ANALYSIS
107–109
(pp. 253–258)

1. Ich bin kein Arzt. Ich kann Ihnen nicht helfen.
2. Wir haben kein Geld. Wir können nicht mit Meyers in die Schweiz fahren.
3. Wir können hier draußen nicht einkaufen. Es gibt kein Einkaufszentrum.
4. Wir müssen den Bus nehmen. Die U-Bahn fährt nicht nach Sondersbach.
5. Ich fahre mit der Bahn. Das Benzin ist zu teuer.
6. Ich komme erst um sieben. Ich muß dreimal umsteigen.

I. Change the following factual statements to irreal wishes. Change from negative to affirmative and vice versa. Start first with **ich wollte**, then with **ich wünschte, es wäre besser gewesen, wenn** . . . , **wenn** (*subject*) **doch nur** . . . .

> **Wir haben das Haus leider nicht gekauft.**
> **Wenn wir das Haus doch nur gekauft hätten.**

SEE
ANALYSIS
110
(p. 259)

1. Sie hat mich nicht angerufen.
2. Wir sind in den Berufsverkehr gekommen.

3. Ich habe meinen Mantel zu Hause gelassen. (Place **nicht** in front of **zu Hause**.)
4. Wir konnten das Haus nicht kaufen. (Watch the position of **hätten**.)
5. Ich habe heute abend zuviel Kaffee getrunken. (Replace **zuviel** by **nicht so viel**.)

J. Change the following factual assertions to irreal preferential statements using first **gerne**, then **lieber**, and then **am liebsten**, all three of them replacing **leider**.

> **Wir haben das Haus in Köln leider nicht gekauft.**
> **Wir hätten lieber das Haus in Köln gekauft.**

1. Wir sind leider nicht in die Berge gefahren.
2. Wir sind leider nicht in den Zoo gegangen.
3. Ich habe heute morgen leider nicht bis neun geschlafen.
4. Ich bin gestern leider nicht mit meinem Freund ins Kino gegangen.

SEE
ANALYSIS
110
(p. 259)

K. Change the following pairs of factual statements to irreal conditions.

> **Rosemarie studierte damals in München. Ich habe sie kennengelernt.**
> **Wenn Rosemarie damals nicht in München studiert hätte, hätte ich sie nie kennengelernt.**

1. Tante Amalie schickte mir jeden Monat fünfhundert Mark. Ich konnte Medizin studieren.
   Ich _____ nie Medizin studieren _____, wenn Tante Amalie mir nicht _____.

SEE
ANALYSIS
110
(p. 259)

2. Auf der Autobahn war viel Verkehr. Wir kamen zu spät in die Oper.
   Wenn auf der Autobahn nicht so viel Verkehr _____ _____, _____ wir nicht zu spät in die Oper _____.

3. Wir sind nicht in die Berge gefahren. Das Wetter war zu schlecht.
   Wir _____ in die Berge _____, wenn das Wetter nicht so schlecht _____ _____.

4. Tante Amalie kam. Ich mußte ins Museum gehen.
   Wenn Tante Amalie nicht . . .

5. Wir saßen bis fünf im Café Schneider und kamen dann in den Berufsverkehr.
   Wenn wir nicht . . .

L. Use the following elements to construct sentences in the past tense; then rewrite these sentences in the perfect tense.

1. Ich / gestern / arbeiten / müssen.
2. Ich / zu Hause / bleiben / wollen // aber / nicht / können.
3. Fridolin / nach Hause / fahren // und / ich / er / folgen.
4. Ich / er / vor Bahnhof / sehen // aber / dann / er / plötzlich / verschwinden.
5. Karin / mit Bahn / nach Stuttgart / fahren // um / ihr Freund / besuchen.
6. Kinder / um eins / aus Schule / kommen.
7. Im Sommer / wir / oft / schwimmen / gehen.
8. Am Abend / wir / noch lange / vor Haus / sitzen.
9. Robert Meyer / später / Arzt / werden.
10. Sommer 1977 / wochenlang / regnen.

M. Express in German.

1. It would be nice if we could go back to Lübeck.
2. If I had not been there twenty years ago, I would never have met him.
3. Frau Enderle would like to there again.
4. But Herr Enderle prefers living in Burgbach. (Use **lieber.**)
5. I wish you would help me in the kitchen.
6. Then we could eat much earlier.
7. How would it be if we drank another bottle of wine?
8. We could have stayed here, but we didn't want to.
9. It would be nice if she would invite me.
10. I would like to visit her. (Use **gern.**)
11. If you'd go to bed early, you wouldn't always be tired.
12. If only the bus would come.
13. If it weren't raining, we could walk.
14. Would you like to have sauerkraut for lunch (**Mittagessen**) today?
15. I'd rather have cauliflower (**Blumenkohl**).

N. Composition.

Turn the conversations of Unit 9 into a simple narrative, starting as follows. Number your sentences.

1. Frau B. telefoniert mit Frau R.
2. Sie will mit Frau R. in die Stadt fahren.
3. . . .

Then rewrite your sentences in the past tense.

1. Frau B. telefonierte mit Frau R.
2. Sie wollte . . .

Finally, have Frau B. tell the story to her family during **Abendessen** of the same day, using the perfect tense, but remember to use the past with **haben, sein,** and the modals.

1. Ich war den ganzen Tag mit Elisabeth in der Stadt.
2. Ich habe sie heute morgen angerufen.
3. Ich wollte mit ihr einkaufen gehen.
4. Wir sind mit der Bahn gefahren, weil . . .
5. . . .

Vocabulary

die Ampel, -n	traffic light	**ausstellen**	to show, exhibit
aufwärts	up, upward	**die Autobahn, -en**	turnpike, freeway
talaufwärts	up the valley	**der Bach, ⸚e**	stream, brook
ausdehnen	to extend	**beinah(e)**	nearly, almost
der Ausflug, ⸚e	excursion	**das Benzin′**	gasoline
der Schulausflug, ⸚e	school excursion,	**betrachten**	to regard, look at
	field trip	**beweisen**	to prove

bilden	to form	**mittelalterlich**	medieval
der Charak′ter, -e	character	**möglich**	possible
dienen	to serve	**unmöglich**	impossible
das Ding, -e	thing	**die Möglichkeit, -en**	possibility
draußen	outside	**der Nachbar, -n**	neighbor
duschen	to shower	**der Nebel, -**	fog
die Dusche, -n	shower	**neblig**	foggy
das Dutzend, -e	dozen	**der Nerv, -en**	nerve
die Ehe, -n	marriage	**das Objekt′, -e**	object
eigen	own	**offen**	open
eng	narrow	**öffentlich**	public (ly)
erhalten	to preserve	**der Ort, -e**	town
erklären	to explain	**prägen**	to form, to impress on
erleben	to experience	**profilieren**	to profile
erledigen	to take care of	**der Rand, ⁼er**	rim, outskirts
erwähnen	to mention	**rechthaben**	to be right
erziehen	to raise, bring up, educate	**ich hatte recht**	I was right
		das Reich, -e	empire, kingdom, realm
das Essen, -	food, meal		
die Fahrt, -en	drive, trip	**die Reichsstadt, ⁼e**	imperial city
die Heimfahrt, -en	trip home	**die Rolle, -n**	the role
das Feld, -er	field	**schlimm**	bad
fließen	to flow	**schneien**	to snow
der Fußgänger, -	pedestrian	**schwer**	difficult; heavy
die Fußgängerzone, -n	pedestrian zone	**der Sinn, -e**	sense
		sparen	to save
die Geburt, -en	birth	**die Spur, -en**	trace
gebürtig	native	**der Stall, ⁼e**	stall, stable
das Gefühl, -e	feeling	**die Stelle, -n**	spot, position
die Gegend, -en	area	**an deiner Stelle**	in your place
die Gemeinde, -n	(religious or civic) community	**die Strafe, -n**	punishment, fine
		der Strafzettel, -	traffic ticket
der Grund, ⁼e	the base, reason	**tatsächlich**	in fact, indeed
gründen	to found	**umsteigen**	to change (trains, buses, etc.)
krumm	bent, crooked		
die Kunde (*no pl.*)	knowledge about	**unbedingt**	absolutely
die Heimatkunde	study of the local area	**der Unfall, ⁼e**	accident
		unterrich′ten	to instruct, teach
die Landwirtschaft (*no pl.*)	agriculture	**das Vergnügen, -**	pleasure
		das Vor′urteil, -e	prejudice
am liebsten (*adv.*)	(I would like) most of all	**vorwärts**	forward
		der Wald, -⁼er	forest
am liebsten wohnten wir in München	we would like most of all to live in Munich	**die Ware, -n**	the goods (to be sold)
		das WC, -s	(water closet) toilet
das Mittel, -	means	**wecken**	to awaken, wake (someone) up
das Verkehrsmittel, -	means of transportation		
		wertvoll	valuable
das Mittelalter	the Middle Ages	**das Zentrum, die Zentren**	center

Additional Vocabulary

das Ackerland	farmland
die Armee', -n	army
ausgraben	to dig out
aussterben	to die out
befestigen	to fortify
die Befestigung, -en	fortification
der Berghang, ⸚e	mountain slope
besiegen	to defeat
der Beton (no pl.)	concrete
der Blumenkohl (no pl.)	cauliflower
die Burg, -en	castle
der Diesel, -	Diesel car
dokumentieren	to document
dokumentierbar	documentable
der Einheimische, -n	native
die Eisenbahn, -en	railroad
entdecken	to discover
die Entdeckung, -en	discovery
existieren	to exist
das Fundament, -e	foundation, basis
die Geographie (no pl.)	geography
gotisch	Gothic
der Händler, -	tradesman
harmonisch	harmonious
häßlich	ugly
der Herzog, ⸚e	duke
hinkommen	to get there
hinstellen	to put up, to place
die Innenstadt, ⸚e	inner city
irr	insane
ein Irrer	an insane person
die Kelten (pl.)	the Celts
der Kern, -e	kernel, center
das Kloster, ⸚	monastery
konzentrisch	concentric

lebhaft	lively
der Millionär, -e	millionaire
der Missionar, -e	missionary
mitten in	in the middle of
das Parkhaus, ⸚er	parking garage
pessimi'stisch	pessimistic
protestan'tisch	protestant
rasen	to race
rationalisieren	to rationalize
der Ratskeller, -	restaurant in city hall
das Reihenhaus, ⸚er	row house
reinlassen (hereinlassen)	to let in
revoltie'ren	to revolt
roma'nisch	Romanesque
der Römer, -	the Roman
römisch	Roman
die Ruine, -n	ruin
die Sage, -n	legend
die Seitenstraße, -n	side road
die Selbständigkeit (no pl.)	independence
siedeln	to homestead, settle
die Stauung, -en	traffic jam
der Stolz (no pl.)	pride
überde'cken	to cover
überle'ben	to survive
um'wandeln	to change
undenkbar	unthinkable
die Urkunde, -n	document
urbanisie'ren	to urbanize
die Urbanisierung	urbanization
die Verteidigung, -en	defense
vollenden	to complete
die Vor'wahl	area code
der Weingärtner, -	vintner
der Zoo, -s	zoo

Strong Verbs

ausgraben	gräbt aus	grub aus	ausgegraben	to dig out
aussterben	stirbt aus	starb aus	ist ausgestorben	to die out
erhalten	erhält	erhielt	erhalten	to preserve
erziehen		erzog	erzogen	to raise, educate
fließen		floß	ist geflossen	to flow
umsteigen		stieg um	ist umgestiegen	to change (trains, buses, etc.)

Wein der Könige   König der Weine !

Die geschützte Qualitätsmarke für
geprüften Original

GUMPOLDSKIRCHNER
SPITZENWEIN

UNIT 10 Prepositions with Dative or Accusative—
The Genitive Case—**ein**-Words without Nouns

If you look up prepositions in a dictionary, you will find neat pairs of cognates, such as *in*-**in,** *for*-**für,** *by*-**bei,** *since*-**seit,** or *from*-**von.** However, these correspondences don't always exist and a German prepositional phrase very often does not use the same preposition as its English equivalent. To be sure, you may live *in* Cologne and a German **wohnt** *in* **Köln,** and the flowers you have bought are *for* Aunt Emily and *für* **Tante Amalie,** but if you live *with* Aunt Emily, your German cousin **wohnt** *bei* **Tante Amalie,** and if you are expected for dinner *at* six, Cousin Fritz is due to arrive **um** sechs. The trouble is, the use of a given preposition is completely unpredictable, and you can never assume that by using the German cognate of an English preposition you use that preposition correctly.

Be sure, therefore, that when you memorize verbs you memorize at least some of the uses of prepositions that can go with them. You will have opportunities to do so in this unit which involves the remaining two groups of prepositions, those with the genitive and those with either dative or accusative. You will now be able to determine why you go **ins Kino,** but are **im Kino.**

With the introduction of the genitive case, we also conclude the description of the German case system. After you have learned the genitive forms we suggest that you go back to the analysis sections describing the nominative, accusative, and dative, and that you review the entire German case system and the functions of each case.

By now, most units provide an opportunity for you to go beyond the printed conversations and to invent small talk of your own. Make the most of these opportunities, especially if you are planning to travel or study in Central Europe. Remember that the Germans you meet in Dresden, or the Austrians in Klagenfurt or the Swiss in Sankt Gallen will not have memorized the other half of your dialogues; in fact, they will, at least initially, speak the way they would to another native German speaker. It is for this reason that we ask you to regard your teacher as a "native" and to have him or her respond to you as though you were already completely bilingual.

The reading selection in this unit is quite different from what you have read so far. It is written in the journalistic style that you find in German weekly magazines such as *Stern* or *Quick.*

Der Wein ist gut hier in Gumpoldskirchen.

Patterns

[1] Review: Prepositions with the Accusative, Prepositions with the Dative

Note the variety of ways and meanings in which these prepositions are used.

SEE
ANALYSIS
118
(p. 287)

In einer halben Stunde fuhren wir durch ganz Liechtenstein. (*preposition*)	In half an hour we drove through all of Liechtenstein.
Wir durch*fuhren** Liechtenstein in einer halben Stunde. (*prefix*)	We drove through (traversed) Liechtenstein in half an hour.
Das Fleisch ist noch nicht ganz *durch*gebraten. (*complement*)	The meat isn't quite well done yet.
Es hat so geregnet, daß wir durch und durch naß wurden. (*adverb*)	It rained so much that we got wet through and through.
Es regnete Tag für Tag.	It rained day in and day out (day after day).
Was hast du denn für den Wein bezahlt?	What did you pay for the wine?
Ich habe gar nichts gegen deinen Bruder.	I have nothing at all against your brother.
Gegen Abend fing es an zu regnen.	As night fell (toward evening) it began to rain.
Karla sagt, sie kommt gegen sechs.	Karla says she'll come around six o'clock.

*Note that **durch** in **durchfahren** is not a verbal complement, but a prefix like **ge-** or **ver-;** hence the stress is on the stem: durch**fahren**. Contrast with **durch**braten. Hence, the participle of **durchfahren** is durch**fahren** (without **-ge-**), the participle of **durch**braten is **durch**gebraten (with **-ge-**).

Ich fahre nie ohne einen Regenmantel in die Berge.	I never go to the mountains without a raincoat.
Der Zug aus Darmstadt kommt um sechs Uhr an.	The train from Darmstadt arrives at six o'clock.
Alle standen um den neuen Porsche herum.	They were all standing around the new Porsche.
Um Weihnachten herum will er wieder hier sein.	He wants to (plans to) be back around Christmas time.
Jetzt habe ich das Glas umgeworfen; schade um den schönen Wein.	Now I've knocked over the glass; too bad about that nice wine.
Die Zeit ist um.	Time is up.
Um um Umstadt herumzufahren, müssen wir auf der Bundesstraße bleiben.	In order to drive around (bypass) Umstadt, we'll have to stay on the federal highway.
Ich komme gerade aus dem Kino.	I'm just coming from the movies.
Wann ist denn heute das Fußballspiel aus?	When is the soccer game over today?
Herr Enderle ist aus Stuttgart, aber seine Frau kommt aus Ostpreußen.	Mr. Enderle is from Stuttgart, but his wife comes from East Prussia.
Der Kalbsbraten ist leider aus, mein Herr, aber wie wäre es mit einem Rippchen mit Kraut?	Sorry, but we are out of the veal roast, sir, but how about smoked rib with sauerkraut?
Das Wort *beef* kommt aus dem Französischen.	The word *beef* comes from the French.
Außer einem Kriminalroman habe ich leider nichts zu lesen mitgebracht.	Except for a detective novel, I unfortunately didn't bring anything to read.
Bei dem Regen bleiben wir lieber zu Hause.	In this rain we'd better stay home.

Wo noch?
NUR BEI MÖBELFABRIK
WALTER MAYER

Ferien für Mutter

Gedanken zur Woche

So kam der Mars zu uns ins Zimmer

... und bei Müllers wird gefeiert

Liebe im Straßenverkehr

Flug über die Grenze

Dem Gulasch gibt man dann noch etwas Paprika bei.	Then you add some paprika to the goulash.
Brötchen kriegen Sie hier bei uns.	Rolls you can get right here from us.
Burgbach liegt bei Stuttgart.	Burgbach is located near Stuttgart.
Er wohnt bei seiner Tante.	He lives with his aunt (at his aunt's).
Er geht mit seiner Tante ins Museum.	He goes to the museum with his aunt.
Bist du mit dem Wagen gefahren?—Nein, mit dem Zug.	Did you go by car?—No, by train.
Nach dem Theater fuhr er noch nach Köln.	After the theater, he still drove to Cologne.
Meine Uhr geht nach.	My watch runs slow.
Geht ihr nur schon; ich komme nach.	You go ahead; I'll come later (I'll follow you).
Seit dem Abitur* habe ich sie nicht mehr gesehen.	I haven't seen her since we graduated.
Seit wir in Hamburg wohnen, kommen wir nur noch selten in die Berge.	Since we've been living in Hamburg, we only rarely get to the mountains anymore.
Vom Denken wird man leicht müde.	Thinking makes you tired very easily.
Die Brötchen sind nicht ganz frisch; sie sind von gestern.	The rolls aren't quite fresh anymore; they're from yesterday.
Ich hätte gerne ein Pfund von dieser Leberwurst.	I'd like to have a pound of this liverwurst.

*Abitur: final examinations after secondary school (**Gymnasium**).

Ich fahre heute zum Mittagessen nach Hause.

I'll go home for lunch today.

Hast du was zu essen hier? —Ja, was denn zum Beispiel?

Have you got something to eat here?—Yes, what, for example?

Die Tür ist zu. Wer hat sie denn zugemacht?

The door is shut. Who's closed it?

[2] Prepositions with either Accusative or Dative

Analyze the use of case after the prepositions. Be prepared to produce the answers orally in class when you hear the questions.

Wo fahrt *ihr* denn hin?—Wir fahren an den *Neck*ar.
   Where are *you* going?—*We* are going to the *Neck*ar.

SEE
ANALYSIS
119
(p. 288)

Wo *wart* ihr denn gestern?—Wir waren gestern am *Neck*ar.
   Where *were* you yesterday?—We were at the *Neck*ar yesterday.

Wohin ist er denn mit seiner Frau gefahren?—Er ist mit ihr in den Schwarzwald gefahren.
   Where did he go with his wife?—He went to the Black Forest with her.

Wo wohnt er denn?—Er wohnt im Schwarzwald.
   Where does he live?—He lives in the Black Forest.

Was hat er denn mit seinem Geld gemacht?—Er hat es auf die Bank gebracht.
Wo hast *du* dein Geld?—*Ich* habe mein Geld *auch* auf der Bank.

Wo hast du den Wagen denn *hin*gestellt?—Hinter das *Haus.*
Wo *steht* denn dein Wagen?—Hinter dem *Haus.*

Was habt *ihr* denn gestern gemacht?—*Wir* sind gestern ins The*a*ter gegangen.
Wo wart ihr denn gestern abend?—Im Theater.

Was haben Sie denn mit meiner Zeitung gemacht?—Ich habe sie neben Ihren Hut gelegt.
Neben meinem Hut liegt sie aber nicht.—Wo kann sie denn sein?

Wie seid ihr nach Deutschland geflogen?—Wir sind nonstop über den Atlantik geflogen.
Und wo habt ihr gefrühstückt?—Über dem Atlantik.

Es regnete, und wir hielten unter der Brücke.
Es regnete, und wir liefen unter die Brücke.

Wo haben Sie Rosemarie denn gesehen?—Vor dem Hotel.
Bringen Sie mir bitte den Wagen?—Ja, ich bringe ihn vor das Hotel.

Wo lag denn der Brief?—Er lag zwischen den Zeitungen, und ich konnte ihn nicht finden.
Er konnte den Brief lange nicht finden; seine Frau hatte ihn zwischen die Zeitungen gelegt.

Vor zehn Jahren stand hier ein Haus.
Sollen wir vor oder nach dem Theater essen?
Vor einem Jahr kam Ingelheim nach Hause.
Ich möchte vor dem Essen noch einen Brief schreiben.

[3] Prepositions with the Genitive

SEE
ANALYSIS
122-123
(pp. 291-293)

Während des Sommers war Schmidt in Tirol.
   During the summer Schmidt was in the Tyrol.

Während der Woche kannst du mich nicht besuchen.
   During the week you can't visit me.

Sie können doch wegen des Regens nicht zu Hause bleiben.
   You can't stay at home because of the rain.

Wir haben trotz des Regens gestern gearbeitet.
   We worked yesterday in spite of the rain.

Wir haben trotz dem Regen gestern gearbeitet.
   We worked yesterday in spite of the rain.

Try to form sentences of your own using **während, wegen,** and **trotz.**

[4] The Attributive Genitive

Rephrase the German sentences by using the elements indicated in parentheses.

SEE
ANALYSIS
123
(p. 293)

Am Abend ihres Geburtstages ging er mit ihr ins Theater.
   On the evening of her birthday he went to the theater with her.
   (on the evening of his birthday)

Gegen Ende des Jahres kam er aus Afrika zurück.
   Toward the end of the year he came back from Africa.
   (toward the end of the week)

Herr Harms ist ein Freund meines Mannes.
   Mr. Harms is a friend of my husband.
   (the son of my friend)

Werners Freundin kenne ich nicht.
   I don't know Werner's girlfriend.
   (Ingrid's aunt)

Schmidts Roman habe ich nicht gelesen.
   I haven't read Schmidt's novel.
   (father's books)

Hast du Mutters Hut gesehen?
   Have you seen mother's hat?
   (Karl's car)

[5] von plus Dative as a Genitive Substitute

SEE
ANALYSIS
123
(p. 293)

Hannelore? Das ist doch die Freundin von Werner Schlosser!
Hannelore? She's Werner Schlosser's friend, isn't she?
(Hans Wagner's wife)

Herr Behrens ist ein Freund von meinem Mann.
Mr. Behrens is a friend of my husband's.
(Mrs. Behrens; of my wife's)

Herr Behrens ist ein Freund von Johannes.
Mr. Behrens is a friend of Johannes's.
(Mrs. Behrens; a friend of Inge's)

Renate ist eine von Dieters Freundinnen.
Renate is one of Dieter's girlfriends.
(Jürgen; Armin's friends)

Note the difference in the use of the genitive and of von plus dative in the following sentences. When is the von-phrase obligatory?

Ingelheims Kinder sind noch klein.
Die Kinder von Ingelheim sind noch klein.
Die Kinder von Ingelheims sind noch sehr klein.
Ingrids Kinder sind noch sehr klein.
Die Kinder von Ingrid sind noch sehr klein.
Sie war eine Freundin von Overhoffs Frau.
Er war der Vater von dreizehn Kindern.
Ich bin kein Freund von Rheinwein.
Jeder Leser von Kriegsromanen weiß, wer Schmidt-Ingelheim ist.

[6] Special Constructions

SEE
ANALYSIS
123
(p. 293)

Er ist ein Freund von mir.

von _____ (du)
von _____ (er)
von _____ (sie)
von _____ (wir)
von _____ (ihr)
von _____ (Sie)
von _____ (meine Mutter)
von _____ (mein Vater)

Möchten Sie noch eine Tasse Tee?
Would you like another cup of tea?

Haben Sie schon gewählt?—Ja, ich hätte gerne ein Glas Mosel.
Have you decided yet?—Yes, I'd like a glass of Moselle.

Meine Frau würde gerne ein Glas Wasser trinken.
My wife would like to drink a glass of water.

[7] ein-Words without Nouns

Form variations of your own.

SEE
ANALYSIS
124
(p. 295)

Ich habe leider kein Buch mitgebracht. Hast du eins bei dir?
    Unfortunately, I didn't bring a book along. Do you have one with you?

Keiner von seinen Freunden hat ihn besucht.
    None of his friends visited him.

Hier ist das Buch von Rolf.—Nein, das ist meins.
    Here is Rolf's book.—No, that's mine.

Mir gehört das Buch nicht; es muß deins sein.
    That book doesn't belong to me. It must be yours.

Wem gehört denn der Porsche? Ist das Ihrer, Frau Kröger?
    Who owns that Porsche? Is it yours, Mrs. Kröger?

Einen Ihrer Romane habe ich gelesen.
    I have read one of your novels.

Einen von Ihren Romanen habe ich gelesen.
    I have read one of your novels.

Eine seiner Töchter studiert jetzt Medizin.
    One of his daughters is studying medicine now.

Eine von seinen Töchtern studiert jetzt Medizin.
    One of his daughters is studying medicine now.

[8] gar nicht, gar kein, gar nichts

Study these sentences carefully. Note that whenever **gar** is stressed, it denies an immediately preceding idea. Be prepared to form your own examples.

SEE
ANALYSIS
125
(p. 296)

Meyer ist gar nicht *dumm*; er weiß immer, was er will.
    Meyer isn't at all stupid; he always knows what he wants.

Was, Heidi will heiraten? Das habe ich gar nicht ge*wußt*.
    What? Heidi wants to get married? I didn't have any idea of that.

Er spricht so leise, daß man ihn gar nicht ver*ste*hen kann.
    He speaks so softly that you can't understand him at all.

Hast du gut geschlafen?—Nein, ich habe *gar* nicht geschlafen.
    Did you sleep well?—No, I didn't sleep at all.

Was habt ihr denn heute gelernt?—*Gar* nichts, wir haben nur gespielt.
    What did you learn today?—Nothing at all, we only played.

Ingelheim *war* gar kein General; er war nur Leutnant.
    Ingelheim wasn't a general at all; he was only a lieutenant.

Analysis

118 Prepositions

Prepositions have a more versatile function than any other type of words, and their use tends to be so idiomatic and idiosyncratic that one English preposition may correspond to ten German prepositions and vice versa. Even when used as genuine prepositions, that is, before a noun or pronoun, it may take a whole dictionary column to describe their semantic range. Take, for example, the preposition **in** in each phrase:

in any case	**auf jeden Fall**	**in die Schule gehen**	to go to school
in the evening	**am Abend**	**im Gras**	on the grass
in German	**auf Deutsch**	**in diesem Augenblick**	at this moment
one in five	**eins von fünf**	**in ärztlicher Behand-**	under medical care
in my opinion	**nach meiner Meinung**	**lung**	
in that rain	**bei dem Regen**	**in guter Absicht**	with good intentions
in time	**zur rechten Zeit**	**im ersten Stock**	on the second floor
in a word	**mit einem Wort**		
in heaven	**im Himmel**		
in the sky	**am Himmel**		

---

topfit im Büro

Trotz Sturz erfolgreich

Gespräch zwischen zwei Schulen

Seit Jahren bewährt,

Prepositions are also widely used as unstressed verbal prefixes (*to overlook*, **übersehen**), as verbal complements (*to go out*, **ausgehen**), with prepositional objects (*to believe in God*, **an Gott glauben**) (see Unit 12). Some prepositions are even used like adjectives:

The light is on.	**Das Licht ist an.**
The door was closed.	**Die Tür war zu.**
Is everybody in?	**Sind alle da?**

In Patterns [1], which reviews those prepositions that always take the accusative or always take the dative, we have used these prepositions in a variety of idiomatic ways.

Remember:

ALWAYS WITH THE DATIVE: **aus, außer, bei, mit, nach, seit, von, zu.**
ALWAYS WITH THE ACCUSATIVE: **durch, für, gegen, ohne.**

Bis (*until; up to; as far as*) and **um** (*at; at about*). These two prepositions are used with the accusative, but very infrequently; either they are not followed by a noun phrase in the accusative or the accusative is not readily identifiable because there is no article. Examples:

Also bis Sonntag.	See you on Sunday.
Also bis nächsten Sonntag.	See you next Sunday.
Er bleibt bis zum* ersten April hier.	He is staying here until April 1.
Ich fahre bis Darmstadt mit.	I'll come along as far as Darmstadt.
Von April bis Oktober regnet es hier nie.	From April until October it never rains here.
Von Stuttgart bis München fährt der Zug etwa zwei Stunden.	The train takes about two hours from Stuttgart to Munich.
Er kam um halb neun.	He came at (exactly) 8:30.
Er kam gegen halb neun.	He came around 8:30.
Fahren Sie hier um die Ecke und dann um den Bahnhof herum.	Turn the corner here, and then drive around the station.

Note that **um** with a local meaning is often followed by **herum** after the noun or pronoun.

119 Prepositions with either Dative or Accusative

Nouns or pronouns following the prepositions **aus, außer, bei, mit, nach, seit, von, zu** must always be in the dative case.

> Ich komme von meiner Tante.
> Ich komme von ihr.

Nouns or pronouns following **durch, für, gegen, ohne, um** must always be in the accusative.

> Ich gehe ohne meinen Freund.
> Ich gehe ohne ihn.

In both groups, it is the preposition alone that determines the case of the following noun or pronoun.

There is, however, a group of prepositions which can be used with either dative or accusative, and the case of the noun or pronoun following these prepositions depends on the particular situation.

These prepositions are:

> **an, auf, hinter, in, neben, über, unter, vor, zwischen**

These nine prepositions are used to describe local areas in relation to some fixed point of reference. Thus, the English phrases *under the sofa* and *behind the sofa* describe different areas in relation to the *sofa*.

*Dative case determined by **zu**, not by **bis**.

To a native speaker of English, the phrase *under the sofa* is not ambiguous; it can be used without danger of confusion in such sentences as

The dog slept under the sofa

and

The dog crawled under the sofa.

However, the same speaker of English will usually distinguish between *in* and *into* in such sentences as

The dog slept in the house.   The dog ran into the house.

A German will argue that the difference between *sleeping in the house* and *running into the house* is exactly parallel to the difference between *sleeping under the sofa* and *crawling under the sofa*.

Germans are very conscious of this difference because their language forces them to distinguish not only between *in*-situations and *into*-situations, but also between the two kinds of *under*-situations. The distinction is made in German not by the use of different prepositions like *in* and *into* but by the use of different cases following one and the same preposition.

If the area described by one of the nine prepositions above functions as the end-point or goal reached by the action (of crawling under the sofa), the noun following this preposition shows the accusative case.

If the area is the place where the entire action (of sleeping under the sofa) goes on from beginning to end, the noun following the preposition shows the dative.

This means that a German will always distinguish between **unter das Sofa** and **unter dem Sofa.**

Der Hund schläft unter dem Sofa.	**Der Hund springt unter das Sofa.**
Der Hund schläft hinter dem Sofa.	**Der Hund springt hinter das Sofa.**
Der Hund schläft auf dem Sofa.	**Der Hund springt auf das Sofa.**

It is important to realize that the distinction between dative and accusative after these nine prepositions is not one of rest versus motion. In both situations there may be motion (*He walked in the garden* and *He walked into the garden*). The determining factor is whether or not, in the course of the verbal action, a border line is crossed by either the subject or the object. If such a border line is crossed, the accusative must be used; if not, the dative must be used. This border line may be real or imagined. Thus, the area **vor dem Haus** does not have a clearly defined border, but there is nevertheless common consent as to the meaning of **vor dem Haus.** If this area **vor dem Haus** is entered in the course of the verbal action, the accusative must be used: **Er fuhr vor das Haus** (*He drove up to the house*). If the entire verbal action takes place within the area **vor dem Haus,** the dative must be used: **Er hielt vor dem Haus** (*He stopped in front of the house*).

On the other hand, after verbs which cannot imply motion, such as **sein** and **bleiben,** the dative is always required with these nine prepositions.

> **Er ist schon im Bett.**
> **Ich bleibe heute im Bett.**

NOTE:

1. The preposition corresponding to English *on* is **auf,** not **an.** German **an** describes an area "leaning against and touching" the point of reference. Thus it is **Frankfurt am Main** and **Köln am Rhein** (cf. *Stratford-on-Avon*). One speaks of a bed which stands **an der Wand** (**an** plus dative) after it has been pushed **an die Wand** (**an** plus accusative).

2. Unless the article is stressed, the following contractions are customary: **an dem = am; an das = ans; in dem = im; in das = ins.** The contractions **aufs, hinterm, übers, unterm** also occur in colloquial German.

3. If used with the accusative, **über** means either *over* with the implication "into the territory across," or it means *via* or *by way of*.

Er sprang über *den* Zaun.	He jumped over the fence (into the neighbor's garden).
Er ist über *die* Schweiz nach Italien gefahren.	He went to Italy via Switzerland.

When **über** means *via*, the corresponding interrogative is **wie?**, not **wohin?**

Wie seid ihr nach Italien gefahren, über Österreich oder über die Schweiz?	How did you go to Italy, via Austria or via Switzerland?

but

Wohin seid ihr gefahren?	Where did you go?
Nach Italien! Und zwar über die* Schweiz!	To Italy—and by way of Switzerland!

4. As you already know, the preposition **vor** frequently means *ago*. If so used, it must be followed by the dative: **vor drei Jahren** (*three years ago*).

120 wo and wohin

The difference between **unter dem Sofa** and **unter das Sofa** reappears in the difference between **wo** and **wohin**. If you ask a **wo**-question, chances are that the answer will contain one of the nine "local area" prepositions with the dative; if you ask a **wohin**-question, chances are that the answer will contain one of those prepositions with the accusative.

> **Wo warst du denn?—In der Stadt.**
> **Wohin willst du denn?—In die Stadt.**

---

*With the names of a few countries, the article *must* be used, for example, **die Schweiz, die Tschechoslowakei, die Türkei.**

121 Splitting **wohin, woher, dahin,** and **daher**

In spoken German, the interrogatives **wohin** (*to which place*) and **woher** (*from which place*) and the demonstratives **dahin** (*to that place*) and **daher** (*from that place*) are usually split in such a way that **hin** and **her** become part of the second prong. They are then treated as if they were complements like **ab** or **an** and thus join a following verb form. Thus, there are two distinct patterns of the types **Wohin . . . gehen** and **Wo . . . hingehen.**

UNSPLIT POSITION	SPLIT POSITION
Wohin *gehst* du?	**Wo** gehst du *hin?*
Wohin willst du *gehen?*	**Wo** willst du denn *hingehen?*
Woher *kommst* du?	**Wo** kommst du *her?*
Woher ist der Brief *gekommen?*	**Wo** ist denn der Brief *hergekommen?*
Dahin *will* ich nicht.	**Da** will ich gar nicht *hin.*
Daher komme ich *auch.*	**Da** komme ich *auch* her.

These "split" forms are very commonly used. When a German unexpectedly meets a friend, he is more apt to ask **Wo kommst du denn her?** than **Woher kommst du?**

122 The Genitive Case

The English phrases *John Miller's house* and *the house of John Miller* are interchangeable. Both forms are *possessives* and answer the question *whose?* But *John Miller's* is called a genitive form, and *of John Miller* is a prepositional phrase used as a substitute for that genitive form. Forms like *John's* are normally used when referring to persons or to personifications; phrases with *of* are used in English when referring to things or ideas. It is normal to say *the purpose of the experiment*, not *the experiment's purpose*. Phrases with *of* are much more prevalent than forms with *-'s.*

In this unit the German genitive case is introduced. It is important to recognize from the very beginning two areas where German differs from English:

1. Phrases like *John's father* as well as phrases like *the purpose of the experiment* can be expressed in German by genuine genitive forms—that is, without the use of a preposition. German, in other words, does not make any distinction between persons and things. For example, **das Haus meines Vaters** and **der Titel meines Romans** correspond to *my father's house* and the incorrect *my novel's title.*

2. There is a growing tendency in German, especially in the spoken language, to avoid the genitive and to replace it with a prepositional phrase with **von,** again without any distinction between persons and things. It is very important, therefore, that you memorize thoroughly the patterns demonstrating

these constructions, and that you keep in mind the fact that quite often the same English phrase can be expressed in two different ways in German.

ein Freund meines Mannes   or   ein Freund von meinem Mann
das Ende dieses Romans   or   das Ende von diesem Roman

Forms of the Genitive Case

INTERROGATIVE PRONOUNS

NOM.	wer	was
ACC.	wen	was
DAT.	wem	was
GEN.	*wessen*	

NOTE: **Was** has no genitive of its own. The dative **was** is used only after prepositions governing the dative, for example. **Von *was* habt ihr geredet?**

***der*-WORDS AND *ein*-WORDS**

	MASC.	FEM.	NEUT.	PLURAL
NOM.	der	die	das	die
	ein	eine	ein	(keine)
ACC.	den	die	das	die
	einen	eine	ein	(keine)
DAT.	dem	der	dem	den
	einem	einer	einem	(keinen)
GEN.	*des*	*der*	*des*	*der*
	eines	*einer*	*eines*	*(keiner)*

NOUNS

Feminine nouns have the same form throughout the singular; there is no special ending for the genitive.

NOM.	die Frau	die Zeitung
ACC.	die Frau	die Zeitung
DAT.	der Frau	der Zeitung
GEN.	der Frau	der Zeitung

The majority of masculine and neuter nouns add the ending **-es** if their stem consists of one syllable, and **-s** if their stem consists of two or more syllables.

NOM.	der Mann	der Bahnhof	das Buch
ACC.	den Mann	den Bahnhof	das Buch
DAT.	dem Mann	dem Bahnhof	dem Buch
GEN.	des Mannes	des Bahnhofs	des Buches

Some masculine nouns, for example, **der Student, der Mensch, der Polizist'** (*the policeman*) have the ending **-en** in the genitive; this ending **-en** in such nouns occurs in all forms but the nominative singular.

	SINGULAR	PLURAL
NOM.	der Student	die Studenten
ACC.	den Studenten	die Studenten
DAT.	dem Studenten	den Studenten
GEN.	des Studenten	der Studenten

There are a few nouns that are irregular in the singular, for example, **das Herz** (*the heart*).

	SINGULAR	PLURAL
NOM.	das Herz	die Herzen
ACC.	das Herz	die Herzen
DAT.	dem Herz(en)	den Herzen
GEN.	des Herzens	der Herzen

The genitive plural of nouns has the same form as the nominative plural and the accusative plural. Remember that the dative plural of most German nouns ends in **-n** (see **55**).

NOM.	die Männer	die Frauen	die Bücher
ACC.	die Männer	die Frauen	die Bücher
DAT.	den Männern	den Frauen	den Büchern
GEN.	der Männer	der Frauen	der Bücher

123 Use of the Genitive

Prepositions Governing the Genitive

There are a number of prepositions which must be used with the genitive, but only three of these are important at this stage of your studies: **während** (*during*), **wegen** (*because of*), and **trotz** (*in spite of*).

> **Während des Krieges war Schmidt in Norwegen.**
> **Wegen des Regens bleiben wir zu Hause.**
> **Trotz des Regens fahren wir nach Köln.**

With **trotz** and **wegen**, there is a tendency to replace the genitive with the dative, but this is still considered colloquial (**trotz dem Regen**). The compound **trotzdem** (*in spite of that*, *nevertheless*) has become standard.

We have now introduced all the major German prepositions. Remember that they *must* be used with specific cases. There are four different groups:

WITH THE GENITIVE:	**während, wegen, trotz**
WITH THE DATIVE:	**aus, außer, bei, mit, nach, seit, von, zu**
WITH THE ACCUSATIVE:	**bis, durch, für, gegen, ohne, um**
WITH EITHER DATIVE OR ACCUSATIVE:	**an, auf, hinter, in, neben, über, unter, vor, zwischen**

The Genitive of Time
___

Occasionally, the genitive is used to express indefinite time. In contrast to English *one day* (past) and *some day* (future), **eines Tages** can be used for both past and future. Similarly: **eines Morgens, eines Abends,** and, by analogy, **eines Nachts** (and not **einer Nacht**). Definite time is expressed in the accusative: **nächsten Sonntag,** *next Sunday* (definite); **eines Sonntags,** *one (some) Sunday* (indefinite).

The Attributive Genitive
___

By far the most common occurrence of the genitive is its use as an attribute. It then modifies a noun in the same way that an adjective does.

> The government's decision did not come unexpectedly.
> (*government's* is an attribute of the subject *the decision*)

> The Thurbers expected Joan's cousin Jill to arrive momentarily.
> (*Joan's* is an attribute of the direct object *cousin Jill*)

In these sentences, the possessive attributes can be eliminated without impairing the basic structure of the sentence; in other words, even without the attributes, the sentences are complete units of thought.

> The decision did not come unexpectedly.
> The Thurbers expected cousin Jill momentarily.

In German, the use of the attributive genitive is considered standard in the written language. It is used in two positions:

1. If the genitive form is a proper name, it *precedes* the noun it modifies. The genitive of all proper names ends in -s.

> **Schmidt-Ingelheims Roman war eine Sensation.**
> **Werners Freundin kannte er nicht.**
> **Das Buch handelt von Deutschlands Rolle in der Weltpolitik.**

Note that German does not use an apostrophe with this personal genitive.

2. If the genitive form is a common noun, it *follows* the noun it modifies.

> **Am Abend ihres Geburtstages ging er mit ihr ins Theater.**

This means that *the woman's husband* must be rendered by **der Mann der Frau** and *the girl's father* by **der Vater des Mädchens.**

In the spoken language, the situation is far more complicated. While the attributive genitive is still considered standard German by most educated speakers, there is a steady erosion of these forms. The genitive most frequently replaced is the real possessive genitive in such forms as *my father's house* (expressing ownership: *My father owns the house*). The German equivalent is **das Haus meines Vaters,** but the variant **das Haus von meinem Vater** also occurs and is used even by many well-educated Germans.

Von plus dative is always used when the genitive would not be recognizable—
that is, primarily in the absence of an article or of a **der-** or **ein**-word.

die Ankunft von Touristen	the arrival of tourists
ein Vater von zehn Kindern	a father of ten children
eine Freundin von Müllers Frau	a friend of Müller's wife

With **Freund** and other nouns expressing similar relationships, **von** plus dative
is used as the equivalent of the English phrases

He is a friend of mine.	**Er ist ein Freund von mir.**
He is a friend of Karl's.	**Er ist ein Freund von Karl.**

The idea *one of* in such sentences as *He is one of my friends* is expressed by
einer (eine, eins) von (see **124**).

> **Er ist einer von meinen Freunden.**
> **Sie ist eine von Karls Freundinnen.**

In such phrases as *a cup of coffee*, *a glass of wine*, *a pound of butter*, where the
first noun denotes a measure and the second something measured, the second
German noun shows no case.

> **eine Tasse Kaffee**
> **ein Glas Wein**
> **ein Pfund Butter**

If more than one measured unit is involved, only feminine nouns are used in
the plural; masculines and neuters retain the singular form.

> **zwei Tassen Kaffee**
> **zwei Glas Wein**
> **zwei Pfund Butter**

Compounding of nouns is another means by which German very frequently
expresses the equivalent of English phrases with *of*, for example, *the production of leather goods:* **die Produktion von Lederwaren** or **die Lederwarenpro-
duktion.** English, of course, uses the same device, but usually without spelling
the compound as one word: *wheat production*, *book publishing*, and so forth.

124 ein-Words without Nouns

When **ein**-words are not followed by nouns, their declension is the same as that
of the **der**-words. The neuter ending is usually **-s** instead of **-es**. Thus **mein
Freund** becomes **meiner; ein Buch** becomes **eins.**

	MASCULINE		FEMININE		NEUTER	
NOM.	**ein Freund**	**einer**	**eine Frau**	**eine**	**ein Kind**	**ein(e)s**
ACC.	**einen Freund**	**einen**	**eine Frau**	**eine**	**ein Kind**	**ein(e)s**
DAT.	**einem Freund**	**einem**	**einer Frau**	**einer**	**einem Kind**	**einem**
GEN.	**eines Freundes**	—	**einer Frau**	—	**eines Kindes**	—

NOTE: The genitive forms are replaced by **von** + dative: **eines Freundes = von einem.**

> **Inges Freund heißt Ulrich, und** *meiner* **heißt Werner.**
> **Ich habe leider kein Buch. Hast du** *eins?*
> **Hier steht ein Wagen, und dort steht noch einer.**

125 gar nicht, gar kein, gar nichts

The particle **gar** is used in connection with a following **nicht, kein,** or **nichts** either to add the idea "contrary to expectation" or to strengthen the negative particle in the same way in which *at all* strengthens the *not* in *not at all.*

> **Meyer ist gar nicht so dumm, wie du denkst.**
> Meyer isn't as stupid as you think.

> **Ich habe heute nacht gar nicht geschlafen.**
> I didn't sleep at all last night.

> **Ingelheim war gar kein General; er war nur Leutnant.**
> Ingelheim wasn't a general at all, he was only a lieutenant.

> **Ich dachte, er würde mir wenigstens Blumen mitbringen; aber er hat mir gar
>   nichts mitgebracht.**
> I thought he would at least bring me flowers; but he didn't bring me any-
>   thing at all.

Nicht, kein, and **nichts** after **gar** are never stressed.

126 Word Formation

The Suffix -ung

The suffix **-ung** is added to many verb stems. It forms feminine nouns, the plural form being **-ungen,** and often corresponds to English *-tion.*

die Einladung	invitation
die Erwartung	expectation
die Erzählung	story, narration
die Hoffnung	hope
die Untersuchung	investigation
die Versuchung	temptation
die Wohnung	living quarters, apartment

The Suffix -ig

The suffix **-ig** may be added to nouns to form adjectives corresponding to English derivatives of the type *stone: stony, cat: catty,* which all express pos-session of the quality typical of the thing denoted by the noun.

der Stein	steinig	stony
der Hunger	hungrig	hungry
die Seite	einseitig	one-sided

The suffix **-ig** is also added to some time expressions to form adjectives which have no equivalents in English.

die Zeit	zeitig	in (good) time
	rechtzeitig	on time, at the right time
das Jahr	-jährig	
	dreijährig	three years old, lasting for three years
	ein dreijähriges Kind	a three-year-old child
	eine dreitägige Wanderung	a three-day hike
heute	heutig	of today
	die heutige Zeitung	today's paper
jetzt	jetzig	of today, present, contemporary
	der jetzige Bürgermeister heißt Böttle	the name of the present mayor is Böttle
damals	damalig	then
	der damalige Bürgermeister hieß Meyer	the then mayor's name was Meyer

Note also:

hier	hiesig	
	die hiesige Bevölkerung	the local population
geboren	gebürtig	native
die Geburt	Herr Schmid ist ein gebürtiger Burgbacher	Mr. Schmid is a native of Burgbach.

The Suffix **-los**

The suffix **-los** corresponds to English *-less*. It is added to nouns to form adjectives.

das Herz	herzlos	heartless
die Arbeit	arbeitslos	unemployed
die Zeit	zeitlos	timeless

Conversations

Ein junges Ehepaar,° Gerd und Sabine Mattes, nach dem Abendessen: couple

I

SABINE: Mach doch mal den Fernseher° an; jetzt kommt gleich der   TV
Wetterbericht.°   weather report

1.PROGRAMM

20.00 Tagesschau — Wetter

20.15 Hits Hits Hits
BR
Die Interpreten: **Hank The Knife**: ›Guitar King‹ / **Peter Maffay**: ›Josie‹ / **Abba**: ›Waterloo‹ / **Udo Jürgens**: ›Griechischer Wein‹ / **Rubettes**: ›Juke Box Jive‹ / **Michael Holm**: ›Tränen lügen nicht‹ / **Albert Hammond**: ›Down by the river…‹ / **Juliane Werding**: ›Wenn du denkst…‹ / **Bay City Rollers**: ›By bye baby‹ / **Howard Carpendale**: ›Deine Spuren im Sand‹ / **Carl Douglas**: ›Kung Fu fighting‹ / **Chris Roberts**: ›Du kannst nicht mehr 17 sein‹ / **Alain Barrière & Noelle Cordier**: ›Tu t'en vas‹ / **Jürgen Marcus**: ›Ein Lied zieht hinaus in die Welt‹ / **Santabarbara**: ›Charly‹ / **Vikky Leandros**: ›Theo, wir fahr'n nach Lodz‹ / **Rod Steward**: ›Sailing‹ / **Gunter Gabriel**: ›Hey Boß‹ / **George Baker Selection**: ›Paloma Blanca‹ und **Ilja Richter**

21.40 Ziehung der Lottozahlen
HR

☐☐☐☐☐☐ / ☐

SDR
**Tagesschau — Wetter
Das Wort zum Sonntag**

Das Wetter

Veränderlich bewölkt und meist niederschlagsfrei. Höchsttemperaturen um 20 Grad. Nachts Tiefstwerte bei zwölf Grad. Schwacher Wind aus nordöstlichen Richtungen.

GERD: In welchem Programm?*

SABINE: Im ersten.

GERD: Wahrscheinlich° wird's morgen sowieso wieder regnen, aber wir können ja mal hören.
      probably

II

SABINE: Das sind noch die Nachrichten,° die habe ich vorhin° schon gehört.
      news   a while ago

GERD: Ja, und dann kommt erst noch zehn Minuten Sport, und dann die Lotto-Zahlen,† und …

SABINE: Nein, die Lotto-Zahlen kommen doch erst nachher,°—nach dem Wetter.
      afterwards

GERD: Ich dachte, die kämen immer vorher.

III

SABINE: Wenn's so bleibt, könnten wir morgen segeln° gehen.
      sailing

GERD: Das wäre eine Idee, obwohl ich eigentlich lieber mit dem Motorboot rausfahren° würde, zum Fischen.
      = hinausfahren

SABINE: Das kannst du doch auch mit dem Segelboot, —und außerdem° sparst° du dabei das Benzin.
      besides   save

GERD: Da hast du natürlich recht. —Sollen wir noch jemand mitnehmen?

SABINE: Ruf doch mal den Heinz an; der kommt sicher mit.

*In the Federal Republic, there are three nationwide TV networks, **das erste Programm, das zweite Programm, das dritte Programm**; in addition, there are regional programs, for example, as indicated in the TV schedule on this page, the **Bayerische Rundfunk (BR)**, the **Hessische Rundfunk (HR)**, and the **Süddeutsche Rundfunk (SDR)**.

†**Lotto-Zahlen** refers to a weekly numbers game, played by millions of people. If you have correctly indicated six out of fifty numbers (from 1–50) on your entry blank, you can win several hundred thousand D-marks when the numbers are drawn on TV every Saturday night.

IV

SABINE: Na, was hat er gesagt?

GERD: Er sagt, er wäre zwar zur Zeit sehr beschäftigt und müßte
eigentlich auch am Sonntag in den Betrieb.*

SABINE: Aber . . . ?

GERD: Aber er würde doch versuchen, mitzukommen.

SABINE: Dann sollten wir auch die Annemarie anrufen. Der würde das
bestimmt Spaß machen.°   she would have fun

V

Construct a telephone conversation between Sabine and Annemarie, using the following elements:

SABINE: morgen, segeln, mitkommen?

ANNEMARIE: müde, lange Woche, schlafen wollen.

SABINE: früh ins Bett gehen, —übrigens: Heinz, mitgehen.

ANNEMARIE: nicht *so* müde, wann wegfahren?

SABINE: nicht sehr früh, neun Uhr.

ANNEMARIE: Heinz anrufen, fragen, ob abholen.°   pick up

VI

Now produce a conversation between Annemarie and Heinz, as outlined. A. tells H. that she has just talked to S. He says that he has talked to Gerd and that Gerd and Sabine have asked him to go sailing tomorrow. A. tells him that they have asked her to go too. H. is delighted and asks A. if he can pick her up. A. says that she was about to ask him to pick her up. They agree that he will come at about 8:30.

VII

After reviewing the reading of Units 7, 8, and 9, let your teacher be a German from Burgbach and ask questions about the village and his or her background. Your teacher, playing the role of a native speaker, will, of course, speak much more involved German than you are capable of using. Slow him or her down ("**Bitte sprechen Sie langsamer**"), mention that you are a foreigner, that you haven't been in Germany very long, etc.

Fragen an Sie persönlich

1. Sehen Sie gern fern? (**fernsehen** to watch TV)
   Was für Programme sehen Sie am liebsten? (**was für** what kinds of)
       Sport?   Krimis? (**der Krimi** cop show)
       Spielfilme (feature films)?   Nachrichten?   Diskussionen?
   In Europa gibt es keine privaten (kommerziellen) Radio- und Fernsehstationen. Radio und Fernsehen werden vom Staat subventioniert, und kein Programm wird durch Reklame unterbrochen. Halten Sie das für gut oder schlecht? (**wird unterbrochen** is interrupted   **die Reklame** advertising)

---

*This use of the subjunctive in indirect discourse will be explained in Unit 11. The sentence means, *He says that he is very busy right now and that he really ought to go to the shop/office on Sunday.*

2. Treiben Sie Sport?

Spielen Sie gern Fußball?

Golf?

Hockey?

Korbball (basketball)?

Können Sie schilaufen?

segeln?

Reading

The following text is of an expository nature. You will find its syntax somewhat more involved than in the texts you have read so far, and you will also notice that the vocabulary is of a different kind.

Wir haben nicht immer gegessen, wie° wir heute essen

Kein Mensch weiß genau, seit wann es wirkliche Menschen gibt, das heißt Wesen,° die aufrecht auf zwei Beinen gehen konnten und daher° zu der Klasse *homo erectus* gehörten. In Afrika hat man Skelette des *homo erectus* gefunden, die 1½ Millionen Jahre alt sind. Nach Nordeuropa ist der *homo erectus* nicht oft gekommen. Aber der 5 Heidelberg-Mensch, von dem man in der Nähe von° Heidelberg 1907 einen 500.000 Jahre alten Kiefer° fand, war ein *homo erectus*. Der erste nordeuropäische Mensch, dessen° Skelette man relativ oft gefunden hat, ist der *Neandertaler*. Der Name stammt von° dem Neandertal bei Düsseldorf, wo man seine Überreste° im Jahre 1856 10 entdeckt hat. Seitdem hat man Neandertalskelette auch in anderen nordeuropäischen Ländern gefunden.

Der Neandertaler erschien in Europa ca. 100.000 v. Chr. Er kannte schon das Feuer, aber man weiß nicht genau, ob er schon gelernt hatte, wie man jederzeit ein Feuer machen kann. Der Neandertaler 15 lebte in Höhlen,° aus denen er wahrscheinlich erst wilde Raubtiere° vertreiben° mußte, bevor er mit seiner Gruppe einziehen konnte.

Die Neandertaler hatten ein schweres Leben. Weniger als 50% der Neandertaler wurden 20 Jahre alt, und von den Menschen über 20 starben 80%, bevor sie 40 waren. Die Neandertaler lebten von wilden 20 Früchten, von Insekten, von Fischen, von Wurzeln° und von wilden Säugetieren,° von denen einige—wie der Mammut—sehr groß wurden. Wenn es ihnen gelang,° in einer Grube einen Mammut zu fangen, dann hatte die ganze Gruppe wahrscheinlich vier Wochen lang genug Fleisch zu essen. Alle mußten helfen, das große Tier mit 25 Steinmessern zu zerschneiden° und die Fleischstücke in die Höhle zu

the way

beings
therefore

in the proximity of, near
jawbone
whose
originates (stems) from
remains

caves   beasts of prey
chase

roots
mammals
when they succeeded

cut up

bringen, wo man das Fleisch dicht° neben einem Feuer braten konnte.   close
Leider konnte man das frische Fleisch nicht konservieren. Nach
einigen Wochen begann das frische Mammutfleisch zu riechen.° Und   smell
wahrscheinlich kommt die hohe Sterblichkeitsziffer° der Neander-   mortality rate
taler daher, daß° sie zu oft zuviel verdorbenes° Fleisch gegessen 5   from the fact that
haben. Kochen konnten die Neandertaler auch noch nicht. Töpfe°   spoiled   pots
gibt es erst seit 6000 v. Chr. Kein Neandertaler, so muß man anneh-
men,° hat also je eine gute Hühnersuppe° mit Nudeln gegessen.   assume   chicken soup

Aus irgendeinem Grunde sind die Neandertaler nach dem Anfang der
vierten Eiszeit ausgestorben. Seit ca. 60.000 v. Chr. gibt es in Europa 10
einen neuen Menschentyp: den Cro-Magnon Typ (benannt nach dem
Fundort Crô Magnon in Frankreich), den *homo sapiens diluvialis.*

Die Cro-Magnons hatten bessere Werkzeuge° als die Neandertaler.   tools
Sie machten ihre Werkzeuge nicht nur aus Steinen, sondern auch aus
Knochen.° Aber der Mensch lebte auch weiterhin° nur dadurch, daß 15   bones   continued to live
er Pflanzen und Früchte sammelte und wilde Tiere jagte.°   **dadurch, daß . . .**
                                                                       sammelte und . . .
                                                                       jagte by gathering
Eine entscheidende Änderung° brachte erst das langsame Verschwin-   . . . and hunting . . .
den des Eises. Als im Nahen Osten die Vereisung° um 10.000 v. Chr.   decisive change
zurückging, entstanden unter günstigen Bedingungen° große Felder   glaciation
von wildem Weizen.° Solche Felder gibt es in manchen Gegenden 20   originated under favor-
noch heute, und die Archäologen haben bewiesen,° daß eine sechs-   able conditions
köpfige prähistorische Familie in drei Wochen etwa 1000 kg Weizen-   wheat
körner ernten° konnte. Natürlich dauerte° es noch lange, bis der   proved
Mensch es lernte, Weizenkörner zu mahlen° und Brot zu backen.   harvest   took
                                                                       grind
Um ca. 9000 v. Chr. lernten die Menschen, die Ziege° und das Schaf° 25 goat   sheep
zu zähmen,° um 7000 v. Chr. erschien das Schwein auf dem Bauern-   tame
hof, und um 6000 v. Chr. erschien das Rind.° Mit Weizen in der   beef cattle
Scheune,° mit Ziegen, Schafen, Schweinen und Rindern im Stall   barn
brauchten die Menschen nicht mehr zu sammeln und zu jagen. Sie
hatten endlich—auch im Winter—genug zu essen „im Hause". Aus 30
den Jägern waren Bauern geworden.

Aber trotz Weizen, trotz gezähmter Schafe, Ziegen, Rinder und
Schweine blieb man in der alten Welt in einem Punkt da stehen, wo
auch der Neandertaler schon gestanden hatte: Man aß immer noch
mit den Fingern. Und das blieb noch 10.000 Jahre so.   35

Wenn um 1250 der König von England oder Frankreich oder der
deutsche Kaiser die Großen des Landes zu einem Festessen einlud,
dann saßen die Gäste immer zu zweien am Tisch. Vor jedem Gast lag
eine etwa 10 cm x 15 cm* große Schnitte° aus dunklem° Brot. Vor   slice   dark
jedes Paar stellten die Diener° ein größeres Stück gebratenes Fleisch. 40 servants
Die Gäste schnitten mit kleinen Messern, die sie mitgebracht hatten,
ein Stück Fleisch von diesem Braten° und legten es auf die Brot-   roast

*Read as: **zehn auf fünfzehn Zentimeter.**

schnitte. Dann zerrte° man das Fleisch mit den Fingern in kleine   tear
Stückchen und aß es. Wenn eine Suppe mit gekochtem Fleisch serviert
wurde, fischte man das Fleisch mit der Hand aus der Suppe und legte
es auf die Brotschnitte. Hatte das Fleisch Knochen, so warf man die
abgenagten° Knochen einfach auf den Boden.° Kleine Eßgabeln, mit 5   gnawed off   ground
denen man ein kleines Stück Fleisch aufspießen° und in den Mund   spear
führen konnte, gab es noch nicht. Sie wurden erst gegen 1800 populär,
aber noch im Jahre 1897 durften die Matrosen° auf englischen Kriegs-   sailors
schiffen keine Gabeln gebrauchen. Die Admiralität hielt das für un-
männlich.   10

Die industrielle Revolution hat dafür gesorgt,° daß Messer, Gabeln   taken care
und Löffel aus Metall so billig wurden, daß heute auch in Familien,
die nicht viel Geld haben, für jedes Familienmitglied° ein „Besteck",   family member
d.h. ein Messer, eine Gabel und ein Löffel im Hause ist.

Wenn in den dreißiger Jahren dieses Jahrhunderts° ein junges Paar° 15   century   couple
beschloß, an einem bestimmten Tage zu heiraten und seine Freunde
zur Hochzeit° einlud, dann wußten die eingeladenen Gäste genau,   wedding
was sie zu tun hatten. Sie fragten die Mutter der Braut, ob die Tochter
schon ein „Besteckmuster"° ausgesucht hätte. Das hatte die Tochter   silverware pattern
natürlich schon getan—bei einem Juwelier. Die Gäste gingen dann zu 20
diesem Juwelier und ließen der Braut, ein oder mehrere Bestecke ins
Haus schicken.° Es gehörte zum guten Ton,° daß man nur Silber   **ließen schicken** had
schickte. Das ist heute anders.° Im Jahre 1930 kostete eine Unze Silber   sent to   good manners
an der New Yorker Börse 22 Cent, heute etwa zwanzig Dollar. Man   different
findet daher Silberbestecke nur noch in älteren Haushalten oder in 25
Familien, die Geld haben wie Heu.° Normale Sterbliche° sind mit   hay   mortals
Bestecken aus rostfreiem° Stahl zufrieden—die auch nicht billig sind.   rustfree, stainless

Es ist noch gar nicht lange her,° daß man, wie heute, von jedem er-   it hasn't been very long
wachsenen Menschen erwartet, daß er weiß, wie man beim Essen
Gabel und Messer gebraucht. In Deutschland hält man die Gabel 30
immer in der linken und das Messer *immer* in der rechten Hand. Man
darf sich, wenn es Erbsen° gibt, die runden Dinger zwar mit dem   peas
Messer und der rechten Hand auf die Gabel schieben, aber dann muß
man die Erbsen mit der linken Hand in den Mund schieben,° was gar   shove, push
nicht leicht ist.   35

> Ich ess' meine Erbsen mit Honig;   I eat my peas with
> Mein Leben lang hab' ich's getan.   honey;
> Die Erbsen, die schmecken zwar komisch,   I've done it all my life.
> Doch sie bleiben am Messer dran.   It makes the peas taste
>   funny,

Seit der Neandertaler ausgestorben ist, haben die Menschen viel ge- 40 but it keeps them on my
lernt. Wir haben heute Hühner,° die fast jeden Tag ein Ei° legen. Wir   knife.
haben Rinder gezüchtet,° die sehr viel mehr Fleisch haben und sehr   chickens   egg
viel mehr Milch geben als die alten „Langhörner". Wir haben   bred
Weizensorten gezüchtet, die soviele Körner° haben, daß man mit   grains

Recht von einer „grünen Revolution" spricht, und der deutsche
Chemiker Haber hat sogar eine Methode erfunden, nach der man
Kunstdünger° aus der Luft herstellen° kann. Nur eins° haben wir
noch nicht gelernt: Wir können noch immer nicht die erzeugten°
Nahrungsmittel° so verteilen,° daß alle Menschen auf der Erde genug 5
zu essen haben. In den weniger entwickelten Ländern sterben jeden
Tag Tausende, weil sie nicht genug zu essen haben. Und wir tun, was
der Neandertaler vor 50.000 Jahren vielleicht nicht getan hätte: wir
lassen sie einfach sterben.

artificial fertilizer
produce   *one thing*
produced
foodstuffs   *distribute*

Exercises

A. Form questions for the following statements, using either **wo** or **wohin** (wo . . . hin).

1. Ich habe den Tisch an die Wand gestellt.
2. Gestern habe ich im Theater Frau Schönberg gesehen.
3. Ich wollte mir auf dem Bahnhof eine Zeitung kaufen.
4. Im Sommer war er mit Rosemarie an der Mosel.
5. Morgen fährt er mit Rosemarie nach Bonn.
6. Seine Tochter war in Mainz.
7. Meine Frau liest die Zeitung immer im Bett.
8. Zu Hause trinkt Anton immer Tee.
9. Meyer hat uns zum Bahnhof gefahren.

SEE
ANALYSIS
119–121
(pp. 288–291)

B. Answer the following questions, using in your answers one of the prepositions that can take either the dative or the accusative.

1. Wohin hat er seinen Hut gelegt?
2. Wo hast du sie gesehen?
3. Wo waren Sie während des Krieges, Herr Schmidt?
4. Wo steht denn euer Wagen?
5. Wo geht ihr heute abend hin?
6. Wo wohnen Sie in München, Herr Schneider?
7. Wie seid ihr nach Italien gefahren?
8. Was hast du denn mit meinem Buch gemacht?
9. Wo hast du heute gefrühstückt?

SEE
ANALYSIS
119–120
(pp. 288–290)

C. Express in German.

1. He is my friend.
2. He is Karl's friend.
3. He is my sister's friend.
4. He is a friend of my sister's.
5. He is one of my sister's friends.
6. He is my father.
7. He is Ursula's father.
8. He is my wife's father.
9. He is her son.
10. He is Jutta's son.
11. He is my brother's son.
12. Karl is one of my brother's sons.
13. Ernst is one of the sons of Mr. Bertram.
14. Fritz is her friend.
15. Fritz is a friend of hers.
16. Fritz is one of her friends.
17. Her daughters are very intelligent.
18. Ingrid's daughter is also very intelligent.
19. Ingelheim's daughters are intelligent.
20. The Ingelheims' daughters are intelligent.

SEE
ANALYSIS
119
(p. 288)

D. Give appropriate answers to the following questions, using either the genitive or **von** plus dative.

1. Wessen Buch ist das?
2. Mit wessen Wagen sind Sie denn nach Aachen gefahren?
3. Mit wessen Freundin warst du im Theater?

SEE
ANALYSIS
119
(p. 288)

    4. Von wessen Roman sprecht ihr denn?

    5. Wessen Haus habt ihr gekauft?

    6. Wessen Tochter hat er geheiratet?

    7. Wessen Freundin ist das?

    8. Wessen Vater hast du besucht?

    9. Für wessen Haus willst du so viel Geld bezahlen?

   10. Durch wessen Freundin hast du ihn kennengelernt?

E. Fill the blanks with appropriate **ein**-words.

SEE
ANALYSIS
124
(p. 295)

    1. Ich habe leider kein Buch. Hast du _____?

    2. Ich habe meinen Wagen nicht hier, Herr Schnitzler. Wo ist denn _____?

    3. Habt ihr schon ein Haus? Nein, wir haben noch _____.

    4. Hast du Zeit? Ich habe _____.

    5. Das ist _____ von den Büchern, die mein Vater mir geschickt hat.

    6. Er ist auch _____ von den Soldaten, die nicht über den Krieg sprechen wollen.

    7. Ich habe nicht _____ von seinen Büchern gelesen.

    8. _____ seiner Romane habe ich mir gekauft.

    9. Mein Hut ist das nicht; es muß _____ sein, Frau Kästner.

F. Supply the missing words.

    1. Ich habe heute morgen meine Frau _____ Bahnhof gebracht.

    2. Ich habe gerade gelesen, daß Sie _____ drei Wochen in München wohnen.

    3. Liegt er immer noch _____ Bett?

    4. Von Ingelheims Kriegsroman spricht heute _____ Mensch mehr.

    5. Ich weiß, daß Anton nach Berlin gefahren _____.

    6. Kannst du mir sagen, _____ Ingelheims Kinder haben?

    7. Er ist einer _____ Ingelheims Söhnen.

    8. Ich möchte wissen, _____ du mich eigentlich geheiratet hast.

    9. Können Sie mir sagen, _____ der Zug nach Bamberg fährt?

   10. _____ der Krieg anfing, studierte Schmidt in Frankfurt Medizin.

   11. Man kann doch nicht im Garten arbeiten, _____ es regnet.

   12. Er fragte mich, ob ich heute abend auch ins Konzert _____.

   13. Ich wollte, ich _____ dich nie gesehen.

   14. Wenn er nicht an die Ostsee gefahren _____, hätte ich ihn nie kennengelernt.

   15. Ich habe das Haus nicht kaufen _____.

G. Express in German.

    1. We really ought to put (**stellen**) that (little) table between our beds.

    2. Do you always have to put your books on the breakfast table?

    3. Why can't they lie on the breakfast table?

    4. During the war Ingelheim was on the western front.

    5. At that time he was happy that he did not have to go to Africa.

    6. It is cold tonight; I wish you hadn't forgotten your overcoat.

    7. If only that woman hadn't been so unfriendly!

    8. If only I hadn't accepted the money!

    9. You should have given him more money.

   10. I wish I weren't so far away from you.

H. Read the following sentences and supply either **nicht** or **nichts**, or the correct form of **kein**.

SEE
ANALYSIS
125
(p. 296)

1. Ich habe seit gestern morgen gar _____ gegessen.
2. Daß du in Italien warst, habe ich gar _____ gewußt.
3. Hast du denn mit deiner neuen Kamera noch gar _____ Aufnahmen gemacht?
4. Es ist doch dumm, daß er uns gar _____ geschrieben hat, wann er ankommt.
5. Aber der Hund hat doch gar _____ gebellt.

I. Fill the blanks with the correct preposition or article, or contracted preposition plus article.

1. Wart ihr gestern _____ Kino?
2. Ja, wir sind _____ Kino gegangen.
3. Helene wohnt immer noch _____ ihren Eltern.
4. Sie will _____ ihren Eltern verreisen.
5. Ich habe ihn _____ zehn Jahren kennengelernt.
6. _____ fünf Jahren habe ich ihn nicht mehr gesehen.
7. Er ist durch _____ Schweiz gefahren.
8. Christian wohnt in _____ Altstadt.
9. Ich komme gerade aus _____ Stadt.
10. Der Zug kam _____ 10.37 Uhr an.
11. _____ des Regens gehen wir heute nicht segeln.
12. Die Maschine fliegt _____ London _____ Frankfurt.
13. Also auf Wiedersehen _____ nächsten Sonntag.
14. Stellen Sie den Wagen doch bitte hinter _____ Hotel.
15. Bitte, kommt _____ Essen.
16. Wir waren gerade _____ Essen, als er kam.
17. Der Junge stand zwischen _____ Lehrer und _____ Lehrerin.
18. Wir fuhren _____ die Stadt _____.
19. Köln liegt _____ Rhein.
20. Er rannte aus _____ Haus und auf _____ Straße.

J. Form derivatives as indicated and guess their meaning.

1. fahren	— der Fahrer		2. der Fluß	— das Flüßchen
anfangen	—		die Glocke	—
besuchen	—		die Hand	—
helfen	—		das Messer	—
kennen	—		das Schild	—
sprechen	—		das Stück	—
3. glücklich	— unglücklich		4. der Freund	— freundlich
bestimmt	—		der Winter	—
sympathisch	—		das Wort	—
modern	—		das Bild	—
die Vernunft	— die		der Tag	—
das Wetter	— das		das Dorf	—
5. brauchen	— brauchbar		6. wohnen	— die Wohnung
zahlen	—		bewundern	—
erreichen	—		erzählen	—
lesen	—		mischen	—
lernen	—		rechnen	—
denken	—		benutzen	—

7. der Berg	— bergig	8. die Arbeit	— arbeitslos
die Ecke	—	das Beispiel	—
das Glas	—	der Geschmack	—
der Saft	—	der Erfolg	—
die Vernunft	—	das Ende	—
die Vorsicht	—	die Zeit	—

K. Try to guess the meaning of the following compounds and derivatives.

1. ein achtjähriges Mädchen
2. er arbeitet nur vormittags
3. er ist ein Bergsteiger
4. das Alleinsein ist schwer
5. kinderlos
6. eine vielköpfige Familie
7. ich bin wunschlos glücklich
8. endlos
9. ein gleichseitiges Dreieck
10. ein vielseitiger Künstler
11. unfreundlich
12. ein Autounglück
13. Zigaretten sind ungesund
14. schlaflos
15. die Dinosaurier sind ausgestorben
16. ein Mittagsschläfchen halten
17. ein Stückchen Seife
18. ein Menschenkenner
19. die Tänzerin
20. die Bahnhofshalle
21. unhörbar
22. in unerreichbarer Ferne
23. unbrauchbar
24. eine winterliche Landschaft
25. du bist herzlich eingeladen
26. eine Kurzgeschichte
27. bildlich gesprochen
28. eine Nacherzählung
29. die Menschwerdung Gottes
30. eine ärztliche Untersuchung

L. Write a brief paragraph in German containing the following ideas. Do *not* translate the passage; just use it as an outline. Use your own words, but do not attempt to use any construction or any vocabulary that you haven't had yet.

During her trip to Germany, Elisabeth Reichmann visited Mr. Schmid, the teacher in Burgbach. Mr. Schmid is a friend of Elisabeth's father, a native of Burgbach, who came to America only fifteen years ago. Elisabeth was born in Germany, too, and speaks German very well. She is studying psychology in America and wanted to learn (**erfahren**) something about life in the village, and especially about the schools. Mr. Schmid told her about the urbanization of the village. Before the war, Burgbach had been way out in the country, and there had been only vintners. After the war came the refugees, then people from North Germany and from the city, and, finally, foreign workers. Today Burgbach, although it is still a "Weinort," has become a suburb of the city.

M. In Unit 9, the conversations are preceded by a list of words pertaining to traffic. Make similar lists for the following topics by going through the vocabulary of Units 1–10. Then write out sentences illustrating the use of each word in a proper context:

1. School and university: die Schule, das Gymnasium, lehren, der Lehrer, etc.
2. Travel: die Reise, verreisen, die Eisenbahn, etc.
3. Food, cooking, eating out: das Menu, kochen, die Wurst, etc.
4. Housing: wohnen, die Wohnung, die Küche, etc.

N. Make a list of German terms that have no exact English equivalent or are not used in the same way as their English cognates. Why and in what way are they different? Examples: **die Bundesstraße, das Mittagessen, das Menu.**

Vocabulary

die Ankunft, ⸚e	arrival
annehmen	to assume
die Aufnahme, -n	photograph, picture, shot
aufrecht	upright
der Augenblick, -e	moment, instant
(einen) Augenblick, bitte	just a moment, please
aus (adj.)	over
das Spiel ist aus	the game is over
aussuchen	to select, pick out
der Ball, ⸚e	ball
Fußball	soccer
das Fußballspiel	soccer game
Korbball	basketball
die Bank, -en	bank
die Bank, ⸚e	bench
die Bedingung, -en	condition
behandeln	to treat
die Behandlung, -en	treatment
das Bein, -e	leg
beschließen	to decide
das Bild, -er	picture
der Boden, ⸚	floor; ground
die Brücke, -n	bridge
dicht	close; tight; dense
dumm	dumb, stupid
das Ehepaar, -e	(married) couple
entscheiden	to decide
entscheidend	decisive
erwarten	to expect
fallen	to fall
zerfallen	to decay; to fall apart
der Finger, -	finger
frühstücken	to (eat, have) breakfast
der Gast, ⸚e	guest
gelingen (impers.)	to succeed
es gelingt mir	I succeed
halten	to stop
halten für	to consider
ich halte ihn für dumm	I think he's stupid
der Haushalt, -e	household

das Jahrhun′dert, -e	century
jederzeit	(at) any time
komisch	funny; odd; comical
legen	to lay (flat), place
liegen	to lie
die Meinung, -en	opinion
na	well
nachher	afterwards, later
nachkommen	to come later, to follow
die Nachricht, -en	report, message
die Nachrichten (pl.)	news (radio, TV, etc.)
naß	wet
die Pflanze, -n	plant
der Punkt, -e	point
die Regierung, -en	government
die Rekla′me	advertising
rennen	to run
rund	round
schieben	to shove, push
segeln	to sail
die Sensation, -en	sensation
sorgen für	to take care of
spielen	to play
das Spiel, -e	game
Sport treiben	to exercise
springen	to jump
der Stahl, ⸚e	steel
stellen	to put, place (upright)
der Ton, ⸚e	tone
der Topf, ⸚e	pot
der Tourist′, -en	tourist
trotz (prep. with gen.)	in spite of
die Tür, -en	door
um (adj.)	up
die Zeit ist um	time is up
um . . . herum	around
unterbrechen	to interrupt
untersuchen	to investigate
die Untersuchung, -en	investigation
verteilen	to distribute
vorhin	a while ago

wählen	to choose, decide, elect	umwerfen	to knock over
während *(prep. with gen.)*	during	das Werkzeug, -e	tool
wahrscheinlich	probably	der Wetterbericht, -e	weather report
die Wand, ⸚e	wall (of a room)	wild	wild
was (= etwas)	something	zu *(adj.)*	closed
wegen *(prep. with gen.)*	because of	die Tür ist zu	the door is closed
werfen	to throw	zumachen	to close, shut

Additional Vocabulary

bellen	to bark	der Krimi, -s	detective novel; TV cop show
beschäftigt sein	to be busy	das Metall', -e	metal
die Bundesstraße, -n	federal road	die Metho'de, -n	method
durch'braten	to roast (well done)	mischen	to mix
durchfah'ren	to drive through, traverse	das Mitglied, -er	member
die Einladung, -en	invitation	das Familienmitglied, -er	family member
die Erbse, -n	pea	nachgehen (of clock)	to be (run) slow
ernten	to harvest	vorgehen	to be (run) fast
erwachsen *(adj.)*	grown	das Nahrungsmittel, -	foodstuff
der Erwachsene, -n	grown-up, adult	die Produktion, -en	production
erzeugen	to produce	das Prozent, -e	percent
fangen	to catch	der Regenmantel, ⸚	raincoat
das Feuer, -	fire	riechen	to smell
die Frucht, ⸚e	fruit	der Saft, ⸚e	juice
das Gras, ⸚er	grass	sammeln	to gather, collect
günstig	favorable	der Sammler, -	collector
der Himmel, -	sky; heaven	das Schaf, -e	sheep
die Hoffnung, -en	hope	die Scheune, -n	barn
jagen	to hunt, chase	die Sorte, -n	kind; variety
der Jäger, -	hunter	der Typ, -en	type; model
der Kaiser, -	emperor	der Weizen	wheat
der König, -e	king	das Wesen, -	being
das Korn, ⸚er	kernel; corn; grain		
der Kriminalroman, -e	detective novel		

Strong Verbs and Irregular Weak Verbs

annehmen	nimmt an	nahm an	angenommen	to assume
beschließen		beschloß	beschlossen	to decide
durch'braten	brät durch	briet durch	durch'gebraten	to roast
durchfah'ren	durchfährt	durchfuhr	durchfah'ren	to drive through
entscheiden		entschied	entschieden	to decide
fallen	fällt	fiel	ist gefallen	to fall

fangen	fängt	fing	gefangen	to catch
gelingen		gelang	ist gelungen	to succeed
halten	hält	hielt	gehalten	to hold
rennen	rennt	rannte	ist gerannt	to run
riechen		roch	gerochen	to smell
schieben		schob	geschoben	to push, shove
springen		sprang	ist gesprungen	to jump
umwerfen	wirft um	warf um	umgeworfen	to knock over
unterbrechen	unterbricht	unterbrach	unterbrochen	to interrupt
werfen	wirft	warf	geworfen	to throw
zerfallen	zerfällt	zerfiel	ist zerfallen	to fall apart

UNIT 11 Indirect Discourse—The Conjunctions als, ob, wann, wenn

For many years, textbook authors have been debating whether or not to include literary readings in introductory German texts. Literature, so an argument goes, is the most significant expression of a language and should be introduced as early as possible. But no writer produces his work with the first six or eight chapters of an American textbook in mind; he limits neither his grammar nor his vocabulary. Most literary works are therefore far too difficult to read with comprehension and enjoyment in the early stages of learning a foreign language.

Some textbooks contain simplified versions of literary works, but such adaptations all but destroy the quality of the originals. On the other hand, adaptations do seem justified in the case of writings in which content and message are more important than literary form, such as the popular science piece in this unit, which has been adapted from a German magazine. However, you should now be able to read, without too much difficulty, a few genuine literary selections. The short prose piece by Bertolt Brecht in this unit is typical of the way Brecht couches social criticism in an ambiguous satirical form. The song which follows is from Brecht's *Threepenny Opera*, which you have probably heard in an English version.

Patterns

[1] Indirect Discourse: Introductory Verb in Present Tense

SEE
ANALYSIS
127–128
(pp. 317–319)

Mein Freund Giovanni sagt: „In Italien ist das Benzin sehr teuer."

Mein Freund Giovanni sagt,
    in Italien ist das Benzin sehr teuer.
    in Italien wäre das Benzin sehr teuer.
    daß in Italien das Benzin sehr teuer ist.
    daß in Italien das Benzin sehr teuer wäre.

Herr Enderle sagt: „Ich komme heute erst spät nach Hause."

Herr Enderle sagt,
    er kommt heute erst spät nach Hause.
    er käme heute erst spät nach Hause.
    daß er heute erst spät nach Hause kommt.
    daß er heute erst spät nach Hause käme.

Christa sagt: „Ich bin die ganze Woche krank gewesen."

Christa sagt,
    sie ist die ganze Woche krank gewesen.
    sie wäre die ganze Woche krank gewesen.
    daß sie die ganze Woche krank gewesen ist.
    daß sie die ganze Woche krank gewesen wäre.

VARIATIONS

Form the same four indirect discourse versions with the following direct statements.
Use introductory verbs in the present tense.

„Das Fußballspiel ist um vier Uhr aus."
„In einer halben Stunde kann man durch ganz Liechtenstein fahren."
„Ich habe nur vier Mark für den Wein bezahlt."
„Ich habe meinen Regenmantel vergessen."

[2] Indirect Discourse: Introductory Verb in Past Tense; Present and Future Time in Original Statement

SEE
ANALYSIS
128
(p. 319)

Hans sagte: „Mein Vater bleibt noch in Salzburg."
    Hans sagte, sein Vater bliebe noch in Salzburg.
    Hans sagte, sein Vater würde noch in Salzburg bleiben.

Inge sagte: „Erika fährt morgen nach Nürnberg."
    Inge sagte, Erika führe morgen nach Nürnberg.
    Inge sagte, Erika würde morgen nach Nürnberg fahren.
    Inge sagte, daß Erika morgen nach Nürnberg führe.
    Inge sagte, daß Erika morgen nach Nürnberg fahren würde.

Restate as indirect discourse, using both present subjunctive and **würde**-forms.

Herr Meyer sagte: „Mein Sohn lernt bald fahren."
Frau Schulz sagte: „Meine Tochter studiert im nächsten Semester in Bonn."
Hans sagte: „Ich gehe mit Inge ins Kino."

[3] Indirect Discourse: Introductory Verb in Past Tense; Past Time in Original Statement (Past, Perfect, or Pluperfect)

Er sagte: „Ich arbeitete damals in Hamburg."
    „Ich habe damals in Hamburg gearbeitet."
    „Ich hatte damals in Hamburg gearbeitet."
Er sagte, er hätte damals in Hamburg gearbeitet.

Er sagte: „Ich fuhr dann nach Hamburg."
    „Ich bin dann nach Hamburg gefahren."
    „Ich war dann nach Hamburg gefahren."
Er sagte, er wäre dann nach Hamburg gefahren.

Er sagte: „Ich wollte damals nach Hamburg fahren."
    „Ich habe damals nach Hamburg fahren wollen."
    „Ich hatte damals nach Hamburg fahren wollen."
Er sagte, er hätte damals nach Hamburg fahren wollen.

SEE ANALYSIS 128 (p. 319)

Restate as indirect discourse, using the past subjunctive; introductory statement: **Sie sagte,** . . .

„Außer mir war niemand da."
„Wegen des Regens bin ich zu spät gekommen."
„Kein Mensch hat es geglaubt."
„Johannes mußte nach Basel fahren."

[4] Indirect Questions

Er fragte: „Ist dein Vater heute abend zu Hause?"
Er fragte, ob mein Vater heute abend zu Hause wäre.
Er fragte: „Wohin geht ihr heute abend zum Essen?"
Er fragte, wohin wir heute abend zum Essen gingen.
Er fragte: „Kommt Fritz morgen?"
Er wollte wissen, ob Fritz morgen käme.

Er fragte, ob ich krank wäre.
Er fragte, ob wir das Haus in Wiesbaden kaufen wollten.
Er fragte, ob er mich zum Bahnhof bringen dürfte.
Er fragte mich, warum ich denn nicht mit nach Bern führe.
Er wollte wissen, ob Maria zu Hause wäre.
Er wollte wissen, warum Hans nicht mitgehen könnte.

SEE ANALYSIS 128 (p. 319)

Er fragte: „Warum sind Sie denn gestern nicht nach Graz gefahren?"
Er fragte, warum ich denn gestern nicht nach Graz gefahren wäre.
Er fragte: „Mit wem warst du denn gestern abend im Theater?"
Er wollte wissen, mit wem ich gestern abend im Theater gewesen wäre.

Er wollte wissen, wieviel die Zigarren gekostet hätten.
Er wollte wissen, wie lange ich für die Lufthansa gearbeitet hätte.

[5] Indirect Discourse: The Alternate Subjunctive

SEE
ANALYSIS
129-130
(pp. 320-321)

„Ich bin nur zwei Tage in München."
Sie sagte, sie wäre nur zwei Tage in München.
Sie sagte, sie sei nur zwei Tage in München.

„Ich habe ein Zimmer im Bayerischen Hof."
Sie sagte, sie hätte ein Zimmer im Bayerischen Hof.
Sie sagte, sie habe ein Zimmer im Bayerischen Hof.

„Wann bist du denn gestern abend nach Hause gekommen?"
Er fragte mich, wann ich gestern abend nach Hause gekommen wäre.
Er fragte mich, wann ich gestern abend nach Hause gekommen sei.

„Ich mußte gestern nach Regensburg fahren."
Er sagte, er hätte gestern nach Regensburg fahren müssen.
Er sagte, er habe gestern nach Regensburg fahren müssen.

„Ihr braucht nicht auf mich zu warten; ich komme erst morgen."
Er sagte, wir brauchten nicht auf ihn zu warten; er käme erst morgen.
Er sagte, wir brauchten nicht auf ihn zu warten; er komme erst morgen.

„Kannst du mit mir frühstücken?"
Er fragte, ob ich mit ihm frühstücken könnte.
Er fragte, ob ich mit ihm frühstücken könne.

München, Ludwigstraße von der Feldherrnhalle.

„Dann können wir zusammen frühstücken."
Er sagte, wir könnten dann zusammen frühstücken.

VARIATIONS

Transform the following statements into indirect discourse in accordance with the examples above. Use appropriate introductory verbs and, if possible, both forms of the subjunctive.

„Er ist schon lange wieder zu Hause."
„Morgen habe ich keine Zeit."
„Ich kann Sie morgen leider nicht besuchen."
„Leider muß ich morgen nach Wiesbaden fahren."
„Fahren Sie morgen nach Mainz, Herr Rombach?"
„Ich darf meinen Mann noch nicht besuchen."
„Ich will nicht studieren."
„Wann fahren Sie nach Essen?"
„Der Mantel ist ganz neu."
„Ich muß mal telefonieren."

Restate all those indirect statements in Patterns [1]–[4] in which the alternate subjunctive can be used.

[6] Indirect Imperative

After studying the examples, form other imperatives and change them to indirect discourse.

SEE
ANALYSIS
131
(p. 322)

„Fahren Sie doch einmal an die Nordsee."
Mein Arzt hat gesagt, ich sollte (solle) doch einmal an die Nordsee fahren.

My doctor said I should go to the North Sea for a change.

„Bleiben Sie mindestens vierzehn Tage* dort."
Er sagte, ich sollte (solle) mindestens vierzehn Tage dort bleiben.

„Bring mir doch bitte etwas zu lesen mit."
Carola sagte, ich sollte (solle) ihr doch bitte etwas zu lesen mitbringen.

„Besucht mich bald wieder."
Tante Amalie sagte, wir sollten sie bald wieder besuchen.

[7] wann

Form other questions with **wann** and transform them into dependent clauses.

SEE
ANALYSIS
132
(p. 322)

„Wann ist Wolfgang denn gestern abend nach Hause gekommen?"
Wolfgang, Vater möchte wissen, wann du gestern abend nach Hause gekommen bist.

---

*vierzehn Tage is commonly used to express *two weeks*; *one week*, oddly enough, turns out to be **acht Tage**. Count them: **Sonntag, Montag, Dienstag, Mittwoch, Donnerstag, Freitag, Samstag, Sonntag.**

„Wann will Heidi denn heiraten?"
Ich weiß nicht, wann sie heiraten will.

[8] ob

Form other yes-or-no questions and transform them into dependent clauses.

SEE
ANALYSIS
132
(p. 322)

„Fährst du nach Bern?"
Mutter will wissen, ob du nach Bern fährst.

„War Erich wirklich in Garmisch-Partenkirchen?"
Ich weiß nicht, ob Erich wirklich in Garmisch-Partenkirchen war.

[9] als with the Comparative

Form parallel sentences with **besser als** and **mehr als.**

SEE
ANALYSIS
132
(p. 322)

Du bist auch nicht besser als er.	You are no better than he is.
Das ist besser als nichts.	That is better than nothing.
In Berlin wohnen mehr Menschen als in Unterzwingenbach.	More people live in Berlin than in Unterzwingenbach.
Meyer hat in Baden-Baden mehr Geld verloren, als er wollte.	Meyer lost more money in Baden-Baden than he intended to.
Er wußte bestimmt mehr, als er uns gesagt hat.	I'm sure he knew more than he told us.

[10] The Conjunction als

Note the difference between the **wenn**-sentences and the **als**-sentences.

SEE
ANALYSIS
132
(p. 322)

Wenn wir in München sind, wohnen wir im Bayerischen Hof.
    When(ever) we are in Munich we stay at the Bayerischer Hof.
Als wir in München waren, wohnten wir im Bayerischen Hof.
    When we were in Munich, we stayed at the Bayerischer Hof.

Wenn ich nach Freiburg komme, besuche ich ihn sofort.
> If (when) I get to Freiburg, I'll visit him immediately.

Als ich nach Freiburg kam, besuchte ich ihn sofort.
> When I got to Freiburg, I visited him immediately.

Als Ingelheim ins Hotel kam, wartete Erich schon auf ihn.

Wir wollten gerade ins Haus gehen, als Meyers kamen.

Als ich ihn sah, wußte ich, daß etwas passiert war.

Frau Enderle studierte in Hamburg, als sie ihren Mann kennenlernte.

[11] als ob, als wenn, als

Er tut, als ob er schliefe (schlafe). Er tut, als schliefe (schlafe) er.	He acts as if he were asleep.	SEE ANALYSIS 132 (p. 322)
Er tat, als ob er schliefe (schlafe). Er tat, als schliefe er.	He acted as if he were asleep.	
Er tut, als ob er geschlafen hätte (habe). Er tut, als hätte (habe) er geschlafen.	He acts as if he had been asleep.	
Er tat, als ob er geschlafen hätte (habe). Er tat, als hätte (habe) er geschlafen.	He acted as if he had been asleep.	
Er tat, als wenn er schliefe (schlafe). Er tat, als wenn er geschlafen hätte (habe).	He acted as if he were asleep. He acted as if he had been asleep.	
Gerda sah aus, als wäre (sei) sie krank.	Gerda looked as if she were sick.	

[12] wenn

Form parallel sentences with **wenn**, in the meaning of *if, when,* and *whenever.*

Wenn es morgen regnet, bleiben wir zu Hause.
Wenn er schon hier wäre, könnten wir ihn besuchen.
Wenn er damals hier gewesen wäre, hätten wir ihn besuchen können.
Wenn der Sommer kam, fuhren unsere Eltern immer mit uns an die Nordsee.
Jedesmal, wenn Tante Amalie uns besuchte, mußte ich mit ihr ins Museum gehen.
Wenn ich in München bin, gehe ich abends immer ins Theater.

SEE
ANALYSIS
132
(p. 322)

Analysis

127 Direct and Indirect Discourse

If a speaker (or writer) wants to report to a second person what a third person has said or written, he can choose between several syntactical patterns.

Direct Discourse

The speaker can repeat verbatim—in quotation marks, as it were—what he has been told. If his friend Fritz told him on the phone, *I have been sick all week*, he can report that Fritz called and said, *I have been sick all week*. Fritz's original statement as well as the speaker's repetition of it are in "direct discourse." This reporting technique presents no grammatical problems in either English or German.

Indirect Discourse

The speaker can also change the original message *I have been sick all week* into a dependent clause which functions as the direct object of some verb of communication such as *to say* or *to write*. He can use this introductory verb in the present tense or in a past tense form. This "second-hand" reporting technique is called "indirect discourse."

Introductory verb in the present tense:

> "I have been sick all week."
> He says he has been sick all week.
> He says that he has been sick all week.

The *I* of the original statement is changed to *he*, but the tense of the original statement, the present perfect, remains the same. The object clause can be un-introduced or introduced by *that*.

Introductory verb in the past tense:

> "I have been sick all week."
> He wrote he had been sick all week.
> He wrote that he had been sick all week.

Now not only is *I* changed to *he*, but the tense may be changed as well: *has been* becomes *had been*, though, strictly speaking, this is not a change of tense, but a change from the indicative to the subjunctive. (See Analysis **108** on the subjunctive in English.) In the same way, a present tense in the original statement is changed to the past tense in the indirect statement. Again, these past tense forms are really subjunctives, though, interestingly, the *was/were* choice does not exist: *he were* is not possible in indirect discourse.

> "I am sick."
> He wrote that he was sick.

There are, however, situations in which English does not change from indicative to the subjunctive even if the introductory verb is in the past tense. For example, if you have just talked to a friend on the phone and somebody asks you what he said, you might reply

> He said that he is sick.
> He said that he has been sick all week.

If you keep these various English possibilities in mind—choice of tense in the introductory verb and presence or absence of subjunctive in the indirect statement—you will have little difficulty in the indicative/subjunctive choice in German indirect discourse.

128 Indirect Discourse in German

In German, the change from direct to indirect discourse frequently involves a change from the indicative to the subjunctive. This subjunctive can be either the "normal subjunctive" introduced in Unit 9 or a second set of subjunctive forms, introduced below in **131**, which is used mainly in indirect discourse and cannot be used in any of the patterns of Unit 9. We call this second set the "alternate subjunctive."

Introductory Verb in the Present Tense

If a direct statement like

In Italien ist das Benzin sehr teuer

is changed to indirect discourse, the opening verb may be in the present tense. If so, the subjunctive *may, but does not have to be,* used:

Mein Freund Giovanni sagt,
(a) **in Italien ist das Benzin sehr teuer.**   (indicative)
(b) **in Italien wäre das Benzin sehr teuer.** (normal subjunctive)
(c) **in Italien sei das Benzin sehr teuer.** (alternate subjunctive)

The use of the subjunctive in (b) and (c) does not express any doubt in the veracity of the original statement; it merely signals that the speaker reports this statement as originating with someone else.

Introductory Verb in a Past Tense

It is, of course, also possible to use an opening verb in the past tense: **sagte** or **hat gesagt** rather than **sagt**. Now the use of the subjunctive is much more frequent than when the introductory verb is in the present tense. For the time being, however, we recommend that you always use the subjunctive when the opening verb is in a past tense.

The tense of the introductory verb never has an influence on the tense of the dependent clause in indirect discourse.

„In Italien ist das Benzin sehr teuer."
Giovanni sagte (hat gesagt),
   in Italien wäre (sei) das Benzin sehr teuer. (pres. subj.)

„In Italien war das Benzin sehr teuer."
Giovanni sagte (hat gesagt),
   in Italien wäre (sei) das Benzin sehr teuer gewesen. (past subj.)

In direct statements referring to the future, either the present or the future tense is used.

> **Ich komme bald wieder.**
> **Ich werde wiederkommen.**

In indirect discourse, the present subjunctive or the future subjunctive (the **würde**-forms) is used.

> **Er sagte, er käme (komme) bald wieder.**
>   **er würde (werde) wiederkommen.**

With modals, however, the future subjunctive is used only very rarely.

Because all indirect discourse statements are dependent clauses, they can also be introduced by **daß** and then have verb-last position.

> **Giovanni sagte,**
> **daß in Italien das Benzin sehr teuer wäre (sei).**
> **daß in Italien das Benzin sehr teuer gewesen wäre (gewesen sei).**

TIME RELATIONSHIP BETWEEN INTRODUCTORY VERB AND INDIRECT STATEMENT

INTRODUCTORY VERB	INDIRECT STATEMENT
Er sagt, **Er sagte,** **Er hat gesagt,**	**er würde nach München fahren.** **er führe nach München.** **er wäre nach München gefahren.**

The choice of subjunctive forms in the indirect statement is *not* determined by the tense of the introductory verb: any subjunctive form can be combined with any introductory verb tense.

1. Use of the future subjunctive frequently indicates that the action of the indirect statement will take place *after* the time of the introductory verb.

2. Use of the present subjunctive indicates that the action of the indirect statement takes place either *at the same time as*, or *after*, the time of the introductory verb.

3. Use of the past subjunctive indicates that the action of the indirect statement took place *prior to* the time of the introductory verb.

129 The Alternate Subjunctive

The second set of subjunctive forms introduced in this unit is used mainly in indirect statements and we refer to it as "alternate subjunctive." These forms have a more literary flavor than the normal subjunctive and are rarely used in colloquial German. For all practical purposes, only the third-person singular forms are in general use, though some first-person singular forms also occur. As usual, **sein** appears to be an exception.

PRESENT TENSE

	sein	haben	werden	können	wollen	wissen	lieben	nehmen	fahren
ich	sei	(habe)	(werde)	könne	wolle	wisse	(liebe)	(nehme)	(fahre)
du	—	—	—	—	—	—	—	—	—
er	sei	habe	werde	könne	wolle	wisse	liebe	nehme	fahre
wir	seien	—	—	—	—	—	—	—	—
ihr	—	—	—	—	—	—	—	—	—
sie	seien	—	—	—	—	—	—	—	—

The past forms of this subjunctive simply add the past participle to the correct forms of **sein** or **haben**:

> **ich sei gefahren**
> **er habe gelesen**
> **er habe kommen wollen**

The forms in active use are the only ones which are clearly recognizable as subjunctives and distinguishable from the corresponding indicative forms. Hence (a) **sein** is not really an exception, (b) the third-person singular forms of *all* verbs can be used because they end in **-e** and not in **-t**, (c) the first-person singular forms of the modals and **wissen** can be used and (d) other first-person forms can be used only if the context makes clear that they are indeed used as subjunctive forms.

130 The Use of the Alternate Subjunctive

The forms of the normal subjunctive can *always* be used in indirect discourse. It is not possible to formulate any definite rule stating when the alternate subjunctive should be used. It simply exists as an alternative preferred by some and almost completely avoided by others.

Those who do use the alternate subjunctive usually follow this rule: The forms not recognizable as subjunctive occur only in indirect questions.

> **Sie fragte mich, ob ich sie liebe.**

In an indirect assertion, the unrecognizable **ich liebe** is replaced by the normal subjunctive **ich liebte**.

> **Ich sagte ihr, daß ich sie liebte.**

To illustrate the range of choice, let us assume that somebody asks the following question:

> **„Liebst du mich denn, und findest du mich schön?"**

By using the normal subjunctive only, this question could be reported in the form

> **Sie fragte mich, ob ich sie denn liebte und schön fände.**

By using the new set only, one could write:

Sie fragte mich, ob ich sie denn liebe und schön finde.

Very likely, one may find a mixture; thus (in Heinrich Böll, *Ansichten eines Clowns*)

Sie fragte mich, ob ich sie denn liebe und schön fände

is followed, at the end of the same paragraph, by:

Ich murmelte [*mumbled*], ja, ja, ich fände sie schön und liebte sie.

NOTE: If the original statement was made in the normal subjunctive, it cannot be changed.

„Es wäre schön, wenn heute die Sonne schiene."
Er sagte, es wäre schön, wenn heute die Sonne schiene.

The alternate subjunctive is also used in sentences with **als ob,** *as if* (see **132** below).

131 Indirect Imperatives

Any imperative constitutes direct discourse. In order to report, by indirect discourse, that a request was made or a command given, **sollen** is used.

IMPERATIVE
Fahren Sie doch einmal an die Nordsee.

INDIRECT DISCOURSE
Der Arzt meinte, ich solle (sollte) doch einmal an die Nordsee fahren.
Der Arzt meinte, er solle (sollte) doch einmal an die Nordsee fahren.
Der Arzt meinte, wir sollten doch einmal an die Nordsee fahren.

The English indirect imperative is exactly parallel:

"Go to the North Sea."
The doctor said I should go to the North Sea.

132 The Conjunctions **als, ob, wann, wenn**

These conjunctions tend to be troublesome for the native speaker of English because their range of use does not correspond exactly to that of their English equivalents and cognates (*as, if, when*). It is important, therefore, that you understand their exact meaning and practice their use thoroughly.

Als is used in the following ways:

1. In comparisons, it means *than* and is used only to compare what is *not* equal. Comparison of adjectives will be discussed in Unit 17.

Er trinkt mehr als du.	He drinks more than you (drink).
Ich habe nicht mehr als hundert Mark.	I don't have more than a hundred marks.

The phrase with **als** always stands in the end field.

> **Er hat mehr getrunken als ich.**
> **Er sagt, daß das Benzin dort viel teurer ist als hier.**

If the **als**-phrase contains its own verb, it is a dependent clause and must be separated from the main clause by a comma. (See also Analysis **37**, p. 70.)

> **Er hat mehr gewußt, als er uns sagen wollte.**

2. As a conjunction, **als** means *when* and introduces dependent clauses referring to *one single event or situation in the past*. English *when* has a much wider usage: It corresponds to German **als** only if it can be replaced by *at the time when* followed by a past tense.

> **Als mein Mann noch lebte, gingen wir oft ins Theater.**
> When (at the time when) my husband was still alive, we often went to the theater.

3. **Als** may be the short version of **als ob** or **als wenn**, both meaning *as if*. When so used, **als** or **als ob** is followed either by the normal subjunctive or, less frequently, by the alternate subjunctive.

If **als** is equivalent to **als ob** (**als wenn**), the verb of the dependent clause follows immediately after **als**.

> **Er tat, als ob er schliefe.**   He acted as if he were asleep.
> **Er tat, als schliefe er.**
> **Er tat, als schlafe er.**
>
> **Er tat, als wenn er alles wüßte.**   He acted as if he knew everything.
> **Er tat, als wüßte er alles.**
> **Er tat, als wisse er alles.**

If the introductory verb is in the present tense, the indicative can also be used, especially in the spoken language, but only with **als ob** and not with **als**.

> **Er tut, als schliefe er.**
> **Er tut, als schlafe er.**
> **Er tut doch nur so, als ob er schläft.**

Ob is a conjunction used to change a yes-or-no question into a dependent clause. **Ob** means *whether*, and it must be used whenever *whether* could be used in the corresponding English sentence.

> **Fährst du nach Berlin?**
> **Mutter will wissen, ob du nach Berlin fährst.**
> Mother wants to know if (whether) you are going to Berlin.

Wann is an interrogative, meaning *when*. It can only be used in situations where English *when* can be replaced by *at what time*. **Wann** is used:

1. To introduce a question.

> **Wann fährst du nach Köln?**
> When (at what time) are you going to Cologne?

2. As an interrogative conjunction when a **wann**-question is changed into a dependent clause (indirect question).

Mutter will wissen, wann du nach Köln fährst.

Mother wants to know when (at what time) you are going to Cologne.

Wenn is troublesome because it introduces both conditional and time clauses.

1. In conditional clauses, **wenn** always corresponds to English *if*, and any *if* which cannot be replaced by *whether* must be rendered by **wenn**.

2. In time clauses, **wenn** can mean *whenever* and presents no difficulties as long as it is used with this meaning.

3. Trouble arises because English *when* is apt to be a source of interference. English *when* is used as an interrogative and then corresponds to German **wann**. English *when* can also be a time conjunction meaning "at the time when." In this latter function, *when* corresponds to **als** if the clause refers to one single event in the past, and it corresponds to **wenn** if the clause refers to present or future time. The following table summarizes the situation:

	IF (condition)	IF (whether)	WHEN-EVER	WHEN (interrog.) (at what time)	WHEN (conj.) (at the time when)
PAST	wenn	ob	wenn	wann	als
PRESENT	wenn	ob	wenn	wann	wenn
FUTURE	wenn	ob	wenn	wann	wenn

NOTE: You can eliminate all interference caused by your own speech habits if you realize that:

(a) In the sentence *I'd like to know when he came home*, *when* is an interrogative replaceable by *at what time*; *when* therefore corresponds to German **wann**.

Ich möchte wissen, wann er nach Hause gekommen ist.

(b) In *When my husband was still alive, we often went to the theater*, *when* is replaceable by *at the time when*; *when* therefore corresponds to German **als**, because it refers to a single event or situation in the past.

Als mein Mann noch lebte, sind wir oft ins Theater gegangen.

(c) In *When he comes home from the war, we will get married*, *when* is also replaceable by *at the time when*. But this time it refers to the future and corresponds to German **wenn**.

Wenn er aus dem Krieg nach Hause kommt, heiraten wir.

Since **wenn** also corresponds to English *if*, this last German sentence is ambiguous; only the context makes the meaning clear. There are no linguistic means in German of distinguishing between *when* and *if* as long as **wenn** refers to the future.

Conversations

I

ERIKA: Du Hans, Tante Amalie hat angerufen.

HANS: Was wollte sie denn?

ERIKA: Sie wollte wissen, ob du heute nachmittag mit ihr ins Museum gehen könntest.

HANS: Du hast ihr doch hoffentlich gesagt, ich wäre heute nicht zu Hause.

ERIKA: Nein, ich dachte, du würdest gerne mit ihr gehen.

HANS: Das hättest du nicht tun sollen.

ERIKA: Ja, wenn ich gewußt hätte, daß du nicht willst, dann hätte ich ihr natürlich gesagt, du könntest heute nicht. Aber ich dachte, . . .

HANS: Du solltest nicht immer so viel denken.

II

TANTE AMALIE: Das war wirklich nett von dir, daß du mit mir ins Museum gegangen bist. Und jetzt würde ich gerne noch eine Tasse Kaffee trinken.

HANS: Das ist mir recht. Wo möchtest du denn hin?

TANTE AMALIE: Ich ginge gerne mal ins Café Schneider; da war ich schon lange nicht mehr.

HANS: Gut, und dann könnten wir Erika anrufen. Sie käme sicher auch gerne.

TANTE AMALIE: Ja, und wie wäre es, wenn ihr dann zum Abendessen zu mir kommen würdet?

HANS: Das wäre sehr nett, Tante Amalie, aber ich kann leider nicht; ich habe zu viel zu tun.

TANTE AMALIE: Wenn du nur nicht immer so viel arbeiten müßtest!

HANS: Ja, aber ohne meine Arbeit wäre das Leben nur halb so schön.

TAXI-FUNK
Berlin e.G.m.b.H.
66 00 22
Berlin 61
Mehringdamm 107

**TAG
UND
NACHT
BEREIT**

66 00 22

Vorbestellung
jederzeit

Willst du mit dem Taxi ins Museum, Tante Amalie?

Die Nummer ist sechs-sechs, null-null, zwo-zwo.

III

ERIKA: Na, Hans, wie war's denn?

HANS: Ach, weißt du, Tante Amalie ist ja eigentlich sehr nett. Wenn sie nur nicht immer so viel reden würde.

ERIKA: Dann wäre sie nicht Tante Amalie.

HANS: Weißt du, sie hat mir erzählt, daß sie gestern bei Overhoffs den Museumsdirektor kennengelernt hat. Sie sagte, er wäre sehr interessant und hätte ihr sehr viel über Picasso erzählt.

ERIKA: Nun, wenn sie jetzt den Direktor kennt, brauchst du vielleicht nicht mehr so oft mit ihr ins Museum zu gehen.

HANS: Ja, und wenn sie den Direktor heiraten würde, brauchte ich nie mehr mit ihr ins Museum zu gehen. Dann könnte sie im Museum wohnen.

ERIKA: Hans, das ist nicht sehr nett von dir.

IV

The following brief exchanges contain characteristic conversational patterns, many using subjunctive forms. By recombining these phrases, construct similar exchanges.

A: Wer war denn das eben am Telefon?
B: Frau Schmidt.
A: Welche Frau Schmidt?
B: Die Mutter von Heinz.
A: Ach so. —Was wollte sie denn?

A: Herr Doktor, Frau Schulz ist am Apparat.°
B: Ja, was ist denn?°

= Telefon
What's the matter?

A: Sie sagt, ihrem Mann ginge es nicht gut.

B: Sagen Sie ihr, ich würde in ein paar Minuten zurückrufen.

A: Hast du nicht gesagt, du müßtest morgen in die Stadt?

B: Ja, ich muß zum Zahnarzt. —Warum fragst du?

A: Ich dachte, du könntest vielleicht etwas für mich erledigen.°   take care of, do

B: Aber gerne. —Was denn?

A: Tante Amalie hat mich gefragt, wo du gestern gewesen wärst. Sie hätte den ganzen Nachmittag auf dich gewartet.

B: Ich hätte natürlich hingehen sollen, aber ich hatte tatsächlich°   indeed, really keine Zeit.

A: Dann hättest du sie aber wenigstens anrufen sollen.

B: Da hast du natürlich recht. Am besten ruf ich sie jetzt gleich mal an und bitte sie um Entschuldigung.

Fragen an Sie persönlich

1. Haben Sie gestern (oder heute) den Wetterbericht gehört oder gelesen?
   Wie soll das Wetter werden?

2. Haben Sie im Radio oder im Fernsehen die Nachrichten gehört?
   Erzählen Sie, was Sie gehört haben. (indirect discourse)

3. Haben Sie in den letzten Tagen interessante Post bekommen?
   Hat Sie jemand angerufen?
   Was hat er/sie gesagt?
   (Hier dürfen Sie auch erfinden—*invent*.)

Reading

I

BERTOLT BRECHT

Bertolt Brecht (born 1898 in Augsburg) was one of the major figures in German literature during the first half of this century, and also one of the most controversial. Though best known in America for his plays, for example, *Mutter Courage, Der gute Mensch von Sezuan, Der kaukasische Kreidekreis,* he also produced poetry and prose. In 1933, he emigrated from National Socialist Germany, first to Denmark, then to Finland, and then, via Siberia, to the United States. He lived in California until 1948, then returned to East Berlin, where he died in 1956. The following story is from his *Geschichten vom Herrn Keuner.*

Bertolt Brecht.

Wenn die Haifische Menschen wären

„Wenn die Haifische Menschen wären", fragte Herrn K. die kleine Tochter seiner Wirtin, „wären sie dann netter zu den kleinen Fischen?" „Sicher", sagte er. „Wenn die Haifische Menschen wären, würden sie 5 im Meer für die kleinen Fische gewaltige Kästen bauen lassen, mit allerhand Nahrung drin, sowohl Pflanzen als auch Tierzeug. Sie würden sorgen, daß die Kästen immer frisches Wasser hätten, und sie würden 10 überhaupt allerhand sanitäre Maßnahmen treffen. Wenn zum Beispiel ein Fischlein sich die Flosse verletzen würde, dann würde ihm sogleich ein Verband gemacht, damit es den Haifischen nicht wegstürbe vor der Zeit. 15 Damit die Fischlein nicht trübsinnig würden, gäbe es ab und zu große Wasserfeste; denn lustige Fischlein schmecken besser als trübsinnige. Es gäbe natürlich auch Schulen in den großen Kästen. In diesen Schulen 20 würden die Fischlein lernen, wie man in den Rachen der Haifische schwimmt. Sie würden zum Beispiel Geographie brauchen, damit sie die großen Haifische, die faul irgendwo liegen, finden könnten. Die Hauptsache 25 wäre natürlich die moralische Ausbildung des Fischleins. Sie würden unterrichtet werden, daß es das Größte und Schönste sei, wenn ein Fischlein sich freudig aufopfert, und daß sie alle an die Haifische glauben 30 müßten, vor allem, wenn sie sagten, sie

If Sharks Were People

"If sharks were people," the landlady's little daughter asked Mr. K., "would they be nicer to the little fishes?"

"Certainly," he said. "If sharks were people 5 they would have enormous boxes built in the sea for the little fishes with all sorts of things to eat in them, plants as well as animal matter.

They would see to it that the boxes always 10 had fresh water and, in general, take hygienic measures of all kinds. For instance, if a little fish injured one of its fins, it would be bandaged at once, so that the sharks should not be deprived of it by an untimely death. 15 To prevent the little fishes from growing depressed there would be big water festivals from time to time, for happy little fishes taste better than miserable ones. Of course there would also be schools in the big boxes. 20 In these schools the little fishes would learn how to swim into the sharks' jaws. They would need geography, for example, so that when the big sharks were lazing about somewhere they could find them.

25 The main thing, of course, would be the moral education of the little fishes. They would be taught that the greatest and finest thing is for a little fish to sacrifice its life gladly, and that they must all believe in the 30 sharks, particularly when they promise a splendid future. They would impress upon

würden für eine schöne Zukunft sorgen. Man würde den Fischlein beibringen, daß diese Zukunft nur gesichert sei, wenn sie Gehorsam lernten. Vor allen niedrigen, materialistischen, egoistischen und marxisti-5 schen Neigungen müßten sich die Fischlein hüten und es sofort den Haifischen melden, wenn eines von ihnen solche Neigungen verriete. Wenn die Haifische Menschen wären, würden sie natürlich auch unter-10 einander Kriege führen, um fremde Fischkästen und fremde Fischlein zu erobern. Die Kriege würden sie von ihren eigenen Fischlein führen lassen. Sie würden die Fischlein lehren, daß zwischen ihnen und 15 den Fischlein der anderen Haifische ein riesiger Unterschied bestehe. Die Fischlein, würden sie verkünden, sind bekanntlich stumm, aber sie schweigen in ganz verschiedenen Sprachen und können einander 20 daher unmöglich verstehen. Jedem Fischlein, das im Krieg ein paar andere Fischlein, feindliche, in anderer Sprache schweigende Fischlein tötete, würden sie einen kleinen Orden aus Seetang anheften und den Titel 25 Held verleihen. Wenn die Haifische Menschen wären, gäbe es bei ihnen natürlich auch eine Kunst. Es gäbe schöne Bilder, auf denen die Zähne der Haifische in prächtigen Farben, ihre Rachen als reine Lustgärten, in denen es 30 sich prächtig tummeln läßt, dargestellt wären. Die Theater auf dem Meeresgrund würden zeigen, wie heldenmütige Fischlein begeistert in die Haifischrachen schwimmen, und die Musik wäre so schön, daß die 35 Fischlein unter ihren Klängen, die Kapelle voran, träumerisch, und in allerangenehmste Gedanken eingelullt, in die Haifischrachen strömten. Auch eine Religion gäbe es ja, wenn die Haifische Menschen wären. Sie 40 würden lehren, daß die Fischlein erst im Bauche der Haifische richtig zu leben begännen. Übrigens würde es auch aufhören, wenn die Haifische Menschen wären, daß

the little fishes that this future could only be assured if they learned obedience. The little fishes would have to guard against all base, materialistic, egotistic, and Marxist tendencies, reporting at once to the sharks if any of their number manifested such tendencies.

If sharks were people they would also, naturally, wage wars among themselves, to conquer foreign fish boxes and little foreign fishes. They would let their own little fishes fight these wars. They would teach the little fishes that there was a vast difference between themselves and the little fishes of other sharks.
Little fishes, they would proclaim, are well known to be dumb,* but they are silent in quite different languages and therefore cannot possibly understand each other. Each little fish which killed a few other little fishes in war—little enemy fishes, dumb in a different language—would have a little seaweed medal pinned on it and be awarded the title of Hero.
If sharks were people they would also have art, naturally. There would be lovely pictures representing sharks' teeth in glorious colors, their jaws as positive pleasure grounds in which it would be a joy to gambol.
The seabed theaters would show heroic little fishes swimming rapturously into sharks' jaws, and the music would be so beautiful that to its strains the little fishes, headed by the band, would pour dreamily into the sharks' jaws, lulled in the most delightful thoughts.
There would also be a religion if sharks were people. It would teach that little fishes only really start to live inside the bellies of sharks. Moreover, if sharks were people, not all little fishes would be equal anymore, as they are now. Some of them would be given positions

---

*German distinguishes between **stumm**, *dumb (incapable of speech)* and **dumm**, *dumb (stupid, simple-minded, lacking intelligence)*.

alle Fischlein, wie es jetzt ist, gleich sind. Einige von ihnen würden Ämter bekommen und über die anderen gesetzt werden. Die ein wenig größeren dürften sogar die kleineren auffressen. Das wäre für die Haifische nur 5 angenehm, da sie dann selber öfter größere Brocken zu fressen bekämen. Und die größern, Posten habenden Fischlein würden für die Ordnung unter den Fischlein sorgen, Lehrer, Offiziere, Ingenieure im Kastenbau 10 usw. werden. Kurz, es gäbe überhaupt erst eine Kultur im Meer, wenn die Haifische Menschen wären."

and be set over the others. The slightly bigger ones would even be allowed to gobble the smaller ones. That would give nothing but pleasure to the sharks, since they would more often get larger morsels for themselves. And the bigger little fishes, those holding positions, would be responsible for keeping order among the little fishes, become teachers, officers, box-building engineers, and so on. In short, the sea would only start being civilized if sharks were people."

The following poem is from Brecht's *Dreigroschenoper* (Threepenny Opera), his 1928 free adaptation of John Gay's *Beggar's Opera* (1728), with music by Kurt Weill. A *Moritat* is traditionally a ballad with a moral, sung by a street singer and often accompanied by a hurdy-gurdy.

Die Moritat von Mackie Messer

Und der Haifisch, der hat Zähne
Und die trägt er im Gesicht
Und Macheath, der hat ein Messer
Doch das Messer sieht man nicht.

Ach, es sind des Haifischs Flossen°   fins
Rot, wenn dieser Blut vergießt!*
Mackie Messer trägt 'nen Handschuh
Drauf man keine Untat° liest.   misdeed

*Die Flossen des Haifischs sind rot, wenn er Blut vergießt. (**Blut vergiessen** to bleed)

An der Themse grünem Wasser
Fallen plötzlich Leute um!°   fall down, keel over
Es ist weder Pest noch Cholera°   neither plague nor cholera
Doch es heißt: Macheath geht um.

An 'nem schönen blauen Sonntag   5
Liegt ein toter Mann am Strand°   beach, bank of a river
Und ein Mensch geht um die Ecke
Den man Mackie Messer nennt.

Und Schmul Meier bleibt verschwunden
Und so mancher reiche Mann   10
Und sein Geld hat Mackie Messer
Dem man nichts beweisen° kann.   prove

Jenny Towler ward gefunden°   was found
Mit 'nem Messer in der Brust
Und am Kai geht Mackie Messer   15
Der von allem nichts gewußt.

Wo ist Alfons Glite, der Fuhrherr°?   carter, merchant
Kommt das je ans Sonnenlicht?
Wer es immer wissen könnte—
Mackie Messer weiß es nicht.   20

Und das große Feuer in Soho
Sieben Kinder und ein Greis°—   old man
In der Menge° Mackie Messer, den   crowd
Man nicht fragt und der nichts weiß.

Und die minderjährige° Witwe°   25   minor, underage   widow
Deren° Namen jeder weiß   whose
Wachte auf und war geschändet°—   woke up raped
Mackie, welches war dein Preis?

II

Fabrik° für frische Fische*   factory

Wenn wir im nächsten Jahrhundert° noch genug zu essen haben   century
wollen, müssen wir neue Nahrungsquellen° suchen, besonders für sources for food
Eiweiß.°   protein (lit.: egg white)

Das Meer ist der ideale Lieferant° für Eiweiß. Doch rücksichtslose   supplier
Massenfangmethoden° haben die riesigen° Fischzahlen stark 5   reckless methods of mass
reduziert, und weil andere Länder deshalb° ihre Fischereigrenzen°   catches   immense
drastisch ausdehnen,° werden für die deutschen Hochseefischer die   for that reason   fishing
Fanggründe° immer kleiner.   limits   extend
                                                                fishing areas

*Adapted from an article by Henning Seehusen in the weekly magazine *Stern*, 28 October 1976.

Ein Ausweg heißt „Aquakultur im Meer",° was soviel bedeutet wie   ocean
„Viehzucht° unter Wasser". An diesem Problem arbeiten deutsche   breeding livestock
Meeresbiologen° in Hamburg, in Kiel und in anderen Städten an der   marine biologists
Nord- und Ostseeküste. Am Kieler Institut für Meereskunde° experi-   oceanography
mentieren die Biologen seit 1972 mit der Aufzucht° von Jungfischen. 5   breeding
Sie konstruierten drehbare Käfige aus Netzen,° die später (bei   rotating cages made
kommerzieller Fischzucht) einen Durchmesser° von 8 Metern und ein   out of nets   diameter
Volumen von 150 Kubikmetern haben sollen. Diese Käfige sind fest
verankert und schwimmen fast wartungsfrei° im Wasser.   maintenance-free

Zur Zeit° produziert diese „Fischfarm" einige zehntausend Lachse 10   at the moment
und Forellen° im Jahr. Zum Glück liegt in der Nähe der Fischfarm   salmon and trout
ein großes Kraftwerk,° das sehr viel warmes Wasser erzeugt° und in   power plant   produces
die Ostsee leitet. Das warme Wasser bekommt° den kleinen Fischen   agree with
sehr gut: Sie wachsen fast dreimal so schnell wie Jungfische in unge-
heizter° See, weil, wie ein Fischexperte erklärt, „die wachstumstote 15   unheated
Winterzeit" ausgeschaltet° ist. Schon nach einem Jahr sind die   eliminated
Forellen reif für den Markt, was sonst° zwei bis drei Jahre dauert°.   otherwise   takes

Nun müssen die Biologen noch das Futterproblem° lösen. Denn bevor   feed problem
die Fische als Eiweißnahrung auf unserem Teller landen, fressen sie
selbst erst viel Eiweiß. Die Kieler Wissenschaftler° versuchen jetzt, 20   scientists
die Jungfische mit gezüchteten Muscheln° zu füttern, die einen   sea mussels
Eiweißgehalt° von 60% haben.   protein content

Wenn der Versuch° gelingt, können bald die ersten Fabriken mit der   experiment
Produktion von Frischfischen beginnen. Die Aussichten° sind gut.   prospects
Japan, die größte Fischfang-Nation der Welt, produziert heute schon 25
jedes Jahr 500.000 Tonnen Fisch in Aquakulturen.

III

A German Tongue Twister

Fischers Fritz frißt* frische Fische; frische Fische frißt Fischers Fritz.
  The Fischer's (son) Fritz eats fresh fish; fresh fish does the Fischer's (son) Fritz eat
  (indeed).

Exercises

A. Change the following sentences to indirect discourse, starting with **Er sagte, daß** . . . . Change pronouns as appropriate. Use both normal and alternate subjunctives, if possible.

SEE
ANALYSIS
127-130
(pp. 317-321)

1. Meyer wohnt in Köln.   4. Ich brauche nicht nach Bonn zu fahren.
2. Ich brauche kein Geld.   5. Ich bleibe heute abend zu Hause.
3. Wir arbeiten heute nicht.   6. Das kann ich Ihnen nicht glauben.

*The verb **fressen, fraß, hat gefressen** is normally used only with animals.

7. Ich will ihn in Berlin besuchen.
8. Ich möchte mit dir ins Kino gehen.
9. Ich muß Ingelheims Roman lesen.

10. Ich darf mit meinem Vater nach Afrika fahren.

B. Change the following sentences to indirect discourse, starting with **Er sagte,** . . . Change pronouns as appropriate.

1. Man hat ihn nach Bayern geschickt.
2. Er ist nicht mit uns nach Berlin gefahren.
3. Ich mußte nach Zürich fliegen.
4. Wir konnten das Haus in Köln nicht kaufen.
5. Ich habe zuviel Kaffee getrunken.
6. Er konnte uns gestern nicht besuchen.
7. Den Roman von Ingelheim habe ich noch nicht gelesen.

SEE ANALYSIS 127–130 (pp. 317–321)

C. Change the following questions to indirect yes-or-no questions. First start with **Ich wüßte gerne, ob** . . . (indicative), and then with **Er fragte mich, ob** . . . (subjunctive).

1. Fährt Erika morgen bestimmt nach Berlin?
2. Sind Sie verheiratet?
3. Wohnen Sie in München?
4. Haben Sie noch ein Zimmer frei?
5. Kennst du meine Freundin?
6. Kannst du mich morgen anrufen?

SEE ANALYSIS 127–130 (pp. 317–321)

D. Change to direct questions. Change pronouns as appropriate.

1. Er wollte wissen, ob ich nach Berlin kommen könnte.
2. Er wollte wissen, ob mein Vater Schriftsteller wäre.
3. Er wollte wissen, was er mir schenken solle.
4. Er wollte wissen, ob mein Vater bald nach Hause käme.
5. Er wollte wissen, ob ich ihm vielleicht zwanzig Mark geben könnte.

E. Change to indirect questions (past time). Start with **Er fragte mich,** . . . Change pronouns as appropriate.

1. Waren Sie damals auch Student?
2. Warst du gestern in der Universität?
3. Hattest du kein Geld bei dir?
4. Stand da drüben nicht früher ein Hotel?
5. Warum hattest du eigentlich nie Geld?
6. Wie lange war Hans denn in Afrika?
7. Warum konntest du nicht kommen?
8. Warum ist Inge nicht mitgegangen?
9. Wen wolltest du denn besuchen?
10. Mußtest du am Sonntag arbeiten?

SEE ANALYSIS 127–130 (pp. 317–321)

F. Change the following imperatives to indirect discourse, starting with **Er sagte,** . . . Use both forms of the subjunctive where possible.

1. Fahren Sie doch mal an die See.
2. Sei nicht so unfreundlich.
3. Schicken Sie mir den Brief nach.
4. Geht doch mit ins Theater.
5. Nimm mich doch bitte mit.
6. Besuchen Sie uns doch mal.

SEE ANALYSIS 131 (p. 322)

G. Change to direct questions.

1. Er fragte, ob viele Leute dagewesen wären.
2. Er fragte, ob ich gestern krank gewesen sei.
3. Er fragte, ob es wahr wäre, daß es im Winter hier immer so kalt ist.
4. Er fragte, ob ich Irene gesehen hätte.
5. Er fragte, wie lange ich in der Schweiz gewesen wäre.
6. Er fragte, warum ich um neun Uhr noch im Bett gelegen hätte.

SEE ANALYSIS 127–130 (pp. 317–321)

7. Er fragte, warum Inge nicht hätte mit nach Italien fahren dürfen.
8. Er fragte, warum Erika gestern abend hätte zu Hause bleiben müssen.
9. Er fragte, warum ich ihr nicht hätte schreiben können.
10. Er fragte, ob sein Sohn nicht hätte zu Hause bleiben können.

H. Restate the following sentences by starting with **Er sah aus, als ob** . . . and **Er sah aus, als.** . . .

SEE
ANALYSIS
132
(p. 322)

1. Er hat die Gelbsucht.   4. Er ist unglücklich.
2. Er hat nicht gut geschlafen.   5. Er war krank.
3. Er hat viel erlebt.

I. Restate the following sentences in the past tense. Note that with the change from present tense to past tense, **wenn** must be changed to **als** in some cases.

SEE
ANALYSIS
132
(p. 322)

1. Wir können erst ins Theater gehen, wenn Else kommt.
2. Jedesmal, wenn Tante Amalie hier ist, muß ich mich zwingen, nett zu ihr zu sein.
3. Wenn mein Zug in München ankommt, bist du schon lange zu Hause.
4. Wenn meine Wohnung groß genug wäre, könnte ich auch fünfundzwanzig Leute einladen.
5. Wenn Hans geht, gehe ich auch.

J. In the following sentences, supply **als, als ob, ob, wann,** or **wenn.**

SEE
ANALYSIS
132
(p. 322)

1. Ich weiß, jemand hat hinter mir gestanden, _____ ich den Brief schrieb.
2. _____ ich gewußt hätte, daß sie nicht schwimmen konnte, wäre ich natürlich nicht mit ihr fischen gegangen.
3. Können Sie mir sagen, _____ der Zug aus Kiel ankommt?
4. Können Sie mir sagen, _____ der Zug aus Kiel schon angekommen ist?
5. Ich wußte nicht, _____ Erich mich erkannt hatte; jedenfalls tat er, _____ hätte er mich nicht gesehen.
6. Ich bin so müde. _____ ich nur endlich einmal lange schlafen könnte!
7. Ich bin nicht sicher, _____ ich das Geschenk annehmen soll oder nicht.
8. Was? Tante Amalie will uns schon wieder besuchen? _____ kommt sie denn?
9. Aber Inge, du tust ja, _____ *du* immer mit ihr ins Museum gehen müßtest.
10. Du weißt doch, ich komme erst um 7 Uhr nach Hause. _____ soll ich denn essen, _____ das Theater schon um 7 Uhr 30 anfängt?

K. Express in German.

1. If it began to rain now, we wouldn't be able to work anymore.
2. If it begins to rain now, we can't work anymore.
3. When it began to rain, we couldn't work anymore.
4. I was often unhappy; but when I saw her, I was always happy.
5. I'd like to know whether he is really a doctor.
6. I wish he weren't a doctor.
7. I don't understand why you always want to eat here.
8. I wish we'd eat at home tonight.
9. It would have been nice if you had stayed at home.
10. I really should (ought to) invite him, but I have no time.
11. I really should have invited him, but I had no time.
12. Not until yesterday did I hear from him.
13. She told me she would go to Bonn with me.
14. If only we could go to Bonn again!

15. He said he had never been in Berlin.
16. I'd like to have a cup of coffee.
17. You should have seen him three years ago.
18. If only she had learned to drive.
19. I shall never be able to forget you.
20. I wish he didn't always forget my birthday.
21. I wish you hadn't forgotten my birthday again.
22. I know Aunt Amalie is unreasonable.
23. In three weeks they saw sixteen cities; now they believe they know Europe.
24. He knows he should have stayed at home.
25. If he hadn't lived in Munich at that time, he would never have met her.

L. Supply the missing words.

1. Wir _____ gestern in die Stadt gefahren, _____ wir einkaufen wollten.
2. _____ habt ihr denn gekauft?
3. Was habt ihr denn _____ den Wein bezahlt?
4. Die Studenten standen alle _____ den Professor herum.
5. Sie wollten in _____ Schweiz fahren.
6. Weil er kein Geld _____, mußte er zu Hause bleiben.
7. Wenn er Geld gehabt _____, _____ er mit uns ins Theater gegangen.
8. Der Arzt sagte mir, ich _____ an die See fahren.
9. Wo waren Sie denn während _____ Sommers?
10. Herr Dr. Schmidt _____ leider verreist.
11. Ich habe Hans einen Brief _____, aber er hat _____ noch nicht geantwortet.
12. Sind Sie _____ einmal in Berlin gewesen? —Nein, noch nie.
13. Ich denke sehr oft _____ dich.
14. Hans lud mich ein, _____ in Köln zu besuchen.
15. Wußtest du, daß Erika Ärztin geworden _____?
16. Kann ich _____ helfen, Fridolin?
17. Nach dem Kino _____ er mich nach Hause.
18. Aber Fritz, _____ doch nicht so unfreundlich!
19. Wir sind gestern schwimmen gegangen, _____ es sehr kalt war.
20. _____ ist schön, _____ du noch eine Woche hierbleiben willst.

Vocabulary*

acht Tage	a week; eight days	**Milch bekommt**	milk does not
als ob	as if	**mir nicht**	agree with me
als wenn		**besser**	better
aufwachen	to wake up	**besser als**	better than
die Ausbildung	training	**blau**	blue
bedeuten	to mean, to signify	**das Blut**	blood
bekommen (*with dat.*)	to agree with	**die Brust, ⸚e**	breast, chest

*Some low-frequency words that occur in texts which are either translated entirely or glossed in the margin do not appear in the unit vocabularies or in the end vocabulary.

das Café, -s	café, coffeehouse
drehen	to turn
drehbar	rotary, revolving
um Entschuldigung bitten	to apologize
die Farbe, -n	color
faul	lazy
fressen	to eat (of animals), feed
das Futter	feed, food, fodder
ganz	all of, entire
durch ganz Deutschland	through all of Germany
der Gedanke, -n	thought
der Gehalt (no pl.)	content
das Gehalt, ¨er	salary
genug	enough
das Geschenk, -e	present
gleich	right away
der Handschuh, -e	glove
die Hauptsache, -n	main thing
der Ingenieur', -e	engineer
irgendwo	somewhere; anywhere
jedesmal	every time
jedesmal, wenn	whenever
der Kasten, ¨	box, case, container
die Kraft, ¨e	strength; force; power
das Kraftwerk, -e	power plant
die Kunst, ¨e	art
landen	to land
leiten	to lead, direct; to pipe
die Wasserleitung	water pipe
mancher (der-word)	many a
das Meer, -e	ocean
melden	to report
die Musik'	music
die Nahrung	nourishment, food
das Netz, -e	net
niemand	nobody
die Ordnung, -en	order
in Ordnung	all right, OK

ein paar	a few
der Preis, -e	price; prize
das Problem', -e	problem
die Quelle, -n	spring, source
die Nahrungsquelle, -n	source of food
das Radio, -s	radio
reif	ripe
die Religion, -en	religion
riesig	huge, gigantic, immense
rot	red
schweigen	to be silent
das Semester,	semester
sichern	to secure, make safe
stark	strong
überhaupt	in general; altogether
überhaupt nicht	not at all
untereinander	among each other, among themselves
verletzen	to hurt
verlieren	to lose
versuchen	to try
der Versuch, -e	experiment; attempt, try
vierzehn Tage	two weeks; fourteen days
vor allem	above all, particularly
wachsen	to grow, increase
das Wachstum	growth
wachstumstot	without growth
der Wirt, -e	innkeeper
die Wirtin, -nen	landlady; innkeeper
die Wissenschaft, -en	science
der Wissenschaftler, -	scientist
der Zahn, ¨e	tooth
der Zahnarzt, ¨e	dentist
die Zigar're, -n	cigar
die Zigaret'te, -n	cigarette

Additional Vocabulary

| der Anker, - | anchor |
| verankern | to fasten, to anchor |

| der Direk'tor, pl. die Direkto'ren | director |
| der Durchmesser, - | diameter |

das Eiweiß	white of egg; protein	ideal'	ideal
eiweißhaltig	containing protein	das Ideal', -e	ideal
der Eiweißgehalt	protein content	der Käfig, -e	cage
die Forelle, -n	trout	der Lachs, -e	salmon
der Haifisch, -e	shark	die Zucht	breeding, rearing
der Hai, -e		die Viehzucht	cattle raising
die Hochsee (no pl.)	high seas		

Strong Verbs

fressen	frißt	fraß	gefressen	to eat
schweigen		schwieg	geschwiegen	to be silent
verlieren		verlor	verloren	to lose
wachsen	wächst	wuchs	ist gewachsen	to grow

München

UNIT 12 Relative Pronouns—da-Compounds—wo-Compounds—Prepositional Objects

Much of the German used in this unit is more formal than in earlier units; that is, it is more highly structured and the syntax is more complex than in the simple drills you started out with. One reason for this is the use of relative clauses, which occur with greater frequency in the written than in the spoken language. Thus, the pattern sections dealing with relative pronouns are as much a reading exercise as they are the basis for oral drills. Because of the relative clauses, the sentences become much longer, and you will find it more difficult at first to repeat these sentences when you hear them without your book in front of you.

The reading selections are also more demanding than earlier ones. They again contain expository prose, but only the first few paragraphs are translated; thereafter, there are only marginal glosses. You should read these pieces for content, even if at first you don't fully comprehend every word and every grammatical construction. The topic is education in the German-speaking countries and a comparison of Central European school systems with that of the United States. Much of the vocabulary for the reading is introduced in the pattern sections to help you find your way through some rather complicated material.

The values and attitudes of a society are often reflected in its schools, just as schools and universities have a major impact on shaping these values and attitudes. Knowing something about how Germans grow up and are educated will help you understand that vague phenomenon sometimes referred to as "national character," and it may help explain some events in history that might have taken a different turn with a different system of education. Recent reforms in both the Federal Republic and the German Democratic Republic have grown at least partly out of such considerations.

On the lighter side, the conversation section of Unit 12 consists of a lengthy string of small talk typical of the way people carry on everyday conversations. It is followed by some suggestions for you to engage in some German chitchat yourselves. By now, you should be reaching the stage where you can break out of structured drills and begin to communicate rather than just reply to stimuli provided by your teacher.

Patterns

[1] Definite Relative Pronouns

SEE
ANALYSIS
133
(p. 345)

Mein Vater hatte nicht studiert.

Er konnte nicht verstehen, warum ich Schriftsteller werden wollte.

Mein Vater, der nicht studiert hatte, konnte nicht verstehen, warum ich Schriftsteller
werden wollte.

> My father, who had not gone to the university, could not understand why I wanted to be a writer.

Meine Mutter war Klavierlehrerin.

Sie wollte immer, daß ich Musik studieren sollte.

Meine Mutter, die Klavierlehrerin war, wollte immer, daß ich Musik studieren sollte.

> My mother, who was a piano teacher, always wanted me to study music.

Hier stand früher das Gymnasium.

Es stammte noch aus dem neunzehnten Jahrhundert.

Das Gymnasium, das früher hier stand, stammte noch aus dem neunzehnten Jahrhundert.

> The Gymnasium (secondary school) which once stood here dated from the nineteenth century.

Meyers Kinder gehen noch aufs Gymnasium.

Sie wollen später alle studieren.

Meyers Kinder, die noch aufs Gymnasium gehen, wollen später alle studieren.

> Meyer's children, who are still in secondary school, all want to go to the university later on.

Studienrat* Meinig war der Lehrer, den ich als Schüler† am meisten bewundert habe.

> Studienrat Meinig was the teacher I admired most when I was in school.

Die Schule, die ich neun Jahre lang besuchte, hieß Wöhler-Realgymnasium.‡

> The school that I attended for nine years was called Wöhler-Realgymnasium.

Das Fach, das ich am liebsten hatte, war Chemie.

> The subject I liked best was chemistry.

Viele von den Jungen (Mädchen), die ich auf der Schule kennengelernt habe, sind heute noch
meine Freunde (Freundinnen).

> Many of the boys (girls) I met in school are still my friends.

Die Grundschule ist der Schultyp, von dem man mit zehn Jahren entweder auf die Hauptschule, auf die Realschule oder auf das Gymnasium geht.

> The Grundschule (basic school) is the school type from which, at age ten, one goes either to the
> Hauptschule (main school), the Realschule (middle school), or the Gymnasium.

Die Prüfung, mit der das Gymnasium abschließt, ist das Abitur.

> The examination with which the Gymnasium terminates, is (called) the Abitur.

Das Abitur, mit dem man das Gymnasium abschließt, besteht aus einer Reihe von schrift-
lichen und mündlichen Prüfungen.

> The Abitur, with which you finish the Gymnasium, consists of a series of written and oral tests.

---

*Studienrat, Studienrätin (literally, *studies counselor*) is the official title for tenured teachers in a Gymnasium.

†Schüler, Schülerin student in a primary or secondary school; the term Student, Studentin is used only for university
students.

‡Realgymnasium a type of secondary school oriented toward the sciences and modern languages, in contrast to the
classical Gymnasium which stressed Greek, Latin, and sometimes Hebrew.

Keine Feier ohne
MEYER

Es gibt heute nur wenige Abiturienten, denen es gelingt, einen Studienplatz in der Medizin zu bekommen.

There are only very few *Gymnasium* graduates who succeed in getting admitted to study medicine.

Meyer, dessen Sohn ein sehr schlechtes Zeugnis bekam, mußte die achte Klasse wiederholen.

Meyer, whose son got a very bad grade report, had to repeat the eighth grade.

Anni Müller, in deren Klasse Fritz Meyer jetzt ist, erzählt immer, wie dumm Fritzchen ist.

Anni Müller, in whose class Fritz Meyer is now, always tells about how dumb Fritzchen is.

Dieses Mädchen Anni, dessen Eltern Herrn Meyer nicht leiden können, ist auch nicht gerade intelligent.

This girl Anni, whose parents can't stand Mr. Meyer, is not exactly intelligent either.

Meyers, deren Kinder, wie wir gehört haben, alle studieren wollen, haben sehr viel Geld.

The Meyers, whose children, as we have heard, all want to go to the university, have loads of money.

[2] Indefinite Relative Pronouns

Wer das Abitur hat, kann die Universität besuchen.
Wer das Abitur hat, der kann die Universität besuchen.

He who has (those who have; whoever has) the *Abitur*, can go to the university.

SEE ANALYSIS 133 (p. 345)

Wer mit 15 Jahren von der Hauptschule abgeht, (der) muß noch drei Jahre die Berufsschule besuchen.

Those who graduate from the *Hauptschule* at age fifteen have to attend a vocational school for another three years.

Was man in der Berufsschule lernt, kann man sofort praktisch im Betrieb verwenden.

What you learn in (the) vocational school you can put to use immediately in your place of work.

Unser Sohn will Automechaniker werden, was ich sehr vernünftig finde.

Our son wants to become an auto mechanic, which I think makes a lot of sense (is very reasonable).

Ich habe leider nicht alles verstanden, was Professor Kunz erklärt hat.

Unfortunately, I did not understand everything Professor Kunz explained.

Professor Bodenstein hat wirklich nichts gesagt, was ich nicht schon wußte.

Professor Bodenstein really didn't say anything that I didn't already know.

Aber Hans, du *mußt* doch etwas gelernt haben, was neu für dich war.

But Hans, you *must* have learned something that was new for you.

[3] da-Compounds with Unstressed da-

SEE
ANALYSIS
134
(p. 347)

Wo ist denn mein Kugelschreiber?—Ich schreibe gerade damit.
  Where is my ballpoint pen?—I'm writing with it.

Wir haben *auch* ein Haus mit einer Garage dahinter.
  We, too, have a house with a garage behind it.

Das ist die Marienkirche, und in dem Haus da*neben* hat früher mein Bruder gewohnt.
  That's St. Mary's, and my brother used to live in the house next to it.

Haben Sie Ingelheims Roman gelesen?—Nur den Anfang davon.
  Have you read Ingelheim's novel?—Only the beginning of it.

[4] Stressed da-Compounds; Split da-Compounds; der hier, der da

SEE
ANALYSIS
135
(p. 349)

Den Kugelschreiber kannst du zurückbringen.
Damit (mit *dem*) kann ich nicht schreiben.
Da kann ich nicht mit schreiben.
Der Kugelschreiber hier ist mir zu schwer. Darf ich mal *den* da versuchen?

In die *Oper* brauchst du mit Tante Amalie *nicht* zu gehen.
Dabei schläft sie immer ein.
Da schläft sie immer bei *ein*.
Sonntag im Kino ist sie *auch* eingeschlafen.—Aber im Gloria-Palast läuft heute abend ein
  Hitchcock-Film. Bei *dem* (*dabei*) schläft sie be*stimmt* nicht ein.

From an ad for
MAIL ORDER KAISER
München 13.

[5] wo-Compounds

SEE
ANALYSIS
136
(p. 350)

Wofür brauchst du denn so viel Geld? Was willst du denn kaufen?
  What do you need so much money for? What do you want to buy?

Für was brauchst du denn das Geld?
  What do you need the money for?

Ich weiß nicht, wofür er das Geld ausgegeben hat.
  I don't know what he spent the money for.

War der Briefträger immer noch nicht da?—Warum fragst du denn schon wieder? Auf was
 (worauf) wartest du denn eigentlich, auf einen Brief von deiner Freundin?
> Hasn't the mailman been here yet?—Why are you asking again? What are you waiting for anyway,
> a letter from your girlfriend?

Ich weiß nicht, worauf er wartet.
> I don't know what he is waiting for.

[6] Prepositional Objects

Most of the verbs in this section are not new, and many have already been used with the
prepositions introduced here. Therefore, use this section as a review of verbs and to
learn some more school and university terminology in small contexts.

Ich glaube, Franziska hat Angst vor dem Abitur. —Aber sie braucht doch wirklich keine
 Angst davor zu haben, daß sie durchfällt.
> I think Franziska is afraid of the *Abitur*. —But she really doesn't need to be afraid of flunking.

SEE
ANALYSIS
137–138
(pp. 351–353)

Ich habe Professor Baumgärtner geschrieben und ihn gebeten, mir eine Empfehlung zu
 schreiben, aber bisher hat er mir noch nicht geantwortet.
> I've written to Professor Baumgärtner and have asked him to write a recommendation for me, but
> so far he hasn't answered me.

Ich habe ihn um eine Empfehlung gebeten.
> I've asked him for a recommendation.

Er hat noch nicht auf meinen Brief geantwortet.
> He hasn't answered my letter yet.

Herr Studienrat, ich möchte Ihnen noch einmal für alles danken, was Sie für unsere Tochter
 getan haben.
> Herr Studienrat, I'd like to thank you once more for all that you have done for our daughter.

Ich denke oft und gern an meine Schulzeit in Frankfurt zurück.
> I often think back with pleasure to my school years in Frankfurt.

Wir denken oft darüber nach, wie man den Fremdsprachenunterricht verbessern könnte.
> We often think (meditate) about how one could improve foreign language instruction.

Darf ich dich nach der Vorlesung* zu einer Tasse Kaffee einladen?
> May I invite you to (have) a cup of coffee after class?

Wir haben Professor Müller zu einem Vortrag* in unserem Institut eingeladen.
> We have invited Professor Müller to give a lecture in our Institute.

Früher war Professor Meyer *der* Spezialist für Chirurgie; heute fragt kein Mensch mehr
 nach ihm.
> Professor Meyer used to be *the* specialist in surgery; today nobody asks about him (mentions him)
> anymore.

Hast du auch danach gefragt, wann nächstes Jahr die Sommerferien anfangen?
> Did you inquire when summer vacation begins next year?

---

*The term **Vorlesung** is used in the sense of *class,* for daily lectures in a university course; **Vortrag** refers to individual public lectures.

Fritzchen Meyer gehört sicher zu denen, die nie das Abitur machen werden.
>   Fritzchen Meyer, I'm sure, is one of those (belongs to those) who will never get their *Abitur*.

Unser Institut gehört zum Fachbereich Angewandte Physik.
>   Our Institute belongs to (is part of) the Department of Applied Physics.

Nein, das sind nicht meine Bücher; die gehören dem Institut.
>   No, those aren't my books; they belong to the Institute.

Viele Leute glauben nicht an den Erfolg der Universitätsreform. Glauben Sie daran?
>   Many people don't believe in the success of the university reform. Do you believe in it?

Ich glaube nicht daran, daß die Universitätsreform das Hochschulsystem* wirklich verbessern wird.
>   I don't believe that the university reform will really improve the system of higher education.

Was halten Sie von den höheren Schulen* in der Bundesrepublik, Mr. Ray? Sind sie besser als in Amerika?
>   What do you think of the secondary schools in the Federal Republic, Mr. Ray? Are they better than in America?

Ich halte sie für sehr gut, Herr Huber; aber man kann sie nicht gut mit der High School* in Amerika vergleichen.
>   I consider them (to be) very good, Mr. Huber. But it is difficult to compare them with the high school in America.

Meyer hofft immer auf Wunder. Zur Zeit hofft er darauf, daß Fritzchen das Abitur bestehen wird.
>   Meyer always hopes for miracles; right now he hopes that Fritzchen will pass the *Abitur*.

Was hören Sie denn von Ihrem Sohn, Herr Schulze?
>   What do you hear from your son, Mr. Schulze?

Ich hatte gar nichts davon gehört, daß er promoviert† hatte.
>   I had heard nothing about his having gotten his Ph.D.

Fritzchen will Kernphysik studieren? Mit einer Fünf‡ in Mathematik? Darüber kann ich nur lachen.
>   Fritzchen wants to study nuclear physics? With a D in math? That's ridiculous. (About that I can only laugh.)

Lacht doch nicht immer über Fritzchen.
>   Don't always laugh about little Fritz.

Auf den Vorschlag der Fakultät haben die Studenten und Assistenten sehr positiv reagiert.
>   To the proposal by the faculty, students and assistants reacted very positively.

Herr Doktor Schmidt, sind Sie *für* die Universitätsreform oder sind Sie da*gegen?*
>   Doctor Schmidt, are you *for* university reform or are you *against* it?

---

*Hochschule does not mean *high school*, but is used for all institutions of higher learning, that is, for the university level. Secondary schools are referred to as **höhere Schulen**, but since they are not really the equivalent of secondary schools in the U.S., it is best to use the term *high school* when speaking of American schools. Also, since there is no equivalent of the American college in Germany, the term *college* should be used as well; thus:
>   **Mein Bruder geht noch auf die High School, aber ich bin schon im College, —in Massachusetts.**

†**promovieren** is used only in the sense of *to receive the Ph.D.*, the noun **die Promotion** is also used only in this sense.
‡German grades go from 1 (highest) to 6 (lowest).

Von wem (von was; wovon) sprecht ihr denn?
    Whom (what) are you talking about?

Wir sprachen gerade davon, daß wir in den Semesterferien nach Schweden fahren wollen.
    We were just talking about going to Sweden during vacation (the semester break).

In seinem Vortrag sprach Professor Schmidtke über die Verschmutzung unserer Flüße durch die Industrie.
    In his lecture, Professor Schmidtke talked about the pollution of our rivers by industry.

Natürlich sind wir stolz auf Fritz. Ich hätte nie gedacht, daß er einmal Arzt werden würde.
    Of course we are proud of Fritz. I would never have thought that he'd be a doctor some day.

Wissen *Sie,* was Endokrinologie ist? —Nein, davon verstehe ich leider gar nichts.
    Do *you* know what endocrinology is? —No, unfortunately I know nothing about it.

Ich warte auf Joachim. Er wollte gleich nach dem Seminar hierher kommen.
    I'm waiting for Joachim. He wanted to come here right after his seminar.

Was wissen Sie vom Schulsystem in der Bundesrepublik? —Davon weiß ich leider nur sehr wenig.
    What do you know about the school system in the Federal Republic?—Unfortunately I know very little about it.

Carola Müller ist mit ihrem Zeugnis sehr zufrieden.
    Carola Müller is very satisfied with her report card.

Analysis

133 Relative Pronouns

The Definite Relative Pronoun

The German relative pronouns are **der, die, das.** Their forms are the same as those of the definite article, except that the singular genitive and the plural genitive and dative add the ending **-en.** This **-en** necessitates doubling the -s in the masculine and neuter forms in order to keep the preceding **-e-** short.

	MASC.	FEM.	NEUT.	PLURAL
NOM.	der	die	das	die
ACC.	den	die	das	die
DAT.	dem	der	dem	denen
GEN.	dessen	deren	dessen	deren

Relative pronouns must agree in gender and number with their antecedent; but their case depends on their function within the relative clause. *The German relative pronouns are never omitted.* All relative clauses are thus introduced dependent clauses and therefore have verb-last position.

NOM.   **Kennst du den Mann, *der* gestern hier war?**
    Do you know the man who was here yesterday?

Kennst du die Frau, *die* gestern hier war?
Kennst du das Mädchen, *das* gestern hier war?

ACC.   **Der Junge, *den* du gestern gesehen hast, ist mein Sohn.**
The boy (whom) you saw yesterday, is my son.
Die Dame, *die* du gestern gesehen hast, ist meine Tante.
Das Mädchen, *das* du gestern gesehen hast, ist meine Schwester.

DAT.   **Wer war denn der Junge, mit *dem* ich dich gestern gesehen habe?**
Who was the boy I saw you with (with whom I saw you) yesterday?
Wer war denn die Dame, mit *der* ich dich gestern gesehen habe?
Wer war denn das Mädchen, mit *dem* ich dich gestern gesehen habe?

GEN.   **Sein Vater, *dessen* Frau aus Leningrad kam, sprach gut Russisch.**
His father, whose wife came from Leningrad, spoke Russian well.
Seine Frau, *deren* Vater aus Leningrad kam, sprach gut Russisch.

PLURAL   **Kennst du die Leute, *die* gestern hier waren?**
Do you know the people who were here yesterday?

Die Mädchen, *die* du gesehen hast, waren meine Schwestern.
The girls (whom) you saw were my sisters.

Wer waren denn die Mädchen, mit *denen* ich dich gestern gesehen habe?
Who were the girls I saw you with (with whom I saw you) yesterday?

Relative clauses do not always follow their antecedents immediately. If only
the second prong is needed to complete the main clause, this clause is not interrupted by a relative clause.

> **Ich wollte Hermann Schneider besuchen, mit dem ich vor zehn Jahren in Afrika gewesen
> war.**

Not

> [**Ich wollte Hermann Schneider, mit dem ich vor zehn Jahren in Afrika gewesen war, be-
> suchen.**]

The Indefinite Relative Pronoun
___

The German indefinite relative pronouns are **wer** and **was**. They are always
used if there is no antecedent.

> *Wer* **Geld hat, hat auch Freunde.**
> Whoever (He who) has money has friends, too.

> *Wer* **nicht für mich ist, ist gegen mich.**
> Whoever is not for me is against me.

> *Was* **er zu erzählen hatte, war nicht viel.**
> What he had to tell was not much.

> **Was er zu erzählen hatte, das war nicht viel.**
> **Wer Geld hat, der hat auch Freunde.**
> **Wer mich liebt, den liebe ich auch.**

Wer Schnupfen hat braucht Rhino Spray

RhinoSpray
macht die Nase frei

Note: Germans pronounce **Spray** to rhyme with **drei.**

In the last three examples, **das, der,** and **den** repeat the relative clause.

Was is also used to refer to an entire clause or to **alles, nichts,** or **etwas.**

Hans hat mich zum Essen eingeladen, was ich sehr nett finde.
Ich habe nicht alles verstanden, was er gesagt hat.
Er hat nichts gesagt, was ich nicht schon wußte.
Er hat mir etwas geschenkt, was ich schon lange haben wollte.

134 da-Compounds with Unstressed da-

All personal pronouns:

		SINGULAR		PLURAL
NOM.	er	sie	es	sie
ACC.	ihn	sie	es	sie
DAT.	ihm	ihr	ihm	ihnen

can be used to replace *any* noun, not just nouns referring to persons. If a noun like **der Wagen** is replaced by a pronoun, the masculine **der Wagen** is replaced by **er, ihm, ihn.**

Er (der Wagen) ist sechs Jahre alt. It is six years old.
Ich habe ihn auch immer gut gepflegt. I've always taken good care of it.
Das sieht man ihm nicht an. It doesn't look it.

But you cannot express

I want to drive to Paris with it

by

[Ich will mit ihm nach Paris fahren]

because **mit ihm** can only mean *with him*.

After a preposition, all pronouns are strictly *personal* pronouns, that is, they can only refer to persons and not to things. The **mit ihm** in the sentence above can therefore refer to your friend, but not to your car.

If **mit meinem Wagen** is to be replaced by something comparable to *with it*, all nouns referring to things (and all the pronouns you are tempted to use) become **da-**, preceding and compounded with the preposition (cf. English *therewith*). Thus **mit meinem Wagen** becomes **damit**.

Ich will damit nach Paris fahren.

This **da-** is a substitute for any noun which does not refer to persons. There is no longer any difference between masculine, feminine, and neuter; no difference between dative and accusative; and no difference between singular and plural. Thus the questions

Was soll *ich* denn	**mit dem Schlüssel?** **mit der Uhr?** **mit dem Buch?** **mit den Büchern?**

all become

Was soll *ich* denn	**damit?**

Similarly, the questions

Was hast du denn	**für diesen Wein** **für diese Uhr** **für dieses Haus** **für diese Blumen**	**be*zahlt*?**

all become

Was hast du denn	**dafür**	**be*zahlt*?**

The **da-** in the examples above is unstressed just as the corresponding articles and the nouns are unstressed. The preposition is usually unstressed, too, but occasionally it may become the stress point of the sentence.

Ich habe nichts da*gegen*, aber ich bin auch nicht da*für*.

Table of **da**-Compounds

If the preposition starts with a vowel, **dar-** is used instead of **da-**.

dadurch	dabei	dahinter
dafür	damit	daneben
dagegen	danach	daran
	daraus	darauf
	davon	darin
	dazu	darüber
		darunter
		davor
		dazwischen

Note that **ohne, außer, seit,** and the prepositions governing the genitive (**während, wegen, trotz**) do not form **da**-compounds. **Außer** forms **außerdem** (*besides*), **seit** forms **seitdem** (*since then*, conj. *since*), and **trotz** forms **trotzdem** (*in spite of that, nevertheless*).

135 da-Compounds with Stressed da-

As long as *unstressed* nouns and pronouns denoting things are replaced after prepositions, you have no choice but to replace them with a **da**-compound. However, if *stressed* nouns and pronouns denoting things and preceded by a preposition are to be replaced, you have a choice. You can use either the stressed demonstrative pronoun *after* the preposition or a stressed **da-** *preceding* the preposition.

Thus

Was soll ich denn	mit *dem* Schlüssel? mit *der* Uhr? mit *dem* Buch? mit *den* Büchern?	or	mit dem *Schlüssel?* mit der *Uhr?* mit dem *Buch?* mit den *Büchern?*

may become either

Was soll ich denn	mit *dem?* mit *der?* mit *dem?* mit *denen?*

or

Was soll ich denn	*da*mit?

In assertions, **da**-compounds with a stressed **da-** usually occupy the front field and carry contrast intonation.

Was soll ich denn mit *dem* Hut? *Da*mit gehe ich *nicht* in die Kirche.
So, Jutta hat ge*hei*ratet? *Da*von habe ich nichts ge*wußt*.

NOTE:

1. The second example above shows that **da**-compounds are used not only to refer to things, but also to refer to entire sentences.

Davon (daß Jutta geheiratet hat) habe ich nichts gewußt.

2. Do not replace directives like **ins Haus, zum Bahnhof, nach Berlin** with **da**-compounds. Such directives are sometimes replaced by **hin** or **dahin**.

Mußt du zum Bahnhof? Ich bringe dich gerne *hin*.
Ich soll nach Kairo fahren? Nein, *da*hin fahre ich nicht.
Sie fahren nach Berlin? Da möchte ich *auch* gerne mal hinfahren.

Split **da**-Compounds

In the spoken language, **da**-compounds may be split. The **da**- (stressed or un-stressed) then stands in the front field, and the preposition becomes the first part of the second prong. This pattern, however, is quite colloquial.

Damit	war	mein Mann *gar* nicht		zufrieden.
Da	war	mein Mann *gar* nicht	mit	zufrieden.

If the preposition begins with a vowel, **daraus** does not become **da . . . aus**, but **da . . . draus; daran: da . . . dran; darauf: da . . . drauf**; and so on.

der hier and **der da**

In spoken German, the contrast *this one: that one* is expressed by **der hier** (or **dieser hier**): **der da** (or **dieser da**).

Dieses Haus hier möchte ich nicht, aber das da hätte ich gerne.
Dieser Kugelschreiber hier ist mir zu schwer. Mit dem kann ich nicht schreiben. Kann ich den da mal versuchen?
Die hier (diese Uhr hier) kostet mir zu viel. Darf ich die da mal sehen?

136 wo-Compounds

If the question word **was** is preceded by a preposition, it may be replaced by **wo** (**wor-** in front of vowels) compounded with and followed by the preposition in question. One may ask:

Ich möchte wissen, auf was du noch wartest.

or

Ich möchte wissen, worauf du noch wartest.

The indefinite relative pronoun **was**, however, must *always* be replaced by **wo-**.

Das ist etwas, worüber ich nicht gern spreche.

137 Prepositional Objects

It was pointed out in Unit 3 that prepositions can be used by themselves as verbal complements. They are joined to a following infinitive or participle and appear in a dictionary under the preposition.

fahren to drive   **abfahren** to leave, depart

(a) **Der Zug fährt (fuhr) sofort *ab*.** *
(b) **Der Zug soll sofort *ab*fahren.**
(c) **Der Zug ist sofort *ab*gefahren.**

English also uses prepositions as verbal complements, but only occasionally do they precede, and are joined to, the infinitive, as, for example, in *to outflank, to overlook, to bypass*. The infinitive belonging to *He went out* is *to go out*, and is listed in a dictionary under *go*. English present participles and nouns occasionally show the "German" arrangement: to be outgoing; the outgoing administration; the incoming mail; the intake, the outflow.

We now introduce another type of verbal complement. Whereas in the type **abfahren** the preposition alone stands as the second prong if the verb is in the present or past tense [(a.) above], this new type consists of a preposition which is *always* followed by a noun or pronoun.

In sentences like

The bartender refused to wait on him

the prepositional phrase *on him* functions just like the direct object *him* in

The bartender refused to serve him.

Therefore, *on him* is called a prepositional object. Prepositional objects always form one single unit of meaning with their verb and are always verbal complements. If the preposition is changed, the meaning of the verb is also changed: *to wait on somebody* and *to wait for somebody* are two separate dictionary entries.

Questions asking for a prepositional object always use the preposition plus a form of **wer** or **was** (or a **wo**-compound):

Auf wen wartest du?	Whom are you waiting for?
Ich warte auf Erika.	I'm waiting for Erika.
Auf was (worauf) wartest du?	What are you waiting for?
Ich warte auf die Post.	I'm waiting for the mail.

Do not confuse prepositional objects with time phrases, place phrases, or directives:

vor einem Jahr	(question: **wann?**)	**nach Leipzig**	(question: **wohin?**)
zu Hause	(question: **wo?**)		

---

*The use of **ab** as a preposition is rather restricted. If a case is recognizable, it is usually the accusative: **ab nächsten Sommer**, *beginning (as of) next summer*; it also occurs in sentences like **Ab Hamburg hat der Zug keinen Speisewagen mehr.**

Both English and German have hundreds of such fixed combinations of verbs plus prepositional objects. Unfortunately, however, the prepositions used with the German verbs hardly ever correspond to the prepositions used with the English verbs. Compare the following sentences:

Ich warte *auf* Meyer.   I'm waiting *for* Meyer.
Ich spreche *von* Meyer.   I'm talking *about* Meyer.

Ich bin *in* sie verliebt.   I'm in love *with* her.
Ich bin *mit* ihr verlobt.   I'm engaged *to* her.

Ich habe Angst *vor* ihr.   I'm afraid *of* her.
Ich bin stolz *auf* sie.   I'm proud *of* her.

Note that the prepositional objects sometimes go with such compound verbs as **Angst haben** or **stolz sein**.

Not all English prepositional objects can be expressed by prepositional objects in German, and vice versa:

He looked *at me.*   **Er sah *mich* an.**
Ich halte es *für gut.*   I consider it *good.*

Frequent Prepositional Objects
___

Memorize the following verbs with their prepositions:

Angst haben vor (*dat.*)	to be afraid of
antworten auf (*acc.*)	to reply to (something)
jemandem antworten	to answer somebody
bitten um (*acc.*)	to ask for (something)
danken für (*acc.*)	to thank (someone) for
denken an (*acc.*)	to think of, to remember
nachdenken über (*acc.*)	to think, meditate about
einladen zu (*dat.*)	to invite to
fragen nach (*dat.*)	to ask about, inquire about
gehören zu (*dat.*)	to be part or a member of, to belong to
glauben an (*acc.*)	to believe in
halten von (*dat.*)	to have an opinion about; to think (highly, a great deal, not much, etc.) of (somebody or something)
halten für (*acc.*)	to think that something (or somebody) is (something)
hoffen auf (*acc.*)	to hope for, to trust in, to look forward to
hören von (*dat.*)	to hear from somebody or about something
lachen über (*acc.*)	to laugh about
jemanden auslachen	to laugh at (make fun of) somebody
reagieren auf (*acc.*)	to react to (something or somebody)
sein für or **sein gegen** (*acc.*)	to be for or against
sprechen von (*dat.*)	to talk of, to mention
sprechen über (*acc.*)	to talk in detail about a topic
stolz sein auf (*acc.*)	to be proud of
verstehen von (*dat.*)	to understand about
warten auf (*acc.*)	to wait for
wissen von (*dat.*)	to know about
zufrieden sein mit (*dat.*)	to be satisfied with

Note: A number of these prepositional objects use the prepositions **an, auf,
über.** In all cases listed, **an, auf,** and **über** are used with the accusative, even
though these phrases are not directives answering the question **wohin.** There
are a few cases where the dative *must* be used—for example, with **Angst haben
vor.** From now on, the correct case will be indicated in the vocabulary. The
importance of using the correct case can be seen in the following:

> **Ich warte auf *die* Straßenbahn**

means

> I am waiting for the streetcar

whereas

> **Ich warte auf *der* Straßenbahn**

could only mean

> I am waiting on top of the streetcar.

138 The Syntax of Prepositional Objects

Preposition plus Noun or Personal Pronoun

The prepositional object constitutes the second prong and is preceded by **nicht.**
Under contrast intonation, it can be placed in the front field.

> **Ich warte auf meinen Mann.**
> **Ich warte nicht auf sie.**
> **Auf Fritz brauchst du heute abend nicht zu warten.**

Replacement of Nouns and Pronouns by Demonstratives

The stressed demonstratives used to replace nouns or names usually occur in
the front field and produce contrast intonation.

> **Erika? Auf die brauchst du nicht zu warten.**
> **Meyers? Von denen haben wir lange nichts gehört.**
> ***Das* ist ein *Wein!* Mit *dem* werden Sie be*stimmt* zufrieden sein! Gegen *den* kann auch ein**
> ***Kenner* nichts sagen.**

Prepositional **da**-Compounds

The **da**-compounds with an unstressed **da**- appear in the first box of the second
prong. The compounds with a stressed **da**- usually appear in the front field,
with contrast intonation.

> ***Daran* glaube ich nicht.**   **Da*rauf* kann ich nicht *warten.***
> **Ich *glaube* noch nicht daran.**   **Ich hoffe, ich brauche nicht da*rauf* zu *warten.***

Prepositional **wo**-Compounds

Like all questions, questions introduced by a **wo**-compound can be changed into dependent clauses.

> **Auf was wartet er denn?**
> **Worauf wartet er denn?**
>
> **Ich weiß nicht, auf was er wartet.**
> **Ich weiß nicht, worauf er wartet.**

da-Compounds with an Anticipatory Function

The prepositional object may be replaced by a dependent clause or an infinitive phrase. If this is the case, a **da**-compound anticipating or repeating this dependent clause frequently appears in the main clause.

> **Ich habe gar nicht daran gedacht, daß du**   It had slipped my mind that you too live in
> **ja auch in Köln wohnst.**   Cologne.

or

> **Daran, daß du ja auch in Köln wohnst,**
> **habe ich gar nicht gedacht.**

or

> **Daran habe ich gar nicht gedacht, daß du**
> **ja auch in Köln wohnst.**
>
> **Ich möchte Ihnen noch einmal dafür**   I would like to thank you once more (for the
> **danken, daß Sie gekommen sind.**   fact that you came) for coming.
>
> **Ich hoffe immer noch darauf, sie wieder-**   I still hope to see her again.
> **zusehen.**

These anticipatory **da**-compounds are especially frequent if the ideas contained in the dependent clause or in the infinitive phrase have been expressed before in some form and are not news either for the speaker or for the listener.

Conversations

The following is one continuous conversation in typical, everyday German, containing quite a few subjunctive constructions. Read it aloud several times to get a feeling for this kind of spoken German; then follow the instructions under **II** below.

I

TELEFONISTIN: Hotel Bayerischer Hof, guten Morgen.
KLAUS: Guten Morgen. Ich hätte gerne Zimmer 641 (sechseinundvierzig).
TELEFONISTIN: Einen Augenblick, bitte.

ROSEMARIE:	Ja, bitte?
KLAUS:	Rosemarie? Guten Morgen.
ROSEMARIE:	Klaus? Guten Morgen. Du hättest aber wirklich nicht so früh anzurufen brauchen. Ich schlafe ja noch.
KLAUS:	Das höre ich.
ROSEMARIE:	Wieviel Uhr ist es denn? Sieben? Oder ist es schon acht?
KLAUS:	Acht? Es ist zwanzig nach zehn.
ROSEMARIE:	Nein, das ist nicht möglich—zwanzig nach zehn?
KLAUS:	Doch, das *ist* möglich. Wenn es *nicht* schon so spät wäre, hätte ich dich nicht angerufen.
ROSEMARIE:	Ja, und wenn wir gestern abend nicht so lange getanzt hätten, wäre ich auch schon lange auf.
KLAUS:	Aber wer wollte denn gestern so lange tanzen, du oder ich?
ROSEMARIE:	Ich, natürlich. Wenn ich nur zwei Tage in München bin, will ich doch auch etwas erleben.
KLAUS:	Na, *so* interessant ist diese Diskothek ja *auch* nicht!
ROSEMARIE:	Du, Klaus, wo bist du denn eigentlich? Hier im Hotel?
KLAUS:	Nein, ich bin noch zu Hause. Aber wenn du willst, komme ich um elf ins Hotel. Dann können wir zusammen frühstücken. Du könntest natürlich auch auf deinem Zimmer frühstücken, und ich komme erst um zwölf—wie du willst.
ROSEMARIE:	Nein, das möchte ich nicht. Wenn ich nur drei Nächte in München bin, will ich mit *dir* frühstücken.
KLAUS:	Gut, Rosemarie—ich bin um elf in der Hotelhalle—und es wäre schön, wenn du nicht erst um zwölf kämst: ich habe Hunger, ich bin schon seit acht Uhr auf.
ROSEMARIE:	Aber Klaus, du weißt doch, daß du nie auf mich zu warten brauchst. Gestern hast du auch gesagt, daß ich um acht Uhr da sein müßte oder wir kämen nicht mehr in das Restaurant—wie hieß es doch?
KLAUS:	Feldherrnkeller.

ROSEMARIE: Ja richtig—wir kämen nicht mehr in den Feldherrnkeller, weil dort immer so viele Leute seien. Na, und wann war ich da? Um zehn vor acht.—Übrigens, Klaus, wie ist denn das Wetter? Ich habe noch nicht aus dem Fenster gesehen, aber es wäre schön, wenn heute die Sonne schiene.

KLAUS: Das Wetter könnte nicht besser sein. Heute morgen sah es ja aus, als ob es wieder regnen würde—und wenn du nicht hier wärst, hätte es heute bestimmt geregnet.

ROSEMARIE: Vielen Dank für das Kompliment, Klaus. Aber wenn es geregnet hätte, das hätte auch nichts gemacht. Wir hätten ja in ein Museum gehen können. Aber weißt du was? Ich ginge nach dem Frühstück gerne durch die Stadt; ich möchte mir doch einen Mantel kaufen, und es wäre nett, wenn wir das zusammen machen könnten.

KLAUS: Gut—und was machen wir, wenn wir den Mantel gekauft haben?

ROSEMARIE: Dann können wir eine Stunde auf einer Bank in der Sonne sitzen.

KLAUS: Im Hofgarten.* Das wäre prima. Wir gehen eine Stunde in den Hofgarten, und dann gehen wir essen.

ROSEMARIE: Du, aber bitte in ein Restaurant, wo keine Touristen sind, ja, Klaus? Ich wollte, in München wären nicht immer so viele Touristen.

KLAUS: Ja, was wäre München ohne die Touristen! Aber ich kenne ein Restaurant bei der Universität; da ist noch nie ein Tourist gewesen, nur Studenten. Wie wäre das, Rosemarie?

ROSEMARIE: Du, das wäre nett. Übrigens, hast du gestern nicht gesagt, daß es heute abend die *Fledermaus*† gibt?

KLAUS: Ja, im Theater am Gärtnerplatz. Das ist eine Idee. Wie wäre es, wenn wir heute abend ins Theater gingen?

ROSEMARIE: Gerne, ich habe die *Fledermaus* noch nie gesehen. Und dann könnten wir nach Schwabing‡ gehen und tanzen, ja?

KLAUS: Und ein Glas Wein trinken,—und jetzt ist es halb elf, und wenn ich jetzt nicht gehe, bist du um elf Uhr *doch* nicht in der Halle. Oder soll ich doch lieber erst um zwölf kommen?

ROSEMARIE: Nein, nein—ich bin bestimmt da.

II

Now construct some brief exchanges based on the conversation above; for example, arrange with a friend to meet at a certain time and place; discuss a proposed shopping expedition or a visit to a museum or theater; or recall something you did the day before.

III

Using the map and information below, talk about topics such as the following:

1. Why do you want to spend your vacation in Strümpfelbach?
2. Where is Strümpfelbach?
3. How does one get there?

*The Royal Gardens, a public park in the center of Munich.
†Operetta by Strauss—literally, *The Bat*; **es gibt** they are playing.
‡Artists' and students' quarter near the University of Munich.

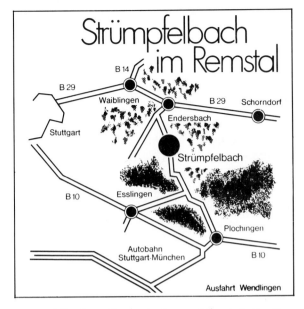

Strümpfelbach im Remstal—Strümpfelbach in the Rems Valley

Well-known excursion and wine place with many historic half-timbered houses (292 meters above sea level, 2000 inhabitants).* Attractive surrounding countryside for relaxing walks.

Open-air pool — indoor pool.

20 km from Stuttgart, 13 km from Esslingen or Waiblingen.

About 20 km to the Autobahn Stuttgart-Munich (exit Wendlingen).

Lodging House Amalie.

Restaurant Lamb.

Owner A. Grötzinger.

IV

1. As you have done before, make a topical list of vocabulary, this time on education; divide into three sections: (1) school, (2) university, (3) general educational terms, such as **lernen** or **die Prüfung.**

2. Once again, ask your teacher to play the role of a "native informant" whom you can question about such topics as (1) his or her own education, (2) the education of his or her children, (3) education reform.

3. Prepare a report, to be given orally before your class, on some aspect of education in Germany. Use the lists you made, as well as the pattern sentences and the reading selections of Unit 12.

Fragen an Sie persönlich

1. Welche Schulen haben Sie bisher besucht°?   attended
2. Was halten Sie vom amerikanischen Schulsystem?
                von der amerikanischen Grade School?
                                High School?
        vom amerikanischen College?
3. Was ist Ihr Hauptfach°?   major
   Warum haben Sie dieses Hauptfach gewählt°?   chosen

*Above sea level: **ü. d. M. = über dem Meeresspiegel;** inhabitants: **Einw. = Einwohner.**

4. Wollen Sie auf die Graduate School?
     Wenn ja, auf welche?
               in welchem Fach?
5. Wollen Sie promovieren°?   get a doctorate (Ph.D.,
6. Was sind Ihre Berufspläne°?   M.D., etc.)
7. Wozu, meinen Sie, soll eine College-Ausbildung dienen, zur All-   career plans
     gemeinbildung° oder zur Vorbereitung° auf einen Beruf?   general education
                                                              preparation

Reading

I

ERICH KÄSTNER

Erich Kästner (1899–1974) is best known in the United States for his children's
story *Emil und die Detektive* (1929). He wrote, especially in the late 1920s and
30s, a large number of humorous and satirical poems, one of which is the following "Sachliche Romanze" (1929). Because of his bitter social criticism,
much of which was directed against German militaristic tendencies, he was
forbidden to write by the Nazis, and his books were burned in 1933. He stayed
in Germany, however, and, after World War II, wrote for the American-
sponsored *Neue Zeitung* in Munich from 1945–48. He refers to his poetry,
most of which is written in the same matter-of-fact style as the "Sachliche
Romanze" as *Gebrauchslyrik* ("utility poetry").

Sachliche Romanze   **sachlich**   matter-of-fact

Als sie einander acht Jahre kannten
(und man darf sagen: sie kannten sich gut),   **abhanden kommen**   to
kam ihre Liebe plötzlich abhanden.   get lost
Wie andern Leuten ein Stock oder Hut.   **der Stock, ̈e**   walking
                                                         stick, cane

Sie waren traurig, betrugen sich heiter,   5   **traurig**   sad
versuchten Küsse, als ob nichts sei,   **betrugen sich heiter**
und sahen sich an und wußten nicht weiter.   acted cheerful
Da weinte sie schließlich. Und er stand dabei.   **der Kuß, Küsse**   kiss
                                                     sich   each other
Vom Fenster aus konnte man Schiffen winken.   **weinen**   to cry
Er sagte, es wäre schon Viertel nach Vier   10   **winken**   to wave at
und Zeit, irgendwo Kaffee zu trinken.
Nebenan übte ein Mensch Klavier.   **nebenan**   next door
                                                     üben   to practice

Sie gingen ins kleinste Café am Ort
und rührten in ihren Tassen.   **rühren**   to stir
Am Abend saßen sie noch immer dort.   15
Sie saßen allein, und sie sprachen kein Wort
und konnten es einfach nicht fassen.   **fassen**   to comprehend

II

Schulen in Deutschland
oder
Wie real ist die Realschule?

Schools in Germany
or
How Real is the *Realschule?*

„Meine Tochter geht seit fünf Jahren aufs Gymnasium", erklärt Herr Hinz dem Besucher aus Amerika. „Oh", sagt der Besucher, „dann ist sie wohl Sportlerin von Beruf." „Nein, sie ist Schülerin, und in Sport 5 hat sie Vier plus." „Vier plus", denkt der Besucher, „das ist doch ein A plus", und er sagt: „Dann ist sie sicher die beste in ihrer Klasse." „Im Gegenteil", sagt Herr Hinz, „sie ist sportlich ganz unbegabt."

"My daughter has been going to the *Gymnasium* for five years," Mr. Hinz explains to the visitor from America. "Oh," says the visitor, "then she must be a professional athlete." "No, she is a (secondary school) student, and in athletics she has a four plus." "Four plus," the visitor thinks, "that's an A plus," and he says: "then she is surely at the top of her class." "On the contrary," says 10 Mr. Hinz, "she is completely untalented athletically."

Als der Besucher mit Frau Kunz über ihre Kinder spricht, erfährt er, daß der Sohn auf der Realschule ist, und er überlegt, ob es in Deutschland wohl auch „unreal schools" 15 gibt. Die Tochter ist 24 Jahre alt und auf der Hochschule für Musik. „So alt", meint der Besucher, „und immer noch auf der High School?" „Nein, nein", sagt Frau Kunz, „ ‚Hochschule' ist das gleiche wie ‚Universi- 20 tät'. Ihre High School in Amerika ist das gleiche wie unsere ‚höhere Schule'." „Aber das ist doch paradox, daß die höhere Schule nicht so hoch ist wie die Hochschule!"

When the visitor talks to Mrs. Kunz about her children, he finds out that the son goes to the *Realschule*, and he wonders if there are "unreal" schools in Germany as well. The daughter is twenty-four years old and goes to the "High School for Music." "So old," says the visitor, "and still in high school?" "No, no," Frau Kunz replies, " 'Hochschule' is the 20 same as 'Universität.' Your high school in America is the same as our 'higher school'." "But how paradoxical that the higher school is not as high as the high school!"

Und als Xaver Schreibmeyer ihm erklärt, in 25 Deutschland gäbe es kein College, aber zehn Minuten später beim Weggehen sagt, er müsse jetzt ins Kolleg, da ist der Besucher aus Amerika ganz verzweifelt.

And when Xaver Schreibmeyer explains to 25 him that there is no (such thing as a) college in Germany, but ten minutes later as he leaves says that he has to go to the *Kolleg*, the visitor from America is in despair.

Unser Besucher aus Amerika ist natürlich 30 eine Fiktion. Aber Amerikaner, die das deutsche Schulsystem kennenlernen wollen, haben am Anfang immer das gleiche° Prob-   same
lem: sie begegnen einem Begriff,° den sie zu   encounter a term
verstehen glauben, aber der Begriff hat im 35
Deutschen eine ganz andere Bedeutung.°   meaning
Das Gymnasium ist nicht *the gymnasium*,
obwohl es das gleiche Wort ist. Griechisch°   Greek
gymnasion, von *gymnos*, *nackt*, war zuerst°   at first
der Ort, wo man Sport trieb, später auch der 40

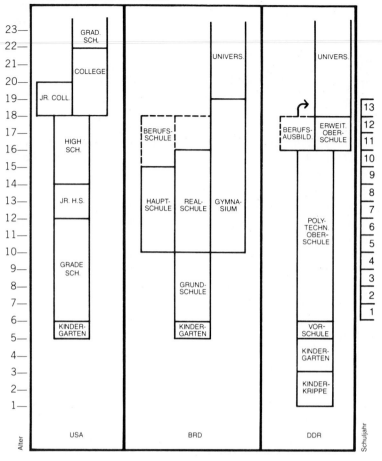

Platz, wo die Philosophen zusammenkamen.
Das Englische hat die erste Bedeutung beibe-
halten,° und im Deutschen benutzt man seit   retained
dem sechzehnten Jahrhundert die zweite
Bedeutung für die höhere Schule, für die 5
Akademie, die·junge Leute auf die Universi-
tät vorbereitet.°   prepares

Statt *höhere Schule* sagt man im Amerika-
nischen *high school*, aber die Übersetzung°   translation
von *high school*, *Hochschule*, entspricht° im 10 corresponds to
Deutschen der *Universität*. Das deutsche
Wort *Kolleg* und das englisch-amerikanische
college gehen beide zurück auf das latein-
ische *collegium*, *Zusammenkunft* oder
Zusammentreffen (aus *con* plus *legere*, 15
zusammenlesen), aber im Deutschen ist ein
Kolleg eine *Vorlesung*, *a lecture*; das
englische *College* ist Teil° einer Universität,   part of
und das amerikanische *College* ist synonym
mit *undergraduate school*.   20

Schließlich° hat *Real*- nichts mit *wirklich* zu   finally
tun, und die *Realschule* ist keine „real
school". Das Wort bedeutet hier eine
Orientierung auf das Praktische und Technische, im Gegensatz° zum Gymnasium, das 5   contrast
mehr auf Theorie und Philosophie hin°   **auf . . . hin** toward
orientiert ist.

An die Bedeutung dieser Begriffe ist man
bald gewöhnt,° aber es ist nicht so leicht,   used to
das System der Schulen in der Bundesrepub- 10
lik zu verstehen, denn es basiert° auf einem   is based
ganz anderen Prinzip als die Schulen in
Amerika.

Die Tradition des Schulsystems in Deutsch-
land ist elitär. Früher gab es° nur die Volks- 15   there used to be
schule, das heißt, die Schule für das „Volk",
für den „gemeinen Mann",° und daneben   common man
das Gymnasium, die Akademie für die
„Gebildeten".° Bis lange nach dem zweiten   educated and cultured
Weltkrieg gingen nur wenige Kinder von 20
Arbeitern aufs Gymnasium, und das, was
man im Englischen „social mobility" nennt,
gab es kaum. Nur wer das Abitur hatte,
„war etwas", und wer die Universität besucht hat, den nennt man auch heute noch 25
einen „Akademiker". Das intellektuelle
Niveau der alten Gymnasien und Universitäten war sehr hoch, und die Zahl der Abi-
turienten° war sehr klein, die Zahl der Dok-   *Gymnasium* graduates
toranden° noch viel kleiner. Aber das System 30   doctoral candidates
war auch sehr ungerecht,° denn die Ent-   unjust
scheidung,° ob Gymnasium oder nicht,   decision
mußten Eltern schon treffen,° wenn ihre   make
Kinder erst zehn Jahre alt waren, das heißt,
nach vier Jahren Volksschule.   35

In der Bundesrepublik, in der Schweiz und
in Österreich stehen die Schulen auch heute
noch vertikal nebeneinander. Neben dem
Gymnasium gibt es die Realschule (oder
Mittelschule) und die Volksschule, die in der 40
Bundesrepublik jetzt Hauptschule heißt.
Von der ersten bis zur vierten Klasse gehen
alle Kinder in die gleiche Schule, die Grundschule.

Im Gegensatz° dazu ist das amerikanische   contrast
Schulsystem horizontal gegliedert° und des-   structured
halb° im Prinzip egalitär und nicht elitär.   therefore
Nach der *grade school* gehen alle Kinder in
die *junior high school* und dann, bis zum 5
Ende der Schulpflicht,° in die *high school*.   compulsory schooling
Jeder, der will, kann auf ein College gehen,
und braucht dazu keine Prüfung wie das
Abitur abzulegen.°   take, pass

Interessanterweise ist das Schulsystem in der 10
DDR dem amerikanischen viel ähnlicher°   more similar
als dem westdeutschen. Alle Kinder be-
suchen von sechs bis sechzehn Jahren eine
,,allgemeinbildende, polytechnische Ober-
schule'',° die Basis des sozialistischen Schul- 15 general-education, polytechnic high school
systems.

III

Schul- und Universitätsreform, Ost und West

In der DDR, damals noch ,,Sowjetische
Besatzungszone'',° sprach man schon 1945   Soviet Zone of Occupation
von einer ,,demokratischen Schulreform'',
gegen die bürgerliche° Tradition, und im   bourgeois
Sinne° des Marxismus-Leninismus. Man 5   spirit

UNIVERSITÄTEN
UND HOCHSCHULEN
IN DER BRD
UND DDR

schuf° eine neue Grundschule, eine Einheits- — created
schule° mit acht Klassen, und darüber die — comprehensive school
Mittel- und Oberschule. Bei der Reform von
1955 erhielt° die zehnklassige Mittelschule — received
eine neue Rolle; sie wurde zur Grundlage° 5 — became the basis
für die Polytechnische Einheitsschule, die
seit 1965, mit dem „Gesetz über das einheit-
liche sozialistische Bildungssystem",° der — "Law for the Unified Socialist Education System"
Mittelpunkt° des Schulsystems der DDR ist. — center, core
„Alle Schüler, Lehrlinge und Studenten", 10 — "All pupils, apprentices, and university students are to
heißt es in diesem Gesetz, „sind zur Liebe — be educated to love the GDR and to be proud of the
zur DDR und zum Stolz auf die Errungen- — achievements of socialism, in order to be ready to place
schaften des Sozialismus zu erziehen, um — all their strength at the disposal of society, to strengthen
bereit zu sein, alle Kräfte der Gesellschaft — and to defend the socialist state."
zur Verfügung zu stellen, den sozialistischen 15
Staat zu stärken und zu verteidigen."

Der polytechnische Unterricht° in der DDR — instruction
verbindet° Schule und praktische Arbeit, er — joins
verbindet Allgemeinbildung° und Berufs- — general education
bildung° und schafft° die wissenschaftliche 20 — vocational education   creates
Grundlage° für die Produktion. Daher be- — scientific basis
tont° die polytechnische Schule besonders — emphasizes
intensiv die gesellschaftswissenschaftlichen
Fächer,° Mathematik und die Naturwissen- — social science disciplines
schaften.° Erste Fremdsprache ist Russisch. 25 — natural sciences
Von der siebten Klasse an findet ein Teil des
polytechnischen Unterrichts in Betrieben der
Industrie° und in Landwirtschaftlichen Pro- — industrial plants
duktionsgenossenschaften° (LPG's) statt.° — agricultural production cooperatives   **findet . . . statt**
Eine erweiterte° Oberschule mit Abitur oder 30 — takes place   expanded, extended
eine dreijährige Berufsausbildung° mit A- — vocational training
bitur führen zur Universität.

Es gibt heute in der DDR 54 Universitäten*
und andere Hochschulen. Die Mehrzahl° — majority
der Studenten sind Kinder von Arbeitern 35
und Bauern, aber die Zahl der Abiturienten,
die studieren dürfen, ist begrenzt.° Das — limited
heißt, es gibt einen „Numerus clausus",° der — limited admission
zwar nicht offiziell ist, den aber der Staat
plant, um die Berufsausbildung zu lenken.° 40 — to guide, control

Das Studium an den Universitäten der DDR
beginnt mit einem Grundstudium° von zwei — basic curriculum
Jahren, in dem wissenschaftliche Forschungs-

---

*But of these, only six are full-fledged universities in the traditional sense: Berlin, Greifswald, Halle, Jena, Leipzig, and Rostock.

methoden° und marxistisch-leninistische | research methods
Weltanschauung° gelehrt werden° und in | world view, philosophy, ideology   are taught
dem alle Studenten weiter Russisch lernen.
Danach folgen zwei Jahre Fachstudium° | specialized study, major
und, für zukünftige° Wissenschaftler, noch 5 | future
ein Jahr Forschungsstudium.° | research studies

Die Reformen in der DDR führten radikale
Veränderungen° und einen totalen Bruch° | changes   break
mit der Vergangenheit° herbei.° Die Schul- | past   **führten . . . herbei**   lead to
und Universitätsreform in der Bundesrepub- 10
lik, die bis heute noch nicht abgeschlossen° | completed
ist, ist dagegen° das Resultat der Spannun- | on the other hand
gen° zwischen der traditionsgebundenen | tensions
alten Ordnung° und den Bedürfnissen° einer | order   needs
modernen Wohlstandsgesellschaft.° Weder 15 | affluent society
das elitäre Gymnasium noch° die elitäre | **weder . . . noch**   neither . . . nor
Universität, die in ihrer modernen Form von
Wilhelm von Humboldt am Anfang des
neunzehnten Jahrhunderts gegründet wurde,*
waren adäquat für die Industriegesellschaft 20
des zwanzigsten Jahrhunderts.

Die alte Universität war insular; sie diente° | served
der „reinen" Wissenschaft° und hatte wenig | "pure" knowledge
Interesse an der Berufsausbildung der Stu-
denten. Es gab nur wenige Ordinarien,† die 25
ihre Institute und Seminare, —und ihre
Assistenten—, autokratisch regierten.° Nach | governed
dem Ende des nationalsozialistischen Re-
gimes sah es jahrelang so aus, als ob die Universität und auch das Gymnasium in der 30
alten Form weiterleben sollten.

Aber dann kam der Baby-Boom der fünfziger
Jahre,° kam das westdeutsche „Wirtschafts- | fifties
wunder",° kam die zunehmende° Techno- | "economic miracle"   increasing
logisierung der Bundesrepublik, und mit 35
wachsendem Wohlstand° schickten immer | growing affluence
mehr Eltern ihre Kinder aufs Gymnasium.
Das Prestige des Akademikers lockte° immer | lured
mehr Abiturienten in die Universität, und
bald waren Klassenzimmer und Hörsäle° 40 | auditoriums
überfüllt. Während 1950 nur 100.000 junge

---

*gegründet wurde *was founded* is a passive form. The German passive will not be introduced until Unit 18, but we will use occasional passive forms in the reading.

†der **Ordinarius**, plural die **Ordinarien** does not quite correspond to the American full professor; an **Ordinarius** of the old type was also director of his institute, and his authority was virtually untouchable.

Leute studierten, waren es 1975 etwa
800.000, und die Zahl wird wohl 1.000.000
erreichen,° bevor sie wieder abnimmt.°   reach   declines

Zunächst° jedoch geschah nur wenig, und   at first
als Georg Picht 1964 von der ,,deutschen 5
Bildungskatastrophe" schrieb, sprach man
zwar viel über sein Buch, aber von der Re-
form war das System noch weit entfernt.°   far removed
Die Gründung° von über 20 neuen Universi-   founding
täten und Fachhochschulen in den sechziger 10
Jahren konnte die Situation zwar verbessern,°   improve
aber im Grunde° nicht verändern.°   basically   change

Dann kam die weltweite Studentenbewe-
gung.° 1966 fand der erste Studentenstreik   student movement
in Deutschland statt,° an der Freien Univer- 15   **fand . . . statt** took place
sität in Berlin, und mit der Studentenbewe-
gung kam auch die Universitätsreform in
Bewegung. Mit der Krise des Vietnam-
Krieges erreichten° die Studentenrevolten in   reached
Europa ihren Höhepunkt.° Trotz der radi- 20   high point, climax
kalen Exzesse hatte die Studentenbewegung
positive Aspekte. Der Slogan
    Unter den Talaren   Beneath the academic gowns
    Muff von tausend Jahren°   the musty odor of a thousand years
enthielt° mehr als einen Kern° von Wahr- 25 contained   kernel
heit;° das überalterte Erziehungssystem   truth
konnte in der traditionellen Form einfach
nicht mehr weiterexistieren, besonders weil
die Zahl der Schüler und Studenten immer
weiter anstieg.°   30 increased

Seit Anfang der siebziger Jahre sind nun
Reformen im Gange,° die aber erst zum Teil   **im Gange . . . sein** to be under way
durchgeführt° sind und über die man über-   carried through
all heftig° debattiert. Reorganisation der   vigorously
Schulformen, Experimente mit Gesamt- 35
schulen und Gesamthochschulen,° Curricu-   comprehensive schools and comprehensive universities
lum-Reform und Reform der Lehrerausbil-
dung,° Einführung° der neuen Gymnasial-   teacher training   introduction
oberstufe° (Sekundarstufe II), die mit ihrem   upper division, upper school
Kurssystem an das amerikanische College 40
erinnert,° Neuordnung° der Fachbereiche   reminds   reorientation
an den Universitäten, Abbau° der alten   dismantling
Ordinarienhierarchie und Mitbestimmungs-
recht° für Assistenten und Studenten, —das   right to codetermination
sind einige der Resultate und Ziele° der Bil- 45   aims
dungsreform.

Das komplizierteste Problem, sowohl mora-
lisch als auch legal, ist wohl der „Numerus
Clausus", das heißt, die Zulassungsbe-
schränkung° in vielen Disziplinen, zum Bei-   limited admission
spiel in der Medizin, wo nur ein Bewerber° 5 applicant
von sechs einen Studienplatz bekommen
kann, oder in Psychologie, Biologie und
Rechtswissenschaft.° Die Zahlen werden erst   jurisprudence, law
wieder kleiner werden, wenn die Ein-
führung° der Anti-Baby-Pille, die den Baby- 10 introduction
Boom abstoppte, eine Wirkung° hat. Aber   effect
das wird erst um 1985 der Fall° sein.   case

Exercises

A. Each of the following incomplete sentences contains a blank for a relative pronoun. Fill in the correct forms.

SEE
ANALYSIS
133
(p. 345)

1. das Haus, aus _____ er kam
2. die Betten, zwischen _____ der Tisch stand
3. der Blick, mit _____ er mich ansah
4. die vielen Aufnahmen, _____ ich von ihm gemacht habe
5. die Leute, _____ zu uns kamen
6. der Herr, nach _____ Sie fragen
7. der Materialismus, gegen _____ wir kämpfen
8. das Haus, in _____ wir wohnen
9. das Theater, vor _____ ich sie treffen wollte
10. die Familie, bei _____ du wohnst
11. das Haus, vor _____ wir unseren Wagen stellten
12. seine Frau, _____ Vater in Berlin Architekt war
13. meine Bücher, ohne _____ ich nicht leben kann
14. der Zug, mit _____ du fahren willst
15. die Blicke, _____ sie mir zuwarf
16. die Ecke, an _____ er stand
17. die Stadt, von _____ wir sprachen
18. ihr Mann, _____ Vater in Berlin Architekt war

B. Determine the case, the antecedent, and the function of each relative pronoun; then insert the correct relative pronoun.

SEE
ANALYSIS
133
(p. 345)

1. Sein Vater, _____ Frau aus Moskau kam, sprach gut Russisch.
2. Seine Frau, _____ Vater aus Leningrad kam, sprach gut Russisch.
3. Kennen Sie meinen Freund Rombach?—Meinen Sie den Rombach, _____ das Corona-Hotel gehört?
4. Ist das der Hut, _____ dir dein Mann aus Paris mitgebracht hat?

5. Habe ich dir schon die Omega gezeigt, _____ ich in Zürich gekauft habe?

6. Das Essen, _____ wir hier bekommen, ist so gut, daß wir noch eine Woche bleiben wollen.

7. Ich wollte Gerd und Liselotte wiedersehen, _____ Gast ich damals in Frankfurt gewesen war.

8. Ist das der Wagen, mit _____ du nach Sylt gefahren bist?

9. Hermann, durch _____ ich meine Frau kennengelernt habe, ist jetzt Bankdirektor in Hamburg.

10. Wer waren denn die drei Herren, Marie-Louise, mit _____ ich Sie gestern abend gesehen habe?

11. Wer sind eigentlich diese Schäufeles, von _____ du immer redest?

12. Ihre Kinder, für _____ sie so schwer gearbeitet hat, wollen heute nichts mehr von ihr wissen.

13. Der Mann, ohne _____ Hilfe ich heute nicht Arzt wäre, ist Professor Bornemann.

14. Studenten, _____ Eltern nicht genug Geld verdienen, bekommen ein Stipendium (*scholarship*) vom Staat.

C. Join the following pairs of sentences by changing one of them into a relative clause.

SEE ANALYSIS 133 (p. 345)

1. Werners Vater sprach gut Englisch. Er hatte lange in Amerika gelebt.
2. Werners Vater sprach gut Englisch. Seine Frau kam aus London.
3. Ich habe dich gestern abend im Theater mit einem jungen Mann gesehen. Wer war denn der junge Mann?
4. In Mainz besuchte ich meinen Freund Emil. Ich bin mit ihm in die Schule gegangen.
5. Ich fuhr nach Hamburg, um Hermann wiederzusehen. Während des Krieges war ich mit ihm in Afrika.
6. Wer ist denn eigentlich dieser Schmidt? Du redest schon seit Tagen von ihm.
7. Der Brief lag vor ihr auf dem Tisch. Ihr Mann hatte ihn aus Rom geschickt.
8. Ich kann diese Vase doch nicht wegwerfen. Tante Amalie hat sie mir geschenkt.

D. Fill in each blank by using a form of the demonstrative **der, die, das.**

1. Sollen Inge und Gerda auch kommen?—Nein, _____ brauchst du nicht einzuladen; _____ können zu Hause bleiben; mit _____ will ich nichts mehr zu tun haben.

2. Kennen Sie _____ Friedrich Bertram?—Aber natürlich; mit _____ war ich doch in Mainz auf der Schule.

3. Diese Schuhe hier möchten Sie also doch nicht, gnädige Frau?—Nein, ich nehme lieber _____ da.

4. Nein, Maria; mit _____ Hut kannst du nicht nach Paris fahren. _____ läßt du besser zu Hause.—Aber Paul, _____ kommt doch aus Paris. _____ hast du mir doch letztes Jahr aus Paris mitgebracht.

5. Dieser Kaffee ist aber gut. Wo hast du _____ denn gekauft?— _____ hat mein Mann gekauft.—Dein Mann? Versteht _____ was von Kaffee?

E. In the following sentences, substitute a **da**-compound for the italicized prepositional phrases.

SEE ANALYSIS 134-135 (pp. 347-349)

1. Der Garten *hinter dem Haus* braucht viel Wasser.
2. *Mit dem Hut* kannst du nicht in die Stadt gehen.
3. Und *vor dem Wohnzimmer* ist eine große Terrasse.
4. Er hat viel Geld *für das Haus* bezahlt.
5. Aber den Namen *unter dem Bild* kann ich nicht lesen.

F. In the following sentences, substitute for the prepositional phrase in the front field (a) a stressed **da**-compound and (b) the preposition plus demonstrative article.

> **Für *den* Wein hast du zuviel bezahlt.**
> (a) *Dafür* hast du zuviel bezahlt.
> (b) **Für *den* hast du zuviel bezahlt.**

SEE
ANALYSIS
135
(p. 349)

1. Mit *dem* Wagen fahre ich nicht.
2. Mit *diese*m Hut kann ich nichts anfangen.
3. In *diese*m Bett kann ich nicht schlafen.
4. Für *den* Wagen bezahle ich keine zehntausend Mark.
5. Mit *meine*r Leica kann ich auch bei Nacht Aufnahmen machen.

G. Write down the questions to which the following sentences would be the answers. Start each question with (a) a **wo**-compound and (b) the preposition plus **was**.

> **Meine Tochter hat Angst vor der Schule.**
> (a) **Wovor hat sie denn Angst?**
> (b) **Vor was hat sie denn Angst?**

SEE
ANALYSIS
136
(p. 350)

1. Wir warten auf schönes Wetter.
2. Ich brauche das Geld für einen neuen Wagen.
3. Wir haben gerade von dem neuen Film gesprochen.
4. Ich denke gerade daran, daß Vater morgen Geburtstag hat.
5. Ich habe ihn an seiner Stimme erkannt.

H. Read the following sentences aloud and supply the missing prepositions.

SEE
ANALYSIS
137
(p. 351)

1. Ich glaube _____ Gott.
2. Wir haben _____ unserer Reise gesprochen.
3. Denkst du auch noch _____ mich?
4. Hast du schon _____ den Brief geantwortet?
5. Hast du auch nicht vergessen, ihn _____ seiner Frau zu fragen?
6. Ich danke Ihnen _____ Ihre Hilfe.
7. Meyer hat mich _____ einem Glas Wein eingeladen.
8. Dürfte ich Sie _____ eine Zigarette bitten?
9. Er spricht nie _____ seiner Frau.
10. _____ wen warten Sie denn?

I. Read the following sentences aloud and supply the missing articles or possessives.

SEE
ANALYSIS
137
(p. 351)

1. Wir warten auf _____ Zug aus Hannover.
2. Wir warten auf _____ Bahnhof.
3. Fritzchen hat Angst vor _____ Abitur.
4. Ingelheim hat viel über _____ Krieg geschrieben.
5. Kurt stand an _____ Ecke und wartete auf _____ Freundin.
6. Ich muß in _____ Universität über _____ Krieg zwischen Rom und Karthago sprechen.
7. Ich halte nicht viel von _____ Film.
8. Wir hoffen sehr auf _____ Mitarbeit Ihres Mannes, Frau Becker.
9. Frau Doktor, als Sie an die Tür kamen, habe ich Sie für _____ Tochter gehalten.
10. Sie hat den ganzen Abend nicht von _____ Mann gesprochen.

J. Using the verbs in parentheses, form main clauses containing a **da**-compound anticipating the dependent clause.

> (schon lange nachdenken), wo ich dieses Jahr hinfahren soll.
> Ich denke schon lange darüber nach, wo ich dieses Jahr hinfahren soll.

1. (sehr hoffen), daß er morgen kommen kann.
2. (gerade sprechen), daß er im Sommer nach Italien fahren will.
3. (warten), daß mein Mann endlich nach Hause kommt.
4. (nicht viel halten), daß meine Tochter Psychologie studieren will.
5. (wohl bitten dürfen), daß Sie um acht Uhr im Büro sind.

SEE
ANALYSIS
137–138
(pp. 351–353)

K. Expand the prepositional objects in the following sentences into dependent clauses.

> Ich warte auf einen Brief von ihr.
> Ich warte darauf, daß sie mir schreibt.

1. Ich möchte Ihnen noch einmal für Ihre Hilfe danken.
2. An seinen Geburtstag gestern habe ich gar nicht gedacht.
3. Er war sehr glücklich über den Erfolg seines Buches.
4. Lacht sie immer noch über seinen Akzent?

SEE
ANALYSIS
138
(p. 353)

L. Expand the prepositional objects in the following sentences into infinitive phrases.

> Erika denkt gar nicht an eine Italienreise.
> Erika denkt gar nicht daran, nach Italien zu fahren.

1. Darf ich Sie zu einem Glas Wein einladen, Herr Rohrmoser?
2. Ich habe meinen Freund um Ingelheims Romane gebeten.
3. Hoffst du immer noch auf ein Wiedersehen mit ihr?
4. Ich hoffe auf ein Wiedersehen mit Ihnen.
5. Ich habe wochenlang auf einen Brief von ihr gewartet.

SEE
ANALYSIS
138
(p. 353)

M. Supply the missing words.

1. Es wäre nett, _____ du mit mir in das Restaurant gehen _____, von _____ du gestern abend gesprochen hast.
2. Ist das der Mantel, _____ du dir in München gekauft hast?
3. Hast du auch _____ gedacht, daß ich morgen Geburtstag _____?
4. Frau Meyer war sehr stolz _____ Fritz, _____ er hatte endlich das Abitur gemacht.
5. Wie lange wartest du schon auf _____ Bus, Karl?
6. _____ Inge kam, _____ wir sofort in die Stadt gefahren, _____ ins Kino zu gehen.
7. Wenn wir nicht ins Kino gegangen _____, _____ wir zu Hause ferngesehen.
8. Er fragte mich, _____ ich der Sohn von Direktor Helbig _____.
9. Das Buch kostet bestimmt nicht mehr _____ öS 200.
10. Möchtest du nicht mitfahren?—_____, aber nur _____ zum Bahnhof.

N. Construct sentences as indicated.

1. The man I saw yesterday is a teacher at the Wöhler-Gymnasium.
   (a) The man is a teacher. (professional status!)
   (b) add: *at the Wöhler-Gymnasium* (Use **am.**)
   (c) I saw him yesterday.
   (d) gender, case of *him*?
   (e) change *him* to *whom* (You *must* use relative pronoun.)
   (f) whom I saw yesterday (Don't forget commas.)
   (g) insert relative clause after *The man*

2. The trip I took was very interesting.
   (a) The trip was interesting.
   (b) I took a trip. (Use **machen.**)
   (c) case, gender, of *trip*?
   (d) which I took (commas!)
   (e) insert relative clause after *The trip*

3. This is Mr. Meyer whose son you met last night.
   (a) This is Mr. Meyer.
   (b) You met his son last night.
   (c) change *his son* to *whose son*
   (d) start (b) with *whose son* (verb-last position!)
   (e) add relative clause to (a)

4. Dr. Scholte is the man I have to fly to Berlin with tomorrow.
   (a) I have to fly to Berlin.
   (b) add: *with him*
   (c) add: *tomorrow*
   (d) change *with him* to *with whom*
   (e) with whom I have to fly to Berlin tomorrow
   (f) Dr. Scholte is the man
   (g) add relative clause

O. Express in German.

1. The man with whom Mrs. Ingelheim is talking is called Behrens.
2. Hans wanted to know whether I could pick him up at the station.
3. When did you pick him up?
4. Can you tell me when you picked him up? (indicative)
5. When I arrived, she was not there yet.
6. He acted as if the house belonged to him.
7. He looked as if he hadn't slept well.
8. You know him better than her, don't you?
9. That was more than I had expected.
10. That was a moment I shall not forget.
11. The man I saw in front of the house was Erich.
12. He said that he had seen nothing at all.
13. If I'm not there at three o'clock, you'll simply have to wait for me.
14. And this is a picture of our house. —And where is your swimming pool? —That's behind it.
15. In front of the house stood a Mercedes; next to it stood a Volkswagen.

P. Using the map above, write a letter to a friend or relative:

> Herrn/Frau/Fräulein
> X.Y.
> Bahnhofstr. 27
> D-000 A-Stadt

You have just arrived for a two weeks' winter vacation at the Hirzingerhof, a resort hotel in Kitzbühel in the Austrian Tyrol. Describe how you got there, how you like the place, and what your plans are for the next two weeks.

Start your letter as follows:
> Lieber Fritz, (Liebe Tante Amalie; Liebe Frau Enderle)

and sign off with
> Mit herzlichen Grüßen
> Dein (Deine, Ihr, Ihre)

Additional Reading

Johannes Schmidt-Ingelheim

Eine unmögliche Geschichte

Dieses Wochenende werde ich nicht vergessen, auch wenn ich noch hundert Jahre leben sollte. Natürlich wird mir kein Mensch glauben, was ich erlebt habe. Aber wahr ist es doch.

Die Geschichte fing Freitag morgen in Tripolis an, das heißt, eigentlich hat sie schon angefangen, als wir noch mit Rommel in Afrika 5 gegen die Amerikaner kämpften.

Mein Schulfreund Hermann Schneider, Erich Karsten und ich wohnten damals in Tripolis bei dem Ägypter Ali und seiner Frau Busuq. Ali war ungefähr sechzig; Busuq war mindestens achtzig. Vor Busuq hatten wir alle Angst. Wenn wir mit ihr sprachen, hatten wir das 10

Wochenende weekend

kämpfen to fight

Gefühl: sie sieht dich nicht nur an, sie sieht durch dich durch. Nur Erich hatte keine Angst vor ihr. Für ihn war diese Frau eine Königin. Er brachte ihr immer etwas mit, wenn er ins Haus kam, und man sah, es machte ihn glücklich, wenn sie seine Geschenke annahm.

ansehen   to look at

Einmal, als wir nicht weit von der Stadt an unserem Wagen arbeiteten, 5 erschienen plötzlich ein paar englische Tiefflieger. Wir warfen uns zu Boden, aber nicht schnell genug. Als wir wieder aufstanden, blieb Erich mit einer Kopfwunde wie tot liegen.

Tiefflieger   strafing plane
Kopfwunde   head injury

Wir fuhren mit ihm nach Tripolis zurück. Als Busuq Erichs Wunde sah, befahl sie uns, ihn ins Haus zu bringen. Wir hatten, wie immer, 10 Angst vor ihr. Darum gehorchten wir und brachten ihn ins Haus. Wir konnten aber nicht bei ihm bleiben und kamen erst nach vierzehn Tagen wieder zurück. Erich war noch schwach, aber die Wunde war gottseidank geheilt.

gehorchen   obey

schwach   weak
heilen   to heal

Doch Erich war nicht mehr unser Erich. Er redete nicht mehr so viel 15 wie früher, und seine Augen schienen sagen zu wollen: Ich weiß etwas, was ihr nicht wißt. Außerdem sah er oft stundenlang irgendwohin in die Ferne und war sozusagen einfach nicht da.

Ferne   distance

Nun, Hermann und ich hatten keine Zeit, Erich zu analysieren. Die Situation in Afrika war damals schon gefährlich, und wir fragten uns 20 oft: Wie kommt ihr nur zurück nach Deutschland?

Zwei oder drei Wochen später saßen Hermann und ich in Alis Haus und schrieben Briefe. Erich saß bei uns und war wieder einmal sozusagen nicht da. Aber plötzlich sah er mich mit seinem Ich-weiß-etwas-was-du-nicht-weißt Blick an und sagte: ,,Weißt du, daß deine Frau 25 dir gerade einen Brief schreibt, um dir zu erzählen, daß deine Tochter schon bis fünf zählen kann?" Niemand lachte. Ich wußte nicht, was ich denken sollte.

zählen   to count

Ungefähr zehn Tage später flog man Hermann und mich nach Deutschland. Erich blieb in Afrika zurück. Wie lange er noch bei der 30 Ägypterin gewesen ist, weiß ich nicht. Ich habe ihn erst dieses Wochenende wiedergesehen.

Kurz vor dem Abflug nach Deutschland aber bekam ich damals noch einen Brief von meiner Frau. Was sie schrieb, machte mich unruhig. ,,Es wäre wirklich nett", schrieb sie, ,,wenn Du* hier wärst. Du 35 hättest sehen sollen, wie Dein Töchterchen heute morgen an den Fingern bis fünf gezählt hat . . . Du, Hans, was ich gerade erlebt habe, ist wirklich unglaublich, und ich muß mich zwingen, ruhig zu bleiben. Ich hatte beim Schreiben plötzlich das Gefühl, daß jemand hinter mir stand. Ich fühlte es. Ich wußte einfach, daß jemand hinter mir stand. 40 Ich saß eine Zeitlang still, dann sprang ich auf. Niemand war im Zimmer. Aber Hans, auf dem Boden waren Fußabdrücke, wie Du sie

Abflug   departure
unruhig machen   to disturb

fühlen   to feel
Zeitlang   short time
Fußabdrücke   footprints

*In letters, all pronouns of direct address must be capitalized (**Du, Dich, Dein, Ihr,** etc.).

machst, wenn Du mit Deinen Militärschuhen nach Hause kommst. Du darfst nicht lachen. Ich weiß, was ich Dir schreibe, kann einfach nicht passieren. Aber es *ist* passiert!—Oder ist es doch nicht passiert? Hans, ich bin einfach zu viel allein."

Militärschuhe army boots

Ich wußte sofort, daß meine Frau diesen Brief an dem Tag ge- 5 schrieben hatte, als ich mit Erich und Hermann bei Ali gesessen hatte und Erich plötzlich sagte: „Du Hans, deine Frau schreibt dir gerade einen Brief." Aber wie gesagt, ich wußte damals nicht, wo Erich war, und habe ihn erst letzten Freitag in Tripolis wiedergesehen.

Ich arbeite gerade an meinem Roman *Ende bei Karthago* und war 10 nach Afrika geflogen, um noch einmal die Gegend zu besuchen, wo wir damals gegen die Amerikaner gekämpft haben. Es war darum ganz natürlich, daß ich, sofort nachdem ich in Tripolis angekommen war, zu Busuqs Haus gehen wollte. Es steht tatsächlich noch. Ich wollte gerade mit meiner Leica eine Aufnahme machen (hätte ich 15 diese Aufnahme doch nur gemacht!), als jemand aus dem Haus kam. Es war Erich.

Erich, der mich jahrelang immer nur in Uniform gesehen hatte, er- kannte mich nicht. Er sah nur einen Mann mit einer Kamera—und war auf einmal verschwunden. Verschwunden, sage ich: er ging nicht 20 um die Ecke, er ging nicht ins Haus zurück, er war plötzlich einfach nicht mehr da. „Diese Sonne", dachte ich, „die macht einen noch ganz verrückt." Dann ging ich ins Haus. Ali saß im Garten. Er war jetzt über achtzig. Er erzählte mir, daß seine Frau kurz nach dem Ende des Krieges gestorben sei und daß mein Freund Erich ihn jedes 25 Jahr einmal besucht habe. Ja, Erich wäre gerade vor ein paar Minuten im Haus gewesen und habe ihm, wie jedes Jahr um diese Zeit, fünf Goldstücke dagelassen. Tatsächlich stand Ali auf, nahm einen Stein aus der Wand des Hauses, griff in ein Loch hinter dem Stein und zeigte mir fünf Goldstücke, fünf Zwanzigmarkstücke. „Also war es 30 wirklich Erich, den du gesehen hast und der dann einfach nicht mehr da war", sagte ich mir; und plötzlich wußte ich: hier ist etwas nicht in Ordnung.

verrückt crazy

Goldstück gold coin
Loch hole

Ich ging ins Hotel zurück, um nachzudenken. Im Hotel wartete ein Brief von Hermann Schneider aus Hamburg auf mich. „Lieber Hans", 35 schrieb Hermann, „ich habe Dich zwar seit Ende des Krieges nicht mehr gesehen, aber ich habe alle Deine Bücher gelesen. Ich gratuliere Dir zu Deinen Detektivromanen, die ich viel besser finde als Deine Kriegsromane. Dein Verleger ist ein Freund von mir und hat mir ver- sprochen, Dir diesen Brief nachzuschicken. Aber da er mir nicht sagen 40 wollte, wo Du bist, weiß ich nicht, wo und wann Dich mein Brief er- reichen wird. Ich habe eine Bitte an den Detektiv in Dir.

Verleger publisher

Bitte request

„Wie Du vielleicht weißt, bin ich in Hamburg Direktor der Hansa- Bank. In unserer Bank verschwinden seit zehn Jahren jedes Jahr um diese Zeit fünf Zwanzigmarkstücke. Natürlich sind hundert Mark in 45

Gold nicht viel Geld. Aber es ist doch seltsam, daß jemand in unserer Bank jedes Jahr fünf Goldstücke stiehlt. Ich will noch nicht die Polizei anrufen, denn ich habe das Gefühl, ich stehe hier vor irgendeinem Geheimnis. Ich bitte Dich daher, die Sache zu untersuchen. Du könntest ein paar Wochen lang in der Bank ‚arbeiten‘ und versuchen, den 5 Dieb zu finden. Mein Privatsekretär ist übrigens unser Freund Erich Karsten.‘‘

seltsam strange

Geheimnis secret
Sache matter
Dieb thief

Erich Karsten!

Erich Karsten! Gerade vor einer Stunde war er bei Ali gewesen und hatte ihm, ,,wie jedes Jahr um diese Zeit‘‘, fünf Goldstücke gegeben. 10 Und damals hatte er mit seinen Militärschuhen hinter meiner Frau gestanden und den Brief gelesen.

Es wäre nicht gerade intelligent gewesen, Hermann Schneider von Tripolis aus anzurufen. Wenn Erich der Dieb war—und er mußte es sein—durfte er auf keinen Fall wissen, daß ich gerade heute in 15 Tripolis war, als er Ali fünf Goldstücke ins Haus getragen hatte.

nicht gerade not exactly

Ich nahm daher ein Taxi zum Flughafen, bekam auf der Maschine nach Paris noch einen Platz und rief Hermann Schneider von Paris aus an. Da ich nicht wußte, ob Erich bei Hermann war oder nicht, erzählte ich Hermann, ich sei ein paar Tage in der Normandie ge- 20 wesen, hätte gerade seinen Brief bekommen und würde gegen sechs in Hamburg ankommen. Ich gab meinem Freund die Flugnummer und bat ihn, mich abzuholen. ,,Natürlich hole ich dich ab‘‘, sagte Hermann. ,,Ich wohne nicht weit vom Hamburger Flughafen. Es ist zwar sehr heiß hier in Hamburg, aber gottseidank habe ich hinter dem 25 Haus ein Schwimmbecken.‘‘

Schwimmbecken swimming pool

Es war ungefähr sieben Uhr, als wir vor Hermanns Haus hielten. Vor dem Haus stand ein Volkswagen. ,,Das ist Gerdas Wagen‘‘, sagte Hermann. ,,Sie hat deine Romane gelesen und wollte dich gerne kennenlernen; übrigens werden wir nächste Woche heiraten. Ich—‘‘   30

Hinter dem Haus schrie eine Frau. Sie schrie, daß mir fast das Herz stillstand. Bevor ich wußte, was geschah, hatte Hermann einen Revolver aus dem Wagen geholt und lief hinter das Haus. Ich folgte ihm. Am Schwimmbecken stand ein Mädchen, blond, schön und mit einer Figur, wie man sie sonst nur im Film sieht. Auf dem Wasser 35 schwamm ein Hut. Sie zitterte, zeigte auf den Hut und sagte: ,,Er ist weg—oh, ich hasse diesen Menschen.‘‘

schreien (schrie, geschrien) to scream
holen to get, fetch

zittern to tremble

,,Wer ist weg?‘‘ fragte Hermann. ,,Herr Karsten‘‘, antwortete das Mädchen. Hermann führte sie zu einem der Gartenstühle, versuchte, ganz ruhig zu sein, und sagte: ,,Gerda, dies ist mein Freund Schmidt- 40 Ingelheim. Ich habe ihn gerade am Flugplatz abgeholt‘‘, und als sie nicht auf seine Worte reagierte, sagte er: ,,Gerda, könntest du dich zwingen, mir und Hans jetzt zu erzählen, was hier geschehen ist?‘‘

führen to lead, take
Stuhl chair

Wort word

Es dauerte doch noch ein paar Minuten, bis Gerda ruhig sprechen konnte. Dann erzählte sie: ,,Ich bin kurz nach fünf mit meiner Mutter hier angekommen. Wir sahen, daß du noch nicht zurück warst. Mutter ist spazierengegangen, und ich wollte schwimmen, bis du kamst. Als ich ins Wasser sprang, war niemand hier, das weiß ich 5 bestimmt. Aber als ich aus dem Wasser wollte, stand Herr Karsten oben und hielt mir die Hand hin, um mir zu helfen. Ich erschrak, schrie laut und sprang zurück. Herr Karsten fiel ins Wasser. Als ich auf dieser Seite aus dem Wasser kam, war Herr Karsten weg. Aber da schwimmt sein Hut." 10

erschrecken (erschrak, erschrocken) to be scared

Hermann, dem ich auf dem Weg vom Flughafen erzählt hatte, was in Tripolis geschehen war, sah mich an, dann ging er ins Wohnzimmer, holte ein Telefon, stellte es auf den Gartentisch beim Schwimmbecken, wählte eine Nummer und wartete. Gerda und ich hörten, wie es am anderen Ende klingelte. Dann gab mir Hermann den Hörer. ,,Hier 15 Karsten", sagte eine Männerstimme. Und obwohl ich seit dem Kriege nicht mit Erich gesprochen hatte, erkannte ich seine Stimme sofort. Ich log und sagte ihm, ich riefe vom Flughafen aus an.

Ich hätte gehofft, Hermann könnte mich abholen, er sei aber nirgends zu sehen, und zu Hause sei er auch nicht. ,,Er wollte dich auch 20 abholen", sagt Erich, ,,aber vielleicht ist er nicht so schnell durch die Stadt gekommen, wie er wollte. Ich rufe ihn trotzdem sofort noch einmal an und sage ihm, daß du da bist. Aber er ist bestimmt nicht mehr zu Hause."

nirgends nowhere

Einen Augenblick später klingelte das Telefon. Wir antworteten nicht. 25 ,,Wie weit ist es von hier bis zu Erichs Wohnung?" fragte ich Hermann. ,,Mit dem Wagen mindestens eine Stunde", war die Antwort. Ich sagte nichts, auch Gerda schwieg; aber ich glaube, sie fühlte, daß Hermann und ich mehr wußten, als wir sagten.

Endlich meinte Hermann: ,,Gerda, die Geschichte, die du uns da 30 erzählt hast, ist einfach unmöglich. Wem der Hut auf dem Wasser gehört, weiß ich nicht. Aber Erich kann er nicht gehören, Erich kann nicht hier gewesen sein. Wenn er hier gewesen wäre, könnte er jetzt nicht zu Hause sein. Weißt du was, wir warten, bis deine Mutter zurückkommt, und dann fahre ich euch beide in meinem Wagen nach 35 Hamburg zurück. Hans kann mit deinem VW hinter uns herfahren."

Es war schon ungefähr neun, als wir Gerda und ihrer Mutter gute Nacht sagten. Gerda hatte versprochen, ein Bad zu nehmen, eine Tasse Tee mit Kognak zu trinken und dann ins Bett zu gehen. Um halb zehn saßen wir bei Hermann, tranken einen Whisky und redeten 40 von den Fußabdrücken hinter dem Stuhl meiner Frau, von den fünf Goldstücken hinter dem Stein in Alis Haus und von Erichs Hut in Hermanns Schwimmbecken. Wir versuchten, etwas zu erklären, was man einfach nicht erklären kann.

Da klingelte das Telefon; Hermann nahm den Hörer ab. Lange sagte
er nichts, und ich wußte nicht, mit wem er sprach. „Wir kommen
sofort, Gerda", sagte er dann, legte den Hörer auf und sprang auf.
„Aber so etwas ist doch einfach unmöglich!" rief er. „Was ist unmöglich?" fragte ich und versuchte, ruhig zu bleiben. Das Telefon 5
klingelte wieder. Diesmal ging ich in Hermanns Arbeitszimmer, wo   **Arbeitszimmer** study
noch ein Telefon stand, und hörte mit.

„Hier ist Elisabeth Meyer", hörte ich eine Frauenstimme sagen. „Bei
mir in der Wohnung wohnt ein Herr Karsten. Soviel ich weiß, ist er
Ihr Privatsekretär. Herr Direktor, Ihrem Sekretär muß irgendetwas 10
passiert sein. Er ist heute noch gar nicht weggewesen. Seit dem Frühstück sitzt er auf seinem Zimmer. Vor ein paar Minuten habe ich an
seine Tür geklopft, um ihn zu fragen, ob er nicht etwas essen wollte.
Während ich klopfte, hörte ich einen lauten Schrei, und dann war es
still im Zimmer. Ich habe die Polizei schon angerufen, aber es wäre 15   **still** quiet, still
vielleicht gut, wenn Sie auch kämen. Er ist doch ein Freund von
Ihnen." „Ich komme sofort, Frau Meyer", sagte Hermann und legte
auf. Dann sagte er zu mir: „Hans, das ist zum Verrücktwerden. Du
mußt sofort zu Gerda fahren. Die zwei Frauen dürfen heute abend
nicht allein in ihrer Wohnung sein. Du kannst meinen Wagen nehmen, 20
und ich fahre mit einer Taxe zu Erichs Wohnung. Ich sehe dich dann
später bei Gerda. Sie soll dir erzählen, was dort passiert ist." „O.K.",
sagte ich. Dann liefen wir aus dem Haus.

Gerda und ihre Mutter waren erstaunt, mich allein zu sehen. „Her-   **erstaunt** astonished
mann ist zu Erich gefahren", sagte ich. „Erichs Wirtin hat ihn vor 25
einer halben Stunde laut schreien hören, und sie meint, ihm sei etwas
passiert."

„Aber Erich war doch vor einer halben Stunde hier", sagte Gerda.
„Hat Ihnen Hermann denn nichts davon erzählt?"—„Unmöglich!
Wie kann er vor einer halben Stunde hier gewesen sein, wenn er vor 30
einer halben Stunde in seinem Zimmer laut geschrien hat? Gerda, ich
glaube, Sie hätten keinen Kognak trinken sollen."

Aber Gerda lachte nicht. „Hans, Sie wissen mehr als Sie sagen",
meinte sie, und dann erzählte sie mir, was passiert war. „Nachdem Sie
beide heute abend weggegangen waren, nahm ich, wie ich ver- 35
sprochen hatte, ein Bad. Als ich nach zehn Minuten aus der Bade-   **Badewanne** bathtub
wanne stieg, stand plötzlich der Karsten wieder vor mir. Wie er ins
Badezimmer gekommen ist, weiß ich nicht. Niemand hat geklingelt,
und meine Mutter hat niemand hereingelassen. Auch durch den
Garten kann er nicht gekommen sein, sonst hätte bestimmt der Hund 40
gebellt. Fitzi schläft nämlich auf der Terrasse, wissen Sie. Aber trotzdem stand Karsten in der Badezimmertür und fragte: ,Wo haben Sie
meinen Hut?' Ich wurde wütend, nahm meinen Schuh und schlug ihm   **wütend** mad, angry
damit auf den Kopf. Und dann war er plötzlich weg, gerade wie heute   **schlagen (schlug,
                                                                      geschlagen)** to hit

nachmittag im Schwimmbecken. Und mein Schuh ist auch weg."—
„Ich glaube, wir sollten jetzt wirklich eine Tasse Tee mit Kognak
trinken", sagte ich zu den Frauen, „oder noch besser einen Kognak
ohne Tee." Dann warteten wir auf Hermann. Es war schon eins, als er
kam. „Eine unglaubliche Geschichte", fing er an, „einfach un- 5
möglich. Als ich vor Erichs Wohnung hielt, war die Polizei gerade
angekommen. ‚Aber ich sage Ihnen doch, er hat laut geschrien', hörte
ich die Wirtin sagen, ‚gerade als ich an die Tür klopfte, um ihn zu
fragen, ob ich ihm etwas zu essen bringen könnte. Als er mir dann
nicht antwortete, habe ich Sie sofort angerufen, und ich habe hier vor 10
der Tür gestanden, bis Sie kamen.'—Es dauerte fast zehn Minuten, bis
die Polizisten endlich die Tür aufmachen konnten. Dann gingen wir   **Polizist**   policeman
alle ins Zimmer. Erich war weg; kein Mensch war im Zimmer, aber
auf dem Tisch stand eine Tasse Kaffee, der noch warm war. Die
Polizisten wußten nicht, was sie von der Sache halten sollten. Ich 15
konnte ihnen nicht helfen, denn wenn ich ihnen erzählt hätte, was seit
gestern geschehen ist, hätten sie bestimmt gedacht, ich wäre
verrückt."

Ich wäre nicht erstaunt gewesen, wenn Gerda jetzt hysterisch geworden wäre, aber sie blieb ruhig, erzählte noch einmal, daß Erich in 20
der Tür zum Badezimmer gestanden und sie nach seinem Hut gefragt
habe, daß sie ihm mit einem Schuh auf den Kopf geschlagen hätte,
und daß Erich plötzlich einfach nicht mehr dagewesen sei.

Hermann, die zwei Frauen und ich redeten, bis es Tag wurde.

Dann frühstückten wir zusammen—Gerdas Kaffee war übrigens un- 25   **unglaublich**   incredibly
glaublich gut—und fuhren nach Hause.

Gestern abend waren Gerda und ihre Mutter wieder bei uns. Wir
saßen gerade beim Abendessen, als das Telefon klingelte. Ich hörte
wieder mit. Es war die Polizei, aber nicht die Hamburger Polizei. Es
war Interpol in Tripolis. Vor dem Haus eines Ägypters habe* man am 30
Morgen einen Mann gefunden, tot und mit einer Wunde im Kopf. Die
Untersuchung durch die Polizei hätte bis jetzt zu nichts geführt. Einen
Paß habe der Mann nicht gehabt; in seiner Tasche wäre ein Brief
gewesen, adressiert an Hermann, aber außer hundert Mark wäre in
dem Brief nichts gewesen. Niemand wisse, wer der Mann sei; in 35
keinem der Hotels in Tripolis kenne man ihn, und so sei nur die eine
Spur da, die zu Hermann führe, und ob er wüßte, wer der Mann sein
könnte. Übrigens habe man neben ihm—wie seltsam—einen Damen-
schuh gefunden, und sonst gar nichts.

---

*Note that the use of the subjunctive is sufficient to indicate indirect discourse; no in-
troductory statement such as **Man sagte uns,** . . . is necessary.

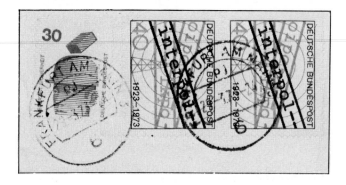

Hermann zitterte. „Das könnte mein Privatsekretär Erich Karsten sein", sagte er, „er ist seit gestern abend spurlos verschwunden. Ich werde sofort die Polizei hier in Hamburg anrufen." Dann legte er auf.

Heute nachmittag fliege ich nach Hause. Meine Frau holt mich, wie immer, am Flughafen ab.   5

Aber was soll ich ihr erzählen?

Vocabulary*

abnehmen	to decrease, decline, diminish; to lose weight; to wane (moon)	bestehen aus	to consist of
		besuchen	to attend (a school)
		bewegen	to move
		die Bewegung, -en	movement
Angst haben vor (*dat.*)	to be afraid of	die Bildung	education, training
antworten auf (*acc.*)	to reply to; to answer (a letter)	bisher (*adv.*)	up to now, so far
		bitten um (*acc.*)	to ask for
anwenden	to use, to apply to	der Blick, -e	look, glance
der Arbeiter, -	(blue-collar) worker, workingman	denken an (*acc.*)	to think of
		einander	each other
aufsein	to be up (and out of bed)	die Einführung, -en	introduction
		enthalten	to contain
die Ausfahrt	exit; off-ramp (railway and *Autobahn*)	die Entscheidung, -en	decision
		eine Entscheidung treffen	to make a decision
die Einfahrt	entrance; on-ramp		
die Bedeutung, -en	meaning, importance	entweder . . . oder	either . . . or
begegnen	to meet	das Fach, ̈-er	(academic) subject, discipline; compartment, box, shelf
der Begriff, -e	term, idea, notion		
der Bereich, -e	sphere, area		
beschränken auf	to limit to		
bestehen	to pass (an examination)	das Fenster, -	window
		die Form, -en	form

*Many verbs that take prepositional objects are listed here even if the verbs were introduced earlier. Be sure to learn prepositions and case of the prepositional object along with the verbs.

die Forschung, -en	research
fragen nach *(dat.)*	to ask about, inquire after
der Gang ⸚e	motion, gear; hallway, corridor
der erste Gang	the first gear
im Gang halten	to keep in motion
die Gara'ge, -n	garage
der Gegensatz, ⸚e	contrast
das Gegenteil, -e	the opposite
im Gegenteil	on the contrary
gehören zu *(dat.)*	to belong to, be a member of, be part of
gerecht *(adj.)*	just
ungerecht	unjust
geschehen *(impers. verb)*	to happen
die Gesellschaft, -en	society
gesellschaftlich	social
die Industriegesellschaft	industrial society
die Wohlstandsgesellschaft	affluent society
gewöhnt sein an *(acc.)*	to be accustomed to
glauben an *(acc.)*	to believe in
Grund	reason; ground
im Grunde	basically
die Grundlage, -n	foundation, basis
die Halle, -n	hall; lobby
halten von *(dat.)*	to have an opinion about
heißen	to be called
das heißt, d.h.	that is, i.e.
hierher *(adv.)*	here (hither); to this place
die Hilfe	help
die Hochschule, -n	university; institution for higher learning
hoffen auf *(acc.)*	to hope for
das Institut', -e	institute
jedoch	however
kämpfen	to fight; struggle
die Kugel, -n	sphere, ball
der Kugelschreiber,-	ballpoint pen
der Kuß, die Küsse	kiss
leiden an *(dat.)*	to suffer from; to tolerate

ich kann sie nicht leiden	I can't stand her
der Mensch, -en	man, human being
kein Mensch	nobody
die Mitbestimmung	codetermination
mündlich	orally
nachdenken über *(acc.)*	to think about, meditate about
nebenan	next door
nebeneinander	next to each other
pflegen	to take care of
die Pflicht, -en	duty
der Plan, ⸚e	plan, aim
planen	to plan
praktisch	practical
die Prüfung, -en	examination
regieren	to govern
schriftlich	in writing
der Sitz, -e	seat
sowohl . . . als auch	as well as
sprechen von *(dat.)*	to talk about
sprechen über *(acc.)*	
stattfinden	to take place
stolz sein auf *(acc.)*	to be proud of
der Streik, -s	strike
das Studium, die Studien	(period of) study
tanzen	to dance
der Teil, -e	part
zum Teil	partly
überlegen	to wonder, consider
überset'zen	to translate
die Übersetzung, -en	translation
der Unterricht	instruction
verbessern	to improve, to make better; to correct
vergleichen mit *(dat.)*	to compare with
verliebt sein in *(acc.)*	to be in love with, to be infatuated
verlobt sein mit *(dat.)*	to be engaged to
verwenden	to use, make use of, put to use
das Volk, ⸚er	people
das deutsche Volk	the German people
die Vorbereitung *(auf)*	preparation (for)
der Vorschlag, ⸚e	proposal
der Vortrag, ⸚e	(formal) lecture
die Wahrheit	truth

warten auf (acc.)	to wait for	zur Zeit	at the moment; right now; for the time being
weder . . . noch	neither . . . nor		
werfen	to throw		
zuwerfen	to cast at, throw at	das Zeugnis, -se	testimony; school report
wiederho'len	to repeat		
die Wirtschaft	economy	zufrieden sein mit (dat.)	to be satisfied with
das Wirtschafts- wunder	economic miracle	zunehmen	to increase; to gain weight; to wax (moon)
Zeit	time		

Additional Vocabulary

abgehen von (dat.)	to leave (a school)	der Hörsaal, -säle	lecture hall in a university
der Abiturient, -en	Gymnasium graduate		
adäquat	adequate, sufficient	die Hotelhalle, -n	lobby
die Allgemeinbildung	general education	interessanterweise	interestingly
ansteigen	to climb, increase (price, popula- tion)	die Katastro'phe, -n	catastrophe
		die Kernphysik	nuclear physics
		das Klavier, -e	piano
baldig (adj.)	soon	lenken	to direct
auf baldiges Wie- dersehen	(hoping to) see you again soon	nackt	naked, nude
		das Niveau	level
basieren auf (dat.)	to be based on	die Oper, -n	opera
das Bedürfnis, -se	need, requirement	orientiert sein	to have a direction or bias
begabt (adj.)	gifted, intelligent		
betonen	to stress, accent	paradox'	paradox
die Chemie	chemistry	positiv	positive
chemisch	chemical	promovieren	to get a Ph. D. degree
der Doktorand, -en	doctoral candidate	die Promotion, -en	awarding of the Ph. D.
durchfallen	to flunk an examina- tion		
		reagieren auf (acc.)	to react to
egalitär	egalitarian	die Spannung, -en	tension
die Einheitsschule, -n	comprehensive school	Hochspannung	high voltage
elitär	elitist, selective	stärken	to strengthen
der Fachbereich, -e	group of academic departments	das Stipendium, die Stipendien	stipend, scholarship, fellowship
der Fremdsprachen- unterricht	foreign language in- struction	überfüllt	overcrowded, over- flowing
der Gruß, ̈-e	greeting	die Verschmutzung	pollution
das Hauptfach, ̈-er	(academic) major (sub- ject)	verteidigen	to defend
		verzweifeln	to despair
herbeiführen	to bring about	verzweifelt	in despair
die Hierarchie', -n	hierarchy	die Vorlesung, -en	lecture (in university class)
der Höhepunkt, -e	high point, climax		
höher	higher	die Weltanschauung, -en	world view
die höhere Schule	secondary school, Gymnasium	der Wohlstand	well-being, prosperity

Wohlstandsgesell- schaft	affluent society	**zunächst** (*adv.*)		first (of all), to begin with
zu 'lassen		to admit	**die Zusammenkunft, ⸚e**	meeting, get-together

Strong Verbs and Irregular Weak Verbs

abnehmen	nimmt ab	nahm ab	abgenommen	to decrease, decline, di- minish; to lose weight; to wane (moon)
anwenden		wendete an	angewandt	to use, to apply
bestehen		bestand	bestanden	to pass (an examination)
enthalten	enthält	enthielt	enthalten	to contain
geschehen	geschieht	geschah	ist geschehen	to happen
leiden		litt	gelitten	to suffer; to tolerate
stattfinden		fand statt	stattgefunden	to take place
vergleichen		verglich	verglichen	to compare
werfen	wirft	warf	geworfen	to throw
zunehmen	nimmt zu	nahm zu	zugenommen	to increase; to gain weight; to wax (moon)

In unseren Betten wird jede Nacht zum Erholungs-Urlaub.

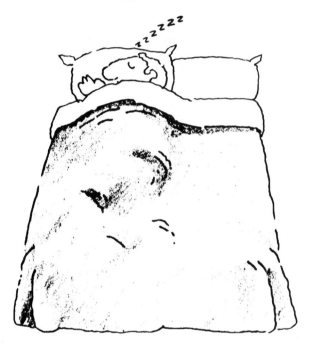

Das ist Holiday Inn-Schlafkomfort: lärmgeschützte, luxuriöse 30-qm-Zimmer mit Bad + WC, franz. Betten, Klimaanlage, TV, Radio, Telefon. Dazu Schwimmbad, Solarium und Sauna.

UNIT 13 Present and Past Infinitives—Subjective and Objective Use of Modals—Negation in the Inner Field—Contrary-to-Fact Conditions without **wenn**

People talk about all sorts of things, and it would be impossible to give you examples containing the vocabulary of *all* common topics of conversation. Therefore, we have selected topics that will help you communicate in German when you first encounter native speakers of the language who know no English. We have had you talk about the weather—always a good opening gambit—about food and drink, about traffic, and about student life. The conversations as well as the patterns of Unit 13 once more pick up the subject of travel, so that you can add to your list of words and phrases on this topic. By the end of the course, you should have quite a number of such topical lists to help you free yourself from the book and to engage in genuine communication, be it with your fellow students, your teacher, or with the real Meyers, Müllers and Schmidts of this world.

There is more to learning a language than speaking and reading. You should now be prepared to work on competence in *writing* German. At the beginning, this will seem to be much more difficult than speaking because the written word has the unpleasant habit of not vanishing into thin air; but as long as your teacher, or your German addressee, can get the message, you are on the right track. A wrong ending, or even a misplaced word, won't make people laugh at you—on the contrary, they will be pleased with your effort.

The reading selections of Unit 13 cover a wide variety of language. The first selection pokes fun at stereotypes, national and sexual, and even at a German headwaiter. The breakfast menu on p. 406 incidentally, shows that Germans don't know their English quite as well as you may think they do. The remaining selections are again literary in character. A Kafka text and a Bible chapter, though written two thousand years apart, deal with an ever recurring literary topic, the prodigal son.

Patterns

[1] Past Infinitives

Er scheint zu schlafen.
Er scheint gut geschlafen zu haben.

SEE ANALYSIS 139 (p. 393)

Er schien zu schlafen.
Er schien gut geschlafen zu haben.

Meyer schien sehr glücklich zu sein.
Meyer scheint sehr glücklich gewesen zu sein.

Wer Arzt werden will, muß sechs Jahre studieren.
Wer Arzt ist, muß sechs Jahre studiert haben.

[2] The Objective and Subjective Use of **müssen**

OBJECTIVE

SEE
ANALYSIS
140
(p. 393)

In Heidelberg mußt du unbedingt das Schloß besichtigen.
   In Heidelberg you've absolutely got to visit the castle.

Er mußte oft Geschäftsreisen in die Schweiz machen.
   He often had to take business trips to Switzerland.

Er sagte, er müßte nächste Woche wieder nach Bern.
   He said he had to go to Berne again next week.

Wenn er nicht krank geworden wäre, hätte er nach Bern fahren müssen.
   If he hadn't gotten sick, he would have had to go to Berne.

SUBJECTIVE

Ich habe ihn schon lange nicht gesehen; er muß wieder in der Schweiz sein.
   I haven't seen him for a long time; he must be in Switzerland again.

Er muß lange in England gelebt haben, denn er spricht Englisch praktisch ohne Akzent.
   He must have lived in England for a long time, because he speaks English practically without an
   accent.

Der Mann, der zur Tür hereinkam, mußte Hans von Hollenbeck sein. Er sah genau so aus,
   wie der Inspektor ihn beschrieben hatte.
   The man who came in through the door had to be Hans von Hollenbeck. He looked exactly the way
   the inspector had described him.

Tante Amalie muß schon wieder im
Museum gewesen sein.

Das muß von Hollenbeck gewesen sein, sagte der Inspektor. Wir wissen, daß er damals in
    Klein-Kleckersdorf war.
> That must have been von Hollenbeck, said the inspector. We know that he was in Klein-Kleckers-
> dorf at that time.

Es ist kurz vor acht. Heinz müßte eigentlich jetzt hier sein.
> It is shortly before eight. Hans really ought to be here now.

Ruf doch mal den Bahnhof an. Der Zug müßte doch schon lange angekommen sein.
> Why don't you call the station? That train ought to have arrived a long time ago.

VARIATIONS

Following the pattern of the examples below, answer the questions by using a subjective form of **müssen**; try to support your conclusion with a sentence starting with **denn**.

> **(a) Ist sie wirklich schon achtzehn?**
> **Sie muß achtzehn sein, denn sie hat einen Führerschein (driver's license).**
>
> **(b) Waren Meyers wirklich im Ausland?**
> **Sie müssen im Ausland gewesen sein, denn sie reden dauernd über Spanien**
>   **und Portugal.**

Hat Meyer wirklich so viel Geld?
War Ingelheim schon oft in Frankreich?
Woher wußtest du, daß er Amerikaner war?

[3] wollen

Determine whether **wollen** is used subjectively or objectively.

Tante Amalie will die Osterferien bei uns verbringen.
> Aunt Amalie wants to spend Easter vacation with us.

SEE
ANALYSIS
140
(p. 393)

Als er über die Grenze fahren wollte, bemerkte er plötzlich, daß er seinen Paß vergessen
    hatte.
> When he wanted to cross the border, he suddenly noticed that he had forgotten his passport.

Er will in Wien studiert haben? Das glaube ich nicht.
> He says he studied in Vienna? I don't believe that.

Als Ingelheim den Preis bekam, wollte natürlich jeder seinen Roman schon gelesen haben.
    Ich hatte ihn *wirk*lich gelesen.—So?—Und ich wollte, ich hätte ihn *nicht* gelesen.
> When Ingelheim got the prize, everybody pretended to have read his novel already, of course. *I*
> really *had* read it.—Really?—And I wish I *hadn't* read it.

VARIATIONS

Change the following sentences according to the pattern of the example.

> **Er behauptet, ein Freund des Direktors zu sein.**
> **Er will ein Freund des Direktors sein.**

Er behauptet, ein Freund des Direktors gewesen zu sein.
Er behauptete, ein Freund des Direktors zu sein.
Er behauptete, ein Freund des Direktors gewesen zu sein.
Er behauptet, ein Haus an der Riviera zu haben.
Er behauptet, ein Haus an der Riviera gehabt zu haben.
Er behauptete, ein Haus an der Riviera zu haben.
Er behauptete, ein Haus an der Riviera gehabt zu haben.

[4] sollen

Decide which sentences express "hearsay about the grammatical subject."

SEE
ANALYSIS
140
(p. 393)

Du sollst nicht stehlen.
> Thou shalt not steal.

Wir sollen morgen um acht auf dem Bahnhof sein.
> We are supposed to be at the station at eight tomorrow.

Er sagte, wir sollten morgen um acht Uhr auf dem Bahnhof sein.
> He said we were to be at the station at eight tomorrow.

Die Brücke sollte schon letztes Jahr fertig werden, aber sie ist immer noch nicht fertig.
> The bridge was to be completed last year, but it still isn't finished.

Wir fahren dieses Mal in den Bayerischen Wald in Urlaub. Dort sollen die Hotels viel billiger
sein als in den Alpen.
> We are going to spend our vacation in the Bavarian Forest this time. The hotels are supposed to be
> much cheaper there than in the Alps.

Wo ist denn der Erich?—Der soll schon wieder an der Riviera sein.
> Where is Erich?—Supposedly he is on the Riviera again.

Hast du etwas von Dietlinde gehört?—Die soll im Juni geheiratet haben. Ihr Mann soll
Ingenieur sein.
> Have you heard anything about Dietlinde?—I've heard that she got married last June. I understand
> her husband is an engineer.

VARIATIONS

Change the following sentences according to the pattern of the example.

> **Ich höre, Meyer wohnt in Berlin.—Meyer soll in Berlin wohnen.**

Ich höre, er ist schon wieder in Tirol.	Er _____ schon wieder in Tirol _____.
Ich höre, er ist noch nie in Afrika gewesen.	Er _____ noch nie in Afrika _____ _____.
Ich höre, seine Frau war krank.	Seine Frau _____ krank _____ _____.
Ich höre, Erika hat geheiratet.	Erika _____ geheiratet _____.
Ich höre, er muß schon wieder nach Amerika fahren.	Er _____ schon wieder nach Amerika _____ müssen.

[5] mögen

This section uses the indicative of **mögen,** both as a nonmodal and as a subjective modal.

Ingelheims Romane sind ja ganz gut, aber als Menschen mag ich ihn gar nicht.
 Ingelheim's novels aren't bad, but as a person I don't care for him at all.

Ich mochte ihn schon nicht, als wir noch auf dem Gymnasium waren.
 I disliked him already when we were still in the *Gymnasium.*

Meine Frau hat ihn auch nie gemocht.
 My wife never liked him either.

Danke, Schweinefleisch mag ich nicht; ich esse lieber ein Steak.
 Thanks, I don't care for pork; I'd rather have a steak.

Wie alt ist seine Tochter eigentlich?—Oh, ich weiß nicht. Sie mag achtzehn oder neunzehn
 sein.
 How old is his daughter?—Oh, I don't know, maybe eighteen or nineteen.

Er mochte damals etwa dreißig sein.
 At that time, he was probably about thirty.

Was mag ihm nur passiert sein?
 I wonder what has happened to him.

Was mochte ihm nur passiert sein?
 I wondered what had happened to him.

Er mag gedacht haben, ich hätte ihn nicht gesehen.
 He may have thought that I hadn't seen him.

SEE
ANALYSIS
140
(p. 393)

VARIATIONS

Change the following sentences according to the pattern of the example.

> **Ich glaube, sie ist etwa zwanzig.—Sie mag etwa zwanzig sein.**

Ich glaube, sie war damals etwa zwanzig.—Sie _____ damals etwa zwanzig _____ _____.
Ich glaube, er hat mich nicht gesehen.—Er _____ mich nicht _____ _____.
Ich glaube, das ist Zufall.—Das _____ Zufall _____.
Ich glaube, das war Zufall.—Das _____ Zufall _____ _____.

[6] können

Determine whether **können** is used objectively (ability) or subjectively (inference).

Klaus ist krank und kann leider nicht kommen.
 Klaus is sick and unfortunately can't come.

Seine Frau sagte, er sei krank und könne leider nicht kommen.
 His wife said he was sick and unfortunately wouldn't be able to come.

Heute ist ja schon Donnerstag. Bis Samstag kann ich den Roman nicht gelesen haben.
 But today is Thursday already. I can't possibly have read the novel by Saturday.

SEE
ANALYSIS
140
(p. 393)

Daß GRUNDIG Cassetten-Autosuper noch und noch gekauft werden, kann nicht nur am Preis liegen!

Intelligent kann er nicht sein. Wenn er intelligent wäre, würde er nicht für Meyer arbeiten.
    He can't be intelligent. If he were intelligent, he wouldn't work for Meyer.

Sie war fast noch ein Kind und konnte nicht älter sein als siebzehn.
    She was still almost a child and couldn't have been any older than seventeen.

Wenn Meyer kein Geld hätte, könnte er keinen Mercedes 450 SE fahren.
    If Meyer didn't have any money, he couldn't drive a Mercedes 450 SE.

Seine Frau sagte, er sei krank und könne leider nicht kommen.
    His wife said he was sick and unfortunately wouldn't be able to come.

Könnte ich vielleicht ein Zimmer mit Bad haben?
    Could I have a room with bath?

Und der Herr, der mich sprechen wollte, hat nicht gesagt, wie er heißt? Wer kann das nur gewesen sein? Er sprach mit einem Akzent, sagen Sie? Hm, das könnte Mr. Taylor gewesen sein.
    And the gentleman who wanted to talk to me didn't tell you his name? Who could that have been? You say he had an accent? Hm, that could have been Mr. Taylor.

Ich glaube, wir sollten heute im Garten arbeiten. Morgen könnte es regnen.
    I think we should work in the garden today. It could (might) rain tomorrow.

Von Hollenbeck hätte fliehen können, aber er wollte nicht.
    Von Hollenbeck could have escaped, but he didn't want to.

Wahrscheinlich ist er noch im Lande, aber er könnte natürlich auch geflohen sein.
    He is probably still in the country, but it is possible, of course, that he has fled.

Natürlich hätte er das Geld stehlen können, aber er ist doch kein Dieb.
    Of course, he could have stolen the money; but he isn't a thief.

Sie können doch gar nicht wissen, ob ihm das Geld wirklich gehört; er könnte es ja auch gestohlen haben.
    You can't know whether the money really belongs to him; it is possible, after all, that he has stolen it.

VARIATIONS

Change the following sentences according to the pattern of the example.

Ist er schon hier?
Nein, er kann noch nicht hier sein. Es ist doch erst acht.

Ist das Herr Meyer dort drüben?

Nein, _____. Der ist doch heute in München.

War er gestern abend im Kino?

Nein, _____. Er war gestern abend bei Meyers.

Bist du sicher, daß es Erich war?

Nein, sicher bin ich nicht, aber _____.

[7] dürfen

Determine whether **dürfen** is used objectively or subjectively.

Darf ich heute abend ins Kino gehen, Mutti?

Kann ich heute abend ins Kino gehen, Mutti?

    May I go to the movies tonight, Mom?

SEE
ANALYSIS
140
(p. 393)

Ich fragte sie, ob ich sie nach Hause bringen dürfte.

    I asked her whether I could (might) take her home.

Rauchen darf man hier leider nicht.

    Unfortunately smoking is not permitted here.

Sie dürfen nicht mehr so viel Kaffee trinken, Frau Emmerich.

    You mustn't (shouldn't) drink so much coffee anymore, Mrs. Emmerich.

Wann ist er denn weggefahren?—Vor zwei Stunden.—Dann dürfte er jetzt schon in Frankfurt sein.

    When did he leave?—Two hours ago.—Then we can assume that he is in Frankfurt by now.

Ich möchte wissen, wer mich gestern abend um elf noch angerufen hat.—Das dürfte Erich gewesen sein; der ruft doch immer so spät an.

    I wonder who called me last night at eleven.—I suppose that was Erich; he always calls that late, doesn't he?

[8] werden

Ich fahre in irgendeinen Badeort an der See, aber ich werde nicht lange bleiben.

    I'm going to some resort on the ocean, but I won't stay long.

SEE
ANALYSIS
140
(p. 393)

Bis Sie zurückkommen, Herr Direktor, werden wir das Büro neu eingerichtet haben.

    By the time you come back, sir, we will have refurnished the office.

From a dictionary of foreign words. Note German transcription of English pronunciation.

Camouflage w (kahmuhflah′sh) Tarnung.
Camp s (kä′mp) Lager.
campen (kä′mpen) mit Zelt oder Wohnwagen Freizeit machen; **Camper** m (kä′mper) mit Zelt oder Wohnwagen reisender Urlauber.
Camping s (kä′mpiñ) Zelten, Leben auf Zeltplätzen (im Zelt oder Wohnwagen).

Ca′mpus m (ka . . . auch kä′mp′s) Gelände einer Universität.
Ca′nnabis bot. Hanf; im engeren Sinne der Indische Hanf, aus dem Haschisch (s. dort) und Marihuana (s. dort) gewonnen werden.
Carava′n m (auch kä′r′w′n) (Reise-)Wohnwagen; auch Kombiwagen; kombinierter

Personen- und Lastkraftwagen; **Carava′ner** m (kär′weh′n′r) mit Wohnwagen Reisender; **Carava′ning** s (kär′weh′niñ) Leben im (Reise-)Wohnwagen.
Cartoon m (kartuh′n) moderne Witzzeichnung; Karikatur.
Cash (kä′sch) Bargeld, Barzahlung.

Wenn diese Perlen so teuer sind, werden sie wohl echt sein.
> If these pearls are that expensive, then I guess they are genuine.

Er wird Schwierigkeiten mit seinem Caravan gehabt haben; sonst hätte er von hier bis nach Mailand keine drei Tage gebraucht.
> He's probably had trouble with his trailer; otherwise he wouldn't have taken three days (to get) from here to Milan.

VARIATIONS

Determine whether **werden** is used to express futurity or probability.

Sei nur ruhig; er wird bestimmt kommen.
Versuchen Sie die Pension Edelweiß; Sie werden bestimmt zufrieden sein.
Bis Ende des Monats werde ich schon zweimal in Berlin gewesen sein.
Meyer wird wohl in Berlin gewesen sein.
Er sagte, er werde wahrscheinlich nicht mitgehen können.
Hans wird wohl noch schlafen.

[9] Position of **nicht**

Determine how much of each sentence is negated by **nicht**.

SEE ANALYSIS 141 (p. 397)

Aber du kannst doch nicht den ganzen Tag schlafen!
> But you can't sleep all day!
> (Question: Was kannst du nicht tun? Answer: Den ganzen Tag schlafen.)

Warum denn nicht? Ich habe die ganze Nacht nicht geschlafen.
> Why not? I didn't sleep all night.
> (Question: Was hast du die ganze Nacht nicht getan? Answer: Geschlafen.)

Meyer war krank und hat lange nicht arbeiten können.
> Meyer was sick, and for a long time he couldn't work.

Heute haben wir nicht lange arbeiten können.
> Today we couldn't work very long.

Du brauchst nicht auf dem Sofa zu schlafen. Wir haben ein Bett für dich.
> You don't have to sleep on the sofa. We have a bed for you.

Ich kann in diesem Bett einfach nicht schlafen. Es ist zu kurz.
> I simply can't sleep in this bed. It is too short.

Geschlafen habe ich. Aber ich habe nicht gut geschlafen.
> I slept all right, but I didn't sleep well.

[10] nicht A, sondern B

SEE
ANALYSIS
143
(p. 399)

Ich wartete nicht auf Inge. Ich wartete auf Erika.
Ich wartete damals nicht auf Inge, sondern auf Erika.
Ich habe nicht auf Inge, sondern auf Erika gewartet.
Ich habe nicht auf Inge gewartet, sondern auf Erika.
Nicht auf Inge, sondern auf Erika habe ich gewartet.

Du weißt doch, daß ich nicht auf Inge, sondern auf Erika gewartet habe.
Du weißt doch, daß ich nicht auf Inge gewartet habe, sondern auf Erika.

Er ist gestern nicht nach Ber*lin*, sondern nach *Ham*burg gefahren.
Er ist nicht *gestern*, sondern erst *heute* nach Berlin gefahren.
Er ist nicht *gestern* nach Berlin gefahren, sondern erst *heute*.
Er ist gestern nicht nach Ber*lin* gefahren, sondern nach *Ham*burg.

Wir sind gestern nicht nach Hamburg ge*flo*gen, sondern ge*fah*ren.

Nicht alle Urlaubsländer sind Käseländer. Und nicht alle Käseländer sind Urlaubsländer. Aber Bayern ist Urlaubsland und Käseland.

[11] entweder . . . oder; weder . . . noch

SEE
ANALYSIS
144
(p. 399)

Wer mag das wohl gewesen sein? Es könnte entweder Liselotte oder Hannelore gewesen sein.
Er kommt entweder überhaupt nicht, oder sein Zug hat Verspätung.
Entweder fahren wir in die Berge, oder wir fahren an die See. Wir wissen es noch nicht.
Herr Meyer trinkt weder Kaffee noch Tee.
Ich habe ihn weder besuchen können, noch hatte ich Zeit, ihn anzurufen.
Weder Meyer noch Kunz konnte damals nach Berlin fahren.

[12] Contrary-to-Fact Conditions without **wenn**

SEE
ANALYSIS
145
(p. 400)

Hätten wir uns dieses Wochenendhaus nicht gekauft, dann könnten wir jetzt jeden Sommer
    nach Italien fahren.
    If we hadn't bought this weekend house, we could go to Italy every summer now.

Hättest du mir doch nur geschrieben, daß du Geld brauchtest! Du weißt doch, daß ich dir
    gerne geholfen hätte.
    If only you had written that you needed money! You know that I would have been glad to help you.

Hätte ich doch nur gewußt, daß Monika krank war! Ich hätte sie gerne besucht.
    Had I only known that Monika was sick! I would have been glad to visit her.

[13] **sonst**

SEE
ANALYSIS
146
(p. 400)

Wir waren ja sonst immer in Italien, aber dieses Mal wollen wir in den Ferien an die
    Nordsee.
    We've always gone to Italy (in former times), but this time we want to go to the North Sea for our
    vacation.

Was ist nur mit Hans los? Der ist doch sonst nicht so unhöflich.
    What's the matter with Hans? He isn't usually so impolite.

Herr Hanfstängl ist noch im Büro, aber sonst ist niemand mehr da.
    Mr. Hanfstängl is still in the office, but nobody else is here anymore.

Hat sonst noch jemand angerufen?
    Has anybody else called?

Erika muß mitgehen, sonst bleibe ich zu Hause.
    Erika has to come along, otherwise I'll stay home.

Er flüchtete, sonst hätte man ihn verhaftet.
    He escaped, otherwise they would have arrested him.

Sie sind leider umsonst gekommen; der Herr Doktor ist heute nicht da.
    Unfortunately you've come for nothing (in vain); the doctor is not in today.

Wenn das Kind noch keine zwei Jahre alt ist, fährt es umsonst.
    If the child isn't two yet, he travels free.

Umsonst ist nur der Tod. (Sprichwort)
    Only death doesn't cost you anything. (proverb)

**B: Findest Du nicht auch, daß ich
ein feiner Scotch bin?**

**W: Sonst hätt´ ich Dich schon
längst verlassen.**

Analysis

139 Present and Past Infinitives

In any sentence containing an infinitive, there is always a time relation between this infinitive and the inflected verb. Consider the sentences

Er scheint zu schlafen.	He seems to be asleep.
Er schien zu schlafen.	He seemed to be asleep.

In both sentences the infinitive (**schlafen**) refers to the same time as the inflected verbs (**scheint** and **schien**).

If the infinitives, compared to the time of the inflected verb, refer to the same time, they are called present infinitives, *even if* (as in **er schien zu schlafen**) both the inflected verb and the infinitive refer to past time compared to the moment of speaking. Up to now, only such present infinitives have been used in this book.

The situation is different in

Er scheint gut geschlafen zu haben.	He seems to have slept well.
Er schien gut geschlafen zu haben.	He seemed to have slept well.

Here the infinitive **geschlafen zu haben** (*to have slept*) refers to a point in time which precedes the time of the inflected verb. The compound infinitives used in such cases are called past infinitives.

In German past infinitives, the participle (**geschlafen**) precedes the infinitive of the auxiliary, which is always either **haben** or **sein.** The **zu** stands between the participle and **sein** or **haben. Zu** is, of course, not used after modals.

PRESENT INFINITIVE	PAST INFINITIVE
schlafen	**geschlafen (zu) haben**
sein	**gewesen (zu) sein**
essen	**gegessen (zu) haben**
abfahren	**abgefahren (zu) sein**
kennenlernen	**kennengelernt (zu) haben**
glücklich sein	**glücklich gewesen (zu) sein.**

140 The Subjective Use of Modals

müssen

In sentences as

Alle Menschen müssen sterben	All human beings must die
Vater muß morgen arbeiten	Father has to work tomorrow

both English *must* and German **müssen** express an unavoidable necessity for the grammatical subjects **alle Menschen** and **Vater.** The speaker can do nothing about this necessity. He simply reports it as an objective fact. He is using *must* and **müssen** *objectively*.

The situation is quite different when a speaker, observing a well-dressed couple getting out of a Rolls Royce, makes the remark

Die Leute müssen Geld haben.   Those people must have money.

This remark still expresses a necessity, but this time not for the grammatical subject **die Leute** (they are not *compelled* to have money). Rather, it is a subjective necessity felt by the speaker: Seeing what he sees he cannot help but come to the conclusion that the Rolls Royce people have money. The speaker is using *must* and **müssen** *subjectively*. Another example: When Meyer, who expects his friend to arrive at 4:30, looks at his watch and sees that it is 4:40, he says:

Gustav muß (müßte) schon angekommen sein.
Gustav must (ought to) have arrived by now.

NOTE: The subjunctive of subjectively used modals does not express irreality but only states an assumption more tentatively.

Up to now, we have avoided using modals subjectively, because they are frequently followed by past infinitives like **angekommen sein**; also, some subjectively used German modals have no parallel in English. It is therefore advisable to look at the most frequently occurring subjective uses of the other modals as well.

wollen

When used objectively, the grammatical subject intends to do something in the future.

Fritz will Medizin studieren und Arzt werden.
Fritz wants to study medicine and to become a doctor.

But if the infinitive following **wollen** is either a past infinitive or does not relate to the future, then the statement with **wollen** expresses not a factual intention of the grammatical subject to do something in the future, but a claim made by the subject which the speaker reports with suspicion.

Fritz will 20 Jahre alt sein.
Fritz says (claims) he is twenty. (But I doubt it.)

sollen

When used objectively, the infinitive following **sollen** expresses an authoritative statement about a future event which does not originate from the speaker but from some authority. Thus, when someone, reading a newspaper, remarks

In Hamburg soll es morgen regnen
It is supposed to rain in Hamburg tomorrow

he is reading the weather report, which predicts rain for the Hamburg area. But when the same speaker, having heard someone talking about the weather in Hamburg, says

> **In Hamburg soll das Wetter sehr schlecht sein; gestern soll es den ganzen Tag geregnet haben**

he is using the infinitives **sein** and **geregnet haben** without reference to the future. This lack of a relation to the future changes the meaning of **sollen**: the infinitives that follow no longer express an authoritative prediction or prescription but simply some information not originating from the speaker and passed on to his audience without any guarantee. The sentence above means: *I hear that the weather in Hamburg is very bad and that it rained all day yesterday*. The same "hearsay" element is present in the sentence:

> **Erika soll geheiratet haben und ihr Mann soll Fotograf sein.**
> I hear that Erika has married and that her husband is a photographer.

mögen

Up to this point, we have used only the forms **ich möchte, du möchtest,** and so on. But although these **möchte**-forms are the ones used most frequently, **mögen**, like the other modals, has a complete set of forms.

PRESENT INDICATIVE	PRESENT SUBJUNCTIVE
ich mag	**ich möchte**
du magst	**du möchtest**
er mag	**er möchte**
wir mögen	**wir möchten**
ihr mögt	**ihr möchtet**
sie mögen	**sie möchten**

PAST INDICATIVE	PAST SUBJUNCTIVE
ich mochte	**ich hätte** . . . (infinitive) **mögen**
du mochtest	**du hättest** " "

PERFECT WITH DEPENDENT INFINITIVE	PERFECT WITHOUT INFINITIVE
ich habe . . . **mögen**	**ich habe gemocht**
du hast . . . **mögen**	**du hast gemocht**
etc.	etc.

The verb **mögen** can be used without a following infinitive. If so used, it is not a modal; it means *to like* and takes an accusative object.

Sie mag ihn nicht.	She doesn't like him.
Wir mögen kein Schweinefleisch.	We don't like pork.
Wir mochten ihn nicht.	We did not like him.
Ich habe sie nie gemocht.	I never liked her.

When used as a modal—that is, with a dependent infinitive, **mögen** has an objective and a subjective meaning.

Used objectively, **mögen** plus infinitive expresses the fact that the grammatical subject has a desire. This use, for all practical purposes, is restricted to the **möchte**-forms.

> **Fritzchen Meyer möchte Arzt werden.**   Fritzchen Meyer would like to become a doctor.

When used subjectively, as in **Das mag sein** (*That may be*), **mögen** means *may* and denotes that the speaker presents his statement with the reservation that what he reports "may be" the case. As a matter of fact, **Mag sein!**, used as a sentence by itself, does mean *Maybe!*

This subjective use of **mögen** occurs quite frequently in modern literature. The present indicative **mag** denotes a present possibility, and **mochte**, the past indicative, a past possibility. The use of the past infinitive is frequent. The following examples are taken from modern literature:

> **Man mag es nicht glauben wollen.**   You may not want to believe it.
> **Das mag einer der Punkte gewesen sein.**   That may have been one of the points.
> **Das mochte wirklich Zufall gewesen sein.**   Perhaps that was really a coincidence.
> **Er mag geglaubt haben, ich verstände ihn.**   He may have thought that I understood him.

können

When used objectively, **können** expresses either the ability of the grammatical subject to do something, or the availability of facilities to do it.

> **Leider konnte sie nicht schwimmen.**
> Unfortunately she couldn't (was not able to) swim.

> **Man kann heute nonstop von Frankfurt nach Los Angeles fliegen.**
> Today you can fly nonstop from Frankfurt to Los Angeles.

When used subjectively, **können** expresses a possibility inferred by the speaker on the basis of observable facts. English expresses such inferred possibility by using *can* or *may* in the present, and *could* or *might* in the past or in the subjunctive.

> **Das kann nicht Frau Müller sein; die ist doch heute in München.**
> That can't be Mrs. Müller; she is in Munich today, you know.

> **Doch, das könnte Frau Müller sein; sie ist doch schon wieder zurück.**
> Yes, that could be Mrs. Müller; she's back again, you know.

dürfen

Of the six modals, **dürfen** has the lowest frequency. When used objectively, **dürfen** means *may* or *to be permitted*.

Hier dürfen wir nicht parken.   We cannot (mustn't) park here.

Ich darf abends keinen Kaffee mehr   I must not drink coffee at night anymore.
trinken.

The only subjective use of **dürfen** is syntactically extremely restricted. You will occasionally hear:

Erika dürfte jetzt schon in Frankfurt sein.
Erika is probably already in Frankfurt by now. (She took a train from Munich.)

scheinen

German **scheinen,** if used with the meaning *to seem,* is followed by an infinitive with **zu** (and is therefore, strictly speaking, not a modal). But we mention it here because it behaves like a subjective modal and can be used in only two tenses, present and past. It can be followed by either a present or a past infinitive.

Er scheint zu schlafen.
Er scheint gut geschlafen zu haben.
Er schien zu schlafen.
Er schien gut geschlafen zu haben.

141 Uses of **werden**

As was pointed out in **103,** the German future tense (**werden** plus infinitive) can also be used to express present probability:

Er wird schon zu Hause sein.
He is probably at home by now.

This use of the future tense represents a subjective judgment by the speaker on a present fact or event:

I am sure (I guess; I think) he's at home by now.

Past probability is expressed by a form of **werden** plus a past infinitive:

Er wird schon nach Hause gegangen sein.
He has probably gone home already.
I assume he's gone home already.

The *objective* use of this construction is the German future perfect.

Weil unser Bus erst um 12.15 Uhr am Bahnhof ankommt, wird der 12-Uhr-Zug schon abgefahren sein.
Because our bus won't arrive at the station until 12:15, the twelve o'clock train will already have left.

NOTE: Just as the future is usually expressed by the present tense, the future perfect is usually expressed by the present perfect:

> Ich fahre morgen nach München.
> Bis wir zum Bahnhof kommen, ist der Zug bestimmt schon abgefahren.

142 Negation in the Inner Field

In 36, we pointed out that **nicht** follows the inner field and precedes the second prong. In 116, we showed that **nicht** can negate "the whole thing":

> Ich wollte, er hätte nicht wieder den ganzen Abend nur von seinem Hobby geredet.

This sentence does not deny that he talked, but only bemoans the fact that he talked so long and only about his hobby. In other words, **nicht** negates only elements in what we normally consider the inner field. Now consider the following two sentences:

> Ich bin oft nicht zu Hause.
> Ich bin nicht oft zu Hause.

The first sentence negates the verbal idea **zu Hause sein** for many instances (**oft**); the second sentence states that I can indeed be found at home, though not very often. If someone says

> Ich habe die ganze Nacht nicht geschlafen

he didn't sleep at all, but if he says

> Ich habe nicht die ganze Nacht geschlafen

then he did sleep, but not all night.

Thus, we can say that as **nicht** moves forward in the sentence, it loses some of its negative force upon the verb and its complement, and it restricts rather than totally negates the verbal idea.

143 nicht . . . , sondern . . .

The English pattern "not A, but B," which occurs in such sentences as

> You are not my friend, but my enemy

is expressed in German by **nicht A, sondern B**.

> **Das war nicht gestern, sondern vorgestern.**
> That was not yesterday, but the day before yesterday.

Usually such sentences use contrast intonation. The element introduced by **nicht** (or **kein**) has a rising stress (⟋), and the element introduced by **sondern** has a falling stress (⟍). The **nicht** (or **kein**) and the **sondern** are normally unstressed.

The element introduced by **sondern** can either stand behind the second prong in the end field, or it can follow immediately upon the **nicht A**-element.

> **Ich war nicht gestern in Berlin, sondern vorgestern.**
> **Ich war nicht gestern, sondern vorgestern in Berlin.**

144 entweder . . . oder; weder . . . noch

These two pairs of connecting conjunctions correspond to English *either . . . or* and *neither . . . nor*. As in English, they can be used in several positions, but note that **entweder, weder** and **noch** (unlike **oder**, which has no influence on word order) can occupy the front field and are then immediately followed by the first prong.

	FRONT FIELD	1ST PRONG	
oder	**Entweder** **ich**	gehe gehe	ich ins Theater, ins Kino.
	Weder **noch**	ging ging	er ins Kino, er ins Theater.

Entweder and **weder** can also be used in the inner field, but **noch** cannot, unless there is only one verb.

	FRONT FIELD	1ST PRONG	
oder	**Ich** **ich**	gehe gehe	entweder ins Theater, ins Kino.
	Er **noch**	ging ging	weder ins Kino er ins Theater.
	Ich **Er**	gehe ging	entweder nach Hause oder ins Kino. weder ins Kino noch ins Theater.

145 Contrary-to-Fact Conditions without **wenn**

In contrary-to-fact conditions, the conjunction **wenn** may be omitted. In contemporary German, and particularly in the spoken language, this pattern occurs almost exclusively in past time.

> **Wenn Ingelheim nicht Soldat gewesen wäre, hätte er keine Kriegsromane schreiben können.**
>
> **Wäre Ingelheim nicht Soldat gewesen, dann hätte er keine Kriegsromane schreiben können.**

The clause with the omitted **wenn** always shows verb-first position and usually precedes the conclusion. The conclusion is usually introduced by **dann** or **so.**

If the condition stands alone to express a wish or desire, the **wenn** can also be omitted, but again primarily in past time.

> **Wenn er mir nur geschrieben hätte!**
> **Hätte er mir doch nur geschrieben!**

NOTE: These wishful **wenn**-clauses are independent syntactical units and almost always contain a **nur** or **doch nur** or a **wenigstens.** Like all sentence adverbs, this **nur** or **wenigstens** shifts position as follows: The elements preceding *nur, doch nur,* or *wenigstens* are unstressed and include all those things which have already been talked about; the elements following *nur, doch nur,* or *wenigstens* are all news items.

> **Ich wollte ja studieren. Wenn ich nur das Geld dazu gehabt hätte!**
> **Jetzt habe ich das Geld. Wenn ich das Geld nur früher gehabt hätte!**

146 sonst

The word **sonst** is very versatile. It is used in a variety of ways:

1. as an adverb meaning *in other times; formerly; in other cases.*

> **Sonst war er immer so fröhlich, aber jetzt lacht er kaum mehr.**
> He always used to be so cheerful, but now he rarely laughs anymore.

2. as an adverb meaning *else, besides, otherwise.*

> **Sonst noch etwas, bitte?**
> Anything else, please?
>
> **Das Essen ist nicht besonders gut, aber sonst gefällt es mir hier.**
> The food is not particularly good, but otherwise I like it here.

3. as a conjunction (which occupies the front field), meaning *otherwise; or else.* In this case, **sonst** replaces a **wenn**-clause.

> **Du mußt deine Medizin nehmen, sonst wirst du nicht gesund.**
> You must take your medicine, or else you won't get well.

> Hat es dir in Salzburg gefallen? —Natürlich, sonst wäre ich doch nicht so
>   lange geblieben.
> Did you like it in Salzburg? —Of course, otherwise I wouldn't have stayed
>   so long.

The adverb **umsonst** means *in vain*; or *free, without charge, for nothing*.

> Ich bin umsonst zu ihm in die Wohnung gefahren; er war gar nicht da.
> Was hast du denn dafür bezahlt? —Gar nichts, ich habe es umsonst be-
>   kommen.

147 ja

The most obvious use of **ja,** of course, is to answer a question. Frequently, however, it is used in the same position and with the same affirmative function, even if there is no question or previous conversation. Similar to English *well*, this **ja** can precede any reaction.

Ja, das ist aber schön, daß ihr doch noch gekommen seid.	Well, how nice that you came after all.
Ja, was machen wir denn jetzt?	Well, what are we going to do now?

It also occurs very frequently as an unstressed sentence adverb in two functions:

1. The speaker wants to express the idea that the facts asserted are well known and accepted by both speaker and listener.

Bei uns regnet es im Sommer ja sehr oft.	As you know, we have lots of rain during the summer.
Wir müssen ja alle einmal sterben.	We've all got to die, you know.

2. In sentences spoken with emphatic stress, **ja** heightens the emotional flavor.

> Das ist ja *himm*lisch.
> Ich *komm*e ja schon.
> Ich bin ja *so* glücklich.
> Das ist ja nicht *mög*lich.

When used as a sentence adverb, **ja** follows items of no news value and precedes items with news value, unless the verb itself is stressed.

148 Word Formation

Adverbs in **-erweise**

These sentence adverbs are formed from adjectives and express a judgment.

glücklicherweise	fortunately, it is fortunate that
möglicherweise	possibly, it is possible that
normalerweise	normally, as a rule, it is normal that

Adverbs in **-ens**

The following derivatives are frequently used:

frühestens	at the earliest	**nächstens**	in the near future
spätestens	at the latest	**mindestens**	at least
höchstens	at most	**wenigstens**	at least
meistens	in most cases, mostly		

Conversations

I

HERR STRAUSS: Wann nimmst du denn dieses Jahr deinen Urlaub,* Kurt?

HERR GSCHEIDLE: Früher als sonst. Unsere Firma macht dieses Jahr schon im Juni Betriebsferien,* und da müssen wir, ob wir wollen oder nicht.

HERR STRAUSS: Na ja, das muß nicht unbedingt ein Nachteil sein. Im Juni haben doch die Schulferien* noch nicht angefangen.

HERR GSCHEIDLE: Da hast du natürlich recht; aber wir wollten eigentlich wieder an die Ostsee, an den Ort, wo wir letztes Jahr waren, und da ist es um die Zeit noch zu kalt.

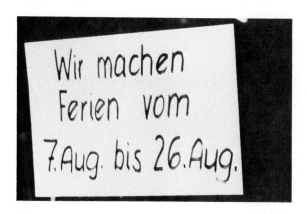

II

An einer Tankstelle:

TANKWART: Voll machen?

HERR GSCHEIDLE: Ja, bitte, mit Super.

TANKWART: Soll ich auch das Öl und das Wasser nachsehen?

HERR GSCHEIDLE: Ja, und sehen Sie doch auch mal nach den Reifen.

---

*The words **der Urlaub** and **die Ferien** (pl. only) both mean *vacation*; generally, **Urlaub** is used in the case of white- or blue-collar workers, and **Ferien** is always used for school vacations. The term **Betriebsferien** is used when an entire firm, whether corner grocery store or industrial plant, shuts down for two or three weeks and all employees have to take their vacation at the same time.

```
Quittung        Gscheidle
Herrn
Frau
Firma

_____ Ltr. Benzin _____

_____ Ltr. Super _____
52   Ltr. Diesel _____              52.—
_____ Ltr. Gemisch _____

_____ Ltr. Motorenöl _____

_____

_____

Wagen-Waschen _____

Abschmieren _____

_____

               Gesamtbetrag DM      52.—

Betrag dankend erhalten

_____        _____
  Tag                Unterschrift

Verkauf der Treibstoffe erfolgt im Namen und auf Rechnung der
         Firma F. G. Förster & Co. KG., Hanau.
    Im Endbetrag sind 11% Mehrwertsteuer enthalten
```

TANKWART (beim Scheibenwaschen):	Das ist ja direkt ein Insektenfriedhof.
HERR GSCHEIDLE:	Ja, wir sind gerade zwei Stunden am Fluß entlanggefahren.
TANKWART:	Ah, *daher.*° *that's why*

TANKWART:	Öl ist O.K., und das Wasser ist auch in Ordnung, aber die Vorderreifen sind ein bißchen niedrig, —nur 1,9.* Die Hinterreifen haben 2,5.
HERR GSCHEIDLE:	Dann machen Sie es vorne doch 2,1, ja?

HERR GSCHEIDLE:	So, was bekommen Sie jetzt von mir?
TANKWART:	118 Schilling. Brauchen Sie eine Quittung?
HERR GSCHEIDLE:	Nein, danke. —Sagen Sie, wie weit ist es noch nach Innsbruck?
TANKWART:	38 Kilometer. In einer halben Stunde sind Sie garantiert da.
HERR GSCHEIDLE:	Na, ich weiß nicht; bei *dem* Verkehr. —Also, Wiedersehen.
TANKWART:	Auf Wiederschaun, —und gute Fahrt.

III

Paßkontrolle und Zoll:

ZOLLBEAMTER:	Darf ich mal Ihren Ausweis sehen?
JOHN RAY:	Ja bitte, —hier ist mein Paß.
ZOLLBEAMTER:	Ah, Sie sind Amerikaner. Und wie lange wollen Sie in Österreich bleiben?
JOHN RAY:	Nur ein, zwei Tage. Ich bin auf der Durchreise nach Italien.
ZOLLBEAMTER:	Haben Sie etwas zu verzollen? Zigaretten? Alkohol?
JOHN RAY:	Nein, gar nichts. So viel Platz habe ich gar nicht in meinem Rucksack.
ZOLLBEAMTER:	Vielen Dank, —und gute Reise.

*In Europe, tire pressure is measured in **atü**; **1,9 atü** stands for **1,9 Atmosphären Überdruck** or 1.9 times normal atmospheric pressure. This corresponds to 27 psi (pounds per square inch). Read **1,9** as "eins komma neun," **2,5** as "zwei komma fünf," etc.

WAS IST ZOLLFREI?

Information für Reisende, die
in Österreich wohnhaft sind.

IV

FRAU SCHUSTER: Wir fahren diesen Sommer überhaupt nicht weg.

FRAU VOGT: Warum denn nicht? Ihr seid doch sonst immer nach Jugoslawien gefahren.

FRAU SCHUSTER: Ja, aber diesmal wollen wir lieber im Winter Urlaub machen.

FRAU VOGT: Aha, zum Schilaufen.

FRAU SCHUSTER: Na klar. Und zwar wollen wir entweder in den Harz oder ins Allgäu.

Iveco: Busse, die einen Fahrgast nie warten lassen.

V

Make another topical vocabulary list, this time on vacation, travel, tourism, etc. Then have your teacher act the role of a policeman, travel agent, customs officer, ticket agent, or just an ordinary Central European with whom you want to talk about traveling.

Fragen an Sie persönlich

1. Wo und wie haben Sie die Sommerferien verbracht?
    Winterferien
    Osterferien
    Weihnachtsferien

2. Wie würden Sie gern Ihre nächsten Ferien verbringen?

    Wo würden Sie hinfahren, wenn Sie viel Zeit und viel Geld hätten? Und warum? (Use subjunctives.)

3. Was wissen Sie über Urlaub, Ferien und Tourismus in Deutschland, Österreich, in der Schweiz, in Europa? (Use subjunctive modals.)

4. Was halten Sie von den Eisenbahnen in Amerika?

    Wie wäre es, wenn die Eisenbahnen in Amerika so gut wären wie in Europa?

5. Wie, meinen Sie, könnte man das Energieproblem im Verkehr lösen?

Reading

I

Woher wußten Sie denn, daß ich Amerikanerin bin?

Ich weiß, mein Deutsch ist gut und fast akzentfrei; und wenn ich nach Deutschland fahre, glaubt man oft, daß ich in Deutschland geboren bin. Aber letztes Jahr habe ich gelernt, daß man mehr als die Sprache können muß, wenn man nicht will, daß jeder sofort weiß, daß man Amerikaner ist. 5

Ich war mit meinem Mann in Hamburg, und wir wohnten in den Vier Jahreszeiten. Morgens im Frühstückszimmer saßen wir kaum an unserem Tisch, als der Kellner kam und uns fragte: "And what would you like for breakfast?" Woher wußte er, daß wir Amerikaner waren?

Vier Jahreszeiten Four Seasons

Mein Kleid hatte ich am Tage vorher in Hamburg gekauft; ich hatte 10 keinen Lippenstift an, und meine Dauerwelle hatte ich mir in Köln machen lassen. Außerdem las mein Mann eine Hamburger Zeitung. Und trotzdem sagte der Kellner: "What would you like for breakfast?" Ich war neugierig und fragte: „Herr Ober, woher wissen Sie, daß wir Amerikaner sind?" 15

der Lippenstift,-e lipstick
die Dauerwelle permanent
neugierig curious

„Wenn man seit dreißig Jahren Kellner ist, dann sieht man das sofort, gnädige Frau", sagte er auf Deutsch. „Als Sie Platz nahmen, hat Ihnen Ihr Mann den Stuhl gehalten,—und das tut man in Deutschland nicht. Und als ich an Ihren Tisch kam, habe ich sofort gesehen, daß Sie Ihren Ring an der linken Hand tragen,—und das tut man in 20 Deutschland nur, solange man verlobt ist."

„Und woher wußten Sie, daß wir verheiratet sind?"

„Gnädige Frau, das darf ich Ihnen wirklich nicht sagen."

„Das brauchen Sie auch nicht", sagte mein Mann, der bis jetzt hinter seiner Zeitung gesessen und nichts gesagt hatte. Er grinste, faltete die 25 Zeitung zusammen, gab sie dem Kellner und sagte: „Herr Ober, Sie sind ein Menschenkenner.—Also: zwei Orangensaft, Spiegeleier mit Schinken, Toast und Kaffee."

grinsen to grin
zusammenfalten to fold
der Saft juice
Spiegelei fried egg, sunny side up
der Schinken ham

"In other words, an American breakfast," sagte der Ober und verschwand. 30

Guten Morgen! Was möchten Sie gern zum Frühstück, bitte?

Portion Kaffee — Nescafé — Tee — Schokolade
mit Butter, Konfitüre, Marmelade, Honig, Brot,
Brötchen, Hörnchen, Zwieback   3,50

Eierspeisen

1 weichgekochtes Ei	—,60
2 Eier im Glas	1,20
2 Stück Rühreier oder Spiegeleier	1,50
2 Spiegeleier mit Schinken oder Speck	2,50

Diverses

Käse nach Wahl	1,30
Porridge mit Sahne und Zucker	1,50
Cornflakes mit Sahne oder Milch	1,50
Joghurt mit Zucker	1,—

Kleine Fleischbeilage

Wurstaufschnitt	1,30
Spezial-Frühstücksteller	1,50
Gekochter Schinken	1,80
Roher Räucherschinken	2,—
Roastbeef	2,—

Fruchtsäfte und Früchte

Orangensaft, frisch gepreßt	1,50
Grapefruitsaft	1,25
Tomatensaft	1,25
Karottensaft, frisch	1,50
Frische halbe Pampelmuse	1,—
Geeiste Melone	nach Jahreszeit
Gemischtes Kompott oder Backpflaumen mit Sahne	2,—
Frisches Obst	zum Tagespreis

15 % Etage · Etagenaufschlag pro Person DM 0,50 · 10 % Service

Good morning! What would you like for breakfast, please?

Coffee — Nescafé — tea — chocolate
compl. with butter, jam, marmelade, honey,
rolls, recent-rolls, bread, biscuits   3,50

Egg - dishes

1 soft boiled egg	—,60
2 boiled eggs in a glass	1,20
Scrambled eggs or fried eggs	1,50
2 fried eggs with ham or bacon	2,50

Sundries

Assorted cheese	1,30
Porridge with cream and sugar	1,50
Cornflakes with cream or milk	1,50
Yoghurt with sugar	1,—

Small meat supplements

Sausages cold meat	1,30
Assorted cold meat	1,50
Boiled ham	1,80
Smoked ham	2,—
Roastbeef	2,—

Fruit and fruit-juices

Orange juice, fresh	1,50
Grapefruit juice	1,25
Tomato juice	1,25
Carrots juice, fresh	1,50
Fresh half grapefruit	1,—
Mixed fruits or stewed prunes with cream	2,—
Fresh fruit	price of day

15 % room-service · room-tax per person DM 0,50 · 10 % service

II

FRANZ KAFKA

Franz Kafka (born 1883 in Prague), though most of his works were published posthumously, was one of the most influential prose writers of this century. Among his best-known works are the novels *Der Prozeß* (The Trial) and *Das Schloß* (The Castle) and such stories as *Das Urteil* (The Judgment), *Die Verwandlung* (Metamorphosis), and *Der Landarzt* (The Country Doctor). He died in 1924. The short piece below was written around 1920–22.

Franz Kafka.

Heimkehr

Ich bin zurückgekehrt, ich habe den Flur durchschritten und blicke mich um. Es ist meines Vaters alter Hof. Die Pfütze in der Mitte. Altes, unbrauchbares Gerät, ineinanderverfahren, verstellt den Weg zur Bodentreppe. Die Katze lauert auf dem Geländer. Ein zerrissenes Tuch, einmal im Spiel um eine Stange gewunden, hebt sich im Wind. Ich bin angekommen. Wer wird mich empfangen? Wer wartet hinter der Tür der Küche? Rauch kommt aus dem Schornstein, der Kaffee zum Abendessen wird gekocht. Ist dir heimlich, fühlst du dich zu Hause? Ich weiß es nicht, ich bin sehr unsicher. Meines Vaters Haus ist es, aber kalt steht Stück neben Stück, als wäre jedes mit seinen eigenen Angelegenheiten beschäftigt, die ich teils vergessen habe, teils niemals kannte. Was kann ich ihnen nützen, was bin ich ihnen und sei ich auch des Vaters, des alten Landwirts Sohn. Und ich wage nicht, an der Küchentür zu klopfen, nur von der Ferne horche ich, nur von der Ferne horche ich stehend, nicht so, daß ich als Horcher überrascht werden könnte. Und weil ich von der Ferne horche, erhorche ich nichts, nur einen leichten Uhrenschlag höre ich oder glaube ihn vielleicht nur zu hören, herüber aus den Kindertagen. Was sonst in der Küche geschieht, ist das Geheimnis der dort Sitzenden, das sie vor mir wahren. Je länger man

Homecoming

I have returned, I have crossed the entranceway and am looking around. It is my father's old place. The puddle in the middle. Old, unusable equipment, shoved into a heap, bars the way to the stairway to the loft. The cat lies in wait on the railing. A torn cloth, wound around a stake once at play, rises in the wind. I have arrived. Who will receive me? Who is waiting behind the kitchen door? Smoke comes from the chimney, coffee for supper is being made. Do you feel at home? I don't know, I am very unsure. My father's house it is, but coldly piece stands by piece, as if each were occupied with its own affairs which partly I have forgotten, partly never knew. Of what use can I be to them, what am I to them, even if I am my father's, the old farmer's, son. And I dare not knock at the kitchen door, only from the distance I listen, only from the distance I listen, standing, not in such a way that I could be surprised as an eavesdropper. And because I listen from a distance, I hear nothing, only the soft ring of a clock do I hear, or perhaps I only imagine hearing it, from the days of my childhood.

What else happens in the kitchen is the secret of those sitting there, which they keep from me. The longer you hesitate in

vor der Tür zögert, desto fremder wird man. Wie wäre es, wenn jetzt jemand die Tür öffnete und mich etwas fragte. Wäre ich dann nicht selbst wie einer, der sein Geheimnis wahren will.

front of the door, the more of a stranger you become. How would it be if someone opened the door now and asked me something. Would I then myself not be like one who 5 wants to keep his secret.

III

AUS DER BIBEL

Das Gleichnis vom verlornen Sohn

Aus dem Evangelium nach Lukas 15:11–32

The Parable of the Prodigal Son

From The Gospel According to Luke 15: 11–32

[11] Er sprach aber: Ein Mann hatte zwei Söhne. [12] Und der jüngere von ihnen sagte zum Vater: Vater, gib mir den Teil des Vermögens, der mir zukommt! Der aber verteilte seine Habe unter sie. [13] Und nicht viele Tage darnach nahm der jüngere Sohn alles mit sich und zog hinweg in ein fernes Land, und dort vergeudete er sein Vermögen durch ein zügelloses Leben. [14] Nachdem er aber alles durchgebracht hatte, kam eine gewaltige Hungersnot über jenes Land, und er fing an, Mangel zu leiden. [15] Und er ging hin und hängte sich an einen der Bürger jenes Landes; der schickte ihn auf seine Felder, Schweine zu hüten. [16] Und er begehrte, seinen Bauch mit den Schoten zu füllen, die die Schweine fraßen: und niemand gab sie ihm. [17] Da ging er in sich und sprach: Wie viele Tagelöhner meines Vaters haben Brot im Überfluß, ich aber komme hier vor Hunger um! [18] Ich will mich aufmachen und zu meinem Vater gehen und zu ihm sagen: Vater, ich habe gesündigt gegen den Himmel und vor dir; [19] ich bin nicht mehr wert, dein Sohn zu heißen; stelle mich wie einen deiner Tagelöhner! [20] Und er machte sich auf und ging zu seinem Vater. Als er aber noch fern war, sah ihn sein Vater und fühlte Erbarmen, lief hin, fiel ihm um den Hals und küßte ihn. [21] Der Sohn aber sprach zu ihm: Vater, ich habe gesündigt gegen den Himmel und vor dir; ich bin nicht mehr wert, dein Sohn zu heißen. [22] Doch der Vater sagte zu seinen Knechten: Bringet schnell das beste Kleid

[11] Again he said: 'There was once a man who had two sons; [12] and the younger said to his father, "Father, give me my share of the property." So he divided his estate between them. [13] A few days later the younger son turned the whole of his share into cash and left home for a distant country, where he squandered it in reckless living. [14] He had spent it all, when a severe famine fell upon that country and he began to feel the pinch. [15] So he went and attached himself to one of the local landowners, who sent him on to his farm to mind the pigs. [16] He would have been glad to fill his belly with the pods that the pigs were eating; and no one gave him anything. [17] Then he came to his senses and said, "How many of my father's paid servants have more food than they can eat, and here am I, starving to death! [18] I will set off and go to my father, and say to him, 'Father, I have sinned, against God and against you; [19] I am no longer fit to be called your son; treat me as one of your paid servants.'" [20] So he set out for his father's house. But while he was still a long way off his father saw him, and his heart went out to him. He ran to meet him, flung his arms round him, and kissed him. [21] The son said, "Father, I have sinned, against God and against you; I am no longer fit to be called your son." [22] But the father said to his servants, "Quick! fetch a robe, my best one, and put it on him; put a ring on his finger and shoes on his feet. [23] Bring the fatted calf and kill it, and let us have a feast to

heraus und ziehet es ihm an und gebet ihm einen Ring an die Hand und Schuhe an die Füße, ²³ und holet das gemästete Kalb, schlachtet es und lasset uns essen und fröhlich sein! ²⁴ Denn dieser mein Sohn war tot ⁵ und ist wieder lebendig geworden, er war verloren und ist wiedergefunden worden. Und sie fingen an, fröhlich zu sein.

²⁵ Sein älterer Sohn aber war auf dem Felde; und als er kam und sich dem Hause 10 näherte, hörte er Musik und Reigentanz. ²⁶ Und er rief einen der Knechte herbei und erkundigte sich, was das sei. ²⁷ Der aber sagte ihm: Dein Bruder ist gekommen, und dein Vater hat das gemästete Kalb ge-15 schlachtet, weil er ihn gesund wiedererhalten hat. ²⁸ Da wurde er zornig und wollte nicht hineingehen. Doch sein Vater kam heraus und redete ihm zu. ²⁹ Er aber antwortete und sagte zum Vater: Siehe, so viele Jahre diene 20 ich dir und habe nie ein Gebot von dir übertreten; und mir hast du nie einen Bock gegeben, damit ich mit meinen Freunden fröhlich wäre. ³⁰ Nun aber dieser dein Sohn gekommen ist, der deine Habe mit Dirnen auf- 25 gezehrt hat, hast du ihm das gemästete Kalb geschlachtet. ³¹ Da sagte er zu ihm: Kind, du bist allezeit bei mir, und alles, was mein ist, ist dein. ³² Du solltest aber fröhlich sein und dich freuen; denn dieser dein Bruder war tot 30 und ist lebendig geworden, und war verloren und ist wiedergefunden worden.

celebrate the day. ²⁴ For this son of mine was dead and has come back to life; he was lost and is found." And the festivities began.

²⁵ 'Now the elder son was out on the farm; and on his way back, as he approached the house, he heard music and dancing. ²⁶ He called one of the servants and asked what it meant. ²⁷ The servant told him, "Your brother has come home, and your father has killed the fatted calf because he has him back safe and sound." ²⁸ But he was angry and refused to go in. His father came out and pleaded with him; ²⁹ but he retorted, "You know how I have slaved for you all these years; I never once disobeyed your orders; and you never gave me so much as a kid, for a feast with my friends. ³⁰ But now that this son of yours turns up, after running through your money with his women, you kill the fatted calf for him." ³¹ "My boy," said the father, "you are always with me, and everything I have is yours. ³² How could we help celebrating this happy day? Your brother here was dead and has come back to life, was lost and is found."

IV

Drei Gedichte

Mathias Schreiber

Demokratie

Ich will
du willst
er will
was wir wollen
geschieht   5
aber was geschieht
will keiner von uns

ARNFRID ASTEL

Ostkontakte°	contacts with the East
Als mein Freund kürzlich°	recently
wieder nach Weimar fuhr,	
bat ich ihn,	
mir den Baum zu fotografieren,	
auf dem wir als Kinder 5	
Burgen° gebaut hatten.	castles
Er brachte mir	
eine Fotographie mit,	
darauf waren Kinder zu sehen,	
die auf unserem Baum 10	
eine Burg bauten.	

Grünanlage°	park
Die Überlebenden°	survivors
planieren° die Erde.	level, smooth
Sie sorgen°	provide
für eine schönere	
Vergangenheit.° 5	past

Exercises

A. This exercise reviews verbs with prepositional objects. Express the twenty sentences in German by using the verbs that follow (but not in the same order). All these verbs were used in earlier units, though not necessarily with prepositional objects.

SEE
ANALYSIS
137–138
(pp. 351–353)

1. Of course we count on you, Mr. Meyer. It wouldn't be a party without you.
2. This rice is very good; it tastes of paprika.
3. You can pay in dollars too, if you want to.
4. I am ready for everything.
5. I wouldn't have expected that of him.
6. On my birthday he surprised me with flowers.
7. That was very nice of him.
8. We'll now begin with the movie.
9. I recommended him to Professor Haudegen.
10. I will talk with Mr. Schulz about it.
11. I wish I could spend my vacation with Rosemarie.
12. Write to Dr. Müller. I'm sure he'll help you.
13. We called out for him, but he didn't hear us.
14. Be nice to her.
15. Why am I so tired? It must be the weather. (**liegen an**)
16. What does one use this machine for?
17. I had always regarded him as my friend.
18. Could you please help me with my work?
19. You should mix your wine with water.
20. Stop this nonsense. (**der Unsinn**)

aufhören mit (*dat.*)   nett sein von (*dat.*) (or: lieb sein von)
beginnen mit (*dat.*)   nett sein zu (*dat.*)
bereit sein zu (*dat.*)   rechnen mit (*dat.*)
benutzen zu (*dat.*)   reden mit (*dat.*) über (*acc.*)
betrachten als (*acc.*)   rufen nach (*dat.*)
empfehlen an (*acc.*)   schmecken nach (*dat.*)
erwarten von (*dat.*)   schreiben an (*acc.*)
helfen bei (*dat.*)   überraschen mit (*dat.*)
liegen an (*dat.*)   verbringen mit (*dat.*)
mischen mit (*dat.*)   zahlen mit (*dat.*)

B. In the following sentences, change the present infinitives to past infinitives; then translate into English.

> **Maria muß schon aufstehen.**
> **Maria muß schon aufgestanden sein.**

1. Meyer muß nach Berlin fahren.
2. Er scheint sehr freundlich zu sein.
3. Er wird wohl nicht zu Hause sein.
4. Sie kann doch nicht schon wieder spazieren-gehen.
5. Ihr Mann muß sehr viel Geld haben.

SEE ANALYSIS 139 (p. 393)

C. Change the following sentences, all containing objective modals, from present indicative to present subjunctive and add **eigentlich** in the place indicated by /. Then translate these sentences into English.

1. Ich soll / um sechs Uhr zu Hause sein.
2. Hans muß / hierbleiben.
3. Wir müssen heute abend / schon wieder ausgehen.
4. Wir können / auch einmal ins Theater gehen.
5. Ich kann ja / auch mit *Inge* spazierengehen.

SEE ANALYSIS 140 (p. 393)

D. Change the following sentences in two ways: (a) Change the modal to the perfect; (b) keep the modal in the present and change the infinitive to a past infinitive. Then translate the two resulting sentences so as to show the difference in meaning.

> **Er soll um acht Uhr zu Hause sein.**
> (a) **Er hat um acht Uhr zu Hause sein sollen.**   He had to be home at eight.
> (b) **Er soll um acht Uhr zu Hause gewesen sein.**   He is said to have been at home at eight.

1. Er kann nicht in Berlin arbeiten.
2. Ingelheim muß Soldat werden.
3. Sie muß in die Stadt fahren.
4. Meyer will ein Haus in Tirol kaufen.
5. Ingelheim soll Arabisch lernen.

SEE ANALYSIS 140 (p. 393)

E. By using the proper forms of modals, express in one sentence each of the following ideas.

1. There is a rumor that he has been sick.
2. Meyer claims that he was in Africa again.
3. I came to the conclusion that he was living in Berlin.
4. I have arrived at the conclusion that he had been in America.
5. You should have gone to Berlin two years ago.
6. There was a rumor that she had gone to Berlin.
7. It is possible that he is still here.

SEE ANALYSIS 140 (p. 393)

8. It is not possible that he was in Berlin.
9. It has never been possible for him to go to Berlin.
10. He tries to give the impression that he was a friend of my father's.

F. Change the following sentences from the past indicative to the past subjunctive. Add **eigentlich** in the place indicated by /.

> **Ich mußte gestern nach Berlin fahren.**
> **Ich hätte gestern eigentlich nach Berlin fahren müssen.**

SEE
ANALYSIS
140
(p. 393)

1. Ich sollte gestern / meine Mutter besuchen.
2. Ich durfte es Ihnen / nicht sagen.
3. Ich brauchte / gar nichts zu sagen.
4. Ich konnte damals / auch nach Rom fliegen.
5. Mir konntest du das ja / erzählen.

G. In the following sentences, change the modals from indicative to subjunctive. Then translate each pair of sentences into English.

SEE
ANALYSIS
140
(p. 393)

1. Er kann, wenn er will.
2. Ich konnte auch mitgehen.
3. Ich muß auch einmal nach Italien fahren.
4. Ich mußte gestern zu Hause bleiben.
5. Sie sollen nicht so viel rauchen.
6. Sein Sohn sollte in Heidelberg studieren.

H. Without changing word order, negate the following sentences by using **nicht** in two different positions. How does the different position of **nicht** change the meaning of the sentence?

SEE
ANALYSIS
142
(p. 398)

1. Ich möchte mit Rosemarie ins Theater gehen.
2. Meyer hat lange arbeiten können.
3. Ich bin oft ins Kino gegangen.
4. Ich kann aber auf dem Sofa schlafen.
5. Sie wollte aber den Meyer heiraten.

I. Using the **nicht A, sondern B** pattern, combine the following pairs of sentences.

> **Wir fahren nicht im Juli nach Berlin. Wir fahren im August.**
> (a) **Wir fahren nicht im Juli, sondern im August nach Berlin.**
> (b) **Wir fahren nicht im Juli nach Berlin, sondern im August.**

SEE
ANALYSIS
143
(p. 399)

1. Ich habe nicht meine Mutter besucht. Ich habe meinen Vater besucht.
2. Er hat nicht acht Stunden gearbeitet. Er hat nur zwei Stunden gearbeitet.
3. Gestern abend hat Erich keinen Wein getrunken. Er hat nur Bier getrunken.
4. Er hat mir kein Buch geschenkt. Er hat mir eine Uhr geschenkt.

J. Connect the following pairs of sentences by means of the words in parentheses. Which of the connecting words are adverbs, which are coordinating conjunctions, and which are subordinating conjunctions?

1. Ich habe nichts davon gewußt. Er hat mir nicht geschrieben. (weil)
2. Er stand lange vor der Tür. Er klopfte endlich an. (dann)
3. Er wollte nicht mit Professor Müller sprechen. Er hatte Angst vor ihm. (denn)
4. Er war krank. Ich konnte ihn nicht besuchen. (daher)
5. Ich konnte ihn nicht besuchen. Er war krank. (da)
6. Ich rief von Paris aus an. Mein Flugzeug hatte Verspätung. (weil)
7. Er fuhr sofort nach Hamburg. Er hatte meinen Brief bekommen. (nachdem)

8. Sollen wir ins Kino gehen? Sollen wir zu Hause bleiben? (oder)
9. Tante Amalie kommt morgen. Wir gehen bestimmt wieder ins Museum. (Wenn . . . , dann)
10. Fritzchen ist Arzt geworden. Ich kann es nicht glauben. (Daß . . . , das)
11. Ich habe Erich nicht mehr gesehen. Wir haben das Abitur gemacht. (seit)
12. Ich war mit Erich zusammen auf der Schule. Ich habe ihn nicht mehr gesehen. (seitdem)
13. Er ist nicht mit ins Kino gegangen. Er hat seiner Frau einen Brief geschrieben. (sondern)
14. Der Meyer will mich heiraten. Ich kann nur lachen. (Daß . . . , darüber)
15. Er hätte eigentlich um zehn nach Hause gehen sollen. Er blieb bis elf. (trotzdem)
16. Er blieb bis elf. Er sollte um zehn zu Hause sein. (obwohl)
17. Ich habe ihn lange gesucht. Ich habe ihn nicht finden können. (aber)
18. Er hat mir nicht geschrieben. Ich habe ihm auch nicht mehr geschrieben. (darum)
19. Gestern habe ich bei Meyers eine Frau kennengelernt. Ihr Mann soll Arabisch sprechen. (deren)
20. Ich kenne Erich nicht. Ich kenne Hans nicht. (weder . . . noch)
21. Wir wollen meine Mutter in Hamburg besuchen. Sie kommt zu uns nach München. (entweder . . . oder)

K. The following sentences contain a dependent clause introduced by **weil.** By changing the **weil**-clause, first into a conditional clause with **wenn** and then without **wenn,** transform the sentences into contrary-to-fact conditions. Start all sentences with the conditional clause.

> **Weil er krank war, konnte er nicht arbeiten.**
> (a) **Wenn er nicht krank gewesen wäre, hätte er arbeiten können.**
> (b) **Wäre er nicht krank gewesen, dann hätte er arbeiten können.**

1. Weil ich nicht so viel Geld hatte wie Meyer, konnte ich nicht an der Riviera wohnen.
2. Weil es mir in Hamburg zu kalt war, bin ich nach Afrika gefahren.
3. Er kam spät nach Hause, weil er ins Kino gegangen war.
4. Wir mußten zu Hause bleiben, weil es so stark regnete.
5. Weil das Essen so schlecht war, fuhren wir nach Hause.

SEE ANALYSIS 144 (p. 399)

L. Change the following statements to wishes contrary to fact, using either **doch nur** or **doch nur nicht** and starting with **wenn** and then without **wenn.** (Like **eigentlich, doch nur** follows the pronouns and elements of no news value.)

> **Er ist nach Italien gefahren.**
> (a) **Wenn er doch nur nicht nach Italien gefahren wäre.**
> (b) **Wäre er doch nur nicht nach Italien gefahren.**

1. Er kam so oft.
2. Er hat mir nicht geschrieben, daß er Geld braucht.
3. Sie hat mir gesagt, daß sie Thusnelda heißt.
4. Vor den Sommerferien ist sie krank geworden.
5. Ich habe nicht gewußt, daß du auch in Berlin warst.

SEE ANALYSIS 144 (p. 399)

M. In the following sentences, change the first clause into a real or irreal **wenn**-clause; leave out **sonst.**

> **Der Wein ist gut. Sonst wäre ich nicht mehr hier.**
> **Wenn der Wein nicht so gut wäre, wäre ich nicht mehr hier.**

SEE
ANALYSIS
145
(p. 400)

1. Du mußt die Medizin regelmäßig nehmen, sonst wirst du nicht gesund.
2. Er ist krank. Sonst wäre er bestimmt gekommen.
3. Du mußt schnell fahren, sonst kommen wir zu spät.
4. Du darfst nicht so spät ins Bett gehen, sonst bist du morgen den ganzen Tag müde.
5. Er fuhr mit dem Wagen, denn sonst hätte er dreimal umsteigen müssen.

N. Express in German.

1. He must have waited for me for three hours.
2. He had to wait for me for three hours.
3. He can't have slept long. I called him up at seven o'clock, but I couldn't reach him anymore.
4. Had he sent the letter to me, I could have answered him immediately.
5. His letter must have arrived when I had already gone to Munich.
6. The man you claim to have seen cannot have been von Hollenbeck.
7. He has always wanted to go to Rome.
8. He cannot have been in Rome.
9. Erich has probably already been here.
10. Erika seems to have arrived already.
11. I don't think much of him.
12. I often think of you.
13. He ought to have arrived an hour ago.
14. Dr. Schmidt was at the Meyers' too; you must have met him there.
15. It could not have been Erich, for I knew that Erich had gone to the airport to pick up Hans.
16. Could I have another cup of coffee, please?
17. Could you work in the garden yesterday?
18. Of course we could have gone to the movies, but we didn't want to.
19. He is said to be seventy years old, but he looks as though he were only fifty.
20. She may have thought that Erich wanted to help her.

O. Composition. Write on the following topic, using as many modals as possible.

Yesterday you saw your friend Fridolin whom you hadn't seen in a long time. Fridolin claims to have become a writer, and that he travels to all sorts of countries. Since you don't believe that, list a number of reasons why it cannot be true.

Vocabulary

der Ausweis, -e	identification paper, I.D. card	**die Energie′, -n**	energy
		entlang	along
behaupten	to claim, maintain, assert	**am Rhein entlang**	along the Rhine
		die Erholung	recreation; recuperation
bemerken	to notice; to remark		
bereit sein zu (*dat.*)	to be ready for	**fliehen**	to flee
beschreiben	to describe	**frühestens**	at the earliest
besichtigen	to visit, look at, inspect	**der Führerschein, -e**	driver's license
betrachten als (*acc.*)	to consider (as)	**garantiert**	guaranteed; I guarantee you
dauernd	constantly, incessantly		
die Demokratie, -n	democracy	**hinten** (*adv.*)	in the back
der Dieb, -e	thief	**höflich**	polite
echt	genuine	**unhöflich**	impolite
einrichten	to furnish	**die Jahreszeit, -en**	season

klar	of course, sure	die Scheibe, -n	(glass) pane, wind-
na klar			shield; slice
das Kleid, -er	dress	der Schinken, -	ham
kürzlich	recently	die Schwierigkeit, -en	difficulty
liegen an	to be due to	die See (*no pl.*)	sea, ocean
merken	to notice	der See, -n	lake
der Monat, -e	month	solange (*conj.*)	as long as
nächstens	in the near future	spätestens	at the latest
der Nachteil, -e	disadvantage	stehlen	to steal
niedrig	low	der Stuhl, ⸚e	chair
das Öl, -e	oil	der Tag, -e	day
(die) Ostern (*pl.*)	Easter	den ganzen Tag	all day
die Osterferien	Easter vacation	umsonst	in vain; for nothing
der Paß, die Pässe	passport	der Urlaub	leave; vacation
pünktlich	on time, punctually,	verzollen	to declare; to pay
	on the dot		duty on
der Reifen, -	wheel (of a car)	voll machen	to fill up
der Vorderreifen, -	front wheel	vorne (*adv.*)	in front
der Hinterreifen, -	rear wheel	wegfahren	to leave, depart (by car,
die Reise, -n	trip		etc.), drive away
die Geschäftsreise, -n	business trip	auf Wiederschaun	Austrian for **auf**
der Ring, -e	ring		**Wiedersehen**
der Rucksack, ⸚e	backpack	das Wochenende, -n	weekend
rufen nach (*dat.*)	to shout, call out for	der Zufall, ⸚e	accident, chance

Additional Vocabulary

anklopfen	to knock (on a door)	die Perle, -n	pearl
der Badeort, -e	resort	die Quittung, -en	receipt
die Dauerwelle, -n	permanent (wave)	das Sofa, -s	sofa
die Durchreise	transit	der Spiegel, -	mirror
ertrinken	to drown	das Spiegelei, -er	fried egg
falten	to fold	das Sprichwort, ⸚er	proverb
fröhlich	cheerful	verhaften	to arrest
grinsen	to grin	das Vermögen, -	fortune, estate
himmlisch	heavenly	er hat ein	he is worth ten
die Lippe, -n	lip	Vermögen von	million
der Lippenstift, -e	lipstick	zehn Millionen	
Mailand	Milan		

Strong Verbs

abfahren	fährt ab	fuhr ab	ist abgefahren	to leave, depart
beschreiben		beschrieb	beschrieben	to describe
ertrinken		ertrank	ist ertrunken	to drown
fliehen		floh	ist geflohen	to flee, escape
stehlen	stiehlt	stahl	gestohlen	to steal

UNIT 14 Reflexive Verbs

Unit 14 introduces reflexive verbs, that is, verbs that are used with reflexive pronouns, as in English *I enjoyed myself.* German uses reflexives far more than English, and you already know many verbs that may be used with reflexive pronouns, but there are also many verbs that *must* be used with reflexive pronouns.

Mastering German reflexives is not difficult, but you will again have to do some memorizing. To facilitate the process, the conversation section of Unit 14 is also arranged around reflexive verbs.

Three verbs, **setzen, stellen,** and **legen,** can be difficult for an American who is used to saying *I'm going to lay down for a while* instead of *I'm going to lie down.* But even if you can keep the forms of *to lie* and *to lay* apart, you'll have to get used to the German way of saying *He sat down,* which is "*He set himself,*" **Er setzte sich.**

The reading selections of Unit 14, following another short prose piece by Kafka, are excerpts from newspapers. German journalese has a style of its own; one of its most prominent features is the "fronting" or "topicalization" of the most newsworthy or most sensational element in the first sentence of a news report. English can achieve the same effect, as, for example, in the change from *Scientists at the Clone Laboratories achieved a great success* to *A great success was achieved by scientists at the Clone Laboratories.* What is not necessary in German, however, is the change from active to passive: **Die Bild-Zeitung bringt heute einen Sex-Skandal** simply becomes **Einen Sex-Skandal bringt heute die Bild-Zeitung.**

Patterns

[1] Reflexive Pronouns

Ich habe mich schon bedient.
  I've already served myself.

Hast du dich schon bedient?
Er hat sich schon bedient.
Wir haben uns schon bedient.
Habt ihr euch schon bedient?
Sie haben sich schon bedient.

SEE
ANALYSIS
149
(p. 425)

417

Ein Selbstbedienungsladen.

Er hat mir ein Auto gekauft.
Er hat sich ein Auto gekauft.

Sie haben uns ein Haus gebaut.
Sie haben sich ein Haus gebaut.

Er konnte es mir einfach nicht erklären.
Er konnte es sich einfach nicht erklären.

Ich halte ihn für dumm, aber er hält sich für sehr intelligent.
Hat er den Porsche für *sich* gekauft oder für seinen Sohn?
Tante Amalie war ganz außer sich (*beside herself*), weil sie keinen Pfennig Geld bei sich hatte.

[2] selbst and selber

SEE
ANALYSIS
150
(p. 426)

Das weiß ich *selbst*.
Ihrer Frau geht es also wieder gut—und wie geht es Ihnen *selbst*?
Ich wollte eigentlich Herrn Meyer nach Berlin schicken; aber ich fahre doch besser *sel*ber hin.
Ich habe nicht mit Meyers Frau gesprochen; ich habe mit ihm *selbst* gesprochen.
Meine Frau hat nicht mit ihm gesprochen; ich habe *selbst* mit ihm gesprochen.

Kaufen Sie Ihr Fleisch doch im Supermarkt; da können Sie sich selbst bedienen.
Dabei brauchst du mir nicht zu helfen; das kann ich *sel*ber machen.
Muß *ich* denn jeden Morgen zuerst aufstehen? Kannst du dir das Frühstück nicht mal *sel*ber machen?

Er *selbst* ist ja ganz *nett*; aber mit seiner *Mut*ter könnte ich nicht *le*ben.
Andere hat er ge*ret*tet, aber sich *selbst kann* er nicht retten.
Uns schickt Vater jeden Sonntag in die *Kir*che, aber er *sel*ber bleibt zu *Hau*se und liest die *Zei*tung.

Ich habe *sel*ber kein Geld.
Ich habe *auch* kein Geld.
Ich kann dir nicht helfen; ich habe *sel*ber viel zu tun.

[3] selbst, sogar, auch meaning *even*

Selbst (sogar, auch) *das* ist ihm zu viel.

Selbst (sogar, auch) Herrn Dr. Müller, der sonst immer da ist, konnte ich diesmal nicht sprechen; der war auch in Berlin.

In Berlin sprechen selbst (sogar, auch) kleine Kinder Deutsch.

Selbst (sogar, auch) von seiner Frau läßt er sich nichts sagen.

SEE ANALYSIS 150 (p. 426)

[4] Reciprocal Pronouns

Note the use of **sich** and **einander**.

Hat er sie zuerst geküßt oder hat sie ihn zuerst geküßt?—Das weiß ich nicht. Aber es ist sicher, daß sie sich geküßt haben.

Wo haben Sie einander denn kennengelernt?—Bei Tante Amalie. Vorher hatten wir uns noch nie gesehen.

Im Sommer hat er ihr das erste Mal geschrieben, und seitdem schreiben sie sich jede Woche zweimal, und mindestens einmal im Monat rufen sie sich an.

Heute abend gehe ich mit ihr ins Theater.—Wo triffst du sie denn?—Wir treffen uns am Bahnhof.

SEE ANALYSIS 151 (p. 428)

[5] Occasional Reflexive Verbs

anziehen: sich anziehen: angezogen sein
to dress (somebody): to get dressed: to be dressed

Hast du den Kleinen schon angezogen?
Der kann sich doch jetzt schon selbst anziehen; den brauche ich nicht mehr anzuziehen.
Ich *bin* schon angezogen, Mutti; ich habe mich *sel*ber angezogen.

beruhigen: sich beruhigen: beruhigt sein
to calm (sb.) down: to calm down: to be calmed down

SEE ANALYSIS 152 (p. 428)

Beruhigen Sie sich, Frau Meyer, Ihrem Mann ist nichts passiert. Ich habe gerade eben mit
ihm telefoniert.
Gottseidank; ich war ja so beunruhigt.
Na, sehen Sie, es ist ja alles in Ordnung, und Sie können ganz beruhigt sein.
Daß Sie mit ihm telefoniert haben, beruhigt mich sehr.

entschuldigen: sich entschuldigen: entschuldigt sein
to excuse: to excuse oneself: to be excused

Ich glaube, Sie sitzen auf meinem Platz.
Oh, entschuldigen Sie, Sie haben recht.
Oh, Entschuldigung, Sie haben recht.
Oh, ich bitte um Entschuldigung.

Entschuldigen Sie, daß ich so spät komme.
Sie brauchen sich gar nicht zu entschuldigen, bei dem Regen ist das ja kein Wunder.—Aber
wo ist denn Herr Schneider?
Schneider kommt nicht; er ist entschuldigt; er mußte nach Berlin.
Entschuldigen Sie mich bitte noch einen Augenblick, bevor wir anfangen, ich muß eben
noch mal telefonieren.

jemanden langweilen: sich langweilen: langweilig
to bore somebody: to be bored: boring

Und dann hat er gesagt: „Ich hoffe, ich langweile Sie nicht."
Wenn der nur gewußt hätte, wie sehr wir uns gelangweilt haben.
War er wirklich so langweilig? Ich muß sagen, ich habe mich in seiner Vorlesung eigentlich
nie gelangweilt.

[6] Mandatory Reflexive Verbs

SEE
ANALYSIS
152
(p. 428)

sich ärgern über (with acc.)
to be annoyed with (by)

Der Meyer ist wirklich ein Dummkopf. Ich habe mich gestern abend furchtbar über ihn
geärgert.
Ich ärgere mich immer darüber, daß er so spät kommt. Gestern abend kam er erst um halb
neun.

sich eilen: sich beeilen
to hurry

Kannst du dich nicht mal ein bißchen beeilen? Wir müssen in zehn Minuten hier wegfahren,
sonst verpassen wir den Zug.
Ich eile mich doch. Ich muß nur eben noch eine Postkarte an Tante Amalie schreiben.

sich irren
to be mistaken, to err

Was, Meyer soll Generaldirektor geworden sein? Bist du sicher, daß du dich da nicht irrst?
Ich weiß, Irren ist menschlich, aber ich irre mich bestimmt nicht; ich habe nämlich gerade
einen Brief von ihm bekommen.

sich wundern über (with acc.)·
to be amazed (surprised) at

Ich habe mich doch gestern abend über den Fritz gewundert. Daß der gar nichts gesagt hat!
　　Früher hat er immer zu viel geredet.
Ich würde mich nicht wundern, wenn er überhaupt nicht mehr zu unserem Stammtisch
　　käme.

[7] Transitional Reflexive Verbs

sich verlieben in (with acc.): **verliebt sein in** (with acc.)
to fall in love with: to be in love with

SEE
ANALYSIS
152
(p. 428)

Fridolin ist schon wieder verliebt.
In wen hat er sich denn diesmal verliebt?—In eine Studentin.

sich verloben mit: verlobt sein mit
to become engaged to: to be engaged to

Weißt du, daß die Emma sich mit einem Zahnarzt verlobt hat?
Ich dachte, die wäre schon lange verlobt. Wie heißt denn ihr Verlobter?—Klaus, —Meyer
　　oder Müller oder so irgendetwas. Und nächsten Sonntag sollen wir zu ihr kommen und
　　Verlobung feiern.

heiraten: sich verheiraten: verheiratet sein mit
to marry: to get married: to be married to

Ich höre, Ihre Tochter will sich verheiraten.
Nein, sie *hat* schon geheiratet, —gestern vor vierzehn Tagen.
Oh, herzlichen Glückwunsch. Mit wem ist sie denn verheiratet?
Mit einem Jungen, mit dem sie schon zusammen auf dem Gymnasium war.

sich scheiden lassen von: geschieden sein
to get a divorce from: to be divorced

Seit ich von Hans geschieden bin, habe ich viel mehr Zeit für mich selbst, und für die Kinder.
Aber damals sagtest du doch immer, du wolltest dich auf keinen Fall scheiden lassen, gerade
　　wegen der Kinder.
Das stimmt; aber nach der Scheidung wußte ich plötzlich, daß es so doch besser war.

[8] Additional Reflexive Verbs*

This section introduces a number of other reflexives: occasional, mandatory, and transitional.

Reg dich doch nicht so furchtbar auf.	Don't get so terribly excited.
Aber ich bin doch gar nicht aufgeregt.	But I'm not excited at all.
Du solltest dich wirklich einmal gut aus- ruhen.	You really ought to get some good rest.

SEE
ANALYSIS
152
(p. 428)

---

*Another group of reflexive verbs is used in the conversations section of this unit. See pp. 432–433.

Wir freuen uns über die Geburt unseres Sohnes

WOLF KRISTOF

11. Februar 1975

*MARGRIT UND
WOLFHARD HOFMANN*

Stuhr, Schwäbisch-Hall-Straße 45

Aber ich habe doch heute morgen bis zehn geschlafen und bin ganz ausgeruht.	But I slept until ten this morning and am completely rested.
Ich freue mich auf eure Party am nächsten Sonntag.	I am looking forward to your party next Sunday.
Ich habe mich wirklich darüber gefreut, daß du an meinen Geburtstag gedacht hast.	I was really pleased that you thought of (remembered) my birthday.
Ich dachte, ich könnte mich nie an dieses Klima gewöhnen, aber jetzt bin ich doch daran gewöhnt.	I thought I could never get used to this climate, but now I'm used to it after all.
Ich habe ihn fast nicht erkannt, so sehr hat er sich verändert.	I almost didn't recognize him, he's changed so much.
Das stimmt. Seit dem Tod seiner Frau ist er ganz verändert.	That's right. Since his wife's death he is completely changed.
Haben Sie sich auch gut vorbereitet?	Have you prepared yourself well?
Ja, Herr Professor, ich glaube, ich bin gut vorbereitet.	Yes, sir, I think I am well prepared.
Na, hast du dich gut erholt?	Well, did you get a good rest?
Ich bin so gut erholt wie noch nie.	I'm as well rested as never before.
Bei Schmidts war es gestern abend so kalt, daß ich mich erkältet habe.	It was so cold at the Schmidts last night that I caught cold.
Hannelore ist auch erkältet. War die auch bei Schmidts?	Hannelore has a cold too; was she at the Schmidts too?
Ich muß mich noch rasieren, bevor wir zu Erdmanns gehen; wenn ich nicht gut rasiert bin, fühle ich mich einfach nicht wohl.	I've got to shave before we go to the Erdmanns; if I'm not well shaven I simply don't feel right.

[9] sich setzen, sich stellen, sich legen

SEE
ANALYSIS
152
(p. 428)

sitzen; setzen: sich setzen

Wer sitzt denn da bei euch am Tisch?—Den kenne ich auch nicht. Der hat sich einfach an unseren Tisch gesetzt.

Nein, unter *diesen* Brief setze ich meinen Namen *nicht*.

Ich wollte mich gerade in die erste Reihe setzen, als ich sah, daß Frau Meier da saß; und da
    habe ich mich in die letzte Reihe gesetzt.

stehen; stellen: sich stellen

Wer steht denn da bei Frau Schmidt? Ist das nicht Dr. Gerhardt?

Diese Cocktailparties machen mich wirklich müde. Ich habe stundenlang stehen müssen und
    war froh, als ich mich endlich setzen konnte.

Ich habe den Wein auf den Tisch gestellt.

Bitte, gnädige Frau, wie wäre es, wenn Sie sich hier auf diesen Stuhl setzten? Und Sie stellen
    sich links neben Ihre Frau, Herr Doktor. Und der Kleine kann rechts von Ihrer Frau
    stehen.—So, und jetzt bitte recht freundlich!

In der Zeitung steht, daß Carola van Dongen wieder geheiratet hat.—So? Auf welcher Seite
    steht das denn?

liegen; legen: sich legen

Ich hatte mich gerade ins Bett gelegt, als Erich anrief. ,,Liegst du etwa schon im Bett?''
    sagte er.

Ich lag noch nicht lange im Bett, als Erich anrief. ,,Hast du dich etwa schon ins Bett gelegt?''
    sagte er.

Wo hast du denn mein Buch hingelegt?—Ich habe es auf deinen Schreibtisch gelegt. Liegt es
    denn nicht mehr dort?

Köln liegt am Rhein. Wolframs-Eschenbach liegt in der Nähe von Nürnberg.

VARIATIONS

Ich habe den Wein auf den Tisch _____.
Der Wein _____ auf dem Tisch.

Ich habe die Kleine schon in ihren Stuhl _____.
Die Kleine _____ schon in ihrem Stuhl.

Ich habe den Kleinen schon ins Bett _____.
Der Kleine _____ schon im Bett.

Warum hast du dich noch nicht ins Bett _____?
Warum _____ du noch nicht im Bett?

Warum hast du dich denn in die letzte Reihe _____?
Warum _____ Reihe?

[10] Dative Reflexives

SEE
ANALYSIS
152
(p. 428)

ich stelle mich vor: ich stelle mir vor
to introduce (socially): to imagine

Darf ich mich vorstellen? Ich bin Dr. Ingelheim.
Gnädige Frau, darf ich Ihnen Herrn Dr. Ingelheim vorstellen?
Ich kann mir nicht vorstellen, daß Ingelheim Soldat gewesen ist.
Ich hatte mir das alles viel leichter vorgestellt.

sich etwas denken
to imagine something

Du kannst dir gar nicht denken, wie ich mich darauf freue, Dich endlich wiederzusehen.
Ich habe mir gar nichts dabei gedacht, als ich sie fragte, wie es ihrem Mann ginge. Wie
    konnte ich denn wissen, daß sie geschieden ist?

sich etwas überlegen
to meditate about something

Ich überlege mir oft, ob es nicht besser wäre, wenn wir nach Heidelberg zögen.
Wie wäre es, wenn Sie auch in die Stadt zögen?—Das muß ich mir erst noch überlegen.

sich etwas ansehen: sich etwas anschauen
to look at something

Ich wollte mir den Hitchcock Film eigentlich gar nicht ansehen; aber du kennst ja Tante
    Amalie. Sie interessiert sich nur noch für Hitchcock und Picasso.
Schau dir das an! Da kommt Edith Maschke mit ihrem neuen Freund.—Die hat sich ja ganz
    verändert! Seit wann ist sie denn blond?

3 Wochen Ferien auf Mallorca
Holen Sie sich das Geld dafür einfach von uns

VARIATIONS

Complete the following sentences.

Petra freut sich _____ Weihnachten.
Das kann ich _____ nicht vorstellen.
Ich habe _____ noch nicht vorgestellt; ich bin Hans Ingelheim.
Ich kann _____ gar nicht denken, was er _____ dabei gedacht hat.
Das solltest du _____ gut überlegen.
Was kann er _____ nur dabei gedacht _____?
Habt ihr _____ schon überlegt, welchen Film _____ euch anschauen wollt?

[11] Household Reflexives

Ich putze mir die Zähne.	I am brushing my teeth.	**SEE ANALYSIS 152** (p. 428)
Sie schneidet sich die Haare selber.	She cuts her own hair.	
Willst du dir nicht die Schuhe putzen?	Don't you want to polish your shoes?	
Kinder, habt ihr euch schon die Hände gewaschen?	Children, have you washed your hands yet?	
Er hat sich den Arm gebrochen.	He broke his arm.	
Er hat sich in den Finger geschnitten.	He cut his finger.	

[12] Impersonal Reflexives

Es freut mich, daß es Ihnen bei uns gefallen hat.
Es ärgert mich, daß Meyer in der Oper immer zu spät kommt.
Es wundert mich, daß Erika immer noch nicht geschrieben hat.

SEE ANALYSIS 152 (p. 428)

Worum handelt es sich denn eigentlich?
Es handelt sich um ein wichtiges Problem.
Mein Vater hat mit Diamanten gehandelt.
Wovon handelt dieser Roman denn?
Ich hatte keine Zeit, darüber nachzudenken; ich mußte sofort handeln.

Analysis

149 Reflexive Pronouns

Very often, the subject and the object of a verb are one and the same person or thing.

I hurt myself.
I bought myself a car.

In all these cases, English uses reflexive pronouns for the object. The use of *myself* rather than *me* is linguistic luxury. *I bought me a car* is just as clear as *I bought myself a car*. This is the reason why German does not use special reflexive pronouns for the first and second persons:

Ich habe mich verletzt.	I hurt myself.
Du hast dich verletzt.	You hurt yourself.
Wir haben uns verletzt.	We hurt ourselves.
Ihr habt euch verletzt.	You hurt yourselves.
Ich habe mir ein Auto gekauft.	I bought myself a car.
Du hast dir ein Auto gekauft.	You bought yourself a car.
Wir haben uns ein Auto gekauft.	We bought ourselves a car.
Ihr habt euch ein Auto gekauft.	You bought yourselves a car.

Whereas the distinction between *I hurt me* and *I hurt myself* is luxury, the distinction between the nonreflexive *him* and the reflexive *himself* in the third person may be the difference between murder and suicide.

He killed him.	He killed himself.

However, while English uses five third-person forms, *himself, herself, themselves, itself,* and *oneself,* German gets by with but one: **sich,** which serves both as a dative and as an accusative, both as a singular and as a plural.

Er hat sie verletzt.	He hurt her.
Sie hat ihn verletzt.	She hurt him.
Er hat sich verletzt.	He hurt himself.
Sie hat sich verletzt.	She hurt herself.
Sie haben sie verletzt.	They hurt her.
Sie haben ihn verletzt.	They hurt him.
Sie haben sich verletzt.	They hurt themselves.
Er hat ihr ein Auto gekauft.	He bought her a car.
Sie hat ihm ein Auto gekauft.	She bought him a car.
Er hat sich ein Auto gekauft.	He bought himself a car.
Sie hat sich ein Auto gekauft.	She bought herself a car.
Sie haben ihr ein Auto gekauft.	They bought her a car.
Sie haben ihm ein Auto gekauft.	They bought him a car.
Sie haben sich ein Auto gekauft.	They bought themselves a car.

150 selbst and selber

1. The English reflexive pronouns *myself, yourself, himself,* and so on, sometimes merely repeat, for emphasis, a preceding noun or pronoun. When so used, they carry the main syntactical stress, but nevertheless they are not independent syntactical units.

He said it him*self*.
They did it them*selves*.

German cannot repeat a preceding noun or pronoun. Instead, German uses the strongly stressed particles **selbst** or **selber** to emphasize these nouns or pronouns. **Selbst** and **selber** are interchangeable. They always follow the word to be emphasized, either immediately or at the end of the inner field.

Das weiß ich *selbst*.	I know that my*self*.
Ich fahre morgen *selbst* nach Berlin.	I am going to Berlin my*self* tomorrow.
Das war der Direktor *selber*.	That was the boss him*self*.

Note that the use of **selbst** is not determined by the presence or absence of a reflexive pronoun, and that **selbst** does not replace the reflexive pronoun when the reflexive is required.

Er sollte auch einmal an *sich* denken.
Er sollte auch einmal an sich *selbst* denken.
He ought to think of himself, too, for a change.

2. When **selbst** (or **selber**) is used at the end of the inner field, it frequently assumes the meaning *without help* or *others don't have to*.

Das kann ich doch selber machen.	I can do that *myself*.
Hänschen kann sich selber anziehen; er ist	
doch schon drei.	

3. If **selbst** (or **selber**) appears in the front field, contrast intonation is used, and a contrast with others, of whom the opposite statement is true, is implied.

Sie *selbst* hat kein Geld; aber ihre *Mut*ter hat *viel* Geld.
Er *selber* bleibt zu *Hause*; *uns* schickt er in die *Kirche*.

4. If **selbst** (or **selber**) appears in the inner field, it may also be a substitute for **auch** and express the notion *just like others*.

Ich bin *selber* arm, so arm wie du.
Ich bin *selbst* nicht glücklich, ich bin so unglücklich wie ihr.

5. **Selbst, sogar,** and **auch,** without stress, may form a syntactical unit with an immediately following stressed word. If so used, they mean *even*.

> **Selbst (sogar, auch)** *das* **ist ihm zu viel.**
>
> **Er** *will* **einfach nicht, und solange jemand nicht** *will*, **kann ihm selbst (sogar, auch)** *Gott* **nicht helfen.**

151 Reciprocal Pronouns

Normally, the reflexive plural pronouns can also be used as reciprocal pronouns, and it is not necessary to make a distinction. No one will misunderstand **Sie küßten sich.** This can only mean *They kissed each other*, not *They kissed themselves*.

If it is desirable to express reciprocity, **einander** can be used. **Einander** is literary and replaces the reflexive, as in the following folk song.

1. Es wa-ren zwei Kö-nigs- kin-der, die hat-ten ein-an-der so lieb, sie konn-ten zu-sàm-men nicht kom-men, das Was-ser war viel zu tief, das Was-ser war viel zu tief.

152 Reflexive Verbs

Occasional Reflexives

As long as it makes sense, any verb that takes an accusative object can also be used with a reflexive pronoun object. For example, it is possible to think of a set of facts that would call for the statement **Meyer hat meinen Pudel vergiftet,** *Meyer has poisoned my poodle*; it is also possible to think of another set of facts that would call for **Meyer hat sich vergiftet,** *Meyer poisoned himself.* Such *occasional* reflexives pose no problem: the reflexive pronoun, which is a genuine object, simply takes the place of the accusative noun. Such occasional reflexives do not, strictly speaking, constitute genuine reflexive verbs.

Mandatory Reflexives

Some German verbs are always used with an accusative reflexive pronoun that can neither be left out nor replaced by a noun. English has only one such verb, *to enjoy oneself*, which, when meaning "to have fun," forms one inseparable unit. If the reflexive *oneself* is replaced by a nonreflexive pronoun or a noun (*I enjoyed them and their hospitality*), *to enjoy* changes its meaning to "to derive pleasure from." These two meanings of *to enjoy* cannot even be accommodated in one and the same sentence without repeating the verb. You cannot say [*Thanks; I enjoyed myself and that good steak.*].

German, on the other hand, has many such mandatory reflexives. They *must* be used with an accusative reflexive pronoun; they cannot take an accusative noun object (though many take a prepositional object), and they all form the perfect tense with **haben.** In the vocabulary, they will be indicated by **sich** before the infinitive: **sich erkälten,** *to catch a cold* or **sich verlieben in,** *to fall in love with.*

Ich habe mich erkältet.	**Ich habe mich in Inge verliebt.**
Du hast dich erkältet.	**Du hast dich in Inge verliebt.**
Er hat sich erkältet.	**Er hat sich in Inge verliebt.**
Wir haben uns erkältet.	**Wir haben uns in Inge verliebt.**
Ihr habt euch erkältet.	**Ihr habt euch in Inge verliebt.**
Sie haben sich erkältet.	**Sie haben sich in Inge verliebt.**

Note again that it is impossible to say either [**Ich habe erkältet**] or [**Ich habe ihn erkältet**].

Transitional Reflexives

This group of verbs includes both occasional (such as **sich entschuldigen**) and mandatory reflexives. Transitional reflexives denote a transition of the subject from one condition or state to another, for example, in

He has fallen in love with her

and a process that ended in a new state:

He is in love with her.

When used in the present tense, these verbs usually have a future meaning:

Ich wette, er verliebt sich in sie.   I bet he'll fall in love with her.

The complete process is expressed in the perfect:

Er hat sich tatsächlich in sie verliebt.   He indeed fell in love with her.

and the new state resulting from the process is expressed by **sein** plus participle:

Er ist in sie verliebt.   He is in love with her.

sich setzen, sich stellen, sich legen

The verbs **sitzen, stehen,** and **liegen** describe a state, not an event. They are intransitive—that is, they cannot take an accusative object—and they are strong verbs.

sitzen, saß, hat gesessen, er sitzt
stehen, stand, hat gestanden, er steht
liegen, lag, hat gelegen, er liegt

Anton und Emma saßen auf der Bank vor dem Haus.
Das Haus stand am Rhein.
Auf dem Tisch lag ein Buch.

The weak verbs (sich) setzen, (sich) stellen, and (sich) legen describe the action
leading to the state of sitzen, stehen, and liegen.

NONREFLEXIVE

Sie hat das Kind auf die Bank gesetzt.   Das Kind sitzt auf der Bank.
Er hat die Flasche auf den Tisch gestellt.   Die Flasche steht auf dem Tisch.
Er hat das Buch auf den Tisch gelegt.   Das Buch liegt auf dem Tisch.

REFLEXIVE

Er hat sich auf die Bank gesetzt;   jetzt sitzt er auf der Bank.
Er hat sich vor die Haustür gestellt;   jetzt steht er vor der Tür.
Er hat sich ins Bett gelegt;   jetzt liegt er im Bett.

If a prepositional phrase is used with these verbs, (sich) setzen, (sich) stellen,
(sich) legen require the accusative and sitzen, stehen, liegen require the dative
with those prepositions that can be used with either case (see 119).

Wohin hat er sich gesetzt? —Auf die Bank.
Wo sitzt er? —Auf der Bank.

Note the principal parts of the English equivalents.

INTRANSITIVE		TRANSITIVE	
sit, sat, sat	**sitzen**	set, set, set	**setzen**
lie, lay, lain	**liegen**	lay, laid, laid	**legen**

Dative Reflexives

Verbs that are used with dative reflexive pronouns take genuine accusative objects in addition to the reflexive pronoun. Sometimes these accusative objects
are expressed by dependent (object) clauses.

Ich hatte mir diesen Job viel leichter vor-   I had imagined this job to be much easier.
   gestellt.

Ich kann mir nicht vorstellen, daß er   I can't imagine that he could· forget my
   meinen Geburtstag vergessen könnte.   birthday.

The most frequently used verbs in this group are what we call *household* reflexives. They all express what the speaker is doing for or to himself.

Ich putze mir die Zähne.   I am brushing my teeth.
Ich habe mir den Arm gebrochen.   I broke my arm.

Impersonal Reflexives

Some reflexives are used with the impersonal subject **es.**

Es zeigte sich, daß . . .	It became apparent that . . .
Es stellte sich heraus, daß . . .	It turned out that . . .
Es erwies sich, daß . . .	It was proved that . . .
Es handelte sich um . . .	It was a matter of, we were dealing with . . .
Es handelt sich um Geld.	It is a matter of money.
Es handelt sich hier um eine wichtige Sache.	We are dealing here with an important problem.

But note:

Er handelt *mit* Bananen.
He sells bananas; he is in the banana business, a banana dealer.

Sein neuer Roman handelt *von* den Kämpfen in der Normandie.
His new novel deals with the battles in Normandy.

Wir haben lange genug geredet. Jetzt müssen wir handeln.
We've talked long enough; now we must act.

Some mandatory reflexives, like **sich ärgern, sich freuen,** and **sich wundern,** also occur in stereotyped phrases with **Es** . . . , followed by a dependent clause, or without **es** if the dependent clause comes first.

Es wundert mich, daß er in Berlin bleiben will.
Daß er in Berlin bleiben will, wundert mich eigentlich.

153 **eben** and **gerade**

If **eben** is used with a full lexical meaning, it means either *flat, even,* or *just (a while ago).*

ebenes (flaches) Land	flat land
die Ebene,-n	the plain

die Norddeutsche Tiefebene	the North German Plain
Er ist eben gekommen.	He just came.

Eben can also be used as a sentence adverb meaning "it won't take long; I hope you won't mind the interruption." In this function, it minimizes the significance of the action, and for this reason is frequently used in connection with the casual **mal**. As a sentence adverb, **eben** is never stressed.

Ich muß mal eben in die Stadt.
I've got to run downtown for a minute. (Nothing important; I'll be right back.)

Entschuldigst du mich einen Augenblick? Ich muß mal eben telefonieren.
Will you excuse me for a minute? I just want to make a quick phone call.

If **gerade** is used with full lexical meaning, it means *straight*.

eine gerade Linie	a straight line

In connection with numbers, one speaks of **gerade Zahlen** and **ungerade Zahlen** (*even and odd numbers*). It can also mean *just then* or *just now* (see **eben** above).

Er ist gerade (eben) gekommen.   He just came.

Ich war gerade (eben) nach Hause gekommen, als das Telefon klingelte.

154 ruhig

German **ruhig** can be used either as an adjective or as a sentence adverb. As an adjective, it means *calm, quiet.*

Seid ruhig, Kinder.   Be quiet, children.

If used as a sentence adverb, **ruhig** denotes that the speaker will remain "quiet" and has no objections.

Bleib du ruhig im Bett; ich frühstücke im Flughafen.
Don't bother to get up for me; I'll have breakfast at the airport.

Ihr könnt ruhig laut sein, Kinder, ich will jetzt *doch* nicht schlafen.
I won't mind your being loud; I don't want to sleep now anyway.

Conversations

Instead of the usual type of conversations, we introduce here another group of reflexive verbs; each verb is presented within a mini-conversation. By using the situations suggested, enlarge these conversations (though not necessarily with the same verbs) until you have four or more exchanges for each. The first set below can serve as a model.

Patterns [5]–[8] can be used in the same way.

I

A: Guten Morgen, Hans. Bist du endlich ausgeschlafen?

B: Mein Gott, es ist ja schon zehn Uhr. Aber so gut habe ich schon lange nicht mehr geschlafen.

A: Kein Wunder. Du warst ja wochenlang jede Nacht bis eins oder zwei im Labor.

B: Ja, ich mußte mich wirklich mal ausschlafen.

A: Bist du denn jetzt fertig mit dem Experiment?

B: Noch nicht ganz; aber in zwei, drei Tagen bin ich so weit.

A: Das beruhigt mich. Dann können wir ja über das Wochenende wegfahren.

B: Ja,—und darauf freue ich mich jetzt schon.

A: So, jetzt wollen wir aber erst mal frühstücken.

sich ausschlafen: ausge-schlafen sein

to get enough sleep: to have had enough sleep

II

Könntest du dich nicht doch noch dazu entschließen, am Sonntag mit nach Heidelberg zu fahren, Irene?

Ja, weißt du, Jürgen, gestern abend war ich ja fast dazu entschlossen, aber heute morgen habe ich an meine Prüfung gedacht,—na ja, ich bleibe doch besser hier.

sich entschließen zu: entschlossen sein zu

to make up one's mind to: to have made up one's mind, to be determined

III

Ich möchte dich nur daran erinnern, daß wir heute abend bei Gerda eingeladen sind. Sie hat gerade angerufen,—Hannelore Ebert kommt auch, mit ihrem Mann.

Hannelore Ebert?

Ja, erinnerst du dich nicht? Die war doch damals mit Gerda zusammen in England.

Natürlich, ich erinnere mich sehr gut an sie; ich hatte nur den Namen nicht mehr in Erinnerung.

jemanden erinnern an (with acc.): sich erinnern an (with acc.)

to remind somebody: to remember

IV

Ist Professor von Embden wirklich Leiter der Prüfungskomission?

Ich fürchte, ja. Weißt du, der ist immer so ironisch, —ich habe direkt Angst vor ihm.

Bis jetzt habe ich mich vor dem Examen ja gar nicht gefürchtet, aber mit von Embden . . . ?

Na, wir wollen mal sehen. Vielleicht ist er gar nicht so.

sich fürchten vor (with dat.): fürchten

to be afraid of: to fear

V

Meinen Glückwunsch, Fräulein Maurer, das war wirklich eine sehr gute Prüfung. —Sie interessieren sich also besonders für den Impressionismus in Frankreich.

Ja, Herr Professor, —und das Thema, das Sie mir für die Dissertation vorgeschlagen haben, interessiert mich sehr.

Das freut mich. Ich bin gerne bereit, Ihnen dabei zu helfen. —Übrigens, wären Sie an einer Assistentenstelle in meinem Institut interessiert?

jemanden interessieren: sich interessieren für: interessiert sein an (with dat.)

to interest somebody: to be interested in: to be interested in (acquiring or doing)

VI

Ich muß mich noch umziehen, bevor wir ins Theater gehen.
Oh, ich dachte, du wärst schon umgezogen.

Meyers sind umgezogen.
Wirklich? Wo sind sie denn hingezogen?
Nach Wiesbaden.

**sich umziehen: umge-
  zogen sein**
*to change (clothes): to
  have changed (clothes)*
umziehen: ziehen
to move (one's residence)

VII

Gib mir doch mal die Straßenkarte. Ich glaube, wir haben uns verfahren.
Was heißt „wir"! Wer verfährt sich denn immer, du oder ich?

In München kann man sich leicht verlaufen.
Wieso denn? Ich habe mich in München noch nie verlaufen.

NOTE: Do not use **sich vergehen,** which means *to commit a crime.*

**sich verfahren: sich ver-
  laufen**
*to lose one's way driv-
  ing: to lose one's way
  walking*

VIII

Wenn du den Mercedes nimmst, kannst du beruhigt sein. Auf den
  kann man sich verlassen.
Ja, aber aufs Wetter kann man sich nicht verlassen, nicht um diese
  Jahreszeit.

Ich muß Sie leider schon verlassen, gnädige Frau, aber der Abend war
  wirklich nett.
Schade, daß Sie schon gehen müssen, Herr Professor.

sich verlassen auf (with
  acc.)
to rely on

verlassen (with acc.
  object)
*to leave (a place or
  person)*

Fragen an Sie persönlich

1. Interessieren Sie sich für Politik?
                              Sport?
                              Musik?
                              Literatur?
   Wofür interessieren Sie sich sonst?
   Was interessiert Sie an der Politik?
                       am Sport?
                       usw. (= **und so weiter** etc.)

2. Langweilen Sie sich oft?
   Ärgern   selten?
                       nie?
   Was langweilt Sie am meisten (most)?
   Worüber ärgern Sie sich am meisten?

3. Worauf freuen Sie sich am meisten, wenn das Semester zu Ende ist?·
                                        die Schule aus ist?
                                        die Ferien beginnen?

4. Sind Sie verlobt?
         verheiratet?
         verliebt?

5. Fürchten Sie sich vor irgendjemand?
                        vor irgendetwas?
                        vor der nächsten Prüfung?
   (Oder sind Sie sehr gut vorbereitet?)

6. Können Sie sich vorstellen,
      daß Sie Präsident der Vereinigten Staaten wären?
                   Präsident der Universität?
                   Bürgermeister von New York?
                                    Berlin?
                                    Burgbach?
                   die Mutter von sieben Kindern?
                   der Vater
   Was würden Sie tun, wenn Sie . . . wären?
   Was möchten Sie sein, wenn Sie sein könnten, was Sie wollten?

Reading

FRANZ KAFKA

Gibs auf!

Es war sehr früh am Morgen, die Straßen rein und leer°, ich ging zum   clean and empty
Bahnhof. Als ich eine Turmuhr° mit meiner Uhr verglich°, sah ich,   tower clock compared
daß es schon viel später war, als ich geglaubt hatte, ich mußte mich

sehr beeilen°, der Schrecken° über diese Entdeckung° ließ mich im   hurry fright, panic
Weg unsicher werden, ich kannte mich in dieser Stadt noch nicht sehr   discovery
gut aus°, glücklicherweise war ein Schutzmann° in der Nähe, ich lief   **sich auskennen** to
zu ihm und fragte ihn atemlos° nach dem Weg. Er lächelte und sagte: know one's way a-
„Von mir willst du den Weg erfahren°?" „Ja", sagte ich, „da ich ihn 5   round policeman
selbst nicht finden kann." „Gibs auf, gibs auf", sagte er und wandte   breathlessly
sich mit einem großen Schwunge ab°, so wie Leute, die mit ihrem   find out
Lachen allein sein wollen.   turned away from me
                                                                         with a big swinging
                                                                         motion

Auch in den Ferien liest Gerd
Weber die Bild-Zeitung.

Aus deutschen Zeitungen

The remaining reading passages of this unit are excerpts from recent issues of German
newspapers. They have been slightly modified, but they are typical of the kind of German you will find in newspapers. We have purposely not deleted attributive adjectives,
that is, adjectives followed by nouns, which will be introduced systematically in Unit
15. For the time being, pay no attention to the endings of these adjectives.

I

The individual sentences in this first section all contain vocabulary and syntactic arrangements used with high frequency in newspapers and magazines.

Ein Sprecher der Bundesregierung teilte mit, daß die Bundesrepublik gemein-
    sam mit den USA versuchen wolle, das Problem zu lösen.
   A speaker for the federal government announced that the Federal Republic, together with the U.S., would attempt to solve the problem.

Die Verhandlungen über den Verkauf von Atomwaffen dauern noch an.   5
   The negotiations about the sale of atomic weapons are continuing.

Weniger als 20% (Prozent) der Bevölkerung erinnern sich an die Konferenz
    von Potsdam. So die Bild-Zeitung.
   Less than twenty percent of the population remember the Potsdam Conference,
   states the Bild-Zeitung.   10

Der Fall Schäfer-Meinhardt ist nach wie vor das Hauptthema von Berichten in
    Presse und Fernsehen.
   The Schäfer-Meinhardt case continues to be the main topic of reports in the press
   and on TV.

Über das tägliche Leben in der Bundeswehr berichtet unser Korrespondent
    Uwe Steiner.
    Our correspondent Uwe Steiner reports on daily life in the armed forces.

Der Unfall passierte in unmittelbarer Nähe der Grenze.
    The accident occurred in the immediate vicinity of the border. 5

Zwei der Opfer des Unglücks sind immer noch in Lebensgefahr.
    Two of the victims of the accident are still in critical condition.

Die Polizei teilt mit, die Terroristengruppe habe geplant, den Angeklagten aus
    dem Gefängnis zu befreien.
    The police report that the group of terrorists had planned to liberate the accused 10
    from jail.

Kurz vor der Explosion konnte sich Flugkapitän Schulte noch in Sicherheit
    bringen.
    Shortly before the explosion, flight captain Schulte succeeded in reaching a safe
    area. 15

Glück im Unglück hatte ein 43-jähriger Münchner Künstler, als er gestern
    gegen 21 Uhr mit seinem Wagen gegen eine Mauer fuhr.
    A 43-year-old Munich artist was pretty lucky when his car hit a wall at about nine
    o'clock last night.

Die Mordwaffe hat die Polizei inzwischen sichergestellt, vom Täter fehlt 20
    jedoch bisher jede Spur.
    In the meantime, the police have secured the murder weapon, but so far there is no
    trace of the murderer (lit.: doer, culprit).

Das Land Niedersachsen steht unmittelbar vor einer Koalition von FDP and
    CDU. 25
    The state of Lower-Saxony stands immediately before a coalition of the Free Demo-
    cratic party and the Christian Democratic Union.

Mit der Verhaftung von etwa 25 Demonstranten endete die Demonstration
    gegen das geplante Atomkraftwerk.
    The demonstration against the planned atomic power plant ended with the arrest of 30
    about twenty-five demonstrators.

Der Ministerpräsident beabsichtigt, einen Teil seines Urlaubs in den Schweizer
    Alpen zu verbringen.
    The prime minister intends to spend part of his vacation in the Swiss Alps.

II

Niedersachsen: FDP will mit CDU gehen

WamS Wolfsburg.* Nieder-
sachsen steht vor der Bildung
einer Koalition† von FDP und
CDU. Damit kommt es zum
ersten Mal seit der Gründung 5
der sozial-liberalen Koalition

*WamS: *Welt am Sonntag*, die Sonntagsausgabe der Zeitung *Die Welt*; Wolfsburg:
Stadt in Niedersachsen, bekannt durch die Volkswagenfabrik.
†Die Endung *-tion* spricht man aus wie *-tsion*: Ko-a-li-*tsion*.

1969 in Bonn wieder auf Lan- | in der die Gegner der Koalition
desebene zu einer Verbindung | meinten, die Verbindung sei
von Freien Demokraten und | „Pendelpolitik" und werde sich
Christdemokraten.   10 | bei der nächsten Landtagswahl
                              | negativ auswirken.   25

Zu diesem Schritt entschloß | Die niedersächsische FDP war
sich gestern nachmittag in | bei der letzten Landtagswahl
Wolfsburg die Mehrheit im | als Koalitionspartner der SPD
FDP-Landeshauptausschuß. 70 | mit elf Abgeordneten ins Lan-
der 125 Delegierten sprachen 15 | desparlament eingezogen. Die 30
sich für offizielle Koalitionsver- | Koalition mit der SPD zerbrach
handlungen mit der CDU aus, | jedoch im Januar dieses Jahres.
55 waren dagegen. | Seitdem regiert die CDU mit

Die Entscheidung kam nach | einer Minderheitenregierung.
einer siebenstündigen Debatte, 20 |

1 **Niedersachsen** Lower Saxony,
  eines der Bundesländer der BRD
3 **FDP = Freie Demokratische Partei**
4 **CDU = Christliche Demokratische**
  Union
5 **die Gründung** founding, establishment
7 **die Ebene** level
13 **die Mehrheit** majority
14 **Landeshauptausschuß** state execu-
  tive committee

23 **Pendelpolitik** swing politics
24 **der Landtag** state parliament
24 **die Wahl** election
25 **sich auswirken** to have an effect
28 **SPD = Sozialdemokratische Partei**
  Deutschlands
29 **der Abgeordnete** representative
34 **die Minderheit** minority

Stellen Sie fest, ob die folgenden Aussagen richtig oder falsch sind.
(Determine whether the following statements are true or false.)

1. In Niedersachsen gibt es nur zwei Parteien.
2. Die FDP und die CDU regieren seit der letzten Wahl gemeinsam.
3. Die Mehrheit der Delegierten war für die FDP-CDU-Verbindung.
4. Die Gegner der Koalition sind Abgeordnete im Landesparlament.
5. „Pendelpolitik" heißt hier, daß die FDP nun nach der Koalition mit der
   SPD eine Verbindung mit der CDU eingehen will.

Nötig wie innere Reformen

Baden-Baden (dpa).* Die Ent- | Bundesrepublik. In einem Inter-
wicklungshilfe ist nach der | view des Südwestfunks erklärte
Meinung des Bundesministers | der Minister gestern, Entwick-
für wirtschaftliche Zusammen- | lungshilfe sei genau so eine In- 10
arbeit genau so nötig und wich- 5 | vestition in die gemeinsame
tig wie innere Reformen in der | Zukunft wie die Investitionen in

*****dpa: Deutsche Presse-Agentur** German Press Agency.

Schulen und Universitäten. Der Minister sagte, die Entwicklungshilfe solle von jetzt an vor 15 allem für solche Projekte zur Verfügung stehen, die den Auf- schwung von ganzen Landstrichen in die Wege leiten können. Außerdem will der Mini- 20 ster mehr als bisher Familienplanungsprogramme fördern.

4 **wirtschaftlich** economic
10 **die Investition,-en** investment
11 **gemeinsam** common
15 **vor allem** above all
16 **zur Verfügung stehen** to be available

17 **der Aufschwung** upswing, improvement
18 **der Landstrich,-e** region
19 **in die Wege leiten** to initiate
22 **fördern** to further

Analysieren Sie die folgenden Komposita:

die Entwicklungshilfe	**die Entwicklung**	development
	die Hilfe	aid
der Bundesminister	**der Bund**	federation
	der Minister	minister
die Bundesrepublik	**der Bund**	federation
	die Republik	republic
die Zusammenarbeit	**zusammen**	together
	die Arbeit	work
der Südwestfunk	**der Südwesten**	southwest
	der (Rund) funk	radio
das Familienplanungsprogramm	**die Familie**	family
	die Planung	planning
	das Programm	program

Protest gegen Atomkraftwerk°

Brokdorf (dpa). Nach friedlichem Beginn endete am Samstag eine Demonstration gegen das geplante Atomkraftwerk in Brokdorf an der Unterelbe mit 5 Tumulten. Etwa 400 Demonstranten konnten in das Gelände eindringen, obwohl die Polizei versuchte, sie mit Wasserwerfern daran zu hindern. Vor dem 10 Gelände waren auch am späten Abend noch etwa 3000 Menschen. Ein großer Teil von ihnen hatte vorher mit Songs und Slogans gegen den Bau des 15 1300-Megawatt-Kraftwerks protestiert, der in der Nacht zum Dienstag überraschend begonnen hatte. Die Aktion war von der Gruppe „Umweltschutz 20 Unterelbe" und anderen, meist linksgerichteten Organisationen ausgegangen.

o **das Kraftwerk** power plant
1 **dpa = Deutsche Presse-agentur**
5 **die Unterelbe** the lower Elbe River
7 **das Gelände** area

8 **eindringen** to penetrate
20 **die Umwelt** environment
20 **der Schutz** protection

Wenn Sie in Brokdorf dabei gewesen wären, wären Sie für oder gegen die Demonstranten gewesen? Machen Sie eine Liste von Argumenten für und gegen Atomkraftwerke.

Scotland Yard untersucht Bombenanschlag°

London (dpa). Ein Spezialteam von Kriminalisten Scotland Yards untersucht seit gestern intensiv die Ursachen der Explosion, die am Vorabend die Woh- 5 nung des Industrieministers zerstört hatte. Der Leiter des Teams ist anonym; man kennt ihn nur als „Commander X", den Spezialisten für die Jagd auf 10 Bombenattentäter. Bis jetzt fehlt von den Tätern jede Spur.

o **der Anschlag,-̈e** attack
10 **die Jagd** hunt, chase

11 **der Attentäter,-** assassin

Setzen Sie die fehlenden Wörter ein:

1. Scotland Yard _____ die Ursachen einer Explosion.
2. Eine Bombe hatte die _____ eines Ministers zerstört.
3. Man weiß nicht, wie der _____ des Teams heißt.
4. Man _____ ihn nur als „Commander X".
5. Commander X ist ein _____ für die Jagd auf Bombenattentäter.
6. Von den Tätern _____ noch jede Spur.

Nebel! Flug- und Straßenverkehr behindert

Dichter Nebel hat am Samstagvormittag den Flugverkehr in Norddeutschland stark behindert. Auf den Flughäfen von Hannover und Bremen kam der 5 Flugbetrieb fast ganz zum Stillstand. In Berlin-Tegel konnten in den Morgenstunden keine Maschinen landen. Die Starts verzögerten sich zum Teil um 10 zwei Stunden.

In der Nacht und gegen Morgen wurde der Nebel in manchen Teilen Niedersachsens so dicht, daß die Autofahrer „nicht die 15 Hand vor den Augen sehen konnten".

Auch in großen Teilen von Baden-Württemberg* war das Autofahren wegen des Nebels 20 bei einer Sichtweite von unter 100 m fast unmöglich. Auf der Autobahn Stuttgart-Ulm kam es zu einem schweren Verkehrsunfall, als zwei Lastwagen aufein- 25 anderfuhren. Erst nach fünf Stunden war die Autobahn wieder frei.

1 **dicht** dense
10 **verzögern** to delay

21 **die Sichtweite** visibility

*Baden-Württemberg: das Bundesland im Südwesten der BRD.

Sonntag auf der Autobahn
relativ störungsfrei

Hamburg (dpa/AP). Der Verkehr auf den Autobahnen und Fernstraßen der Bundesrepublik war am Sonntag zwar lebhaft und dicht, aber im allge-[5] meinen störungsfrei, während am Samstag die Rückreisewelle des Ferienverkehrs von Süden nach Norden noch einmal sehr intensiv gewesen war. [10]

Der starke Rückreiseverkehr, den die Polizei von Nordrhein-Westfalen für dieses Wochenende erwartet hatte, da dort am Montag die Schule wieder [15] beginnt, blieb aus. Am Sonntagmittag war der Verkehr normal; nur auf der Autobahn Frankfurt-Köln gab es infolge eines Unfalls bei Limburg noch [20] einmal einen Verkehrsstau.

Auf den Autobahnen in Bayern und Hessen war der Verkehr dicht, aber relativ reibungslos. In Rheinland-Pfalz, Saarland, [25] Niedersachsen und in Nord-deutschland war es am Sonntag ruhig. Fünf Tote und zwei Schwerverletzte gab es bei einem Verkehrsunfall auf der [30] Bundesstraße 80 in der Nähe von Gertenbach (Kreis Witzenhausen). Beim Überholen eines Traktors stieß ein Personenwagen mit einem Kleinbus aus [35] Göttingen zusammen. Dabei kamen zwei zehnjährige Kinder und drei Erwachsene ums Leben.

Ein glückliches Ende nahm am [40] Samstagvormittag ein Zwischenfall auf der Autobahn Köln-Aachen, wo ein Autofahrer die Gegenfahrbahn befuhr. Die Polizei warnte über [45] den Rundfunk alle Benutzer der Autobahn, konnte aber den „Linksfahrer" erst nach 15 km zum Halten bringen. Der Fahrer hatte die falsche Einfahrt [50] benutzt.

4 **lebhaft** lively
7 **die Welle,-n** wave
16 **blieb aus** did not materialize
19 **infolge** (*with gen.*) as a consequence of
21 **der Stau** back-up
23 **Hessen** Hesse
24 **reibungslos** smooth
25 **Rheinland-Pfalz** Rhineland-Palatinate

26 **Niedersachsen** Lower Saxony
32 **der Kreis,-e** county
33 **überholen** to pass
34 **zusammenstoßen** to collide
37 **ums Leben kommen** to be fatally injured
41 **der Zwischenfall,-̈e** incident
44 **die Fahrbahn,-en** lane
50 **falsch** wrong, false

Schreiben Sie die folgenden Sätze zu Ende.

1. Am Sonntag war der Verkehr relativ störungsfrei, aber am Samstag

   _____.

2. Der Verkehr war so intensiv, weil viele Leute _____

   _____.

3. Viele reisen nach Nordrhein-Westfalen zurück, denn dort _____

_____.

4. Der Unfall auf der Bundesstraße 80 passierte, weil _____

_____.

5. Der Zwischenfall auf der Autobahn Köln-Aachen nahm wahrscheinlich
   deshalb ein glückliches Ende, weil die Polizei _____

_____.

6. Der Bericht nennt den Autofahrer einen „Linksfahrer", weil er _____

_____.

7. Der Autofahrer fuhr auf der Gegenfahrbahn, weil er _____

_____.

Vom Duschen und Frühstücken wird man noch lange nicht fahrtüchtig.

Mit einem kräftigen Schwips war er nach Hause gekommen. Per Taxi. Denn, vernünftig wie er ist, seinen Wagen hatte er in der Garage gelassen.

Vier Stunden Schlaf. Die heiße Dusche und das kräftige Frühstück machen wieder richtig munter, fit für die Autofahrt zur Arbeit – denkt er.

Ein gefährlicher Irrtum.

Nach ein paar Stunden Schlaf fühlt man sich zwar wieder einigermaßen in Ordnung. Nur – fahrtüchtig ist man noch lange nicht. Denn der Körper baut pro Stunde nur 0.1 Promille ab. Der Faschingsheld, der um 3 Uhr nachts mit 1.4 Promille ins Bett sinkt, hat morgens um 7 Uhr immer noch 1,0 Promille.

Aber selbst zwei Stunden mehr Schlaf ändern nicht viel. Denn immer noch sind 0.8 Promille Alkohol im Blut.

In beiden Fällen viel zu viel, um sich selbst ans Steuer zu setzen.

Deshalb heißt nach feucht-fröhlichem Fest die Formel für die Sicherheit:

Auch am nächsten Morgen bleibt's Auto zu Hause.

Über 3.500 Menschen sterben jährlich auf der Straße, weil Alkohol im Spiel war. Und weil viele Fahrer glaubten, zum Fahren noch stark genug zu sein.

Eine Information des Bundesministers für Verkehr
Kurt Gscheidle
FÜR MEHR VERKEHRSSICHERHEIT

duschen   to shower
tüchtig   capable
kräftig   strong, hearty, hefty
der Schwips   state of being drunk (*colloq.*)
  einen Schwips haben to be drunk

munter   fit, awake
der Irrtum   error
einigermaßen   relatively
der Körper   body
abbauen   to eliminate
der Faschingsheld   carnival hero
das Steuer   steering wheel

Warnsignal: Vorsicht Betrunkener°

Stuttgart (dpa). Auf einer Straße bei Heiningen (Kreis Göppingen) fand die Polizei am Mittwoch zwei Warndreiecke, zwischen denen ein Betrunkener schlief. 5 Ein Autofahrer mit Sinn für Humor wollte den Betrunkenen, der auf der Straße seinen Rausch ausschlief, nicht wecken, sondern stellte vor und hinter 10 dem alkoholisierten Hindernis einfach die Warnzeichen auf. Die Autos kurvten so lange um den gut markierten Straßen-Schläfer herum, bis die Polizei 15 kam und den Betrunkenen und die Warndreiecke einsammelte.

o **betrunken** drunk
9 **der Rausch** stupor

11 **das Hindernis,-se** obstacle
17 **einsammeln** to collect

Erzählen Sie die Geschichte vom Standpunkt des Autofahrers. Beginnen Sie wie folgt:

Gestern ist mir etwas Komisches passiert. Ich fuhr auf der Straße nach Heiningen. . . .

Die Berlinerin, die den Vater ihres Kindes nicht heiraten darf

Er ist Grieche, sie wohnt im anderen Teil der Stadt, und zwischen ihnen steht nicht nur die Mauer . . .

Da sind ein Mann und eine Frau. Ein Kind haben sie auch. Da sind aber auch zwei verschiedene Staatsangehörigkeit-en, und eine Mauer, die diese 5 Stadt zerschneidet. Und schon ist der Wirrwarr komplett.

Der griechische Elektriker Spyridon Nicolis (34) kam vor acht Jahren nach West-Berlin. 10 Er suchte Anerkennung als politischer Flüchtling, aber das akzeptierte die Polizei nicht, weil er keine guten Gründe hatte. Acht Jahre lang versuchte 15 er alle rechtlichen Möglichkeiten, aber nun sollte er nach Athen zurück.

Doch die Ausländerpolizei wollte ihm eine Brücke bauen: 20 Wenn er eine Deutsche heiratet, kann er den gewünschten Daueraufenthalt bekommen.

Diese Deutsche ist da: es ist die Arzthelferin Erna Knauft aus 25 der Albrechtstraße in Ostberlin.

Die beiden sind seit 1968 verlobt und haben eine Tochter, Tatjana, fünf Jahre alt. Sie möchten heiraten. 30

Die Verlobte hat ihre Umsiedlung nach West-Berlin beantragt, und man würde sie und das Kind gehen lassen, wenn sie vorher heiratete. 35

Es ergibt sich nun folgendes Kuriosum:

Die Westberliner Behörden verlangen eine Heirat, wenn Nicolis nicht nach Griechenland 40 zurückgehen soll.

Die Ostberliner Behörden verlangen auch eine Heirat, wenn Erna Knauft mit dem Kind ausreisen will. 45

Heiratet Nicolis jedoch in Ostberlin, dann darf er nicht nach West-Berlin zurück und müßte mit Familie in Ostberlin bleiben. Und das will er nicht. 50

4 **die Staatsangehörigkeit** citizenship
6 **zerschneiden** to cut in half
7 **der Wirrwarr** confusion
11 **die Anerkennung** recognition
14 **der Grund** reason
16 **rechtlich** legal

23 **der Daueraufenthalt** permanent residency
31 **die Umsiedlung** resettlement
32 **beantragen** to apply for
38 **die Behörden** (*pl.*) authorities

Exercises

A. In the following sentences, insert **selbst** or **selber** in as many places as possible and translate the resulting sentences into English. The number of possibilities is indicated in parentheses.

SEE
ANALYSIS
150
(p. 426)

1. Erika fährt nicht. (4)
2. Ich wollte, ich könnte einmal mit Meyer reden. (4)
3. Warum denkst du eigentlich nie an dich? (1)
4. Meyer geht jeden Sonntag in die Kirche. (3)
5. Ich habe Angst gehabt. (3)
6. Mit Tante Amalie könnte ich, wenn nötig, ins Museum gehen. (5)

B. Restate the following sentences by using the subjects indicated in parentheses. Be sure to distinguish between dative and accusative reflexives.

SEE
ANALYSIS
151
(p. 428)

1. Natürlich haben sie sich schon einmal geküßt. (wir)
2. Kann er sich schon selber anziehen? (du)
3. Und dann sah er sich im Spiegel. (ich)
4. Ich muß mir morgen eine Wohnung suchen. (wir) (ihr)
5. Das können sie sich nicht kaufen. (ich) (du) (er) (Erika)
6. Sie trafen sich am Bahnhof. (wir)
7. Du mußt auch einmal an dich selbst denken. (Sie)
8. Kannst du dir das Frühstück nicht einmal selber machen? (er)
9. Sie hat sich in ihn verliebt. (er)
10. Hat er sich schon umgezogen? (du)

C. Restate the following sentences by using the corresponding perfect of the reflexive.

SEE
ANALYSIS
152
(p. 428)

1. Ich bin gut ausgeruht.
2. Er ist schon rasiert.
3. Er ist in Rosemarie verliebt.
4. Ich bin schwer erkältet.
5. Er ist seit einer Woche mit meiner Schwester verlobt.

D. Restate the following sentences by replacing the reflexives with a form of **sein** plus participle.

SEE
ANALYSIS
152
(p. 428)

1. Mit wem hat er sich denn verlobt?
2. Warum hat er sich denn so aufgeregt?
3. Hat Hans sich vorbereitet?
4. Hast du dich schon wieder erkältet?
5. Ich habe mich entschlossen, das Haus zu kaufen.

E. In the following sentences, fill in the blanks by using the correct form of **setzen, sitzen; stellen, stehen; legen, liegen.**

SEE
ANALYSIS
152
(p. 428)

1. Als ich nach Hause kam, _____ meine Frau schon im Bett.
2. Als ich nach Hause kam, hatte meine Frau sich schon ins Bett _____.
3. Hast du die Weinflasche auf den Tisch _____?
4. Meine Frau geht nur dann ins Theater, wenn sie in der ersten Reihe _____ kann.
5. Ich hatte einen guten Platz. Aber dann _____ sich der dicke Meyer vor mich, und ich konnte nichts mehr sehen.
6. Gestern im Theater habe ich neben Rosemarie _____.
7. Heute möchte ich eigentlich gern im Garten _____.
8. Ich habe deinen Mantel aufs Bett _____.
9. Der Zug war so voll, daß ich keinen Sitzplatz finden konnte, und ich mußte von Köln bis nach Frankfurt _____.
10. Wir haben den Tisch jetzt an die Wand _____.

F. In the following sentences, replace the transitives **setzen, stellen, legen** or the reflexives **sich setzen, sich stellen, sich legen** with the intransitives **sitzen, stehen, liegen,** or vice versa. Observe the difference in tense and, in some cases, the change of subject; remember also that you have to change case in the prepositional phrase.

Sie liegt schon im Bett.	**Sie hat sich schon ins Bett gelegt.**

1. Er hat sich neben sie gesetzt.
2. Wir saßen in der ersten Reihe.
3. Sie sitzen alle im Garten.
4. Warum hast du dich denn noch nicht ins Bett gelegt?
5. Er muß sich schon ins Bett gelegt haben.
6. Sie hatte sich direkt neben die Tür gestellt.
7. Er stand am Fenster.
8. Er hat das Buch auf den Nachttisch gelegt.
9. Ich habe die Flasche auf den Tisch gestellt.
10. Er saß schon am Frühstückstisch.
11. Vor ihm stand eine Tasse Kaffee. (New subject: Ingrid)
12. Er legte die Bibel vor sich auf den Tisch.
13. Wo hast du denn meinen Hut hingelegt?
14. Wo sitzt denn deine Frau? (Start new question with **Wo** and use **sich hinsetzen.**)
15. Wo steht denn mein Wagen? (Start question with **Wohin**; new subject: **du.**)

SEE ANALYSIS 152 (p. 428)

G. Change the following actions into states.

1. Sie hat sich in ihren Lehrer verliebt.
2. Sie hat sich mit ihm verlobt.
3. Sie soll ihn geheiratet haben.
4. Hast du dich schon angezogen?
5. Meyer soll sich furchtbar darüber aufgeregt haben.
6. Ich hoffe, du hast dich gut ausgeruht.

SEE ANALYSIS 152 (p. 428)

H. Change the following states into action; use the perfect.

1. An das Klima bin ich schon gewöhnt.
2. Ich bin davon überzeugt, daß sie gut Englisch spricht.
3. Mein Mann ist wirklich überarbeitet.
4. Ist er schon wieder nicht rasiert?

I. Complete the following sentences.

sich ärgern
Hast du _____ heute im Büro wieder _____ müssen?
Über _____ hast du _____ denn heute _____?
Ja, heute habe ich _____ über Meyer geärgert.
Ich glaube, du bist nicht glücklich, wenn du dich nicht _____ kannst.

SEE ANALYSIS 152 (p. 428)

sich freuen
Ich habe mich sehr _____ gefreut, daß sie gekommen ist. (Use **da**-compound.)
Ich freue mich sehr _____, daß sie morgen kommt. (Use **da**-compound.)

sich verfahren
Wo bleibt er denn? Ob er sich schon wieder _____ hat?
Ich brauche keine Straßenkarte; ich _____ mich nie.

J. Express in German by using reflexive verbs.

SEE
ANALYSIS
152
(p. 428)

1. Why don't you go to bed?
2. Did you shave this morning?
3. They got engaged.
4. They got a divorce.
5. Can't Fritzchen take a bath by himself now?
6. You ought to change before Aunt Amalie comes.
7. I broke my arm and I can't undress myself.
8. Have you had enough sleep?
9. Did you have a good rest?
10. He always gets so excited.
11. Did she finally calm down?

K. Express the following sentences in German. These sentences all contain reflexives. Do not use **sein** plus participle.

SEE
ANALYSIS
152
(p. 428)

1. Are you still interested in her?
2. Think of yourself for a change.
3. I was really mad at him last night.
4. She fell in love with her teacher.
5. We have never been so bored.
6. I've bought myself a new coat.
7. They want to get a divorce.
8. May I introduce myself?
9. Just imagine: after twenty years he still remembered me.
10. I know she has nothing against you; you just imagine that.
11. I am looking forward to seeing her again.
12. We want to have a look at Meyer's new house.
13. I haven't changed yet, and I still have to shave.
14. Hurry up!
15. Don't get so excited.
16. Has she calmed down again?
17. I simply can't get used to his Russian accent.
18. Did you lose your way again? (hiking) (driving)
19. His new novel deals with a woman and her daughter.
20. We are dealing with people, gentlemen, and not with machines.

Vocabulary

allgemein	general	**sich** (*acc.*) **bedienen**	to serve (oneself)
im allgemeinen	generally	**Selbstbedienung**	self-service
sich (*acc.*)* **anziehen**	to get dressed	**sich** (*acc.*) **beeilen**	to hurry
sich (*acc.*) **ärgern über** (*acc.*)	to be annoyed by	**berichten**	to report
		sich (*acc.*) **beruhigen**	to calm down
arm	poor	**beunruhigt sein**	to be worried
der Arm, -e	arm	**brechen**	to break
sich (*acc.*) **aufregen**	to get excited	**sich** (*dat.*) **den Arm brechen**	to break one's arm
sich (*acc.*) **ausruhen**	to rest		
sich (*acc.*) **ausschlafen**	to get enough sleep	**sich** (*dat.*) **denken**	to imagine
sich (*acc.*) **ausziehen**	to undress	**ich denke mir etwas**	I imagine

*Since **sich** can be either dative or accusative, the case of the reflexive pronoun is indicated in parentheses.

eben	flat, even; just	es handelt sich um (acc.)	it is a matter of
die Ebene, -n	plain, flatland	sich (acc.) interessieren	to be interested in
sich (acc.) eilen	to hurry	für (acc.)	
sich beeilen		sich (acc.) irren	to err, be in error
sich (dat.) etwas ein-	to imagine something	die Karte, -n	card; map
bilden		die Postkarte, -n	postcard
eingebildet sein	to be conceited	die Straßenkarte, -n	road map
sich (acc.) entscheiden	to decide	der Künstler, -	artist
die Entscheidung,	decision	küssen	to kiss
-en		(sich) (acc.) langweilen	to bore (to be bored)
sich (acc.) entschließen	to decide, to make up	sich (acc.) legen	to lie down
	one's mind	die Li′nie, -n	line
entschlossen sein	to be determined	menschlich	human
sich (acc.) entschuldigen	to excuse (oneself)	mitteilen	to announce, report,
die Entschul-	excuse		convey
digung, -en			
(ich bitte um)	(I am) sorry; excuse	nach wie vor	as always
Entschuldigung	me	nötig	necessary
sich (acc.) erholen	to get a rest	putzen	to clean
erholt sein	to be well rested	sich (acc.) rasieren	to shave
erinnern an (acc.)	to remind of	retten	to save
sich (acc.) erinnern	to remember	richten	to direct, orient
an (acc.)		die Richtung, -en	direction
sich (acc.) erkälten	to catch a cold	die Sache, -n	matter; thing
erkältet sein	to have a cold	scheiden	to separate, divide
sich (acc.) freuen auf	to look forward to	sich (acc.) scheiden	to get a divorce
(acc.)		lassen	
sich (acc.) freuen über	to be happy (glad)	die Scheidung, -en	divorce
(acc.)	about	der Schreibtisch, -e	desk
der Frieden	peace	der Schritt, -e	step
friedlich	peaceful	der Schuh, -e	shoe
früher	earlier; formerly	ich putze mir die	I clean (polish) my
früher war er . . .	he used to be . . .	Schuhe	shoes
furchtbar	terrible	selbst	-self
sich (acc.) fürchten vor	to be afraid of	selber	
(dat.)		sich (acc.) setzen	to sit down
die Gefahr, -en	danger	die Sicherheit	safety, security
gefährlich	dangerous	sich (acc.) stellen	to place oneself; to
sich (acc.) gewöhnen an	to get used to		stand (up)
(acc.)		stimmen (impers.)	to be correct
gewöhnt sein an	to be used to	das stimmt	that is correct
(acc.)		das Thema, die Themen	theme; topic
der Gott, ″er	god	sich (acc.) treffen	to meet
die Göttin, -nen	goddess	sich (dat.) überlegen	to think (meditate); to
sich (dat.) die Haare	to cut one's hair		wonder
schneiden		überzeugen	to convince
sich (dat.) die Hände	to wash one's hands	sich (acc.) umziehen	to change (clothes)
waschen		umziehen	to move (from one
handeln	to act		place to another)
handeln mit (dat.)	to deal in	usw. (und so weiter)	and so on
		sich (acc.) verändern	to change

die Verbindung, -en	connection; coalition	sich (*acc.*) vorbereiten auf (*acc.*)	to prepare for
sich (*acc.*) verfahren	to get lost (driving)	vorschlagen	to suggest, propose
verhandeln	to negotiate	sich (*acc. or dat.*) vorstellen	to introduce; to imagine
die Verhandlung, -en	negotiation	ich stelle mich vor	I introduce myself
sich (*acc.*) verheiraten (mit)	to get married (to)	ich stelle mir vor	I imagine
verheiratet sein mit	to be married to	die Wahl, -en	election
verlassen (*plus acc.*)	to leave	sich (*acc.*) wohl fühlen	to feel well
sich (*acc.*) verlassen auf (*acc.*)	to rely on	sich (*acc.*) wundern	to be amazed
		das Wunder, -	miracle
sich (*acc.*) verlaufen	to get lost walking	der Zahn, ̈e	tooth
sich (*acc.*) verlieben in (*acc.*)	to fall in love with	sich (*dat.*) die Zähne putzen	to brush one's teeth
verliebt sein in (*acc.*)	to be in love with	das Zeichen, -	sign
		sich zeigen	to become apparent, to turn out
sich (*acc.*) verloben mit (*dat.*)	to get engaged to	es zeigte sich, daß . . .	it turned out that . . .
verlobt sein mit (*dat.*)	to be engaged to	zerbrechen	to break (to pieces), come apart
verpassen	to miss	zerstören	to destroy
verzeihen	to forgive	die Zusammenarbeit	cooperation

Additional Vocabulary

sich (*acc.*) amüsieren	to amuse oneself	sich erweisen	to turn out, to prove
anklagen	to accuse	es erwies sich, daß . . .	it was proved that . . .
der Angeklagte, -n	the accused	das Experiment', -e	experiment
der Assistent', -en	assistant	das Gefängnis, -se	prison, jail
die Assisten'tin, -nen	assistant	der Gegner, -	opponent
die Assistentenstelle, -n	assistantship	der Generaldirektor, -en	director general
		der Glückwunsch, ̈e	congratulation
außer sich	beside oneself	die Haustür, -en	front door
ich bin außer mir	I am beside myself	sich herausstellen	to turn out
beabsichtigen	to intend	es stellte sich heraus, daß . . .	it turned out that . . .
die Absicht, -en	intention	der Kapitän, -e	captain
befreien	to liberate	das Klima	climate
die Befreiung	liberation	das Kraftwerk, -e	power plant
die Demonstration', -en	demonstration	das Atomkraftwerk	atomic power plant
der Demonstrant, -en	demonstrator	das Labor', -s	lab
das Dreieck, -e	triangle	das Laborato'rium, *pl.* die Laborato'rien	laboratory
der Dummkopf, ̈e	stupid person, dumbbell, dunce		

der Leiter, -	head, chief, leader	der Täter, -	culprit, criminal
der Ministerpräsident, -en	prime minister	unmittelbar	immediate, direct
		die Ursache, -n	cause
der Mord, -e	murder	zur Verfügung stehen	to be available
das Opfer, -	victim	vergiften	to poison
der Stammtisch, -e	regular table (in a restaurant)	die Waffe, -n	weapon
		wetten	to bet

Strong Verbs

(sich)* anziehen		zog an	angezogen	to dress
sich ausschlafen	schläft aus	schlief aus	ausgeschlafen	to sleep one's fill
(sich) ausziehen		zog aus	ausgezogen	to undress
brechen	bricht	brach	(ist) gebrochen	to break
(sich) entscheiden		entschied	entschieden	to decide
sich entschließen		entschloß	entschlossen	to make up one's mind
scheiden		schied	geschieden	to separate, divide
(sich) treffen	trifft	traf	getroffen	to meet
(sich) umziehen		zog um	umgezogen	to change clothes (refl.); to move
sich verfahren	verfährt	verfuhr	verfahren	to lose one's way
(sich) verlassen	verläßt	verließ	verlassen	to depend (refl.); to leave
sich verlaufen	verläuft	verlief	verlaufen	to lose one's way
verzeihen		verzieh	verziehen	to forgive
vorschlagen	schlägt vor	schlug vor	vorgeschlagen	to propose
zerbrechen	zerbricht	zerbrach	(ist) zerbrochen	to break

*sich in parentheses indicates occasional reflexive verbs.

UNIT 15 Adjectives

You have already encountered many German adjectives, but up to now you have been using only predicate adjectives (*the sky is blue*) rather than attributive adjectives, that is, adjectives preceding nouns (*the blue sky*). Many of the earlier reading selections contain German attributive adjectives, which, unlike their English counterparts, have endings resembling the endings of **der-** and **ein-**words.

We can't blame you if you consider these endings a needless complication, and well they might be, because the language could, almost, get along without them. But unfortunately, they are a fact of life and have to be dealt with. Actually, the system of adjective endings is quite simple; what you will find difficult is to acquire enough fluency to use these forms correctly and without thinking. The problem is compounded, of course, because you must also automatically come up with the correct gender of the noun that the adjective goes with. But you should not let these adjective endings deter you from speaking and writing German—as long as you can communicate your ideas, you have achieved a great deal. Germans are tolerant in this respect: there are so many foreigners in Germany, in Austria, and in Switzerland that people are used to foreign accents and grammatical mistakes—and some foreigners don't get all their adjective endings straight after years of living there.

**Wunderbare
Nebentätigkeit**

für den erkrankten Fischer-Dieskau

beim Europäischen Patentamt

Blutiger Terror

Schwierige Geburt

Totes Kind

The reading selection of this unit should provide ample opportunity for conversations in which you can use your new acquisition, the adjective endings. Once more you will be reading about German education, but from a much more personal point of view. Let your teacher play the role of Frau Anni Schneider or of her divorced husband, and see what either side has to say about the education of the children.

Patterns

[1] Attributive Adjectives, Nominative Singular

SEE
ANALYSIS
155–156
(p. 460)

Der neue Schüler hieß Bodenstein.	The name of the new student was Bodenstein.
Ein junger Mann wartete auf ihn.	A young man was waiting for him.
Die junge Frau hieß Petra.	The young woman's name was Petra.
Eine junge Frau stand neben ihm.	A young woman was standing next to him.
Das kleine Mädchen hieß auch Petra.	The little girl's name was also Petra.
Petra war noch ein kleines Mädchen, als ich sie kennenlernte.	Petra was still a little girl when I met her.
Mein lieber Vater!	My dear Father: (Salutation)
Meine liebe Mutter!	My dear Mother:
Mein liebes Kind!	My dear Child:
Lieber Vater!	Dear Father:
Liebe Mutter!	Dear Mother:
Liebes Kind!	Dear Child:
Das ist wirklich ein guter Wein!	That is really a good wine!
Guter Wein ist teuer.	Good wine is expensive.
Klare Fleischsuppe ist eine Spezialität unseres Hauses.	Clear broth is a specialty of the house.
Eine gute Suppe gehört zu jeder Mahlzeit.	A good soup belongs with every meal.
Unsere italienische Gemüsesuppe ist auch nicht schlecht.	Our Italian vegetable soup isn't bad either.
Frisches Obst ist immer gut.	Fresh fruit is always good.
Das italienische Obst ist nicht mehr so teuer wie früher.	Italian fruit is no longer as expensive as it used to be.
Ich empfehle Ihnen Dortmunder Union; das ist ein gutes Bier.	I recommend Dortmunder Union; that's a good beer.

das Germanische Nationalmuseum

auf vollen Touren

PATTERNS

Eigenes Telefon gehört zum Leben.

VARIATIONS

Der Mann war sehr alt. Es war ein sehr _____ Mann.

Sie ist intelligent. Sie ist ein _____ Mädchen.

Der Wein ist wirklich gut. Das ist wirklich ein _____ Wein.

Sie ist immer noch schön. Sie ist immer noch eine _____ Frau.

Das Wasser ist aber kalt. Das ist aber _____ Wasser.

Das Bier hier ist gut. Das ist wirklich ein _____ Bier.

So klein ist eure Barbara nicht mehr. Sie ist kein _____ Kind mehr.

Gestern war es kalt. Gestern war ein _____ Tag.

[2] Attributive Adjectives, Accusative Singular

Hast du den alten Mann gesehen?	Did you see the old man?	**SEE ANALYSIS 156** (p. 460)

Hast du den alten Mann gesehen? — Did you see the old man?

Nein, einen alten Mann habe ich nicht gesehen. — No, I haven't seen an old man.

Ich kenne die junge Dame leider nicht. — I don't know the young lady, unfortunately.

Ich habe das junge Mädchen lange nicht gesehen. — I haven't seen the young girl for a long time.

Schmidts haben gestern ein kleines Mädchen bekommen. — The Schmidts had a little girl yesterday.

Nehmen Sie ein heißes Bad und gehen Sie früh ins Bett. — Take a hot bath and go to bed early.

VARIATIONS

Gestern war das Wetter schlecht. Gestern hatten wir _____ Wetter.

Gestern war es kalt. Gestern hatten wir einen _____ Tag.

Der Wein war gut. Wir haben einen _____ Wein getrunken.

Das Bier ist wirklich gut. Wo habt ihr denn dieses _____ Bier gekauft.

Meyers Frau ist jung. Meyer hat eine _____ Frau.

[3] Attributive Adjectives, Dative Singular

Mit *dem* alten Wagen fahre ich aber nicht an den Bodensee. — I won't drive to the Lake of Constance with *that* old car.

Was soll ich denn mit einem alten Wagen? — What am I supposed to do with an old car?

Wir wohnten damals in einer kleinen Stadt. — At that time we lived in a small town.

SEE ANALYSIS 156 (p. 460)

Wir wohnten damals in einem kleinen Städtchen an der Elbe.

We then lived in a small town on the Elbe
River.

Ingrid ist aus guter Familie.

Ingrid comes from a good family.

VARIATIONS

Gibt es hier warmes Wasser?—Ja, wir haben nur Zimmer mit _____ Wasser.

Das Haus ist alt. Wir wohnen in einem _____ Haus.

Die Stadt ist klein. Wir wohnen in einer _____ Stadt.

Das Wetter ist schlecht. Bei dem _____ Wetter bleibe ich zu Hause.

[4] Attributive Adjectives, Genitive Singular

Ingrid war die Tochter eines bekannten
Architekten in Berlin.

Ingrid was the daughter of a well-known
architect in Berlin.

Der Besuch der alten Dame ist ein Stück von
Dürrenmatt.

The Visit of the Old Lady is a play by
Dürrenmatt.

Wegen des schlechten Wetters konnten wir
in Frankfurt nicht landen.

Because of the bad weather we couldn't land
in Frankfurt.

Innerhalb* eines einzigen Tages verkauft unsere Firma oft zwanzig bis fünfundzwanzig Wagen.

Within a single day our firm often sells
twenty to twenty-five cars.

Außerhalb* der inneren Stadt gibt es noch
viel offenes Land.

Outside (of) the inner city there is still much
open space.

VARIATIONS

Die Reise war lang, aber trotz der _____ Reise war ich gar nicht müde.

Ein intelligenter Mann raucht PRIVAT. PRIVAT, die Zigarette des _____ Mannes.

Denken Sie modern? Der Preis eines _____ Hauses ist nicht so hoch, wie Sie denken.

[5] Attributive Adjectives, Plural

SEE
ANALYSIS
156
(p. 460)

Die jungen Leute gehen ins Kino.

The young people go to the movies.

Unsere deutschen Freunde wohnen in Freiburg.

Our German friends live in Freiburg.

Liebe Eltern!

Dear Parents:

Petra ist die Mutter der beiden Kinder.

Petra is the mother of two children.

Eines der kleinen Mädchen hieß Petra.

One of the little girls was called Petra.

Was halten Sie von den italienischen Autos?

What do you think of the Italian cars?

Für seine neuen Brieftauben hat Ingelheim
viel Geld bezahlt.

Ingelheim paid a lot of money for his new
carrier pigeons.

Niemand liest seine letzten Romane.

Nobody reads his last novels.

Er brachte ihr rote Rosen.

He brought her red roses.

Sie hat zwei intelligente Kinder.

She has two intelligent children.

---

*The prepositions **innerhalb** (*within, inside of*) and **außerhalb** (*outside of*) take the genitive, like **trotz, während, wegen.**

Meyers Kinder sind intelligent. Meyer hat _____ Kinder.

Rot ist meine Lieblingsfarbe; daher bringt er mir immer _____ Rosen.

Ich habe Freunde in Amerika. Ich fliege morgen zu meinen _____ Freunden.

Sie kennen doch Amerika, nicht wahr? Was halten Sie denn von den _____ Schulen?

[6] Series of Attributive Adjectives

		SEE ANALYSIS 156 (p. 460)

Der blonde junge Mann da drüben heißt Kleinholz.

The name of the blond young man over there is Kleinholz.

Zuerst kam ein blonder junger Mann aus dem Haus.

First a blond young man came out of the house.

Die blonde junge Dame ist seine Frau.

The blonde young lady is his wife.

Zuerst kam eine blonde junge Dame aus dem Haus.

First a blonde young lady came out of the house.

Das kleine blonde Mädchen hieß Petra.

The name of the blonde little girl was Petra.

Vor dem Haus saß ein blondes kleines Mädchen.

A blonde little girl was sitting in front of the house.

Die Eltern des netten jungen Mannes kamen aus Leipzig.

The parents of the nice young man came from Leipzig.

Mit deinem alten grauen Mantel kannst du doch nicht nach Baden-Baden fahren.

With your old gray coat you can't go to Baden-Baden.

Ich nehme an, Sie kennen den netten jungen Mann da drüben.

I assume you know the nice young man over there.

Die hellen, kurzen Sommernächte Norwegens hat er nie vergessen können.

He has never been able to forget the bright, short summer nights of Norway.

Helle kurze Sommernächte wie in Norwegen gibt es in Afrika nicht.

In Africa, there are no bright, short summer nights as in Norway.

Mit seinen langen, sentimentalen Romanen hat er viel Geld verdient.

He has made a lot of money with his long, sentimental novels.

From an exhibit in East Berlin.

VARIATIONS

Insert the adjectives **neu** and **automatisch** in the following sentences.

Ich wollte, ich hätte eine Waschmaschine.
Der Preis einer Waschmaschine ist gar nicht so hoch.
Die Preise unserer Waschmaschinen sind gar nicht so hoch.
Mit dieser Waschmaschine ist Ihre Frau bestimmt zufrieden.
Ist das eure Waschmaschine?
Diese Waschmaschinen sind gar nicht teuer.
Waschmaschinen sind gar nicht teuer.
Wir können nur noch Waschmaschinen verkaufen.

[7] der-Words

SEE
ANALYSIS
158
(p. 464)

Bei diesem schlechten Wetter bleibe ich zu Hause.

In this bad weather I'll stay home.

Welche deutschen Städte haben Sie denn gesehen?

Which German cities did you see?

Jeder junge Mensch sollte einmal ein Jahr lang im Ausland leben.

Every young person ought to live abroad for a year.

Von hier aus fährt jede halbe Stunde ein Zug nach Stuttgart.

From here, a train goes to Stuttgart every half hour.

Dort haben wir schon manchen schönen Tag verbracht.

We've spent many a beautiful day there.

Mancher von den jungen Soldaten wußte gar nicht, wofür er kämpfte.

Many a young soldier didn't know at all what he was fighting for.

VARIATIONS

Express in German.

Who is this young man?
Which young man? (*nom.*)
Who are these young men?
Which young men?
In which hotel does he live?
He always lives in this old hotel.
These old hotels are not expensive.
Every good hotel should have a garage.

[8] solcher, solch, so

SEE
ANALYSIS
159
(p. 464)

So einen guten Freund finde ich so bald nicht wieder.

Such a good friend I will not find again soon.

Wie kann ein so intelligenter Mensch nur so blöd sein!

How can a man who is that intelligent be so stupid!

Für einen so alten Wagen bekommst du bestimmt keine tausend Mark.

I'm sure you won't get a thousand marks for a car as old as that.

Für solch einen Wagen muß man mindestens zwanzigtausend Mark bezahlen.	For such a (fancy) car you'll have to pay at least twenty thousand marks.
Ich wußte gar nicht, daß er noch so kleine Kinder hat.	I didn't know that his children are still that little.
Solche Kinder wie die möchte ich auch haben.	I'd like to have children like that too.

[9] Numbers

Am ersten und zweiten Februar waren wir in Berlin, am dritten und vierten in Hamburg und vom fünften bis zum zehnten in Bonn.

SEE ANALYSIS 160 (p. 465)

Berlin, den 1.2.1978 (den ersten Februar 1978)

Hamburg, 8.9.77 (den achten September 1977)

Read the following dates.

13.1.27	7.7.29	18.6.1962
8.2.25	20.8.54	22.2.1732
25.10.04	1.9.39	7.12.1941

Heinrich I. (Heinrich der Erste)

Friedrich Wilhelm IV. (Friedrich Wilhelm der Vierte)

Er war ein Sohn Friedrichs II. (Er war ein Sohn Friedrichs des Zweiten.)

Read the following.

Leo XIII. (1887–1903) (1887 bis 1903)

Pius X. (1903–1914)

Benedict XV. (1914–1922)

Pius XI. (1922–1939)

Pius XII. (1939–1958)

Johannes XXIII. (1958–1963) (der Dreiundzwanzigste)

Und hier, meine Damen und Herren, sehen Sie ein Bild von Herzog August III., der, wie Sie wissen, der Vater Sigismunds II. war. Seine Frau Mechthild, eine Tochter Augusts V. von Niederlohe-Schroffenstein, soll die schönste Frau ihrer Zeit gewesen sein.

Nein, nach Italien fahren will ich nicht. Erstens habe ich kein Geld, zweitens habe ich keine Lust, drittens mag ich Meyers nicht, und viertens ist meine Frau dagegen.

Nein, soviel kann ich nicht essen. Die Hälfte davon ist mehr als genug.

Hat Tante Amalie schon ihr Testament gemacht?—Ja, und ein Drittel von ihrem Geld bekommt das Museum.

Seine Frau erhielt zwei Drittel seines Vermögens, und das dritte Drittel ging an seine beiden Söhne.

Ich hätte gerne ein halbes Pfund Butter.

Geben Sie mir bitte ein viertel Pfund Schinken.

Read aloud:

$\frac{1}{2}$ $\frac{1}{3}$ $\frac{2}{7}$ $\frac{6}{8}$ $\frac{5}{12}$

[10] The Rhetorical **nicht**

SEE
ANALYSIS
161
(p. 466)

Haben Sie einen *Bru*der?	Do you have a brother?
Haben Sie keinen *Bru*der?	Don't you have a brother?
Haben Sie nicht *ei*nen *Bru*der?	Don't you have a single brother?
Haben Sie nicht einen *Bru*der?	You have a brother, haven't you?

Ist Manfred Schmidtke nicht ein netter junger Mann?

Habe ich nicht einen intelligenten Sohn?

Ist sie nicht ein hübsches Mädchen?

Warst du nicht gestern abend mit Inge im Kino?

Haben Sie nicht früher bei der Hansa-Bank gearbeitet?

Bin ich nicht schon immer dagegen gewesen?

Hat nicht unsere Partei seit Jahren immer wieder bewiesen, daß sie allein den Weg weiß in
eine bessere Zukunft?

Change the following statements into rhetorical questions.

Sie haben ihn schon vor dem Krieg kennengelernt, nicht wahr?

Seine Tochter hat den Fritz Müller geheiratet, nicht wahr?

Sie haben schon immer einmal nach Amerika fahren wollen, nicht wahr?

[11] **hin** and **her**

Be prepared to produce orally the sentences on the left when you hear the sentences on
the right, and vice versa.

SEE
ANALYSIS
162
(p. 467)

Ich fahre sofort hin.	Er kommt sofort her.
Kannst du hinfahren?	Kannst du herkommen?
Ich bin sofort hingefahren.	Er ist sofort hergekommen.
Ich brauche nicht hinzufahren.	Er braucht nicht herzukommen.
Wer hat dich denn dahingebracht?	Wer hat dich denn hierhergebracht?
Wie bist du denn dahingekommen?	Wie bist du denn hierhergekommen?
Sie fahren nach Tirol? Dahin fahre ich auch.	Sie kommen aus Tirol? Daher komme ich auch.

VARIATIONS

Form variations with the following pattern:

> **Den kenne ich noch von früher her.**
> (Literally: I've known him from an earlier time on.)

von der Schule	von der Tanzstunde
vom Kriege	von München

Form variations of the following situations with **vorher** and **nachher**:

> **Gestern abend waren wir im Theater. Vorher haben wir im Regina gegessen, und nach-
> her waren wir bei Schmidts.**

Letzten Mittwoch war ich in Salzburg.
Um sieben haben wir zu Abend gegessen.
Morgen mittag besuche ich Tante Amalie.

Memorize the following sentences.

Weißt du was? Rosemarie hat vorhin angerufen.
Ich war vorhin bei Schmidts.
Diese Uhr hier ist hin,—die ist kaputt.
Meine Ruh' ist hin, mein Herz ist schwer. (Goethe)

Be prepared to produce the sentences on the left when you hear the sentences on the
right, and vice versa.

Wohin gehst du denn?	Wo gehst du denn hin?
Woher kommst du denn?	Wo kommst du denn her?
Wohin ist er denn gegangen?	Wo ist er denn hingegangen?
Woher ist er denn gekommen?	Wo ist er denn hergekommen?
Dahin gehe ich auch.	Da gehe ich auch hin.
Daher komme ich auch.	Da komme ich auch her.

In the following examples, note the difference in meaning between the forms with **hin-**
and **her-** and the forms without **hin-** and **her-**.

Die Titanic ist untergegangen.
    The Titanic sank.

Ich gehe ins Eßzimmer hinunter.
    I'm going down to the dining room.

Die Sonne geht unter.
    The sun sets.

Er kommt sofort herunter.
    He'll be down in a minute.

Wo seid ihr denn untergekommen?
    Where did you find a place to stay?

Ist er schon heruntergekommen?
    Has he come down yet?

Das Licht ist ausgegangen.
    The light went out.

Er ist gerade hinausgegangen.
    He just went out.

Die Sonne geht auf.
    The sun rises.

Er ist schon hinaufgegangen.
    He has already gone up.

Ich konnte ihn nicht mehr einholen.
    I couldn't catch up with him anymore.

Hast du die Zeitung schon hereingeholt?
    Have you brought the paper in yet?

Mit zweihundert Mark im Monat kann ich
    nicht auskommen.
    I can't get along on two hundred marks a
    month.

Ich habe ihn noch nicht herauskommen
    sehen.
    I haven't seen him come out yet.

Note the "prepositional brackets" in the following sentences.

Er kam aus dem Haus heraus.
Er ging ins Haus hinein.
Wir fahren durch den Panamakanal hindurch.
Wir stiegen auf den Berg hinauf.
Er sprang über den Zaun hinüber.

155 Predicate Adjectives and Adverbs

Most English adjectives can be transformed into adverbs by adding the suffix
-ly, for example, *high, highly; beautiful, beautifully;* for some others, there is a
separate adverbial form, for example, *good, well;* and only a few have the
same form both as adjectives and as adverbs, for example, *fast.* In German, on
the other hand, predicate adjectives and adverbs always have the same form.

> **Seine Frau soll sehr *schön* sein.**
> His wife is supposed to be very *beautiful.*

> **Sie soll auch sehr *schön* singen können.**
> Supposedly she can also sing very *beautifully.*

156 Strong (Primary) and Weak (Secondary) Adjective Endings

Predicate adjectives are verbal complements; they constitute the second prong
and never have any ending.

> **Meyer ist leider nicht intelligent.**

Attributive adjectives belong to a following noun and always have an ending
which depends on the case, gender, and number of that noun, and on the presence or absence of a **der**-word or **ein**-word (see Analysis **22–23**, pp. 42–43).

> **Wir haben einen intelligenten Sohn.**   **Wir haben ein   intelligentes Kind.**
> **Wir haben eine intelligente Tochter.** **Wir haben   intelligente Kinder.**

The endings of attributive adjectives are the bane of German grammar. They
are a bothersome anachronism, and you will sympathize with Mark Twain,

who said he would rather decline two glasses of German beer than one German adjective.

The trouble is that attributive adjectives use not just one set of endings but two: a set of primary (or *strong*) endings and a set of secondary (or *weak*) endings.

The strong endings are the endings of the **der**-words. Because these endings are unstressed (as in **jeder, jede, jedes**), the long **-ie** of **die** becomes **-e** and the **-as** of **das** becomes **-es.**

Strong Endings

***der*-WORD ENDINGS (ALL STRONG)**

	MASC.	FEM.	NEUT.	PLURAL
NOM.	**-er**	**-e**	**-es**	**-e**
ACC.	**-en**	**-e**	**-es**	**-e**
DAT.	**-em**	**-er**	**-em**	**-en**
GEN.	**-es**	**-er**	**-es**	**-er**

***ein*-WORD ENDINGS (EITHER ZERO OR STRONG)**

ein-words (**ein, kein, mein,** etc.) have the same endings as **der**-words except for the three forms that have no ending at all.

	MASC.	FEM.	NEUT.	PLURAL
NOM.	Ø	**-e**	Ø	**-e**
ACC.	**-en**	**-e**	Ø	**-e**
DAT.	**-em**	**-er**	**-em**	**-en**
GEN.	**-es**	**-er**	**-es**	**-er**

Weak Endings

There are only two weak endings, **-e** and **-en.** Note that only the masculine singular distinguishes between nominative and accusative.

	MASC.	FEM.	NEUT.	PLURAL
NOM.	**-e**	**-e**	**-e**	**-en**
ACC.	**-en**	**-e**	**-e**	**-en**
DAT.	**-en**	**-en**	**-en**	**-en**
GEN.	**-en**	**-en**	**-en**	**-en**

Attributive adjectives use both strong and weak endings. The trick is to learn (and to overlearn until you can do it automatically) when to use a strong ending and when to use a weak ending.

You *must* observe the following two rules. Study these rules before you proceed to the sentences in the table on page 462. The table has four slots, marked

		SLOT 0 NO ENDING	SLOT 1 STRONG ENDING	SLOT 2 WEAK ENDING	SLOT 3 NOUN		RULE TO BE APPLIED
1	NOM.	Dies (das) ist	guter		Kaffee.		1
2	SING.	Dies (das) ist	gute		Butter.		1
3		Dies (das) ist	gutes		Bier.		1
4		Das (dies) ist ein	guter		Kaffee.		1
5	NOM. SING.	Das (dies) ist	eine	gute	Suppe.		2
6		Das (dies) ist ein	gutes		Bier.		1
7			Der	junge	Mann	blieb zu Hause.	2
8	NOM. SING.		Die	junge	Dame	blieb zu Hause.	2
9			Das	kleine	Kind	blieb zu Hause.	2
10		Gegen	hohen		Blutdruck	nehmen Sie Vitalin.	1
11	ACC. SING.	Gegen	große		Nervosität	nehmen Sie Vitalin.	1
12		Gegen	hohes		Fieber	nehmen Sie Vitalin.	1
13		Siehst du	den	jungen	Mann	da drüben?	2
14		Ich sehe	keinen	jungen	Mann.		2
15	ACC. SING.	Siehst du	die	junge	Frau	da drüben?	2
16		Ich sehe	keine	junge	Frau.		2
17		Siehst du	das	kleine	Mädchen	da drüben?	2
18		Ich sehe kein	kleines		Mädchen.		1
19		Bei	dichtem		Nebel	bleiben wir zu Hause.	1
20	DAT. SING.	Bei	großer		Hitze	bleiben wir zu Hause.	1
21		Bei	schlechtem		Wetter	bleiben wir zu Hause.	1
22		Mit	dem	alten	Wagen	fahre ich nicht.	2
23	DAT. SING.	Mit	der	alten	Kutsche	fahre ich nicht.	2
24		Mit	dem	alten	Auto	fahre ich nicht.	2
25		Ich bin die Frau	eines	intelligenten	Mannes.		2
26	GEN. SING.	Ich bin der Mann	einer	intelligenten	Frau.		2
27		Sie ist die Mutter	eines	intelligenten	Kindes.		2
28	NOM. PL.		Gute		Menschen	lügen nicht.	1
29	ALL GENDERS		Die	guten	Menschen	lügen nicht.	2
30	ACC. PL.	Wir haben	gute		Kinder.		1
31		Wir haben	unsere	guten	Kinder.		2
32	DAT. PL.	Die Eltern von	intelligenten		Kindern	sind meistens auch intelligent.	1
33		Die Eltern von	diesen	intelligenten	Kindern	sind auch intelligent.	2
34	GEN. PL.	Die Eltern	intelligenter		Kinder	sind meistens auch intelligent.	1
35		Die Eltern	dieser	intelligenten	Kinder	sind auch intelligent.	2

0, 1, 2, and 3 respectively. The zero-slot is reserved for the three endingless forms of the **ein**-words; slot 1 contains words with strong endings; slot 2 words with weak endings; and slot 3 the noun that follows. The last column in the table indicates which rule applies to the particular sentence.

RULE 1   If no strong ending (on a **der**-word or **ein**-word) precedes the adjective, the adjective itself takes a strong ending and is placed in slot 1.

RULE 2   If slot 1 is occupied either by a **der**-word or by one of the **ein**-words *with* an ending, the adjective goes into slot 2 and takes a weak ending.

You can add a second adjective to each sentence in the table, and it will take the same ending as the first. For example:

> **dieser intelligente junge Mann**
> **dieses intelligente junge Mädchen**
> **ein intelligenter junger Mann**
> **ein intelligentes junges Mädchen**

These rules are easy to learn. However, it will take time and lots of practice to acquire the facility to apply them automatically. We seriously urge you to memorize the thirty-five sentences in the table so that you can recite them without using a wrong ending.

To sum up: Slot 1 *must be filled* as long as there is a word that can take a strong ending. If there is no word that *has* to take strong endings (like **der**), the adjective "moves forward" and takes strong endings.

157 Adjective Endings: Variants

1. In the dative masculine and neuter, the sequence **-em -en** is so ingrained that of two or more adjectives not preceded by an **ein**-word or **der**-word only the first tends to take the strong ending **-em.**

	SLOT 0	SLOT 1	SLOT 2	SLOT 3
Bei		diesem	nebligen kalten	**Wetter**
Bei		nebligem	kalten	**Wetter**

2. In the genitive masculine and neuter, with adjectives not preceded by a **der**-word or an **ein**-word, the strong endings have been replaced by weak endings. These forms, however, do not, as a rule, occur in the spoken language.

	SLOT 0	SLOT 1	SLOT 2	SLOT 3
Trotz			starken	**Nebels**
Trotz			schlechten	**Wetters**

The spoken language prefers the regular pattern with the dative.

	SLOT 0	SLOT 1	SLOT 2	SLOT 3
Trotz		starkem		Nebel
Trotz		schlechtem		Wetter

3. Adjectives ending in **-el** and **-er** drop the **-e-** if an attributive ending is added.

Das Zimmer war dunkel.	The room was dark.
Sie saßen in einem dunklen Zimmer.	They sat in a dark room.
Die Zimmer hier sind aber sehr teuer.	The rooms here are very expensive.
Wir wohnten in einem teuren Zimmer.	We lived in an expensive room.

4. The adjective **hoch** drops the **-ch**-sound if an ending is added and substitutes a silent **-h-**.

Der Baum war sehr hoch.	The tree was very tall.
Vor dem Haus stand ein hoher Baum.	A tall tree stood in front of the house.

158 der-Words

The following are declined like the definite article; that is, they take strong endings:

dieser   this
jeder   each, every
welcher   which, what
mancher   many a; *plural:* some

(a) The neuter singular **dieses** may be used without an ending (**dies**) in the nominative and accusative.

Dies Buch hier ist wirklich gut.

In sentences identifying or introducing persons or objects, **dies** must be used.

Gerda, dies ist mein Freund Hans.
Und dies, meine Damen und Herren, war das Schlafzimmer des Königs.

(b) **Jeder** has no plural forms. The plural of **jeder Mensch** is **alle Menschen**.

(c) **Welcher** is normally used as an interrogative: **in welcher Stadt?** (*in which (what) city?*).

159 so, solch

In the singular, **so ein** may be and **ein so** must be followed by adjectives.

Sie ist doch so ein intelligentes Mädchen.   She is such an intelligent girl.

Das Bier, das unsere Sprache spricht

So ein Bier...

So ein Bier, so wunderschön wie Hofbräu!

Ein so intelligentes Mädchen findet sicher eine gute Stellung.	A girl who is that intelligent will certainly find a good job.

In the plural, **so** is immediately followed by an adjective.

Ich wußte gar nicht, daß er noch so kleine Kinder hat.	I didn't know that his children are still so little.

It is advisable to use **solch** only with a strong ending and without a following adjective; it then means "such a degree of" or "that kind of" (cf. English *with such force*).

Warum hast du denn immer solche Angst? (so große Angst?)	Why are you always so afraid?
Mit solchen Menschen will ich nichts zu tun haben.	I don't want to have anything to do with that kind of people.

160 Ordinal Numbers; Fractions

German *ordinal numbers* are attributive adjectives.

der erste	der neunzehnte
der zweite	der zwanzig*ste*
der *dritte*	der einundzwanzig*ste*
der vierte	der dreißig*ste*
der fünfte	etc.
der sechste	
der siebte	
etc.	

To make a figure indicate an ordinal number, German uses a period.

der 4. Juli	the Fourth of July

NOTE:

Heinrich I. (Heinrich der Erste)
Friedrich Wilhelm IV. (Friedrich Wilhelm der Vierte)
Er war ein Sohn Friedrichs II. (Friedrichs des Zweiten)

Series are expressed as follows:

1.	erstens	5.	fünftens
2.	zweitens	6.	sechstens
3.	drittens	7.	siebtens
4.	viertens		etc.

„Erstens bin ich zu alt, und zweitens bin ich zu müde."

Fractions:

die Hälfte,-n	das Sechstel,-
das Drittel,-	das Siebtel,-
das Viertel,-	etc.
das Fünftel,-	

All fractions are uninflected, except for **halb**, which is usually used with endings.

$^1/_3$ **ein drittel**
$^3/_4$ **drei viertel**
$^7/_8$ **sieben achtel**

Ich hätte gerne ein viertel Pfund Butter.
Ich hätte gerne ein halbes Pfund Butter.

But:

eineinhalb Pfund Butter

161 The Rhetorical **nicht**

If a speaker asks for a positive confirmation of a statement he makes, he adds
don't you?, aren't you?, haven't you? and so on in English and **nicht?** or **nicht
wahr?** in German.

Du warst doch gestern abend mit Inge im Kino, nicht?
You and Inge were at the movies last night, weren't you?

This rhetorical **nicht** can be moved forward, usually behind the last pronoun if
the statement is transformed into a rhetorical question. The normal question

Warst du gestern abend mit Inge im Kino?

thus becomes the rhetorical

Warst du nicht gestern abend mit Inge im *Kino?*

This rhetorical **nicht** appears only in yes-or-no questions. It is never stressed; it is always followed by the stress point of the sentence; and if followed by **ein**, it cannot be replaced by **kein**. An affirmative answer to such rhetorical questions can be either **Ja** or **Doch**. However, even though the speaker always expects a confirmation, the answer can, of course, also be **Nein**.

Haben Sie nicht einen Bruder? Answer: *Ja, Doch,* or *Nein.*	You have a brother, don't you?
Haben Sie keinen Bruder? Answer: *Doch* or *Nein,* but never *Ja.*	Don't you *have* a brother?
Haben Sie einen Bruder? Answer: *Ja* or *Nein,* but never *Doch.*	Do you have a brother?

Further examples:

Warum hast du denn den *Meyer* nicht besucht?
(Real question; stress point precedes *nicht.*)

Hast du den Meyer letzte Woche *nicht* besucht?
(Real question; *nicht* is stressed.)

Hast du nicht letzte Woche den *Meyer* besucht?
(Rhetorical question; stress point follows unstressed *nicht.*)

162 hin and her

Hin and **her** are both directional adverbs denoting motion. **Hin** indicates motion away from the speaker or the speaker's position, **her** refers to motion toward the speaker.

hin and her as Verbal Complements

Hin and **her** can both be used by themselves as complements of certain verbs denoting various methods of traveling or change of location.

Thus a person told to visit his father immediately might say:

Ich fahre (gehe, reise) sofort hin

or he might say:

Ich werde sofort hinfahren.
Ich bin sofort hingefahren.
Ich brauche nicht sofort hinzufahren.
Ich weiß nicht, ob ich sofort hinfahren kann.

The father might say:

Mein Sohn ist sofort hergekommen.
Kannst du sofort herkommen?

hin and **her** with Adverbs of Place and of Time

Since **hin** implies no specific goal and since **her** implies no specific point of origin, they are frequently found after more specific terms like **da, dort, hier,** and after prepositional phrases expressing goal or origin.

>Wer hat dich denn hierhergebracht?
>Du willst sofort zum Flughafen? Wer bringt dich denn dahin?
>Im nächsten Dorf gibt es ein Hotel? Wie weit ist es denn bis dahin?—Zehn
>   Kilometer. Wir kommen gerade daher (dorther, von dorther).

Her may also be used with a temporal meaning.

>Das ist ein alter Freund von mir. Den kenne ich noch *von der Schule her.*
>Den kenne ich noch *von früher her.*
>Gestern abend waren wir im Theater. *Vor*her haben wir im Regina gegessen,
>   und *nach*her waren wir bei Schmidts.

Hin may be used as a predicate adjective meaning *gone* or *beyond repair.*

>Alles ist hin.

Vorhin is an adverb of time meaning *just a little while ago.*

>Vorhin hat Rosemarie angerufen.

hin and **her** Following **wo**

In many cases, the use of **her** and **hin** stems from the "splitting" of **wohin** and **woher.**

>Wohin *gehst* du denn?
>Wo gehst du denn *hin?*
>Wo willst du denn *hin?*
>Wo ist er denn *hin*gegangen?
>Wo *du* hingehst, da will ich *auch* hin.
>Woher *kommen* Sie denn?
>Wo kommen *Sie* denn her?
>Wo kann *der* denn hergekommen sein?
>Wo hast du denn den neuen *Man*tel her?

The unseparated **wohin** and **woher** are today slightly literary in character. They *may* be used in conversation, but the separated forms are heard much more frequently.

hin and **her** Preceding Another Verbal Prefix

Certain English compound verbs have developed special meanings which are apt to trap a foreigner. It is, for instance, a surprise to a German-speaking person to find out that *he threw in the towel* cannot always be replaced by *he threw the towel in.*

In German, the verbal prefixes **ein-**, **unter-**, **auf-**, and **aus-**, if used without **hin-** or **her-**, are apt to develop nonliteral meanings. To express a strictly *spatial* meaning **hinein-** or **herein-**, **hinunter-** or **herunter-**, **hinauf-** or **herauf-**, **hinaus-** or **heraus-** must be used.

For example, **untergehen** may mean not only *to sink*, but also *to come to an end*, *to vanish*, *to perish*. Note the difference:

Die Titanic ging unter.	The Titanic sank.
Die Inkakultur ging unter.	The Inca civilization vanished.
Er ist schon hinuntergegangen.	He has already gone down.

Compare also:

Das Licht ging aus.	The light went out.
Wir sind ausgegangen.	We went out (theater, restaurant, etc.).
Wir sind hinausgegangen.	We went out (of a room).

There are no definite rules governing the use of **hin-** and **her-** in these cases, but in general it can be said that verbs with **hin-** and **her-** in the complement have a strictly spatial meaning, whereas verbs with the simple complements **ein-**, **unter-**, **auf-**, and **aus-** tend to have figurative meanings.

Kommst du mit dem Geld aus?
Can you get along with the money you have?

Er kam heraus.
He came out (of a room).

Ich konnte mit meinem VW den Mercedes nicht einholen.
With my VW I could not catch up with the Mercedes.

Hast du die Zeitung schon hereingeholt?
Have you brought the paper in yet?

Die Sonne ging auf.
The sun rose.

Wollen Sie bitte in den zweiten Stock hinaufgehen? *
Would you please go up to the third floor?

Wir haben Sie im Hotel Zeppelin untergebracht.
We've put you up at the Hotel Zeppelin.

Ihre Koffer habe ich schon hinunterbringen lassen.
I've already had your suitcases taken down.

hin and **her** in "Prepositional Brackets"

The sentence

Wir fuhren durch den Panamakanal

*Since **Stock** means upper story, **der erste Stock** corresponds to the second floor, **der zweite Stock** to the third floor, etc.

expresses the idea

> We went through the Panama Canal.

In order to strengthen the feeling of spatial motion, the preposition **durch** can be reinforced by adding the verbal complement **hindurch**.

> **Wir fuhren *durch* den Panamakanal *hindurch*.**

This **durch . . . hindurch** acts as a prepositional bracket enclosing the noun. Other frequently used brackets are:

> **Er kam *aus* dem Haus *heraus*.**
> **Er ging *in* das Haus *hinein*.**
> **Er stieg *auf* den Turm** (*tower*) ***hinauf*.**

Frequently **her,** without a preposition, forms the second bracket; it then expresses continuous motion.

> **Er lief hinter mir her.**
> **Er lief neben mir her.**
> **Er lief vor mir her.**

This tendency to "bracket" is so strong in German that it is found even in such syntactical units as **von Berlin aus** (*from Berlin*); **von da an** (*from then on*); **von mir aus** (*as far as I'm concerned*).

Conversations

The following exchanges could take place as you arrive in Germany after an overnight flight from the United States.

I

HOSTESS:	(Vor der Landung): Meine Damen und Herren, wir werden in wenigen Minuten in Frankfurt landen und möchten Sie bitten, sich nun wieder anzuschnallen und das Rauchen einzustellen.

wenige a few
sich anschnallen to fasten seat belt
einstellen to stop

(Nach der Landung): Wir sind soeben in Frankfurt gelandet. Die Ortszeit ist 7 Uhr 35. Wir bitten Sie, sitzenzubleiben, bis die Maschine völlig zum Stillstand gekommen ist. Flugkapitän Bauer und seine Besatzung wünschen Ihnen einen angenehmen Aufenthalt in der Bundesrepublik Deutschland.

soeben just
die Ortszeit local time
völlig completely
die Besatzung crew
angenehm pleasant
der Aufenthalt stay

II

SCHLÄFRIGER FLUGGAST:	Wieviel Uhr, sagten Sie, ist es jetzt hier in Frankfurt?
HOSTESS:	Sieben Uhr fünfunddreißig, mitteleuropäische Zeit. Sie müssen Ihre Uhr fünf Stunden vorausstellen.

der Fluggast passenger

vorausstellen set ahead

FLUGGAST: Fünf? Ich dachte, der Zeitunterschied wäre sechs
              Stunden.

HOSTESS: Das stimmt,° —aber nur im Winter. Wir haben in   that's correct
              Deutschland keine Sommerzeit; das heißt, so lange Sie
              in Amerika Daylight Saving Time haben, ist der Unter-
              schied nicht sechs, sondern fünf Stunden. In New York
              ist es kurz nach halb drei nachts.

FLUGGAST: (sieht auf die Uhr.) Stimmt. Mein Gott, bin ich müde.

III

Vor dem Zoll, bei der Auskunft: **der Zoll** customs
                                                                   die Auskunft informa-
AMERIKANISCHER   tion
STUDENT: Bitte, was für Papiere brauche ich beim Zoll?   **was für** what kind of
                                                                   Das kommt darauf an
DEUTSCHER   that depends
ZOLLBEAMTER: Das kommt darauf an. Sie sind Amerikaner, nicht   **der Zollbeamte**
              wahr?   customs official

STUDENT: Ja, ich komme gerade aus New York.

ZOLLBEAMTER: Haben Sie etwas zu verzollen?

STUDENT: Ich habe 200 amerikanische Zigaretten, für meine   **die Kusine** cousin
              deutsche Kusine, . . .   (female)

ZOLLBEAMTER: Die sind zollfrei, bis zu 400 Stück. Haben Sie Whis- **zollfrei** duty-free
              key, Wein, Kaffee? Sie dürfen einen Liter Whiskey
              oder zwei Liter Wein einführen, und ein halbes
              Pfund Kaffee.

STUDENT: Ich habe eine Flasche kalifornischen Wein in
              meinem Rucksack; die habe ich für einen deutschen
              Freund mitgebracht.

ZOLLBEAMTER: Geschenke dürfen Sie bis zu hundert Mark einführen.
              —Sonst haben Sie nichts?

STUDENT: Nein, nur was ich für die Reise brauche.

ZOLLBEAMTER: Wenn Sie nichts zu verzollen haben, können Sie
              gleich hier rechts durchgehen.

STUDENT: Und meinen Rucksack brauche ich gar nicht aufzu-
              machen?

ZOLLBEAMTER: Nein, —und viel Spaß in Europa.   **viel Spaß** have fun

STUDENT: So einfach müßte das beim amerikanischen Zoll
              sein!

IV

Bei der Bank* im Flughafen:

STUDENT: Würden Sie mir bitte einen Reisescheck
              wechseln°?   change

---

*Note: **die Bank** pl. **die Banken**   the bank
       die Bank pl. **die Bänke**   the bench

DER JUNGE MANN

HINTER DEM SCHALTER°:	(sagt nichts.)	counter
STUDENT:	Bitte, was ist heute der Wechselkurs° für den Dollar?*	exchange rate
DER JUNGE MANN:	Zwei elf.	
STUDENT:	Zwei Mark elf für den Dollar?	
DER JUNGE MANN:	(sagt nichts.)	
STUDENT:	Dann wechseln Sie mir bitte 20 Dollar.	
DER JUNGE MANN:	(sagt nichts, füllt ein Formular° aus und gibt dem Studenten DM 40,70.)	form
STUDENT:	Wieso?° Zwanzig mal zwei Mark elf ist zwei-undvierzig Mark zwanzig.	How come?
DER JUNGE MANN:	Eins fünfzig Spesen°.	service charge
STUDENT:	Das hätten Sie mir aber vorher sagen sollen!	
DER JUNGE MANN:	Der nächste!°	Who's next?

V

Am Zeitungsstand°:		newsstand
STUDENT:	Haben Sie den *Spiegel*?†	
VERKÄUFER:	Nur den von der letzten Woche; der neue ist noch nicht da.	
STUDENT:	Dann geben Sie mir den alten,—und die *Herald Tribune* von heute.	
VERKÄUFER:	Tut mir leid,° aber ich habe gerade die letzte verkauft.	I'm sorry
STUDENT:	Dann nehme ich die *Frankfurter Rundschau* und die *Süd-deutsche Zeitung* und dann möchte ich noch einen guten Kriminalroman.	
VERKÄUFER:	Bitte hier drüben°. Suchen Sie sich doch etwas aus, —vielleicht den ganz neuen von Schmidt-Ingelheim, *Der Spion° im Rosengarten*?	over there / spy

VI

Gespräch mit einem Polizisten:		
STUDENT:	Bitte, würden Sie mir wohl sagen, wie ich am besten in die Innenstadt komme?	
POLIZIST:	Wie wollen Sie fahren, schnell° oder billig°?	fast cheap
STUDENT:	Wie teuer° ist schnell?	expensive

*In the "good old days," the dollar was worth about DM 4.00 or sFr. 4.00. It started slipping against the mark, the schilling, and the franc around 1970. The rate given here pertained in January 1978; by August 1978, the dollar had fallen below DM 2.00 and to about sFr. 1.50. One hundred schillings, once worth $4.00, cost over $7.00 in September 1978. You can look up the foreign currency listing in a daily paper, or call a bank, to find out what today's value of these currencies is.
†*Der Spiegel* is a West German news magazine like *Time* or *Newsweek*; the **Frankfurter Rundschau** and the **Süddeutsche Zeitung** are daily papers.

POLIZIST: Ein Taxi kostet Sie zwischen zwanzig und fünfundzwanzig
            Mark, und für Ihren Rucksack° bezahlen Sie auch noch   backpack
            mal 'ne Mark, und dann noch zwei oder drei Mark Trink-
            geld°. Aber in zwanzig Minuten sind Sie da.   tip
STUDENT: Danke, dann fahre ich lieber billig und langsam°.   slow
POLIZIST: Nehmen Sie die Bahn° für eine Mark zehn. Hier vorne° die   = Eisenbahn
            linke Treppe° hinunter und dann durch den langen Tunnel.   over there   stairs
            Die Bahn fährt alle halbe Stunde, —und hier rechts ist der
            Fahrkartenautomat.
STUDENT: Vielen Dank.

DEUTSCHE BUNDESBAHN

01829699   031 1905   R   1.10

DB Standort Tag   Uhrzeit   Preis

Nicht übertragbar. Es gelten die Gemeinsamen Beförderungsbedingungen
und Tarifbestimmungen. Fahrscheine sind nach Beendigung der Fahrt bis
nach Verlassen des Haltestellenbereichs aufzubewahren.

VII

As in previous units, let your teacher play the role of a native German. Have him/her be the friendly
person behind an information counter at the airport in Frankfurt with whom you have struck up a conversation. You have just arrived from the United States and are insatiably curious: where do you
change money; what is the dollar worth today; how do you get downtown; where should you go to buy
(soap, shoes, a dictionary, —what else?); how has the weather been (is it always so hot?), etc.

Or have your teacher be your Kusine* Emma or your Vetter* Fritz who has come to pick you up.
Report about the trip, about your parents and your brothers and sisters; ask about their family, their
new house, etc.

Fragen an Sie persönlich

1. Halten Sie es für wichtig°, daß man als Student nach Europa   important
   fährt?
2. Was würden Sie von Europa (von Deutschland) erwarten? Oder,
   wenn Sie schon einmal dort waren, was hatten Sie vor ihrer Reise
   erwartet, und wie war die Wirklichkeit°?   reality
3. Glauben Sie, daß es für einen Amerikaner wichtiger ist, nach
   Europa zu fahren (wegen der „westlichen Tradition" Amerikas),
   als etwa nach Afrika oder Asien?
4. Woher kamen Ihre eigenen Vorfahren°? Seit wievielen Genera-   ancestors
   tionen ist Ihre Familie in Amerika? Betrachten° Sie sich als Mit- consider
   glied° einer ethnischen Gruppe oder einfach als Amerikaner?   member

*die Kusine female cousin; der Vetter male cousin.

5. Halten Sie „ethnisches Bewußtsein°" für besser oder schlechter   consciousness
   als die alte Idee von den USA als „Schmelztiegel°"?   melting pot
6. Glauben Sie, daß alle Amerikaner zweisprachig° sein sollten,   bilingual
   und wenn ja, warum?

Reading

I

ERICH KÄSTNER

Die Entwicklung der Menschheit

Einst haben die Kerls auf den Bäumen gehockt,
behaart und mit böser Visage.
Dann hat man sie aus dem Urwald gelockt
und die Welt asphaltiert und aufgestockt,
bis zur dreißigsten Etage.   5

Da saßen sie nun, den Flöhen entflohn,
in zentralgeheizten Räumen.
Da sitzen sie nun am Telefon.
Und es herrscht noch genau derselbe Ton
wie seinerzeit auf den Bäumen.   10

Sie hören weit. Sie sehen fern.
Sie sind mit dem Weltall in Fühlung.
Sie putzen die Zähne. Sie atmen modern.
Die Erde ist ein gebildeter Stern
mit sehr viel Wasserspülung.   15

Sie schießen die Briefschaften durch ein Rohr.
Sie jagen und züchten Mikroben.
Sie versehn die Natur mit allem Komfort.
Sie fliegen steil in den Himmel empor
und bleiben zwei Wochen oben.   20

Was ihre Verdauung übrigläßt,
das verarbeiten sie zu Watte.
Sie spalten Atome. Sie heilen Inzest.
Und sie stellen durch Stiluntersuchungen fest,
daß Cäsar Plattfüße hatte.   25

So haben sie mit dem Kopf und dem Mund
den Fortschritt der Menschheit geschaffen.
Doch davon mal abgesehen und
bei Lichte betrachtet sind sie im Grund
noch immer die alten Affen.   30

(1932)

der Kerl,-s guy
hocken to squat
der Urwald,⸚er jungle
locken to lure
aufstocken to build up
die Etage,-n floor
der Floh,⸚e flea
entfliehen to flee from
heizen to heat
der Raum,⸚e room
herrschen to prevail
seinerzeit formerly
das Weltall universe
putzen to brush
die Erde earth
der Stern,-e star
gebildet educated
die Wasserspülung toilet flushing
schießen to shoot
die Briefschaften mail
das Rohr,-e pipe
jagen hunt
züchten breed
versehen to supply
steil steep
der Himmel sky
empor up
die Verdauung digestion
übriglassen leave over
verarbeiten transform
die Watte cotton
spalten to split
feststellen to ascertain
die Untersuchung,-en investigation
der Plattfuß,⸚e flat foot
der Mund,⸚er mouth
der Fortschritt progress
schaffen to create
die Menschheit mankind
absehen von to disregard
betrachten to look
im Grund basically
der Affe,-n ape

II

Bertolt Brecht

Freundschaftsdienste

Als Beispiel für die richtige Art, Freunden einen Dienst zu erweisen, gab Herr K. folgende Geschichte zum besten. „Zu einem alten Araber kamen drei junge Leute und sagten ihm: ‚Unser Vater ist gestorben. Er 5 hat uns siebzehn Kamele hinterlassen und im Testament verfügt, daß der Älteste die Hälfte, der zweite ein Drittel und der Jüngste ein Neuntel der Kamele bekommen soll. Jetzt können wir uns über die Teilung nicht ein- 10 igen; übernimm du die Entscheidung!' Der Araber dachte nach und sagte: ‚Wie ich es sehe, habt ihr, um gut teilen zu können, ein Kamel zu wenig. Ich habe selbst nur ein ein- ziges Kamel, aber es steht euch zur Ver- 15 fügung. Nehmt es und teilt dann, und bringt mir nur, was übrigbleibt.' Sie bedankten sich für diesen Freundschaftsdienst, nahmen das Kamel mit und teilten die achtzehn Kamele nun so, daß der Älteste die Hälfte, das sind 20 neun, der Zweite ein Drittel, das sind sechs, und der Jüngste ein Neuntel, das sind zwei Kamele bekam. Zu ihrem Erstaunen blieb, als sie ihre Kamele zur Seite geführt hatten, ein Kamel übrig. Dieses brachten sie, ihren 25 Dank erneuernd, ihrem alten Freund zurück.“

Herr K. nannte diesen Freundschaftsdienst richtig, weil er keine besonderen Opfer verlangte. 30

Good Turns

As an example of how to do friends a good turn Mr. K. obliged with the following story. "Three young men came to an old Arab and said: 'Our father has died. He has left us seventeen camels and stipulated in his will that the eldest should have half, the second a third, and the youngest a ninth of the camels. Now we can't agree among our- selves on the division: you decide the mat- ter.' The Arab thought about it and said: 'As I see it, you have one camel too few to share them out properly. I've only got one camel myself, but it's at your disposal. Take it and share them out, and give me back only what's left over.' They thanked him for this good turn, took the camel with them, and then divided the eighteen camels in such a way that the eldest got half—that is, nine— the second a third—that is, six—and the youngest a ninth—that is, two—of the camels. To their amazement when they had each led their camels aside, there was one left over. This they took back to their old friend with renewed thanks."

Mr. K. called this the right sort of good turn, since it demanded no special sacrifice.

III

Frau Anni Schneider und ihre Kinder

Anni Schneider, 45 Jahre alt und geschieden°, lebt mit ihren vier Kindern in M., einer kleinen Stadt im Land Rheinland-Pfalz°. In Koblenz geboren, war sie 15 Jahre lang mit dem Kraftfahrzeug- meister° Peter Schneider verheiratet. Seit ihrer Scheidung° arbeitet sie als Verkaufsleiterin° in einem Kaufhaus in Koblenz. Monatliches 5

divorced

Rhineland-Palatinate

master auto mechanic
divorce
sales manager

Staatliches Gymnasium Mayen

Mainzer Studienstufe

HALBJAHRESZEUGNIS

Schuljahr 19 *76* / *77*

Name: *Schlich*   Vorname: *Jürgen*

besuchte das *1.* Halbjahr der *12.* Jahrgangsstufe

Leistungen in den einzelnen Fächern:

		Note	Punkte
Leistungsfächer:	Deutsch	befriedigend	7
	Englisch	befriedigend	9
	Erdkunde	gut	10
Facharbeit in:			
Verpflichtende Grundfächer:			
Deutsch:		—	—
Fremdsprachen:	Latein	gut	10
		—	—
	—	—	
Gemeinschaftskunde:			
Mathematik:		ausreichend	5
Naturwissenschaften:	Biologie	gut	11
	Physik	mangelhaft	3
			—
Künstlerische Fächer:	Bildende Kunst	sehr gut	13
(in 12)			—
Religion/~~Ethikunterricht~~:		sehr gut	14
Sport:		ausreichend	6

Freigewählte Grundfächer (in Überschreitung der Pflichtstundenzahl)

Bemerkungen:

Versäumnisse: *13* Std.

Auf Beschluß der Jahrgangsstufenkonferenz/Gesamtkonferenz vom _____ 19 ____ in die

12. Jahrgangsstufe versetzt/nicht versetzt.

Mayen, den *15. 2. 77*

Der Schulleiter

Handel
Der Leiter der Mainzer Studienstufe

Die Erziehungsberechtigten

Bedeutung der Noten und Punkte:

Note:	1 = sehr gut	2 = gut	3 = befriedigend	4 = ausreichend	5 = mangelhaft	6 = ungenügend
Punkte:	15, 14, 13	12, 11, 10	9, 8, 7	6, 5, 4	3, 2, 1	0

Einkommen: etwa DM 2.400. (,,Wenn die Kinder erst mal alle aus
dem Hause sind, ist das nicht schlecht.") Sie gehört zu den vielen ge-
schiedenen Frauen, die heute in der Bundesrepublik allein und ohne
Hilfe für die Erziehung ihrer Kinder verantwortlich° sind, und sie   responsible
denkt viel darüber nach, was aus den Kindern werden soll und werden 5
wird. ,,Aber", sagt sie, ,,ich komme heute besser zurecht° als vor zehn   **zurechtkommen** to get
Jahren. Die dauernden Schwierigkeiten° mit meinem Mann haben   along
mir damals das ganze Leben sauer gemacht."   constant troubles

Als sich Frau Schneider vor zehn Jahren scheiden ließ, war Tobias,
ihr Jüngster, gerade zwei Jahre alt. Heute ist er in der sechsten Klasse 10
im Gymnasium, in der sogenannten ,,Orientierungsstufe":* In M.
schickt man heute fast alle Kinder nach der Grundschule aufs Gym-
nasium. ,,Die Hauptschule ist eine Hilfsschule° geworden", sagen die   school for the retarded
Lehrer, ,,aber was soll man machen? Die meisten Eltern glauben, daß
sie die intelligentesten Kinder haben, für die nur die beste Erziehung 15
gut genug ist, und welcher Lehrer will da schon Gott spielen und für
das Schicksal° von zehnjährigen Kindern verantwortlich sein? Also   fate
geben wir fast allen ein positives Gutachten° und schicken sie aufs   evaluation
Gymnasium."

In der Orientierungsstufe, das heißt, in der fünften und sechsten 20
Klasse, bestimmt° man dann, welche Kinder auf dem Gymnasium   determines
oder auf der Realschule bleiben sollen und welche in die Hauptschule
zurück müssen. Frau Schneider ist nicht sicher, ob ihr Tobias wirklich
aufs Gymnasium gehört. Erstens, meint sie, ist er gar nicht so intelligent; er arbeitet lieber mit den Händen als mit dem Kopf. Und zwei- 25
tens haben die jungen Akademiker heute doch gar keine gute
Zukunft°. Tobias interessiert sich für Maschinen, für Motoren, für   future
Autos. (,,Das hat er von seinem Vater", sagt Frau Schneider.) Trotzdem bekommt er gute Noten, und wenn er auf dem Gymnasium
bleibt, könnte er ja nach dem Abitur auf eine Technische Hochschule 30
gehen und Ingenieur werden. Wer weiß?

Annemarie ist vier Jahre älter als Tobias. Sie hatte gerade ihren sechzehnten Geburtstag und ist vor ein paar Wochen von der Realschule
abgegangen°. Als sie zehn Jahre alt war, gab es noch keine Orientie-   has graduated
rungsstufe, und die Kinder blieben entweder in der Hauptschule, oder 35
sie gingen auf die Realschule oder aufs Gymnasium. Anni Schneider
schickte ihre Tochter Annemarie auf die Realschule. ,,Und das war
gut so", meint sie jetzt. ,,Aus der Annemarie wäre nie eine Akademi-
kerin geworden; sie war schon immer ein praktisches Kind, und auf
der Realschule hat sie genau° das lernen können, was für sie das 40 exactly

---

*Orientierungsstufe: the first two years of secondary school, during which a final deter-
mination is made as to the school type to which a youngster will be assigned (see
diagram on p. 360).

FRÖHLICHE FAHRT INS BLAUE

**EINMALIG° IN BERLIN –
STIMMUNGS-KREUZFAHRT°
MIT EINEM BVG - DOPPELDECKER
PANORAMABUS.
AB MAI
JEDEN 2. SAMSTAG
IM MONAT.**

1. Fahrt	15. Mai
2. Fahrt	12. Juni
3. Fahrt	10. Juli
4. Fahrt	14. Aug.
5. Fahrt	11. Sep.
6. Fahrt	9. Okt.
7. Fahrt	13. Nov.
8. Fahrt	11. Dez.
9. Fahrt :	Neujahrs-Sonder-fahrt 1. Jan.

PREIS PRO PERSON : 34.50DM (Endpreis)

Erleben Sie Berlin einmal so, wie Sie
es wahrscheinlich noch nicht erlebt haben—
in einem BVG - Doppeldecker - Panoramabus
auf einer Fahrt kreuz und quer durch Berlin.
   Wir starten um 13⁰⁰Uhr vor dem
HOTEL BERLIN, Kurfürstenstr. 62 (am Lützow-
platz), und um 13¹⁵Uhr vor dem
SCHULTHEISS BRÄUHAUS am Kurfürsten-
damm 220, Ecke Meinekestr.
Es erwartet Sie während der Fahrt typische
Berliner Kost°: wie Schusterjungen und Pfann-
kuchen, Schultheiss Bier,
Malteser-Kreuz und
natürlich auch
Heimbs Kaffee.
Für Musik und
Stimmung
sorgt ein
Akkordeon-
Spieler.
Die gute
Laune° sollten Sie
mitbringen.

fröhlich happy, joyous
einmalig unique
**die Stimmungs-Kreuz-
  fahrt** spirited cruise
die Kost (*no pl.*) food
  and drink, dishes
die Laune mood

Richtige war." Für die Fähigkeiten° ihrer Kinder hat Frau Schneider
einen guten Instinkt, und bei ihrer jüngeren Tochter hatte sie ganz
bestimmt recht. Annemarie ist jetzt in der Lehre° in einem großen
Werk° in der Nähe von M., und sie will Verwaltungsbeamtin°
werden.

Die meisten Firmen nehmen lieber Lehrlinge auf, die von der Realschule kommen, als solche, die nach sechs Jahren das Gymnasium verlassen. Die Realschüler haben eine abgeschlossene°, praxis-orientierte
Erziehung hinter sich, während Schüler, die nach der zehnten Klasse
vom Gymnasium abgehen, in den meisten Fällen° unfreiwillig° abgehen, weil sie zu schlechte Noten haben.

Hannelore Schneider, Annis ältere Tochter, ist achtzehn und in der
zwölften Klasse (der Unterprima) auf dem Gymnasium in M. Aber seit
der Oberstufenreform gibt es eigentlich keine „Klassen" mehr auf der
Oberstufe (die jetzt Sekundarstufe II heißt). Die Schüler haben nach
der zehnten Klasse vier Jahre Zeit, um die „Abiturqualifikation" zu
erwerben.

„Ich verstehe das alles nicht mehr", sagt Frau Schneider, —und mit
ihr sagen das die meisten Eltern, deren Kinder sich auf das Abitur vorbereiten. „Früher war das alles so einfach: man kam von einer Klasse
in die andere, —wenn man nicht sitzenblieb°—, und dann machte
man das Abitur, —oder man fiel durch°. Jetzt redet die Hannelore
von Punkten, die sie braucht; Noten gibt es nicht mehr, und sie hat
Grundkurse und Leistungskurse°, und . . . na ja, wenn die Deutschen
etwas reformieren, dann ist es nachher immer komplizierter als es
vorher war."

capabilities

in der Lehre sein to be
  an apprentice
5 plant, factory
  administration official

completed

10 cases involuntarily

15

20

sitzenbleiben to stay
  behind, to have to
  repeat a year
flunked
basic courses and
25 achievement courses

Unsere feucht-fröhliche Fahrt endet gegen 17-18 Uhr wieder vor dem Schultheiss Bräu-haus oder dem Hotel Berlin.
Die richtige Zeit, in gemütlicher Atmos-phäre bei einem Drink den Samstag-Nachmittag zu beenden.

feucht-fröhlich
animated (literally:
moist-happy; i.e.,
happy because of the
drinking)

Buchungen und Kartenverkauf
im **HOTEL BERLIN**
Kurfürstenstr. 62
1 Berlin 30

Tel. (030) 269291
Telex 0184332

Seit der Oberstufenreform gibt es in den Bundesdeutschen Gymnasien das „Kurssystem"; das heißt, jeder Schüler kann wählen°, welche Fächer° er als Leistungsfächer oder als Grundfächer nehmen will. Deutsch, Mathematik, Gemeinschaftskunde und eine Fremdsprache sind Pflichtfächer°, alle anderen sind Wahlfächer°, und statt Noten bekommt man von null bis fünfzehn Punkte. Wer 300 Punkte hat, hat die Abiturqualifikation und kann dann die Abiturprüfungen machen.

Hannelore findet das neue System sehr gut, obwohl ihre Mutter es nicht versteht. Sie will Jura° studieren und Rechtsanwältin° werden. Sie interessiert sich sehr für die Probleme der Gastarbeiter und hofft, daß sie als Anwältin den ausländischen Arbeitern wird helfen können. „Ob sie das schafft°, weiß ich nicht", meint Frau Schneider skeptisch. „Aber sie soll es nur versuchen. Energie hat sie genug."

Klaus, der Älteste, ist 21 und studiert Volkswirtschaft° an der Mainzer Universität. Er hat ein Zimmer in der Rheinstraße, der Hauptstraße von Mainz, und ißt fast alle seine Mahlzeiten in der Mensa°. Finan-ziell ist er ziemlich unabhängig°, denn er bekommt eine recht gute BAFöG*-Unterstützung°, genug für ein einfaches Studentenleben.

Eigentlich hatte er Studienrat werden und Deutsch, Englisch und Geschichte studieren wollen, aber er sieht keine Zukunft als Lehrer. „Es gibt schon genug stellungslose° Leute mit Staatsexamen und sogar

choose
subjects

required courses
electives

law, jurisprudence
attorney

makes

economics

university cafeteria
rather independent
support

unemployed

*BAFöG is the abbreviation for the monstrous compound noun **Bundesausbildungs-förderungsgesetz**, Federal Law for the Support of Educational Training, through which all students whose parents earn less than a certain amount are supported by the federal government.

mit Promotion°, sagt er, da studiere ich doch lieber etwas Praktisches,   doctorates
womit ich hinterher° auch etwas anfangen kann." Wenn er übers   afterwards
Wochenende nach Hause kommt, spricht er oft von seinen Freunden,
zum Beispiel von Sigrid, die Veterinärmedizin studieren will, und von
Joachim, der Chemiker werden will. Beide wurden nicht zugelassen°, 5   were not admitted
wegen des „Numerus Clausus",* und studieren jetzt Germanistik, bis
ein Platz für sie frei wird.

Klaus hat schon zweimal in den Sommerferien bei Opel in Rüssels-
heim† gearbeitet, am Fließband°, aber er hat dabei sehr gut ver-   assembly line
dient°. Wenn er mit dem Studium fertig ist und seinen Diplom- 10   earned money
Volkswirt gemacht hat, hofft er, bei Opel als Industriekaufmann°   industrial economist
unterzukommen.

„Ich bin sehr neugierig°", meint Anni Schneider, „was aus meinen   curious
vier Kindern werden wird."

Wie weit geht der amerikanische Einfluß? Aufgenommen in einer
bayerischen Kleinstadt.

Exercises

A. Insert the adjectives given in parentheses into the following sentences.

SEE
ANALYSIS
156
(p. 460)

1. Meyer ist mit einer Frau verheiratet. (sehr intelligent)
2. Eine Frau ist sie *nicht*. (intelli*gent*)
3. Er ist dumm, aber er hat eine Frau geheiratet. (intelligent)
4. Sie ist dumm, aber sie hat einen Mann geheiratet. (intelligent)

*The **Numerus Clausus** limits enrollment in many disciplines, particularly in medicine,
law, and the natural sciences. Only those with extremely high grade-point averages in
the *Abitur* have a chance to get into these disciplines.
†**Opel,** the General Motors subsidiary in Germany, has its main plant in Rüsselsheim,
between Mainz and Frankfurt.

5. Er ist ein Mensch. (intelligent)
6. Wer *ist* denn der Mann, von dem ihr da sprecht? (intelligent)
7. Sie ist ein Kind. (intelligent)
8. Wer *ist* denn das Mädchen, von dem ihr da sprecht? (intelligent)
9. Mein Sohn hat ein Mädchen geheiratet. (intelligent)
10. Meyers haben drei Kinder. (intelligent)
11. Frauen wissen immer, was sie wollen. (intelligent)
12. Mit Studenten kann man gut arbeiten. (intelligent)

B. Restate the following sentences, leaving out the italicized **der-** or **ein-**words.

1. *Jeder* gute Wein ist teuer.
2. *Alle* intelligenten Frauen wissen, was sie wollen.
3. *Dieses* deutsche Bier ist sehr gut.
4. *Mein* lieber Vater!
5. *Das* frische Obst ist jetzt zu teuer.
6. Bei *dem* starken Regen fahre ich nicht in die Stadt.

SEE
ANALYSIS
156
(p. 460)

C. Place the word in parentheses in front of the adjective.

1. Für intelligente Kinder tun wir viel zu wenig. (unsere)
2. Automatische Uhren sind teuer. (diese)
3. Nach kurzer Pause fuhren wir weiter. (einer)
4. Beide Kinder gingen damals schon in die Schule. (seine)
5. Westfälischer Schinken ist eine Spezialität unseres Hauses. (dieser)

SEE
ANALYSIS
156
(p. 460)

D. Restate the following sentences by changing the italicized nouns to the singular and by making the corresponding changes in the **der-**words and adjectives.

1. Siehst du *die jungen Mädchen* da drüben?
2. Woher hast du denn *die schönen Bücher?*
3. *Diese neuen Maschinen* fliegen tausend Kilometer in der Stunde.
4. Wir fragten *die jungen Männer*, wo sie herkämen.
5. *Die kleinen Dörfer* lagen im Schwarzwald.

SEE
ANALYSIS
156
(p. 460)

E. Restate the following sentences by changing the nouns to the singular. Change the adjective ending as required and place an **ein-**word before the adjective.

1. Ich habe gute Freundinnen in Frankfurt.
2. Bei uns wohnen jetzt amerikanische Studenten.
3. Vor ihm saßen zwei blonde Mädchen.
4. Er rauchte österreichische Zigaretten.
5. Meyers sind gute Freunde von mir.

SEE
ANALYSIS
156
(p. 460)

F. In the following sentences, insert an appropriate **der-** or **ein-**word (if necessary) and the correct form of the adjective in parentheses.

1. Mit _____ _____ Roman hat er viel Geld verdient. (letzt)
2. Wir wohnen in _____ _____ Haus. (neu)
3. Gestern abend habe ich _____ _____ Professor kennengelernt. (deutsch)
4. Ich freue mich auf _____ Sonntag. (nächst)
5. Mein Mann ist gerade von _____ _____ Reise zurückgekommen. (lang)
6. Mit _____ _____ Schreibmaschine kann ich nicht schreiben. (alt)
7. Wann soll _____ _____ Brücke denn fertig sein? (neu)

SEE
ANALYSIS
156
(p. 460)

8. Mit _____ _____ Mantel kannst du nicht nach Paris fahren. (alt)
9. Bist du mit _____ _____ Sekretärin zufrieden? (neu)
10. Die Mutter _____ _____ Kinder hieß Alexandra. (beide)
11. Ich möchte ein Zimmer mit _____ Wasser. (fließend)
12. Er hat zwei _____ Romane geschrieben. (gut)

G. Insert the adjectives in parentheses in the appropriate place in each sentence.

1. Wir sehen einen Mann. (jung)
2. Es ist ein Amerikaner. (jung)
3. Er kommt aus einer Stadt im Nordosten. (groß)
4. Nach dem Flug ist er müde. (lang)
5. Er wartet auf seine Kusine. (deutsch)
6. Ein Mädchen kommt auf ihn zu. (hübsch, jung)
7. Er erkennt° sie an ihrem Haar. (lang, blond)   recognizes by
8. Sie hat ihren Vetter gefunden. (amerikanisch)
9. Er erzählt von seinem Großvater. (alt)
10. Sie erzählt von ihrer Tante Amalie. (komisch)
11. Tante Amalie ist eine Köchin. (gut)
12. Am besten ist ihr Schweinebraten. (bayrisch)
13. Er freut sich auf Tante Amalies Essen. (gut)
14. Die Kusine heißt Emma. (deutsch)
15. Der Vetter heißt Jimmy. (amerikanisch)
16. Emma wohnt in einem Dorf. (klein)
17. Dort lebt man besser als in einer Stadt. (groß)
18. Sie fahren in Emmas Wagen nach Oberroden. (alt)
19. So ein Wagen ist gar nicht schlecht. (alt)
20. Emma will kein Auto kaufen. (neu, teuer)
21. Oberroden ist ein Dorf. (ruhig)
22. Es hat eine Kirche. (schön, alt)
23. Tante Amalie wohnt neben der Kirche. (alt)
24. Jimmy hat ihr eine Flasche Wein mitgebracht. (amerikanisch)
25. Sie freut sich sehr über den Wein. (amerikanisch)

H. Supply the missing words.

1. Er sagte, seine Frau _____ gestern nach Hamburg gefahren.
2. Er konnte leider nicht kommen _____ des Regens.
3. Er wollte wissen, mit _____ ich telefoniert hätte.
4. Er sagte mir, ich _____ ihn in Berlin besuchen.
5. Es kostet viel weniger, _____ ich dachte.
6. _____ Andreas mitgeht, gehe ich auch mit.
7. Sie sah aus, _____ hätte sie nicht geschlafen.
8. Ich habe _____ ganzen Nachmittag auf dich gewartet.
9. Die Dame, _____ gestern hier war, ist Amerikanerin.
10. Meyer, _____ Frau aus New York kam, sprach gut Englisch.
11. Fritzchen Meyer hat Angst _____ dem Abitur.
12. Wenn Ihnen dieser Wein zu sauer ist, versuchen Sie doch mal _____ da.
13. Ich möchte Ihnen noch einmal _____ danken, daß Sie mir geholfen haben.
14. Kann ich _____ helfen, Herr Schmitz?
15. Ja, danke; ich trinke gerne _____ eine Tasse Kaffee.
16. Wann fangen denn dieses Jahr die Ferien _____?

17. Fridolin, wir sind alle sehr stolz _____ dich.
18. Sie scheint schon wieder in England _____ zu sein.
19. Er _____ Schriftsteller sein, aber das glaube ich ihm nicht.
20. Das war nicht meine Freundin, _____ meine Schwester.

I. Construct a conversation between yourself and your cousin Emma, who has come to pick you up at the Frankfurt Airport. This is not an exercise in translation, but you should nevertheless follow the English outline. Use your imagination, but avoid using patterns that you are not thoroughly familiar with. Be prepared to produce a similar conversation orally in class.

Emma, of course, wants to know how you are, how the flight was, whether you are tired, and whether you would like to have breakfast before driving into town. You try to figure out what time it is in New York and you talk a bit about time differences. When Emma mentions MEZ°, you are puzzled because you've never heard the term. Emma explains. Then you decide that you are really tired and ought to get to your hotel. She wants to know whether you have ordered a room, which, of course, you have done. Emma thinks it might be a good idea to call the hotel to be sure that you have the room. Since you have never made a phone call in Germany, you ask her whether she would please do that for you. While she telephones, you want to get some German money. She asks you to come to the exit in ten minutes, and she will get her car in the meantime.

° mitteleuropäische Zeit

Now, here is your first sentence: Emma: „Da bist du ja endlich."

Vocabulary

angenehm	pleasant	**grau**	gray
ankommen auf	to depend on	**die Hälfte, -n**	half
das kommt darauf an	that depends	**die Hitze**	heat
		hübsch	pretty
atmen	to breathe	**inner-**	inner
der Aufenthalt, -e	stay, residence	**innerhalb** (*prep. with gen.*)	inside of
auskommen mit	to get along with		
die Auskunft, ⸚e	information	**der Kampf, ⸚e**	fight, fighting, struggle
ausreichend	sufficient	**die Kusine, -n**	(female) cousin
außerhalb (*prep. with gen.*)	outside of	**die Laune, -n**	mood, frame of mind
		leid tun (*impers.*)	to be sorry
die Butter	butter	**es tut mir leid**	I'm sorry
daher	from there; therefore, for that reason, that's why	**lieb**	dear
		Liebe Mutter!	Dear mother:
		ich habe dich lieb	I'm in love with you
dritt-	third		
das Einkommen, -	income	**die Lust**	desire
einzig	single, sole; solitary	**ich habe keine Lust**	I don't feel like it
erst-	first	**die Mahlzeit, -en**	meal
die Fahrkarte, -n	ticket (train, etc.)	**die Note, -n**	grade, mark
das Fieber	fever	**die Partei, -en**	(political) party
freiwillig	voluntary	**die Pause, -n**	pause, stop, break, intermission
das Gespräch, -e	conversation		

die Pflicht, -en	duty	der Vetter, -n	(male) cousin
das Pflichtfach, ¨er	required course	völlig	completely
der Polizist, -en	policeman	wechseln	to change (money)
der Reisescheck, -s	traveler's check	zweit-	second
schaffen	to accomplish, manage		
die Schreibmaschine, -n	typewriter	der Januar	January
sitzenbleiben	to stay seated	der Februar	February
sogenannt	so-called	der März	March
die Stimmung, -en	mood, spirits, atmosphere	der April'	April
		der Mai	May
in guter Stimmung	in high spirits	der Ju'ni	June
das Stück, -e	(theatrical) play	der Ju'li	July
tausend	thousand	der August'	August
die Treppe, -n	stairs; staircase	der September	September
verantwortlich	responsible	der Oktober	October
verdienen	to earn	der November	November
Geld verdienen	to make money	der Dezember	December

Additional Vocabulary

aufgehen	to open; to rise (sun, moon)	mitteleuropäisch	Central European
automatisch	automatic	mitteleuropäische Zeit (MEZ)	Central European time
befriedigen	to satisfy; to pacify	die Ortszeit	local time
blöd(e)	stupid	soeben	just (now); this moment
blond	blond, blonde	stellen	to set (a watch, clock)
einführen	to import; to introduce	still	quiet; still
einholen	to catch up with	der Stillstand	standstill
einst	once (upon a time)	zum Stillstand kommen	to (come to a) stop
einstellen	to stop, discontinue		
erwerben	to acquire, gain	die Stufe, -n	step, level
heilen	to heal	das Testament', -e	testament; (last) will
Jura studieren	to study law, jurisprudence	untergehen	to sink, vanish; to set (sun, moon)
kreuz und quer	back and forth; crisscross	unterkommen	to find a place to stay
		das Wahlfach, ¨er	elective
die Kutsche, -n	coach, buggy, jalopy	die Waschmaschine, -n	washing machine
der Liebling, -e	favorite; darling	der Zaun, ¨e	fence
Lieblings-	favorite		

Strong Verbs

erwerben	erwirbt	erwarb	erworben	to acquire
schaffen		schuf	geschaffen	to accomplish, manage
sitzenbleiben		blieb sitzen	ist sitzengeblieben	to remain seated

Stuttgart Hbf

Zeit	Zug-Nr.	aus Richtung	Gleis
		0⁰⁰ – 8⁰⁰	

Zeit	Zug-Nr.	aus Richtung	Gleis
0.01	4352	Stuttgart-Bad Cannstatt 23.56 - ⑦, nach † Esslingen 23.41	4
:0.03 Konsul	D 591	Kiel 15.23 - Hamburg-Altona 16.49 - Hannover 18.34 - Frankfurt 22.00 - Heidelberg 22.50	14
0.29	4355	Bietigheim 23.57	5
:0.35	D 1218	Salzburg 19.55 - München 21.58 - Augsburg 22.39 - Ulm 23.31 ➡ verk nur 2. VII. bis 29. VIII.	9
0.41	4104	Esslingen 0.21	4
0.59	4103	Ludwigsburg 0.40	5
1.02 Vorarlberg-Express	E 418	Innsbruck 18.04 - Bludenz 20.18 - Lindau 21.42 - Friedrichshafen Stadt 22.17 - Ulm 23.55 (🚃 Oberstdorf 21.16 über Kempten 22.19) ➡ verk nur ⑦, tägl 27. VI. bis 5. IX. 🚲	10
:1.08	D 1416	Innsbruck 18.53 - Garmisch-P 20.47 - Augsburg 23.15 (🚃 Berchtesgaden 19.06 über München 22.21) - Ulm 0.06 ➡ verk nur ⑦ ab 13. VI., auch 8. VI.	9
:1.57 Austria-Express	D 216	Klagenfurt 16.05 - Villach 16.57 - Bischofshofen 19.35 - Salzburg 20.45 - München 23.06 - Augsburg 23.52 - Ulm 0.48	9
1.59	4109	Bietigheim 1.27	5
:2.01	D 212	München 23.02 (🚃 Graz 14.40, ← Klagenfurt 16.05 über Salzburg 20.45) - Augsburg 23.47 - Ulm 0.54 (außer ⑦ bis 26. VI. und ab 6. IX. 🚃 Oberstdorf 21.16) (🚃 Innsbruck 18.04)	10
2.04	4108	Esslingen 1.44	4
:2.15	D 566	München 23.20 - Augsburg 0.05 - Ulm 1.09	11
⑥:2.32	D 1417	Dortmund 19.08 - Essen Hbf 19.35 - Düsseldorf 20.13 - Köln 20.55 - Bonn-Beuel 21.16 - Koblenz 22.03 - Wiesbaden 23.20 - Frankfurt 0.01 - Heidelberg 1.13	15
:2.53	D 567	Saarbrücken 23.11 (🚃 Trier 21.51) - Kaiserslautern 0.02 - Heidelberg 1.28 (🚃 Frankfurt 23.39)	16
3.04	4115	Ludwigsburg 2.46	5
3.10	4112	Esslingen 2.52	4
3.51	4116	Plochingen 3.17	4
:3.58	D 213	Nijmegen 21.00 - Krefeld 22.30 - Köln 23.24 - Bonn 23.48 - Koblenz 0.29 - Mainz 1.27 - Mannheim 2.21 - Heidelberg 2.39	15
3.59	4119	Ludwigsburg 3.40	5
:4.09 Austria-Express	D 217	Hoek van Holland 19.30 - Rotterdam 19.57 - Venlo 21.54 - Köln 23.29 (🚃 Nijmegen 21.00) - Bonn 23.54 - Koblenz 0.34 - Mainz 1.33 - Mannheim 2.26 - Heidelberg 2.45	16
:4.21 Vorarlberg-Express	D 419	Dortmund 21.22 - Essen Hbf 21.48 - Duisburg 22.14 (26. VI. bis 4. IX. 🚃 Amsterdam 18.57) - Düsseldorf 22.34 - Köln 23.18 - Bonn-Beuel 23.38 - Koblenz 0.20 - Mainz 1.39 - Mannheim 2.31 - Heidelberg 2.59 ➡ verk nur ⑥, tägl 26. VI. bis 4. IX. 🚲	15
4.39 ✕ außer ⑥	4125	Ludwigsburg 4.20	5
4.51	4124	Esslingen 4.31 - ✕ außer ⑥ Plochingen 4.13	4
5.13 ✕ außer ⑥	4501	Leonberg 4.45	6
5.13	E 2364	München 1.19 - Augsburg 2.32 - Ulm 3.52	10
✕5.16	4129	Bietigheim 4.44	5
✕5.21	4130	Göppingen 4.23	4
✕5.24	4702	Backnang 4.46	3
5.36	4133	Bietigheim 5.04 - † Vaihingen 4.48	5
5.41	4134	Esslingen 5.21	4
✕5.43	4503	Leonberg 5.13 - ✕ außer ⑥ Weil der Stadt 4.59	6

Zeit	Zug-Nr.	aus Richtung	Gleis
7.51	4426	Schorndorf 7.08 - ✕ außer ⑥ Lorch 6.53	✕3 / †1
7.55	E 3444	Aalen 6.48	2
✕7.58	4956	Horb 6.49	8

		8⁰⁰ – 12⁰⁰	
✕8.01	4162	Esslingen 7.41	4
✕8.02	5224	Ulm 5.53	13
8.03	6153	Weil der Stadt 7.19 (⑥, † Zug-Nr 4519)	✕7 / †6
†8.06	6218	Tübingen 6.35	9
✕8.06	E 2350	Tübingen 7.05	9
✕8.09	4167	Ludwigsburg 7.50 - ⑥ Bietigheim 7.34	✕5 / †7
8.10	6216	Tübingen 6.33	3
8.17	4734	Backnang 7.32	12
8.21	4166	Esslingen 8.01	4
8.23 ✕ außer ⑥	4521	Weil der Stadt 7.39	6
⑦:8.26	D 1498	Rimini 19.22 - Brennero 2.17 - Innsbruck 3.09 - München Ost 5.42 - Augsburg 6.32 - Ulm 7.23 mit Autobeförderung, Rimini - München als D 1488 ➡ ab 6. VI.	10
†8.28	4736	Backnang 7.45	1
8.29	4171	Ludwigsburg 8.10	5
8.29	E 3723	Heilbronn 7.40 - ✕ Osterburken 6.40	✕ außer ⑥ 15 / ⑥, † 13
8.34	4434	Schorndorf 7.50	3
:8.37	D 599	Kiel 20.21 - Hamburg-Altona 21.44 - Hannover 0.20 - (🚃 Oldenburg 21.28 - ⑦, nach † Wilhelmshaven 20.23 über Bremen 22.25) (🚃 ← Bremerhaven-Lehe 20.51) - Kreiensen 1.40 (🚃 Braunschweig 22.50) - Kassel 3.07 - Frankfurt 6.11 - Heidelberg 7.16	16
:8.37	5139	Mühlacker 7.37	6
8.40	E 3304	Konstanz 5.38 - Singen 6.05 - Rottweil 6.56 - Eutingen 7.55 (🚃 Freudenstadt 7.15)	9
8.40 ✕ außer ⑥	4738	Backnang 8.03	13
8.41	4170	Esslingen 8.21 - ✕ außer ⑥ Plochingen 8.06	4
8.43	4523	Weil der Stadt 7.59	7
8.44	E 3002	Friedrichshafen Stadt 5.56 - Ulm 7.34	12
✕8.46 Neckar-City	E 3061	Würzburg 6.26 - Heilbronn 8.04	14
8.48	E 3604	Albstadt-Ebingen 6.26 - Tübingen 7.47	2
8.48	E 2852	Bayreuth 4.27 (🚃 Rostock 16.41 über Leipzig 22.28 - Gutenfürst 1.41) - Nürnberg 6.00 (🚃 Berlin-Friedrichstr 20.53 über Probstzella 3.05) - Crailsheim 7.14 - Aalen 7.48	10
✕8.49	4175	Ludwigsburg 8.30 - ⑥ Bietigheim 8.15	5
†8.49	5143	Mühlacker 7.37	5
8.55	E 3770	Crailsheim 7.24 - ✕ Lauda 6.03 - Backnang 8.25	1a
8.57	E 3021	Mannheim 7.10 - Heidelberg 7.26	7
:9.01 Rembrandt	🚃 10	München 6.46 - Augsburg 7.18 - Ulm 8.02 nur 1. Kl	9
9.01	4174	Esslingen 8.41	4
✕9.03	4525	Weil der Stadt 8.19 (⑥ Zug-Nr 6155)	6
:9.03 ① bis ⑥ Enztal	🚃 963	Karlsruhe 8.02	14
:9.07 ① bis ⑤ Hessen-Kurier	🚃 163	Wiesbaden 6.44 - Mainz 6.54 - Mannheim 7.45 - Heidelberg 7.57 nur 1. Kl ➡ verk nicht 7. VI.	13
✕9.09	5230	Ulm 6.56	2
9.09	4179	L... ...50	5

UNIT 16 Dependent Infinitives—Comparison of Adjectives

From Unit 16 on, you will find a change in the usual unit format. There are no longer any "Fragen an Sie persönlich" and complete conversations are discontinued. Instead, topics are suggested, and some vocabulary is given, for you to construct your own conversations. In addition, we have put together short lists of standard phrases for use in many conversations, for example, phrases to express agreement and disagreement. These changes should help you move away from memorized exchanges and guide you toward free expression in German.

The first reading selection presents some more everyday cultural information. If you are planning to travel in Europe by rail, you might consider purchasing a Eurailpass, which is only available in the United States, or an Interail Pass, which you can buy in any European country (except in the Eastern European socialist countries). With the Interail Pass, you get fifty percent off in the country in which you purchased it, and you travel free in all other countries. (Some students have been known to purchase their Interail Pass in Luxemburg.)

The short text by Peter Handke, *Zugauskunft*, at first seems to be merely a tongue-in-cheek description of a traveler's attempt to get from here to there. But it can also be read as a parable, not too dissimilar from Erich Kästner's *Eisenbahngleichnis*, which concludes the reading section of the unit.

Patterns

[1] bleiben, gehen, lernen plus Infinitive

Bitte bleiben Sie doch sitzen, Herr Schmidt.
    Please stay seated (don't get up).

Ich glaube, Fritzchen Meyer bleibt wieder sitzen.* —Wirklich? Er ist doch vor zwei Jahren erst sitzengeblieben.
    I think Fritzchen Meyer is going to be kept behind again. —Really? He just repeated a grade two years ago, didn't he?

Du brauchst noch nicht aufzustehen; du kannst noch liegen bleiben.
    You don't have to get up yet; you can still stay in bed.

SEE ANALYSIS 163-164 (pp. 495-497)

---

*It is not unusual for German students, from grade school through the *Gymnasium*, to have to repeat a grade if they fail in a certain number of subjects. Thus **sitzenbleiben,** quite literally, means "to remain seated" in your classroom while your classmates move up to the next grade.

Wann kommt der Zug aus München an?

Wem gehört denn das Buch da?—Das weiß ich nicht; es ist gestern abend hier liegenge-
    blieben.
    To whom does that book belong?—I don't know; it was left here last night.

Meine Uhr ist gestern abend plötzlich stehengeblieben.
    My watch suddenly stopped last night.

Bitte gehen Sie weiter; Sie dürfen hier nicht stehenbleiben.
    Please go on, you mustn't stop here.

Wie wäre es, wenn wir jetzt essen gingen?
Andreas ist auch schon essen gegangen.
Können wir bald essen gehen?
Du brauchst doch nicht schon wieder essen zu gehen; du hast doch gerade erst gefrühstückt.
Wie wär's denn, wenn wir Sonntag baden gingen?

Ingelheim kannte ich schon vor dem Kriege, aber seine Frau lernte ich erst kennen, als er mit
    ihr nach München zog.
Ingelheim kenne ich schon lange, aber seine Frau habe ich leider noch nicht kennengelernt.
    Ich möchte sie gerne kennenlernen.

Sein Urgroßvater war sehr intelligent, aber er hatte nie lesen gelernt.
Viele Kinder lernen schon mit fünf Jahren lesen.
Bevor Sie nach Kalifornien gehen, müssen Sie unbedingt Auto fahren lernen.
Es wäre besser, wenn Sie Auto fahren gelernt hätten.

VARIATIONS

Complete the following sentences, using the verbs in parentheses, then give the English
equivalents.

Bitte _____, Herr Vollmer (sitzen bleiben).
Ich hoffe, meine Uhr _____ (stehenbleiben).
Ich glaube, meine Uhr _____ (stehenbleiben).
Ich dachte, meine Uhr _____ (stehenbleiben).
Er kommt heute nicht zum Frühstück. Er _____ (liegen bleiben).

Es wäre nett, wenn wir morgen _____ (schwimmen gehen).
Er soll jeden Tag mit Erika _____ (schwimmen gehen).
Ist Hans schon im Bett?—Ja, er _____ (schlafen gehen).
Ich wollte, wir _____ (schlafen gehen).

Es wäre besser, wenn sie _____ (kochen lernen).
Ich möchte wissen, ob sie _____ (kochen lernen).
Ich dachte, du _____ (schwimmen lernen).
Sie soll tatsächlich _____ (Auto fahren lernen).
Ich hoffe, daß er hier jemanden _____ (kennenlernen).

[2] hören and sehen plus Infinitive

Observe how **hören** and **sehen** behave like modals in these sentences.

Ich hörte ihn gestern abend nach Hause kommen.	I heard him come home last night.	SEE ANALYSIS 164 (p. 497)
Ich habe ihn gestern abend nach Hause kommen hören.		
Ich habe ihn gehört, als er gestern abend nach Hause kam.		
Wir sahen sie in Berlin die Desdemona spielen.	We saw her play Desdemona in Berlin.	
Wir haben sie die Desdemona spielen sehen.		

VARIATIONS

Form sentences with the following phrases, using modals, subjunctives, and various tenses.

Emma einmal (noch nie) lachen sehen
den Kleinen schreien hören
die Maria nach Hause kommen hören

[3] lassen

lassen: *to leave (behind)*

Heute regnet es bestimmt nicht. Deinen Regenmantel kannst du zu Hause lassen.
    I'm sure it won't rain today. You can leave your raincoat at home.

SEE ANALYSIS 164 (p. 497)

Heute regnet es bestimmt nicht. Du hättest deinen Mantel zu Hause lassen können.
    I'm sure it won't rain today. You could have left your raincoat at home.

Bitte lassen Sie mich jetzt allein.	Please leave me alone now.
Ich wollte, er ließe mich in Ruhe.	I wish he'd leave me alone (in peace).

Jetzt habe ich schon wieder meinen Mantel im Hotel hängenlassen.
    Now I've left my coat at the hotel again.

Und wo ist deine Handtasche?—Die habe ich bei Tante Amalie auf dem Tisch stehenlassen.
    Where is your bag?—I left it on the table at Aunt Amalie's.

Und deine Handschuhe hast du wohl auch irgendwo liegenlassen?
    And I suppose you left your gloves somewhere too?

Express in German (note that the infinitives **hängen, liegen, stehen** behave like prefixes and do not change).

I hope you won't leave your coat in the hotel again.
I have left my gloves at Aunt Amalie's.
You can't leave your car in front of the hotel.

lassen: *to cause or permit somebody to do something*

Ich lasse dich nicht nach Berlin fahren.
> I will not let you go to Berlin alone.

Ich habe ihn *doch* nach Berlin fahren lassen.
> I let him go to Berlin after all.

Ich wollte, ich hätte ihn nicht nach Berlin fahren lassen.
> I wish I had not let him go to Berlin.

Du kannst mich doch nicht ohne Geld nach Berlin fahren lassen.
> You certainly cannot let me go to Berlin without money.

Wir ließen den Arzt kommen.
> (We let the doctor come.)
> (We caused the doctor to come.)
> We had the doctor come.
> We called (for) the doctor.

Lassen Sie mich das mal sehen!
> Let me see that!

Lassen Sie mich doch erst meinen Kaffee trinken!
> Let me first drink my coffee!

Lassen Sie den Meyer diese Arbeit machen.
> Let Meyer do that job.

Wir lassen gerade unser Dach reparieren.
> (Literally: We are just letting [somebody] repair our roof.)
> We are just having our roof repaired.

Wir müssen unser Auto reparieren lassen.
Wir haben den Motor noch nie reparieren lassen müssen.
Mein Freund Egon muß sich operieren lassen.

Ich habe ihm ein Telegramm schicken lassen.
> I had (somebody) send him a telegram.
> (I had a telegram sent to him.)

Ich habe ihm sagen lassen, daß er mich morgen anrufen soll.
> I had (somebody) tell him that he should give me a ring tomorrow.
> (I sent word to him to give me a ring tomorrow.)

Frau Lenz hat sich einen Mantel machen lassen.
> Mrs. Lenz had (somebody) make her a coat.
> (Mrs. Lenz has had a coat made.)

Ich lasse mir eine Tasse Kaffee aufs Zimmer bringen.
> I request that (somebody) bring me a cup of coffee to my room.
> (I have a cup of coffee brought to my room.)

Warum hat sie sich das Frühstück denn nicht aufs Zimmer bringen lassen?
> Why didn't she have her breakfast sent to her room?
> (Literally: Why didn't she tell somebody to send her the breakfast to the room?)

Wo hast du dir die Haare schneiden lassen?
> Where did you get your hair cut?

Ich lasse mir immer die Haare von meiner Frau schneiden.
> I always let my wife cut my hair.

François? Nein, von dem lasse ich mir nie wieder die Haare schneiden.
> François? No, I'll never have my hair cut again by him.

Wir lassen unseren Kindern von Overhoff ein Haus bauen.
> We are having Overhoff build a house for our children.

Wir lassen uns von Overhoff ein Haus bauen.
> We are having Overhoff build us a house.

Früher haben wir uns immer die Brötchen vom Bäcker ins Haus schicken lassen.
> We used to have the baker deliver our breakfast rolls.

Ich lasse meine Frau von Dr. Meinecke operieren.
> I shall ask Dr. Meinecke to operate on my wife.

Petra läßt sich von ihrem Mann verwöhnen.
> Petra lets her husband pamper her.

Ich ließe mich auch gerne von dir verwöhnen!
> I would like it if you pampered me too!

English *leave*: German **verlassen** or **gehen**

Jeden Abend verließ Meyer sein Büro um 5 Uhr 30.	Every evening Meyer left his office at 5:30.
Frau Meyer hatte nie erwartet, daß Gustav sie je verlassen würde.	Mrs. Meyer had never expected that Gustav would ever leave her.
Ich kann nur bis acht Uhr bleiben; dann muß ich gehen.	I can only stay until eight o'clock; then I'll have to leave.
Fritz ist nicht mehr hier; er ist schon gegangen.	Fritz isn't here anymore; he has already left.

[4] End-Field Infinitives

Es fing an zu regnen.
Als es anfing zu regnen, gingen wir nach Hause.
Es hat angefangen zu regnen.
Es fing an, sehr stark zu regnen.
Als es anfing, sehr stark zu regnen, gingen wir nach Hause.
Kannst du nicht endlich aufhören zu arbeiten?
Weil ich vergessen hatte, ihm zu schreiben, kam er nicht zum Bahnhof.
Hast du denn nicht versucht, sie anzurufen?

SEE
ANALYSIS
165
(p. 500)

Change the following sentences to infinitive clauses and use the verbs in parentheses to form introductory clauses.

> **Es regnet nicht mehr. (aufhören)**
> **Es hat aufgehört zu regnen.**

Er will in Davos gewesen sein. (behaupten)
Ich habe ihr nicht geschrieben. (vergessen)
Meyer will seiner Frau ein Auto schenken. (versprechen)
Ich möchte sie bald wiedersehen. (hoffen)
Ich wollte dich gestern abend anrufen. (versuchen)

Observe the identity of the personal dative and the unmentioned subject of the end-field infinitive. Then complete the variations.

Er schlug mir vor, an die Nordsee zu fahren.
> He suggested that I go to the North Sea.

Wenn Sie mir nicht vorgeschlagen hätten, an die Nordsee zu fahren, hätte ich meinen Mann nie kennengelernt.
> If you hadn't suggested that I go to the North Sea, I would never have met my husband.

Ich rate dir, nicht mehr so viel zu rauchen.
> I advise you not to smoke so much anymore.

Wir erlauben unseren Kindern nicht, jede Woche zweimal ins Kino zu gehen.
> We don't allow our children to go to the movies twice a week.

In Deutschland ist es verboten, im Kino zu rauchen.
> In Germany it is forbidden to smoke in the movie theater.

Niemand kann mir befehlen, einen Mann zu heiraten, den ich nicht liebe.
> Nobody can order me to marry a man I don't love.

Change the following sentences to infinitive clauses and use the verbs in parentheses to form introductory clauses. Use **Er** and the perfect tense throughout.

> **Fahren Sie doch mal an die See. (raten)**
> **Er hat mir geraten, einmal an die See zu fahren.**

Trinken Sie jeden Abend vor dem Schlafengehen ein Glas Wein. (empfehlen)
Bleiben Sie morgen zu Hause. (erlauben)
Fahren Sie doch mit mir nach München. (vorschlagen)

[5] End-Field Infinitives after Predicate Adjectives

SEE
ANALYSIS
165
(p. 500)

After studying these sentences, complete the variations.

Inge war froh, ihren Mann wiederzusehen.
> Inge was glad to see her husband again.

Ich wußte, Inge wäre froh gewesen, ihren Mann wiederzusehen.
>I knew Inge would have been glad to see her husband again.

Ich bin immer bereit gewesen, ihm zu helfen.
>I have always been ready to help him.

Ich war sehr erstaunt, Erich so bald wiederzusehen.
>I was very astonished to see Erich again so soon.

VARIATIONS

Change the following sentences to infinitive clauses. Use the subjects of these sentences and the adjectives in parentheses to form introductory clauses.

> **Inge sah ihren Mann wieder. (froh)**
> **Inge war froh, ihren Mann wiederzusehen.**

Gottseidank sind wir wieder zu Hause. (glücklich)
Erich half uns immer. (bereit)
Ich sah ihn letztes Wochenende in Hamburg wieder. (erstaunt)

[6] End-Field Infinitives after **da**-Compounds

Note that the subject of the inflected verb is also the unmentioned subject of the infinitive.

Ich denke nicht daran, mit Inge schwimmen zu gehen.
Du weißt doch, daß ich gar nicht daran denke, mit Inge schwimmen zu gehen.
Ich habe ja gar nicht daran gedacht, mit Inge schwimmen zu gehen.
Ich hätte nie daran gedacht, mit Inge schwimmen zu gehen.

SEE
ANALYSIS
165
(p. 500)

[7] End-Field Infinitives with **um . . . zu, ohne . . . zu, statt . . . zu**

Note how the German construction changes if the subject of the infinitive is not also the subject of the inflected verb.

Wir bleiben heute zu Hause, um endlich einmal arbeiten zu können.
>We're going to stay at home today in order to get some work done finally.

SEE
ANALYSIS
166
(p. 500)

Wir bleiben heute zu Hause, damit mein Mann endlich einmal arbeiten kann.
>We're going to stay at home today in order that my husband can finally get some work done (so that my husband can finally get some work done).

Ohne auch nur einen Augenblick nachzudenken, gab er die richtige Antwort.
>Without a moment's thought, he gave the right answer.

Mit Meyer kann man nie sprechen, ohne daß Müller dabei ist.
>You can never talk to Meyer without Müller being there too.

Hast du schon wieder die ganze Nacht gelesen, statt zu schlafen?
>Have you read all night again instead of going to sleep?

Statt daß man *Mey*er nach Berlin geschickt hätte, muß *ich* schon wieder fahren.
>Instead of their having sent Meyer to Berlin (which they should have done and didn't), I have to go again.

[8] Comparative Forms of Adjectives

SEE
ANALYSIS
167
(p. 502)

Sie ist so alt wie ich.	Sie ist älter als ich.
Hier ist es so kalt wie in Hamburg.	Hier ist es kälter als in Hamburg.
Leider ist sie nicht so jung wie er.	Leider ist er jünger als sie.
Hier ist es nicht so warm wie bei euch.	Bei euch ist es viel wärmer als bei uns.
Die Alpen sind nicht so hoch wie die Sierras.	Die Sierras sind höher als die Alpen.
Ingelheim ist nicht ganz so interessant wie Thomas Mann.	Thomas Mann ist etwas interessanter als Ingelheim.
Du bist doch nicht so groß wie ich.	Doch, ich bin größer als du.
Das Bier hier ist wirklich gut.	Ja, aber das Bier in München ist noch besser.
Tante Dorothea redet genau so viel wie Tante Amalie.	Nee, nee, die redet noch mehr als Tante Amalie, noch viel mehr.
Hier ist das frische Obst nicht so teuer wie bei uns.	Bei uns ist das Obst viel teurer als bei euch.
Inges Haar war schon immer so dunkel wie meins.	Aber seit sie vierzig ist, wird es immer dunkler.
Möchtest du dir gern den Faustfilm ansehen?	Nein, ich ginge viel lieber in einen Wildwestfilm.

Form similar pairs with the following adjectives.

schnell, schneller	hart, härter	oft, öfter
freundlich, freundlicher	kurz, kürzer	stark, stärker
arm, ärmer	lang, länger	nah, näher

[9] Superlative Form of Adjectives

Read the following sentences and complete the variations.

SEE
ANALYSIS
167
(p. 502)

Die Frau mit dem Flamingo ist sein bester Roman.
Ich halte *Die Frau mit dem Flamingo* für _____.

Monika ist die interessanteste Frau, die ich kenne.
Von allen Frauen, die ich kenne, ist sie die _____.

Im Dezember sind die Tage am kürzesten.
Der 21. Dezember ist der _____ Tag des Jahres.

In dieser Show sehen Sie Giganto, den stärksten Mann der Welt.
Giganto ist von allen Männern der _____.

Was ist Ingelheims bester Roman?
Mir gefällt *Die Frau mit dem Flamingo* am _____.

Hier ist es ja das ganze Jahr sehr schön, aber im Mai ist es hier doch am _____.

Spieglein, Spieglein an der Wand,
wer ist die Schönste im ganzen Land?
Frau Königin, Ihr* seid die Schönste hier,
    aber Schneewittchen hinter den Bergen,
    bei den sieben Zwergen,
    ist noch tausendmal schöner als Ihr.

[10] Comparatives and Superlatives in Advertising

SEE
ANALYSIS
167
(p. 502)

Sie können natürlich mehr Geld ausgeben, aber es ist nicht sicher, ob Sie einen besseren Waschautomaten bekommen.

Gesünder und darum besser ist ein Cottona-Hemd.

Sie sollten nicht weniger für ihr Geld verlangen. Sie sollten mehr verlangen: Ein VW ist der beste Kauf.

Cinzano on the rocks: der beste Anfang einer guten Sache.

Was trinken Sie am liebsten, wenn Sie mit Ihrer Frau abends fernsehen? Natürlich Löwenbräu.

Wie gern essen wir ein Steak. Noch lieber ist es uns mit einem Schuß Ketchup. Am liebsten essen wir es aber mit Thomy's Tomaten-Ketchup. Es gehört zu den neun Thomy's Delikatessen.

Statt für jeden etwas, etwas Besonderes für alle: Triumpf, die beste Schreibmaschine.

Jede moderne Frau weiß, wie man sich interessanter macht. Die interessantesten Frauen tragen Elastiform.

GUTER WEIN
AUS BESTEM HAUSE

JOSEF MILZ KG

WEINGÜTER · WEINGROSSKELLEREI
NEUMAGEN · DHRON/MOSEL

Analysis

163 Dependent Infinitives

As you know, the two-pronged predicate is the most characteristic feature of German syntax. The first prong is always a finite (conjugated) verb form, and the second prong contains verbal complements and infinitives or participles.

*Ihr is an obsolete polite form now replaced by **Sie**.

In the "two-box" second prong, the complement or the dependent infinitive precedes the infinitive or participle of the main verb. Examples:

FRONT FIELD	1ST PRONG	INNER FIELD	2ND PRONG		
Ich	gehe	jetzt	nach Hause.		
Ich	bin	bald	nach Hause		gegangen.
Er	fährt	bald	ab.		
Er	ist	sofort	ab-		gefahren.
Er	will	morgen			arbeiten.
Er	hat	nie	arbeiten		wollen.*
Er	hat	nie	zu arbeiten		brauchen.*
Er	hat	es nie			gewollt.*
Er	hat	es nicht			gebraucht.*
Er	scheint	heute	nach Berlin		zu fliegen.
Er	scheint	gestern	nach Berlin		geflogen zu sein.
Er	soll	gestern	nach Berlin		geflogen sein.
Er	hat	leider	nach Berlin	fliegen	müssen.†
Er	scheint	heute	nach Berlin	fliegen	zu müssen.†
Er	hat	heute nicht	nach Berlin	zu fliegen	brauchen.†

Since dependent infinitives with modals (without **zu**) and with **brauchen** or **scheinen** (with **zu**) always appear in the second prong, we can refer to them as

*Remember that the "infinitive" forms **wollen** and **brauchen** in these sentences are really participles; the participles **gewollt** and **gebraucht** are used when there is no dependent infinitive.
†If a dependent infinitive with a complement precedes a modal, then the first box in turn contains two boxes.

second-prong infinitives. A number of other German verbs also take such second-prong infinitives, without **zu**. Many other verbs can be followed by infinitives in the end field, with **zu**.

164 Second-Prong Infinitives

bleiben, gehen, lernen

These verbs often appear with dependent infinitives, but since they are not modals, they use the regular participles **geblieben**, **gegangen**, and **gelernt**. Only a few of these constructions have literal equivalents in English.

1. **bleiben** is most frequently used with **sitzen**, **stehen**, and **liegen**.

Sie dürfen ruhig sitzen bleiben.	You may remain seated.
Nur ein Haus ist stehen geblieben.	Only one house remained standing.
Er wollte noch eine Weile liegen bleiben.	He wanted to stay in bed a while longer.

When used with nonliteral meanings, these combinations are written as one word. For example:

sitzenbleiben	not to be promoted to the next higher class in school
stehenbleiben	to stop (of a watch or clock)
liegenbleiben	to be left behind (of an object)

2. **gehen** is used with such common verbs as **essen**, **schlafen**, and **baden**.

Wir wollen um zwölf essen gehen.	We want to go to lunch at twelve.
Hans ist schon schlafen gegangen.	Hans has already gone to bed.
Sollen wir morgen baden gehen?	Shall we go swimming tomorrow?

3. With the exception of the nonliteral **kennenlernen**, combinations with **lernen** (*to learn to do something*) are written as two words.

Erika lernt jetzt fahren.	Erika is learning to drive.
Wann haben Sie denn fahren gelernt?	When did you learn to drive?

hören and sehen

In contrast to **bleiben**, **gehen**, and **lernen**, these verbs do behave like modals in that they replace the participles **gehört** and **gesehen** by the infinitive form. In these sentences, the direct object is also the subject of the dependent infinitive.

Er sang. Wir hörten ihn.
        Wir hörten ihn singen.
        Wir haben ihn singen hören.
        Wir haben ihn   gehört; er sang.
Er kam. Ich sah ihn.
        Ich sah ihn kommen.
        Ich habe ihn kommen sehen.
        Ich habe ihn   gesehen; er kam.

lassen

Lassen is one of the verbs most frequently used with a second-prong infinitive. Like the modals, it uses the infinitive form as a participle when there is a dependent infinitive.

Er hat mich nicht in Ruhe gelassen.
Ich habe meinen Mantel im Café hängen lassen.

Unfortunately, this high-frequency **lassen** is one of the nastiest verbs in the German language, not because of its forms, but because of the many constructions in which it is used that have no literal English equivalent. Also, while **lassen** often corresponds to English *let* and *leave*, *let* and *leave* cannot always be expressed by **lassen**.

lassen has two quite separate meanings:

1. **lassen** *to let, to leave* (behind)

   Hast du deinen Mantel zu Hause **gelassen?**
   Did you leave your coat at home?

   Nein, ich habe ihn im Café **hängen lassen.**
   No, I left it (hanging) in the café.

   Ich habe meine Handschuhe irgendwo **liegen lassen.**
   I left my gloves (lying) somewhere.

   Ich habe meinen Schirm im Hotel **stehen lassen.**

   I left my umbrella (standing) in the hotel.

2. **lassen** *to let, to cause* (by request or permission) *somebody to do something*

(a) with the subject of the dependent infinitive as an accusative:

Wir lassen ihn allein.
(Er will allein sein. Wir lassen ihn [allein sein].)

Wir haben ihn gehen lassen.
(Er wollte gehen. Wir haben ihn gelassen.)

(b) with the subject (in the accusative) plus an accusative object of the dependent infinitive:

Ich will einen Sportwagen kaufen. Mein Vater läßt mich nicht.
Mein Vater läßt mich keinen Sportwagen kaufen.
Mein Vater hat mich noch nie einen Sportwagen kaufen lassen.

By way of contrast: In the following sentence, **mein Vater** is the *subject* of both **kaufen** and **hat können:**

> **Mein Vater hat mir keinen Sportwagen gekauft. Er konnte es nicht.**
> **Mein Vater hat mir keinen Sportwagen kaufen können.**

(c) with only the accusative object (but not the subject) of the dependent infinitive:

> **Unser Mechaniker wird morgen unseren Wagen waschen. Wir lassen ihn.**
> **Wir lassen morgen unseren Wagen waschen.**
> **Wir haben gestern unseren Wagen waschen lassen.**

Compare again with the following sentence, in which **wir** is the *subject* of both **waschen** and **haben müssen:**

> **Wir haben gestern unseren Wagen waschen müssen.**

(d) again with an accusative object of the dependent infinitive (but no subject), plus a personal dative denoting the person for whose benefit some other person (the unmentioned subject) is doing something:

> **Architekt Schmidt will meinem Sohn ein Haus bauen.**
> **Ich lasse ihn (den Architekten).**
> **Ich lasse meinem Sohn ein Haus bauen.**
> I am having a house built for my son.

The dative object in the first sentence and the subject of the second sentence may be identical; this results in a reflexive in the **lassen**-sentence.

> **Architekt Schmidt baut meinem Sohn ein Haus.**
> **Mein Sohn läßt ihn (den Architekten).**
> **Mein Sohn läßt sich ein Haus bauen.**

> > **Ich lasse mir ein Haus bauen.**
> > I am having a house built for myself.

(e) with the subject now mentioned in the form of a **von**-phrase with the dative:

> **Architekt Müller wird mir ein Haus bauen. Ich lasse ihn.**
> **Ich lasse mir von Architekt Müller ein Haus bauen.**
> I am having a house built for myself by the architect Müller.

> **Ich lasse meinem Sohn von Architekt Müller ein Haus bauen.**
> **Er läßt sich von Architekt Müller ein Haus bauen.**
> **Wir lassen das Haus von Architekt Müller bauen.**

(f) again with the subject of the dependent infinitive as a **von**-phrase, plus a direct object (which may be a reflexive):

> **Sie lädt mich ein. Ich lasse sie gern.**
> **Ich lasse mich gern von ihr einladen.**
> I am delighted to have her invite me.

Ich habe ihn von meiner Freundin zu ihrer Party einladen lassen.
I've had my girlfriend invite him to her party.

English *to leave*: German **verlassen, (weg)gehen**

English *to leave* is also used with the meaning *to depart (from)*.

He left the city in 1960.
I have to leave now.

In both these cases, German cannot use **lassen.** If there is a direct object, **ver-lassen** can be used:

Er verließ die Stadt im Jahre 1960.

If there is no direct object, neither **lassen** nor **verlassen** can be used:

Ich muß jetzt gehen.
Ich muß jetzt weg.
Ich muß jetzt nach Hause.

165 End-Field Infinitives

In all the constructions above, the dependent infinitive (as part of the second prong) stands at the end of the sentence. A number of German verbs, however, require infinitive phrases (always with **zu**) in the end field. We have already used a number of such end-field infinitives, for example, in connection with prepositional objects.

Ich hoffe nicht mehr darauf, daß er wiederkommt.
Ich hoffe nicht mehr darauf, ihn wiederzusehen.

The infinitive phrase **ihn wiederzusehen** has the same syntactic function as the **daß**-clause, but in the first sentence, the subject of the two clauses is not the same, and in the second it is.

Bei uns hat jeder
die Freiheit,
seine Lektüre
selbst zu wählen

z. B.
DIE ZEIT

The following verbs are among those used with end-field infinitives with identical subjects:

anfangen	to begin	**vergessen**	to forget
aufhören	to stop, cease	**versprechen**	to promise
behaupten	to claim	**versuchen**	to try

Ich rufe sie heute an. Ich habe es ihr gestern versprochen.

Ich habe es ihr gestern versprochen,

      ⌊→ = sie heute anzurufen.

Ich habe ihr gestern versprochen, sie heute anzurufen.

NOTE:

1. The word order in these infinitive phrases is the same as in normal sentences, that is, the infinitive stands in second-prong position at the end of the phrase.

2. End-field infinitives must be separated by a comma unless preceded only by **zu.**

Es hat angefangen, sehr stark zu regnen.
Es hat angefangen zu regnen.

The following verbs all take a personal *dative object* which is the same as the subject of the infinitive clause that follows it.

befehlen	to give an order to somebody
empfehlen	to make a recommendation to somebody
erlauben	to give permission to somebody
helfen	to give help to someone in doing something
raten	to give somebody advice
verbieten	to forbid someone to do something
vorschlagen	to make a suggestion to somebody

Ich fahre einmal an die See. Mein Arzt hat es mir geraten.

Mein Arzt hat es mir geraten,

      ⌊→ = einmal an die See zu fahren.

Mein Arzt hat mir geraten, einmal an die See zu fahren.

The End-Field Infinitive after Predicate Adjectives

The following predicate adjectives are frequently used with end-field infinitives:

bereit	ready	**froh**	glad
erstaunt	astonished	**schön**	nice
glücklich	happy		

Sie wissen doch, daß ich immer bereit gewesen bin, Ihrem Mann zu helfen.
Warum sind Sie denn so erstaunt, mich hier zu sehen?
Inge war froh, ihren Mann endlich wiedersehen zu dürfen.

Replacement of Prepositional Objects

Verbs which take a prepositional object frequently replace this complement
with a **da**-compound which anticipates an infinitive phrase in the end field (see
138).

Ich denke ja gar nicht daran,
Du weißt doch, daß ich gar nicht daran denke,   } den Meyer zu heiraten.
Ich habe ja nie daran gedacht,
Du weißt doch, daß ich nie daran gedacht habe,

166 um . . . zu, ohne . . . zu, statt . . . zu

We have already used infinitives with **um . . . zu** in the end-field position. The
same construction is possible with **ohne . . . zu** and **statt (anstatt) . . . zu**. All of
these infinitives appear most frequently in either end-field or front-field position.

Er fuhr nach Afrika, um dort einen Roman zu schreiben.
Er fuhr nach München, ohne seine Frau mitzunehmen.
Er fuhr nach Afrika, statt zu Hause zu bleiben.
Statt zu Hause zu bleiben, fuhr er nach Afrika.

English uses an infinitive as the equivalent of the **um . . . zu** forms (*in order to
write a novel*), but for the **ohne . . . zu** and **statt . . . zu** forms, English must use
the gerund (*without taking his wife along; instead of staying at home*).

In the above examples, the subject of the infinitive clause is the same as the
subject of the main clause. If there is a different subject, the infinitive constructions must be replaced by dependent clauses.

um . . . zu	damit
ohne . . . zu	ohne daß
statt . . . zu	statt daß

Wir bleiben zu Hause, um endlich einmal arbeiten zu können.
Wir bleiben zu Hause, damit mein Mann endlich einmal arbeiten kann.

167 Comparison of Adjectives and Adverbs

Forms of the Comparative and the Superlative

Both German adjectives and adverbs form their comparative and superlative
forms by adding **-er** and **-(e)st** to the stem, parallel to the English pattern in
fast, fast-er, fast-est.

schnell, schneller, schnellst-

The English patterns *interesting, more interesting, most interesting,* and *quickly, more quickly, most quickly* are not possible in German.

interessant, interessanter, interessantest-

The **-e-** in the superlative forms is added whenever the **-st-** ending alone would be hard to pronounce—for example, **weitest-, ältest-, kürzest-.** An exception is the superlative form of **groß.**

groß, größer, größt-

Many monosyllable adjectives add an umlaut in both the comparative and superlative.

alt, älter, ältest-	old
arm, ärmer, ärmst-	poor
hart, härter, härtest-	hard
jung, jünger, jüngst-	young
kalt, kälter, kältest-	cold
kurz, kürzer, kürzest-	short
lang, länger, längst-	long
oft, öfter, öftest-	often
schwarz, schwärzer, schwärzest-	black
stark, stärker, stärkst-	strong

Adjectives ending in **-el** and **-er** lose the **-e-** in the comparative.

dunkel, dunkler, dunkelst-
teuer, teurer, teuerst-

The adjective **hoch** replaces the **-ch** by a silent **-h-** in the comparative:

hoch, höher, höchst-

and the adjective **nah** changes the silent **-h** to a **-ch-** in the superlative.

nah, näher, nächst-

Rotlackiert schwimmt man am schnellsten

Gut and **viel** have irregular forms:

> gut, besser, best-
> viel, mehr, meist-

and the adverb **gern**, which has no comparative and superlative forms of its own, substitutes the forms of the adjective **lieb.**

> gern, lieber, liebst-

To indicate that superlatives cannot be used without an ending, the superlative forms above are followed by hyphens.

Use of Comparison

In comparisons implying equality, **so . . . wie** is used.

> **Er ist so alt wie ich.**
> **Er ist nicht so alt wie ich.**
> **Er ist nicht so alt, wie ich dachte.**

If the comparison expresses inequality, the comparative form of the adjective is used, followed by **als.**

> **Er ist älter als ich.**
> **Er kann nicht älter sein als ich.**
> **Er ist älter, als ich dachte.**

As *attributive adjectives*, comparative and superlative forms are treated like any other adjective; that is, they add normal adjective endings to the **-er** and **-st** suffixes:

> **Einen interessanteren Roman habe ich nie gelesen.**
> **Ein interessanteres Buch habe ich nie gelesen.**
> **Das ist die interessanteste Geschichte, die ich kenne.**

As *adverbs*, comparative forms do not take an ending, and superlative forms always use the pattern **am** (adjective)**-sten.**

> **Mit deinem Mercedes kommen wir bestimmt schneller nach München als
>   mit meinem VW-Bus.**
> **Können Sie mir sagen, wie ich am schnellsten zum Flughafen komme?**
> **Da nehmen Sie am besten ein Taxi.**

As *predicate adjectives*, comparative forms do not take an ending. Superlatives use attributive forms preceded by an article if a noun can be supplied; otherwise they follow the **am** (adjective)**-sten** pattern.

Meyers finde ich ja ganz nett, aber Schmidts sind doch netter.
Von seinen drei Töchtern ist Ingrid zwar die intelligenteste, aber nicht die
schönste (Tochter).
Ich reise ja sehr gerne, aber zu Hause ist es doch am schönsten.

Some Special Forms

1. A few comparatives are used with reference to their opposites. For example,

Wir haben längere Zeit in Berlin gewohnt

means: we did not live there a long time, but longer than a short time. Similarly, **eine ältere Dame** (*an elderly lady*) does not mean that the lady is old, but that she is no longer young.

2. To express a high degree of a certain quality, German can use **höchst** as the equivalent of English *most*. Observe the degrees:

Das war ganz interessant.   (quite *interesting*)
Das war interessant.   (*interesting*)
Das war sehr interessant.   (*very* interesting)
Das war aber höchst interessant.   (*most* interesting)

3. Where English repeats the comparative to indicate an increase in degree, German uses **immer** with the comparative.

It was getting warmer and warmer.   **Es wurde immer wärmer.**

168 Word Formation: Nouns Derived from Adjectives

German, like English, has a number of suffixes which can be used to derive nouns from adjectives.

The Suffix -e

A number of adjectives may be changed into feminine nouns by adding the suffix **-e** and by umlauting when possible. These nouns correspond in meaning to English nouns in *-th* (*strong, strength; long, length*), *-ness* (*weak, weakness; great, greatness*), or *-ity* (*brief, brevity*).

breit	die Breite	breadth
groß	die Größe	greatness; size
hart	die Härte	hardness
heiß	die Hitze	heat
hoch	die Höhe	height
kalt	die Kälte	cold(ness)*
kurz	die Kürze	shortness, brevity
lang	die Länge	length
nah	die Nähe	nearness, proximity
schwach	die Schwäche	weakness
stark	die Stärke	strength
still	die Stille	peacefulness, calm, quiet
warm	die Wärme	warmth

The Suffixes -heit, -keit, -igkeit

Many feminine abstract nouns, also corresponding to English derivatives in *-ity* and *-ness*, can be formed by adding one of these three suffixes; they form their plurals in **-en.** Feel free to use the nouns listed, but do not try to invent your own: they may not exist. Of high frequency are the formations in **-keit** added to derivatives in **-bar, -ig,** and **-lich,** and formations in **-igkeit** added to **-los.**

	dunkel	die Dunkelheit	darkness
	frei	die Freiheit	freedom
	gesund	die Gesundheit	health
	krank	die Krankheit	sickness
	möglich	die Möglichkeit	possibility
	müde	die Müdigkeit	tiredness
	neu	die Neuheit	newness, novelty
		die Neuigkeit	news
	schön	die Schönheit	beauty
	sicher	die Sicherheit	security
	vergangen	die Vergangenheit	past
	wahr	die Wahrheit	truth
	wahrscheinlich	die Wahrscheinlichkeit	probability
	wirklich	die Wirklichkeit	reality
	zufrieden	die Zufriedenheit	contentment
	unfähig	die Unfähigkeit	inability
	unzufrieden	die Unzufriedenheit	discontent
	unsicher	die Unsicherheit	insecurity
der Freund,-e	freundlich	die Freundlichkeit	friendliness
der Hof,-̈e	höflich	die Höflichkeit	politeness
der Mensch,-en	menschlich	die Menschlichkeit	humaneness
die Sache,-n	sachlich	die Sachlichkeit	objectivity,
(thing, fact, cause)	(objective)		matter-of-factness

*But *cold* in the medical sense: **die Erkältung.**

sterben	sterblich	die Sterblichkeit	mortality
	unsterblich	die Unsterblichkeit	immortality
die Hoffnung	hoffnungslos	die Hoffnungslosigkeit	hopelessness
der Schlaf	schlaflos	die Schlaflosigkeit	sleeplessness, insomnia
der Dank	dankbar	die Dankbarkeit	gratitude
halten (to last, to hold up)	haltbar (durable)	die Haltbarkeit	durability
teilen (to divide)	teilbar (divisible)	die Teilbarkeit	divisibility
	unteilbar (indivisible)	die Unteilbarkeit	indivisibility

Note the following special cases:

die Kindheit	childhood
die Menschheit	mankind
die Flüssigkeit	liquid
die Seltenheit	rarity

The following compounds are all derived from the stem **ein**:

die Einheit	unit, unity
die Einigkeit	accord, being of one mind, unity
einig	in agreement, in accord
vereinigt	united
die Vereinigten Staaten	the United States
einsam	lonely
die Einsamkeit	loneliness, solitude
einzeln	single (apart from the rest)
die Einzelheit	detail
einzig	single, unique, sole
einfach	simple
die Einfachheit	simplicity

Conversations

I

How to Express What?

The following groups of expressions are arranged topically. Each group lists characteristic reactions in conversational situations. You are familiar with most of them; some others we have translated into near English equivalents. In your conversations from now on, use as many of these expressions as possible and try to develop a feeling for the "social register" for which each expression is adequate and acceptable.

AGREEMENT

Ja.
Natürlich.

DISAGREEMENT

Nein. (Nee.)
Leider nein.

Aber natürlich.
Gern(e).
Richtig.
Genau.
Da haben Sie recht.
   hast Du
Stimmt.
Sicher.
Na klar.
O.K.
Ach so! (reconfirmation: "Now I get it.")

nicht.
Das glaube ich Dir nicht.
                Ihnen
Das stimmt nicht.
Da haben Sie (aber) nicht recht.
   hast Du
Mensch, hör auf. ("Come off it.")
Rede doch nicht so'n Unsinn.
Quatsch. (Nonsense.)

REQUESTS

Bitte.
Ich bitte sehr.
Darf (dürfte) ich um X bitten?
Bitte, geben Sie mir X.
Gib mir doch mal X.
Ich hätte gerne X.
Wie wär's mit X?
Ich möchte (gerne) X.
Könnte (dürfte) ich wohl mal . . .
Es wäre nett, wenn . . .
Bitte, seien Sie so gut und . . .
Würdest Du bitte mal . . .

THANKS

Danke (sehr).
Vielen Dank.
Dankeschön.
Herzlichen Dank.
Ich bedanke mich.
Das ist (war) sehr nett von Dir.
Ich bin Ihnen sehr dankbar dafür, daß . . .
Das war aber nicht nötig.
Das hätten Sie aber nicht zu tun brauchen.

II

Construct conversations around the topics below; as before, your teacher can play the role of the native speaker of German.

AUF DER POST

das Postamt post office
die Post post office; mail
der Postbeamte,-n postal clerk
   die Postbeamtin,-nen
der Brief,-e letter
   einen Brief aufgeben to post (mail) a
   letter
   der Luftpostbrief* airmail letter
   der Eilbrief special-delivery letter
die Postkarte,-n postcard
der Einschreibebrief; das Einschreiben registered letter

die Briefmarke,-n stamp
das Paket,-e package
das Telegramm,-e telegram, cable
   ein Telegramm (nach Übersee) aufgeben
das Telefongespräch,-e phone call
   das Ferngespräch long-distance call
die Auskunft information
selbst wählen to dial direct
   das Selbstwählferngespräch direct-dial
   long-distance call
die Postleitzahl zip code
die Vorwahlnummer area code

*The Austrian term for airmail is **Flugpost**.

CONVERSATIONS

Briefmarken aus vier Ländern.

	VORWAHL*	POSTLEITZAHL†
Frankfurt	0611	6000
Wiesbaden	06121	6200
Berlin	030	1000
München	089	8000
Augsburg	0821	8900
Wasserburg am Inn	08071	8090
Weil über Landsberg am Lech	08195	8911

KINO, THEATER, OPER, KONZERT

das Kino,-s
das Theater,-
die Oper,-n
das Konzert,-e
die Vorstellung,-en; die Aufführung,-en
  performance

die Karte,-n ticket
die Kinokarte
Theaterkarte
Opernkarte
Konzertkarte
Karten bestellen to order tickets

*To dial outside of Germany, an additional area code is used; for example, Austria's code is 0043, and to get Vienna (0222), you dial 0043-222- and the local number.
†All zeros at the end of the zip code can be left out; thus 6 Frankfurt, or 809 Wasserburg.

der Akt,-e act
die Szene,-n scene
die Pause,-n intermission
der Beifall; der Applaus applause

III

Berichten° Sie über einen Film (ein Theaterstück, eine Oper, ein Konzert).   report
Was hat Ihnen gut (schlecht) gefallen?

Reading

Eisenbahnterminologie

Es ist nicht leicht, einen deutschen Fahrplan zu lesen. Die folgende
Tabelle (siehe Seite 512) ist eine Seite aus einem deutschen Kursbuch,
und wir wollen versuchen, einen Zug von Frankfurt nach Koblenz zu
finden.

der Fahrplan,-̈e
timetable
die Tabelle,-n table
das Kursbuch,-̈er
complete book of
timetables

Zunächst suchen wir Frankfurt (Zeile 11) und Koblenz (Zeile 23). 5
Hbf. steht für Hauptbahnhof. Der erste Zug hat die Nummer D 1269,
d.h. es ist ein D-Zug oder Schnellzug, der nur auf größeren Bahnhöfen
hält. Dieser Zug kommt um 13.57 Uhr in Koblenz an, aber er fährt
nicht über Frankfurt, sondern direkt von Mannheim nach Mainz.
Auch der nächste Zug, D 463, aus Basel in der Schweiz, fährt nicht 10
über Frankfurt. Jetzt kommt ein Eilzug (E 721), ab Frankfurt Hbf.
um 12.32 Uhr und an Koblenz um 14.27 Uhr.

die Zeile,-n line
das Haupt,-̈er head;
  Haupt- (in com-
  pounds) main
d.h. = das heißt that
  is (i.e.)

eilen to hurry

Eilzüge halten öfter als Schnellzüge, aber nur Nahverkehrzüge halten auf allen Bahnhöfen. Außerdem gibt es noch IC-Züge, d.h. InterCity-Züge und TEE (Trans-Europ-Express)-Züge. TEE- und IC-Züge haben nur 1. Klasse, alle anderen Züge haben 1. und 2. Klasse. Fahrkarten für die 1. Klasse kosten etwa 50% (Prozent) mehr als für 5 die 2. Klasse. Außerdem gibt es Rückfahrkarten mit 10 bis 40% Ermäßigung. In IC-Zügen und D-Zügen bezahlt man zum Fahrpreis noch einen besonderen Zuschlag.

Zurück zum Fahrplan: Die nächsten beiden Züge sind wieder Eilzüge (E 590 und E 297), aber der erste fährt von Bingerbrück aus nach 10 Saarbrücken, der zweite fährt rechtsrheinisch, d.h. auf der östlichen Seite des Rheins, und Koblenz liegt auf der westlichen Rheinseite, wo die Mosel in den Rhein mündet. Der D 203 (von München nach Dortmund) fährt nicht über Frankfurt, aber der D 1114, ab Frankfurt um 14 Uhr, hat in Mainz Anschluß an diesen Zug. Allerdings muß man 15 dabei umsteigen und hat zwischen den beiden Zügen nur acht Minuten Zeit.

Der letzte Zug auf unserem Fahrplan ist die beste Verbindung von Frankfurt nach Koblenz und auch der interessanteste Zug. Es ist der Hellas-Expreß, und er kommt aus Athen. Deshalb hat er allerdings 20 auch oft sehr viel Verspätung.

Europ- shortened form of **Europa**

die Ermäßigung,-en reduction, reduced price
der Zuschlag,-̈e surcharge

münden to flow into

der Anschluß,-̈e connection
umsteigen to change (trains)

die Verbindung,-en connection

Hellas Greece

AUS DEM FAHRPLAN DER BUNDESBAHN

10 KARLSRUHE und FRANKFURT (Main)—KÖLN—DORTMUND°

	Station		D1269	D463	E721	E590	E297	D203	D1114	D455
1	München Hbf.	ab	....	....	....	....	....	9.00	....	8.42
2	Stuttgart Hbf.	ab	....	....	....	....	....	11.55	....	
3	Basel Bad. Bf.	ab	....	9.18	....					
	ZUG NR.		**D1269**	**D463**	**E721**	**E590**	**E297**	**D203**	**D1114**	**D455**
4	Karlsruhe Hbf.	ab	11.30	11.36						....
5	Heidelberg Hbf.							13.15		(von Athen)
6	Mannheim Hbf.		12.06	12.13				13.34		
7	Ludwigshafen (Rh.)							13.50		
8	Worms Hbf.	ab								....
9	Nürnberg Hbf.	ab			....	....			....	10.59
10	Würzburg Hbf.	ab			10.09	....			....	12.10
11	Frankfurt Hbf.	ab			12.32	12.42	13.14		14.00	14.04
12	Rüsselsheim				12.51	13.01				
13	Mainz Hbf.	ab	12.53	13.03	13.07	13.17		14.37	14.29	
14	Mainz-Kastel	ab					13.40		an	
15	Wiesbaden Hbf.						13.55		....	14.42
16	Eltville						14.07		....	
17	Rüdesheim (Rh.)						14.20		....	15.06
18	Niederlahnstein	ab		(von Freiburg)		(von Hof)	15.10		....	(Hellas-Express)
19	Bingen (Rhein)	ab	13.12		13.30	13.41			....	
20	Bingerbrück				13.33	13.43		14.58	....	
21	St. Goar				13.57				....	
22	Boppard			13.40	14.10				....	
23	Koblenz Hbf.		13.57	14.03	14.27		(nach Saarbrücken)	15.40	....	15.57
24	Andernach				14.40				....	
25	Remagen				14.58				....	
26	Bad Godesberg				15.08				....	
27	Bonn	an	14.35	14.40	15.14			16.17	....	16.34
28	Neuwied	ab					15.29		....	
29	Linz (Rhein)						15.48		....	
30	Königswinter					....	16.01		....	
31	Beuel					....	16.09		....	
32	Troisdorf					....	16.16		....	
33	KÖLN Hbf.	an	15.00	15.05	15.41	....	16.35	16.40	....	17.00
34	Aachen Hbf.	an	....	....	....			....	....	....
35	Mönchengladb. Hbf.	an	....	....	....		17.38	....	....	....
36	Krefeld Hbf.	an	....	....	....			....	....	....
	ZUG NR.					**E441**			**E315**	
37	Köln Hbf.	ab	15.05	15.10	15.47	16.13	....	16.45	16.48	17.10
38	Solingen-Ohligs	an	15.23			16.38			17.15	
39	Wuppertal-Elberf.	an	15.38			16.55			17.32	
40	Hagen	an	16.03			17.20			18.03	
41	Münster (Westf.)	ab	....				....	....	....	....

° Abbreviations

Hbf.—Hauptbahnhof	Nr.—Nummer	Mönchengladb.—Mönchengladbach
Bf.—Bahnhof	Rh.—am Rhein	Elberf.—Elberfeld
Bad. Bf.—Badischer Bahnhof	St. Goar—Sankt Goar	Westf.—Westfalen

See also the page facing Unit 16, from the schedule of arrivals at **Stuttgart Hauptbahnhof.**

Fahrkarten bekommt man am Fahrkartenschalter. Man sagt: „Eine Fahrkarte erster Klasse nach Koblenz", oder als alter Eisenbahn- fahrer: „Einmal erster Koblenz."

„Einfach oder hin und zurück?"

„Einfach, bitte. Und einen D-Zug-Zuschlag." 5

„So, mein Herr, das macht 17,88 und 2 Mark für den Zuschlag: 19 Mark 88, bitte."

Der Zug soll um 13.47 auf Gleis 12 ankommen, aber kurz vorher hört man über den Lautsprecher: „Der Schnellzug aus München, plan- mäßige Ankunft 13.47 Uhr, hat voraussichtlich 30 Minuten Ver- 10 spätung." Aber es dauert etwas länger als eine halbe Stunde, und um halb drei heißt es endlich: „Der verspätete Schnellzug aus München läuft soeben auf Gleis 12 ein. Bitte von der Bahnsteigkante zurück- treten." Der Zug ist nicht stark besetzt, und es ist leicht, in einem Nichtraucherabteil einen Fensterplatz zu bekommen. Der Zug hat 15 eine elektrische Lokomotive; in großen Teilen Deutschlands ist die Eisenbahn elektrifiziert, aber man sieht auch Diesellokomotiven und manchmal sogar noch eine alte Dampflokomotive. Der Zug hat Wagen erster und zweiter Klasse; in jedem Wagen gibt es zwölf Ab- teile mit je sechs Sitzplätzen. In den meisten D-Zügen kann man sich 20 einen Platz reservieren lassen. Außerdem hat der Zug einen Post- wagen, einen Gepäckwagen und einen Speisewagen, aber keinen Schlafwagen, denn er kommt schon um 19.06 in Dortmund an, fährt also nicht mehr über Nacht.

einfach (here) one way
hin und zurück round trip

das Gleis,-e track
planmäßig scheduled, according to plan
voraussichtlich probably
Verspätung haben to be late (not on schedule)
heißt es it is announced
die Kante,-n the edge

der Dampf steam
das Abteil,-e compart- ment
je (here) each, apiece

das Gepäck baggage
speisen to dine

PETER HANDKE

Zugauskunft

»Ich möchte nach Stock.«

Sie fahren mit dem Fernschnellzug um 6 Uhr 2.
Der Zug ist in Alst um 8 Uhr 51.
Sie steigen um in den Schnellzug nach Teist.
Der Zug fährt von Alst ab um 9 Uhr 17.
Sie fahren nicht bis nach Teist, sondern steigen aus in Benz.
Der Zug ist in Benz um 10 Uhr 33.
Sie steigen in Benz um in den Schnellzug nach Eifa mit dem Kurs- wagen nach Wössen.

der Fernschnellzug,-̈e long-distance express train
umsteigen to change 5 trains
aussteigen to get off

der Kurswagen through-car

Der Schnellzug nach Eifa fährt ab um 10 Uhr 38.

Der Kurswagen wird in Aprath abgehängt und an den Schnellzug   **abhängen** to uncouple
Uchte-Alsenz gekoppelt.

Der Zug fährt in Aprath ab um 12 Uhr 12.

Ab Emmen fährt der Zug als Eilzug.

Sie fahren nicht bis nach Wössen, sondern steigen um in Bleckmar.   5

Der Zug ist in Bleckmar um 13 Uhr 14.

In Bleckmar können Sie sich umsehen bis 15 Uhr 23.   **sich umsehen** to look

Um 15 Uhr 23 fährt von Bleckmar ein Eilzug ab nach Schee.   around

(Dieser Zug verkehrt nicht am 24. und 25. 12. und führt nur sonn- 10 **verkehren** to run (of
tags 1. Klasse.)   trains)

Sie kommen in Schee-Süd an um 16 Uhr 59.

Die Fähre nach Schee-Nord geht ab um 17 Uhr 5.   **die Fähre,-n** ferry

(Bei Sturm, Nebel und unvorhergesehenen Ereignissen kann der   **das Ereignis,-se** event
Fährverkehr ausfallen.)   15 **ausfallen** to be

Sie sind in Schee-Nord um 17 Uhr 20.   canceled

Um 17 Uhr 24 fährt vom Bahnhof Schee-Nord der Personenzug ab
nach Sandplacken.

(Dieser Zug führt nur 2. Klasse und verkehrt nur an Werktagen
*und verkaufsoffenen Samstagen.)** 20

Sie steigen aus in Murnau.

Der Zug ist in Murnau ungefähr um 19 Uhr 30.

Vom gleichen Bahnsteig fährt um 21 Uhr 12 ein Personen- und   **gleich** same
Güterzug weiter nach Hützel.   **der Güterzug,̈e** freight

(In Murnau gibt es einen Warteraum.)   25   train

Sie sind in Hützel um 22 Uhr 33. *(Diese Zeiten sind ohne Gewähr.)* **ohne Gewähr** not

Da der Personenverkehr von Hützel nach Krün eingestellt ist, neh-   guaranteed
men Sie den am Bahnhofsvorplatz wartenden Bahnbus *(ohne Ge-*   **einstellen** discontinue
währ).

Sie steigen aus in Vach gegen 1 Uhr.   30

Der erste Straßenbus von Vach geht ab um 6 Uhr 15.

(In Vach gibt es keinen Mietwagen.)   **der Mietwagen** rental

Sie sind in Eisal um 8 Uhr 9.   car

Der Bus um 8 Uhr 10 von Eisal nach Weiden verkehrt nicht in den
Schulferien.   35

Sie sind in Weiden um 8 Uhr 50.

*On Saturdays, stores normally close at 1:00 or 2:00 P.M., but are open in the afternoon of the first Saturday
of every month.

```
┌─────────────────────────────────┐
│ GEÖFFNET:                       │
│ MONTAG-FREITAG                  │
│              8 30 – 18 30        │
│ SAMSTAG   8 30 – 14 00           │
│ jeden 1. Samstag des Monats      │
│              8 30 – 18 00        │
└─────────────────────────────────┘
```

Um 13 Uhr geht der Bus eines Privatunternehmens von Weiden   **das Unternehmen** firm
über Möllen-Forst-Ohle nach Schray.
(Nach Schray und Ohle fährt der Bus weiter nur nach Bedarf.)   **nach Bedarf** if needed
Sie sind in Schray um 14 Uhr 50.
Zwischen Schray und Trompet verkehrt um diese Zeit ein Milch- 5
wagen, der bei Bedarf auch Personen befördert.
In Trompet können Sie gegen 16 Uhr sein.
Zwischen Trompet und Stock gibt es keine Kraftverkehrslinie.   **die Kraftverkehrslinie,-n**
Zu Fuß können Sie gegen 17 Uhr 30 in Stock sein.   bus line

»Im Winter ist es dann schon wieder dunkel?«   10
»Im Winter ist es dann schon wieder dunkel.«

                                                                 (1967)

ERICH KÄSTNER

Das Eisenbahngleichnis

das Gleichnis,-se
parable

Wir sitzen alle im gleichen Zug
und reisen quer durch die Zeit.   **quer durch** straight
Wir sehen hinaus. Wir sahen genug.   across
Wir fahren alle im gleichen Zug.
Und keiner weiß, wie weit.   5

Ein Nachbar schläft, ein andrer klagt,   **klagen** to complain
ein dritter redet viel.
Stationen werden angesagt.
Der Zug, der durch die Jahre jagt,   **jagen** to rush
kommt niemals an sein Ziel.   10   **das Ziel,-e** destination

Wir packen aus. Wir packen ein.   **auspacken** to unpack
Wir finden keinen Sinn.   **einpacken** to pack
Wo werden wir wohl morgen sein?   **der Sinn** sense
Der Schaffner schaut zur Tür herein
und lächelt vor sich hin.   15   **der Schaffner,-**
                                                                   conductor

Auch er weiß nicht, wohin er will.
Er schweigt und geht hinaus.
Da heult die Zugsirene schrill!   **heulen** to howl
Der Zug fährt langsam und hält still.
Die Toten steigen aus.   20

Ein Kind steigt aus. Die Mutter schreit.
Die Toten stehen stumm   **stumm** silent
am Bahnsteig der Vergangenheit.   **die Vergangenheit** past
Der Zug fährt weiter, er jagt durch die Zeit,
und niemand weiß, warum.   25

Die 1. Klasse ist fast leer.
Ein feister Herr sitzt stolz   **feist** fat
im roten Plüsch und atmet schwer.   **stolz** proud

Er ist allein und spürt das sehr.
Die Mehrheit sitzt auf Holz.

Wir reisen alle im gleichen Zug
zur Gegenwart in spe.
Wir sehen hinaus. Wir sahen genug. 5
Wir sitzen alle im gleichen Zug
und viele im falschen Coupé.

(1932)

spüren   to feel
die Mehrheit   majority
das Holz   wood

Gegenwart in spe
   present-in-the-future
falsch   wrong
das Coupé,-s   train
   compartment

Exercises

A. Express in German, using **lassen** in each case. The sections of this exercise follow the description of the second meaning of **lassen**. In (5) and (6), express the subject of the infinitive with **von**.

SEE
ANALYSIS
164
(p. 497)

1. Why don't you let me study medicine?
   I wish you would let me study medicine.
   I wish we had let him study medicine.
   We can't let him study medicine.
   We shall let her study medicine.

2. Shall we let Fritz wash the car?
   Why don't you let me wash the car, Father?
   Could you let me finish reading this letter? (Use **zu Ende lesen**.)

3. We should have (somebody) paint (**anstreichen**) our house.
   Why don't you have an operation (let [somebody] operate on you)?

4. I must get a haircut today.
   I got a haircut yesterday.
   Why didn't you get a haircut today?

5. I always have him cut my hair.
   I'll never have him make me a coat again.
   Why don't you let François cut your hair?

6. I won't have Dr. Meinecke operate on me.
   Did you let him take you home?

B. Express in German. All German sentences must contain a form of **lassen**.

SEE
ANALYSIS
164
(p. 497)

1. That leaves me cold.
2. Why didn't you leave your books at home?
3. I don't want to let him take me home. (Use reflexive pronoun plus **von ihm**.)
4. He has his letters written by his wife. (Use reflexive pronoun plus **von seiner Frau**.)
5. You shouldn't let him go to Hamburg.
6. I must get myself a haircut.
7. Why don't you have your hair cut?
8. He went downtown to get a haircut.
9. She has left her coat here again.
10. You should leave her in peace.
11. We are having a house built in Cologne.

12. We want to have Overbeck build us a house.
13. I wish we had had Overbeck build us a house.

C. Restate the following sentences in the perfect.

SEE
ANALYSIS
164
(p. 497)

1. Ich blieb oft vor Erikas Haus stehen.
2. Er riet mir, an die Nordsee zu fahren.
3. Wir ließen gestern abend den Arzt kommen.
4. Er braucht *doch* nicht nach Berlin zu fahren.
5. Wir dachten damals daran, nach Köln zu ziehen.
6. Um sechs Uhr gingen wir essen.
7. Der Müller war einfach nicht zu verstehen.
8. Gegen Abend fing es dann an zu regnen.
9. Er lief aus dem Haus, ohne ein Wort zu sagen.

D. Transform the following pairs of sentences into sentences with **ohne . . . zu** or **statt . . . zu.** Note that the negation disappears in the infinitive phrase.

Er fuhr nach Afrika. Er nahm seine Frau nicht mit.—ohne
Er fuhr nach Afrika, ohne seine Frau mitzunehmen.

1. Er fuhr nach Afrika. Er blieb nicht zu Hause.—statt
2. Er schrieb ihr einen Brief. Er rief sie nicht an.—statt
3. Er war in Berlin. Er hat mich nicht besucht.—ohne
4. Er kaufte sich einen Wagen. Er hatte nicht das Geld dafür.—ohne

SEE
ANALYSIS
166
(p. 502)

E. Express in German.

1. Where is your coat?—Oh, I left it (hanging) at the Meyers.
2. Perhaps you should try once more to call him.
3. This chair you must leave (standing) in the living room.
4. Now the apartment is in order again at last.—No, you have forgotten to put the chairs back into the living room.
5. He finally had to promise his wife not to go to Africa again.
6. He suggested that my wife should go to the North Sea this year.

F. Change to comparatives.

Ich bin nicht so alt wie er. Er ist älter als ich.

1. Unser Haus ist nicht so groß wie eures.
2. Bei uns ist es nicht so kalt wie bei euch.
3. Glas ist nicht so hart wie ein Diamant.
4. Der Weg war nicht so lang wie ich dachte. (Use **kurz.**)
5. Ich gehe nicht so oft ins Theater wie du.
6. Amerikanisches Bier ist nicht so stark wie deutsches Bier.
7. Von Köln bis Bonn ist es nicht so weit wie von Frankfurt bis Bonn.
8. Ich kann nicht so viel essen wie du.
9. Bier trinke ich nicht so gerne wie Wein.
10. Ich finde ihn nicht so interessant wie seine Frau.

SEE
ANALYSIS
167
(p. 502)

G. Change the adjectives to superlatives.

SEE
ANALYSIS
167
(p. 502)

1. Hans hat viel getrunken.
2. München ist eine schöne Stadt.
3. In München gibt es gutes Bier.
4. Im Dezember sind die Tage kurz.
5. Im Juni sind die Tage lang.

6. Der 21. Juni ist ein langer Tag.
7. Giganto ist ein starker Mann.
8. Ich wäre jetzt gern in Deutschland.
9. In Alaska ist das Obst teuer.

H. Imagine that you have a cousin, Hildegard, who lives in Munich and knows no English. You want to visit her during your stay in Germany, so you decide to write her a letter while on the train to Koblenz. For lack of anything profound to say (owing to your lack of that kind of German), you tell her about your adventures at the Frankfurt railroad station.

The envelope, incidentally, would be addressed as follows: Fräulein
Hildegard Pfeilguth
Tengstraße 40
8 München 13

After duly addressing her as "Liebe Hildegard!" you tell her that you arrived in Frankfurt after a good flight. Because you wanted to go to Koblenz on the same day, you took the train from the airport to the main railroad station. Then you describe what happened to you until the Hellas-Express finally started moving.

You sign off by writing:

Viele herzliche Grüße
Deine Jane

Vocabulary

aufführen	to perform, put on (a play)	**damit** (*conj.*)	so that, in order that
die Aufführung, -en	performance	**dankbar**	grateful
aussteigen	to get off (a train, etc.), deplane, disembark	**deshalb** (*adv.*)	because of that
		einsteigen	to get on (a train, etc.), board, embark
sich (*acc.*) **bedanken**	to thank	**sich ereignen**	to occur, happen
befördern	to transport	**das Ereignis, -se**	event, occurrence
bestellen	to (place an) order	**erlauben**	to allow, permit
breit	broad	**erst** (= **zuerst**)	first (*adv.*)
der Brief, -e	letter	**erstaunt sein**	to be astonished
einen Brief aufgeben	to post (mail) a letter	**die Fahrkarte, -n**	ticket (train, plane, etc.)
der Luftpostbrief, -e	airmail letter	**die Rückfahrkarte, -n**	round-trip ticket
der Eilbrief, -e	special-delivery letter	**der Fahrplan, ∴e**	timetable
		die Handtasche, -n	handbag
der Einschreibebrief, -e	registered letter	**hängen (hängte, gehängt)** (*with acc.*)	to hang (something)
das Einschreiben, -			
die Briefmarke, -n	stamp	**er hängte das Bild an die Wand**	he hung the picture on the wall
		(hing, gehangen)	to hang, be suspended

das Bild hing an der Wand	the picture hung on the wall	sich (*acc.*) umsehen	to look around
hart	hard	der Unsinn	nonsense
die Härte	hardness	verboten	forbidden, not allowed, not permitted
die Höhe, -n	height; altitude		
der Lautsprecher, -	loudspeaker	Eingang verboten	do not enter
leer	empty	Rauchen verboten	no smoking
operieren	to operate	die Vorstellung, -en	introduction; (theater) performance; idea, representation
sich (*acc.*) operieren lassen	to have an operation		
das Paket, -e	package		
das Postamt, ¨er	post office	die Vorwahlnummer, -n	area code
die Post (*no pl.*)	mail; post office; postal service	abhängen	to detach a (railway) car, to uncouple
die Postkarte, -n	postcard	der Beifall	applause
die Postleitzahl, -en	zip code	der Kauf, ¨e	buy, purchase
raten	to advise; to guess	koppeln an	to connect, attach to; to couple
der Rat (*no pl.*)	advice		
reparieren	to repair	der Quatsch (*colloq.*)	nonsense
der Schalter, -	(ticket) window, counter	der Schuß, ¨e	shot
		sitzenbleiben	to stay seated; to stay behind (in school), to have to repeat a grade
der Lichtschalter, -	light switch		
der Schirm, -e	umbrella		
schreien	to scream		
schwach	weak	der Sportwagen, -	sportscar
die Schwäche, -n	weakness	verwöhnen	to spoil, pamper (someone); to take good care (of someone)
stehenbleiben	to stop; to remain standing		
der Sturm, ¨e	storm	die Weile	while, short time
das Telegramm, -e	telegram	der Zwerg, -e	dwarf

Strong Verbs

aussteigen		stieg aus	ist ausgestiegen	to get off
einsteigen		stieg ein	ist eingestiegen	to board
hängen		hing	gehangen	to hang
raten	rät	riet	geraten	to advise; to guess
schreien		schrie	geschrien	to scream
stehenbleiben		blieb stehen	ist stehengeblieben	to stop
sich umsehen	sieht um	sah um	umgesehen	to look around

UNIT 17 Adjectives (Continued)

Europe on $5 a Day used to be almost everybody's favorite travel guide, but no longer. Due to the decline of the dollar's value and the increase in prices of practically everything, traveling on a shoestring today allows fewer luxuries than ten or twenty years ago. Nevertheless, with careful planning, you can still travel in Europe without undue burden on your pocketbook. You can make use of Germany's superb rail system for relatively little money; by train you can reach even the remotest parts of Germany, Austria, or Switzerland. Or, still cheaper, you can travel by rented bicycle and use byways instead of highways.

Travel in the DDR is still relatively inexpensive, but there are many restrictions, and visas must be obtained well in advance, except for visits to East Berlin and for transit trips on the Autobahn from West Germany to West Berlin. A minimum amount of Western currency per day must also be changed to East German marks, which cannot be reconverted. The exchange rate of West and East marks is 1:1, and the dollar thus fluctuates in the East just as it does in the West. Visitors "aus dem nicht-sozialistischen Ausland" can stay in *Interhotels*, where only Western currency is accepted; and both foreigners and citizens of the DDR can use nonsocialist money in the chain of *Intershops* which are owned and operated by the state, as are almost all other business establishments, from newsstands to the steel industry.

The large international hotels in West Germany are more expensive today than American luxury hotels, but you can still find bargains in many a country inn, away from the urban centers. Here, you can also find hearty and tasty meals for less than what you have to pay at McDonald's in Vienna or a Burger King in Berlin; and, of course, you can always put together a lunch or supper of bread, sausage, cheese, and beer or wine.

Small-town hotels and country inns by and large are very clean and well-kept, but you can also try hosteling or camping. German youth hostels, many of them quite modern and rather like American college dormitories, are so numerous that you can hike or cycle from the North Sea to the Alps and find tonight's hostel at just the right distance from yesterday's. Campgrounds, totally unknown in Germany until years after World War II, now dot the countryside. During the summer, they tend to be overcrowded, but in spring and autumn they provide another set of inexpensive accommodations, especially if you travel with a small group and have a car—perhaps an ancient secondhand Volkswagen bug.

INTERHOTELS
DRESDEN

INTERHOTEL NEWA	INTERHOTEL LILIENSTEIN	INTERHOTEL KÖNIGSTEIN
801 Dresden Leningrader Straße Telefon 496271	801 Dresden Prager Straße Telefon 48560	801 Dresden Prager Straße Telefon 48560

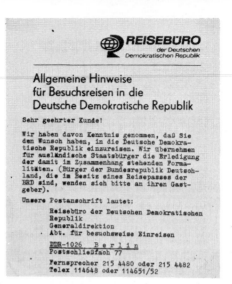

REISEBÜRO
der Deutschen
Demokratischen Republik

Allgemeine Hinweise
für Besuchsreisen in die
Deutsche Demokratische Republik

Sehr geehrter Kunde!

Wir haben davon Kenntnis genommen, daß Sie
den Wunsch haben, in die Deutsche Demokratische Republik einzureisen. Wir übernehmen
für ausländische Staatsbürger die Erledigung
der damit im Zusammenhang stehenden Forma-
litäten. (Bürger der Bundesrepublik Deutschland, die im Besitz eines Reisepasses der
BRD sind, wenden sich bitte an ihren Gast-
geber).

Unsere Postanschrift lautet:

   Reisebüro der Deutschen Demokratischen
   Republik
   Generaldirektion
   Abt. für besuchsweise Einreisen

   DDR-1026 B e r l i n
   Postschließfach 77

   Fernsprecher 215 4480 oder 215 4482
   Telex 114648 oder 114651/52

R 771722

Quittung für
Visagebühren
im Werte von
5,- Mark

Deutsche
Demokratische
Republik

Übernachtungen

Hohen Komfort, Behaglichkeit und gepflegte Gastronomie bieten die Interhotels, z. B. „Stadt Berlin" (39 Etagen, 2000 Betten), „Berolina", aber auch kleinere Hotels wie das Reisebürohotel „Newa" oder die Hotels „Sofia" und „Adlon".

Ein angenehmer Aufenthalt erwartet Sie jedoch auch in den vom Reisebüro unter Vertrag genommenen Privatzimmern im gesamtem Stadtgebiet, die bereits ab 7,– Mark pro Übernachtung zu bekommen sind.

Reading selections in Unit 17, dealing with German hotels, youth hostels, and the intricacies of long-distance telephoning, are followed by two literary selections—a story by the Swiss author Peter Bichsel, much of whose work you can read as easily as this story, and one of the famous fairy tales that were collected by the brothers Grimm early in the nineteenth century.

The conversations in this unit follow the new format established in Unit 16, and the analysis sections introduce a number of adjective patterns of high frequency, such as constructions with **was für**, adjectives used as nouns, and participles used as adjectives. In spite of what we said earlier about not needing complete control of these endings for adequate communication, you should still make every effort to master them, so that you can correctly ask for **ein kleines helles Bier** and inquire about **den nächsten Weg nach Garmisch-Partenkirchen.**

Patterns

[1] Adjectives Used as Nouns

SEE
ANALYSIS
169
(p. 527)

In dem Zimmer lag ein Toter.
Die Polizei fand einen Toten im Zimmer.
Kein Mensch wußte, wer der Tote war.

A dead man was lying in the room.
The police found a dead man in the room.
Nobody knew who the dead man was.

Wer ist denn die Blonde da drüben?	Who is the blonde over there?
Der junge Deutsche auf Zimmer Eins ist erst gestern angekommen.	The young German in room 1 arrived only yesterday.
Auf Zimmer Eins wohnt ein junger Deutscher.	A young German lives in room 1.
John wohnt mit einem jungen Deutschen auf Zimmer Eins.	John lives in room 1 with a young German.
Den jungen Deutschen habe ich noch nicht kennengelernt.	I haven't met the young German yet.
Auf Zimmer Eins wohnen zwei junge Deutsche.	Two young Germans are living in room 1.
Die beiden jungen Deutschen habe ich noch nicht kennengelernt.	I haven't met the two young Germans yet.
Er spricht ein gutes Deutsch.	He speaks good German.
Sie haben recht, er spricht wirklich gut Deutsch.	You are right, he really does speak German well.
Auf Wiedersehen, und alles Gute.	Good-bye, and all the best.
Er hat viel Gutes getan.	He has done much good.
Könnte ich noch etwas Warmes zu essen bekommen?	Could I still get something hot to eat?
Ich habe etwas sehr Schönes erlebt.	I've experienced something very beautiful.
Ich hoffe, ich habe nichts Wichtiges vergessen.	I hope I haven't forgotten anything important.

[2] Participles Used as Adjectives and Nouns

Es war nicht leicht, in einer zerstörten Stadt zu leben.	It was not easy to live in a destroyed city.	SEE ANALYSIS 170 (p. 529)
Er kam mit einem gebrochenen Bein vom Schilaufen zurück.	He returned from skiing with a broken leg.	
Sie kam mit gebrochenem Herzen vom Schilaufen zurück.	She returned from skiing with a broken heart.	
Er war bei uns immer ein gern gesehener Gast.	He was always a welcome guest at our house. (Literally: he was a gladly seen guest.)	
Erich Merkle ist ein guter Bekannter von uns.	Erich Merkle is a close acquaintance of ours.	
Frau Merkle ist eine gute Bekannte von meiner Frau.	Mrs. Merkle is a close acquaintance of my wife's.	
Haben Sie Bekannte hier in der Stadt?	Do you have acquaintances here in town?	
Haben Sie Verwandte in Westfalen?	Do you have relatives in Westphalia?	
Otto Müller ist ein Verwandter von mir.	Otto Müller is a relative of mine.	
Heidi ist eine entfernte Verwandte von mir.	Heidi is a distant relative of mine.	
Das ist der amerikanische Gesandte.	That is the American ambassador.	
Sein Vater war ein hoher Beamter bei der Bundesregierung.	His father was a high official in the federal government.	
Alle deutschen Lehrer sind Beamte.	All German teachers are civil servants.	

Hier auf der Post arbeiten über hundert Beamtinnen.

More than a hundred women civil servants work here at the post office.

Auch Frau Meyer ist eine Beamtin.

Mrs. Meyer is a civil servant too.

[3] -d Adjectives

SEE ANALYSIS 171 (p. 529)

Wer war denn der gut aussehende junge Mann gestern abend?

Who was the good-looking young man last night?

Er hatte so ein gewinnendes Lächeln.

He had such a winning smile.

Alles um sich her vergessend, saßen sie mit klopfendem Herzen unter der blühenden Linde; und ihre vielsagenden Blicke aus leuchtenden Augen sagten mehr als ihre zurückhaltenden Worte.

(from Schmidt-Ingelheim, *Die Frau mit dem Flamingo*, p. 97)

Forgetting everything around them, they sat under the blooming linden tree, with their hearts pounding, and the meaningful glances of their shining eyes said more than their reserved words.

[4] derselbe

SEE ANALYSIS 172 (p. 530)

Ist das derselbe Wein, den wir gestern abend getrunken haben?

Is that the same wine that we drank last night?

Wir wohnen in demselben Hotel, in dem Fürstenbergs gewohnt haben.

We are staying in the same hotel in which the Fürstenbergs stayed.

Wir saßen gestern mit Fürstenbergs am selben Tisch.

Yesterday we sat at the same table with the Fürstenbergs.

Seit Jahren trägt sie jeden Sonntag dasselbe Kleid.

For years she's been wearing the same dress every Sunday.

[5] was für

SEE ANALYSIS 173 (p. 530)

Was ist denn das für ein Wagen?
Was für ein Wagen ist das?

What kind of car is that?

Was hast du dir denn für einen Wagen gekauft?
Was für einen Wagen hast du dir denn gekauft?

What kind of car did you buy?

Mit was für einem Wagen bist du denn gefahren?

What kind of car did you go in?

Ich muß noch immer daran denken, was für wunderbare Tage wir an der Ostsee verbracht haben.

I still remember what wonderful days we spent at the Baltic Sea.

Hast du gesehen, was für einen unmöglichen Hut Tante Amalie schon wieder aufhat?

Did you see what an impossible hat Aunt Amalie has on again?

Weißt du noch, mit was für einem unmöglichen Hut sie damals im Theater war?

Do you remember what an impossible hat she came to the theater with?

Was ist denn das für ein Wagen?

[6] all, ganz

Alles Gute zum neuen Jahr wünscht Dir Deine Luise.	All good wishes for the New Year. Yours, Louise.	**SEE ANALYSIS 174** (p. 531)
Was hilft ihm jetzt all sein schönes Geld?	What good does all his lovely money do him now?	

Was hilft ihm denn jetzt das ganze Geld?　What good does all that money do him now?
Ich habe alle meine alten Freunde besucht.　I visited all my old friends.
All meine Freunde sind Ärzte.　All my friends are doctors.
Ich habe alle seine Romane gelesen.　I have read all his novels.
Ich habe seine Romane alle gelesen.　I have read all his novels.
Kannst du für uns alle *Kar*ten kaufen?　Can you buy tickets for all of us?
Kannst du Karten für uns *al*le kaufen?　Can you buy tickets for all of us?
Ich habe alle Karten gekauft, die noch zu haben waren.　I've bought all the tickets that were still to be had.
Alle guten Karten waren schon ausverkauft.　All the good tickets were sold out already.
Wir alle sind dir dankbar.　We are all grateful to you.
Wir sind dir alle dankbar.　We are all grateful to you.
Er hat den ganzen Tag auf mich gewartet.　He waited for me all day.
Fritzchen hat einen ganzen Apfel gegessen.　Fritzchen has eaten a whole apple.
Sie war ganz allein.　She was all alone.
Wie geht's dir denn?—Danke, ganz gut.　How are you?—Thanks, pretty well.
Wir sind durch ganz Österreich gefahren.　We drove through all of Austria.

[7] viel, wenig

Meyer hat viel Geld.	Meyer has a lot of money.	**SEE ANALYSIS 175** (p. 532)
Ja, aber das viele Geld macht ihn auch nicht glücklich.	Yes, but all that money doesn't make him happy either.	

Sein vieles Geld macht ihn nicht glücklich.　All his money doesn't make him happy.
Heute ist Sonntag, und viele Leute fahren heute spazieren.　Today is Sunday, and many people go for a ride today.
Was haben Sie denn während der vielen langen Winternächte gemacht?　What did you do during the many long winter nights?

Ich habe viel zu wenig Geld, um jedes Jahr
   in die Schweiz fahren zu können.

I have far too little money to be able to go to
   Switzerland every year.

Mit dem wenigen Geld, das du mir schickst,
   kann ich nicht viel kaufen.

With the little money you send me I can't
   buy much.

Wir haben dieses Wochenende nur wenige
   Gäste im Hause. Bei dem Wetter bleiben
   die Leute zu Hause.

We have only a few guests here this weekend.
   In this weather, people stay at home.

VARIATIONS

Insert the correct form of **viel.**

Ich habe nicht _____ Geld.
Was tut sie denn mit ihrem _____ Geld?
Wie _____ Kinder habt ihr denn?
Wie _____ Bier habt ihr denn getrunken?
Was machst du denn jetzt mit deinen _____ Büchern?
Er hat schon immer _____ gelesen.

[8] ander-

SEE
ANALYSIS
176
(p. 534)

So geht das nicht; das mußt du anders
   machen.

It won't work that way; you'll have to do it
   differently.

Aber Erich, du bist ja ganz anders als früher.

But Erich, you are so different from the way
   you used to be.

Erich soll ein ganz anderer Mensch geworden sein.

Erich supposedly has become a completely
   different person.

Er spricht von nichts anderem als von seiner
   Amerikareise.

He talks about nothing (else) but his trip to
   America.

Den einen Herrn kannte ich, aber wer war
   denn der andere?

One of the gentlemen I knew, but who was
   the other one?

Den anderen Herrn kenne ich auch nicht.

I don't know the other gentleman either.

Das muß jemand anders gewesen sein.

That must have been somebody else.

Das kann niemand anders gewesen sein als
   Meyer.

That can have been nobody (else) but Meyer.

Anderen hat er geholfen; sich selbst kann er
   nicht helfen.

Others he has helped; himself he cannot help.

VARIATIONS

Insert the correct form of **ander-.**

Es war ganz _____, als ich gedacht
   hatte.

Dieses Buch war es nicht; es war ein
_____.

Wer waren denn die _____ Herren?
Sie wohnen in einem _____ Hotel.
Ich war es nicht; es war jemand _____.

Ich habe leider keinen _____ Mantel.
Alle _____ gingen nach Hause.
Ich hätte lieber etwas _____.

[9] ein paar, einige, mehrere

„In ein paar Tagen bin ich wieder hier", hatte er gesagt. Aber dann wurden aus den paar Tagen ein paar Jahre.

"I'll be back in a few days," he had said. But then the few days turned into a few years.

SEE ANALYSIS 177 (p. 534)

Es waren nur ein paar Leute da.

Only a few people were there.

Mit den paar Mark kannst du doch nicht nach Davos fahren.

You can't go to Davos with those few marks.

Ein paar schöne Tage haben wir ja gehabt, aber die meiste Zeit hat es geregnet.

We did have a few nice days, but most of the time it rained.

Ich hätte gerne ein paar kleine Würstchen zum Frühstück.

I'd like to have a few sausages for breakfast.

Bringen Sie mir doch bitte ein Paar Würstchen.

Could I have a couple of sausages (frankfurters), please?

Ich habe nur zwei Paar gute Schuhe mitgebracht.

I've only brought two pairs of good shoes.

Anton und Emma waren ein schönes Paar.

Anton and Emma were a lovely couple.

Einige von unseren Lesern möchten wissen, ob Ingelheim noch in Konstanz wohnt.

Some of our readers would like to know whether Ingelheim still lives in Constance.

Wir kamen durch mehrere alte Dörfer.

We came through several old villages.

Im Löwen kann man für ein paar Mark gut essen.

At the Lion Inn one can eat well for a few marks.

Ich habe auch schon einige Male da gegessen.

I've eaten there several times, too.

Letzte Woche habe ich mehrere Male im Löwen gegessen.

Last week I ate at the Lion several times.

Analysis

169 Adjectives Used as Nouns

In such English phrases as

the idle rich   *Gentlemen Prefer Blondes*
he helped the poor   *The Naked and the Dead*

the adjectives *rich*, *poor*, *blonde*, *naked*, and *dead* are used as plural nouns. In German, many more adjectives can be used as nouns than in English, and, unlike English, they very often occur in the singular. If so used, they are capitalized, but are otherwise treated like attributive adjectives; thus, **der reiche Mann** becomes **der Reiche.**

SLOT 0	SLOT 1	SLOT 2	SLOT 3	
	der	Reiche		the rich man
	die	Alte		the old woman
	das	Gute		the good
mein	Alter			my old man
	die	Armen		the poor
	der	Tote		the dead man
	die	Tote		the dead woman
	die	Toten		the dead
ein	Toter			a dead man

When an adjective follows **nichts, etwas, viel,** as in English *nothing new* or *something important,* the German adjective is capitalized and has a strong neuter singular ending.

> **Es gibt leider nichts Neues.**
> **Ich habe etwas Wichtiges vergessen.**
> **Das führt zu nichts Gutem.**
> **Er hat viel Gutes getan.**

NOTE: Of all nouns indicating nationality, **Deutsch** is the only one declined like an adjective.

der Deutsche	the German (man)
die Deutsche	the German (woman)
die Deutschen	the Germans

170 Participles Used as Adjectives and Nouns

In German, as in English, participles can be used as attributive adjectives.

SLOT 0	SLOT 1	SLOT 2	SLOT 3	
	die	zerstörte	Stadt	the destroyed city
	eine	zerstörte	Stadt	a destroyed city
	zerstörte		Städte	destroyed cities
ein	gestohlenes		Goldstück	a stolen gold coin
	das	gestohlene	Goldstück	the stolen gold coin
mein	geliebter		Sohn	my beloved son

Both German and English can use participles as plural nouns.

die Verwundeten   the wounded
die Besiegten   the conquered

Unlike English, however, German can also use participles as singular nouns.

SLOT 0	SLOT 1	SLOT 2	SLOT 3
	der	Verwundete	
ein	Verwundeter		
	der	Gekreuzigte*	
	der	Erwählte†	
	die	Betrogene‡	

Similarly:

der Bekannte   acquaintance—from: **bekannt sein**   to be (well) known
die Bekannte
der Verwandte   relative—from: **verwandt sein**   to be related
die Verwandte
der Beamte   official, civil servant—from: **das Amt**   office
    (originally: **der Beamtete**   one who is given an office)

but

die Beamtin, plural: **die Beamtinnen**

171 -d Adjectives

In principle, any German verb can form an adjective corresponding to English adjectives in *-ing* simply by adding the suffix **-d** to the infinitive. These **-d** derivatives can be used safely only as attributive adjectives. Both the English

*The crucified one (Christ).
†The chosen one (title of Thomas Mann's novel *The Holy Sinner*).
‡The deceived one (title of Thomas Mann's novel *The Black Swan*).

-*ing*-form and the German **-d**-form are often referred to as "present participles."

	SLOT 0	SLOT 1	SLOT 2	SLOT 3
mit	ein	das lachendes klopfendem ihre	lachende leuchtenden	Kind Kind Herzen Augen

172 derselbe

There are two German adjectives to express English *the same:* **der gleiche** and **derselbe.** The forms of **derselbe** are written as one word unless the article is contracted with a preposition. Both **der-** and **selb-** must be declined.

> **Ist das derselbe Wein wie gestern?**
> **Ist das der gleiche Wein wie gestern?**
> **Wir trinken heute wieder denselben Wein wie gestern.**
> **Wir wohnen in derselben Stadt.**
> **Wir wohnen im selben Hotel.**
> **Wir wohnen im gleichen Hotel.**
> **Wir wohnen in demselben Hotel.**

Strictly speaking, **der gleiche** expresses similarity (the same kind), and **derselbe** expresses identity (the very same). However, this distinction is rapidly disappearing.

173 was für

There is no English structural equivalent for the very frequently used construction with **was für.** The **für** in this fixed phrase does not have any influence on the case of the following adjective or noun. **Was für** means *what kind of* or *what.*

In the nominative and accusative, **was** occupies the front field; **für** plus the noun or pronoun may either follow the **was** immediately or stand in the inner field, usually right before the second prong.

Was für ein Wagen ist denn das da drüben?
Was ist denn das *für ein Wagen* da drüben?
Was ist denn das da drüben *für ein Wagen?*

Was für einen Wagen hast du dir denn gekauft?
Was hast du dir denn *für einen Wagen* gekauft?

Was für Bücher hast du mir denn mitgebracht?
Was hast du mir denn *für Bücher* mitgebracht?

In the dative, the **was für** construction cannot be split. Nor can it be split if it is preceded by a preposition.

Was für einem Mann gehört denn der Wagen?
Mit was für einem Wagen bist du denn gefahren?
Durch was für Dörfer seid ihr denn gefahren?
Auf was für einen Mann wartest du denn?

174 all, ganz

All is used with or without endings. When there is an ending, it is always strong; that is, it behaves like a **der**-word.

SINGULAR

(a) Forms with an ending are not used very frequently. They occur, immediately followed by a noun, in stereotyped phrases.

Ich wünsche dir alles Gute

and in proverbial expressions:

Aller Anfang ist schwer.

(b) If used without an ending, **all** must be followed by a **der**-word or a possessive adjective.

all das schöne Geld
all mein Geld

Such phrases express bulk quantity, and **all** can be replaced by the attributive adjective **ganz.**

das ganze schöne Geld
mein ganzes Geld

PLURAL

(a) **All** with an ending is the plural of **jeder** and means "every single one of them"; it precedes nouns and follows pronouns.

Alle meine Brüder sind im Krieg gefallen.
Wir alle haben ihn gestern besucht.

In the spoken language, it is usually separated from its noun or pronoun and placed in the inner field preceding the first item of news value.

Meine Brüder sind im Krieg alle gefallen.
Wir haben ihn gestern alle besucht.
Gestern haben wir ihn alle besucht.

(b) **All** without an ending refers again to bulk quantity and means "the whole bunch of them." Again, it must be followed by a **der-** or an **ein-**word, but it cannot be separated from its noun.

Ich habe all meine Bücher verloren.

Again, this "bulk" meaning of **all** can be replaced by the attributive adjective **ganz.**

Ich habe meine ganzen Bücher verloren.

Ganz, if not used as a replacement for **all,** is used in the following ways:

(a) As an attributive adjective meaning *whole* or *entire.*

Er hat den ganzen Tag auf mich gewartet.   He waited for me all day.

(b) As an adverb, meaning *completely,* modifying an adjective.

Sie war ganz allein.   She was all alone.

(c) As an *unstressed* adverb, meaning *quite* or *rather,* modifying such "praising" adjectives as **gut, glücklich, intelligent.**

Das Wetter war ja ganz gut, aber es hätte   The weather wasn't bad, but it could have
    besser sein können.   been better.

Do not thank your hostess by saying **Das Essen war ganz gut.** This would mean that the food wasn't bad, but certainly nothing to rave about.

(d) Without an ending and preceding geographical names. It then means *all of.*

Wir sind durch ganz Österreich gefahren

but

Wir sind durch die ganze Schweiz gefahren.

175 viel, wenig

Viel (*much*; plural: *many*) and **wenig** (*little*; plural: *few*) have the same characteristics. Their use is in a state of flux, but it is safe to use them in the following ways.

(a) In the singular, **viel** and **wenig** express bulk and are usually used without endings.

> **Wieviel Fisch habt ihr gegessen?** (wieviel—one word)
> **Wir haben damals viel Fisch und wenig Fleisch gegessen.**

Adjectives used after these endingless forms have strong endings.

> **Ich habe noch viel deutsches Geld.**
> **Ich habe nur noch wenig deutsches Geld.**

After definite articles, **viel** and **wenig**, still indicating bulk, take normal attributive adjective endings.

> **das viele Geld**
> **mit dem wenigen Geld**

NOTE: **Vielen Dank** (*thank you very much*) is an exception.

(b) In the plural, **viele** means *many* and **wenige** *few*. They are treated as attributive adjectives.

	SLOT 1	SLOT 2	SLOT 3
	viele junge		**Leute**
	die	**vielen jungen**	**Leute**
mit	**wenigen**		**Worten**

(c) **Viel** and **wenig** may be used as adverbs preceding comparatives.

> **Er war viel älter als sie.**
> **Er war nur wenig älter als sie.**
> **Er hatte viel mehr Geld als ich.**

Viel must not be confused with the adverb **sehr** (*very*), which sometimes corresponds to an English *very much*.

Ich habe sie sehr geliebt.	I loved her very much.
Ich ginge sehr gerne mit nach Köln.	I'd like very much to go along to Cologne.
Er war sehr krank.	He was very sick.
Die Amerikaner essen sehr viel Fleisch.	Americans eat a lot of (very much) meat.
Ich war sehr dagegen.	I was very much against it.
Es waren sehr viele Leute dort.	There were very many people there.

English *very* usually precedes *much, many,* or some other adjective or adverb. German **sehr,** on the other hand, is an independent adverb and does not have to be followed by anything.

> **Sie liebte ihn sehr.**

176 ander-

Ander- means *other*, *different*, or *else*. If used attributively or after **etwas** or **nichts**, it takes the same endings as any other attributive adjective and is often preceded by **ganz**.

> Das eine Buch kenne ich, aber das andere habe ich noch nicht gelesen.
> Erika kenne ich ja, aber wer war denn die andere Dame?
> Dieser Herr war es nicht, es muß ein anderer gewesen sein.
> Das ist natürlich etwas anderes. (*something else*)
> Das ist etwas ganz anderes. (*something quite different*)

NOTE: For some unfathomable reason, no form of **ander-** is capitalized.

If **ander-** is used as an adverb or a predicate adjective, it always has the form **anders**.

> Ich hätte das ganz anders gemacht.   I would have done that quite differently.
> Er ist anders, als er früher war.   He is different than he used to be.

Note also the following frequently used phrases:

> Das kann nicht mein Bruder gewesen sein, das muß *jemand anders* (*somebody else*) gewesen sein.
> Das kann *niemand anders* (*nobody else*) gewesen sein als Anton Meyer.

177 mehrere, einige, ein paar

All three of these terms mean "more than two, but not many."

Mehrere and **einige** are never used with an article, as is possible with English *the several states*. They therefore take strong endings.

Mehrere means *several*, **einige** and **ein paar** mean *a few* or *some*.

SLOT 0	SLOT 1	SLOT 2	SLOT 3
	mehrere junge		Leute
	einige deutsche		Bücher
ein paar	junge		Leute
ein paar	deutsche		Bücher

Do not confuse **wenige**, meaning *few* in the sense of *not many*, with **ein paar**, meaning *a few* in the sense of *some*.

> Wenige Menschen wußten, wer er wirklich war.
> Ein paar Menschen wußten, wer er wirklich war.
> Bring mir doch bitte ein paar Zigaretten mit.
> Ich komme in ein paar Minuten.
> Er wollte in Berlin ein paar Freunde besuchen.
> Er ist ein paar Tage in Berlin gewesen.
> Wir haben ein paar schöne Tage an der Riviera verbracht.

After the definite article, **ein paar** becomes **paar.**

> **Die paar schönen Tage an der Riviera waren viel zu kurz.**

Note the difference between **ein paar** (*a few*) and **ein Paar** (*a pair, a couple*):

> **Wir aßen Suppe mit ein paar Würstchen.**
> **Wir aßen Suppe mit einem Paar Würstchen.**
> **Anton und Emma waren ein schönes Paar.**

178 Word Formation: Nouns Derived from Weak Verbs

The stem of some weak verbs appears as a noun of action—that is, a noun denoting the activity expressed by the verb. Feel free to use the nouns listed, but do not try to invent your own—they may not exist. Most of these nouns are masculine, but there are also a few feminines.

antworten	die Antwort,-en	das war eine gute Antwort
baden	das Bad,⸚er	ein heißes Bad
besuchen	der Besuch,-e	Der Besuch der alten Dame (Dürrenmatt)
blicken	der Blick,-e	ein vielsagender Blick
danken	der Dank (*no pl.*)	vielen Dank
fragen	die Frage,-n	das kommt nicht in Frage (*that's out of the question*)
glauben	der Glaube, *gen.* des Glaubens (*no pl.*)	Glaube, Hoffnung, Liebe
grüßen	der Gruß,⸚e	viele Grüße aus den Bergen
hassen	der Haß (*no pl.*)	Ohne Liebe kein Haß (Ingelheim)
heiraten	die Heirat,-en	ich bin gegen diese Heirat
kaufen	der Kauf,⸚e	ein guter Kauf
küssen	der Kuß, die Küsse	mit Gruß und Kuß, Dein Julius
lieben	die Liebe (*no pl.*)	Liebe macht blind
reden	die Rede,-n	er hielt eine lange Rede
suchen	die Suche (*no pl.*)	die Suche nach dem Dieb
tanzen	der Tanz,⸚e	der Tanz um das goldene Kalb
versuchen	der Versuch,-e	ein chemischer Versuch
wünschen	der Wunsch,⸚e	alle guten Wünsche zum Neuen Jahr

The most common nouns of action are the feminine nouns in **-ung** (see **126**).

179 Word Formation: Nouns Derived from Strong Verbs

Theoretically, any one of the various forms of the stem of a strong verb can occur as a noun denoting the action of the verb, or the result of such action, or the thing used for such action.

> Action: **der Schlaf** sleep
> Result of action: **der Fund** the find
> Thing used for action: **der Sitz** the seat

Again, it is safe to use the nouns listed, but do not invent your own. Note that
of the nouns ending in -t and -e, most are feminine.

abfahren	die Abfahrt,-en	departure
anfangen	der Anfang,⸗e	beginning
ankommen	die Ankunft,⸗e	arrival
annehmen	die Annahme,-n	assumption
anrufen	der Anruf,-e	phone call
ansehen	die Ansicht,-en	view; sight
ausgeben	die Ausgabe,-n	expense; delivery
aufnehmen	die Aufnahme,-n	reception; photograph
ausgehen	der Ausgang,⸗e	exit
aussehen	die Aussicht,-en	expectation; view
befehlen	der Befehl,-e	order, command
beginnen	der Beginn (no pl.)	beginning
bitten	die Bitte,-n	request
brechen	der Bruch,⸗e	break, fracture; fraction
fahren	die Fahrt,-en	drive, trip
fallen	der Fall,⸗e	fall; case
geben	die Gabe,-n	gift
	das Gift,-e	poison
	die Mitgift (no pl.)	dowry
gehen	der Gang,⸗e	gait; corridor; gear (in a motor)
gewinnen	der Gewinn,-e	profit, gain
greifen	der Griff,-e	handle; grasp
helfen	die Hilfe,-n	help
lesen (to read;	die Weinlese,-n	grape harvest
to gather)	„Spätlese"	a wine made from overripe grapes
liegen	die Lage,-n	situation
raten	der Rat,⸗e	advice, counsel; counselor
scheinen	der Schein (no pl.)	appearance; light
	der (Geld) schein,-e	bank note
schlafen	der Schlaf (no pl.)	sleep
schlagen	der Schlag,⸗e	strike, stroke, hit
schneiden	der Schnitt,-e	cut
schreiben	die Schrift,-en	(hand)writing
	die Heilige Schrift	Bible, Holy Writ
sehen	das Gesicht,-er	face
sitzen	der Sitz,-e	seat
sprechen	die Sprache,-n	language, speech
springen	der Sprung,⸗e	jump
stehen	der Stand,⸗e	stand
trinken	das Getränk,-e	beverage
tun	die Tat,-en	deed
	die Tatsache,-n	(actual) fact
verbieten	das Verbot,-e	prohibition
verlieren	der Verlust,-e	loss
verstehen	der Verstand (no pl.)	reason, intelligence
ziehen	der Zug,⸗e	train

Conversations

I

How to Express What?

Below you will find colloquial, and mostly stereotypical phrases that are used with high frequency in everyday conversation, to express such sentiments as astonishment, surprise, disbelief, doubt, anger, pleasure, urgency, etc. Almost all of these expressions have been used before; the list, therefore, can serve as a vocabulary review. They are arranged in vaguely alphabetical sequence; as you go through them, try to determine on what level of discourse—from fairly formal to highly colloquial—they may be used. In class, practice all of them in sentences or brief exchanges to make sure you use them right, and then, as you continue with the conversations of Units 17 and 18, use them as much as possible.

Aha!	I see; I get it.
Ach so.	Oh; now I get it.
Na also.	I told you so; why all the fuss?
Guten Appetit.	(said at beginning of a meal)
Mahlzeit.	
(Ganz) bestimmt.	Certainly; definitely.
So was Blödes.	How stupid; what a stupid (dumb) thing to
Dummes.	have happened, to do.
Wie kann man/ein Mensch nur so blöd sein?	How can anybody be so stupid?
Sei mir nicht böse, aber . . .	Don't be angry (mad at me, offended),
	but . . . .
Danke ja/nein.	Thank you, yes/no.
Danke ebenfalls.	Thanks, and the same to you.
Dann ja!	If (X) is the case, then I agree.
Also doch!	So (X) is happening/going to happen after all.
Also gut!	OK, I give in; I'll go along.
Oh doch!	Oh yes! (contrary to expectation)
Ehrlich.	Honest, I mean it. (used mostly by young
	people)
Entschuldigung, entschuldigen Sie.	(I'm) sorry; beg your pardon; forgive me.
Verzeihung.	
Ich bitte um Verzeihung/Entschuldigung.	
Ich bin total fertig.	I'm done in; I've had it.
Ich bin ganz mit den Nerven fertig/runter.	My nerves are shot.
Das ist ja alles falsch.	It's all wrong.
stimmt nicht.	
Das freut mich.	I'm glad/delighted (about that); I like that.
Ich fürchte, ja	I'm afraid so.
nein.	not.
Ganz gut.	Not bad; so-so; OK.
Nicht schlecht.	
(Aber) (sehr) gerne.	Sure; I'll be glad to.
Genau.	Exactly.
(So) ein Glück!	Boy, are we lucky!
Da haben Sie aber Glück (gehabt).	What luck; you sure were lucky.

Das glaubt (dir) doch kein Mensch.	Nobody is going to believe that, is going to buy that.
Gottseidank.	Thank God; thank goodness.
Mein Gott!	(Oh) My God; heavens! (unpleasant surprise)
Um Gottes willen!	For God's sake!
Um Himmels willen!	For heaven's sake!
Was hältst du denn davon?	What do you think of it/make of it?
Was soll denn das heißen?	What's that all about?
	What's going on (around here)?
Hören Sie, . . . hör mal . . .,	Listen, . . .
Gute Idee.	Good idea.
So ein Idiot.	What an idiot.
Na ja.	Well, I don't know, maybe; OK, it's all right with me, I don't care.
Na klar.	Sure; of course.
Das klingt gut.	That sounds good; that's all right (with me).
(Nun) komm schon.	Come on. (impatient)
Ich komm ja schon.	I'm coming.
Ich komme sofort/gleich.	I'll be with you in a minute.
Da kann ich nur lachen.	That (really) makes me laugh.
Leider nicht.	I'm sorry (but I can't . . .).
nein.	
(Das/Es) tut mir leid, aber . . .	
Lieber nicht.	(You'd) better not; (I'd) rather not.
Was ist (denn) los?	What's the matter?
Was ist denn los mit dir?	What's wrong with you?
Jetzt/Gleich geht's los.	Ready to go.
Nun mach schon.	Come on, hurry up.
Eil dich.	
Natürlich.	Sure; of course.
(Das ist doch) nicht möglich.	(That's) not possible/true; you don't mean it.
Nicht wahr?	Right?
(Da habe ich halt) Pech gehabt.	It didn't work out; too bad; I lost that one.
So ein Pech.	Too bad; such bad luck.
Da haben Sie recht.	You are *right* there.
Das ist mir recht.	That's all right with me.
Mir soll's recht sein.	
Wenn's dir recht ist, dann . . .	If it's OK with you, then . . .
Laß mich in Ruhe.	Leave me alone.
Sagen Sie, . . . sag mal . . .	Say; tell me, . . .
(Das ist) schade.	Too bad.
Sehen Sie, . . .	You see, . . .
(Austrian: schaun Sie)	
Na, wir wollen mal sehen.	Well, let's see (how it'll turn out).
(Aber) sicher.	Sure.
Ja/Na, so was.	Well what do you know; I'll be darned.
(Das) stimmt.	(That's) right/correct.
(Das ist) richtig.	

Viel Spaß.	Have fun.
Das macht Spaß/Freude.	That's fun.
Das ist (ja) interessant.	Isn't that interesting.
großartig.	great; marvelous.
prima.	great; first-rate.
echt gut.	real good.
Na, wie wär's?	Well, how about it?
Na, wie war's?	Well, how was it?
Was ist denn?	What's the matter/wrong?
(Bitte,) sei so nett/lieb, und . . .	(Please) do me a favor, and . . .
Das war aber gar nicht nett von dir.	That really wasn't nice of you.
Tu (doch) nicht so.	Don't be funny; oh stop it; don't pretend.
Übrigens.	By the way.
Du bist wohl verrückt?	Are you out of your mind?
wahnsinnig?	crazy?
Verdammt (noch mal).	Dammit; damn.
Aber warum denn?	But why?
Weißt du, was?	(Do) you know what?
Wirklich.	Really.
Auf Ihr Wohl!	Here's to you. (said when raising glasses, but
Prosit!	only with alcoholic beverages)
Prost!	
Kein Wunder.	No wonder.
Nun macht aber (mal) Schluß.	Stop it; come off it; cut it out;
Nun ist aber Schluß.	no more of this;
Nun hört aber mal auf.	I've had enough.

II

Have your class decide on some topics for conversation, discussion, and debate. With the aid of a dictionary and the help of your teacher, put together lists of appropriate vocabulary; then, as usual, have your teacher be the native speaker.

Some suggestions:

1. Kinder, Küche, Kirche, —oder: die Ehe° früher und heute.   (institution of) marriage
2. Die Frauenbewegung: pro's und contra's.
3. Moderne Technologie: Hilfe oder Hindernis?
4. Atomkraft oder Sonnenenergie?
   Die Energiekrise und die Zukunft der Menschheit.°   mankind
5. Bevölkerungszuwachs°: null?   population increase
   oder: was soll mit all den Menschen werden?
6. Der industrialisierte Norden und die „Dritte Welt.''
7. Linksradikalismus, Rechtsradikalismus und Terrorismus.

I

Ein Wort über deutsche Hotels

Wie überall in der Welt, gibt es in Deutschland teure und billige
Hotels, große und kleine, gute und weniger gute. In den Großstädten
gibt es internationale Hotels, in denen man so komfortabel wohnen
kann wie in internationalen Hotels der ganzen Welt. Im Berlin Hilton
oder im Hotel Berlin, im Frankfurter Hof oder im Hotel Interconti- 5
nental in Frankfurt, im Hotel Vier Jahreszeiten in Hamburg und im
Hotel Vier Jahreszeiten in München brauchen Sie kein Deutsch zu
können, um sich Ihr Frühstück aufs Zimmer bringen zu lassen oder
um einen Luftpostbrief nach Chicago aufzugeben. Wenn Sie aber in
einem kleineren Hotel wohnen wollen oder in einer Pension, oder 10
wenn Sie in einer Kleinstadt oder auf dem Land in einem Dorfgasthof
ein Zimmer haben wollen, dann ist das schon etwas anderes. Sie
können dann natürlich mit den Händen reden, aber besser ist es doch,
wenn Sie Deutsch sprechen. Doch dazu brauchen Sie ein bißchen
Hotel-Jargon.

Wir wollen annehmen, daß Sie in Koblenz übernachten wollen, denn
dorthin haben wir Sie ja mit dem Hellas-Express geschickt. In Koblenz
gibt es etwa 30 Hotels und 25 Gasthöfe und Pensionen. Es ist nicht
immer ganz einfach, den Unterschied zwischen einem Hotel und
einem Gasthof zu sehen. Hotels sind größer als Gasthöfe, und Gast- 20
höfe sind kleiner als Hotels. (Aber das ist natürlich keine Definition.)
Das größte Hotel in Koblenz hat 120 Betten, der kleinste Gasthof hat
5 oder 6 Betten. Eine Pension ist etwas, was es in Amerika nicht gibt.

die Jahreszeit,-en
    season

einen Brief aufgeben
    to mail a letter
die Pension,-en tourist
    home
der Gasthof,⸚e inn

15 **der Jargon′** pro-
    nounced as in French

Im Intershop können Sie Ihre
Diners-Club-Karte benutzen.

Die meisten Pensionen sind Privathäuser, in denen man, ganz ähnlich
wie in Gasthöfen, übernachten kann und in denen man Frühstück
bekommt. Zum Gasthof gehört noch eine Gaststätte, ein Restaurant
(oft ähnlich wie in England die *neighborhood pubs*), wo man abends
hingeht, um ein Glas Wein oder ein Bier zu trinken. Die „Gaststätten“ 5
heißen in vielen Gegenden Deutschlands „Wirtschaften“ oder „Wirts-
häuser“. Auf dem Land haben solche Gasthäuser oft Namen wie
„Zum Löwen“, „Zum Ochsen“, „Zum Goldenen Lamm“, „Zum
Deutschen Kaiser“.

der Löwe,-n lion
der Ochse,-n ox
das Lamm,-̈er lamb

Außer den Hotels, Gasthöfen und Pensionen gibt es in Koblenz auch 10
eine Jugendherberge mit 540 Betten und einen Campingplatz für etwa
1000 Personen, aber da Sie Ihre erste Nacht in Deutschland weder in
einer Jugendherberge noch auf einem Campingplatz verbringen
wollen, so gehen Sie in eines der besseren Hotels. In Ihrem Hotelführer
haben Sie eins gefunden: Zimmerpreis DM 62,00–66,00, Frühstück 15
DM 5,00. Frühstück ist in vielen deutschen Hotels obligatorisch; d.h.,
man muß dafür bezahlen, ob man frühstückt oder nicht. Zum
Standard-Frühstück in Deutschland gehören Brötchen, Butter, Marmelade und Kaffee oder Tee.

die Jugendherberge,-n
youth hostel

das Brötchen,- (hard)
roll
die Marmelade,-n any
kind of jam

So, jetzt haben Sie Ihren Reiseführer lange genug studiert; Sie geben 20
dem Gepäckträger, der Ihre Koffer vor den Bahnhof getragen hat,
eine Mark Trinkgeld und nehmen ein Taxi zum Hotel. Der Mann, der
Ihnen am Hotel mit Ihrem Gepäck hilft, ist aber kein Gepäckträger,
sondern ein Hausdiener. Er bringt Ihre Koffer zum Empfang, und der
Mann, der Sie dort empfängt, ist der Portier (oder in manchen 25
größeren Hotels der Empfangschef).

der Gepäckträger,-
porter
das Trinkgeld,-er tip
der Hausdiener,-
bellhop
der Portier,-s desk clerk
der Empfangschef,-s
head clerk

Es folgt ein imaginäres Gespräch zwischen Ihnen und dem Portier.

„Ich habe für heute nacht ein Zimmer bestellt.“

„Auf welchen Namen, bitte?“

„Ray, aus New York.“   30

„Einen Augenblick, bitte,—und würden Sie inzwischen schon das
Anmeldeformular ausfüllen?“

anmelden to register
das Formular,-e form
ausfüllen to fill out

„Sie wollten ein Zimmer mit Bad, Mr. Ray? Leider habe ich nur ein
Zimmer mit Dusche, wenn Sie nichts dagegen haben?“

die Dusche,-n shower

„Das ist mir schon recht. Wie teuer ist denn das Zimmer?“   35

„62 Mark, plus 15% Bedienung; die Mehrwertsteuer ist eingeschlos-
sen.“

bedienen to wait on,
serve; **die Bedienung**
service charge
die Mehrwertsteuer
value added tax

„Gut. Und gibt es ein Telefon auf dem Zimmer? Ich muß nämlich
noch ein paar Ferngespräche führen.“

„Aber sicher. Rufen Sie nur die Zentrale an; die Telefonistin verbindet 40
Sie dann. So, hier ist Ihr Schlüssel,—Zimmer 318. Der Aufzug ist hier
drüben links, bitte. Das Gepäck lasse ich Ihnen nach oben bringen.“

ein Ferngespräch führen
to make a long-
distance call
die Zentrale,-n switchboard

Sie gehen zum Aufzug, einem Aufzug mit Selbstbedienung. Im dritten
Stock gehen Sie einen langen Korridor hinunter und suchen Zimmer

318. Nach Zimmer 315 kommt eine Tür mit „H", dann eine mit „D"
und dann kommt erst 316. (Statt H und D finden Sie vielleicht auch
nur eine Tür mit 00.) Zimmer 318 ist ganz nett, vielleicht ein bißchen
altmodisch, aber doch komfortabel. Am interessantesten finden Sie
das Federbett, aber wir müssen Sie warnen: Solche Federbetten sind 5   **die Feder,-n** feather
für die meisten Amerikaner erstens zu warm und zweitens zu kurz;
wenn man unter einem Federbett schläft, hat man entweder kalte
Füße oder kalte Schultern. Sie klingeln also dem Zimmermädchen
und bitten sie, Ihnen statt des Federbettes eine Wolldecke zu bringen.   **die Wolle** wool **die**
Dann wollen Sie telefonieren; zuerst Köln, und dann Ihre Freundin 10   **Wolldecke** blanket
Barbara, die in Augustdorf bei Detmold wohnt.

II

Ferngespräche

Sie nehmen also den Hörer ab, und dann hören Sie die Stimme der
Telefonistin: „Zentrale."
„Ja, Fräulein, ich hätte gerne Köln, 20 37 88 (zwo-null, drei-sieben,
acht-acht)."
Am Telephon sagt man immer „zwo" statt „zwei."   5
„Köln, 20 37 88—bitte legen Sie wieder auf; ich rufe Sie zurück."   **(den Hörer) auflegen**
Nach zwei Minuten klingelt das Telefon.   to put down the re-
„Die Nummer ist leider besetzt. Soll ich es in ein paar Minuten noch   ceiver
einmal versuchen?"
„Ja, bitte."   10
Fünf Minuten später klingelt es wieder.
„Ihr Gespräch nach Köln. Einen Augenblick, bitte; ich verbinde."
Dann hören Sie am anderen Ende eine Frauenstimme: „Hier bei
Doktor Fischer", und weil die Stimme „bei Doktor Fischer" sagt,
wissen Sie, daß das nicht Frau Fischer sein kann. Sie sagen also: 15
„Kann ich bitte Herrn Doktor Fischer sprechen?"
„Darf ich Sie um Ihren Namen bitten?"
„John Ray,—aus New York."
„Einen Augenblick, bitte, Herr Reh."

Ihr Gespräch mit Herrn Fischer ist natürlich Ihre Privatsache, und 20
wir wollen es hier nicht abdrucken. Aber nachdem das Gespräch zu   **abdrucken**   to print
Ende ist, sprechen Sie wieder mit der Telefonistin, denn Sie wollen ja
Ihre Freundin Barbara auch noch anrufen.

„Sagen Sie, Fräulein, kennen Sie Augustdorf bei Detmold?"
„Nein, nie davon gehört; das muß irgendein Dorf sein."   25
„Ich hatte den Namen auch noch nie gehört, aber so klein kann es
nicht sein, denn die Telefonnummer ist eine Meile lang."   **die Meile,-n**   mile
„Was ist denn die Nummer?"
„05237258."
„Nein, nein", lacht die Telefonistin. (Lacht sie über Ihren ameri- 30
kanischen Akzent oder darüber, daß Sie über deutsche Telefon-
nummern nicht Bescheid wissen?) „Da haben Sie die Vorwahlnummer   **Bescheid wissen**   to
mit dazu genommen. Augustdorf ist bestimmt ein Dorf, denn die   know, be informed
Nummer ist 258. Die Vorwahl ist 05237. Ihre Kölner Nummer ist mit   **die Vorwahlnummer,-n**
der Vorwahlnummer noch länger. Köln hat die Vorwahl 0221; das 35   area code
heißt, die Nummer, die ich vorhin gewählt habe, war 0221203788."
„Das wußte ich nicht—unsere amerikanischen Vorwahlnummern
haben nur drei Zahlen. Aber versuchen Sie doch jetzt mal Augustdorf."
„Gut,—und bleiben Sie doch bitte gleich am Apparat."   40 **am Apparat**   on the line
Aber Sie haben kein Glück. Die Nummer ist zwar nicht besetzt, aber

GASTSTÄTTE
W. und K. Ripps

„Zum Hirsch"

Frankfurt am Main-Hausen   Obergasse 14
Telefon 78 22 69

es antwortet auch niemand. „Da meldet sich leider niemand", sagt
die Telefonistin. „Soll ich es später noch mal versuchen?"
„Nein danke. Ich möchte mir jetzt erst einmal ein bißchen die Stadt
ansehen."
„Dann können Sie es ja von der Post aus noch mal versuchen."   5
„Gute Idee. Ich will sowieso noch einen Brief aufgeben. Vielen Dank,
Fräulein."

sich melden to answer (the phone)

III

PETER BICHSEL

Peter Bichsel (born 1935 in Luzern) is a Swiss writer whose short stories,
though simple in vocabulary and syntax, are highly sophisticated images of
the human condition. They are sometimes tragicomic, often witty, and always
poignant.

Ein Tisch ist ein Tisch

Ich will von einem alten Mann erzählen, von einem Mann, der kein
Wort mehr sagt, ein müdes Gesicht hat, zu müd zum Lächeln und zu
müd, um böse zu sein. Er wohnt in einer kleinen Stadt, am Ende der
Straße oder nahe der Kreuzung. Es lohnt sich fast nicht, ihn zu be-
schreiben, kaum etwas unterscheidet ihn von andern. Er trägt einen 5
grauen Hut, graue Hosen, einen grauen Rock und im Winter den
langen grauen Mantel, und er hat einen dünnen Hals, dessen Haut
trocken und runzelig ist, die weißen Hemdkragen sind ihm viel zu
weit.

Im obersten Stock des Hauses hat er sein Zimmer, vielleicht war er 10
verheiratet und hatte Kinder, vielleicht wohnte er früher in einer
andern Stadt. Bestimmt war er einmal ein Kind, aber das war zu einer
Zeit, wo die Kinder wie Erwachsene angezogen waren. Man sieht sie
so im Fotoalbum der Großmutter. In seinem Zimmer sind zwei

die Kreuzung,-en intersection
es lohnt sich nicht it doesn't pay
unterscheiden to distinguish
der Hals,-̈e neck
die Haut,-̈e skin
runzelig shriveled up
der Hemdkragen,- shirt collar
im obersten Stock on the top floor

Stühle, ein Tisch, ein Teppich, ein Bett und ein Schrank. Auf einem   **der Teppich,-e** rug
kleinen Tisch steht ein Wecker, daneben liegen alte Zeitungen und das
Fotoalbum, an der Wand hängen ein Spiegel und ein Bild.

Der alte Mann machte morgens einen Spaziergang und nachmittags
einen Spaziergang, sprach ein paar Worte mit seinem Nachbarn, und 5
abends saß er an seinem Tisch.

Das änderte sich nie, auch sonntags war das so. Und wenn der Mann
am Tisch saß, hörte er den Wecker ticken, immer den Wecker ticken.

Dann gab es einmal einen besonderen Tag, einen Tag mit Sonne, nicht
zu heiß, nicht zu kalt, mit Vogelgezwitscher, mit freundlichen Leuten, 10 **das Vogelgezwitscher**
mit Kindern, die spielten—und das Besondere war, daß das alles dem   twittering of birds
Mann plötzlich gefiel.

Er lächelte.

„Jetzt wird sich alles ändern", dachte er. Er öffnete den obersten   **der Knopf,-̈e** button
Hemdknopf, nahm den Hut in die Hand, beschleunigte seinen Gang, 15   **beschleunigen** to
wippte sogar beim Gehen in den Knien und freute sich. Er kam in   accelerate
seine Straße, nickte den Kindern zu, ging vor sein Haus, stieg die   **in den Knien wippen**
Treppe hoch, nahm die Schlüssel aus der Tasche und schloß sein   to walk with a spring
Zimmer auf.   **zunicken** (*with dat.*)
                                                                              to nod at

Aber im Zimmer war alles gleich, ein Tisch, zwei Stühle, ein Bett. 20
Und wie er sich hinsetzte, hörte er wieder das Ticken. Und alle Freude
war vorbei, denn nichts hatte sich geändert.

Und den Mann überkam eine große Wut.   **die Wut** anger
                                                                            rot anlaufen to turn red
Er sah im Spiegel sein Gesicht rot anlaufen, sah, wie er die Augen   **zukneifen** to squeeze
zukniff; dann verkrampfte er seine Hände zu Fäusten, hob sie und 25   shut
schlug mit ihnen auf die Tischplatte, erst nur einen Schlag, dann noch   **verkrampfen** to tighten
einen, und dann begann er auf den Tisch zu trommeln und schrie   **die Faust,-̈e** fist
dazu immer wieder: **trommeln** to drum

„Es muß sich ändern, es muß sich ändern!"

Und er hörte den Wecker nicht mehr. Dann begannen seine Hände zu 30
schmerzen, seine Stimme versagte, dann hörte er den Wecker wieder,   **schmerzen** to hurt
und nichts änderte sich.   **versagen** to fail

„Immer derselbe Tisch", sagte der Mann, „dieselben Stühle, das Bett,
das Bild. Und dem Tisch sage ich Tisch, dem Bild sage ich Bild, das   **French: lit** bed
Bett heißt Bett, und den Stuhl nennt man Stuhl. Warum denn eigent- 35   **table** table
lich? Die Franzosen sagen dem Bett ‚li‘, dem Tisch ‚tabl‘, nennen das   **tableau** picture
Bild ‚tablo‘ und den Stuhl ‚schäs‘, und sie verstehen sich. Und die   **chaise** chair
Chinesen verstehen sich auch."

„Weshalb heißt das Bett nicht Bild", dachte der Mann und lächelte,
dann lachte er, lachte, bis die Nachbarn an die Wand klopften und 40
„Ruhe" riefen.

„Jetzt ändert es sich", rief er, und er sagte von nun an dem Bett „Bild".

„Ich bin müde, ich will ins Bild", sagte er, und morgens blieb er oft lange im Bild liegen und überlegte, wie er nun dem Stuhl sagen wolle, und er nannte den Stuhl „Wecker".

überle′gen to meditate

5

Er stand also auf, zog sich an, setzte sich auf den Wecker und stützte die Arme auf den Tisch. Aber der Tisch hieß jetzt nicht mehr Tisch, er hieß jetzt Teppich. Am Morgen verließ also der Mann das Bild, zog sich an, setzte sich an den Teppich auf den Wecker und überlegte, wem er wie sagen könnte.

stützen to put

10

Dem Bett sagte er Bild.
Dem Tisch sagte er Teppich.
Dem Stuhl sagte er Wecker.
Der Zeitung sagte er Bett.
Dem Spiegel sagte er Stuhl.
Dem Wecker sagte er Fotoalbum.
Dem Schrank sagte er Zeitung.
Dem Teppich sagte er Schrank.
Dem Bild sagte er Tisch.
Und dem Fotoalbum sagte er Spiegel.

15

20

Also:

Am Morgen blieb der alte Mann lange im Bild liegen, um neun läutete das Fotoalbum, der Mann stand auf und stellte sich auf den Schrank, damit er nicht an die Füße fror, dann nahm er seine Kleider aus der Zeitung, zog sich an, schaute in den Stuhl an der Wand, setzte sich dann auf den Wecker an den Teppich und blätterte den Spiegel durch, bis er den Tisch seiner Mutter fand.

läuten to ring

blättern to page, leaf
  through

25

Der Mann fand das lustig, und er übte den ganzen Tag und prägte sich die neuen Wörter ein. Jetzt wurde alles umbenannt: Er war jetzt kein Mann mehr, sondern ein Fuß, und der Fuß war ein Morgen und der Morgen ein Mann.

sich etwas einprägen
  to memorize some-
  thing
wurde umbenannt
  was renamed

30

Jetzt könnt ihr die Geschichte selbst weiterschreiben. Und dann könnt ihr, so wie es der Mann machte, auch die anderen Wörter austauschen:

läuten heißt stellen,
frieren heißt schauen,
liegen heißt läuten,
stehen heißt frieren,
stellen heißt blättern.

35

So daß es dann heißt:

Am Mann blieb der alte Fuß lange im Bild läuten, um neun stellte das Fotoalbum, der Fuß fror auf und blätterte sich auf den Schrank, damit er nicht an die Morgen schaute.

40

Der alte Mann kaufte sich blaue Schulhefte und schrieb sie mit den
neuen Wörtern voll, und er hatte viel zu tun damit, und man sah ihn
nur noch selten auf der Straße.

das Heft,-e notebook

Dann lernte er für alle Dinge die neuen Bezeichnungen und vergaß
dabei mehr und mehr die richtigen. Er hatte jetzt eine neue Sprache, 5
die ihm ganz allein gehörte.

die Bezeichnung,-en
designation

Hie und da träumte er schon in der neuen Sprache, und dann über-
setzte er die Lieder aus seiner Schulzeit in seine Sprache, und er sang
sie leise vor sich hin.

hie und da now and
then
träumen dream
übersetʹzen to translate

Aber bald fiel ihm auch das Übersetzen schwer, er hatte seine alte 10
Sprache fast vergessen, und er mußte die richtigen Wörter in seinen
blauen Heften suchen. Und es machte ihm Angst, mit den Leuten zu
sprechen. Er mußte lange nachdenken, wie die Leute zu den Dingen
sagen.

das Lied,-er song
vor sich hin to himself
schwerfallen to prove
difficult

    Seinem Bild sagen die Leute Bett.   15
    Seinem Teppich sagen die Leute Tisch.
    Seinem Wecker sagen die Leute Stuhl.
    Seinem Bett sagen die Leute Zeitung.
    Seinem Stuhl sagen die Leute Spiegel.
    Seinem Fotoalbum sagen die Leute Wecker.   20
    Seiner Zeitung sagen die Leute Schrank.
    Seinem Schrank sagen die Leute Teppich.
    Seinem Tisch sagen die Leute Bild.
    Seinem Spiegel sagen die Leute Fotoalbum.

Und es kam so weit, daß der Mann lachen mußte, wenn er die Leute 25
reden hörte.

Er mußte lachen, wenn er hörte, wie jemand sagte:

„Gehen Sie morgen auch zum Fußballspiel?“ Oder wenn jemand
sagte: „Jetzt regnet es schon zwei Monate lang.“ Oder wenn jemand
sagte: „Ich habe einen Onkel in Amerika.“   30

Er mußte lachen, weil er all das nicht verstand.

Aber eine lustige Geschichte ist das nicht. Sie hat traurig angefangen
und hört traurig auf.

lustig funny
traurig sad

Der alte Mann im grauen Mantel konnte die Leute nicht mehr ver-
stehen, das war nicht so schlimm.   35

Viel schlimmer war, sie konnten ihn nicht mehr verstehen.

Und deshalb sagte er nichts mehr.

Er schwieg,
sprach nur noch mit sich selbst,
grüßte nicht einmal mehr.   40

IV

Der Wolf und die sieben Geißlein*

Es war einmal eine alte Geiß, die hatte sieben junge Geißlein, und hatte sie lieb, wie eine Mutter ihre Kinder lieb hat. Eines Tages wollte sie in den Wald gehen und etwas zu essen holen. Da rief sie alle sieben ins Haus und sprach: „Liebe Kinder, ich will in den Wald. Wenn der Wolf kommt, dürft ihr ihn nicht ins Haus lassen. Wenn er herein- 5 kommt, so frißt er euch alle. Der Bösewicht verstellt sich oft, aber an seiner Stimme und an seinen schwarzen Füßen werdet ihr ihn gleich erkennen." Die Geißlein sagten: „Liebe Mutter, du brauchst keine Angst zu haben." Da meckerte die Alte und ging in den Wald.

eine alte Geiß an old goat

Der Bösewicht . . . oft the rascal often disguises himself

meckern to bleat

Es dauerte nicht lange, so klopfte jemand an die Haustür und rief: 10 „Macht auf, ihr lieben Kinder, eure Mutter ist da und hat jedem von euch etwas mitgebracht." Aber die Geißlein hörten an der Stimme, daß es der Wolf war. „Wir machen nicht auf", riefen sie, „du bist nicht unsere Mutter, die hat eine feine und liebliche Stimme, aber deine Stimme ist rauh; du bist der Wolf." Da ging der Wolf fort und 15 kaufte ein Stück Kreide; die aß er und machte damit seine Stimme fein. Dann kam er zurück, klopfte an die Haustür und rief: „Macht auf, ihr lieben Kinder, eure Mutter ist da und hat jedem von euch etwas mitgebracht." Aber der Wolf hatte seinen schwarzen Fuß in das Fenster gelegt; das sahen die Kinder und riefen: „Wir machen nicht 20 auf, unsere Mutter hat keinen schwarzen Fuß, wie du; du bist der Wolf." Da lief der Wolf zu einem Bäcker und sprach: „Ich habe etwas an meinem Fuß, kannst du etwas Teig auf meinen Fuß streichen?" Und als der Bäcker den Teig auf seinen Fuß gestrichen hatte, so lief er zum Müller und sprach: „Kannst du etwas Mehl auf meinen Fuß 25 streuen?" Der Müller dachte: „Der Wolf will einen betrügen", und wollte es nicht tun; aber der Wolf sprach: „Wenn du es nicht tust, so fresse ich dich." Da bekam der Müller Angst und machte ihm den Fuß weiß. Ja, so sind die Menschen.†

rauh rough

der Teig dough

streuen sprinkle
betrügen deceive

Nun ging der Bösewicht wieder zu der Haustür, klopfte an und 30 sprach: „Macht auf, Kinder, euer liebes Mütterchen ist zurück und hat jedem von euch etwas aus dem Wald mitgebracht." Die Geißlein riefen: „Du mußt uns erst deinen Fuß zeigen, sonst wissen wir nicht, ob du unser liebes Mütterchen bist." Da legte er den Fuß ins Fenster, und als sie sahen, daß er weiß war, so glaubten sie, es wäre alles 35 wahr, was er sagte, und machten die Tür auf. Wer aber hereinkam, das war der Wolf.

---

*This story is taken, with very few changes, from the famous collection of fairy tales by the brothers Grimm. The German of these fairy tales is highly sophisticated and yet of classic simplicity. Every German child grows up with Grimm. The standard introduction to German fairy tales, **Es war einmal . . .** , corresponds to the English *Once upon a time, there was . . . .*

†Observe the change of tense: this sentence is not part of the story.

Da bekamen sie alle Angst. Das eine sprang unter den Tisch, das
zweite ins Bett, das dritte in den Ofen, das vierte in die Küche, das
fünfte in den Schrank, das sechste unter die Waschschüssel, das siebte **die Waschschüssel**
in den Kasten der Wanduhr. Aber der Wolf fand sie alle und fraß sie washbowl
eins nach dem andern; nur das jüngste in dem Uhrkasten fand er nicht. 5
Als der Wolf die Sechs gefressen hatte, ging er fort, legte sich draußen
vor dem Haus unter einen Baum und fing an zu schlafen.

Es dauerte nicht lange, da kam die alte Geiß aus dem Wald wieder
nach Hause. Ach, was mußte sie da sehen! Die Haustür stand auf,
Tisch, Stühle und Bänke waren umgeworfen. Sie suchte ihre Kinder, 10
aber sie konnte sie nicht finden. Sie rief sie alle bei Namen, aber
niemand antwortete. Endlich, als sie an das jüngste kam, da rief eine
feine Stimme: „Liebe Mutter, ich bin im Uhrkasten." Sie holte es
heraus, und es erzählte ihr, daß der Wolf gekommen wäre und die
anderen alle gefressen hätte. Da könnt ihr denken, wie sie über ihre 15
armen Kinder geweint hat.*

Endlich ging sie hinaus, und das jüngste Geißlein lief mit. Als sie vor
das Haus kam, so lag da der Wolf unter dem Baum und schnarchte,
daß die Äste zitterten. „Ach Gott", dachte sie, „vielleicht leben meine
Kinder doch noch." Da mußte das Geißlein ins Haus laufen und 20
Schere, Nadel und Zwirn holen. Dann schnitt sie dem Bösewicht den **Schere, . . . Zwirn**
Bauch auf, und kaum hatte sie einen Schnitt getan, so steckte schon scissors, needle, and
ein Geißlein den Kopf heraus, und als sie weiter schnitt, so sprangen thread
sie alle sechs heraus, und waren noch alle am Leben. Das war eine
Freude! Die Alte aber sagte: „Jetzt wollen wir Steine suchen, mit 25
denen füllen wir dem Bösewicht den Bauch, solange er noch schläft."
Da brachten die sieben Geißlein Steine herbei und steckten sie ihm in
den Bauch. Dann nähte ihn die Alte wieder zu.

Als der Wolf endlich ausgeschlafen hatte, stand er auf, und weil ihn
die Steine in seinem Bauch durstig machten, so wollte er zu einem 30
Brunnen gehen und trinken. Als er aber an den Brunnen kam und
trinken wollte, da zogen ihn die Steine in den Brunnen hinein, und er
mußte ertrinken. Als die sieben Geißlein das sahen, da kamen sie
herbeigelaufen, riefen laut: „Der Wolf ist tot! der Wolf ist tot!" und **da . . . herbeigelaufen**
lachten und tanzten mit ihrer Mutter um den Brunnen. 35 they came running

Exercises

A. Insert the words italicized in the first sentence as adjectives into the second sentence.

1. Der Wind hatte die Brücke *zerstört*. Wir konnten nicht über die _____ Brücke fahren. **SEE**
2. Wir alle hatten unsere Großmutter sehr *geliebt*. Unsere _____ Großmutter ist mit 89 **ANALYSIS**
   Jahren gestorben. **110**
   (p. 529)

*Observe the change of tense: this sentence is not part of the story.

3. Der Dieb hatte DM 50.000 *gestohlen*. Mit dem _____ Geld fuhr er nach Italien.
4. Die Maschine aus London ist gerade *gelandet*. Die gerade _____ Maschine hat 35 Minuten Verspätung.

B. Change the italicized inflected form of the verb into a **-d** adjective and insert it into the second sentence.

SEE
ANALYSIS
171
(p. 529)

1. Der *sieht* aber gut *aus*. Er ist ein gut _____ junger Mann.
2. Die Linden *blühten* noch; sie saßen unter einer _____ Linde.
3. Das Kind *schlief*, als er abfuhr. Er sah noch einmal auf das _____ Kind und fuhr dann ab.
4. Die Kinder *spielten* auf der Straße, aber der alte Mann sah die _____ Kinder nicht.

C. Change singular nouns in the following sentences to plurals.

SEE
ANALYSIS
173
(p. 530)

1. Was für einen herrlichen Tag wir gehabt haben!
2. Was für ein Buch möchtest du denn gerne haben?
3. Was für eine schöne Tochter Sie haben!
4. Was ist denn das für ein Haus?

D. Change the plural nouns in the following sentences to singulars.

1. Was für schöne Kinder sind das!
2. Was müssen das für Menschen sein!
3. Was für schöne Tage waren das!
4. Was für interessante Kleider die Anita anhat!

E. Express in German.

SEE
ANALYSIS
155–159,
169–177
(pp. 460–464,
527–534)

1. We have two small children.
2. He lived with his old mother.
3. I hope you'll marry an intelligent woman.
4. She wrote him a long letter.
5. She never read his long letters.
6. Good coffee is very expensive.
7. He is an old friend of mine.
8. She is a good friend of mine.
9. Is that the new hotel?
10. Last week I was in Berlin.
11. Last Monday I was in Berlin.
12. I am living with my German relatives.
13. I have a German aunt.
14. Do you know that we have a new director?
15. Dear Hans!
16. Our dear old Aunt Amalie died last week.
17. In which hotel did you live?
18. She really is a very interesting woman.
19. In this city we don't have one single good hotel.
20. We all went to the movies last night.
21. I have read all his novels.
22. This is really a good wine.
23. My old friends are all dead.
24. All my old friends are dead.
25. She has married a young German.
26. He married a young German.
27. In the room above me lives a young German (man).
28. I have forgotten something very important.
29. Today I experienced something very beautiful.
30. When a man is thirty-nine, he is no longer a young man in the eyes of a young girl.

F. Try to guess the meaning of the following compounds and derivatives.

1. der Telefonanruf
2. der Gastarbeiter
3. auf baldiges Wiedersehen
4. der Besuch der alten Dame
5. das sogenannte Böse
6. eine achtstellige Zahl
7. eine alte Handschrift aus dem fünfzehnten Jahrhundert
8. ein Bilderbuch
9. ich kann es nicht mit Bestimmtheit sagen

10. wir haben eine Dreizimmerwohnung
11. die Zusammenarbeit
12. Reden ist Silber, Schweigen ist Gold
13. ein eintüriges Badezimmer
14. du stehst mir im Wege
15. mit größter Zufriedenheit
16. das Zwischendeck eines Schiffes
17. nur ein Wunschbild
18. in Wirklichkeit war es anders
19. weitblickend
20. wir hatten in diesem Monat viele Ausgaben
21. Gepäckannahme
22. Gepäckausgabe
23. ein weitgereister Mann
24. die Handschuhe
25. die Krankenpflegerin
26. die Natürlichkeit
27. Meyers sind sehr gastfreundlich
28. handgearbeitet
29. das Rädchen
30. mein Fahrrad
31. er ist ein Tunichtgut
32. die Wanduhr
33. ich trinke auf deine Gesundheit
34. er kennt keine Müdigkeit
35. bei Beginn des Konzertes
36. eine große Frage
37. jemandem einen Befehl geben
38. eine dreitägige Konferenz
39. wir sehen uns täglich
40. die Jungsozialisten
41. der damalige Bürgermeister
42. das ist gesetzlich verboten
43. Professorenphilosophie für Philosophieprofessoren
44. die Schönheitskönigin
45. das macht ein guter Arbeiter mit Leichtigkeit
46. wir werden in Kürze bei euch sein
47. für Meyer sind tausend Mark eine Kleinigkeit
48. die Weimarer Republik hatte eine Hunderttausendmannarmee
49. die Haltestelle der Straßenbahn
50. jede Tür hat einen Griff

G. Composition.

After you have spent your first night in a German hotel, you decide to write to your cousin Hildegard again. This time, describe what happened to you after your arrival in Koblenz; how you took a taxi to your hotel, and how surprised you were at the difference between this German hotel and American hotels. Tell her what an American motel is like; are there any motels in Germany at all? Then tell her that you have tried to call your friend Barbara, but haven't been able to reach her yet. You will try again and you hope that you'll be able to visit her. Ask Hildegard to write to you in Augustdorf and to let you know whether it is all right with her if you come to Munich in about two weeks. Ask her some questions about youth hostels and camping, and would she perhaps be interested in joining you for a hosteling/camping tour through the Alps.

Vocabulary

sich (*acc.*) ändern	to change
(sich) anmelden	to announce; to place (a phone call); to register (in a hotel)
sich (*dat.*) etwas ansehen	to look at something
die Antwort, -en	answer
der Apfel, ¨	apple
der Aufzug, ¨e	elevator
der Ausgang, ¨e	exit
austauschen	to exchange
der Austausch	exchange
der Beginn (*no pl.*)	beginning
der (die) Bekannte, -n	acquaintance
Bescheid wissen	to know, be informed
die Bitte, -n	request
blühen	to bloom, blossom, flower
derselbe, dieselbe, dasselbe	the same
dünn	thin
durstig	thirsty
der Durst	thirst
ich habe Durst	I am thirsty
duschen	to shower
die Dusche, -n	shower
ehrlich	honest
der Eingang, ¨e	entry
einschließen	to include; to lock in
empfangen	to receive
der Empfang, ¨e	reception
etwas anderes	something else
fein	fine, delicate
die Frage, -n	question
die Freude, -n	joy
frieren	to freeze
die Gaststätte, -n	restaurant
das Gepäck (*no pl.*)	baggage, luggage
der Gepäckträger, -	porter
gewinnen	to win
die Großstadt, ¨e	large city, metropolis
grüßen	to greet, say hello
herrlich	splendid, magnificent
die Hilfe,	help
holen	to get, fetch
die Hose, -n	pants, trousers

jemand anders	somebody else
niemand anders	nobody else
die Jugendherberge, -n	youth hostel
der Koffer, -	suitcase
lächeln	to smile
das Lächeln	smile
sich lohnen (*impers.*)	to be of use; to pay
das lohnt sich nicht	it doesn't pay
lustig	funny; merry
mehrere	several
sich (*acc.*) melden	to answer (the phone)
nähen	to sew
zunähen	to sew shut
die Näherin, -nen	seamstress
der Ofen, ¨	oven, stove
der Onkel, -	uncle
die Pension', -en	tourist home
recht	right
das ist mir recht	that's OK with me
die Rede, -n	speech
eine Rede halten	to give a speech
der Reiseführer, -	guidebook
der Rock, ¨e	jacket; skirt
schlagen	to hit, strike, beat
der Schlag, ¨e	hit, strike; stroke; bang
der Schluß, die Schlüsse	conclusion, end
der Schrank, ¨e	cupboard
der Spaziergang, ¨e	walk
einen Spaziergang machen	to take (go for) a walk
springen	to jump
stecken	to stick; to put
streichen	to spread
das Trinkgeld, -er	tip
üben	to practice
übernachten	to spend the night
unterscheiden	to distinguish
verbinden	to connect
verrückt	crazy
verwandt	related
der (die) Verwandte, -n	relative
wählen	to dial (telephone)
wahnsinnig	insane, crazy
warnen	to warn

der Wecker, -	alarm clock	der Wind, -e	wind
weinen	to cry, shed tears, weep	wunderbar	wonderful
weshalb	why, for what reason		

Additional Vocabulary

altmodisch	old-fashioned	die Mehrwertsteuer	value added tax
der Ast, ⸚e	branch (of a tree)	der Müller, -	miller
ausverkauft	sold out	die Mühle, -n	mill
der Bauch, ⸚e	stomach, belly	der Portier, -s	desk clerk (in a hotel)
der Brunnen, -	well		
der Campingplatz, ⸚e	campsite	schauen	to look
die Feder, -n	feather	schnarchen	to snore
das Federbett, -en	feather bed	der Schnitt, -e	cut
das Formular, -e	form, blank	die Schulter, -n	shoulder
geliebt	beloved	der Tanz, ⸚e	dance
der Gesandte, -n	ambassador	die Tischplatte, -n	tabletop
das Hindernis, -se	hindrance, obstacle	verwunden	to wound
der Hotelführer, -	hotel guide; guidebook	der Wolf, ⸚e	wolf
der Idiot, -en	idiot, fool	die Wolle	wool
der Kauf, ⸚e	purchase, buy	die Wolldecke, -n	blanket
die Kreide	chalk	die Wut	anger
die Krise, -n	crisis	die Zentrale, -n	switchboard
leuchten	to shine	das Zimmermädchen, -	chambermaid
die Linde, -n	linden tree	zittern	to tremble
die Marmelade, -n	(any kind of) jam	zurückhalten	to hold back
die Orangenmarmelade	orange marmelade	zurückhaltend	reserved

Strong Verbs

einschließen		schloß ein	eingeschlossen	to include
empfangen	empfängt	empfing	empfangen	to receive
frieren		fror	gefroren	to freeze
gewinnen		gewann	gewonnen	to win
schlagen	schlägt	schlug	geschlagen	to beat
springen		sprang	ist gesprungen	to jump
streichen		strich	gestrichen	to spread
unterscheiden		unterschied	unterschieden	to distinguish
verbinden		verband	verbunden	to join, connect

UNIT 18 The Passive—**es** in the Front Field—
Pre-Noun Inserts

The grammatical topics introduced in this final unit round out the presentation of the most important structures of the German language.

The passive voice, though less frequently used than the English passive, nevertheless has important functions, particularly in expository prose, as used, for example, in scientific writings and newspapers. The forms of the German passive present no problems, but its two manifestations, as actional and as statal passive, are hard to get used to for a native speaker of English, since English cannot formally make those distinctions.

The last analysis sections deal with pre-noun inserts, a "for German very characteristic and in English not an equivalent having structural pattern," which works exactly like the words in quotation marks you just read. Like the passive, pre-noun inserts occur with great frequency in expository prose, and you would find it difficult to read any serious German nonfiction without having a thorough grasp of this striking pattern.

The conversation section of Unit 18 encourages you to leave the realm of the post office, the railroad station, and the restaurant and, as in Unit 17, to attempt some serious conversations about serious topics. We started "liberating" your conversations in Unit 16, and in this last unit of the book, we also try to liberate your reading. There are more reading selections, mostly from newspapers and magazines, than you will probably be asked to read, but we encourage you to peruse them all to prove to yourself that you can now read German texts of moderate difficulty with fairly good comprehension.

Your skills in understanding and speaking, in reading and in writing German should now be sufficient to enter a second-year course with confidence. In the process of acquiring these skills, we hope that you have also begun to gain an understanding of the culture of Central Europe, a culture similar to your own in many ways, but also sufficiently different to challenge your curiosity and to encourage you to learn more about it.

Patterns

[1] The Active Voice of Transitive and Intransitive Verbs; Actional and Statal Forms of the Passive Voice

555

This is a presentation of basic forms. Study these examples *after* you have read 180–184.

SEE
ANALYSIS
180–184
(pp. 563–567)

PRESENT

INTRANSITIVE   Kochen die Kartoffeln schon?

TRANSITIVE   Mutter kocht jeden Tag Kartoffeln.

ACTIONAL PASSIVE   Bei uns werden jeden Tag Kartoffeln gekocht.

STATAL PASSIVE   Sind die Kartoffeln schon gekocht?

PAST

INTRANSITIVE   Als ich nach Hause kam, standen die Kartoffeln schon auf dem Herd und kochten.

TRANSITIVE   Mutter kochte damals jeden Tag fünf Pfund Kartoffeln.

ACTIONAL PASSIVE   Bei uns wurden früher jeden Tag fünf Pfund Kartoffeln gekocht.

STATAL PASSIVE   Als ich nach Hause kam, waren die Kartoffeln schon gekocht.
Wenn die Kartoffeln schon gekocht gewesen wären, hätten wir sofort essen können.

PERFECT

INTRANSITIVE   Die Kartoffeln haben noch gar nicht gekocht.

TRANSITIVE   Hast du auch genug Kartoffeln gekocht?

ACTIONAL PASSIVE   Bei uns sind noch nie soviel Kartoffeln gekocht worden wie in den letzten Tagen.

INFINITIVES

Ingelheim will *Die Frau mit dem Flamingo* an den Exotica-Verlag verkaufen.
Ingelheim soll *Die Frau mit dem Flamingo* an den Exotica-Verlag verkauft haben.
In Kanada darf *Die Frau mit dem Flamingo* nicht verkauft werden.
Im letzten Jahr sollen über 100.000 Exemplare verkauft worden sein.
Die ganze erste Auflage soll schon verkauft sein.
Haben Sie gehört, die ganze erste Auflage soll schon nach vier Wochen verkauft gewesen sein.

[2] Distinction between Actional and Statal Passive Forms

SEE
ANALYSIS
181
(p. 565)

Bei uns werden alle Briefe mit der Maschine geschrieben.
Diese Briefe sind mit der Maschine geschrieben.

Wann ist das Pulver denn erfunden worden?
Das weiß ich nicht. Als ich geboren wurde, war es schon erfunden.

Dieses Zimmer ist aber kalt. Ist es nicht geheizt, oder kann es nicht geheizt werden?

Ich höre, das Haus neben der Kirche soll verkauft werden.
Es ist schon verkauft.

SEE
ANALYSIS
180
(p. 563)

VARIATIONS

Change the following statal passive sentences to the actional passive.

Das Haus ist schon verkauft.
Ist die Stadt wiederaufgebaut?
Das müßte verboten sein.
Ist meine Schreibmaschine schon repariert?

[3] "Transformations" from Active Voice to Actional Passive

Wer hat denn den Bunsenbrenner erfunden?
Der Bunsenbrenner ist von Bunsen erfunden worden.
Bunsen soll den Bunsenbrenner erfunden haben.
Der Bunsenbrenner soll von Bunsen erfunden worden sein.
Wer hat Amerika entdeckt?
Amerika ist von Kolumbus entdeckt worden.
Schon die Wikinger sollen Amerika entdeckt haben.
Amerika soll schon von den Wikingern entdeckt worden sein.

Die Polizei sucht ihn.
Die Polizei soll ihn suchen.
Er wird von der Polizei gesucht.
Er soll von der Polizei gesucht werden.
Die Polizei suchte ihn überall.
Er wurde von der Polizei gesucht.
Hat ihn die Polizei nie gefunden?
Ist er nie gefunden worden?
Doch! Die Polizei soll ihn gestern gefunden haben.
Doch! Er soll gestern gefunden worden sein.

Eine einzige Bombe hat das Haus zerstört.
Das Haus ist durch eine einzige Bombe zerstört worden.
Das Haus soll durch eine einzige Bombe zerstört worden sein.
Eine einzige Bombe soll das ganze Haus zerstört haben.

*Die Trans-Pacific-Eisenbahn
wurde nicht an einem Tag gebaut*

**Auch die
Frankfurter Stadtbahn
braucht ihre Bauzeit**

VARIATIONS

Transform the following sentences to the statal and the actional passive. Leave out the agent.

Man hat die ganze Stadt zerstört.
Er hat das Haus verkauft.
Er soll das Haus schon verkauft haben.
Wir haben ihn gerettet.

Energie muss gespart werden

Das ist Gesetz

[4] Dative Objects

SEE
ANALYSIS
182
(p. 566)

Wir konnten ihm nicht helfen.
Dem Manne kann geholfen werden. (Schiller, *Die Räuber*)
Ihm ist nicht zu helfen.
Man half ihm sofort.
Ihm wurde sofort geholfen.

Jemand hat mir gesagt, ich sollte um drei Uhr hier sein.
Mir wurde gesagt, ich sollte um drei Uhr hier sein.
Es wurde mir gesagt, ich sollte um drei Uhr hier sein.

[5] Passive Forms to Express Activity as Such

SEE
ANALYSIS
183
(p. 566)

Wir waschen nur mit Persil.
Bei uns wird nur mit Persil gewaschen, denn Persil bleibt Persil.
Hier wird gearbeitet.
Jeden Samstag abend wird dort getanzt.
In meinem Elternhaus ist viel musiziert worden.
In Kalifornien wird fast nur mit Gas geheizt.
Bei euch im Büro wird viel zu viel geredet.
Wann wird denn hier morgens gefrühstückt?
In diesem Hotel wird nur vom 15. September bis zum 1. Mai geheizt.
Ingelheim ist mir zu sentimental; in seinen Romanen wird auf jeder dritten Seite geweint.
Es wird gebeten, nicht zu rauchen.

VARIATIONS

Change to actional passive, expressing "activity as such."

Wir arbeiten hier schwer.
Man hat hier noch nie getanzt.
Und um eins essen wir hier zu Mittag.
In unserer Familie lachen wir viel.

[6] Syntactical Variations

zeigen

Der neue schwedische Film wird jetzt auch in Deutschland gezeigt.
Könnte man ihn nicht auch in den Vereinigten Staaten zeigen?
Während der internationalen Filmfestspiele in Berlin wurde auch der neue schwedische
  Film gezeigt.
Der Film soll sehr gut sein, aber in Amerika ist er noch nicht gezeigt worden.
Es wäre besser, wenn dieser Film auch in Berlin nicht gezeigt worden wäre.
Es tut mir leid, daß der Film gezeigt wird. Ich wollte, er würde nicht gezeigt.

SEE
ANALYSIS
180–184
(pp. 563–567)

Express in German.

When is it supposed to be shown here?   _____
It can never be shown here.   _____

einladen

So, ihr seid schon wieder bei Schultes eingeladen?
So, Schultes haben euch schon wieder eingeladen?

Ich werde leider nie eingeladen.
Mich haben sie noch nie eingeladen.

Warum warst du denn gestern abend nicht bei Schultes?
Ich war nicht eingeladen.

Ich wollte, ich würde auch einmal eingeladen.
Ich wollte, ich wäre damals auch eingeladen gewesen.

Den Eugen Wilke treffe ich wahrscheinlich heute bei Schultes. Er soll auch eingeladen sein.
Karola Kirchhoff soll eingeladen worden sein, in Stuttgart die Desdemona zu spielen.
Natürlich freue ich mich darüber, daß ich eingeladen bin, hier in Stuttgart die Desdemona
    zu spielen. Aber ich bin nicht überrascht. Ich wäre sehr enttäuscht gewesen, wenn ich
    nicht eingeladen worden wäre.

Express in German.

I wish they would invite us.	Ich wollte, _____.
I wish we were invited.	Ich wollte, _____.
I wish Ingrid had invited us.	Ich wollte, _____.
I wish we had been invited by Ingrid.	Ich wollte, _____.
I wish we had been invited.	Ich wollte, _____.

reden

Meine Herren, Sie wissen, ich bin hier neu; aber eines habe ich schon festgestellt. Hier wird
    zu viel geredet, zu viel geraucht, zu viel Kaffee getrunken und zu wenig gearbeitet.

Auf dem Weg nach Hause redeten wir kaum ein Wort miteinander.
Auf dem Weg nach Hause wurde kaum geredet.
Auf dem Weg nach Hause wurde kaum ein Wort geredet.

Express in the actional passive.

Wir haben genug geredet; jetzt müssen wir etwas tun.

lösen

Es wurde zwar schon im Altertum angenommen, daß sich die Materie aus gewissen
    „Elementen" zusammensetzt, aber das Problem, aus welchen Elementen die Materie
    tatsächlich zusammengesetzt ist, konnte viele Jahrhunderte lang nicht gelöst werden.

Man konnte das Problem lange nicht lösen.
Das Problem war einfach nicht zu lösen.
Man glaubte, das Problem wäre nicht zu lösen.
Das Problem ließ sich lange nicht lösen.
Das Problem ist erst vor wenigen Jahren gelöst worden.
Das Problem konnte erst vor wenigen Jahren gelöst werden.
Ohne die Entdeckung des Radiums hätte das Problem nie gelöst werden können.
Im Mittelalter war das Problem noch nicht gelöst.
Erst die moderne Wissenschaft hat das Problem gelöst.
Heute ist das Problem gelöst.

ändern   *to change something, to enforce change*
sich ändern   *to become different, to change in nature or character*
sich verändern   *to change in physical appearance or behavior*

Ich habe meine Meinung geändert.

Der Mantel ist mir viel zu groß; den muß ich ändern lassen.

Haben Sie meinen Mantel schon geändert?

Ja, der Mantel ist schon geändert.

Bei uns gibt es nichts Neues; bei uns ändert sich nie etwas.

Der Marktplatz ist noch immer der alte, und nichts scheint sich hier geändert zu haben.

Morgen soll sich das Wetter endlich ändern.

Du hast dich aber verändert, Otto.

Gnädige Frau, Sie haben sich gar nicht verändert.

Die Maria hat sich aber verändert; die muß ja mindestens fünfundzwanzig Pfund abgenommen haben.—Ja, verändert hat sie sich, aber geändert hat sie sich nicht; es ist immer noch dieselbe alte Maria.

Express in German.

Of course I've changed; I'm ten years older.	Natürlich _____.
Karl has really changed; he doesn't drink anymore.	Karl hat _____ _____.

[7] The Impersonal es

Be prepared to produce these and similar sentences orally.

Niemand war zu Hause.
Es war niemand zu Hause.

Jemand hat heute nachmittag nach Ihnen gefragt.
Es hat heute nachmittag jemand nach Ihnen gefragt.

Leider meldete sich niemand.
Es meldete sich leider niemand.

Jetzt werden wieder Häuser gebaut.
Es werden jetzt wieder Häuser gebaut.

Viele Leute waren nicht *da*.
Es waren nicht viele *Leu*te da.

Ach Emma, du bist's!
Wer ist denn da?—Ich bin's, Emma.
Meyer kann es nicht gewesen sein.

Es regnet schon seit Tagen.
Hier regnet es schon seit Tagen.

SEE ANALYSIS 185 (p. 567)

Es sorgt für Sie

HERR MEYER

Es hat schon wieder gehagelt.
Hier hat es heute schon wieder gehagelt.

Es hat die ganze Nacht geschneit.
Heute morgen hat es ein bißchen geschneit.

Es hat stundenlang gedonnert und geblitzt, aber geregnet hat es nicht.

Wie geht es denn deinem Vater?—Danke, es geht ihm gut.
Dem Anton geht's immer gut.
Mir geht es heute gar nicht gut; mir geht's schlecht.
Guten Tag, Herr Müller. Ich habe Sie lange nicht gesehen; wie geht's Ihnen denn?

Vor hundert Jahren gab es noch keine Flugzeuge.
Da oben ist ein Flugzeug.

Was gibt's denn zum Mittagessen?
Es gibt jeden Tag Schweinebraten.
Das ist doch kein Schweinebraten, das ist Kalbsbraten.

Wieviele Hotels gibt es denn hier?
Heute gibt es nicht mehr viele Familien mit neun Kindern.

[8] The Impersonal es Anticipating a Subject Clause

SEE
ANALYSIS
185
(p. 567)

Es ist nicht gestattet, während der Fahrt mit dem Wagenführer zu sprechen.
Natürlich ist es nicht gestattet, während der Fahrt mit dem Wagenführer zu sprechen.

Es ist leider nicht erlaubt, vor dem Rathaus zu parken.
Leider ist es nicht erlaubt, vor dem Rathaus zu parken.

Es ist verboten, die Türen während der Fahrt zu öffnen.
Ist es verboten, die Türen während der Fahrt zu öffnen?

Es muß leider angenommen werden, daß er nicht mehr am Leben ist.
Leider muß angenommen werden, daß er nicht mehr am Leben ist.

Es wurde vorgeschlagen, eine neue Brücke über den Rhein zu bauen.
Von allen Seiten wurde vorgeschlagen, eine neue Brücke über den Rhein zu bauen.

Es wird oft behauptet, daß Männer besser Auto fahren können als Frauen.
Früher wurde oft behauptet, daß Männer besser Auto fahren könnten als Frauen.

Es wurde beschlossen, endlich eine neue Klinik zu bauen.
Gestern abend wurde beschlossen, endlich eine neue Klinik zu bauen.

Leider konnte nicht festgestellt werden, wer der Dieb ist.
Es konnte nicht festgestellt werden, wer der Dieb ist.
Wer der Dieb ist, konnte bis jetzt nicht festgestellt werden.

Invent anticipating clauses with es for the following subject clauses.

_____, das Kind in eine Privatschule zu schicken.
_____, Schmidtke hätte sich scheiden lassen.
_____, daß er nicht gerettet worden ist.
_____, hier ein Bürohaus zu bauen.

[9] Pre-Noun Inserts

Note that the parentheses are added here only to indicate the pre-noun inserts; they are
not normally written.

Mein Chef, der gottseidank nicht sehr intelligent ist, weiß gar nicht, daß es in Berlin auch
    billigere Hotels gibt.
Mein (gottseidank nicht sehr intelligenter) Chef weiß gar nicht, daß es in Berlin auch
    billigere Hotels gibt.

SEE
ANALYSIS
187
(p. 571)

Der Winter, der selbst für Norwegen ungewöhnlich kalt war, wollte gar kein Ende nehmen.
Der (selbst für Norwegen ungewöhnlich kalte) Winter wollte gar kein Ende nehmen.

Die Fluggäste, die soeben mit Lufthansa Flug Nummer 401 aus Frankfurt angekommen
    sind, werden gebeten, den Warteraum nicht zu verlassen.
Die (soeben mit Lufthansa Flug Nummer 401 aus Frankfurt angekommenen) Fluggäste
    werden gebeten, den Warteraum nicht zu verlassen.

Karthago, das von den Römern zerstört wurde, ist nicht wiederaufgebaut worden.
Das (von den Römern zerstörte) Karthago ist nicht wiederaufgebaut worden.

Aloys Hinterkofer, der seit Wochen von der Polizei gesucht wird, soll gestern in der Regina-
    Bar gesehen worden sein.
Der (seit Wochen von der Polizei gesuchte) Aloys Hinterkofer soll gestern in der Regina-Bar
    gesehen worden sein.

Die Züge, die im Sommer von München nach Italien fahren, sind meistens überfüllt.
Die (im Sommer von München nach Italien fahrenden) Züge sind meistens überfüllt.

Alle Studenten, die an dem Projekt interessiert waren, das Professor Behrens vorgeschlagen
    hatte, wurden gebeten, sich am nächsten Tag auf dem Sekretariat zu melden.
Alle (an dem von Professor Behrens vorgeschlagenen Projekt interessierten) Studenten
    wurden gebeten, sich am nächsten Tag auf dem Sekretariat zu melden.

If you can figure out the next sentence, you have really mastered the last few units:

Meine Damen und Herren, es handelt sich hier um ein (von der Wissenschaft bis heute noch
    kaum beachtetes und, soweit ich das aufgrund meiner Untersuchungen beurteilen kann,
    immer wichtiger werdendes) mathematisches Problem.

Analysis

180 The Passive Voice

Both English and German verbs have an active voice (*John Miller played the
lead role*) and a passive voice (*The lead role was played by John Miller*). The
main difference in their use is the center of the speaker's focus of attention.
Thus, for example, the active sentence *Titus destroyed Jerusalem in* A.D. *70*
focuses on the Roman emperor Titus and might be from a history of the
Roman Empire, whereas the passive sentence *Jerusalem was destroyed by*

Titus in A.D. *70* focuses on the city of Jerusalem and might appear in a history of Palestine.

Very often, active verb forms are used with a direct object. When such active sentences are transformed into passive sentences, direct objects become nominative subjects:

> She fed him (the dog) regularly.
> He (the dog) was fed regularly (by her).

The object *him* has become the subject *he*, and the subject *she* has become the prepositional phrase *by her*, which, however, in most instances is simply left out.

English verbs form their passive by using forms of *to be* as an auxiliary, followed by a participle:

	ACTIVE VOICE	PASSIVE VOICE
PRESENT	she feeds him regularly	he is fed regularly
PAST	she fed him regularly	he was fed regularly
PRES. PERF.	she has fed him regularly	he has been fed regularly
FUTURE	she will feed him regularly	he will be fed regularly
PRES. INFIN.	she must feed him regularly	he must be fed regularly
PAST INFIN.	she must have fed him regularly	he must have been fed regularly

German verbs form their passive by using forms of **werden** as an auxiliary, followed by a participle in second-prong position. If used in passives, the participle of **werden** is **worden** rather than **geworden**.

	ACTIVE VOICE	PASSIVE VOICE
PRESENT	sie füttert ihn regelmäßig	er wird regelmäßig gefüttert
PAST	sie fütterte ihn regelmäßig	er wurde regelmäßig gefüttert
PERFECT	sie hat ihn regelmäßig gefüttert	er ist regelmäßig gefüttert worden
FUTURE	sie wird ihn regelmäßig füttern	er wird regelmäßig gefüttert werden
PRES. INFIN.	sie muß ihn regelmäßig füttern	er muß regelmäßig gefüttert werden
PAST INFIN.	sie muß ihn regelmäßig gefüttert haben	er muß regelmäßig gefüttert worden sein

NOTE: Not every direct (accusative) object can become the subject of a passive sentence. Thus, we cannot transform the active sentence

Last year we lost our mother

into the passive sentence

[Last year our mother was lost (by us)]

or

John had a new book

into

[A new book was had by John].

181 Action and State

The phrase *was fed* in the two sentences

The dog was fed well
The dog was well fed

refers to two fundamentally different situations; *was fed well* refers to the repeated action of feeding the dog, and *was fed* is an "actional" passive; *was well fed*, on the other hand, refers to the state resulting from the action of feeding the dog well, and *was fed* in this case is a "statal" passive. The distinction is clear and depends here on word order. English passive forms, however, are ambiguous, for English has never developed a system which forces a speaker at all times to distinguish between actional and statal passive forms. Thus, the sentence

The house was built on a hill

can refer both to the action of building the house "from scratch" and to the accomplished fact that the house had been built and was sitting on a hill.

In German, the speaker must *always* distinguish between action and state, and ambiguous passive forms simply do not exist. The actional passive, as shown above in **180**, is expressed by a form of **werden** plus a participle; the statal passive, on the other hand, is expressed by a form of **sein** plus a participle which functions like a predicate adjective. Statal passives in the perfect are rather rare.

Though the German statal passive looks like a "translation" of *all* English passives, you must be careful to use it only when the English equivalent is also a statal passive.

Der Hund wird jeden Tag gefüttert.
The dog is fed every day.

Der Hund ist schon gefüttert.
The dog is fed already.

182 Dative Objects and the Passive Voice

The event reported in the English sentence *They gave him a pill* can also be reported as *He was given a pill*, even though *him* is not a direct object but an indirect object.

In German, indirect (dative) objects can *never* become the subject of passive sentences; the use of dative objects in this way results in Americanisms, as in

[**Ich wurde sofort geholfen**]
I was helped immediately.

However, even verbs like **helfen**, which require objects in the dative, can form passives, but the dative object is retained and the subject of the passive sentence is either expressed by an impersonal **es** (to preserve verb-second position) or it is left out entirely.

Es wurde mir sofort geholfen.
Mir wurde sofort geholfen.

The same idea, however, is more frequently expressed by an active sentence with the impersonal **man** as the subject:

Man half mir sofort.
They helped me immediately.

183 Use of the Actional Passive to Express Activity as Such

German verbs like **arbeiten, tanzen, schießen, warten** do not normally have an accusative object which can become the subject of a passive sentence, but they can form a passive nevertheless.

The question *What is going on here?* is frequently answered in German by a form of the actional passive.

QUESTION   **Was ist denn hier los?**   ANSWER   **Hier wird gearbeitet.**
                                                        Hier wird getanzt.

Für unsere betriebsärztliche Dienststelle suchen wir zum
1. Oktober 1978 oder wenn möglich früher

examinierte
Krankenschwester

Für unser Altenheim „Lutherheim" (50 Plätze) suchen
wir zum 1. 10. 1978 oder früher

geprüfte Altenpflegerin
als stellvertretende Heimleiterin

Bekanntes Berliner Automobil-Handelshaus

Note that such sentences do not contain a grammatical subject. The form **wird gearbeitet**, structurally not possible in English, denotes the activity of **arbeiten** as such. **Hier wird gearbeitet** means "The activity of working is going on here."

Further examples:

> **In meinem Elternhaus wurde viel musiziert.**
> **Bei uns wird auch sonntags gearbeitet.**
> **Seit heute morgen wird zurückgeschossen.** (Hitler, on September 1, 1939)

184 The Use of **von, durch,** and **mit** in Passive Sentences

A large percentage of German passive sentences contain only the "passive patient" (the grammatical subject) and no active agent.

If a personal agent is mentioned, **von** is used.

> **Jerusalem wurde von den Römern zerstört.**
> Jerusalem was destroyed by the Romans.

Mit is used for things "handled" by a personal agent.

> **Abel wurde von Kain mit einem Stein erschlagen.**
> Abel was slain by Cain with a rock.

> **Das ganze Zimmer war mit Blumen geschmückt.**
> The whole room was decorated with flowers.

Abstract causes, impersonal causes, and impersonal means of destruction are introduced by **durch.**

> **Sie wurden durch ein neues Gesetz gezwungen, das Land zu verlassen.**
> They were forced by a new law to leave the country.

> **Lissabon wurde durch ein Erdbeben zerstört.**
> Lisbon was destroyed by an earthquake.

> **Dresden wurde durch Bomben zerstört.**
> Dresden was destroyed by bombs.

185 The Impersonal **es** in the Front Field

Remember that an **es** in the front field cannot be a normal accusative object, for if the **es** in the sentence

> **Ich weiß es nicht**

is shifted into the front field, it becomes **das.**

> **Das weiß ich nicht.**

The impersonal **es** in the front field has one of three functions: It can (a) be a meaningless filler to preserve verb-second position; it can (b) be the grammatical subject of impersonal verbs; and it can (c) be used to anticipate a following dependent clause.

The Use of **es** as a Filler

In a short sentence like

> **Niemand war zu Hause**

the inner field is empty. Both **war,** the first prong, and **zu Hause,** the second prong, are position-fixed. If the speaker, in order to put greater news value on **niemand,** decides to put **niemand** in the inner field, he must put something else in the front field; otherwise he would come up with the question

> **War niemand zu Hause?**

Verb-second position, in these cases, can be preserved by filling the front field with a meaningless **es.**

> **Es war niemand zu Hause.**
> **Es hat niemand angerufen.**

This use of **es** as a filler is rather frequent in connection with the passive voice.

> **Es werden wieder Häuser gebaut.**
> **Es wird wieder gearbeitet.**

In all these cases, **es** disappears when the front field is occupied by another unit.

> **Gestern war niemand zu Hause.**
> **Gestern hat niemand angerufen.**
> **Hier werden wieder Häuser gebaut.**
> **Hier wird wieder gearbeitet.**

NOTE:
1. The **es** used in identification sentences is not a meaningless filler that disappears when the front field is filled; it can appear either in the front field or immediately behind the first prong.

> **Es war nicht mein Bruder.**
> **Mein Bruder war es nicht.**

The **es** in such sentences means "the thing to be identified." **Ich bin's** corresponds to *it's me,* which cannot be expressed by [**Es bin ich**] or [**Es ist ich**]. Similarly: **Du bist's, er ist's,** and so on.

2. **Es** as a filler is also used in the standard introduction of German fairy tales and folk songs. **Es war einmal ein König** corresponds to *Once upon a time there was a king*. Since the entire news value is concentrated in **ein König**, the subject cannot stand in the front field.

Es war einmal eine alte Geiß.
Es war ein König in Thule.
Es waren zwei Königskinder.
Es steht ein Baum im Odenwald.

es as the Grammatical Subject of Impersonal Verbs

The verbs most frequently used with the impersonal subject **es** are:

Es regnet, es schneit, es donnert, es hagelt.
Es geht mir (ihm, ihr, etc.) gut.
Es geht mir (ihm) schlecht.
Es ist mir zu warm (zu kalt, zu heiß).
Es ist zehn Uhr (schon spät, noch früh).
Es gelingt mir.

In all these cases, the **es** must appear in the inner field if the front field is occupied by some other unit.

Es hat gestern geregnet.	**Gestern hat es geregnet.**
Es schneit schon wieder.	**Schneit es schon wieder?**
Es ist mir hier zu warm.	**Hier ist es mir zu warm.**

Also, the idiom **es gibt** belongs to this group of impersonal verbs. **Es gibt**, translatable by either *there is* or *there are*, and roughly meaning "the situation provides," governs the accusative. In connection with a food term, it expresses what will be served. In other cases, it expresses that certain things exist as a permanent part of the environment or of nature.

Heute mittag gibt es Kartoffelsuppe.
In Afrika gibt es noch immer wilde Elefanten.
Gibt es hier ein Hotel?

Unlike the English *there is*, **es gibt** can never be used to point at a specific thing or person.

[Da oben gibt es ein Flugzeug.]

But:

Da oben ist ein Flugzeug.

The Anticipating es

The use of **es** to anticipate a following dependent clause is comparable to the use of English *it* in

I have *it* on good authority that Smith will be our next boss
It simply is not true that she has gone to college

where the *it*, which cannot be left out, anticipates the following *that*-clause.

The German anticipatory **es** refers forward to a dependent (subject) clause, and **es** is the grammatical subject of the main clause.

> **Es ist möglich, daß Ingelheim noch lebt.**
> **Es tut mir leid, daß ich gestern nicht kommen konnte.**
> **Es wird berichtet, daß Ingelheim spurlos verschwunden ist.**
> **Es freut mich, daß Sie kommen konnten.**

As long as this anticipatory **es** precedes the clause it anticipates, it does not disappear when the front field is occupied by some other unit.

> **Natürlich ist es auch möglich, daß Ingelheim nicht mehr lebt.**
> **Natürlich tut es mir leid, daß ich gestern nicht kommen konnte.**

Only the actional passive in such phrases as **Es wird berichtet, daß** . . . becomes **Gestern wurde berichtet, daß** . . .

If the dependent clause precedes the main clause, the anticipatory **es** disappears, because there is nothing left to anticipate.

> **Daß Ingelheim noch lebt, ist ganz unwahrscheinlich.**

186 jetzt and nun

Though both **jetzt** and **nun** are frequently equivalent to English *now*, they are not always interchangeable. **Jetzt** is an adverb of time without any implications.

> **Es ist jetzt zwölf Uhr fünfzehn.**
> **Meyer wohnt jetzt in München.**

Nun, on the other hand, always implies a reference to something which precedes; it therefore contains the idea that one state of affairs is superseded by another.

> **Und nun wohnt er in München.**
> (He used to live elsewhere.)

> **Und nun ist er schon drei Jahre tot.**
> (He used to be so full of life.)

> **Bist du nun zufrieden?**
> (I know you were dissatisfied before.)

> **Und nun hören Sie zum Abschluß unserer Sendung „Eine kleine Nacht-**
> **musik" von Wolfgang Amadeus Mozart.**
> And now we conclude our broadcast with Mozart's "Eine kleine Nacht-
> musik."

Because of the connotation "this is something new," **nun mal (nun einmal)** has the flavor "you might as well get used to it."

Das *ist* nun einmal so.
That's the way it is.

Ich *bin* nun mal nicht so intelligent wie du.
You might as well accept the fact that I'm not as intelligent as you are.

187 Pre-Noun Inserts

Syntactical units like *a child* can be separated by adjectives, which are placed between the article and the noun. We shall call such inserted adjectives *pre-noun inserts*. For the sake of clarity and illustration, pre-noun inserts are placed within parentheses in this section.

In English, one can speak of *a (healthy) child* or even of *a (healthy but somewhat retarded) child*. However, one cannot speak of *a (by a series of unfortunate childhood experiences somewhat retarded, but otherwise quite healthy) child*.

English speakers don't have that long a syntactical breath. In German, pre-noun inserts of considerable length are a standard characteristic of expository prose and academic lectures.

> **Man sollte dieses (durch eine Reihe von unglücklichen Kindheitserlebnissen leider etwas zurückgebliebene, aber sonst ganz gesunde) *Mädchen nicht der Gefahr aussetzen, von* (gleichaltrigen, nicht zurückgebliebenen) *Kindern unfreundlich behandelt zu werden.***

> *One should not expose this girl,* (who, though quite healthy, is unfortunately retarded by a number of unhappy childhood experiences,) *to the danger of being treated in an unfriendly way by children* (of the same age who are not retarded).

Both in English and in German, pre-noun adjective inserts can be viewed as shorthand versions of dependent clauses, usually relative clauses. Thus

This . . . . child, who is   really very beautiful

becomes

This   really very beautiful   child

and

Dieses . . . . Kind, das   wirklich sehr schön   ist

becomes

Dieses   wirklich sehr schöne   Kind

The example shows that

(a) When a German dependent clause is transformed into a pre-noun insert, it drops its subject and the inflected verb belonging to it.

(b) Since this transformation changes a predicate adjective or a participle into an attributive adjective, the adjective acquires an ending.

As far as German is concerned, pre-noun inserts, with the exception of (5) below, consist of an inner field plus a second prong. The usual word order is preserved. Pre-noun inserts can originate in the following ways:

1. The second prong is a predicate adjective.

> Dieses . . . . Mädchen, das │ sehr intelligent │ ist

becomes

> Dieses │ sehr intelligente │ Mädchen

2. The second prong is the participle of an intransitive verb like **ankommen, fallen, sterben,** or **zurückbleiben,** which forms its compound tenses with **sein.**

> Dieses . . . . Kind, das │ leider etwas zurückgeblieben │ ist

becomes

> Dieses │ leider etwas zurückgebliebene │ Kind

3. The second prong is the participle used to form the actional or statal passive.

> Diese Stadt, die │ während des letzten Krieges zerstört │ wurde (Actional Passive)

becomes

> Diese │ während des letzten Krieges zerstörte │ Stadt

> Diese Stadt, die │ noch nicht wiederaufgebaut │ ist (Statal Passive)

becomes

> Diese │ noch nicht wiederaufgebaute │ Stadt

> **Diese (während des letzten Krieges zerstörte) und (noch nicht wiederaufgebaute) Stadt war einmal ein wichtiges Kulturzentrum.**

4. The second prong is the participle belonging to a reflexive verb.

Der Gast, der sich betrunken **hat** (event)

The guest who got drunk

and

Der Gast, der betrunken **ist** (state)

The guest who is drunk

become

Der betrunkene **Gast**

5. As long as it makes sense, any present and past form of the *active* voice may be changed into a **-d** adjective. This **-d** adjective, preceded by its inner field, can then be used as a pre-noun insert.

Das Kind, das laut schrie

becomes

Das laut schreiende **Kind**

Die Bevölkerung Chinas, die (immer schneller wächst)
The population of China, which is growing faster and faster
　Die (immer schneller wachsende) Bevölkerung Chinas

Der Weg, der (vom Dorf aus in den Wald) führt
The path which leads from the village to the forest
　Der (vom Dorf aus in den Wald führende) Weg

Conversations

I

Vierundzwanzig Aphorismen

Use as many of these aphorisms as time permits for discussions of their meaning and of their applicability in various situations.

1. Wirkliche Führer werden kaum gespürt.° (Lao-Tse)　　　noticed, felt
2. Es ist einfacher, ein Atom zu spalten, als ein Vorurteil° zu zer-　prejudice
   stören. (Einstein)

3. Gewalt° kann Paläste zerstören, aber noch keinen Schweinestall erbauen.   *force, might*

4. Es gibt wirklich sehr viele Menschen, die nur lesen, damit sie nicht zu denken brauchen. (Lichtenberg)

5. Jeder Künstler° ist so groß wie sein größtes Werk. (Schopenhauer)   *artist*

6. Wirtschaftswissenschaft° ist besonders nützlich° für Wirtschaftswissenschaftler. (Galbraith)   *(the study of) economics*   *useful*

7. Nichts ist so verantwortlich° für die „gute alte Zeit" als unser schlechtes Gedächtnis.° (Anatole France)   *responsible*   *memory*

8. Das Leben ist so einfach, aber die Menschen sind so kompliziert.

9. Niemand ist reich genug, um seine Vergangenheit zurückzukaufen.

10. Kunst beginnt da, wo Nachahmung° aufhört. (Wilde)   *imitation*

11. Wer in sich selbst verliebt ist, liebt einen kranken Menschen.

12. Genug ist mehr als viel.

13. Ein Spiegel ist besser als eine Ahnengalerie.   **der Ahne** *ancestor*

14. Zuviel Vertrauen° ist oft eine Dummheit; zuviel Mißtrauen ist immer ein Unglück.   *trust*

15. Erzähle mir die Vergangenheit, und ich werde die Zukunft erkennen. (Konfuzius)

16. Alles was heute selbstverständlich ist, war einmal revolutionär.

17. Es ist besser, einen intelligenten Feind zu haben als einen dummen Freund. (Ben-Gurion)

18. Tu es heute! Morgen könnte es verboten sein.

19. Das Lächeln ist die kürzeste Entfernung° zwischen zwei Menschen.   *distance*

20. Ewige Freizeit—das müßte die Hölle° auf Erden sein. (Shaw)   *hell*

21. Wenn man nicht hat, was man liebt, muß man lieben, was man hat.

22. Wenn es keine schlechten Menschen gäbe, gäbe es keine guten Advokaten. (Dickens)

23. Es ist wichtiger, Menschen zu studieren statt Bücher.

24. Die letzte Stimme, die gehört wird, bevor die Welt auseinanderfliegt, wird von einem Sachverständigen° kommen, der sagt: „Das ist unmöglich!" (Peter Ustinov)   *specialist*

II

Vorschläge für weitere Gespräche und Diskussionen

As in Unit 17, decide on one or more topics to discuss with your fellow students and select appropriate vocabulary with the help of your teacher.

1. Wie wäre das Leben im Staat Oregon, der genau so groß ist wie die BRD, wenn er 60 mio Einw. und über 20 mio Kfz hätte?

   What would life be like in the state of Oregon, which is exactly the size of the FRG, if it had 60 million inhabitants and over 20 million motor vehicles?

2. Verbrechen im Fernsehen: Haben Crime-Shows einen Einfluß auf die zunehmende Kriminalität in den Industrieländern?

   Crime on TV: Do crime shows have an influence on the increasing criminality in the industrial countries?

3. Was sind die Vorteile und Nachteile der modernen Reklame in Zeitungen und Zeitschriften und im Fernsehen?

   What are the advantages and disadvantages of modern advertising in newspapers and magazines, and on television?

Reading

I

Tagesnachrichten

117 Fahrzeuge°
in Unfallserie
verwickelt°

Frankfurt/Main (ap). Nach einem Massenunfall von insgesamt 117 Fahrzeugen ist die Autobahn Frankfurt-Kassel am Dienstag für fast fünf Stunden 5 gesperrt worden. Bei dem bisher schwersten Serienunfall auf dieser Strecke wurde nach Angaben der Polizei ein Kraftfahrer getötet, 31 Menschen 10 wurden verletzt. Zum ersten Zusammenstoß war es am Vormittag in dichtem Nebel gekommen, als ein Stuttgarter Lastzug auf einen Lastzug aus 15 Iserlohn auffuhr. Dabei wurde der Beifahrer aus Stuttgart tödlich verletzt. Innerhalb weniger Sekunden rasten sechs Personenwagen in die Last- 20 wagentrümmer. Ehe die Polizei den nachfolgenden Verkehr warnen konnte, fuhren immer mehr Wagen in den riesigen Schrotthaufen hinein.   25

° **das Fahrzeug** vehicle
  das Kraftfahrzeug = Auto
° **verwickeln** to wrap up
2 **insgesamt** a total of
9 **der Kraftfahrer** driver
11 **verletzen** to hurt, wound
15 **der Lastzug** truck-trailer rig

20 **die Last** load; **der Lastwagen** truck
21 **die Trümmer** (*pl. only*) the wreck(s), ruins
24 **riesig** gigantic
25 **der Schrotthaufen** scrap heap

1. Expand the headline "117 Fahrzeuge in Unfallserie verwickelt" into a complete sentence. What kind of verbal constructions are possible?

2. Identify and analyze the passive forms in the passage.

Einbruch° in Museum

Noch Unbekannte haben bei einem Einbruch in das Hamelner* Heimatmuseum 40 eiserne Ofenplatten im Wert von etwa 12.000 Mark gestohlen. Nach† ₅ Angaben der Polizei müssen die Einbrecher in der Zeit vom Freitag bis Montag in das Museum eingedrungen sein. Außer den zum größten Teil ₁₀ mit biblischen Motiven dekorierten Platten ließen sie zwei Spinnräder und einen Webstuhl mitgehen.

° **ein·brechen** to break in	9 **ein·dringen** to penetrate, enter
2 = **das Heimatmuseum von Hameln**	12 **mitgehen lassen** euphemism for
3 **eisern** = **aus Eisen; der Ofen** stove	**stehlen**
6 **die Angabe** = **die Information**	13 **weben** to weave, **der Webstuhl**
7 **der Einbrecher** = **der Dieb**	loom

1. Complete the following sentences:
   Über das Wochenende _____ hier _____ worden.
   Noch Unbekannte = Menschen, die _____.
   Nach Angaben der Polizei = Die Polizei _____.
   Sie ließen . . . mitgehen = Sie haben _____.

2. What kind of a phrase is **müssen eingedrungen sein?**

3. Identify the pre-noun insert in the passage; then rewrite it as a relative clause.

Auch BMW will
einen Diesel bauer
H. C. Hamburg

Nach Daimler-Benz, Opel und VW werden nun auch die Bayerischen Motorenwerke (BMW) als vierte deutsche Automobilfabrik Dieselwagen bauen. Der ₅ bayerische Diesel—der Vierzylinder-Motor für Wagen der kleinen 3er- und mittleren 5er-Serie‡ wird zur Zeit in München entwickelt—soll möglicher- ₁₀ weise schon auf der nächsten Frankfurter Automobil-Ausstellung im September vorgestellt werden. Spekulationen über eine neue Zwölfzylinder-Limousine ₁₅ dementierte BMW jedoch: ,,Mit Sicherheit wird es in den nächsten Jahren keinen Serien-BMW mit Zwölfzylinder-Motor geben.''   ₂₀

12 **die Ausstellung** exhibition	16 **jedoch** however
16 **dementieren** to deny	

*The ending **-er** added to the name of a city creates an uninflected adjective with the meaning *from (that city)*. Best-known example: **Frankfurter Würstchen**, the original hot dog. (But don't ask for a ''heisser Hund'' in a German restaurant.)

†The preposition **nach** often means *according to*.

‡**die Serie** series, pronounced *Se'-ri-e* (cf. **Fa-mi-li-e**).

1. The preceding passage contains four sentences with forms of **werden.** Which of these are future and which are passive constructions?

Gotthard-Strecke°*
gesperrt

dp Bern. — Durch einen Erdrutsch auf der Gotthard-Strecke und einen Tunneleinsturz auf der Simplon-Strecke ist seit Samstag der Verkehr in Richtung 5 **Süden stark behindert.**

● Wie ein Sprecher der Generaldirektion der Schweizerischen Bundesbahnen (SBB) in Bern mitteilte, wurde die Unterbre- 10 chung auf dem Gotthard zwischen Chiasso und Mailand durch einen Erdrutsch infolge strömenden Regens verursacht. Die Strecke wurde gesperrt.   15

° **die Strecke**   stretch, line
1 **rutschen**   to slide
3 **einstürzen**   to collapse
10 **mitteilen** = **informieren**
10 **brechen**   to break, rupture

12 **Mailand** = **Milan**
13 **infolge** (*prep. with gen.*)   in consequence of, following
15 **sperren** = **zumachen**

1. Classify the forms **ist . . . behindert**
   wurde . . . verursacht
   wurde . . . gesperrt

2. Rewrite as follows: Ein Erdrutsch behindert _____.
   Die Unterbrechung ist durch _____.
   Die Strecke ist jetzt _____.

3. What is the complete subject of **wurde . . . verursacht?**

1860 Volleyball-Meister†

Schon zwei Spieltage vor Saisonende sicherte sich die Mannschaft von 1860 München† den Titel eines Deutschen Meisters im Volleyball. München liegt 5 uneinholbar und ungeschlagen mit 26:0 Punkten vor dem SSF Bonn† (16:6 Punkte).

2 **sichern**   to secure
2 **die Mannschaft**   team

6 **einholen**   to catch up with
7 **26:0**   read 26 zu 0

*The Gotthard line is the main rail connection between Germany and Italy via Switzerland.
†1860 München and SSF Bonn are names of sports clubs; thus, the title as a complete sentence would read: **Sportverein 1860 München ist Volleyball-Meister.**

II

The following items (information on today's events, a weather report, some soccer scores, and a TV program) are unglossed. You can use these bits of information as the basis for conversations or for short compositions.

Seite 12 · Mittwoch, 12. Februar 1975 · Bremer Nachrichten

Was - Wo - Wann

Heute

Theater: Goetheplatz: „Der Freischütz", 20 Uhr; Kammerspiele: „Meister Pathelin", 20 Uhr; Niederdeutsches Theater: „De Deern is richtig", 20 Uhr; Bremer Zimmertheater: „Warum Haustiere", 20.30 Uhr.

Misere im Städtebau? Diskussion mit Thema „Planung und Ausführung — Architekt und Generalunternehmer" im Gewerbehaus, 18 Uhr.

Konzert der Gitarrenklasse des Konservatoriums, Osterdeich 17, 20 Uhr.

Gemeindenachmittag in St. Martini mit Lichtbildervortrag „Christliche Mission in Mexiko" von Frau Poetsch, 16 Uhr.

Vortrag über Camille Pissarro und Alfred Sisley von Frau Dr. Ulrike Köcke in der Kunsthalle, Am Wall, 20 Uhr.

Knabenchor der Christianskirche Fredericia (Dänemark) singt in Unser Lieben Frauen Kirche unter der Leitung von Poul Johansen, 20 Uhr.

„Elektrisches Kochen an neuzeitlichen Herden", Vortrag in der Hauswirtschaftlichen Beratungsstelle, Carl-Ronning-Straße (Anmeldung Tel. 31 12 03), 15 Uhr,

Das Wetter

Voraussichtliche Wetterlage heute, 7 Uhr

Wetterlage:
Nachdem die europäische Hochdruckzone jetzt weitgehend abgebaut ist, können Ausläufer atlantischer Tiefdruckstörungen auf Nordwestdeutschland übergreifen. Mit ihnen werden feuchte und verhältnismäßig milde Meeresluftmassen herangeführt.

Vorhersage:
Im Weser-Ems-Gebiet heute bei schwachen bis mäßigen Winden aus südlichen Richtungen zu-

meist stark bewölkt bis bedeckt mit kurzen Auflockerungen und gelegentlich etwas Regen. Morgens gebietsweise Nebel. Höchste Tagestemperatur 7 bis 10 Grad, örtlich bei länger anhaltendem Nebel etwa 5 Grad. Nachts frostfrei.

Wetterbeobachtungen auf dem Bremer Flughafen vom 11. Februar, 19.00 Uhr: Ostwind Stärke 2; Luftdruck 1009 Millibar (757 Millimeter); relative Luftfeuchtigkeit 91 Prozent bei 7 Grad; kein Niederschlag; höchste Tagestemperatur 8 Grad; tiefste Temperatur in der Nacht zum Dienstag 3 Grad, am Erdboden 2 Grad.

WINTERSPORT-WETTERBERICHT

Alpen: Kleinwalsertal: fester Altschnee, Ski sehr gut, Schneehöhe 60 cm, —2 Grad; Garmisch: keine Schneedecke, —4 Grad; Zugspitzplatt: Pulverschnee, Ski sehr gut, Schneehöhe über 400 cm, —7 Grad; Mittenwald: aper am Ort, Schneereste, 0 Grad; Wendelstein: Firnschnee, Ski sehr gut, Schneehöhe 80 cm, 0 Grad.

Schwarzwald: Feldberg: Südhänge aper, Ski und Rodel gut, Schneehöhe 150 cm, 2 Grad; Herzogenhorn: Südhänge aper, Ski und Rodel gut, 150 cm, 2 Grad; Schauinsland: fester Altschnee, Ski gut, 50 cm, 2 Grad; Todtnauberg: fester Altschnee, Ski gut, Rodel möglich, 20 cm, 0 Grad.

Sonne: 13. Februar A. 07.48, U. 17.31
Mond: 13. Februar A. 08.02, U. 20.26

Hochwasser:	Bremerhaven	Brake	Vegesack	Bremen
13. Februar	02.39	03.33	04.22	04.34
	15.07	16.01	16.45	16.57

(Deutsches Hydrographisches Institut Hamburg)

DONNERSTAG

 4. November

20.00 **Tagesschau**
20.15 **Pro und Contra**
      Leitung: Emil Obermann
21.00 **Detektiv Rockford: Anruf genügt**
      Täglich eine gute Tat.
      Kriminalfilm mit James Garner, Noah Beery u. a.
21.45 **Titel, Thesen, Temperamente**
      Ein Kulturmagazin
22.30 **Tagesschau**
22.50 **Tischtennis-Europaliga in Trier: Bundesrepublik Deutschland — Schweden**

 4. November

19.00 **heute**
19.30 **Artisten-Cocktail 76**
      Bühne frei für eine internationale Show
21.00 **heute**
21.15 **Journalisten fragen — Politiker antworten**
22.15 **Das kleine Fernsehspiel — Kamerafilm**
      Innenstadt
22.50 **heute**

Bochum – Frankfurt	**3:1**	Saarbrücken – Schalke	**2:3**	Karlsruhe – Köln	**2:1**	München – Hamburg	**6:2**

III

Geld liegt
auf der Piste°

„Ich mache mit, weil es Geld bringt", sagt der Engländer James Hunt, der diese Woche in Japan die Weltmeisterschaft der Formel-I-Rennfahrer gewann. 5

Es bringt ganz gutes Geld. Das Jahres-Salär der Rennfahrer liegt zwischen 120.000 und 150.000 Mark. Das aber ist nur der geringste Teil ihrer Einkommen. Sie verdienen noch 10 mehr, weil sie nicht einfache Rennwagen fahren, sondern Reklametafeln auf Rädern, und

weil sie selber wandelnde Litfaßsäulen sind. 15

Weltmeister James Hunt macht gleichzeitig Reklame für die Zigarettenmarke Marlboro und die Ölfirma Texaco. Die 20 gleichen Verträge wie er hat der Deutsche Jochen Mass. Der Franzose Jacques Lafitte läuft und fährt Reklame für die Zigarettenmarke Gitanes. Der Amerikaner Mario Andretti wirbt 25 für die Zigarettenmarke John Player. Exweltmeister Niki

Lauda und der Schweizer Clay Regazzoni machen mit ihren 30 Ferrari-Rennwagen Reklame für Ferrari. Bei den meisten kommt noch die Werbung für eine Reifenfirma (Goodyear) oder eine Mineralölgesellschaft (Texaco) 35

hinzu.

Insider schätzen, daß die Zigarettenfirma John Player etwa drei Millionen Mark an ihr Rennteam zahlt und die Firma 40 Ferrari sogar noch weitaus mehr.

0 **die Piste** race track; runway
4 **die Meisterschaft** championship
5 **der Rennfahrer** racing driver
10 **gering = klein**
13 **die Reklame = die Werbung** advertisement

15 **die Litfaßsäule** billboard (in the shape of a pillar)
21 **der Vertrag** contract
26 **werben** to advertise for
33 **der (Auto)reifen** tire
37 **schätzen** to estimate

Eine Litfaßsäule in Berlin.

IV

After reading this text, outline the main points in English. You need not produce an exact translation, but merely show that you have understood the gist of the article.

Das Leid der Frau

Wenn es um Frauen im Beruf geht, dann zeigt jede neue Untersuchung die alten unbefriedigenden Zustände. Jede dritte Frau in der Bundesrepublik ist 5 erwerbstätig, doch 77 Prozent von ihnen arbeiten in nur 16 Berufen. 20 Prozent sind Bürofachkräfte oder sogar nur Bürohilfskräfte, und 13 Prozent sind 10

„Warenkaufleute" (also Verkäuferinnen). Den größten An-
teil von Frauen gibt es mit 79
Prozent in der Textil- und Be-
kleidungsbranche (Näherinnen 15
und Verkäuferinnen). Das zeigt
jetzt eine neue Untersuchung
des Nürnberger Instituts für
Arbeitsmarkt- und Berufsfor-
schung. Daraus geht weiter her- 20
vor, daß Frauen in qualifizier-
ten Facharbeiterberufen (Mechaniker, Ingenieure, Chemiker)
unterrepräsentiert sind.

Auch die Zukunftserwartun- 25
gen der Nürnberger Berufsfor-
scher sind für die Frauen kaum
erfreulich. Sie sind der Ansicht,
daß sich die berufliche Situation
der Frauen auch in den nächsten 30
Jahren kaum verbessern wird.
Sie schließen das aus der Tatsache, daß sich in den letzten Jah-

ren mehr als zwei Drittel der
jungen Frauen in ihrer Ausbil- 35
dung auf nur 17 Ausbildungs-
berufe beschränkten. Selbst an
den Hochschulen war die über-
wiegende Mehrheit der Studentinnen in weniger als zehn Pro- 40
zent der möglichen Studienfä-
cher eingeschrieben.

Die geringeren Chancen von
berufstätigen Frauen, in leiten-
de oder aufsichtsführende Posi- 45
tionen aufzusteigen, werden
denn auch von den Nürnberger
Berufsforschern auf mangelnde
Voraussetzungen in der Ausbildung zurückgeführt. So habe 50
nur jede dritte berufstätige Frau
eine betriebliche Ausbildung
absolviert; nur eine von hundert
Frauen verfüge über einen
Hochschulabschluß.   55

2 **die Untersuchung** investigation;
  study
3 **befriedigen** to satisfy
6 **erwerbstätig** employed
28 **die Ansicht** opinion
32 **schließen** to conclude

37 **beschränken** to limit
42 **einschreiben** to matriculate
48 **mangelnde Voraussetzungen** lacking prerequisites
49 **die Ausbildung** training

V

Zunft ohne Zukunft?

This article deals with the plight of small neighborhood retail grocers in the Federal
Republic who are fighting a losing battle against retail chains and branch stores of
major retailers. Using the example of one **Einzelhändler**, a man named Herbert Bondas
in Hamburg, the author discusses advantages and disadvantages of this vanishing kind
of small business.

You should be able to comprehend the text quite readily even without glosses. The following, somewhat specialized vocabulary will help. The words are listed in the order of
their occurrence in the text.

die Zunft,⸚e	guild, trade, profession
der Einzelhandel	retail trade
der Einzelhändler,-	independent retailer
der Lebensmittelladen,⸚	grocery store
die Lebensmittel (*pl. only*)	food, groceries, victuals

die Filiale,-n	branch
der Kettenladen,:	chain store
die Ladenkette,-n	chain of stores
der Kunde,-n	customer
der Großhändler,-	wholesaler
die Buchhaltung	bookkeeping
die Branche,-n	line of business
der Unternehmer,-	entrepreneur
der Arbeitnehmer,-	employee
der Arbeitgeber,-	employer
der Angestellte,-n	(white-collar) employee
der Rentner,-	pensioner
abhängig	dependent
das Griebenschmalz	lard
Pleite gehen	to go bankrupt, to fold (*colloq.*)
die Gemeinde,-n	community
der Nachwuchs	young generation going into the same line of business (from **nach** + **wachsen**)
der Umsatz	turnover, sales
die Baugenehmigung,-en	building permit
der Wettbewerb	competition
die Steuer,-n	tax

WELT am SONNTAG · Nr. 44 · Seite 9 Sonntag, 31. Oktober 1976

Zunft ohne Zukunft?
In dieser Woche fordern die
Einzelhändler Hilfe fürs Überleben
Von HANS JÜRGEN TROCHA **Hamburg/Bonn**

Morgens um 7, wenn anderswo der Wecker schellt, ist für Herbert Bondas, 48, der Arbeitstag schon zwei Stunden alt— auch samstags. Kurz nach fünf 5 Uhr steht er auf. Wenn er um sieben die Tür seines Lebensmittelladens an der Osterstraße im Hamburger Stadtteil Elmsbüttel aufschließt, dann hat er schon 10 vom Milch- und Brotlieferanten die Ware für den Tag entgegengenommen.

Um neun Uhr, wenn die meisten der sechs Supermärkte, 15 Warenhausfilialen, Ketten- und Discountläden in seiner Umgebung gerade öffnen, dann hat Herbert Bondas schon ein halbes Hundert Kunden bedient. 20

Abends um sechs, freitags um halb acht, wenn er seine Ladentür wieder verschließt, ist für ihn der Arbeitstag noch lange nicht zu Ende. Dreimal in der 25 Woche besteigt er anschließend seinen Kombiwagen, um bei Großhändlern einzukaufen. Später und an den anderen Abenden muß er sich um die 30 Buchhaltung kümmern. Und am Samstag ist sein Laden auch

noch einmal bis 12 Uhr geöff-
net.

Herbert Bondas ist der typische Vertreter eines allmählich
aussterbenden freien Berufes. 5
Sein Geschäft ist das, was innerhalb und außerhalb der Branche
eher liebevoll als verächtlich
ein „Tante-Emma-Laden" ge-
nannt wird.   10

Die Freiheit, sein eigener Un-
ternehmer zu sein, verlangt von
Herbert Bondas und seinesglei-
chen härtere Opfer als Arbeitnehmer für ihren Beruf zu er-   15
bringen pflegen. 70 und mehr
Arbeitsstunden pro Woche sind
die Regel—wie bei Herbert Bondas. Bei ihm ist das so, seit er
hinter der Ladentheke steht—   20
seit 1954, also schon 22 Jahre
lang. Urlaub hat er nie gemacht.

Solche Opfer zahlen sich für
die meisten Einzelhändler nicht
einmal aus. Zwischen 20 000 25
und 30 000 Mark im Jahr bleibt
dem Einzelhändler im Durch-
schnitt als Überschuß. Die meisten können das gleiche auch als
Angestellte verdienen. Und da- 30

bei ist in dem Verdienst die
Mitarbeit der Familie nicht einmal berücksichtigt.

Denn ohne deren Mithilfe
könnten die Tante-Emma-Läden 35
gar nicht existieren. Bei Herbert
Bondas sind es die Eltern, die
mitarbeiten. Beide sind Rentner.
Die Mutter steht mit im Laden,
der Vater ordnet das Lager. 40
Auch Bondas' Frau muß dreimal in der Woche im Laden aus-
helfen. Sohn Gregor, 6, geht
dann zur anderen Oma.

Trotz allem gibt Herbert Bon- 45
das seinen Laden nicht auf, er
schließt sich nicht einmal einer
der großen Ladenketten an.
„Ich will nicht abhängig, will
nicht Filialleiter sein", sagt er. 50
Drei Angebote von Großunter-
nehmen hat er schon abgelehnt.

So wie auch in allen anderen
Tante-Emma-Läden wird in
Bondas' Geschäft jeder Kunde 55
beraten und immer freundlich
bedient. Bondas hat stets Zeit
für ein Gespräch mit seinen
Kunden. Bei ihnen schnarrt
auch keine eilige Computer- 60

Nach einem zwölfstündigen Arbeitstag erledigt Herbert Bondas im Zimmer
hinter seinem Laden die Buchhaltung.

Ein deutscher Einzelhändler: Herbert Bondas mit seiner Frau vor seinem Lebensmittelgeschäft in Hamburg-Elmsbüttel. Er ist typisch für 100 000 Ladenbesitzer in der Bundesrepublik: FOTOS: JURGEN WIECHMANN

Registrierkasse, über der Tür bimmelt wie anno 1900 die Ladenglocke.

Feuerholz gibt es bei ihm immer noch, auch lose Butter und 5 lose Milch. Früher verkaufte er davon 300 Liter am Tag, heute sind es nur noch 20. ,,Aber da kann der Kunde auch mal einen Viertelliter kaufen und muß 10 nicht immer gleich einen ganzen im Plastikschlauch mitnehmen'', meint Bondas. 15 Pfennig billiger pro Liter ist die lose Milch außerdem noch. Grieben- 15 schmalz ist immer vorrätig, es wird in der Küche hinter dem Laden ausgelassen. Und Käse, den er fünf Monate hat lagern lassen, damit er mild ist und 20 nicht so schmeckt wie der aus dem Paket im Supermarkt.

Natürlich kommt es vor, daß Kunden klagen, weil sie im Supermarkt billigere Waren ent- 25 deckt haben. ,,Doch im Grunde wissen die Leute, daß sie bei mir reell bedient werden'', sagt Herbert Bondas.

Bislang hat sich die Bundesre- 30 gierung geweigert, in den Wettbewerb im Einzelhandel einzugreifen. Inzwischen aber fordern auch neutrale Marktbeobachter, nicht nur die Interessenvertreter 35 des Einzelhandels, eine Intervention des Staates. So plädiert der Augsburger Professor Paul W. Meyer für einen staatlichen Schutz der kleinen Einzelhänd- 40 ler gegen die Macht der großen, durch die der Wettbewerb tatsächlich verhindert werde.

Inzwischen schließen in diesem Jahr wieder 8000 Kollegen 45 von Herbert Bondas ihre Ladentür—endgültig.

Exercises

A. Change the following short sentences from the active voice to the actional passive. Do not change the tense. Omit the subject (**man**) of the active sentence.

> **Man brachte ihn zurück.**   **Er wurde zurückgebracht.**

SEE
ANALYSIS
180
(p. 563)

1. Man führte uns durch den Garten.
2. Man trennte die Kinder von ihren Eltern.
3. Um acht Uhr schloß man das Tor.
4. Mich nimmt man nie mit.
5. Man suchte ihn, aber man fand ihn nicht.
6. Man schickte ihn nach Hause.
7. Man hielt ihn für einen Spion und erschoß ihn.
8. Man brachte uns im Löwen unter.
9. Man hat uns wieder im Löwen untergebracht.
10. Man hat ihn schon wieder gebeten, eine Rede zu halten.

B. In the following sentences, change the present actional passive forms into (a) present statal passive forms and (b) perfect actional passive forms.

> **Die Stadt wird zerstört.**   (a) **Die Stadt ist zerstört.**
>   (b) **Die Stadt ist zerstört worden.**

SEE
ANALYSIS
181
(p. 565)

1. Die Brücke wird schon gebaut.
2. Die Schweine werden gefüttert.
3. Der Brief wird schon geschrieben.
4. Es wird beschlossen.
5. Es wird gefunden.
6. Die Tür wird geschlossen.

C. Change the following active sentences into actional passive sentences. Omit the subject of the active sentence.

> **Wir zeigen den Film jetzt auch in Deutschland.**
> **Der Film wird jetzt auch in Deutschland gezeigt.**

SEE
ANALYSIS
180–181
(pp. 563–565)

1. In den Vereinigten Staaten trinkt man mehr Bier als in Deutschland.
2. Mich lädt nie jemand ein.
3. In unserem Elternhaus haben wir viel musiziert.
4. Kolumbus hat Amerika 1492 entdeckt.
5. Sie konnten nur wenige retten.
6. Wann hat Ihr Vater denn dieses Haus gebaut?

D. In the following sentences, supply **von**, **mit**, or **durch**.

1. Die Stadt wurde _____ ein Erdbeben völlig zerstört.
2. Die Stadt wurde _____ einen Bombenangriff völlig zerstört.
3. Die Stadt wurde _____ den Russen zerstört.

4. Er ist _____ einem Stein erschlagen worden.
5. Er ist _____ seinem Bruder erschlagen worden.
6. Der Brief ist mir _____ meinem Vater nachgeschickt worden.
7. Er hat den Brief zwar unterschrieben, aber der Brief ist nicht _____ ihm selbst geschrieben worden.
8. Er hat alle seine Briefe _____ der Schreibmaschine geschrieben.
9. Ich wurde _____ meinem Chef nach Afrika geschickt.
10. Amerika ist _____ Kolumbus _____ Zufall entdeckt worden.

SEE ANALYSIS 184 (p. 567)

E. In the following sentences, supply either a form of **werden** or a form of **sein.**

1. Daß die Erde sich um die Sonne bewegt, _____ schon lange bewiesen.
2. Die Stadt _____ im Jahre 1944 zerstört.
3. Im Jahre 1950 _____ die Stadt noch nicht wieder aufgebaut.
4. Der weiße Mercedes _____ schon verkauft.
5. Das Haus neben der Kirche soll nächste Woche verkauft _____.
6. Der Film hat mir gar nicht gefallen. Ich _____ wirklich enttäuscht.

SEE ANALYSIS 181 (p. 565)

F. Change the following relative clauses into pre-noun inserts.

1. Der Zug, der soeben aus München angekommen ist, fährt in zehn Minuten weiter.
2. Für einen jungen Menschen, der in einem Dorf in den bayerischen Alpen großgeworden ist, ist es nicht leicht, sich an die Großstadt zu gewöhnen.
3. Hans ist jetzt Arzt, aber sein Bruder, der viel intelligenter ist, hat nie seinen Doktor gemacht.
4. Ingrids Vater war ein Architekt, der auch in Amerika bekannt war.
5. Die Städte, die während des Krieges zerstört wurden, sind heute fast alle wieder aufgebaut.
6. Die Boeing-Maschinen, die in Amerika gebaut werden, sieht man heute auf allen deutschen Flughäfen.
7. Der Juwelendieb, der seit Wochen von der Polizei gesucht wird, soll gestern in München gesehen worden sein.
8. Der Preis, der für diesen Rembrandt bezahlt worden ist, ist nach meiner Meinung viel zu hoch.
9. Seine Mutter, die noch immer in Berlin wohnte, hatte er seit Jahren nicht gesehen.
10. Er sah sie mit einem Blick an, der viel sagte.

SEE ANALYSIS 187 (p. 571)

G. Composition.

Pick one of the topics you discussed in the conversation sections of Unit 17 or 18 and write a brief summary.

Vocabulary

abhängig	dependent	**aufgrund** (*prep. with gen.*)	on the basis of
ändern	to change, to alter		
das Angebot, -e	offer; supply	**aufschließen**	to open, unlock
Angebot und Nachfrage	supply and demand	**beachten**	to notice, take note of
		beob'achten	to observe
der Arbeitnehmer, -	employee	**beraten**	to advise, counsel
der Arbeitgeber, -	employer	**beurteilen**	to judge

sich (*acc.*) bewegen	to move	lose Butter	butter in bulk
blitzen	to lighten	lösen	to solve; to dissolve
der Blitz, -e	lightning	die Macht, ⸚e	might; power
der Chef, -s	boss; chief; chef	der Marktplatz, ⸚e	market square
der Küchenchef, -s	chef	mio (*abbrev. for*	million
der Einfluß, die	influence	Million)	
Einflüsse		der Nachteil, -e	disadvantage
der Einwohner, -	inhabitant	nun	now
(*abbr.* Ew.)		nützen	to be of use
endgültig	final(ly), for good	nützlich	useful
enttäuschen	to disappoint	die Oma, -s	grandma
entwickeln	to develop	der Opa, -s	grandpa
erfinden	to invent	das Rathaus, ⸚er	town hall, city hall
der Fahrgast, ⸚e	passenger	der Raum, ⸚e	room; space
feststellen	to notice, find out; to	die Regel, -n	rule
	determine	in der Regel	as a rule, normally
der Flug, ⸚e	flight	regelmäßig	regular
der Fluggast, ⸚e	(airline) passenger	schätzen	to estimate
füllen	to fill	schließen	to close; to end; to
überfüllt	overcrowded		conclude
das Gas, -e	gas	schützen	to protect
gebären	to give birth to	der Schutz	protection
geboren werden	to be born	senden	to send; to broadcast
er ist 1962 geboren	he was born in	der Sender, -	radio station,
	1962		transmitter
gering	small	die Sendung, -en	broadcast, trans-
geringer	smaller, lesser		mission
geringst-	least	soweit (*conj.*)	as far as
gestatten	to permit	sperren	to close, shut off
gewöhnlich	usual	die Steuer, -n	tax
gleichzeitig	at the same time,	stoßen	to push, to shove; to
	simultaneous		strike
der Handel, ⸚e	trade	zusammenstoßen	to collide
der Einzelhandel	retail trade	die Strecke, -n	stretch, section
der Einzelhändler, -	retailer	die Tafel, -n	(bill)board, blackboard
der Großhändler, -	wholesaler	die Tatsache, -n	fact
heizen	to heat	trennen	to separate
infolge (*prep. with*	as a result of, following	überraschen	to surprise
gen.)		das Unglück, -e	bad luck, misfortune,
insgesamt	a total of; all in all		adversity,
der Kaufmann, *pl.* die	merchant; business-		calamity
Kaufleute	man; business	unterschreiben	to sign (a letter, docu-
	administrator		ment, etc.)
der Kunde, -n	customer	sich (*acc.*) verändern	to change
der Laden, ⸚	store, shop	das Verbrechen, -	crime
die Last, -en	load	der Verbrecher, -	criminal
der Lastwagen, -	truck	der Vertrag, ⸚e	contract; treaty
der Lastzug, ⸚e	trailer rig	vertrauen	to trust
am Leben sein	to be alive	das Vertrauen	trust
lose	loose, unpackaged	das Mißtrauen	distrust

der Vertreter, -	representative	das Werk, -e	work; opus; factory
der Vorteil, -e	advantage	das Kunstwerk, -e	work of art
werben	to advertise	die Zeitschrift, -en	magazine; journal
die Werbung, -en	advertisement	der Zustand, ¨e	state (of affairs)

Additional Vocabulary

der Abschluß, die	conclusion	das Festspiel, -e	festival
Abschlüsse		großwerden	to grow up
angreifen	to attack	hageln	to hail
der Angriff, -e	attack	der Herd, -e	stove
die Ansicht, -en	view, opinion	der Kombiwagen, -	station wagon
aufbauen	to construct	musizieren	to make music
wiederaufbauen	to reconstruct	das Pulver, -	(gun)powder
die Auflage, -n	printing (of a book)	reell'(pronounced	honest, reputable
auslassen	to render (fat)	re-ell')	
sich (acc.) betrinken	to get drunk	reell bedient	to get good value
die Bombe, -n	bomb	werden	for your money
dementieren	to deny	die Saison	season
das Erdbeben, -	earthquake	der Spion, -e	spy
erschießen	to shoot (dead); to	das Tor, -e	gate
	execute	der Überschuß	(net) gain
erschlagen	to slay, kill	der Warteraum, ¨e	waiting room, lounge

Strong Verbs

angreifen		griff an	angegriffen	to attack
aufschließen		schloß auf	aufgeschlossen	to unlock
beraten	berät	beriet	beraten	to advise
sich betrinken		betrank	betrunken	to get drunk
erfinden		erfand	erfunden	to invent
erschießen		erschoß	erschossen	to shoot
erschlagen	erschlägt	erschlug	erschlagen	to slay
gebären	gebiert	gebar	geboren	to bear
schließen		schloß	geschlossen	to close
stoßen	stösst	stieß	gestoßen	to push
unterschreiben		unterschrieb	unterschrieben	to sign
werben	wirbt	warb	geworben	to advertise

Appendix

Principal Parts of Strong Verbs and Irregular Weak Verbs

This table does not contain most compound verbs, since their principal parts are the same as those of the basic verbs. Thus, if you want to look up the forms of **ausgehen,** look under **gehen** and supply the additional information yourself:

gehen	**ging**	**ist gegangen**	to go
ausgehen	**ging aus**	**ist ausgegangen**	to go out

The table also does not show which verbs can or must be used with reflexive pronouns, nor does it show the use of prepositions with these verbs. For all such information, refer to the vocabulary beginning on p. **A6.**

Present-tense forms are listed only for those verbs that change the stem vowel in the second- and third-person singular or, as with the modals and **wissen,** in all three singular forms. The word **ist** indicates that **sein** is used as the auxiliary in the perfect tense. All other verbs use **haben.** Words in parentheses are alternate forms.

INFINITIVE	PRESENT	PAST	AUX.	PERFECT	
anbieten		**bot an**		**angeboten**	to offer
anfangen	**fängt an**	**fing an**		**angefangen**	to start
angreifen		**griff an**		**angegriffen**	to attack
backen	**(bäckt)**	**backte (buk)**		**gebacken**	to bake
befehlen	**befiehlt**	**befahl**		**befohlen**	to command
beginnen		**begann**		**begonnen**	to begin
bekommen		**bekam**		**bekommen**	to receive
beraten	**berät**	**beriet**		**beraten**	to advise
beschließen		**beschloß**		**beschlossen**	to decide
beschreiben		**beschrieb**		**beschrieben**	to describe
bestehen		**bestand**		**bestanden**	to consist
beweisen		**bewies**		**bewiesen**	to prove
bitten		**bat**		**gebeten**	to ask
bleiben		**blieb**	ist	**geblieben**	to stay
braten	**brät**	**briet**		**gebraten**	to roast
brechen	**bricht**	**brach**	(ist)	**gebrochen**	to break
bringen		**brachte**		**gebracht**	to bring
denken		**dachte**		**gedacht**	to think
dürfen	**darf**	**durfte**		**gedurft**	to be permitted
einladen	**lädt ein**	**lud ein**		**eingeladen**	to invite
empfangen	**empfängt**	**empfing**		**empfangen**	to receive
empfehlen	**empfiehlt**	**empfahl**		**empfohlen**	to recommend
enthalten	**enthält**	**enthielt**		**enthalten**	to contain

INFINITIVE	PRESENT	PAST	AUX.	PERFECT	
entscheiden		entschied		entschieden	to determine
entschließen		entschloß		entschlossen	to decide
entstehen		entstand	ist	entstanden	to originate
erfahren	erfährt	erfuhr		erfahren	to find out
erfinden		erfand		erfunden	to invent
erhalten	erhält	erhielt		erhalten	to receive
erkennen		erkannte		erkannt	to recognize
erscheinen		erschien	ist	erschienen	to appear
erschießen		erschoß		erschossen	to shoot
erschlagen	erschlägt	erschlug		erschlagen	to slay
erschrecken	erschrickt	erschrak	ist	erschrocken	to be scared
ertrinken		ertrank	ist	ertrunken	to drown
erwerben	erwirbt	erwarb		erworben	to acquire
erziehen		erzog		erzogen	to educate
essen	ißt	aß		gegessen	to eat
fahren	fährt	fuhr	ist	gefahren	to drive
fallen	fällt	fiel	ist	gefallen	to fall
fangen	fängt	fing		gefangen	to catch
finden		fand		gefunden	to find
fliegen		flog	ist	geflogen	to fly
fliehen		floh	ist	geflohen	to flee
fließen		floß	ist	geflossen	to flow
fressen	frißt	fraß		gefressen	to eat
frieren		fror		gefroren	to freeze
gebären	gebiert	gebar		geboren	to give birth
geben	gibt	gab		gegeben	to give
gefallen	gefällt	gefiel		gefallen	to be pleasing
gehen		ging	ist	gegangen	to go
gelingen		gelang	ist	gelungen	to succeed
gelten	gilt	galt		gegolten	to be valid
geschehen	geschieht	geschah	ist	geschehen	to happen
gewinnen		gewann		gewonnen	to win
gießen		goß		gegossen	to pour
graben	gräbt	grub		gegraben	to dig
haben	hat	hatte		gehabt	to have
halten	hält	hielt		gehalten	to hold
hängen		hing		gehangen	to hang
heben		hob		gehoben	to lift
heißen		hieß		geheißen	to be called
helfen	hilft	half		geholfen	to help
kennen		kannte		gekannt	to know
klingen		klang		geklungen	to sound
kommen		kam	ist	gekommen	to come
können	kann	konnte		gekonnt	to be able
lassen	läßt	ließ		gelassen	to let
laufen	läuft	lief	ist	gelaufen	to run
leiden		litt		gelitten	to suffer
leihen		lieh		geliehen	to lend
lesen	liest	las		gelesen	to read

INFINITIVE	PRESENT	PAST	AUX.	PERFECT	
liegen		lag	(ist)*	gelegen	to lie
lügen		log		gelogen	to tell a lie
messen	mißt	maß		gemessen	to measure
mögen	mag	mochte		gemocht	to like
müssen	muß	mußte		gemußt	to have to
nehmen	nimmt	nahm		genommen	to take
nennen		nannte		genannt	to call
raten	rät	riet		geraten	to advise
rennen		rannte	ist	gerannt	to run
riechen		roch		gerochen	to smell
rufen		rief		gerufen	to call
schaffen		schuf		geschaffen	to create
scheiden		schied	(ist)	geschieden	to separate
scheinen		schien		geschienen	to appear
schieben		schob		geschoben	to push
schlafen	schläft	schlief		geschlafen	to sleep
schlagen	schlägt	schlug		geschlagen	to beat
schließen		schloß		geschlossen	to close
schneiden		schnitt		geschnitten	to cut
schreiben		schrieb		geschrieben	to write
schreien		schrie		geschrien	to scream
schweigen		schwieg		geschwiegen	to be silent
schwimmen		schwamm	ist	geschwommen	to swim
sehen	sieht	sah		gesehen	to see
sein	ist	war	ist	gewesen	to be
senden		sandte (sendete)		gesandt (gesendet)	to send
singen		sang		gesungen	to sing
sinken		sank	ist	gesunken	to sink
sitzen		saß	(ist)*	gesessen	to sit
sprechen	spricht	sprach		gesprochen	to speak
springen		sprang	ist	gesprungen	to jump
stehen		stand	(ist)*	gestanden	to stand
stehlen	stiehlt	stahl		gestohlen	to steal
steigen		stieg	ist	gestiegen	to climb
sterben	stirbt	starb	ist	gestorben	to die
stoßen	stößt	stieß		gestoßen	to push
streichen		strich		gestrichen	to spread
tragen	trägt	trug		getragen	to carry
treffen	trifft	traf		getroffen	to meet
treten	tritt	trat		getreten	to step
trinken		trank		getrunken	to drink
tun		tat		getan	to do
unterbrechen	unterbricht	unterbrach		unterbrochen	to interrupt
unterscheiden		unterschied		unterschieden	to distinguish
verbieten		verbot		verboten	to forbid
verbinden		verband		verbunden	to connect

*Austrians tend to use **liegen**, **sitzen**, and **stehen** with **sein** rather than with **haben**.

INFINITIVE	PRESENT	PAST	AUX.	PERFECT	
verbringen		verbrachte		verbracht	to spend time
verderben	verdirbt	verdarb	(ist)	verdorben	to spoil
vergessen	vergißt	vergaß		vergessen	to forget
verlassen	verläßt	verließ		verlassen	to leave
verlieren		verlor		verloren	to lose
verschwinden		verschwand	ist	verschwunden	to disappear
versprechen	verspricht	versprach		versprochen	to promise
verstehen		verstand		verstanden	to understand
vertreiben		vertrieb		vertrieben	to displace
verwenden		verwandte (verwendete)		verwandt (verwendet)	to use
verzeihen		verzieh		verziehen	to forgive
vorschlagen	schlägt vor	schlug vor		vorgeschlagen	to propose
wachsen	wächst	wuchs	ist	gewachsen	to grow
waschen	wäscht	wusch		gewaschen	to wash
werben	wirbt	warb		geworben	to advertise
werden	wird	wurde	ist	geworden	to become
werfen	wirft	warf		geworfen	to throw
wissen	weiß	wüßte		gewußt	to know
zerbrechen	zerbricht	zerbrach		zerbrochen	to break
ziehen		zog		gezogen	to pull
ziehen		zog	ist	gezogen	to move
zwingen		zwang		gezwungen	to force

Vocabulary: German-English

This vocabulary is intended primarily for quick reference; it is not meant to be a substitute for a dictionary of the German language. The English equivalents given here do not include all the meanings of the corresponding German words that are found in a German dictionary. Most of the translations are limited to the meanings in which the German words are used in this book. Some low-frequency words which occur in the reading sections and are translated there have not been included here.

NOUNS

All nouns are listed with the definite article to indicate their gender:

der Mann, ̈er   die Frau, -en   das Kind, -er

Nouns for which no plural form is shown are not normally used in the plural.

ACCENTUATION

Accent marks are used whenever the pronunciation of a word deviates from the standard German stress pattern (e.g., **das Thea′ter**). If the stress shifts to another syllable in the plural, the entire plural form is given (e.g., **der Dok′tor, die Dokto′ren**). Stress is not indicated for words in which the first syllable is an unaccented prefix such as **be-** or **er-**.

VERBS

All strong verbs and irregular weak verbs are indicated by an asterisk (e.g., ***kommen**). Their principal parts can be found in the list of strong verbs and irregular weak verbs (p. **A2**), but note that not all verbs are listed there; compounds such as **mitfahren** can be looked up under **fahren**.

In compound verbs written as one word, a dot between complement and verb (e.g., **aus•gehen, nach•denken**) indicates that the two parts are separated in the present and past tenses (**er geht aus, er denkt nach**).

With reflexive verbs, the case of the pronoun is given, as with **sich** (*acc.*) **freuen**; most occasional reflexives such as **zeigen** are not indicated.

ABBREVIATIONS

abbrev.	= abbreviation	*conj.*	= conjunction
acc.	= accusative	*dat.*	= dative
adv.	= adverb	*demonstr.*	= demonstrative
colloq.	= colloquial	*gen.*	= genitive

impers.	= impersonal	*refl.*	= reflexive
indef.	= indefinite	*rel. pron.*	= relative pronoun
intrans.	= intransitive	*sent. adv.*	= sentence adverb
pers.	= person, personal	*sing.*	= singular
pl.	= plural	*trans.*	= transitive
prep.	= preposition		

ab off

ab und zu now and then, occasionally

der Abend, -e evening

abends in the evening, evenings

Guten Abend good evening

das Abendessen, - supper

aber but, however

*****ab•fahren** to leave, depart (on schedule)

die Abfahrt, -en departure (by car, train, etc.)

der Abflug, ̈e departure (by plane)

*****ab•gehen von** (*dat.*) to leave (school), to graduate

ab•hängen to detach a (railway) car, to uncouple

*****ab•hängen von** to depend upon

abhängig dependent

ab•holen to pick up (at station, airport)

das Abitur' final examination in secondary school

der Abiturient', -en *Gymnasium* graduate

die Abkürzung, -en abbreviation

*****ab•nehmen** to decrease, decline, diminish; to lose weight; to wane (moon)

ab•reisen to leave, depart

*****ab•schließen** to close, to lock up; to terminate; to conclude

der Abschluß, die Abschlüsse conclusion

die Absicht, -en intention

ach oh

ach so oh, I see

acht eight

acht Tage a week; eight days

achtzehn eighteen

achtzig eighty

der Acker, ̈e field

das Ackerland farmland

adäquat' adequate, sufficient

(das) Afrika Africa

(das) Ägyp'ten Egypt

ähnlich similar

alemannisch Alemannic

der Akade'miker, - university graduate

der Akt, -e act

der Akzent', -e accent

akzeptieren to accept

alle all, all of us

allein alone

allerdings however

alles everything, all

das Allgäu region in the German Alps

allgemein general

im allgemeinen generally

die Allgemeinbildung general education

die Alpen Alps

das Alphabet', -e alphabet

als as; when; than

als ob, als wenn as if

also (*sent. adv.*) therefore; well; in other words

alt old

das Altenheim, -e old-age home

altmodisch old-fashioned

die Altstadt, ̈e old city

(das) Amerika America

amerikanisch American

der Amerikaner, - American (male)

die Amerikanerin, -nen American (female)

die Amerikanis'tik American Studies

die Ampel, -n traffic light

sich (*acc.*) **amüsieren** to amuse oneself, have fun

an (*prep.*) at, on

*****an•gehen** to go on

die Ananas, - pineapple

*****an•bieten** to offer

ander- different, other

ändern to change; to alter

sich (*acc.*) **ändern** to change

*****an•fangen** to begin, start

der Anfang, ̈e beginning

der Anfänger, - beginner

das Angebot, -e offer; supply

Angebot und Nachfrage supply and demand

angenehm pleasant

die Anglis'tik English Studies

*****an•greifen** to attack

der Angriff, -e attack

die Angst, ̈e fear, anxiety

Angst haben vor (*dat.*) to be afraid of

der Anker, - anchor

verankern to fasten; to anchor

an•klagen to accuse

der Angeklagte, -n the accused

an•klopfen to knock (on a door)

*****an•kommen** to arrive

*****an•kommen auf** to depend on

das kommt darauf an that depends

die Ankunft, ⸚e arrival

an•machen to switch on (light)

an•melden to announce; to place (a phone call)

sich (*acc.*) **anmelden** to register (in a hotel)

*an•nehmen** to assume

*an•rufen** to call (on the telephone)

sich (*acc.*) **an•schnallen** to fasten (seatbelt), to buckle in

*an•sehen** to look at

*sich** (*dat.*) **etwas an•sehen** to look at something

die Ansicht, -en view, opinion

*an•steigen** to climb, increase (prices, population)

anstrengend strenuous

der Anthropolo'ge, -n anthropologist

antworten to answer

antworten auf (*acc.*) to reply to, to answer (a letter)

die Antwort, -en answer

*an•wenden** to use, to apply

*sich** (*acc.*) **anziehen** to dress; to get dressed

der Apfel, ⸚e apple

die Apothe'ke, -n pharmacy

der Apparat', -e apparatus; instrument; machine

am Apparat speaking (phone)

der Photoapparat, -e camera

der Appetit' (*no pl.*) appetite

die Apriko'se, -n apricot

der April' April

ara'bisch Arabian, Arabic

arbeiten to work

die Arbeit, -en work

der Arbeiter, - (blue-collar) worker; workingman

der Arbeitgeber, - employer

der Arbeitnehmer, - employee, worker

arbeitslos unemployed

der Arbeitsplatz, ⸚e place of work

das Arbeitszimmer, - study

die Archäologie' archaeology

der Architekt', -en architect

die Architektur', -en architecture

sich (*acc.*) **ärgern über** to be annoyed by, put out; to be mad at

arm poor

der Arm, -e arm

die Armee', -n army

der Arti'kel, - article

der Arzt, ⸚e physician, doctor (male)

die Ärztin, -nen physician (female)

(das) Asien Asia

der Assistent', -en assistant

die Assisten'tin, -nen assistant

die Assistentenstelle, -n assistantship

der Ast, ⸚e branch (of a tree)

atmen to breathe

die Aubergine, -n eggplant (pronounced as in French)

auch also, too

auf on

auf•bauen to construct

wiederauf•bauen to reconstruct

*auf•bleiben** to stay up; to stay awake

der Aufenthalt, -e stay, residence

auf•führen to perform, put on (a play)

die Aufführung, -en performance

*auf•gehen** to open; to rise (sun, moon)

aufgeregt excited

aufgrund (*prep. with gen.*) on the basis of

auf•hören to stop, cease

die Auflage, -n printing (of a book)

die Aufnahme, -n photograph, picture, shot

aufrecht upright

sich (*acc.*) **auf•regen** to get excited

*auf•schliessen** to open, unlock

*auf•sein** to be up (and out of bed)

*auf•stehen** to get up (out of bed), to rise

auf•wachen to wake up

aufwärts up, upward

talaufwärts up the valley

auf•weichen to soften

*auf•weisen** to show, to present

der Aufzug, ⸚e elevator

das Auge, -n eye

der Augenblick, -e moment, instant

(einen) Augenblick, bitte just a moment, please

der August' (month of) August

im August' in August

Au'gust (*pers. name*) Augustus, Gus

aus (*prep.*) out of

aus (*adj.*) over

das Spiel ist aus the game is over

die Ausbildung, -en training

die Ausfahrt, -en exit, off-ramp

aus•dehnen to extend

der Ausflug, ⸚e excursion

der Schulausflug, ⸚e school excursion, field trip

der Ausgang, ⸚e exit

*aus•geben** to give out; to spend (money)

*aus•gehen** to go out

mir war das Geld ausgegangen I had spent all my money

*aus•graben** to dig out

*aus•kommen mit** (*dat.*) to get along with

die Auskunft, ⸚e information

das Ausland (*no pl.*) foreign countries

im Ausland abroad; out of the country

der Ausländer, - foreigner

ausländisch foreign

*aus•lassen** to render (fat)

aus•machen to switch off (light)

aus•probieren to try out

ausreichend sufficient

sich (*acc.*) **aus•ruhen** to rest

*sich** (*acc.*) **aus•schlafen** to get enough sleep

*aus•sehen** to appear, look

außer (*prep. with dat.*) besides, except for

außer sich beside oneself

ich bin außer mir I am beside myself

außerdem moreover, in addition

außerhalb (*prep. with gen.*) outside of

*aus•sprechen** to pronounce

die Aussprache, -n pronunciation

die Ausspracheübung, -en pronunciation exercise

*aus•steigen** to get off (a train, etc.), deplane, disembark

aus•stellen to show, to exhibit

*aus•sterben** to die out

aus•suchen to select, pick out

aus•tauschen to exchange

der Austausch, -e exchange

(das) Australien Australia

ausverkauft sold out

der Ausweis, -e identification paper, I.D. card

aus•wischen to wipe out

*aus•ziehen** to move out

*sich** (*acc.*) **ausziehen** to undress

das Auto, -s car, automobile

das Automobil, -e car

die Autobahn, -en super-highway, freeway, turn-pike

der Autobus, -se bus

der Autounfall, -̈e car accident

automatisch automatic

der Bach, -̈e stream, brook

backen to bake

der Bäcker, - baker

die Bäckerei, -en bakery

baden to bathe, to swim

baden gehen to go swimming

das Bad, -̈er bath; bathroom

der Badeort, -e resort, spa

die Badewanne, -n bathtub

die Bahn, -en track; car (on track)

die Autobahn, -en freeway

die Eisenbahn, -en railroad

die Straßenbahn, -en streetcar

der Bahnhof, die Bahnhöfe railway station

der Bahnsteig, -e platform (in station)

bald soon

baldig (*adj.*) soon

auf baldiges Wiedersehen (hoping to) see you again soon

der Ball, -̈e ball

Fußball soccer

das Fußballspiel, -e soccer game

Korbball basketball

die Banane, -n banana

die Bank, -̈e bench

die Bank, -en bank

die Bar, -s bar, tavern

basieren auf (*dat.*) to be based on

der Bauch, -̈e stomach, belly

bauen to build

der Bau, die Bauten construction; building

das Bauwerk, -e building

die Baufirma, die Baufirmen construction firm

der Ackerbau agriculture

der Weinbau wine-growing, viticulture

der Bauer, -n farmer

die Bäuerin, -nen farmer's wife

bäuerlich rural

der Bauernhof, -̈e farm

der Baum, -̈e tree

(das) Bayern Bavaria

bayerisch Bavarian

der Bayer, -n Bavarian (man)

die Bayerin, -nen Bavarian (woman)

beabsichtigen to intend

die Absicht, -en intention

beachten to notice, take note of

der Beamte, -n civil servant (male)

die Beamtin, -nen civil servant (female)

sich (*acc.*) **bedanken** to thank

bedeuten to mean; to signify

die Bedeutung, -en meaning, importance

bedienen to wait on, to serve

sich (*acc.*) **bedienen** to serve oneself

Selbstbedienung self-service

die Bedingung, -en condition

das Bedürfnis, -se need, requirement

sich (*acc.*) **beeilen** to hurry

beerdigen to bury

die Beerdigung, -en funeral

*befehlen** to command, to order

befestigen to fortify

die Befestigung, -en fortification

befördern to transport

befreien to liberate

die Befreiung, -en liberation

befriedigen to satisfy; to pacify

begabt (*adj.*) gifted, intelligent

begegnen to meet (by chance)

*beginnen** to start, begin

der Beginn (*no pl.*) beginning

begrenzen to border; to limit

der Begriff, -e concept, idea, notion; term

behandeln to treat

　　die Behandlung, -en treatment

behaupten to claim, maintain, assert

bei at; with, at the home of; near; while

　　Potsdam bei Berlin Potsdam near Berlin

　　beim Essen while eating, during a meal

beide both, both of; two

der Beifall applause

*__bei•geben__ to add

das Bein, -e leg

beinah(e) nearly, almost

das Beispiel, -e example

　　zum Beispiel for example

bekannt (well) known

　　unbekannt unknown

der (die) Bekannte, -n acquaintance

*__bekommen__ to get, to receive

　　*__bekommen__ (*with pers. dat.*) to agree with

　　Milch bekommt mir nicht milk does not agree with me

beliebt well-liked

bellen to bark

bemerken to notice; to remark

　　bemerkenswert noteworthy

benutzen to use

das Benzin' gasoline

beob'achten to observe

*__beraten__ to advise, counsel

der Bereich, -e sphere, area

bereit sein zu (*dat.*) to be ready for

der Berg, -e mountain

　　in die Berge to the mountains

　　der Berghang, ⁻e mountain slope

berichten to report

　　der Bericht, -e report

der Beruf, -e job, profession

sich (*acc.*) **beruhigen** to calm down

　　beunruhigt sein to be worried

beschäftigen to employ

　　beschäftigt sein to be busy

Bescheid wissen to know, be informed

*__beschließen__ to decide

beschränken auf (*acc.*) to limit to

*__beschreiben__ to describe

besetzt busy; occupied

besichtigen visit; look at; inspect

besiegen to defeat

besonders especially

besser better

　　besser als better than

best- (*adj. or adv.*) best

　　am besten (*adv.*) best

*__bestehen__ to pass (an examination)

　　*__bestehen aus__ to consist of

bestellen to (place an) order

bestimmt certain

besuchen to visit; to attend (a school)

　　der Besuch, -e visit

der Beton (*no pl.*) concrete

betonen to stress, accent

betrachten to regard, to look at

　　betrachten als to consider as

der Betrieb, -e place of work, plant, factory

*__sich__ (*acc.*) **betrinken** to get drunk

das Bett, -en bed

beurteilen to judge

die Bevölkerung, -en population

　　der Bevölkerungszuwachs population growth

bevor before

sich (*acc.*) **bewegen** to move

　　die Bewegung, -en movement

*__beweisen__ to prove

bewundern to admire

bezahlen to pay (a bill)

der Bezirk, -e district

die Bibel, -n Bible

die Bibliothek', -en library

das Bier, -e beer

das Bild, -er picture

bilden to form; to educate

　　die Bildung education, training

billig cheap

der Biolo'ge, -n biologist

bis until; up to, as far as

　　bis morgen until tomorrow; see you tomorrow

bißchen bit, little, little bit

bisher (*adv.*) up to now, so far

bitte, bitte sehr please; OK, go ahead

*__bitten um__ (*acc.*) to ask for, request

　　die Bitte, -n request

das Blatt, ⁻er leaf

　　das Lorbeerblatt, ⁻er bay leaf; laurel leaf

blau blue

*__bleiben__ to stay, remain

der Blick, -e look, glance

blitzen to lighten

　　der Blitz, -e lightning

blöd(e) stupid, dumb

blond blond, blonde

blühen to bloom, blossom, flower

die Blume, -n flower

der Blumenkohl cauliflower

das Blut blood

　　der Blutdruck blood pressure

der Boden, ⁻e floor; ground

　　sich zu Boden werfen to throw oneself on the ground

der Bodensee Lake Constance

die Bohne, -n bean

　　die Bohnensuppe, -n bean soup

die Bombe, -n bomb

das Boot, -e boat

das Segelboot, -e sailboat
böse angry, mad; evil
   ich bin ihm böse I am
     mad at him
*braten to roast
   der Schweinebraten, -
     pork roast
brauchen to need; to use
   er braucht nicht zu
     arbeiten he doesn't
     have (need) to work
   brauchbar usable
die Braut, ⸚e bride
der Bräutigam, -e groom
*brechen to break
   sich (dat.) den Arm brechen
     to break one's arm
breit broad
   die Breite, -n breadth,
     latitude
der Brief, -e letter
   einen Brief aufgeben to
     post (mail) a letter
   der Luftpostbrief, -e air-
     mail letter
   der Eilbrief, -e special-
     delivery letter
   der Einschreibebrief, -e,
     das Einschreiben, -
     registered letter
   die Briefmarke, -n stamp
   die Brieftaube, -n carrier
     pigeon
   der Briefträger, - mailman
*bringen to bring
das Brot, -e bread; loaf of
   bread
   das Brötchen, - (hard)
     roll
die Brücke, -n bridge
der Bruder, ⸚ brother
brüllen to yell
der Brunnen, - well
die Brust, ⸚e breast; chest
das Buch, ⸚er book
   der Buchstabe, -n letter
     (of alphabet)
die Bulette, -n meat patty
   (Berlin)
der Bund, ⸚e federation

das Bundesland, ⸚er
   federal state
die Bundespost federal
   post office
der Bundesrat Federal
   Council (upper house of
   parliament)
die Bundesregierung
   federal government
die Bundesrepublik
   Deutschland Federal
   Republic of Germany
die Bundesstraße, -n
   federal road
der Bundestag Federal
   Parliament (lower
   house)
der Bundeswehr federal
   army
die Burg, -en castle
das Büro', -s office
der Bus, -se bus
die Butter (no pl.) butter

das Café, -s café, coffeehouse
der Campingplatz, ⸚e campsite
der Charak'ter, die
   Charakte're character
der Chef, -s boss; chief; chef
   der Küchenchef, -s chef
(das) China China
   chinesisch Chinese
   der Chinese, -n Chinese
     (man)
   die Chinesin, -nen Chinese
     (woman)
die Chemie' chemistry
   che'misch chemical
circa (abbrev. ca) circa,
   about, approximately

da there; then; under these
   circumstances; (conj.)
   since
dabei' (adv.) moreover,
   besides
das Dach, ⸚er roof
dagegen in comparison with
   that; on the other hand
daher from there; therefore,

   for that reason, that's
   why
damals at that time; then
   damalig (adj.) then
die Dame, -n lady
damit' (conj.) so that, in order
   that
danken to thank
   danke thanks; thank you
   der Dank gratitude,
     thanks
   vielen Dank thank you
     very much
   dankbar grateful
dann then
darum therefore; for that
   reason
das the (neuter); that
   (demonstr.); which,
   that (rel. pron.)
daß (conj.) that
das Datum, die Daten date
   (calendar)
   die Daten data
   die Datenverarbeitung
     data processing
   der Datenverarbeiter, -
     data processor
dauern to last; to take (time)
   dauernd constantly,
     incessantly
   die Dauerwelle, -n perma-
     nent (wave)
definieren to define
dementieren to deny
die Demokratie', -n democracy
die Demonstration', -en
   demonstration
   der Demonstrant', -en
     demonstrator
*denken to think
   denken an (acc.) to think
     of
   sich (dat.) denken to
     imagine
   ich denke mir etwas I
     imagine
   die Denkweise, -n way of
     thinking
denn (see 16)

dennoch yet; though, nevertheless
der the (*masc.*); that
(*demonstr.*); which,
that (*rel. pron.*)
derselbe, dieselbe, dasselbe, *pl.*
dieselben the same
deshalb (*adv.*) because of that
(das) Deutschland Germany
deutsch German
(das) Deutsch(e) German
(language)
der Deutsche, -n German
(man)
die Deutsche, -n German
(woman)
der Dezember December
der Dialekt', -e dialect
der Diamant', -en diamond
dicht close; tight; dense
dick thick, fat
die the (*fem.*); that
(*demonstr.*);
which, that (*rel. pron.*)
der Dieb, -e thief
dienen (*with dat.*) to serve, be
used for
der Diener, - servant
Dienstag Tuesday
der Diesel, - Diesel car
der Dieselmotor, -en
Diesel engine
dieser, diese, dieses, *pl.* **diese**
this; that
diesmal this time
das Ding, -e thing
direkt direct
der Direk'tor, die Direkto'ren
director
die Diskothek', -en discotheque
doch (*sent. adv.*) (*see* **41**)
der Dok'tor, die Dokto'ren
doctor, physician
der Doktorand', -en doctoral candidate (male)
die Doktoran'din, -nen
doctoral candidate
(female)
dokumentieren to document

dokumentierbar docu-
mentable
der Dom, -e cathedral
die Domglocke, -n
cathedral bells
dominieren to dominate
die Donau the Danube
donnern to thunder
der Donner, - thunder
Donnerstag Thursday
das Dorf, ̈-er village
dort there
draußen outside
drehen to turn
drehbar rotary, revolving
drei three
das Dreieck, -e triangle
dreiviertel sieben 6:45
dreizehn thirteen
dreißig thirty
dritt- third
die Drogerie, -n drugstore
drüben on the other side
da (dort) drüben over there
du you (*sing.*)
dumm dumb, stupid
der Dummkopf, die
Dummköpfe stupid per-
son, dunce, blockhead,
dumbbell
dunkel dark
die Dunkelheit darkness
dünn thin
dünsten to braise
durch (*prep. with acc.*)
through
***durch•braten** to roast (well
done)
***durchfah'ren** to drive
through, traverse
***durch•fallen** to flunk (an
examination)
durch•machen to go through,
suffer
der Durchmesser, - diameter
die Durchreise transit
***dürfen** to be permitted to
das darfst du nicht you
mustn't do that
durstig thirsty

der Durst thirst
ich habe Durst I am
thirsty
duschen to shower
die Dusche, -n shower
das Dutzend, -e dozen

eben flat, even; just
ebensogut just as well
die Ebene, -n plain, flat-
land
ebenfalls likewise, too
danke, ebenfalls thanks,
and the same to you
echt genuine
die Ecke, -n corner
um die Ecke around the
corner
eckig cornered
dreieckig triangular
viereckig rectangular
egalitär egalitarian
egoi'stisch egotistic
die Ehe, -n marriage
das Ehepaar, -e (married)
couple
eher rather, sooner
ehren to honor
Sehr geehrter Herr Meyer!
Very honored Mr.
Meyer: (standard form
of address)
ehrlich honest
das Ei, -er egg
das Eiweiß egg white;
protein
eiweißhaltig containing
protein
der Eiweißgehalt protein
content
eigen own
eigentlich actually
eilen to hurry
sich (*acc.*) **eilen** to hurry
sich beeilen to hurry
ein, eine, ein a; one (*indef.
article*)
eins one (number)
einander each other

sich (*dat.*) etwas einbilden to imagine something (falsely); to fancy

eingebildet sein to be conceited

einfach easy, simple

die Einfahrt entrance (way); driveway

der Zug hat Einfahrt the train is arriving

der Einfluß, die Einflüsse influence

ein•führen to import; to introduce

die Einführung, -en introduction

der Eingang, ¨e entry; entrance

kein Eingang don't enter

der Einheimische, -n native; local person

die Einheit, -en entity; unit

einheitlich uniform, homogeneous

die Einheitsschule, -n comprehensive school

ein•holen to catch up with

einige some; any; a few

ein•kaufen to shop; to purchase

einkaufen gehen to go shopping

das Einkaufen shopping

das Einkommen, - income

ein•laden to invite

die Einladung, -en invitation

einmal once; at some time

zweimal twice

dreimal three times

viermal four times

nicht einmal not once

noch einmal once more

nur einmal just once

ein•ordnen to get into the correct lane; to merge

ein•richten to furnish

ein•schlafen to fall asleep

ein•schließen to include; to lock in

einst once (upon a time)

ein•steigen to get on (a train, etc.), board, embark

ein•stellen to stop, discontinue

ein•treten to enter

ein•wandern to immigrate

der Einwanderer, - immigrant

der Einwohner, - (*abbr.* Ew.) inhabitant

ein•ziehen to move in

einzig single; sole; solitary

das Eis ice; ice cream

die Eiskrem ice cream

die Eisenbahn, -en railroad

die Eiszeit, -en ice age

elf eleven

elitär' (*adj.*) elitist, selective

die Eltern (*pl. only*) parents

empfangen to receive

der Empfang, ¨e reception

empfehlen to recommend

die Empfehlung, -en recommendation

das Ende, -n end

endlich finally

endgültig final(ly), for good

die Energie', -n energy

eng narrow

(das) England England

englisch English

(das) Englisch(e) English (language)

der Engländer, - Englishman

die Engländerin, -nen Englishwoman

das Enkelkind, -er grandchild

der Enkel, - grandchild, grandson

die Enkelin, -nen granddaughter

entdecken to discover

die Entdeckung, -en discovery

entfernt distant

die Entfernung, -en distance

enthalten to contain

entlang along

am Rhein entlang along the Rhine

sich (*acc.*) entscheiden to decide

die Entscheidung, -en decision

eine Entscheidung treffen to make a decision

entscheidend decisive

sich (*acc.*) entschließen to decide, to make up one's mind

entschlossen sein to be determined

sich (*acc.*) entschuldigen to apologize; to excuse (oneself)

die Entschuldigung, -en excuse

um Entschuldigung bitten to apologize

(ich bitte um) Entschuldigung (I am) sorry; excuse me

entschuldigen Sie excuse me

entstehen to originate

enttäuschen to disappoint

entweder . . . oder either . . . or

entwickeln to develop

die Entwicklung, -en development

er he; it

die Erbse, -n pea

die Erde, -n earth

das Erdbeben, - earthquake

sich ereignen to occur, happen

das Ereignis, -se event, occurrence

erfahren to find out, learn; experience

erfinden to invent

der Erfolg, -e success, result

erhalten to preserve

sich (*acc.*) erholen to get a rest

erholt sein to be well rested

die **Erholung** recreation; recuperation
erinnern an to remind of
  sich (*acc.*) **erinnern an** to remember
sich (*acc.*) **erkälten** to catch a cold
  erkältet sein to have a cold
  die **Erkältung, -en** cold
*****erkennen** to recognize
erklären to explain
erlauben to allow, permit
erleben to experience
erledigen to take care of
ernten to harvest
erreichen to reach (a destination)
*****erscheinen** to appear
*****erschießen** to shoot (dead); to execute
*****erschlagen** to slay, kill
*****erschrecken** *intrans.* (*strong verb*) to be scared; *trans.* to scare (someone)
erst only, not until
erst- first
erst (= **zuerst**) first (*adv.*)
erstaunt sein to be astonished
*****ertrinken** to drown
erwachsen (*adj.*) grown
  der **Erwachsene, -n** grown-up, adult
erwähnen to mention; to reveal
erwärmen to warm (up)
erwarten to expect
  die **Erwartung, -en** expectation
*****sich erweisen** to turn out, to prove
  es **erwies sich, daß** . . . it was proved that . . .
*****erwerben** to acquire, gain
erzählen to tell (a story)
  der **Erzähler, -** narrator
  die **Erzählung, -en** story; narration
erzeugen to produce
*****erziehen** to raise, educate
  die **Erziehung** education

es it
*****essen** to eat
  das **Essen, -** food; meal
der **Essig** vinegar
etwa about; by any chance
etwas something, somewhat
  etwas langsamer a little more slowly
  etwas anderes something else
Euro'pa Europe
  europä'isch European
ewig eternal, forever
das **Examen, -** examination
existieren to exist
das **Experiment', -e** experiment

die **Fabrik', -en** factory
das **Fach, ¨er** (academic) subject, discipline; compartment, box, shelf
  der **Fachbereich, -e** group of academic departments
das **Fachwerkhaus, ¨er** frame(work) house; half-timbered house
fähig capable
*****fahren** to drive, to go (by car, train, boat, plane)
  der **Fahrer, -** driver
  der **Fahrgast, ¨e** passenger
  die **Fahrkarte, -n** ticket (train, etc.)
  die **Rückfahrkarte, -n** round-trip ticket
  der **Fahrplan, ¨e** timetable
  die **Fahrt, -en** drive, trip
  die **Ausfahrt, -en** driveway, exit
  die **Einfahrt, -en** driveway, entrance
  die **Heimfahrt, -en** trip home
der **Fall, ¨e** case
  auf jeden Fall at any case
  auf keinen Fall in no case
*****fallen** to fall

*****zerfallen** to decay; to fall apart
falsch wrong, false
falten to fold
die **Fami'lie, -n** family
*****fangen** to catch
die **Farbe, -n** color
fast almost
faul lazy
der **Februar** February
die **Feder, -n** feather
  das **Federbett, -en** featherbed
der **Fehler, -** mistake
feiern to celebrate
fein fine, delicate
  feingeschnitten finely sliced, chopped
der **Feind, -e** enemy
das **Feld, -er** field
das **Fenster, -** window
die **Ferien** (*pl.*) vacation
die **Ferne** distance
  das **Ferngespräch, -e** long-distance call
  der **Fernsprecher, -** telephone
  fernsehen to watch TV
  das **Fernsehen** (*no pl.*) television
  der **Fernseher, -** television set
fertig ready, complete, finished
das **Fest, -e** celebration, party, festivity
  das **Festessen, -** gala dinner, banquet
  das **Festspiel, -e** festival
feststellen to notice, find out; to determine
fett fat
das **Feuer, -** fire
das **Fieber** fever
der **Film, -e** film
*****finden** to find
der **Finger, -** finger
die **Firma, die Firmen** firm, company
der **Fisch, -e** fish

die Fläche, -n area
die Flasche, -n bottle
   eine Flasche Bier a bottle
     of beer
das Fleisch (no pl.) meat
*fliegen to fly
   der Flieger, - flier, pilot
*fliehen to flee
*fließen to flow
   fließend fluent; flowing
flüchten to flee; to escape
   der Flüchtling, -e refugee
der Flug, ⁻e flight
   der Fluggast, ⁻e (airline)
     passenger
   der Flughafen, ⁻ airport
   der Flugkapitän, -e flight
     captain
   das Flugzeug, -e airplane
die Flunder, -n flounder
der Fluß, die Flüsse river
folgen to follow
die Forelle, -n trout
formen to form, mold
   die Form, -en form
   die Formel, -n formula
   das Formular, -e form,
     blank
die Forschung, -en research
fort away
   fort•gehen to go away,
     leave
   fort•leben to live on; to
     survive
   die Fortsetzung, -en con-
     tinuation
der Fotohändler, - photo-
   dealer
fragen to ask
   fragen nach (dat.) to ask
     about, inquire after
   die Frage, -n question
der Franken, - (sFr) franc
   (Swiss)
(das) Frankreich France
   französisch French
   der Franzose, -n French-
     man
   die Französin, -nen
     Frenchwoman

die Frau, -en woman; wife;
   Mrs., Ms.
   Frau Meyer Mrs. Meyer,
     Ms. Meyer
   das Fräulein, - young (un-
     married) woman, Miss,
     Ms.
   Fräulein Meyer Miss
     Meyer, Ms. Meyer
frei free
   freiwillig voluntary
Freitag Friday
fremd strange, foreign
   das Fremdwort, ⁻er foreign
     word, non-German
     word
   der Fremdenverkehr
     tourism
   der Fremdsprachenunter-
     richt foreign language
     instruction
*fressen to eat (of animals),
   feed
die Freude, -n joy
sich (acc.) freuen auf to look
   forward to
sich (acc.) freuen über to be
   happy (glad) about
der Freund, -e friend (male)
   die Freundin, -nen friend
     (female)
   freundlich friendly
   unfreundlich unfriendly
der Frieden peace
   der Friedhof, ⁻e cemetery,
     graveyard
   friedlich peaceful
*frieren to freeze
frisch fresh
froh glad, happy
   fröhlich cheerful
die Frucht, ⁻e fruit
früh early
   früher earlier; formerly
   früher war er . . . he used
     to be . . .
   frühestens at the earliest
der Frühling spring
frühstücken to (eat, have)
   breakfast

das Frühstück, -e breakfast
fühlen to feel
führen to lead, take
   der Führerschein, -e
     driver's license
füllen to fill
   überfüllt overcrowded
das Fundament, -e founda-
   tion, basis
fünf five
   fünfzehn fifteen
   fünfzig fifty
funktionieren to function; to
   work
   es funktioniert nicht it
     doesn't work
für (prep. with acc.) for
furchtbar terrible
fürchten to fear
   sich (acc.) fürchten vor
     (dat.) to be afraid of
der Fürst, -en prince
   das Fürstentum, ⁻er prin-
     cipality
der Fuß, ⁻e foot
   der Fußabdruck, ⁻e foot-
     print
   der Fußgänger, - pedes-
     trian
   die Fußgängerzone, -n
     pedestrian zone
füttern to feed
   das Futter feed, food,
     fodder

die Gabel, -n fork
die Gans, ⁻e goose
die Gefahr, -en danger
   gefährlich dangerous
der Gang, ⁻e motion, gear;
   hallway, corridor
   der erste Gang first gear
   im Gang halten to keep in
     motion, to keep going
ganz all of; entire; quite
   durch ganz Deutschland
     through all of Germany
   ganz gut not bad
gar fully, even; quite, very
   gar nicht not at all

die Gara′ge, -n garage
garantiert guaranteed; I guarantee you
der Garten, ⁼ garden
das Gas, -e gas
der Gast, ⁼e guest
   der Gastarbeiter, - foreign worker
   der Gasthof, ⁼e inn, restaurant
   die Gaststätte, -n restaurant
*gebären to give birth to
   geboren werden to be born
   er ist 1962 geboren he was born in 1962
*geben to give
   es gibt there is, there are
das Gebiet, -e area
das Gebilde, - structure
geboren born
   gebürtig native
   die Geburt, -en birth
   der Geburtstag, -e birthday
gebrauchen to use
   der Gebrauch, ⁼e use; custom, habit
der Gedanke, -n thought
das Gedicht, -e poem
gefährlich dangerous
*gefallen (with dat.) to be pleasing to
   du gefällst mir I like you
*gefangen•nehmen to capture, take prisoner
   das Gefängnis, -se prison, jail
das Gefühl, -e feeling
gegen (prep. with acc.) against; around
   gegen neun around nine o'clock
   gegenüber (prep. with dat.) opposite
   gegenüber dem Bahnhof or dem Bahnhof gegenüber opposite (across from) the station
die Gegend, -en area

der Gegensatz, ⁼e contrast
das Gegenteil, -e the opposite
   im Gegenteil on the contrary
der Gegner, - opponent
der Gehalt (no pl.) content
   das Gehalt, ⁼er salary
das Geheimnis, -se secret
*gehen to go; to walk
   wie geht's? wie geht es dir/euch/Ihnen? how are you? how are things going?
gehorchen to obey
gehören (dat.) to belong to (possession)
   gehören zu (dat.) to belong to, be a member of, be part of
die Gelbsucht jaundice
das Geld, -er money
geliebt beloved
*gelingen (impers.) to succeed
   es gelingt mir I succeed
*gelten to be valid
die Gemeinde, -n (religious or civic) community
gemeinsam common, mutual
die Gemeinschaft, -en community
   die Europäische Gemeinschaft (E.G.) European Community (E.C.)
das Gemüse, - vegetable
gemütlich cozy
genau exact(ly)
der General′, -e general
   der Generaldirektor, -en director general, top manager
die Generation, -en generation
die Geographie′ geography

genug enough
das Gepäck (no pl.) baggage, luggage
   der Gepäckträger, - porter
gerade straight; just
   geradeaus straight, straight ahead

gerecht just
   ungerecht unjust
das Gericht, -e dish, course (food)
gering small
   geringer smaller, lesser
   geringst- least
germanisch Germanic
   der Germanist′, -en Germanist
gern(e) (adv.) gladly
   ich esse gern I like to eat
der Gesandte, -n ambassador
das Geschäft, -e business, store
   das Sportgeschäft, -e sporting goods store
   der Geschäftsmann, pl. die Geschäftsleute businessman
*geschehen (impers.) to happen
das Geschenk, -e present
die Geschichte, -n story; history
der Geschmack taste
geschweige not to mention
die Geschwindigkeit, -en speed
   die Höchstgeschwindigkeit maximum speed, speed limit
die Geschwister (pl. only) brothers and sisters, siblings
die Gesellschaft, -en society
   gesellschaftlich social
   die Industriegesellschaft industrial society
   die Wohlstandsgesellschaft affluent society
das Gesetz, -e law
das Gesicht, -er face
das Gespräch, -e conversation
   das Ferngespräch, -e long-distance call
gestatten to permit
gestern yesterday
   gestern abend last night
   gestern morgen yesterday morning
gesund healthy
   die Gesundheit health

Gesundheit! (said when someone sneezes)

das Getränk, -e beverage

das Getreide, - grain

das Getreidefeld, -er grainfield

das Gewicht, -e weight

***gewinnen** to win

gewiß certainly

sich (*acc.*) **gewöhnen an** (*acc.*) to get used to

gewöhnt sein an (*acc.*) to be used to

gewöhnlich usual

der Gigant', -en giant

die Gitar're, -n guitar

das Glas, ̈er glass

glauben an (*acc.*) to believe in

gleich equal, same, like; right away

gleich hier um die Ecke right here around the corner

ich komme gleich I'm coming right away

gleichzeitig at the same time, simultaneous

gliedern to arrange, to divide

die Glocke, -n bell

das Glück luck, fortune

glücklich happy

Glück haben to be lucky

der Glückwunsch, ̈e congratulation

gnädig gracious

gnädige Frau Madam (formal address)

das Gold (*no pl.*) gold

das Goldstück, -e gold coin

gotisch Gothic

der Gott, ̈er god

die Göttin, -nen goddess

gottseidank thank goodness

der Grad, -e degree

das Gramm (*no pl.*) (metric) gram

500 g = fünfhundert Gramm

das Gras, ̈er grass

gratulieren to congratulate

grau gray

die Grenze, -n border, limit

die Grenzpolizei border police

der Grenzübergang, ̈e border crossing

(das) Griechenland Greece

griechisch Greek

der Grieche, -n Greek (man)

die Griechin, -nen Greek (woman)

grillen to grill, to barbecue

grinsen to grin

groß large, big

die Größe, -n size; greatness

großartig wonderful, great, magnificent, marvelous

die Großeltern grandparents

die Großmutter, ̈ grandmother

der Großvater, ̈ grandfather

die Großfamilie, -n extended family

die Großstadt, ̈e large city, metropolis

***großwerden** to grow up

die Grube, -n pit; hole; ditch

grün green

der Grund, ̈e base; reason

im Grunde basically

die Grundlage, -n foundation, basis

die Grundschule, -n elementary school

gründen to found; to start

die Gruppe, -n group

grüßen to greet, say hello

der Gruß, ̈e greeting

das Gulasch goulash

die Gulaschsuppe, -n goulash soup

günstig favorable

gut good; OK

das Gymnasium, die Gymnasien German secondary school, grades 5–13

das Haar, -e hair

sich (*dat.*) **die Haare schneiden** to cut one's hair

sich (*dat.*) **die Haare schneiden lassen** to have one's hair cut, to get a haircut

***haben** to have

hacken to chop

das Gehackte ground meat

hageln to hail

der Haifisch, -e, der Hai, -e shark

halb half

halb zehn half past nine, 9:30

die Hälfte, -n half

die Halde, -n slope

die Halle, -n hall; lobby

***halten** to hold; to stop, halt

halt just

halten für (*acc.*) to consider

ich halte ihn für dumm I think he's stupid

halten von (*dat.*) to have an opinion about

was halten Sie von Meyer? what do you think of Meyer?

die Hand, ̈e hand

sich (*dat.*) **die Hände waschen** to wash one's hands

der Handschuh, -e glove

die Handtasche, -n handbag

handeln to act

handeln mit to deal in

handeln von to deal with

sich handeln um (*impers.*) to be a matter of

der Handel, ̈ trade

der Einzelhandel retail trade

der Händler, - tradesman

der Einzelhändler, - retailer

der Großhändler, - wholesaler

der Hang, ̈e slope

hängen (hängte, gehängt) (*with acc.*) to hang (something)

    er hängte das Bild an die Wand he hung the picture on the wall

    ***hängen (hing, gehangen)** to hang, be suspended

    das Bild hing an der Wand the picture hung on the wall

(der) Hans Jack; John (*abbrev.* for **Johannes**)

harmonisch harmonic

hart hard

    die Härte hardness

der Harz the Harz Mountains

hassen to hate

häßlich ugly

Haupt- (prefix) main

    das Hauptfach, ⸚er (academic) major (subject)

    die Hauptsache, -n main thing

    hauptsächlich mainly, primarily

    die Hauptstadt, ⸚e capital (city)

das Haus, ⸚er house

    ich bin zu Hause I am at home

    ich gehe nach Hause I am going home

    die Hausfrau, -en housewife

    der Haushalt, -e household

    die Haustür, -en front door

***heben** to lift; to raise

heilen to heal

die Heimat home, native land

heimlich secret, hidden

heiraten to marry; to get married

heiß hot

***heißen** to be called

    wie heißen Sie? what's your name?

    ich heiße Meyer my name is Meyer; I am Mr. Meyer

    das heißt (d.h.) that is, i.e.

heizen to heat

***helfen** (*with dat.*) to help, give help to

hell light, bright

die Hepatitis hepatitis

her from (toward the speaker)

    wo kommst du her? where do you come from?

***heraus•finden** to find out

sich heraus•stellen (*impers.*) to turn out

    es stellte sich heraus, daß . . . it turned out that . . .

herbei•führen to bring about

der Herbst autumn

    im Herbst in the autumn

der Herd, -e stove

der Hering, -e herring

der Herr, -en man, gentleman, Mr.

    Herr Meyer Mr. Meyer

herrlich splendid, magnificent

das Herz, -en, (*gen.*) **des Herzens** heart

    das Herzklopfen palpitation of the heart

    herzlich cordial

der Herzog, ⸚e duke

heterogen' heterogeneous

das Heu (*no pl.*) hay

heute today

    heute abend tonight; this evening

    heute morgen this morning

    heutig (*adj.*) of today

    die heutige Zeitung today's paper

hier here

    hiesig (*adj.*) local

    hierher (*adv.*) here (hither); to this place

die Hierarchie', -n hierarchy

die Hilfe help, aid

der Himmel, - sky; heaven

    himmlisch heavenly

hin there (away from the speaker)

    ich gehe hin I am going there

    hin und her back and forth

    hin und zurück round-trip

***hin•kommen** to get there

das Hindernis, -se hindrance, obstacle

hin•stellen to put up, to place

hinten (*adv.*) in the back

hinter behind

    hintereinander her one behind the other

***hinunter•rennen** to run down (a street)

historisch historical

die Hitze heat

das Hobby, -s hobby

hoch high

    (das) Hochdeutsch High (Standard) German

    die Hochschule, -n university; institution for higher learning

    die Hochsee (*no pl.*) high seas

    höher higher

    die höhere Schule secondary school, *Gymnasium*

    höchst- highest

    höchstens at the most

    die Höhe, -n height; altitude

    der Höhepunkt, -e high point, climax

die Hochzeit, -en wedding

    die Hochzeitsgesellschaft, -en wedding party

hoffen auf (*acc.*) to hope for

    hoffentlich (*sent. adv.*) I hope

    die Hoffnung, -en hope

höflich polite

    unhöflich impolite

die Höhle, -n cave

holen to get, fetch

homogen' homogeneous

    die Homogenität' homogeneity

der Honig honey

hören to hear
  der Hörer, - telephone receiver; listener
  der Hörsaal, die Hörsäle lecture hall (in a university)
die Hose, -n pants, trousers
das Hotel', -s hotel
  die Hotelhalle, -n lobby
  der Hotelführer, - hotel guide; guidebook
hübsch pretty
der Hügel, - hill
das Huhn, -er chicken
der Hund, -e dog
hundert hundred
der Hunger hunger
  ich habe Hunger I am hungry
  hungrig hungry
  ich bin hungrig I am hungry
der Hut, -e hat

ich I
ideal' ideal
  das Ideal', -e ideal
die Idee', die Ide'en idea
identisch identical
  die Identität', -en identity
der Idiot', -en idiot, fool
ihr you (pl.)
immer always
  immer noch, noch immer still
in in
die Industrie', -n industry
  das Industriegebiet, -e industrial area
infolge (prep. with gen.) as a result of, following
der Ingenieur', -e engineer
der Inhalt, -e content
innen (adv.) inside
  die Innenstadt, -e inner city
inner- inner
  innerhalb (prep. with gen.) inside of
das Insekt', -en insect

insgesamt a total of; all in all
instinktiv' instinctive
das Institut', -e institute
intelligent' intelligent
  die Intelligenz' intelligence
interessant interesting
  uninteressant uninteresting
  interessanterweise interestingly
  das Interesse, -n interest
  sich (acc.) **interessieren für** to be interested in
inzwischen meanwhile, in the meantime
irgendetwas anything; something
irgendwo somewhere; anywhere
(das) Irland Ireland
  irisch Irish
  der Ire, -n Irishman
  die Irin, -nen Irishwoman
sich (acc.) **irren** to err, be in error
  irr(e) insane
  der (die) Irre, -n insane person
(das) Ita'lien Italy
  italie'nisch Italian
  der Italiener, - Italian (man)
  die Italienerin, -nen Italian (woman)

ja yes
die Jacht, -en yacht
jagen to rush, race; to chase; to hunt
  der Jäger, - hunter
das Jahr, -e year
jahrelang for years
  die Jahreszeit, -en season
  das Jahrhun'dert, -e century
der Januar January
je ever
jeder, jede, jedes, pl. **alle** each, every, pl. all
  jederzeit (at) any time

jedesmal every time
  jedesmal, wenn whenever
jedoch however
jemand somebody, someone
  jemand anders somebody else
  niemand anders nobody else
jetzt now
  jetzig (adj.) of today, present, contemporary
der Job, -s job
die Jugend (time of) youth
  die Jugendherberge, -n youth hostel
  das Jugendzentrum, die Jugendzentren youth center
(das) Jugoslawien Yugoslavia
  jugoslawisch Yugoslavian
  der Jugoslawe, -n Yugoslavian (man)
  die Jugoslawin, -nen Yugoslavian (woman)
der Ju'li July
jung young
der Junge, -n boy
der Ju'ni June
Jura studieren to study law, jurisprudence
juris'tisch legal

der Kaffee coffee
der Käfig, -e cage
der Kaiser, - emperor
das Kalb, -er calf
  das Kalbfleisch veal
  der Kalbsbraten, - veal roast
kalt cold
  die Kälte cold(ness)
die Kamera, -s camera
kämpfen to fight, struggle
  der Kampf, -e fight, fighting, struggle
der Kapitän', -e captain
kaputt (colloq.) busted, broken
der Karneval carnival, season before Lent
die Karotte, -n carrot

die Karte, -n card; map; ticket
die Postkarte, -n postcard
die Straßenkarte, -n road
  map
die Theaterkarte, -n
  theater ticket
die Kartoffel, -n potato
der Käse, - cheese
die Kasse, -n cash register;
  cashbox
die Kassette, -n cassette
der Kasten, ⁓ box, case, con-
  tainer
die Katastro'phe, -n catastro-
  phe
katho'lisch Catholic
die Katze, -n cat
kaufen to buy, purchase
der Kauf, ⁓e buy, purchase
der Käufer, - buyer, pur-
  chaser
das Kaufhaus, ⁓er depart-
  ment store
der Kaufmann, die Kauf-
  leute merchant; busi-
  nessman; business ad-
  ministrator
kaum hardly
kein, keine, kein, pl. keine no,
  not any
der Kellner, - waiter
die Kellnerin, -nen
  waitress
die Kelten (pl.) the Celts
*kennen to know
der Kenner, - connoisseur
kennenlernen to meet, to
  get acquainted with, to
  get to know
das Kennzeichen identifi-
  cation symbol; license
  plate
der Kern, -e kernel, center
die Kernphysik nuclear
  physics
kichern to giggle
der Kiefer, - jaw(bone)
der Kilometer, - kilometer
der Quadratkilometer, -
  square kilometer

das Kind, -er child
kindlich childlike
kindisch childish
das Kino, -s movie theater
wir gehen ins Kino we are
  going to the movies
die Kirche, -n church
klappern to rattle
klar clear
na klar of course, sure
die Klasse, -n class
das Klavier, -e piano
Klavier spielen to play the
  piano
kleiden to dress
das Kleid, -er dress
die Kleider (pl.) clothes
klein small
das Klima climate
klingeln to ring (the bell)
*klingen to sound
klopfen to knock, to pound;
  to beat
das Kloster, ⁓ monastery
knapp scarce, tight
knapp bei Kasse low on
  cash
kneten to knead
der Knochen, - bone
der Kalbsknochen, - veal
  bone
der Knödel, - dumpling
der Leberknödel, - liver
  dumpling
die Leberknödelsuppe
  liver dumpling soup
knusprig crispy
kochen to boil; to cook
der Koch, ⁓e cook (male)
die Köchin, -nen cook
  (female)
der Koffer, - suitcase
der Kohl cabbage
der Rotkohl red cabbage
der Kombiwagen, - station
  wagon
komforta'bel comfortable
komisch funny; odd; comical
*kommen to come
komplex' complex

das Kompliment', -e compli-
  ment
kompliziert complicated
der König, -e king
*können to be able to
konservativ' conservative
konzen'trisch concentric
das Konzert', -e concert
der Kopf, ⁓e head
die Kopfwunde, -n head
  injury
das Kopftuch, ⁓er scarf,
  kerchief
koppeln an (acc.) to connect,
  attach to; to couple
  (railroad cars)
der Korkzieher, - corkscrew
das Korn, ⁓er kernel; corn;
  grain
der Korridor, -e corridor
kosten to cost
die Kraft, ⁓e strength; force;
  power
das Kraftfahrzeug, -e
  motor vehicle
das Kraftfahrzeugkenn-
  zeichen, - license plate
das Kraftwerk, -e power
  plant
das Atomkraftwerk, -e
  atomic power plant
krank sick
das Krankenhaus, ⁓er hos-
  pital
das Kraut, ⁓er herb
das Kraut (no pl.) cabbage
das (Sauer)kraut sauer-
  kraut
das Unkraut weed
die Kreide chalk
kreisen to revolve; to circle
der Kreis, -e circle; county
der Landkreis, -e rural
  county
kreuz und quer back and
  forth; crisscross
der Krieg, -e war
kriegen to get
der Krimi, -s detective novel;
  TV cop show

der **Kriminalroman, -e** detective novel
die **Krise, -n** crisis
die **Krone, -n** crown
krumm bent, crooked
die **Küche, -n** kitchen
der **Kuchen, -** cake
die **Kugel, -n** sphere; ball
   der **Kugelschreiber, -** ballpoint pen
die **Kuh, ̈e** cow
die **Kultur, -en** culture
   die **Subkultur, -en** subculture
   kulturell cultural
der **Kunde, -n** customer
   der **Stammkunde, -n** regular customer
die **Kunde** (*no pl.*) knowledge about
   die **Heimatkunde** study of the local area
die **Kunst, ̈e** art
   der **Künstler, -** artist
kurz short
   die **Kürze** shortness; brevity
   kürzlich recently
die **Kusine, -n** cousin (female)
küssen to kiss
   der **Kuß, die Küsse** kiss
die **Küste, -n** coast
   die **Nordseeküste** North Sea coast
die **Kutsche, -n** coach; buggy, jalopy

das **Labor′, -s** lab
   das **Labora′torium, die Labora′torien** laboratory
   der **Laborant, -en** lab technician (male)
   die **Laborantin, -nen** lab technician (female)
lächeln to smile
   das **Lächeln** smile
lachen to laugh
   das **Lachen** laugh, laughter

der **Lachs, -e** salmon
der **Laden, ̈** store, shop
die **Lage, -n** site (particular location of a vineyard)
landen to land
das **Land, ̈er** country; land
   er wohnt auf dem Land he lives in the country
   die **Landschaft, -en** landscape
   die **Landwirtschaft** (*no pl.*) agriculture
   landwirtschaftlich agricultural
lang long
   lange for a long time
   die **Länge, -n** length
langsam slow
langweilen to bore
   langweilig boring
   sich (*acc.*) **langweilen** to be bored
der **Lärm** (*no pl.*) noise; din
*****lassen** leave; let, allow; cause
die **Last, -en** load
   der **Lastwagen, -** truck
   der **Lastzug, ̈e** trailer rig
die **Laterne, -n** lantern, (street) light
*****laufen** to run; to walk
   der **Läufer, -** runner
die **Laune, -n** mood, frame of mind
laut loud
   der **Lautsprecher, -** loudspeaker
läuten to ring
lauwarm lukewarm
leben to be alive, live
   das **Leben** life
   am Leben sein to be alive
   der **Lebensinhalt** content of life
   die **Lebensmittel** (*pl.*) groceries, food
   das **Lebensmittelgeschäft, -e** grocery store
die **Leber** liver
   die **Leberwurst, ̈e** liverwurst

lebhaft lively, vivid
die **Lederwaren** (*pl. only*) leather goods
leer empty
legen to lay (flat), place
   sich (*acc.*) **legen** to lie down
   *****liegen** to lie
lehren to teach, instruct
   der **Lehrer, -** teacher (male)
   die **Lehrerin, -nen** teacher (female)
   der **Lehrling, -e** apprentice
leicht easy; light
*****leid tun** (*impers.*) to be sorry
   es tut mir leid I'm sorry
   er tut mir leid I feel sorry for him
*****leiden an** (*dat.*) to suffer from
   leiden to tolerate
   ich kann sie nicht leiden I can't stand her
   leider (*sent. adv.*) unfortunately
*****leihen** to lend; to borrow
   ich leihe ihm ein Buch I lend him a book
   er leiht das Buch von mir he borrows the book from me
leise quiet(ly)
leiten to lead, direct; to pipe
   die **Wasserleitung, -en** water pipe
   der **Leiter, -** head; chief; leader
lenken to direct, to steer
lernen to learn
*****lesen** to read
   der **Leser, -** reader
letzt- last
   letzten Sommer last summer
   letzte Woche last week
   letztes Jahr last year
leuchten to shine
die **Leute** (*no sing.*) people
der **Leutnant, -s** lieutenant
das **Licht, -er** light

lieben to love
 lieb dear
 ich habe dich lieb I'm in love with you
 die Liebe love
 der Liebesbrief, -e love letter
 der Liebling, -e favorite; darling
 Lieblings- favorite
 lieber (*adv.*) rather, preferably
 am liebsten (*adv.*) (would like) most of all
 am liebsten wohnten wir in München we would like most of all to live in Munich
*liegen to lie (flat); to be situated
 *liegen an (*dat.*) to be due to
die Linde, -n linden tree
die Li'nie, -n line
link- left
 links to the left
die Lippe, -n lip
 der Lippenstift, -e lipstick
der Liter, - liter (1,000 cu. cm.)
das Loch, ⸚er hole
der Löffel, - spoon
sich lohnen (*impers.*) to be of use; to pay
 das lohnt sich nicht it doesn't pay, it isn't worth it
das Lokal, -e restaurant
los loose; going on; unpackaged
 was ist hier los? what's going on here?
 was ist los mit dir? what's the matter with you?
 lose Butter butter in bulk
lösen to solve; to dissolve
der Löwe, -n lion
*lügen to lie
 der Lügner, - liar
die Lust desire
 ich habe keine Lust I don't feel like it
lustig funny

machen to do; to make
 mach's gut so long; take care; see you
die Macht, ⸚e might; power
das Mädchen, - girl
mahlen to grind
die Mahlzeit, -en meal
der Mai May
Mailand Milan
mal once; times; for a change
 mal (= **einmal**) once
 diesmal, dieses Mal this time
 ein mal zwei ist zwei one times two is two
 ich bleibe mal zu Hause I'll stay home for a change
man you, we, people, they, one
 einem (*dat.*), **einen** (*acc.*) (indef. third-person pron.)
mancher (**der**-word) many a
manchmal sometimes
der Mann, ⸚er man; husband
der Mantel, ⸚ coat
die Mark (*no pl.*) the mark (money)
 DM = die Deutsche Mark (basic unit of West German currency)
der Markt, ⸚e market
 der Supermarkt, ⸚e supermarket
 der Marktplatz, ⸚e market square
die Marmelade, -n (any kind of) jam
 die Orangenmarmelade orange marmalade
der März (month of) March
die Maschi'ne, -n machine
 die Schreibmaschine, -n typewriter
das Maß, -e measure, measurement
die Mathematik' mathematics
der Matrose, -n sailor
die Mauer, -n (outside) wall
die Maus, ⸚e mouse

der Mechaniker, - mechanic
die Medizin' medicine; science of medicine
 er studiert Medizin he is in medical school
das Meer, -e ocean
das Mehl flour
 die Mehlspeise, -n dish made with flour; dessert (Austrian)
mehr more
 nicht mehr no longer
mehrere several
die Mehrwertsteuer, -n value added tax
die Meile, -n mile
 die Quadratmeile, -n square mile
meinen to think, express an opinion; to say
 die Meinung, -en opinion
meist- most
 meistens in most cases
melden to report
 sich (*acc.*) **melden** to answer (the phone)
die Menge, -n lot; crowd
der Mensch, -en human being
 kein Mensch nobody
 menschlich human
die Mentalität', -en mentality
das Menü, -s complete dinner (i.e., not à la carte)
merken to notice
*messen to measure
das Messer, - knife
das Metall', -e metal
der (*or* **das**) **Meter, -** meter
 der Kilome'ter, -(km) kilometer
 das Thermome'ter, - thermometer
 das Barome'ter, - barometer
die Metho'de, -n method
der Metzger, - butcher
 die Metzgerei, -en butcher shop
 die Metzgersfrau, -en butcher's wife
die Milch (*no pl.*) milk

die **Militärregierung**, -en military government
die **Milliar'de**, -n billion
der **Millimeter**, - (mm) millimeter
die **Million**, -en million
der **Millionär**, -e millionaire
mindestens at least
der **Ministerpräsident**, -en prime minister; minister president
die **Minu'te**, -n minute
mio (abbrev. for **Million**) million
mischen to mix
der **Missionar**, -e missionary
mit with
*mit•bringen to bring
*mit•fahren to ride with, accompany
*mit•gehen to go with, come along
die **Mitbestimmung** co-determination
das **Mitglied**, -er member
das **Familienmitglied**, -er family member
der **Mitmensch**, -en fellow human
der **Mittag**, -e noon
der **Nachmittag**, -e afternoon
das **Mittagessen**, - noonday meal, dinner
die **Mitte** middle, center
(das) **Mitteleuropa** Central Europe
der **Mitteleuropäer**, - Central European
mitteleuropäisch Central European
mitteleuropäische Zeit (**MEZ**) Central European time
mitten in in the middle of
mit•teilen to announce, report, convey
das **Mittel**, - means
das **Verkehrsmittel**, - means of transportation

das **Mittelalter** the Middle Ages
mittelalterlich medieval
Mittwoch Wednesday
möblieren to furnish (a room)
modern' modern
*mögen to like to
möglich possible
unmöglich impossible
die **Möglichkeit**, -en possibility
der **Monat**, -e month
der **Mond**, -e moon
der **Montag** Monday
der **Mord**, -e murder
der **Mörder**, - murderer
der **Morgen**, - morning
Guten Morgen good morning
heute morgen this morning
morgen tomorrow
morgen abend tomorrow night
morgen früh tomorrow morning
der **Moselwein**, -e Moselle wine
der **Motor'**, -en motor
müde tired
der **Müller**, - miller
die **Mühle**, -n mill
mündlich orally
das **Muse'um**, die **Muse'en** museum
die **Musik'** music
musizieren to make music
*müssen to have to
die **Mutter**, ⸗ mother
mütterlich motherly

na well
nach to, toward; after
nach Deutschland to Germany
nach zwei Uhr after two o'clock
nach wie vor as always
der **Nachbar**, -n neighbor
nachdem (conj.) after
*nach•denken to reflect
*nach•denken über (acc.)

to think about, meditate about
*nach•gehen to be (run) slow (of a clock)
*vor•gehen to be (run) fast
nachher afterwards
*nach•kommen to come later, to follow
die **Nachricht**, -en report, message
die **Nachrichten** (pl.) news (radio, TV, etc.)
*nach•sehen to check, investigate
nächst- next
nächsten Sommer next summer
nächste Woche next week
nächstes Jahr next year
nächstens in the near future
die **Nacht**, ⸗e night
nachts at night
der **Nachtzug** night train
der **Nachteil**, -e disadvantage
der **Nachtisch**, -e dessert
nackt naked, nude
nah near, close by
die **Nähe** vicinity, proximity, closeness, nearness
in der Nähe nearby
der **Nahe Osten** Middle East
nähen to sew
zunähen to sew shut
die **Näherin**, -nen seamstress
die **Nahrung** nourishment, food
das **Nahrungsmittel**, - foodstuff
der **Name**, -n name
nämlich to be specific; you see; namely
naß wet
die **Natur'** nature
natür'lich natural, naturally; of course
der **Nebel**, - fog
neblig foggy

neben beside, next to
　nebenan next door
　nebeneinander next to
　　each other, side by side
*****nehmen** to take
nein no
der Nekrolog, -e necrology;
　obituary notice
*****nennen** to call; to name
der Nerv, -en nerve
　nervös nervous
　die Nervosität nervousness
nett nice
das Netz, -e net
neu new
neugierig curious
neun nine
　neunzehn nineteen
　neunzig ninety
neutral′ neutral
nicht not
　der Nichtraucher, - non-
　　smoker
nichts nothing
nie never, not ever
　nie mehr never again
niedrig low
niemand nobody
das Niveau, -s level
nirgends nowhere
noch still
　noch nicht not yet
　noch nie never yet
der Norden north
　nördlich northern
　(das) Nordafrika North
　　Afrika
　die Nordsee North Sea
(das) Norwegen Norway
　norwegisch Norwegian
　der Norweger, - Nor-
　　wegian (man)
　die Norwegerin, -nen
　　Norwegian (woman)
die Note, -n grade, mark
nötig necessary
der November November
die Nudel, -n noodle
die Null, -en zero
die Nummer, -n number

das Nummernschild, -er
　number plate, license
　plate
nun now; *sent. adv.* well
nur only
nützen to be of use
　nützlich useful

ob whether; if
oben (*adv.*) up, above
der Ober, - waiter
das Objekt, -e object
das Obst (*no pl.*) fruit (collec-
　tive noun)
　wir essen viel Obst we eat
　　a lot of fruit
obwohl even though, although
der Ochse, -n ox
　das Ochsenfleisch beef
oder or
der Ofen, ⁚ oven, stove
offen open
öffentlich public
offiziell official
öffnen to open
oft often
ohne (*prep. with acc.*)
　without
das Ohr, -en ear
der Oktober October
das Öl, -e oil
　das Salatöl, -e salad oil
die Oma, -s grandma
　der Opa, -s grandpa
der Onkel, - uncle
die Oper, -n opera
operieren to operate
　sich (*acc.*) **operieren lassen**
　　to have an operation
das Opfer, - victim
die Orange, -n orange
　der Orangensaft orange
　　juice
die Ordnung, -en order
　in Ordnung all right, OK
orientieren to orient
　orientiert sein to be ori-
　　ented; to have a direc-
　　tion or bias
der Ort, -e town

der Ortsrand, ⁚er edge of
　town
　die Ortszeit, -en local time
der Osten east
　der Ostblock East Bloc
　die Ostsee Baltic Sea
(die) Ostern (*pl.*) Easter
　die Osterferien Easter
　　vacation
　der Ostermontag Monday
　　after Easter
(das) Österreich Austria
　österreichisch Austrian
　der Österreicher, -
　　Austrian (man)
　die Österreicherin, -nen
　　Austrian (woman)

das Paar, -e pair, couple
　ein Paar Schuhe a pair of
　　shoes
　ein paar a few, some
das Paket, -e package
paradox′ paradoxical
der Park, -s park
parken to park
　das Parkhaus, ⁚er parking
　　garage
die Partei, -en (political) party
die Party, -s party
der Paß, die Pässe passport
　die Paßkontrolle, -n pass-
　　port control
passieren to happen
die Pause, -n pause, stop,
　break, intermission
das Pech bad luck
die Pension′, -en tourist home
die Perle, -n pearl
die Person, -en person
　der Personenzug, ⁚e local
　　train
　persön′lich personal
pessimistisch pessimistic
die Petersilie parsley
pfeffern to pepper
　der Pfeffer pepper
　das Pfefferkorn, ⁚er pep-
　　percorn
der Pfennig, -e penny

Pfingsten Pentecost
   Pfingstmontag Monday after Pentecost
die Pflanze, -n plant
pflegen to take care of
die Pflicht, -en duty
   das Pflichtfach, ¨er required subject
das Pfund, -e pound
das Phänomen', -e phenomenon
die Philosophie', -n philosophy
photographie'ren (also: fotografieren) to photograph
planen to plan
   der Plan, ¨e plan, aim
die Platte, -n (music) record
   der Plattenspieler, - record player
der Platz, ¨e place; seat
   Platz nehmen to sit down, have a seat
plaudern to chat
plötzlich suddenly
(das) Polen Poland
   polnisch Polish
   der Pole, -n Pole (man)
   die Polin, -nen Pole (woman)
die Politik' politics
   poli'tisch political
die Polizei' (no pl.) police
der Polizist, -en policeman
der Portier, -s desk clerk (in a hotel)
positiv positive
die Post mail; post office
   das Postamt, ¨er post office
   die Postkarte, -n postcard
   die Postleitzahl, -en zip code
prägen to form, to impress on
praktisch practical
der Preis, -e price; prize
prima excellent, tops, first-rate
primitiv' primitive
privat' private
das Problem', -e problem
die Produktion, -en production

der Profes'sor, die Professo'ren professor
profilieren to profile
das Programm', -e program
   der Programmierer programmer
   programmieren to program
das Projekt', -e project
promovieren to get a Ph.D. degree
   die Promotion, -en awarding of the Ph.D.
Prosit cheers! here's to you!
protestantisch protestant
provinziell provincial
das Prozent, -e per cent
die Prüfung, -en examination
die Psychologie' psychology
der Pudel, - poodle
das Pulver, - (gun)powder
der Punkt, -e point, dot
   pünktlich on the dot, on time; punctually
das Püree purée
   das Kartoffelpüree mashed potatoes
putzen to clean

der Quatsch (colloq.) nonsense
die Quelle, -n spring, source
   die Nahrungsquelle, -n source of food
die Quittung, -en receipt

das Rad, ¨er wheel; bicycle
   das Fahrrad, ¨er bicycle
   das Motorrad, ¨er motorcycle
das Radio, -s radio
der Rand, ¨er rim, edge
rapid' rapid
rasen to race, to speed
sich (acc.) rasieren to shave
*raten to advise, counsel; to guess
   der Rat (no pl.) advice, counsel; council
   'der Rat, ¨e counselor

das Rathaus, ¨er town hall, city hall
   der Ratskeller, - restaurant in city hall
rationalisieren to rationalize
das Raubtier, -e beast of prey
rauchen to smoke
räuchern to smoke (meat)
der Raum, ¨e room; space
reagieren auf (acc.) to react to
rechnen to figure, to calculate
recht- right
   rechts to the right
   das ist mir recht that's OK with me
   rechteckig rectangular
   *recht●haben to be right
   ich hatte recht I was right
   rechtzeitig on time
reden to talk, speak
   der Redner, - speaker
   die Rede, -n speech
   eine Rede halten to give a speech
reell' (pronounced re-ell') honest, reputable
   reell bedient werden to get good value for your money
die Regel, -n rule
   in der Regel as a rule, normally
   regelmäßig regular
regieren to govern
die Regierung, -en government
regnen to rain
   der Regen (no pl.) rain
   der Regenmantel, ¨ raincoat
der Rehrücken, - saddle of venison
reich rich
das Reich, -e empire, kingdom, realm
   die Reichsstadt, ¨e imperial city
reif ripe
der Reifen, - wheel (of a car)
   der Vorderreifen, - front wheel

der Hinterreifen, - rear wheel
die Reihe, -n row; series
das Reihenhaus, ¨er row house; condominium
***rein•lassen** (= **herein•lassen**) to let in
der Reis rice
reisen to travel
die Reise, -n trip
die Geschäftsreise, -n business trip
eine Reise machen to take a trip
der Reiseführer, - guidebook
der Reisescheck, -s traveler's check
die Rekla´me advertising
relativ relatively
die Religion´, -en religion
religiös religious
***rennen** to run
reparieren to repair
die Republik´, -en republic
die Bundesrepublik Deutschland Federal Republic of Germany
die Deutsche Demokratische Republik German Democratic Republic
das Restaurant, -s restaurant
retten to save
revoltieren to revolt
das Rezept, -e recipe
der Rhein Rhine River
richten to direct, orient
die Richtung, -en direction
richtig correct, right
***riechen** to smell
riesig huge, gigantic, immense
das Rind, -er (head of) cattle
das Rindfleisch beef
die Rindsleber beef liver
der Ring, -e ring
das Rippchen, - cured and smoked pork chop
der Rock, ¨e skirt; jacket
die Rolle, -n role

der Roman, -e novel
romanisch Romanesque
der Romanist, -en Romanist
romantisch romantic
der Römer, - Roman
römisch Roman
die Rose, -n rose
rosig rosy
rot red
der Rucksack, ¨e backpack
***rufen nach** (*dat.*) to shout, call out for
die Ruhe peace, quietude
laß mich in Ruhe leave me alone
ruhig quiet, restful; (*sent. adv.*) it won't bother me, I'll stay calm about it
die Ruine, -n ruin
(das) Rumänien Romania
rund round
runter (*adv.*) (= **hinunter, herunter**) down
die Straße runter down the street
(das) Rußland Russia
russisch Russian
der Russe, -n Russian (man)
die Russin, -nen Russian (woman)

die Sache, -n matter; thing
der Sack, ¨e sack; bag
der Saft, ¨e juice
die Sage, -n legend
sagen to say; to tell
sag mal tell me, say
die Saison season
der Salat, -e salad
salzen to salt
sammeln to gather; to collect
der Sammler, - collector
der Samstag, -e, der Sonnabend, -e Saturday
sarkastisch sarcastic
sauer sour
das Sauerkraut sauerkraut
das Säugetier, -e mammal

schade too bad, what a shame
schaden to damage
das Schaf, -e sheep
der Schafskäse sheep's cheese
***schaffen** to create, to make; to accomplish, to manage
der Schall sound, ring
die Schallplatte, -n record
die Schallplattenmusik record music
schalten to switch (electrical)
um•schalten to switch over (to a different station)
der Schalter, - (ticket) window, counter
der Lichtschalter, - light switch
schätzen to estimate
schauen to look
auf Wiederschauen goodbye (Bavarian, Austrian)
die Scheibe, -n (glass) pane, windshield; slice
***scheiden** to separate; to divide
***sich** (*acc.*) **scheiden lassen** to get a divorce
die Scheidung, -en divorce
***scheinen** to seem; to shine
es scheint zu regnen it seems to be raining
die Sonne scheint the sun is shining
schenken to give (as a present)
die Scheune, -n barn
schicken to send
***schieben** to shove; push
das Schiff, -e ship
***schi•laufen** to ski
das Schild, -er sign
der Schilling, -e (öS) schilling (Austrian currency)
der Schinken, - ham
der Schirm, -e umbrella
schlachten to slaughter, butcher
der Schlachter, -, der Schlächter, - butcher

*schlafen to sleep
  *schlafen gehen to go to bed
  der Schläfer, - sleeper
*schlagen to hit, strike, beat
  der Schlag, ⁓e hit, strike; stroke; bang
  der Schlager, - (musical) hit, popular song
schlecht bad
*schließen to close; to end; to conclude
schließlich finally, after all
schlimm bad
der Schluß, die Schlüsse conclusion, end
der Schlüssel, - key
  der Hausschlüssel, - house key
schmecken to taste
der Schmerz, -en pain
  die Kopfschmerzen (pl.) headache
schnarchen to snore
*schneiden to cut
schneien to snow
schnell fast
der Schnitt, -e cut
die Schnitte, -n slice
schon already, earlier than expected
schön pretty, beautiful
der Schrank, ⁓e cupboard; closet
*schreiben to write
  die Schreibmaschine, -n typewriter
  der Schreibtisch, -e desk
*schreien to scream
schriftlich in writing
der Schriftsteller, - writer, author
die Schrippe, -n (hard) roll (Berlin)
der Schritt, -e step
der Schuh, -e shoe
  ich putze mir die Schuhe I clean (polish) my shoes
  der Militärschuh, -e army boot
die Schule, -n school

der Schüler, - pupil, (Gymnasium) student
die Schulter, -n shoulder
der Schuß, die Schüsse shot
schütteln to shake
  den Kopf schütteln to shake one's head
schützen to protect
  der Schutz protection
  das Schutzblech, -e (bicycle) fender, mud guard
(das) Schwaben Swabia
  schwäbisch Swabian
  der Schwabe, -n Swabian (man)
  die Schwäbin, -nen Swabian (woman)
schwach weak
  die Schwäche, -n weakness
schwarz black
  der Schwarzwald Black Forest
(das) Schweden Sweden
  schwedisch Swedish
  der Schwede, -n Swede (man)
  die Schwedin, -nen Swede (woman)
*schweigen to be silent
das Schwein, -e pig, swine
  das Schweinefleisch pork
die Schweiz Switzerland
  schweizerisch Swiss
  der Schweizer, - Swiss (man)
  die Schweizerin, -nen Swiss (woman)
schwer heavy; difficult, hard
die Schwester, -n sister
schwierig difficult, hard
  die Schwierigkeit, -en difficulty
*schwimmen to swim
  *schwimmen gehen to go swimming
  das Schwimmbecken, - swimming pool
sechs six
  sechzehn sixteen
  sechzig sixty

der See, -n lake
die See (no pl.) sea, ocean
segeln to sail
*sehen to see
sehr very
*sein to be
seit since
  seit einer Woche for a week
  seit dem since then, since that time
  seitdem (conj.) since
die Seite, -n page, side
  einseitig one-sided
  die Seitenstraße, -n side road
der Sekretär, -e secretary (male)
  die Sekretärin, -nen secretary (female)
die Sekun'de, -n second
selbst, selber -self
selbständig independent
  die Selbständigkeit (no pl.) independence
selbstverständlich self-evident, obvious, of course
der Sellerie celery (root), celeriac
selten rare, rarely
seltsam strange
das Semester, - semester
das Seminar', -e seminar
die Semmel, -n (hard) roll
*senden (sandte, gesandt) to send
  senden (sendete, gesendet) to broadcast
  der Sender, - radio station, transmitter
  die Sendung, -en broadcast, transmission
der Senf mustard
die Sensation, -en sensation
sentimental' sentimental
der September September
serbisch Serbian
servieren to serve
setzen to set; to seat

sich (*acc.*) **setzen** to sit
down

sich (*refl. pron.*) himself; herself; itself; oneself;
themselves

sichern to secure, make safe
sicher certain, certainly;
sure
die Sicherheit safety,
security

sie she; they; it
Sie you

sieben seven
siebzehn seventeen
siebzig seventy

siedeln to settle
das Silber (*no pl.*) silver
*****singen** sing
der Sinn, -e sense
die Sitte, -n custom
*****sitzen** to sit
*****sitzen•bleiben** to stay
seated; to stay behind
(in school), to have to
repeat a grade
der Sitz, -e seat
das Skelett', -e skeleton
so so
soeben just (now); this
moment
das Sofa, -s sofa
sofort right away,
immediately
sogar even
sogenannt so-called
der Sohn, ˝e son
solange (*conj.*) as long as
solch- such
der Soldat', -en soldier
sollen to be supposed to
der Sommer, - summer
nächsten Sommer next
summer
sondern but
die Sonne, -n sun
der Sonntag, -e Sunday
sonntags on Sundays
sonst otherwise
sonst nichts nothing else
sorgen für to take care of
die Sorte, -n kind; variety

soweit (*conj.*) as far as
sowieso anyhow, in any case
sowohl . . . als auch as well as
sozial social
sozialistisch socialist
sozusagen so to speak, as it
were
(das) Spanien Spain
spanisch Spanish
der Spanier, - Spaniard
die Spanierin, -nen
Spanish woman
die Spannung, -en tension
die Hochspannung high
voltage
sparen to save
der Spaß, ˝e fun; joke
Spaß haben to have fun
Spaß machen to joke
spät late
spätestens at the latest
die Spätzle (*pl.*) kind of noodle
(Swabian specialty)
*****spazieren•gehen** to go for a
walk
der Spaziergang, ˝e walk
einen Spaziergang machen
to take (go for) a walk
der Speck bacon
speisen to eat (formal)
die Speisekarte, -n menu
der Speisewagen, - dining
car
sperren to close, shut off
die Spezialität, -en specialty
der Spiegel, - mirror
das Spiegelei, -er fried egg
spielen to play
das Spiel, -e game
der Spieler, - player
der Plattenspieler, - record
player
der Spion, -e spy
der Sport (*no pl.*) sport
Sport treiben to exercise
der Sportwagen, - sports car
die Sprache, -n language
deutschsprachig German-
speaking
der Sprachraum, ˝e
language area

*****sprechen** to speak
*****sprechen von** (*dat.*),
*****sprechen über** (*acc.*) to
talk about
das Sprichwort, ˝er proverb
*****springen** to jump
die Spur, -en trace
spurlos without a trace
der Staat, -en state
die Stadt, ˝e town, city
die Stadtverwaltung, -en
city administration
der Stahl, ˝e steel
der Stall, ˝e stall, stable
stammen aus to come from,
be a native of
der Stammtisch, -e regular
table (in a restaurant)
stärken to strengthen
stark strong
die Stärke, -n strength
starten to start
*****statt•finden** to take place; to
occur
die Stauung, -en traffic jam,
back-up, congestion
stecken to stick; to put
*****stehen** to stand
*****stehen•bleiben** to stop; to
remain standing
*****stehlen** to steal
*****steigen** to climb
*****ein•steigen** to get on
(train, car, etc.)
*****aus•steigen** to get off
(train, car, etc.)
*****um•steigen** to change
(train, bus, etc.)
der Stein, -e stone
steinig stony
stellen to put, place (upright);
to set (a watch, clock)
sich (*acc.*) **stellen** to place
oneself; to stand (up)
aus•stellen to exhibit
hin•stellen to put up
die Stelle, -n place, spot,
position
an deiner Stelle in your
place
*****sterben** to die

sterblich mortal
die Sterblichkeitsziffer mortality rate
die Steuer, -n tax
still quiet; still
 die Stille quietness
 der Stillstand standstill
 zum Stillstand kommen to (come to a) stop
die Stimme, -n voice
stimmen (impers.) to be correct
 das stimmt that is correct
die Stimmung, -en mood, spirits, atmosphere
 in guter Stimmung in high spirits
das Stipen'dium, die Stipen'- dien stipend, scholar- ship, fellowship
der Stock, ˙e stick; floor (of a building)
 achtstöckig with eight stories
stolz proud
 stolz sein auf (acc.) to be proud of
 der Stolz (no pl.) pride
stören to disturb
 nicht stören! do not disturb!
*stoßen to push; to shove; to strike
 *zusammen•stoßen to collide
die Strafe, -n punishment, fine
 der Strafzettel, - traffic ticket
die Straße, -n street
die Strecke, -n stretch, section, route
*streichen to spread
der Streik, -s strike
der Strom, ˙e stream; large river; (electrical) current
die Struktur, -en structure
das Stück, -e piece; (theatrical) play
 ein Stück Kuchen a piece of cake
studie'ren to study, to attend

a university, to be a student (at a university)
der Student', -en univer- sity student (male)
die Studen'tin, -nen uni- versity student (female)
das Studentenheim, -e student residence, dor- mitory
das Studium, die Studien (period of) study
der Studienrat, ˙e Gym- nasium teacher (male)
die Studienrätin, -nen Gymnasium teacher (female)
die Stufe, -n step, level
der Stuhl, ˙e chair
die Stunde, -n hour
der Sturm, ˙e storm
suchen to look for, seek, search
(das) Südamerika South America
der Süden south
die Suppe, -n soup
süß sweet
sympa'thisch likeable
das System', -e system
die Szene, -n scene

die Tafel, -n (bill)board, blackboard
der Tag, -e day
 den ganzen Tag all day
 tagelang for days
das Tal, ˙er valley
die Tante, -n aunt
tanzen to dance
 der Tanz, ˙e dance
die Tasche, -n pocket
die Tasse, -n cup
 eine Tasse Kaffee cup of coffee
die Tat, -en action, deed
 der Täter, - culprit, crimi- nal
die Tatsache, -n fact
 tatsächlich in fact, indeed
die Taufe, -n baptism
tausend thousand

die Taxe, -n or das Taxi, -s taxi
der Techniker, - engineer, technician
 die Technische Hochschule institute of technology
der Tee (no pl.) tea
der Teig, -e dough
teilen to divide
 geteilt durch divided by
 der Teil, -e part, piece
 zum Teil partly
telefonie'ren to talk on the telephone, to make a telephone call
 das Telefon, -e telephone
das Telegramm, -e telegram
der Teller, - plate
die Temperatur, -en tempera- ture
das Tennis tennis
 der Tennisschuh, -e tennis shoe
das Testament', -e testament; (last) will
teuer expensive
das Thea'ter, - theater
das Thema, die Themen theme; topic
tief deep; low
 der Tiefflieger, - strafing plane
das Tier, -e animal
der Tisch, -e table
 die Tischplatte, -n tabletop
der Titel, - title
die Tochter, ˙ daughter
der Tod death
 tot dead
toll crazy; great
die Tomate, -n tomato
der Ton, ˙e tone
der Topf, ˙e pot
das Tor, -e gate
der Tourist', -en tourist
die Tradition, -en tradition
 traditionell traditional
*tragen to carry; to wear (clothes)
die Tragik tragedy
träumen to dream

traurig sad
die Trauung, -en marriage ceremony, wedding
*__treffen__ to hit; to meet
  *__sich__ (*acc.*) **treffen** to meet
  der Treffpunkt, -e meeting place
trennen to separate
die Treppe, -n stairs; staircase
*__trinken__ to drink
das Trinkgeld, -er tip
trotz (*prep. with gen.*) in spite of
  trotzdem nevertheless
*__tun__ to do
die Tür, -en door
die Türkei Turkey
  türkisch Turkish
  der Türke, -n Turk (man)
  die Türkin, -nen Turk (woman)
der Turm, ⁀e tower
der Typ, -en type; model
  typisch typical

die U-Bahn, -en (= **die Untergrundbahn**) subway
üben to practice
über over
überall everywhere
überdecken to cover
überfüllt overcrowded, overflowing
*__übergießen__ to pour over
überhaupt in general; altogether
  überhaupt nicht not at all
überleben to survive
überlegen to wonder, consider
  sich (*dat.*) **überlegen** to think (meditate); to wonder
übernachten to spend the night
überraschen to surprise
  überraschend surprisingly
der Überschuß (net) gain
übersetzen to translate
  die Übersetzung, -en translation

überzeugen to convince
übrigens by the way, incidentally
die Übung, -en exercise; practice
die Uhr, -en clock, watch
  um ein Uhr, um eins at one o'clock
  der Uhrmacher, - watchmaker
um at; around
  um ein Uhr at one o'clock
  um . . . herum around
  um (*adj.*) up
  die Zeit ist um time is up
die Umgebung surroundings
umgekehrt vice versa, conversely
um•rechnen to convert
*__sich__ (*acc.*) **um•sehen** to look around
umsonst in vain; for nothing
*__um•steigen__ to change (trains, etc.)
um•wandeln to change
*__sich__ (*acc.*) **um•ziehen** to change (clothes)
  *__um•ziehen__ to move (from one place to another)
unbedingt absolutely
und and
undenkbar unthinkable
der Unfall, ⁀e accident
(das) Ungarn Hungary
  ungarisch Hungarian
  der Ungar, -n Hungarian (man)
  die Ungarin, -nen Hungarian (woman)
ungeduldig impatient
ungefähr approximately
unglaublich unbelievable, incredible
das Unglück, -e bad luck, misfortune, adversity, calamity; accident
  unglücklich unhappy
die Universität, -en university
unmittelbar immediate, direct
unruhig restless

unruhig machen to disturb
der Unsinn nonsense
unten (*adv.*) down, down below, downstairs
unter under
*__unterbrechen__ to interrupt
untereinander among each other, among themselves
*__unter•gehen__ to sink; vanish; to set (sun, moon)
*__unter•kommen__ to find a place to stay
unter•mischen to mix, blend in
unterrichten to instruct, teach
  der Unterricht instruction
*__unterscheiden__ to distinguish
  der Unterschied, -e difference
*__unterschreiben__ to sign (a letter, document, etc.)
untersuchen to investigate
  die Untersuchung, -en investigation
unverheiratet unmarried
unvernünftig unreasonable
die Unze, -n ounce
unzugänglich impenetrable
urbanisieren to urbanize
  die Urbanisierung urbanization
die Urkunde, -n (official) document
der Urlaub leave; vacation
die Ursache, -n cause
usw. (und so weiter) and so on, etc.

die Variante, -n variation, variant
der Vater, ⁀ father
sich (*acc.*) **verändern** to change
  die Veränderung, -en change
verantwortlich responsible
verarbeiten to process
  die Verarbeitung processing
verbessern to improve, make better; to correct
*__verbieten__ to prohibit

verboten forbidden, not allowed, not permitted, prohibited

Eingang verboten do not enter

Rauchen verboten no smoking

*__verbinden__ to connect

die Verbindung, -en connection; coalition

das Verbrechen, - crime

der Verbrecher, - criminal

*__verbringen__ to spend (time)

verdammt damned

verdammt noch mal dammit

*__verderben__ to spoil, go bad

verdienen to earn

Geld verdienen to make money

vereinigen to unify, unite

die Vereinigten Staaten United States

*__sich__ (*acc.*) **verfahren** to get lost (driving)

*__zur Verfügung stehen__ to be available

die Vergangenheit past

*__vergessen__ to forget

vergeßlich forgetful

unvergeßlich unforgettable

vergiften to poison

vergleichen mit (*dat.*) to compare with

der Vergleich, -e comparison

das Vergnügen (*no pl.*) pleasure

verhaften to arrest

verhandeln to negotiate

die Verhandlung, -en negotiation

sich (*acc.*) **verheiraten** (**mit**) to get married (to)

verheiratet sein (**mit**) to be married (to)

verkaufen to sell

der Verkauf, ⸗e sale

der Verkäufer, - salesman

die Verkäuferin, -nen saleswoman

der Verkehr traffic

verlangen to demand

*__verlassen__ (*with acc.*) to leave

*__sich__ (*acc.*) **verlassen auf** to rely on

*__sich__ (*acc.*) **verlaufen** to get lost (walking), to lose one's way

der Verleger, - publisher

verletzen to hurt (someone)

sich (*acc.*) **verlieben in** (*acc.*) to fall in love with

verliebt sein in (*acc.*) to be in love with, to be infatuated

*__verlieren__ to lose

sich (*acc.*) **verloben mit** to get engaged to

verlobt sein mit to be engaged to

vermissen to miss

das Vermögen, - fortune, estate

er hat ein Vermögen von zehn Millionen he is worth ten million

die Vernunft (*no pl.*) (power of) reason

vernünftig reasonable

verpassen to miss, to fail to make a connection

verreisen to go on a trip

verrückt crazy

verschieden different

die Verschmutzung pollution

*__verschwinden__ to disappear

die Versicherung, -en insurance; assurance

die Verspätung, -en delay

Verspätung haben to be late (train, plane, etc.)

*__versprechen__ to promise

*__verstehen__ to understand

versuchen to try

der Versuch, -e experiment; attempt, try

die Versuchung, -en temptation

verteidigen to defend

die Verteidigung, -en defense

verteilen to distribute

der Vertrag, ⸗e contract, treaty

vertrauen to trust

das Vertrauen trust

das Mißtrauen distrust

*__vertreiben__ to displace, chase away

der (die) Vertriebene, -n expellee

der Vertreter, - representative

verwalten to administer

die Verwaltung, -en administration

der Verwaltungsbezirk, -e administrative district

verwandt related

der (die) Verwandte, -n relative

*__verwenden__ to use, make use of, put to use

verwöhnen to spoil, pamper (someone); to take good care (of someone)

verwunden to wound

*__verzeihen__ to forgive

Verzeihung! excuse me, I'm sorry

verzollen to declare; to pay duty on

verzweifeln to despair

verzweifelt in despair

der Vetter, -n cousin (male)

viel much

vielen Dank thank you very much

vielleicht perhaps

vier four

vierzehn fourteen

vierzehn Tage two weeks; fourteen days

vierzig forty

das Viertel, - quarter

das Volk, ⸗er people

das deutsche Volk the German people

voll full; crowded

voll machen to fill up

vollenden to complete
völlig completely
von from
    von . . . aus from (and out of)
    von Wien aus from Vienna
vor in front of
    vor allem above all, particularly
voraus ahead
    *****voraus•fahren** to drive ahead
*****vorbei•gehen** to pass by
sich (*acc.*) **vor•bereiten auf** (*acc.*) to prepare for
    die Vorbereitung (auf) preparation (for)
vorgestern the day before yesterday
vorher before; earlier
    ein Jahr vorher a year earlier
vorhin a while ago
die Vorlesung, -en lecture (university)
vorne (*adv.*) in front
der Vorort, -e suburb
*****vor•schlagen** to suggest, propose
    der Vorschlag, ⁀e proposal
die Vorsicht precaution
    Vorsicht! careful! watch out!
    vorsichtig careful
(sich) (*acc. or dat.*) **vor•stellen** to introduce; to imagine
    ich stelle mich vor I introduce myself
    ich stelle mir vor I imagine
    die Vorstellung, -en introduction; (theater) performance; idea, representation
der Vorteil, -e advantage
der Vortrag, ⁀e (formal) lecture
das Vorurteil, -e prejudice
die Vorwahl(nummer), -n area code
vorwärts forward

wach awake
*****wachsen** to grow, increase
    das Wachstum growth
die Waffe, -n weapon
der Wagen, - car; cart
    PKW = Personenkraftwagen passenger car
    LKW = Lastkraftwagen truck
wählen to choose, decide; elect; dial (telephone)
    die Wahl, -en election
    das Wahlfach, ⁀er elective
wahnsinnig insane, crazy
wahr true
    nicht wahr? isn't that so? aren't you? don't you?, etc.
    die Wahrheit truth
während (*prep. with gen.*) during
    während (*conj.*) while
wahrscheinlich probably
der Wald, ⁀er forest
die Wand, ⁀e wall (of a room)
wandern to hike
    die Wanderung, -en hike
wann at what time, when
die Ware, -n goods
warm warm
    die Wärme warmth
warnen to warn
warten auf (*acc.*) to wait for
    der Warteraum, ⁀e waiting room, lounge
warum why
was (= **etwas**) something
was what
    was für ein what kind of
*****waschen** to wash
    die Waschmaschine, -n washing machine
das Wasser water
das WC, -s (water closet), toilet
wechseln to change (money)
der Weck, -e (hard) roll
wecken to awaken (someone)
    der Wecker, - alarm clock

weder . . . noch neither . . . nor
weg away
    *****weg•gehen** to go away, leave
    *****weg•fahren** to leave, depart (by car, etc.), drive away
der Weg, -e way; path
wegen (*prep. with gen.*) because of
weich soft
(die) Weihnachten Christmas
weil because
die Weile while, short time
der Wein, -e wine
    der Weinbau wine-making, viticulture
    der Weinberg, -e vineyard
    der Weingärtner, - vintner
    der Weinkenner, - judge of wines, wine connoisseur
weinen to cry, shed tears, weep
weit far
    weiter further
der Weizen wheat
die Welt, -en world
    die Weltanschauung, -en world view
    weltbekannt world-famous
    der Weltkrieg, -e world war
    weltlich worldly, secular
wenig little
    weniger less; minus
    weniger als less than; fewer than
    wenigstens at least
wenn when; if
wer who
*****werben** to advertise
    die Werbung, -en advertisement
*****werden** to become
*****werfen** to throw
    *****um•werfen** to knock over
    *****zu•werfen** to cast at, throw at

das Werk, -e work; opus; factory

das Kunstwerk, -e work of art

das Werkzeug, -e tool

werktags weekdays

wertvoll valuable

das Wesen, - being

weshalb why, for what reason

der Westen west

die Westfront western front

wetten to bet

das Wetter (*no pl.*) weather

der Wetterbericht, -e weather report

wichtig important

wie how

wieder again

auf Wiedersehen see you again; good-bye

auf Wiederschaun *Austrian for* auf Wiedersehen

auf Wiederhören good-bye (telephone)

wiederholen to repeat

die Wiese, -n meadow

wieviel how much

wieviel Uhr what time

der Wiking, -er viking

wild wild

der Wind, -e wind

der Winter, - winter

im Winter during the winter

wir we

wirklich real; really

die Wirklichkeit, -en reality

der Wirt, -e innkeeper

die Wirtin, -nen landlady, innkeeper

das Wirtshaus, ̈er inn, restaurant

die Wirtschaft, -en restaurant, pub

die Wirtschaft (*no pl.*) economy

das Wirtschaftswunder economic miracle

*wissen to know (facts)

das Wissen (*no pl.*) knowledge

das Unwissen ignorance

die Wissenschaft, -en science

der Wissenschaftler, - scientist

wo where

die Woche, -n week

wochenlang for weeks

das Wochenende, -n weekend

wohin where (to)

wohl (*sent. adv.*) probably

sich (*acc.*) **wohl fühlen** to feel well

das Wohl well-being, good health

auf Ihr Wohl to your health

der Wohlstand wealth, affluence, prosperity

die Wohlstandsgesellschaft affluent society

wohnen to live, to reside

die Wohnung, -en apartment

der Wolf, ̈e wolf

die Wolle wool

die Wolldecke, -n blanket

wollen to intend to

das Wort, ̈er (*or* -e) word

die Wunde, -n wound; injury

die Kopfwunde, -n head injury

das Wunder, - miracle

das Wirtschaftswunder economic miracle

wunderbar marvelous, wonderful

wunderschön wonderful, very beautiful

sich (*acc.*) **wundern** to be amazed

wünschen to wish

die Wurst, ̈e sausage

die Wurzel, -n root

würzen to season, to spice

die Wut anger

wütend mad, angry

die Zahl, -en number, figure

zahlen, bezahlen to pay

zählen to count

zähmen to tame

zahm tame

der Zahn, ̈e tooth

sich (*dat.*) **die Zähne putzen** to brush one's teeth

der Zahnarzt, ̈e dentist

der Zaun, ̈e fence

zehn ten

das Zeichen, - sign

zeigen to show

sich zeigen to become apparent, to turn out

es zeigte sich, daß . . . it turned out that . . .

die Zeit, -en time

zeitig in (good) time

rechtzeitig on time, at the right time

eine Zeitlang a short time

zur Zeit at the moment; right now; for the time being

das Zeitalter, - age, epoch

die Zeitschrift, -en magazine; journal

die Zeitung, -en newspaper

das Zelt, -e tent

die Zentrale, -n switchboard

das Zentrum, die Zentren center

*zerbrechen to break (to pieces), come apart

zerren to tear, pull

*zerschneiden to cut up, cut into pieces

zerstören to destroy

das Zeugnis, -se report card, school report

die Ziege, -n goat

*ziehen to pull; to move (from one place to another)

nach München ziehen to move to Munich

*aus•ziehen to move out

*ein•ziehen to move in
ziemlich rather
die Zigar're, -n cigar
   die Zigaret'te, -n cigarette
das Zimmer, - room
   das Wohnzimmer, - living room
   das Schlafzimmer, - bedroom
   das Zimmermädchen, - chambermaid
der Zirkus, -se circus
zittern to tremble
der Zoll, ⸚e customs; duty
   die Zollnummer, -n customs plate (for car)
der Zoo, -s zoo
zu to; at; too
   es scheint zu regnen it seems to be raining
   zu Hause at home
   zu warm too warm
   zu (adj.) closed
   die Tür ist zu the door is closed
züchten to breed

die Zucht breeding, rearing
   die Viehzucht cattle raising
der Zucker sugar
zu•decken to cover
zuerst' at first
der Zufall, ⸚e accident, chance
zufällig by coincidence, by chance, accidentally
zufrieden sein mit (dat.) to be satisfied with
der Zug, ⸚e train
der (die) Zugewanderte, -n immigrant
*zu•gießen to add (liquid)
zugleich at the same time, simultaneously
die Zukunft (no pl.) future
*zu•lassen to admit (to an educational institution)
zuletzt last, lastly, finally
zu•machen to close, shut
zunächst (adv.) first (of all), to begin with
*zu•nehmen to increase; to gain weight; to wax (moon)

zunehmend increasing
zurück back
   *zurück•halten to hold back
zurückhaltend reserved
zusammen together
   sich (acc.) zusammen•setzen aus (dat.) to be composed of
   die Zusammenarbeit cooperation
   die Zusammenkunft, ⸚e meeting, get-together
der Zustand, ⸚e state (of affairs)
der Zustrom, ⸚e influx
zuviel too much
zwanzig twenty
zwar indeed, to be sure
zwei two
   zweit- second
der Zwerg, -e dwarf
die Zwiebel, -n onion
*zwingen to force
zwischen between
zwölf twelve

Vocabulary: English-German

able: to be able to können
to accept annehmen
accidentally zufällig
to act (as if) tun (als ob)
afraid: to be afraid (of)
    Angst haben (vor)
after all doch
again wieder
airport der Flughafen
alone allein
along mit
already schon
also auch
although obwohl
always immer
to answer antworten
apartment die Wohnung
approximately ungefähr
arm der Arm
to arrive ankommen
to ask fragen
aunt die Tante
away weg

back zurück
bank die Bank, –en
to bathe, take a bath (sich)
    baden
beautiful schön
because weil
to become werden
bed das Bett
to begin anfangen
    beginning der Anfang
to believe glauben; denken
    to believe in glauben an
to belong to gehören
bench die Bank, ¨e
birthday der Geburtstag
book das Buch
bored: to be bored sich
    langweilen

to break brechen
breakfast das Frühstück
brother der Bruder
to build bauen
but aber; sondern
to buy kaufen

to call (up) anrufen
called: to be called heißen
to calm down sich beruhigen
car der Wagen
to catch a cold sich erkälten
chair der Stuhl
to change (sich) ändern;
    (sich) verändern
to change (clothes) sich
    umziehen
child das Kind
church die Kirche
city die Stadt
coat der Mantel
coffee der Kaffee
cold kalt
to come kommen
correct: to be correct
    stimmen
to count zählen
of course natürlich
cup die Tasse

darling Liebling
daughter die Tochter
day der Tag
dead tot
to deal with sich handeln um
    (impers.)
dear lieb
to decide sich entschließen
to die sterben
different(ly) ander–; anders

dinner das Essen; das
    Mittagessen; das
    Abendessen
to disappear verschwinden
divorce: to get a divorce sich
    scheiden lassen
to do tun
doctor der Arzt; der Doktor
dog der Hund
door die Tür
downtown in die Stadt
to drink trinken
to drive fahren
dumbbell der Dummkopf

each jeder, jede, jedes
early früh
to eat essen
end das Ende
engaged: to get engaged
    sich verloben
every jeder, jede, jedes
everything alles
excited: to get excited (about)
    sich aufregen (über)
to expect erwarten
expensive teuer
to experience erfahren
eye das Auge

far weit
father der Vater
to feel fühlen
few wenige
    a few ein paar; einige
to fight kämpfen
finally endlich; schließlich
flower die Blume
to fly fliegen
footprint der Fußabdruck
for (conj.) denn
to forget vergessen

free frei
friend der Freund, die Freundin

garden der Garten
girl das Mädchen
to give geben
to go gehen
gold piece das Goldstück
good gut
haircut: to get a haircut sich die Haare schneiden lassen
to happen geschehen; passieren
happy glücklich
hat der Hut
to have haben
   to have to müssen
healthy gesund
to hear hören
to help helfen
here hier
hole das Loch
home (adv.) nach Hause
   at home zu Hause
to hope hoffen
hot heiß
hour die Stunde
house das Haus
how wie
human being der Mensch
hungry hungrig
to hurry up sich eilen; sich beeilen
husband der Mann

if wenn
to imagine sich vorstellen; sich (etwas) einbilden
immediately sofort
important wichtig
instead of statt . . . zu
intelligent intelligent
to intend to wollen
interested: to be interested in sich interessieren für
interesting interessant
to introduce (oneself) (sich) vorstellen
to invite einladen

just gerade

key der Schlüssel
to knock klopfen
to know (a person) kennen
   to know (facts) wissen

large groß
last letzt–; zuletzt
at last endlich
late spät
law das Gesetz
to learn lernen
least: at least mindestens, wenigstens
to leave lassen; abfahren
to let lassen
letter der Brief
to lie liegen
life das Leben
light das Licht
little klein; wenig
to live wohnen; leben
living room das Wohnzimmer
long lang; (adv.) lange
to look aussehen
to look forward to sich freuen auf
to lose one's way sich verlaufen; sich verfahren
to love lieben
to fall in love with sich verlieben in

mad: to be mad at sich ärgern über
to make machen
many viele
married: to be married verheiratet sein
to marry, to get married heiraten
to meet kennenlernen
mistake der Fehler
moment der Augenblick
money das Geld
more mehr
mother die Mutter
movie (house) das Kino
much viel

to need brauchen
never nie
new neu
newspaper die Zeitung
nice nett

nobody niemand
not nicht
   not until erst
   not yet noch nicht
nothing nichts
novel der Roman
now jetzt

o'clock: at (three) o'clock um (drei) Uhr
often oft
old alt
once einmal; früher
only nur; erst
order: in order in Ordnung
in order to um . . . zu
other ander–
overcoat der Mantel

to pay bezahlen
people die Leute
perhaps vielleicht
permitted: to be permitted to dürfen
to pick up, meet abholen
picture das Bild
please bitte
to prepare (oneself) for (sich) vorbereiten auf
to promise versprechen
to put setzen; stellen; legen

quite ganz

to rain regnen
rather lieber
to reach erreichen
to read lesen
really wirklich
to remember sich erinnern an
to rest sich ausruhen
restless unruhig
to ring (a telephone) klingeln
reason die Vernunft
   reasonable vernünftig
to recognize erkennen
relative der Verwandte
room das Zimmer

shoe der Schuh
school die Schule
to scream schreien
to see sehen
to seem scheinen

to send schicken
several mehrere
to shave sich rasieren
to show zeigen
sick krank
silent: to be silent schweigen
simple einfach
sister die Schwester
to sit sitzen
to sleep schlafen
   to get enough sleep (sich)
   ausschlafen
small klein
to smoke rauchen
soldier der Soldat
some einige; ein paar;
   manche; etwas
somebody jemand
something etwas
somewhere irgendwo;
   irgendwohin
son der Sohn
to speak sprechen
to stand stehen
station der Bahnhof
to stay bleiben
still noch
stone der Stein
stop halten; stehenbleiben
story die Geschichte
student der Student, die
   Studentin
to study studieren

such solch
suddenly plötzlich
to suggest vorschlagen
Sunday der Sonntag
supposed: to be supposed to
   sollen
swimming pool das
   Schwimmbecken
to switch off ausmachen

table der Tisch
to take nehmen
to talk reden; sprechen
teacher der Lehrer
to tell sagen; erzählen
to thank danken
thief der Dieb
to think (of) denken (an)
time die Zeit
   at the time damals
tired müde
today heute
tomorrow morgen
tonight heute abend
too auch
trace die Spur
   without a trace spurlos
train der Zug
to try versuchen
to turn off (light) ausmachen
to turn out sich herausstellen
   (impers.)

to understand verstehen
to undress sich ausziehen
unfortunately leider
until bis
to get used to sich gewöhnen
   an

very sehr
to visit besuchen

to wait for warten auf
wall die Wand
to want to wollen
war der Krieg
watch die Uhr
week die Woche
weekend das Wochenende
well gesund; gut
when wann
where wo; wohin
whether ob
why warum
wife die Frau
wine der Wein
winter der Winter
without ohne
woman die Frau
to work arbeiten
writer der Schriftsteller

year das Jahr
yesterday gestern
young jung

Index

This index provides quick references to the grammar topics treated in the analysis sections. Numbers refer to pages.

Mitteleuropa

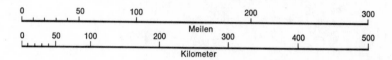

Mitteleuropa und die Vereinigten Staaten
(drawn at the same scale)